Mathematical Methods *for* ECONOMICS

The Addison-Wesley Series in Economics

Abel/Bernanke
Macroeconomics

Bade/Parkin
Foundations of Economics

Bierman/Fernandez
Game Theory with Economic Applications

Binger/Hoffman
Microeconomics with Calculus

Boyer
Principles of Transportation Economics

Branson
Macroeconomic Theory and Policy

Bruce
Public Finance and the American Economy

Burgess
The Economics of Regulation and Antitrust

Byrns/Stone
Economics

Carlton/Perloff
Modern Industrial Organization

Caves/Frankel/Jones
World Trade and Payments: An Introduction

Chapman
Environmental Economics: Theory, Application, and Policy

Cooter/Ulen
Law and Economics

Eaton/Mishkin
Online Readings to Accompany The Economics of Money, Banking, and Financial Markets

Ehrenberg/Smith
Modern Labor Economics

Ekelund/Tollison
Economics: Private Markets and Public Choice

Fusfeld
The Age of the Economist

Gerber
International Economics

Ghiara
Learning Economics: A Practical Workbook

Gordon
Macroeconomics

Gregory
Essentials of Economics

Gregory/Stuart
Russian and Soviet Economic Performance and Structure

Hartwick/Olewiler
The Economics of Natural Resource Use

Hubbard
Money, the Financial System, and the Economy

Hughes/Cain
American Economic History

Husted/Melvin
International Economics

Jehle/Reny
Advanced Microeconomic Theory

Klein
Mathematical Methods for Economics

Krugman/Obstfeld
International Economics: Theory and Policy

Laidler
The Demand for Money: Theories, Evidence, and Problems

Leeds/von Allmen
The Economics of Sports

Lesser/Dodds/Zerbe
Environmental Economics and Policy

Lipsey/Courant/Ragan
Economics

McCarty
Dollars and Sense: An Introduction to Economics

Melvin
International Money and Finance

Miller
Economics Today

Miller/Benjamin/North
The Economics of Public Issues

Mills/Hamilton
Urban Economics

Mishkin
The Economics of Money, Banking, and Financial Markets

Parkin
Economics

Parkin/Bade
Economics in Action Software

Perloff
Microeconomics

Phelps
Health Economics

Riddell/Shackelford/Stamos/Schneider
Economics: A Tool for Critically Understanding Society

Ritter/Silber/Udell
Principles of Money, Banking, and Financial Markets

Rohlf
Introduction to Economic Reasoning

Ruffin/Gregory
Principles of Economics

Sargent
Rational Expectations and Inflation

Scherer
Industry Structure, Strategy, and Public Policy

Schotter
Microeconomics: A Modern Approach

Sherman/Kolk
Business Cycles and Forecasting

Smith
Case Studies in Economic Development

Studenmund
Using Econometrics: A Practical Guide

Su
Economic Fluctuations and Forecasting

Tietenberg
Environmental and Natural Resource Economics

Tietenberg
Environmental Economics and Policy

Todaro
Economic Development

Waldman/Jensen
Industrial Organization: Theory and Practice

Williamson
Macroeconomics

Mathematical Methods *for* ECONOMICS

SECOND EDITION

MICHAEL W. KLEIN

The Fletcher School of Law and Diplomacy, Tufts University

Addison Wesley

Boston San Francisco New York
London Toronto Sydney Tokyo Singapore Madrid
Mexico City Munich Paris Cape Town Hong Kong Montreal

Mathematical Methods for Economics, Second Edition
Michael W. Klein

Editor-in-Chief: Denise Clinton
Acquisitions Editor: Victoria Warneck
Associate Editor: Roxanne Hoch
Senior Production Supervisor: Nancy H. Fenton
Marketing Manager: Adrienne D'Ambrosio
Manufacturing Supervisor: Hugh Crawford
Design Manager: Gina Hagen
Cover Designer: Gina Hagen
Cover Image: Photo Disc
Project Coordination: Thompson Steele, Inc.

Library of Congress Cataloging-in-Publication Data

Klein, Michael W.
Mathematical methods for economics / Michael W. Klein. — 2nd ed.
p. cm. — (Addison-Wesley series in economics)
Includes index.
ISBN 0-201-72626-2 (alk. paper)
1. Economics, Mathematical. I. Title. II. Series.

HB135 .K583 2001
330′.01′51—dc21 2001033359

1 2 3 4 5 6 7 8 9 10—HT—05 04 03 02 01

To Susan, Gabriel and Noah

Contents

Detailed Contents

Preface

Economic analysis lends itself to mathematical frameworks. These mathematical frameworks provide a powerful set of analytic tools. While elementary economic concepts are typically taught with only a modicum of mathematics, more advanced concepts require a broader set of mathematical skills. This book presents the mathematics required for studying economics at the advanced undergraduate level and at the graduate level.

The focus of this book is to teach the mathematical tools that are of central importance in economics in the context of economic examples. This second edition includes many new applications, thus expanding the economic context used in the teaching of mathematics. The economic context is important for four reasons. First, the economic context motivates economics students to learn the mathematical material by explicitly showing the use of the mathematical tools and techniques in economics. To appeal to a wide audience, examples in this book are drawn from a range of fields in economics, including microeconomics, macroeconomics, economic growth, international trade, international finance, labor economics, environmental economics, industrial organization, devlopment economics, and finance. Second, this book provides an explicit link between mathematical tools and their uses in economics. This link is often not obvious to students who are approaching this material for the first time. Third, abstract mathematical concepts can be more easily understood and the intuition behind them becomes more accessible when they are presented in a concrete context. Mathematical concepts in this book are developed in the context of economic examples. Finally, students will hone their economic intuition through the study of the formal mathematical models presented in this text.

Pedagogically, many chapters introduce an economic example at the outset of the chapter and then reference it, or closely related examples, throughout the rest of the chapter to develop students' comprehension of both economics and mathematics. Repeated use of some important economic models, such as the Solow growth model, across chapters also serves to develop the students' knowledge of economics and reinforce the lessons learned in earlier chapters. Many chapters include separate applications sections, while in other chapters applications are included within sections that develop mathematical concepts and tools. Many of the applications are drawn directly from recent research published in leading journals. Each chapter includes a large number of exercises designed to reinforce the concepts of the chapter and to build students' ability to conduct economic analysis. This second edition includes more than twenty-five new exercises. Both mathematical exercises and word problems drawn from economics are included. Short answers to odd-numbered problems are provided in the back of the book. A solutions manual with more detailed answers to all exercises is available for instructors.

The book's modular structure affords instructors a good deal of flexibility in designing courses. Application sections often do not require students to cover the most advanced material in chapters. Thus this book is appropriate for a wide range of audiences. An undergraduate course can make use of most of the applications in a chapter even if that course does not cover the more advanced material presented in the sections of that chapter. Undergraduate students will find that the material presented in this book provides them access to a wide range of economic research. Masters-level courses can include some of the more advanced topics in the text. Students who are studying for a Masters of Business Administration will benefit from the link between material covered elsewhere in their programs and applications on the pricing of bonds, the volatility of bond prices, the pricing of stocks, present value, advertising, exchange-rate determination, and strategic pricing. Students enrolled in masters programs in public policy or international affairs will find that many of the applications with a policy focus, such as the sustainability of deficits, the incidence of a tax, the inflation tax, the international pattern of women's work, measuring inequality, income and the environment, and the Golden Rule, are especially relevant. The most advanced material is appropriate for doctoral students. Such applications as elements of probability and statistics, the Golden Rule, wage gaps and international trade, sources of comparative advantage, rules versus discretion in monetary policy, the price of stocks, exchange-rate determination, exchange-rate overshooting, the constant elasticity of substitution production function, utility functions and risk aversion, optimal growth, and life-cycle consumption tie in with material covered by doctoral students in their other courses. These students will also benefit from the advanced material on dynamic analysis, including the material on systems of difference equations, systems of differential equations, and dynamic optimization.

Structure

The book consists of five parts. Part One, Introduction, consists of three chapters that should be read by all students. Chapter 1 sets the stage for the book by introducing reasons for the use of mathematical modeling in economics and providing some basic definitions. Chapter 2 introduces important concepts that are used throughout the rest of the book, including properties of functions, graphical representation of functions, necessary and sufficient conditions, and concavity. This chapter also has a "menu" of functions to introduce different functional forms used throughout the rest of the book. Chapter 3 focuses on exponential and logarithmic functions, which have a very wide range of uses in economic analysis. The discussion of exponential functions focuses on the important concepts of growth and present value. The section on logarithmic functions discusses the "Rule-of-70," a rule-of-thumb for calculating doubling times, and also shows how the logarithmic transformation is helpful for graphing time series of data. Students with more preparation may spend little time on these chapters, and for them the chapters serve as a review of some basic concepts. Even doctoral students with prior mathematical training, however, will find some of the applications in Chapter 3 useful.

Part Two, Matrix Algebra, consists of two chapters. Professors who want to review basic techniques of solving systems of equations (like demand and supply models or the basic macroeconomic IS/LM model) can cover only the beginning of Chapter 4.

The rest of Chapter 4 serves as an introduction to the concepts and basic results of matrix algebra. This chapter can stand alone as an introduction to the basic terminology, concepts, and tools of matrix algebra. Chapter 5 includes a more thorough presentation of some of the topics in Chapter 4 as well as the more advanced topic of characteristic roots. The material in Chapter 5 is important for the more advanced treatment of topics like optimization and dynamic analysis.

Part Three, Differential Calculus, consists of three chapters. Chapter 6 is a basic introduction of the concepts behind differential calculus. This chapter develops the central concepts of differential calculus in the context of economic examples, including the link between tax rates and tax revenues and the link between exchange rates and the volume of imports. Equations, numerical examples, and graphical analysis are all used to develop the concept of differentiation. Chapter 7 develops the rules of differentiation that are needed to put into practice the concepts introduced in the previous chapter. Applications motivate the study of these rules, show their importance in economic contexts, and provide concrete examples of the use of the rules. These applications include the analysis of the sustainability of government budget deficits and the mathematical framework for thinking about risk aversion. This chapter also introduces the important economic concept of an elasticity. Elasticities are used in two application sections in this chapter: the relationship between a nation's income per capita and its infant mortality rate and the incidence of a tax. Chapter 8 presents multivariate calculus. This chapter demonstrates that partial differentiation is the mathematical analogue to the concept used in economic analysis of *ceteris paribus*, that is, "holding all else equal." Application sections in this chapter focus on returns to education, the puzzling lack of international capital flows to developing countries, means and outliers, and the division of national income. For more advanced students, this chapter has a discussion of properties of homogeneous and homothetic functions. The correspondence between the mathematical concepts and important economic concepts like the effect of changes "at the margin" are emphasized throughout.

A central economic paradigm is that people do the best they can while facing certain constraints. Part Four, Optimization, shows how the tools of differential calculus can be used to determine the optimal actions undertaken by consumers, producers, or governments. Each of the chapters in this section begins by developing the key mathematical techniques, often in the context of an economic problem. Each chapter then includes a section on economic applications, some of which are standard textbook applications and some of which are drawn from recent research. The concept of an extreme value of a univariate function that is briefly introduced in Chapter 7 is revisited in Chapters 9 and 10. Application sections in Chapter 9 include an analysis of an empirical study of the link between income and pollution levels, some standard microeconomic problems like factor demands and the behavior of a monopolist, and three macroeconomic applications, rules versus discretion in monetary policy, the tax raised by governments through printing money, and the optimal savings rate. Chapter 10 extends the discussion in the previous chapter to functions with several arguments. The second section of this chapter presents second-order conditions in the bivariate case to develop students' intuition. The more general case is presented in the third section. This part concludes with Chapter 11, which presents techniques for solving constrained optimization problems. The chapter begins with a simple consumption problem that is referenced throughout the chapter in increasingly more advanced ways. In the development of the Lagrangian method, there is a discussion of the economic interpretation of the Lagrange multiplier and the envelope theorem. The third section of this chapter includes five economic applications. The chapter ends with the more advanced topic of optimization with inequality constraints. Throughout the chapter, analytical methods are illustrated with numerical results. Undergraduate, masters, and doctoral students will all cover these three chapters, although there are sections of Chapters 10 and 11 that may be omitted for undergraduate or masters students.

Time plays a central role in many areas of economics, including finance, macroeconomics, monetary economics, international economics, economic growth, and environmental economics. Part Five, Integration and Dynamic Analysis, presents tools and techniques of dynamic analysis, that is, the analysis of variables over time. Chapter 12, which presents integral calculus, begins with a discussion of the concept of integration and shows how it can be interpreted as an area under a curve. The economic example of valuing a stream of payments (for example, finding the price of a bond that offers a stream of payments) is used to illustrate this concept. Rules of integration are presented. The final section of this chapter includes five applications of integration: consumer's surplus, the relationship between the maturity of a bond and the volatility of its price, a discussion of the cost of inflation, a look at measuring inequality, and a discussion of some basic concepts of probability and statistics. Difference equations, the subject of Chapter 13, link the value of a variable in one period to its value in another period as well as to the value of other variables. This chapter presents techniques for analyzing difference equations and also introduces some important concepts in dynamic analysis. The first two sections of this chapter may serve as a useful introduction to dynamic analysis in undergraduate courses. Applications include a dynamic Keynesian macroeconomic model, a macroeconomic model of inflation, a determination of the half-life of exchange rate misalignments, and a model of stock prices. The third section of this chapter presents more advanced topics, including systems of difference equations and second-order difference equations. Chapter 14 presents an analysis of differential equations which are the continuous time analogue to difference equations. Undergraduate courses may study the first two sections of this chapter, which consist of an introduction to the simplest types of differential equations and a set of applications of these types of equations. More advanced courses may also study the final section that presents systems of differential equations. Applications include the determination of inflation, two models of exchange-rate determination, a mathematical presentation of an eighteenth century theory of the balance of payments, and a presentation of the well-known Dornbusch overshooting model of exchange rates. The book's concluding chapter presents dynamic optimization. This is a more advanced topic, and this chapter is most appropriate for doctoral students. The chapter begins by drawing a link between the constrained optimization methods presented in Chapter 11 and dynamic optimization. The chapter then presents the central results of dynamic optimization. The chapter includes a number of extensions of the basic results. It also includes a number of applications that students are likely to encounter in advanced theory courses, such as optimal growth, the life-cycle theory of consumption, and the optimal rate of depletion of a natural resource.

Some suggested course outlines, corresponding to courses taught at different levels, are presented below. Instructors may choose to include a subset of applications for class presentation.

Suggested Course Outlines

Undergraduate	Masters	Doctoral
Part One	Part One	Part One
Section 4.1	Chapter 4	Part Two
Part Three	Part Three	Part Three
Part Four, except section 10.3, part of section 11.2, and section 11.4	Part Four, except section 10.3 and part of section 11.2	Part Four
Sections 13.1 and 13.2 or sections 14.1 and 14.2	Sections 13.1 and 13.2 and sections 14.1 and 14.2	Part Five

Acknowledgments

The second edition of this book builds on the foundation of the first edition, adding new material and refining the presentation. Accordingly, it is appropriate to acknowledge both those people who helped launch the first edition and those whose help and suggestions contributed to the improvements found in this edition.

My initial interest in writing this book grew out of the encouragment of Denise Clinton, Editor-in-Chief of Economics and Finance, Addison Wesley. The first edition of this book benefitted greatly from the editorial suggestions and detailed comments of Lena Buonanno, also at Addison Wesley, and Deirdre Savarese. Deirdre developed most of the end-of-section exercises for the first edition. Patrick Morton, John Brown (Clark University), Robert Murphy (Boston College), Jay Shambaugh and Toshihiro Ichida (both of whom were students at the Fletcher School) also offered very important, and very welcome, assistance to me while I was writing the first edition. The first edition also benefitted from comments and suggestions from Steven Block and Carsten Kowalczyk (both of the Fletcher School, Tufts University), as well as from Gilbert Metcalf and Dan Richards (both of the Economics Department of Tufts University). The second edition reflects suggestions offered by, among others, Brian

Binger (University of Illinois at Chicago), Kristin Forbes (Sloan School, Massachusetts Institute of Technology), Herve Jacquet (Columbia University), Matthew Kahn (Fletcher School, Tufts University), Frans Kerstholt (Tilburg University), Zbigniew Nitecki (Tufts University), Lynne Pepall (Tufts University), Basel Saleh, and Knut Sydsaeter (University of Oslo).

Reviews helped me improve this book, and I thank the reviewers, including Richard Anderson (Texas A & M University), Daniel G. Arce M. (University of Alabama), Susan Begsemer (Syracuse University), Daniel Bernhofen (Clark University), Vic Brajer (California State University, Fullerton), Michael Donihue (Colby College), Jeffrey Ely (Northwestern University), Adrian Fleissig (University of Texas, Arlington), John M Harrington, Jr. (Johns Hopkins University), Frank Hsiao (University of Colorado), Gary Hunt (University of Maine), James Holcomb (University of Texas, El Paso), Manfred Keil (Claremont McKenna College), S. Henry Kim (Brandeis University), William Lott (University of Connecticut), Gerald Miller (Miami University), Stephen Schmidt (Union College), Robert Sorensen (University of Missouri, St. Louis), Louis Sosa S. (Colorado School of Mines), Mark Tomljanovich (Colgate University), Chris Veendorp (Clark University), Eleanore T. von Ende (Texas Tech University), John Wall (University of Surrey), and Xinghe Wang (University of Missouri, Columbia).

My deepest appreciation goes, as always, to my wife, Susan Cohen, and our sons, Gabriel and Noah. I can acknowledge, but cannot fully express, my debt to them.

Part One

Introduction

Chapter 1
The Mathematical Framework of Economic Analysis

Chapter 2
An Introduction to Functions

Chapter 3
Exponential and Logarithmic Functions

This book begins with a three-chapter section that introduces some important concepts and tools that are used throughout the rest of the book. Chapter 1 presents background on the mathematical framework of economic analysis. In this chapter we discuss the advantages of using mathematical models in economics. We also introduce some characteristics of economic models. The discussion in this chapter makes reference to material presented in the rest of the book to put this discussion in context as well as to give you some idea of the types of topics addressed by this book.

Chapter 2 discusses the central topic of functions. The chapter begins by defining some terms and presenting some key concepts. Various properties of functions first introduced in this chapter appear again in later chapters. The final section of Chapter 2 presents a menu of different types of functions that are used frequently in economic analysis.

Two types of functions that are particularly important in economic analysis are exponential and logarithmic functions. As shown in Chapter 3, exponential functions are used for calculating growth and discounting. Logarithmic functions, which are related to exponential functions, have a number of properties that make them useful in economic modeling. Applications in this chapter, which include the distinction between annual and effective interest rates, calculating doubling time, and graphing time series of variables, demonstrate some of the uses of exponential and logarithmic functions in economic analysis. Later chapters make extensive use of these functions as well.

Chapter 1

The Mathematical Framework of Economic Analysis

What are the sources of long-run growth and prosperity in an economy? How does your level of education affect your lifetime earnings profile? Has foreign competition from developing countries widened the gap between the rich and the poor in industrialized countries? Will economic development lead to increased environmental degradation? How do college scholarship rules affect savings rates? What is the cost of inflation in an economy? What determines the price of foreign currency?

The answers to these and similar economic questions have important consequences. The importance of economic issues combined with the possibility for alternative modes of economic analysis result in widespread discussion and debate. This discussion and debate takes place in numerous forums including informal conversations, news shows, editorials in newspapers, and scholarly research articles addressed to an audience of trained economists. Participants in these discussions and debates base their analyses and arguments on implicit or explicit frameworks of reasoning.

Economists are trained in the use of explicit economic models to analyze economic issues. These models are usually expressed as sets of relationships that take a mathematical form. Thus an important part of an economist's training is acquiring a command of the mathematical tools and techniques used in constructing and solving economic models.

This book teaches the core set of these mathematical tools and techniques. The mathematics presented here provides access to a wide range of economic analysis and research. Yet a presentation of the mathematics alone is often insufficient for students who want to understand the use of these tools in economics because the link between mathematical theory and economic application is not always apparent. Therefore this book places the mathematical tools in the context of economic applications. These applications provide an important bridge between mathematical techniques and economic analysis and also demonstrate the range of uses of mathematics in economics.

The parallel presentation of mathematical techniques and economic applications serves several purposes. It reinforces the teaching of mathematics by providing a setting for using the techniques. Demonstrating the use of mathematics in economics helps develop mathematical comprehension as well as hone economic intuition. In this way, the study of mathematical methods used in economics as presented in this book complements your study in other economics courses. The economic applications in this book also help motivate the teaching of mathematics by emphasizing the practical use of mathematics in economic analysis. An effort is made to make the applications reference a wide range of topics by drawing from a cross section of disciplines within economics, including microeconomics, macroeconomics, economic growth, international trade, labor economics, environmental economics, and finance. In fact, each of the questions posed at the beginning of this chapter is the subject of an application in this book.

This chapter sets the stage for the rest of the book by discussing the nature of economic models and the role of mathematics in economic modeling. Section 1.1 discusses the link between a model and the phenomenon it attempts to explain. This section also discusses why economic analysis typically employs a mathematical framework. Section 1.2 discusses some characteristics of models used in economics and previews the material presented in the rest of the book.

1.1 ECONOMIC MODELS AND ECONOMIC REALITY

Any economic analysis is based upon some framework. This framework may be highly sophisticated, as with a multiequation model based on individuals who attempt to achieve an optimal outcome while facing a set of constraints, or it may be very simplistic and involve nothing more complicated than the notion that economic variables follow some well-defined pattern over time. An overall evaluation of an economic analysis requires an evaluation of the framework itself, a consideration of the accuracy and relevance of the facts and assumptions used in that framework, and a test of its predictions.

A framework based on a formal mathematical model has certain advantages. A mathematical model demands a logical rigor that may not be found in a less formal framework. Rigorous analysis need not be mathematical, but economic analysis lends itself to the use of mathematics because many of the underlying concepts in economics can be directly translated into a mathematical form. The concept of determining an economic equilibrium corresponds to the mathematical technique of solving systems of equations, the subject of Part Two of this book. Questions concerning how one variable responds to changes in the value of another variable, as embodied in economic concepts like price elasticity or marginal cost, can be given rigorous form through the use of differentiation, the subject of Part Three. Formal models that reflect the central concept of economics—the assumption that people strive to obtain the best possible outcome given certain constraints—can be solved using the mathematical techniques of constrained optimization. These are discussed in Part Four. Economic questions that involve consideration of the evolution of markets or economic conditions over time—questions that are important in such fields as macroeconomics, finance, and resource economics—can be addressed using the various types of mathematical techniques presented in Part Five.

While logical rigor ensures that conclusions follow from assumptions, it should also be the case that the conclusions of a model are not too sensitive to its assumptions.

It is typically the case that the assumptions of a formal mathematical model are explicit and transparent. Therefore a formal mathematical model often readily admits the sensitivity of its conclusions to its assumptions. The evolution of modern growth theory offers a good example of this.

A central question of economic growth concerns the long-run stability of market economies. In the wake of the Great Depression of the 1930s, Roy Harrod and Evsey Domar each developed models in which economies either were precariously balanced on a "knife-edge" of stable growth or were marked by ongoing instability. Robert Solow, in a paper published in the mid-1950s, showed how the instability of the Harrod–Domar model was a consequence of a single crucial assumption concerning production. Solow developed a model with a more realistic production relationship, which was characterized by a stable growth path. The Solow growth model has become one of the most influential and widely cited in economics. Applications in Chapters 8, 9, 13, and 15 in this text draw on Solow's important contribution. More recently, research on "endogenous growth" models has studied how alternative production relationships may lead to divergent economic performance across countries. Drawing on the endogenous growth literature, this book includes an application in Chapter 8 that discusses research by Robert Lucas on the proper specification of the production function as well as an application that presents a growth model with "poverty traps" in Chapter 13.[1]

Once a model is set up and its underlying assumptions specified, mathematical techniques often enable us to solve the model in a straightforward manner even if the underlying problem is complicated. Thus mathematics provides a set of powerful tools that enable economists to understand how complicated relationships are linked and exactly what conclusions follow from the assumptions and construction of the model. The solution to an economic model, in turn, may offer new or more subtle economic intuition. Many applications in this text illustrate this, including those on the incidence of a tax in Chapters 4 and 7, the allocation of time to different activities in Chapter 11, and prices in financial markets in Chapters 12 and 13. Optimal control theory, the subject of Chapter 15, provides another example of the power of mathematics to solve complicated questions. We discuss in Chapter 15 how optimal control theory, a mathematical technique developed in the 1950s, allowed economists to resolve long-standing questions concerning the price of capital.

A mathematical model often offers conclusions that are directly testable against data. These tests provide an empirical standard against which the model can be judged. The branch of economics concerned with using data to test economic hypotheses is called econometrics. While this book does not cover econometrics, a number of the applications show how to use mathematical tools to interpret econometric results. For example, in Chapter 7 we show how an appropriate mathematical function enables us to determine the link between national income per capita and infant mortality rates in

[1] Solow's paper, "A contribution to the theory of economic growth," is published in the *Quarterly Journal of Economics,* 70, no. 1 (February 1956): 65–94. The other papers cited here are Roy F. Harrod, "An essay in dynamic theory," *Economic Journal,* 49 (June 1939): 14–33; Evsey Domar, "Capital expansion, rate of growth, and employment," *Econometrica,* 14 (April 1946): 137–147; and Robert Lucas, "Why doesn't capital flow from rich to poor countries?" *American Economic Review,* 80, no. 2 (May 1990): 92–96.

a cross section of countries. An application in Chapter 9 discusses some recent research on the relationship between pollution and income in a number of countries, which bears on the question of the extent to which rapidly growing countries will contribute to despoiling the environment. Chapter 8 includes an application that draws from a classic study of the financial returns to education.

It is natural to begin a book of this nature with a discussion of the many advantages of using a formal mathematical method for addressing economic issues. It is important, at the same time, to recognize possible drawbacks of this approach. Any mathematical model simplifies reality and, in so doing, may present an incomplete picture. The comparison of an economic model with a map is instructive here. A map necessarily simplifies the geography it attempts to describe. There is a trade-off between the comprehensiveness and readability of a map. The clutter of a very comprehensive map may make it difficult to read. The simplicity of a very readable map may come at the expense of omitting important landmarks, streets, or other geographic features. In much the same way, an economic model that is too comprehensive may not be tractable, while a model that is too simple may present a distorted view of reality.

The question then arises of which economic model should be used. To answer this question by continuing with our analogy to maps, we recognize that the best map for one purpose is probably not the best map for another purpose. A highly schematic subway map with a few lines may be the appropriate tool for navigating a city's subways, but it may be useless or even misleading if used aboveground. Likewise, a particular economic model may be appropriate for addressing some issues but not others. For example, the simple savings relationship posited in many economic growth models may be fine in that context but wholly inappropriate for more detailed studies of savings behavior.

The mathematical tools presented in this book will give you access to many interesting ideas in economics that are formalized through mathematical modeling. These tools are used in a wide range of economic models. While economic models may differ in many ways, they all share some common characteristics. We next turn to a discussion of these characteristics.

1.2 CHARACTERISTICS OF ECONOMIC MODELS

An economic model attempts to explain the behavior of a set of variables through the behavior of other variables and through the way the variables interact. The variables used in the model, which are themselves determined outside the context of the model, are called **exogenous variables.** The variables determined by the model are called **endogenous variables.** The economic model captures the link between the exogenous and endogenous variables.

A simple economic model illustrates the distinction between endogenous and exogenous variables. Consider a simple demand and supply analysis of the market for the familiar mythical good, the "widget." The endogenous variables in this model are the price of a widget and the quantity of widgets sold. The exogenous variables in this example include the price of the input to widget production and the price of the good that consumers consider as a possible substitute for widgets.

In this example there is an apparently straightforward separation of variables into the categories of exogenous and endogenous. This separation actually represents a central assumption of this model—the assumption that the market for the input used in producing widgets and the market for the potential substitute for widgets are not affected by what happens in the market for widgets. In general, the separation of variables into those that are exogenous and those that are endogenous reflects an important assumption of an economic model. Exogenous variables in some models may be endogenous variables in others. This may sometimes reflect the fact that one model is more complete than another in that it includes a wider set of endogenous variables. For example, investment is exogenous in the simplest Keynesian cross diagram and endogenous in the more complicated IS/LM model. In other cases the purpose of the model determines which variables are endogenous and which are exogenous. Government spending is usually considered exogenous in macroeconomic models but endogenous in public choice models. Even the weather, which is typically considered exogenous, may be endogenous in a model of the economic determinants of global warming. In fact, much debate in economics concerns whether certain variables are better characterized as exogenous or endogenous.

An economic model links its exogenous and endogenous variables through a set of relationships called **functions.** These functions may be described by specific equations or by more general relationships. Functions are defined in Chapter 2. In that chapter we describe different types of equations that are frequently used as functions in economic models. For now we identify three categories of relationships used in economic models: definitions, behavioral equations, and equilibrium conditions.

A **definition** is an expression in which one variable is defined to be identically equal to some function of one or more other variables. For example, profit (Π) is total revenue (TR) minus total cost (TC), and this definition can be written as

$$\Pi \equiv TR - TC,$$

where "$\equiv$" means "is identically equal to."

A **behavioral equation** represents a modeling of people's actions based on economic principles. The demand equation and supply equation in microeconomics, as well as the investment, money demand, and consumption equations in macroeconomics, all represent behavioral equations. Sometimes these equations reflect very basic economic assumptions such as utility maximization. In other cases, behavioral equations are not derived explicitly from basic economic assumptions but reflect a general relationship consistent with economic reasoning.

An **equilibrium condition** is a relationship that defines an **equilibrium** or **steady state** of the model. In equilibrium there are no economic forces within the context of the model that alter the values of the endogenous variables.

We use our example of the market for widgets to illustrate these concepts. The two behavioral equations in this model are a demand equation and a supply equation. We specify the demand equation for widgets as

$$Q^D = \alpha - \beta P + \gamma G$$

and the supply equation as

$$Q^S = \theta + \lambda P - \phi N,$$

where Q^D is the quantity of widgets demanded, Q^S is the quantity of widgets supplied, P is the price of widgets, G is the price of goods that are potential substitutes for widgets, and N is the price of inputs used in producing widgets. The Greek letters in these equations, $\alpha, \beta, \gamma, \theta, \lambda$, and ϕ, represent the **parameters** of the model. A parameter is a given constant. A parameter may be some arbitrary constant, as is the case here, or a specific value like 100, $\frac{1}{2}$, or -7.2.

A simple example of an equilibrium condition sets the demand for widgets equal to the supply of widgets. This gives us the equilibrium condition

$$Q^D = Q^S.$$

A simultaneous solution of the demand equation, supply equation, and equilibrium condition gives a solution to this model. The **solution** to a model is a set of values of its endogenous variables that correspond to a given set of values of its exogenous variables and a given set of parameters. Thus, in this case, the solution will show how the endogenous variables P and Q (where, in equilibrium, Q equals both quantity demanded and quantity supplied) depend upon the values of the exogenous variables N and G, as well as the values of the six parameters of the model. The values of the endogenous variables in equilibrium are their **equilibrium values.**[2]

The structure of this model is quite simple. One reason for this is that the behavioral equations are each linear functions since they take the form

$$y = a + bx + cz,$$

where y, x, and z are variables and a, b, and c are parameters. In this equation y is the **dependent variable,** and the variables x and z are the **independent variables.** The linearity of the behavioral equations enables us to find a solution for the model using the techniques of **linear algebra** (also called **matrix algebra**) presented in Part Two of this book (Chapters 4 and 5). The techniques in these chapters show how to determine easily whether a model consisting of several linear equations has a **unique solution.** Matrix algebra can be used to conduct **comparative static analysis,** which evaluates the change in the equilibrium values of a model when the value of one or more exogenous variables changes. For example, an evaluation of the change in the equilibrium value of the price of widgets and the quantity of widgets bought and sold in response to a change in the price of the input to widget production would be a comparative static analysis. While the requirement of linearity may seem restrictive, the discussion of logarithmic functions and exponential functions in Chapter 3 shows that certain nonlinear functions can be expressed in linear form. Also material presented in Chapter 7 shows how to obtain a linear approximation of a nonlinear function.

The determination of the solution to this simple linear model may be only the beginning of a deeper economic analysis of the widget market. Such an analysis may

---

[2] We return to this model in Chapter 4 where we show how to solve it.

require a broader set of mathematical techniques. For instance, suppose a tax is imposed on the sale of widgets. The tax revenues from the sale of widgets, T, is given by the definition

$$T \equiv \tau \cdot (Q \cdot P),$$

where τ is the tax rate and $(Q \cdot P)$ is the value of total widget sales. How does a change in the price of potential substitutes for widgets affect the tax revenues received from the sale of widgets? Questions of this nature require the use of **differential calculus,** which is the subject of Part Three (Chapters 6 through 8). Differential calculus offers a set of tools for analyzing the responsiveness of the dependent variable of a function to changes in the value of one or more of its independent variables. These tools are useful in addressing questions such as the responsiveness of the demand for widgets to changes in their price. Chapter 6 provides an intuitive introduction to this subject. Rules of univariate calculus are presented in Chapter 7. Chapter 8 presents the techniques of multivariate calculus. This chapter builds your intuition for multivariate calculus by demonstrating the link between it and the important economic concept of *ceteris paribus,* that is, "all else held equal." The techniques presented in this chapter enable you to address the question of the responsiveness of tax revenues from the sale of widgets to a change in the price of the inputs to widget production.

An important application of differential calculus in economics is the identification of **extreme values,** that is, the largest or smallest value of a function. Part Four, consisting of Chapters 9 through 11, shows how to apply differential calculus in order to identify extreme values of functions. Chapter 9 illustrates how to use the tools of calculus to identify extreme values of functions that include only one independent variable. An example of an economic application of this technique is the identification of the optimal price set by a widget monopolist. Chapter 10 extends this analysis to functions with more than one independent variable. An application in that chapter illustrates how the widget monopolist could optimally set prices in two separate markets. Chapter 11 shows how to determine the extreme value of functions when their independent variables are constrained by certain conditions. This technique of **constrained optimization** explicitly captures the core economic concept of obtaining the best outcome in the face of trade-offs among alternatives. Given a target level of widget production, constrained optimization would be used to determine the optimal amounts of various inputs.

The book concludes with a discussion of **dynamic analysis** in Part Five. Dynamic analysis focuses on models in which time and the time path of variables are explicitly included. This part begins with Chapter 12, which presents **integral calculus.** A common use of integral calculus in economics is the valuation of streams of payments over time. For example, the widget manufacturer, recognizing that a dollar received today is not the same as a dollar received tomorrow, might want to value the stream of payments from selling widgets at different times. Another application of integral calculus, one not related to time, is the determination of consumer's surplus from the sale of widgets. We discuss consumer's surplus in two applications in Chapter 12. Chapters 13 and 14 show how to solve economic models that explicitly include a time dimension. In its discussion of **difference equations,** Chapter 13 focuses on models in which time is treated as a series of distinct periods. In its discussion of **differential equations,** Chapter 14 focuses on models in which time is treated as a continuous flow. Many common themes arise in the discussion of difference equations and of differential equations. Chapter 15 concludes this section with a presentation of **dynamic optimization,** a technique for solving for the optimal time path of variables. Dynamic optimization would enable us to analyze questions like the optimal investment strategy over time for a widget maker.

A Note on Studying This Material

As you study the material in this book, it is important to engage actively with the text rather than just to read it passively. When reading this book, keep a pencil and paper at hand, and replicate the chains of reasoning presented in the text. The problems presented at the end of each chapter section are an integral part of this book, and working through these problems is a vital part of your study of this material. It is also useful to go beyond the text by thinking yourself of examples or applications that arise in the other fields of economics that you are studying. An ability to do this demonstrates a mastery of the material presented here.

Chapter 2

An Introduction to Functions

Functions are the building blocks of explicit economic models. You have probably encountered the term "function" already in your economics education. Basic macroeconomic theory uses, for example, the *consumption function,* which shows how consumption varies with income. Basic microeconomic theory presents, among others, the *production function,* which shows how a firm's output varies with the level of its inputs. Just as M. Jourdain, the title character in Molière's *Le Bourgeois Gentilhomme,* remarked that he had been speaking prose all his life without knowing it, the material presented in this chapter may make you realize that you have been using mathematical functions during your entire economics education.

An ability to analyze and characterize functions used in economics is important for a complete understanding of the theory they are used to express. The concepts and tools introduced in this chapter provide the basis for analyzing and characterizing functions. Later chapters of this book will build on the concepts first introduced in this chapter.

This chapter opens with definitions of terms that are important for discussing functions. This section also includes an introduction to graphing functions. Section 2.2 discusses properties and characteristics of functions. Many of these characteristics are discussed in the context of graphs. There is also a discussion in this section of the logical concept of necessary and sufficient conditions. The final section of this chapter introduces some general forms of functions used extensively in economics.

2.1 A LEXICON FOR FUNCTIONS

A discussion of functions must begin with some definitions. In this section we define some basic concepts and terms. We also introduce the way in which functions can be depicted using graphs.

Variables and Their Values

As discussed in Chapter 1, economic models link the value of exogenous variables to the value of endogenous variables. The variables studied in economics may be qualitative or quantitative. A **qualitative variable** represents some distinguishing characteristic, such as male or female, working or unemployed, and Republican, Democrat or Independent. The relationship between values of a qualitative variable is not numerical. **Quantitative variables,** on the other hand, can be measured numerically. Familiar economic quantitative variables include the dollar value of national income, the number of barrels of imported oil, the consumer price level, and the dollar-yen exchange rate. Some quantitative variables, like population, may be expressed as an integer. An **integer** is a whole number like 1, 219, −32, or 0. The value of other variables, like a stock price, may fall between two integers. **Real numbers** include all integers and all numbers between the integers. Some real numbers can be expressed as ratios of integers, for example, $\frac{1}{2}$, 2.5, or $-3\frac{2}{5}$. These numbers are called **rational numbers.** Other real numbers, such as $\pi = 3.1415\ldots$ and $\sqrt{2}$, cannot be expressed as a ratio and are called **irrational numbers.**

In discussing functions we often refer to an **interval** rather than a single number. An interval is the set of all real numbers between two endpoints. Types of intervals are distinguished by the manner in which endpoints are treated. A **closed interval** includes the endpoints. The closed interval between 0 and 1.5 includes these two numbers and is written [0, 1.5]. An **open interval** between any two numbers excludes the endpoints. The open interval between 7 and 10 is written (7, 10). A **half-closed interval** or a **half-open interval** includes one endpoint but not the other. Notation for half-closed or half-open intervals follows from the notation for closed and open intervals. For example, if an interval includes the endpoint $-\frac{3}{2}$ but not the endpoint 1, it is written as $[-\frac{3}{2}, 1)$ An **infinite interval** has negative infinity, positive infinity, or both as endpoints. The closed interval of all positive numbers and zero is written as $[0, \infty)$. The open interval of all positive numbers is written as $(0, \infty)$. The interval of all real numbers is written as $(-\infty, \infty)$.

Sets and Functions

A **set** is simply a collection of items. The items included in a set are called its **elements.** Some examples of sets include "economists who have won a Nobel Prize by 2001," a set consisting of 46 elements, and "economists who would have liked to have won the Nobel Prize by 2001," a set with a membership that probably numbers in the thousands. Sets are represented by capital letters. To show that an item is an element of a set, we use the symbol ∈. For example, if we denote the set of all Nobel Prize–winning economists by N, then

$$\text{Paul Samuelson} \in N \qquad \text{Milton Friedman} \in N.$$

To show that elements are not members of a set, we use the symbol ∉. For example,

$$\text{Adam Smith} \notin N.$$

The set N can be described either by listing all its elements or by describing the conditions required for membership. Sets of numbers with a finite number of elements can be described similarly. For example, consider the set of all integers between $\frac{1}{2}$ and $5\frac{1}{2}$. We can describe this set by simply listing its five elements

$$S = \{1, 2, 3, 4, 5\}$$

Alternatively, we can describe the set by describing the conditions for membership

$$S = \left\{x \,\middle|\, x \text{ is an integer greater than } \frac{1}{2} \text{ and less than } 5\frac{1}{2}\right\}.$$

This statement is read as "S is the set of all numbers x such that x is an integer greater than $\frac{1}{2}$ and less than $5\frac{1}{2}$." Sets that have an infinite number of elements can be described by stating the condition for membership. For example, the set of all real numbers x in the closed interval $\left[\frac{1}{2}, 5\frac{1}{2}\right]$ can be written as

$$S = \left\{x \,\middle|\, \frac{1}{2} \leq x \leq 5\frac{1}{2}\right\}.$$

The elements of one set may be associated with the elements of another set through a **relationship.** A particular type of relationship, called a **function,** is a rule that associates each element of one set with a single element of another set. A function is also called a **mapping** or a **transformation.** A function f that unambiguously associates with each element of a set X one element in the set Y is written as

$$f : X \mapsto Y.$$

In this case, the set X is called the **domain** of the function f, and the set of values that occur is called the **range** of the function f.

An example of a function is the rule d that associates each member of the Nobel Prize–winning set N with the year in which he won the prize, an element of the set T:

$$d : N \mapsto T.$$

As shown in Figure 2.1, this function maps James Tobin, a member of N, to 1981, an element of the set T. This function also maps both Kenneth Arrow and Sir John Hicks, each a member of N, to 1972, an element of T, since Arrow and Hicks jointly shared the Nobel prize in that year. Note that the reverse relationship that associates the elements of the set T to the elements of the set N is not a function since there are cases where an element of T maps to two or more separate elements of N. For example, the year 1972, an element of T, is associated with two elements of N, Arrow and Hicks.

Univariate Functions

A **univariate function** maps one number, which is a member of the domain, to one and only one number, which is an element of the range. A standard way to represent a univariate function that maps any one element x of the set X to one and only one element y of the set Y is

$$y = f(x),$$

which is read as "y is a function of x" or "y equals f of x." In this case the variable y is called the **dependent variable** or the **value of the function,** and the variable x is called the **independent variable** or the **argument of the function.**

The Set of Nobel Laureates in Economics (N)			The Set of Years in Which the Nobel Prize was Awarded (T)
Ragnar Frisch	Jan Tinbergen		1969
Paul Samuelson			1970
Simon Kuznets			1971
Kenneth Arrow	John Hicks		1972
Wassily Leontief			1973
Gunnar Myrdal	Friedrich von Hayek		1974
Tjalling Koopmans	Leonid Kantorovich		1975
Milton Friedman			1976
Bertil Ohlin	James Meade		1977
Herbert Simon			1978
Theodore Schultz	Arthur Lewis		1979
Lawrence Klein			1980
James Tobin			1981
George Stigler			1982
Gerard Debreu			1983
Richard Stone			1984
Franco Modigliani			1985
James Buchanan			1986
Robert Solow			1987
Maurice Allais			1988
Trygve Haavelmo			1989
Harry Markowitz	William Sharpe	Merton Miller	1990
Ronald Coase			1991
Gary Becker			1992
Robert Fogel	Douglass North		1993
John Harsanyi	John Nash	Reinhard Selten	1994
Robert Lucas			1995
William Vickrey	James Mirrlees		1996
Robert Merton	Myron Scholes		1997
Amartya Sen			1998
Robert Mundell			1999
James Heckman	Daniel McFadden		2000

FIGURE 2.1 The Sets N and T

The term $f(x)$ can represent any relationship that assigns a unique value to y for any value of x, such as

$$y = \frac{1}{2}x^2 \quad \text{or}$$

$$y = \alpha + \beta x.$$

The numbers $\frac{1}{2}$ and 2 in the first function and the Greek letters α and β in the second function represent parameters. As discussed in Chapter 1, a **parameter** may be either a specific numerical value, like 2, or an unspecified constant, like β.

Given numerical parameter values, we can find the value of a univariate function for different values of its argument. For example, consider a basic Keynesian consumption function that relates consumption, C, to income, I, as

$$C = 300 + 0.6I, \tag{2.1}$$

TABLE 2.1 A Consumption Function

I	0	1000	2500	5000	9000
C	300	900	1800	3300	5700

where all variables represent billions of dollars and "300" stands for $300 billion. Table 2.1 reports the value of consumption for various values of income consistent with (2.1).

Graphing Univariate Functions

Table 2.1 illustrates the behavior of the consumption function by providing some values of its independent variable along with the associated value of its dependent variable. This table presents numbers that can be used to construct some ordered pairs of the consumption function. An **ordered pair** is two numbers presented in parentheses and separated by a comma, where the first number represents the argument of the function and the second number represents the corresponding value of the function. Thus each ordered pair for the function $y = f(x)$ takes the form (x, y). Some ordered pairs consistent with the consumption function presented previously are (1000, 900), (2500, 1800) and (5000, 3300).

Ordered pairs can be plotted in a **Cartesian plane** (named after the seventeenth-century French mathematician and philosopher René Descartes). A Cartesian plane, like the one presented in Figure 2.2, includes two lines, called axes, which cross at a right angle. The **origin** of the plane occurs at the intersection of the two axes. Points along the **horizontal axis,** also called the ***x*-axis,** of the Cartesian plane in Figure 2.2 represent values of the level of income, which are the arguments of this function. Points along the **vertical axis,** also called the ***y*-axis,** represent values of the level of consumption, which are the values of this function. The **coordinates** of a point are the values of its ordered pair and represent the address of that point in the plane. The x-coordinate of the pair (x, y) is called the **abscissa,** and the y-coordinate is called the **ordinate.** Thus the origin of a Cartesian plane is represented by the coordinates (0, 0). Two ordered pairs for the univariate consumption function are represented by points labeled with their coordinates in Figure 2.2.

We could continue this exercise by filling in more and more points consistent with the consumption function. Alternatively, we can plot the **graph** of the function.

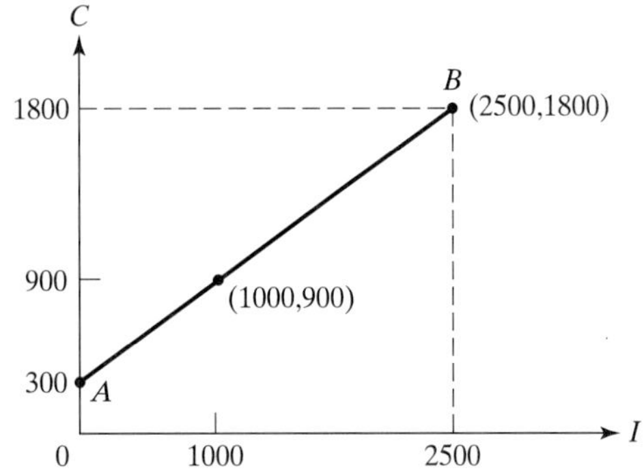

FIGURE 2.2 A Consumption Function

The graph of a function represents all points whose coordinates are ordered pairs of the function. The graph of the consumption function for the domain [0, 2500] is represented by the line *AB* in Figure 2.2. This graph goes through the first three points identified in Table 2.1 as well as all other points consistent with the consumption function over the relevant domain.

The consumption function depicted in Figure 2.2 is a particular example of a **linear function.** A linear function takes the form[1]

$$y = f(x) = a + bx. \tag{2.2}$$

The parameter a is the **intercept** of the function and represents the value of the function when its argument equals zero. In a graph, the intercept is the point where the function crosses the y-axis. The intercept of the consumption function is 300. The parameter b is the **slope** of the graph of the function. The slope of a univariate linear function represents the change in the value of the function associated with a given change in its argument. The slope of the linear function (2.2) evaluated between any two points x_A and x_B (for $x_A \neq x_B$) is

$$\left[\frac{f(x_B) - f(x_A)}{x_B - x_A}\right] = \frac{(a + bx_B) - (a + bx_A)}{x_B - x_A} = b,$$

where $f(x)_B - f(x_A)$ is the change in the value of the function associated with the change in its argument $x_B - x_A$. This result shows that the slope of a linear function is constant and equal to the parameter b. For example, the slope of the consumption function presented above is 0.6.

Figure 2.2 presents a plane with only one quadrant since the domain and the range of the consumption function are restricted to include only positive numbers. Many economic functions include both positive and negative numbers as arguments and values. Graphs of these functions can be represented with other quadrants of the Cartesian plane. In Figure 2.3 the function

$$y = -4 - 2x + 2x^2$$

is presented. You can verify that this function includes the four ordered pairs $(-2, 8)$, $(-\frac{1}{2}, -2\frac{1}{2})$, $(\frac{1}{2}, -4\frac{1}{2})$, and $(3, 8)$. Each of these ordered pairs is in a different quadrant of the Cartesian plane, which indicates that the graph of this function passes through all four quadrants.

Multivariate Functions

A **multivariate function** has more than one argument. For example, the general form of a multivariate function with the dependent variable y and the three independent variables x_1, x_2, and x_3 is

$$y = f(x_1, x_2, x_3).$$

[1]Strictly speaking, a univariate linear function takes the form $y = bx$ and a function of the form $y = a + bx$ is called an **affine function.** Following convention, we use the term linear function to mean an affine function.

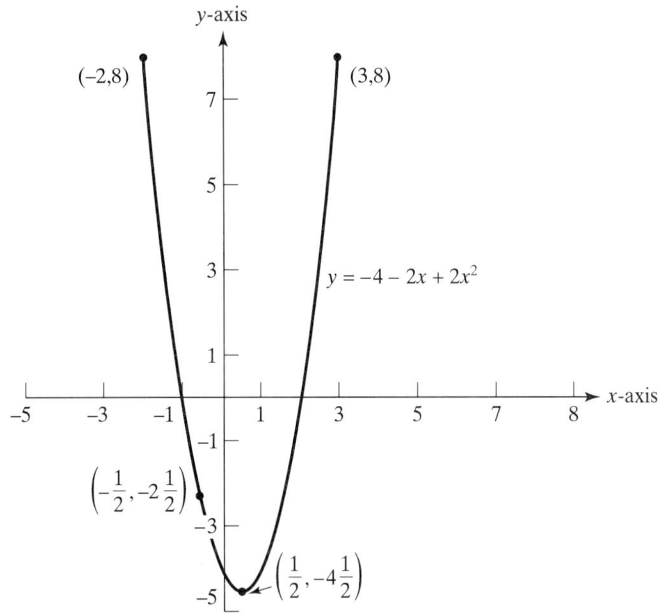

FIGURE 2.3 Graph of Function Filling Four Quadrants

Note that here we have used subscripts to distinguish among the different independent variables. Even more generally, a multivariate function with n independent variables denoted x_1, x_2, and so on, can be written as

$$y = f(x_1, x_2, \ldots, x_n).$$

A multivariate function with two independent variables is called a **bivariate function.** Some specific bivariate functions include

$$j = 5 + 4k^3 + 7h \quad \text{and}$$
$$Q = \lambda K^{\alpha} L^{\beta}.$$

The first function includes the dependent variable j, the independent variables k and h, and the parameters 5, 4, 3, and 7. The second function includes the dependent variable Q, the independent variables K and L, and the parameters λ, α, and β.

The set of arguments and the corresponding value of a multivariate function can also be represented by ordered groupings of numbers. For example, the bivariate consumption function

$$C = 300 + 0.6I + 0.02W, \tag{2.3}$$

where W represents wealth and all variables are expressed in billions of dollars, generates **ordered triples** of the form (I, W, C). Two of the ordered triples for this bivariate consumption function are (5000, 60000, 4500) and (8000, 40000, 5900).

It is also possible to depict a bivariate function in a figure, although this demands greater drafting skills than the depiction of a univariate function since the surface of a piece of paper has only two dimensions. Nevertheless, we can give the illusion of three

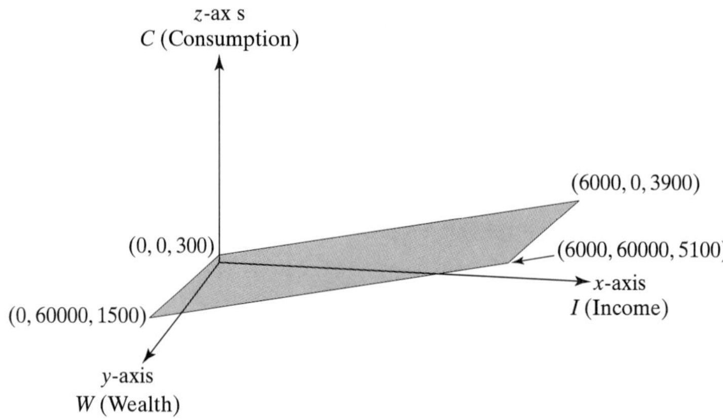

FIGURE 2.4 A Multivariate Consumption Function

dimensions when depicting a function of the form $z = f(x, y)$ by drawing the x-axis as a horizontal line to the right of the origin, the y-axis as a line sloping down and to the left from the origin, and the z-axis as a vertical line rising from the origin as shown in Figure 2.4. This figure depicts the multivariate consumption function (2.3). The x- and y-axes of this graph represent the values of income and wealth, respectively. The values of the function, which are the consumption values, are represented by the heights of the points in the graphed plane above the I-W surface.

Limits and Continuity

It is often necessary in economics to evaluate a function as its argument approaches some value. For example, in the next chapter we will learn how to find the value today of an infinitely-long stream of future payments. In the dynamic analysis presented in Part Five of this book, we solve for the long-run level of a variable. In these cases the argument of the function is time, and we evaluate the value of the function as time approaches infinity. In Part Three of this book we will learn how to evaluate the effect of a very small change in the argument of a function. We show that there is a correspondence between this mathematical technique and the economic concept of evaluating the effect "at the margin." In this section we show how to evaluate a function as its argument approaches a certain value by introducing the concept of a **limit.**

The limit of a function as its argument approaches some number a is simply the number that the function's value approaches as the argument approaches a, either from smaller values of a, giving the **left-hand limit,** or from larger values of a, giving the **right-hand limit.**

Left-Hand Limit The left-hand limit of a function $f(x)$ as its argument approaches some number a, written as

$$\lim_{x \to a^-} f(x),$$

exists and is equal to L^L if, for any arbitrarily small number ϵ, there exists a small number δ such that

$$|f(x) - L^L| < \epsilon$$

whenever $a - \delta < x < a$. ■

Right-Hand Limit The right-hand limit of a function $f(x)$ as its argument approaches some number a, written as

$$\lim_{x \to a^+} f(x),$$

exists and is equal to L^R if for any arbitrarily small number ϵ, there exists a small number δ such that

$$|f(x) - L^R| < \epsilon$$

whenever $a < x < a + \delta$. ■

When the left-hand limit equals the right-hand limit, we can simplify the notation by suppressing the superscripts and defining

$$\lim_{x \to a} f(x) = \lim_{x \to a^-} f(x) = \lim_{x \to a^+} f(x).$$

The limit of a function as its argument approaches some number a equals positive infinity if the value of the function increases without bound, and the limit equals negative infinity if the value of the function decreases without bound. Formally,

$$\lim_{x \to a} f(x) = +\infty$$

if, for every $N > 0$, there is a $\delta > 0$ so that

$$f(x) > N$$

whenever $a - \delta < x < a + \delta$. Also, we have

$$\lim_{x \to a} f(x) = -\infty$$

if, for every $N < 0$, there is a $\delta > 0$ so that

$$f(x) < N$$

whenever $a - \delta < x < a + \delta$.

Evaluating the limits used in this book involves the following two simple rules.

Rules for Evaluating Limits The following two rules are used in evaluating limits:

$$\lim_{x \to 0^+} m(k + x) = \lim_{x \to 0^-} m(k + x) = mk$$

and

$$\lim_{x \to \infty} \frac{k}{(m \cdot x) + h} = 0,$$

where k, m, and h are arbitrary real numbers and m $\neq 0$.

Two applications of these rules are shown below:

$$\lim_{n \to 0^+} \left(\frac{6n - 4n^2}{2n} \right) = \lim_{n \to 0^+} (3 - 2n) = 3$$

and

$$\lim_{t \to \infty} \left(\frac{1}{t - 3} + 5 \right) = 5.$$

The limits in these two examples are finite. The following are examples of limits that are infinite:

$$\lim_{n \to 5^-} \left(\frac{1}{5 - n} \right) = +\infty$$

and

$$\lim_{t \to 7^+} \left(\frac{-2}{t - 7} + 10 \right) = -\infty.$$

One use of limits in the context of the material presented in this book is to determine whether a function is **continuous.** Intuitively, a continuous univariate function has no "breaks" or "jumps." A more formal definition follows.

Continuity A function $f(x)$ is continuous at $x = a$, where a is in the domain of f, if the left- and right-hand limits at $x = a$ exist and are equal,

$$\lim_{x \to a} f(x) = \lim_{x \to a^-} f(x) = \lim_{x \to a^+} f(x),$$

and the limit as $x \to a$ equals the value of the function at that point,

$$\lim_{x \to a} f(x) = f(a).$$

Figure 2.5(a) presents a function that is not continuous at $x = x_0$ since, at that value, there is a "hole" in the function and the limit there does not equal the value of the function at x_0. When both a left-hand limit and a right-hand limit exist, the first part of the definition requires that each approach the same value for the function to be continuous. Figure 2.5(b) presents a total cost curve that is not continuous at

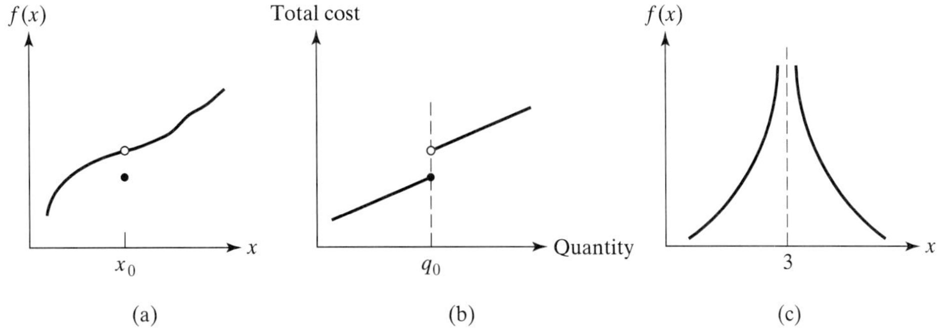

FIGURE 2.5 Functions That Are Not Continuous

$q = q_0$ since the purchase of an additional piece of capital, like a new factory or new equipment, which requires a large one-time cost, is required to increase output above q_0.

The second part of the definition shows that even if the left-hand limit and the right-hand limit of a function exist and are equal at a, it is also necessary for the function to be defined at a for the function to be continuous. This requirement is made clear by considering the function $f(x) = [1/(x - 3)]^2 + 5$ as x approaches 3. The left-hand limit and the right-hand limit are the same since

$$\lim_{x \to 3^-} \left(\frac{1}{x - 3}\right)^2 + 5 = \lim_{x \to 3^+} \left(\frac{1}{x - 3}\right)^2 + 5 = \infty.$$

However, this function is not defined at $x = 3$ since the term $\frac{1}{0}$ is not defined. Figure 2.5(c) illustrates that this function has a **vertical asymptote** at $x = 3$. A vertical asymptote of a function occurs at a point when either a left-hand limit or a right-hand limit approaches positive infinity or negative infinity at that point. A function is discontinuous at a point where there is a vertical asymptote.

Exercises 2.1

1. Use the notation for intervals to represent each of the following specified intervals of x
   (a) $-5 < x < 0$
   (b) $-5 \leq x < 0$
   (c) $x < 100$
   (d) $100 \geq x$
   (e) x is a positive number greater than zero
   (f) x is a real number
2. Determine which of the following relationships represent functions. Assume that the interval is the set of real numbers unless otherwise indicated.

(a) $y = 5x$

(b) $y \leq x$

(c) $y = a + \sqrt{x}$; $(0, \infty)$

(d) $y = -x^2$

(e) $y^2 = x$

(f) $y = \dfrac{1}{x - 3}$; $(0, \infty)$

(g) $y^2 = x^4$; $(0, \infty)$

3. In the following problems, set X represents the domain and Y is the set of values that occur with a potential function, f. Confirm whether the function f can be defined according to the mapping $f: X \to Y$.
   (a) Set X consists of all the alumni of Anycollege University; set Y is each alumnus' alma mater.
   (b) Set X consists of the workers at Busy Firm; set Y is each worker's social security number.
   (c) Set X consists of all the people who have shared the prize for Best-Dressed Celebrity in any given year; set Y consists of the years in which the Best-Dressed Celebrity prize was shared.
   (d) Set X is a set of fathers; set Y is the set of their sons.
4. Consider again the functional mapping $d: N \to T$ where N is the set of Nobel Prize winners and T is the set of years in which the prizes were won. If an economist wins the prize for a second time, would this still be a valid function? Explain.
5. The total cost of a firm can be expressed as a simple univariate function in which cost, C, is a function of the firm's daily output, Q. Assume that the total cost function is $C = 75 + 5Q$.
   (a) Calculate the firm's total cost when $Q = 10$ and $Q = 25$. What are the firm's costs if there is no production?
   (b) Graph this firm's total cost function based on your answers to question 5(a).
   (c) Now assume that the firm faces a capacity constraint and cannot produce more than 50 units of output a day. What are the domain and range of the cost function in this scenario?
6. Identify and graph four ordered pairs for each of the following functions. Sketch a graph of each of the functions.
   (a) $y = 100 - 20x$ over the interval $[-2, 6]$
   (b) $y = -x - x^3$ over the interval $(-5, 5)$
   (c) $y = x^2 + 1$ over the interval $[-100, 100]$
7. Evaluate the following limits.
   (a) $y = \lim_{x \to \infty} \dfrac{1}{x - 7} + 2$
   (b) $y = \lim_{x \to 7^+} \dfrac{1}{x - 7} + 2$

(c) $y = \lim_{x \to 1^+} \sqrt{x - 1} + 7$

(d) $y = \lim_{x \to 1} \dfrac{1 - 2x + x^2}{1 - x}$

(*Hint*: Transform the ratio to remove x from the denominator.)

8. Which functions are continuous over the given intervals?

(a) $y = 8 + \dfrac{1}{x - 7}$; $(0, \infty)$

(b) $y = \dfrac{4 - ax}{7}$; $(-\infty, \infty)$

(c) $y = -3 + \dfrac{1}{x + 7}$; $(0, \infty)$

(d) $y = |2x - 4|$; $[-3, 3]$

9. Is the function presented in question 8(c) continuous over the domain $(-\infty, 0]$? Explain. If the function is not continuous, at what point (or points) in this domain is the function discontinuous?

2.2 PROPERTIES OF FUNCTIONS

Much of the analysis of economic functions involves characterizing these functions and understanding the economic relevance of these mathematical characteristics. In this section we introduce a number of properties of functions. Many of these properties are illustrated through the use of graphs, and thus we define and illustrate these properties in the context of univariate functions. In later chapters we return to these properties, sometimes presenting alternative (though equivalent) definitions and sometimes generalizing the definitions to multivariate functions. Later chapters also stress the economic interpretation of these properties.

Increasing Functions and Decreasing Functions

The graph of the consumption function in Figure 2.2 shows that consumption consistently rises as income rises. The value of other functions used in economics may consistently decrease as the argument of the function increases. For example, most specifications of demand functions have the quantity demanded of a good steadily decrease as the price of that good increases. A function $y = f(x)$ is **increasing, strictly increasing, decreasing,** or **strictly decreasing** if it meets the following criteria for any two of its arguments, x_A and x_B, where $x_B > x_A$.

A function is **increasing** if $f(x_B) \geq f(x_A)$.
A function is **strictly increasing** if $f(x_B) > f(x_A)$.
A function is **decreasing** if $f(x_B) \leq f(x_A)$.
A function is **strictly decreasing** if $f(x_B) < f(x_A)$.

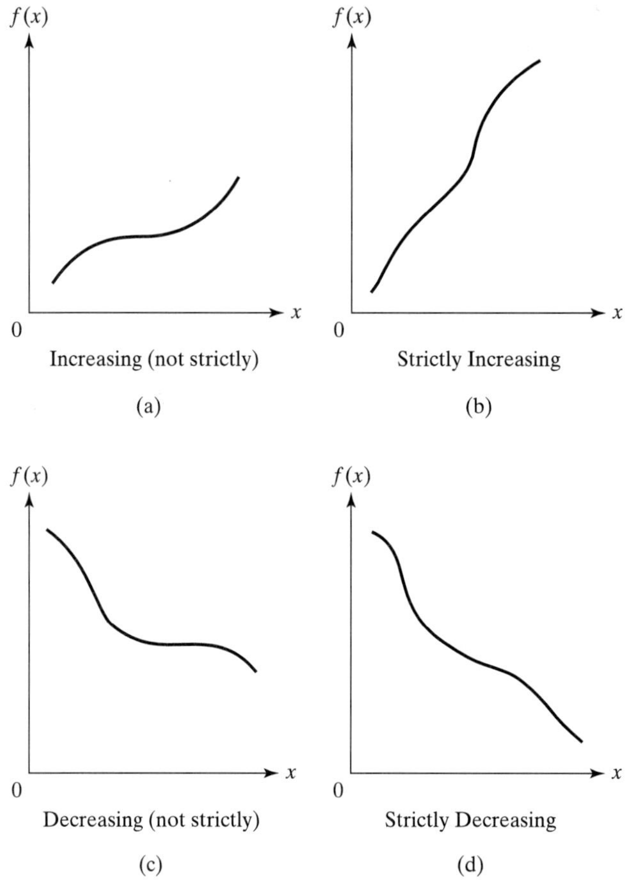

FIGURE 2.6 Increasing Functions and Decreasing Functions

These definitions show that any strictly increasing function is also an increasing function, and any strictly decreasing function is also a decreasing function. An increasing function, however, may not be a strictly increasing function since an increasing function may have a section where $f(x_B) = f(x_A)$. This is illustrated in Figure 2.6. The increasing function in Figure 2.6(a) has a horizontal section, which precludes it from being a strictly increasing function. Figure 2.6(b) is strictly increasing. Figures 2.6(c) and 2.6(d) present graphs of a decreasing and a strictly decreasing function, respectively.

Closely related to these definitions of increasing and decreasing functions are the definitions of a **monotonic function, a strictly monotonic function,** and a **non-monotonic function.**

A function is:

monotonic if it is increasing or if it is decreasing.

strictly monotonic if it is strictly increasing or if it is strictly decreasing.

non-monotonic if it is strictly increasing over some interval and strictly decreasing over another interval.

Non-monotonic functions can have the same value for more than one argument. For example, the value of the non-monotonic function $y = x^2$ is 4 for both $x = 2$ and $x = -2$. In contrast, strictly monotonic functions unambiguously assign only one value to any argument. Therefore, strictly monotonic functions are **one-to-one functions** and have the following property.

One-to-One Function A function $f(x)$ is one-to-one if for any two values of the argument x_1 and x_2,

$$f(x_1) = f(x_2) \quad \text{implies} \quad x_1 = x_2.$$

Any one-to-one function has an **inverse function.** The inverse of the function $y = f(x)$ is written as $y = f^{-1}(x)$.[2] We find the inverse of a function $y = f(x)$ by solving for x in terms of y and then interchanging x and y to obtain $y = f^{-1}(x)$. For example, the inverse of the one-to-one function

$$y = f(x) = 4 + 2x \tag{2.4}$$

can be found by solving this for x in terms of y to get

$$x = -2 + \frac{1}{2}y$$

and then interchanging x and y to obtain the inverse function

$$y = f^{-1}(x) = -2 + \frac{1}{2}x.$$

An important property of a function $f(x)$ and its inverse $f^{-1}(x)$ is

$$f(f^{-1}(x)) = x \quad \text{and} \quad f^{-1}(f(x)) = x.$$

The term $f(f^{-1}(x))$ represents a **composite function.** The argument of a composite function is itself a function. For example,

$$y = g(h(x))$$

is a composite function with the **inside function** $h(x)$ and the **outside function** $g(\bullet)$ where the symbol $\bullet$ is a placeholder for the argument of the function g. The outside function for the composite function

$$f(f^{-1}(x))$$

is $f(\bullet)$, and the inside function is its inverse. For example, using the function (2.4), we have

$$f(f^{-1}(x)) = 4 + 2\left(-2 + \frac{1}{2}x\right) = x$$

---

[2]It is important to note that $f^{-1}(x)$ does *not* mean $1/f(x)$.

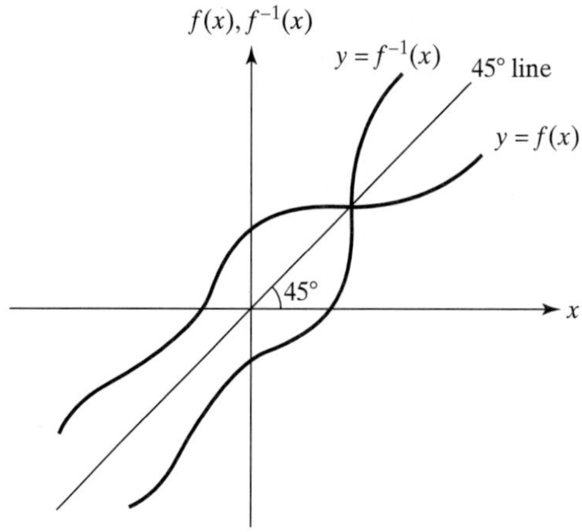

FIGURE 2.7 A Function and Its Inverse

and

$$f^{-1}(f(x)) = -2 + \frac{1}{2}(4 + 2x) = x.$$

There is a simple method for graphing the inverse of a function, $y = f^{-1}(x)$ given the graph of the function $y = f(x)$. This method makes use of the fact that for any given ordered pair (a, b) associated with a one-to-one function, there will be an ordered pair (b, a) associated with its inverse function. For example, one ordered pair associated with the function (2.4) is (2, 8), and an ordered pair associated with its inverse is (8, 2). To graph $y = f^{-1}(x)$, we make use of the **45° line,** which is the graph of the function $y = x$ that passes through all points of the form (a, a). The graph of the function $y = f^{-1}(x)$ is the **reflection** of the graph of $f(x)$ across the line $y = x$. This is illustrated in Figure 2.7. You can think of the reflection across $y = x$ as the graph that is created when you fold the original figure along the 45° line. The coordinates (a, b) of the original function become the coordinates (b, a) of the inverse function. This property of inverse functions will be important in our study of logarithmic and exponential functions in Chapter 3.

Extreme Values

It is often important in economic analysis to identify and characterize the largest or smallest value of a function. For example, we may want to know what price a monopolist should charge to obtain the largest amount of profits or what combination of inputs offers a producer the lowest level of average cost. The **extreme value** of a function within some interval is the largest or smallest value of that function within that interval. The largest value of a function over its entire range is called its **global maximum,** and the smallest value of a function over its entire range is called its **global minimum.** The largest value within a small interval is called a **local maximum.** The smallest value within a small interval is called a **local minimum.**

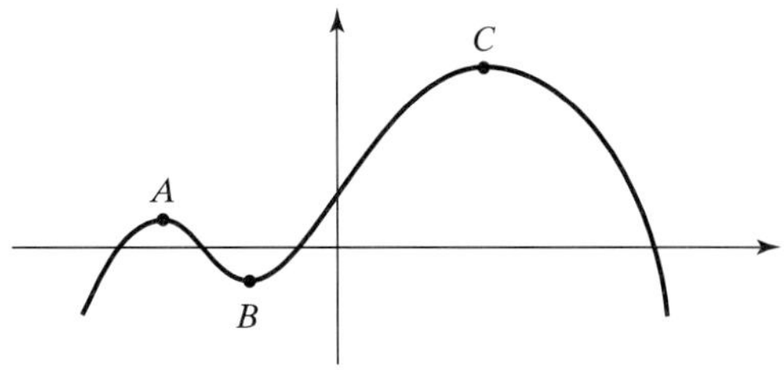

FIGURE 2.8 A Function with Extreme Values

The maximum and minimum of a monotonic function within some closed interval occurs at that interval's endpoints. An illustration of this is provided by the consumption function in Figure 2.2, which has as its domain the closed interval [0, 2500]. The range of this function is then the closed interval [300, 1800]. The global minimum of this strictly increasing function is the y-value of its left endpoint, 300, and its global maximum is the y-value of its right endpoint, 1800.

A continuous function that is non-monotonic over some interval has at least one local minimum or at least one local maximum within that interval. For example, the function presented in Figure 2.3 has a global minimum at the point $(\frac{1}{2}, -4\frac{1}{2})$. The function depicted in Figure 2.8 has a local maximum at point A, a local minimum at point B, and a global maximum at point C.

In Chapters 9 and 10 we will learn how to use calculus to identify and characterize extreme values of functions. The applications in that chapter illustrate a number of uses of these techniques in economic analysis.

The Average Rate of Change of a Function

There are many concepts in economics that concern the extent to which one variable changes in response to a change in another variable. When these two variables are linked by a function, as with consumption and income or quantity demanded and price, the average rate of change can be calculated using that function.

The **average rate of change** of a function over some interval is the ratio of the change of the value of the dependent variable to the change in the value of the independent variable over that interval.

Average Rate of Change The average rate of change of the function $y = f(x)$ over the closed interval $[x_A, x_B]$ is

$$\frac{\Delta y}{\Delta x} = \frac{f(x_B) - f(x_A)}{x_B - x_A}.$$

We can use this formula to calculate the average rate of change of the univariate consumption function (2.1),

$$C = C(I) = 300 + 0.6I,$$

over the closed interval [1000, 9000] of the domain. It is straightforward to show that $C(1000) = 900$ and $C(9000) = 5700$. Therefore the average rate of change is

$$\frac{\Delta C}{\Delta I} = \frac{C(9000) - C(1000)}{9000 - 1000} = \frac{4800}{8000} = 0.6.$$

Notice that this average rate of change is constant and equal to the slope of the function. In general, the average rate of change of any linear function

$$y = a + bx$$

over any nonzero interval equals the slope of that function, b. This can be shown by using the average rate of change formula over the arbitrary closed interval $[x_A, x_B]$. The average rate of change is equal to

$$\frac{\Delta y}{\Delta x} = \frac{(a + bx_B) - (a + bx_A)}{x_B - x_A} = \frac{bx_B - bx_A}{x_B - x_A} = \frac{b(x_B - x_A)}{x_B - x_A} = b.$$

The average rate of change of a nonlinear function is not constant, but instead depends upon the interval over which the rate of change is defined. For example, consider the function

$$y = \frac{1}{3}x^2.$$

The average rate of change of this function over the closed interval [0, 3] is

$$\frac{\Delta y}{\Delta x} = \frac{(1/3)(3^2) - (1/3)(0^2)}{3 - 0} = \frac{3}{3} = 1.$$

The average rate of change of this function over the closed interval [0, 6] is

$$\frac{\Delta y}{\Delta x} = \frac{(1/3)(6^2) - (1/3)(0^2)}{6 - 0} = \frac{12 - 0}{6} = 2,$$

while the average rate of change of this function over the closed interval [−3, 0] is

$$\frac{\Delta y}{\Delta x} = \frac{(1/3)(0^2) - (1/3)(-3^2)}{0 - (-3)} = \frac{0 - 3}{3} = -1.$$

The average rate of change of a function over some interval can be depicted using a **secant line.** A secant line connects two points on the graph of a function with a straight line. Any point (x', y') on the secant line connecting the two points (x_A, y_A) and (x_B, y_B) will satisfy the equation

$$(y' - y_A) = \left[\frac{f(x_B) - f(x_A)}{x_B - x_A}\right](x' - x_A), \tag{2.5}$$

where $y_A = f(x_A)$ and $y_B = f(x_B)$. For any point (x', y') on the line, x' is within the interval $[x_A, x_B]$, and y' is within the interval $[y_A, y_B]$. Note that the term in square brackets in the equation is the slope of the secant line. The value of the slope of the secant line represents the average rate of change of the function over the interval

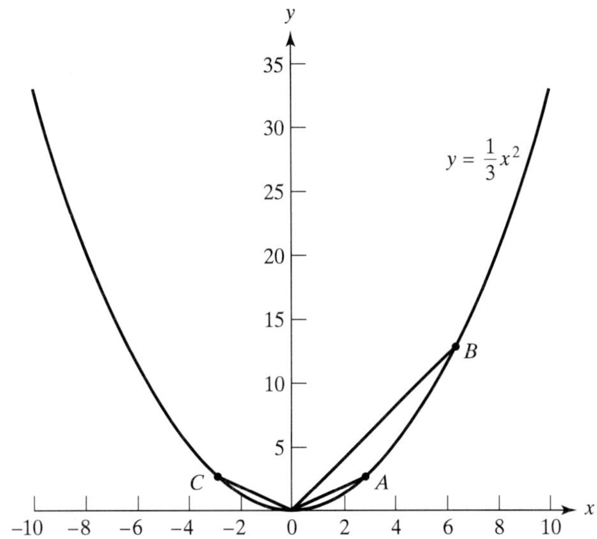

FIGURE 2.9 Secant Lines

defined by the two endpoints of the secant line. For example, Figure 2.9 is a graph of the equation $y = (1/3)x^2$. The secant line $0A$ connects points 0 and 3 on the graph, and the slope of this line is 1. The secant line $0B$ connects the points 0 and 6 in this figure, and the slope of this line is 2. The secant line $C0$ connects points -3 and 0, and its slope equals -1.

Concavity and Convexity

An important concept in economics is "diminishing marginal utility." A simple example of this is that you would get more pleasure from the first cookie than from the fifth cookie at a particular sitting. A utility function that reflects this type of preference cannot be linear, however, since the constant slope in a linear function implies that each cookie provides the same amount of utility. Instead, utility functions are typically drawn as bowed, as in Figure 2.10(a) where utility is measured along the y-axis and number of cookies is measured along the x-axis.

The **concavity** of a univariate function is reflected by the shape of its graph, and different categories of concavity can be illustrated through the use of secant lines. The functions depicted in Figures 2.10(a) and 2.10(b) are each **strictly concave** in the interval $[x_A, x_B]$ since any secant line drawn in that interval lies wholly below the respective function. The functions depicted in Figures 2.10(c) and 2.10(d) are each **strictly convex** in the interval $[x_A, x_B]$ since any secant line drawn in that interval lies wholly above the function. These graphs illustrate that whether a function is strictly concave or strictly convex is distinct from whether that function is strictly increasing or strictly decreasing.

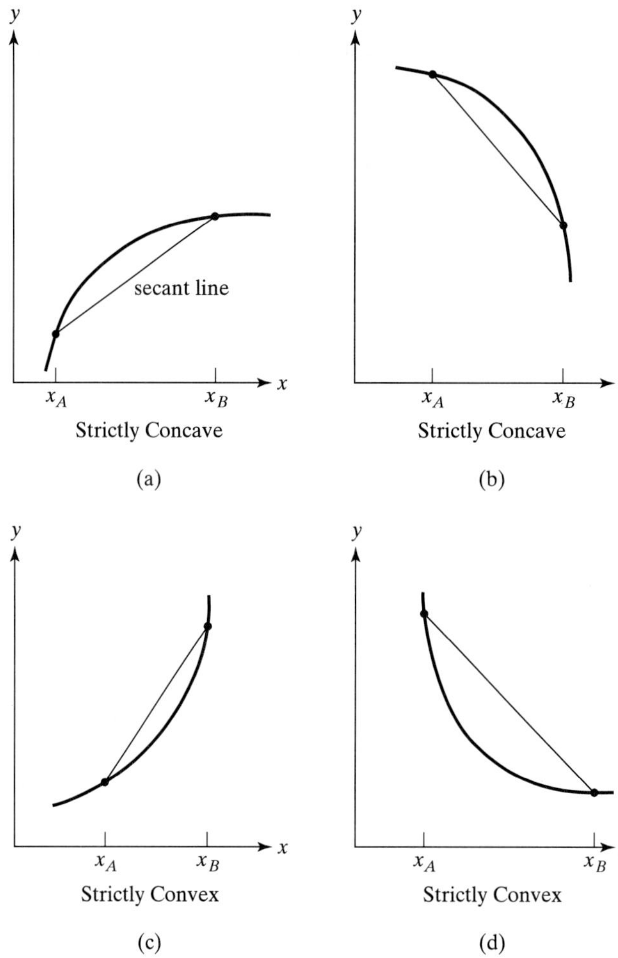

FIGURE 2.10 Strictly Concave and Strictly Convex Functions

A formal set of definitions for concavity and convexity are given here.

Strictly Concave The function $f(x)$ is strictly concave in an interval if, for any two distinct points x^A and x^B in that interval, and for all values of λ in the open interval $(0, 1)$,

$$f(\lambda x^A + (1 - \lambda)x^B) > \lambda f(x^A) + (1 - \lambda)f(x^B).$$

Strictly Convex The function $f(x)$ is strictly convex in an interval if, for any two distinct points x^A and x^B in that interval, and for all values of λ in the open interval $(0, 1)$,

$$f(\lambda x^A + (1 - \lambda)x^B) < \lambda f(x^A) + (1 - \lambda)f(x^B).$$

How are these definitions linked to the descriptions using secant lines? We can demonstrate that the two definitions are identical by using some algebra and the equation for a secant line (2.5) given previously. There are three steps.

1. For any given value of λ within the interval $(0, 1)$, the value of a particular argument of the function in the interval (x_A, x_B) is $x' = \lambda x_A + (1 - \lambda)x_B$, where $x_A < x' < x_B$. The value of the function at the point x' equals
$$f(x') = f(\lambda x_A + (1 - \lambda)x_B).$$
2. Using the definition for the secant line, we find that the value of the secant line at x', which we call y', can be found with (2.5). Using the definition for x', we have
$$\begin{aligned}(y' - y^A) &= \left[\frac{f(x_B) - f(x_A)}{x_B - x_A}\right]([\lambda x_A + (1 - \lambda)x_B] - x_A)\\ &= \left[\frac{f(x_B) - f(x_A)}{x_B - x_A}\right](1 - \lambda)(x_B - x_A)\\ &= (1 - \lambda)[f(x_B) - f(x_A)].\end{aligned}$$
Since $y_A = f(x_A)$, if we add $f(x_A)$ to each side, we have
$$y' = \lambda f(x_A) + (1 - \lambda)f(x_B).$$
3. The definition of a function that is strictly concave within an interval requires that the value of the function at any point within that interval, $f(x')$, is greater than the value of the secant line at that point, y'. Likewise, the definition for a strictly convex function within an interval requires that the value of the function at any point within that interval, $f(x')$, is less than the value of the secant line at that point, y'. Examining the solution for y' demonstrates that the algebraic definitions for a strictly concave interval and a strictly convex interval are identical to the respective definitions based on the secant line in a graph.

A numerical example illustrates this definition. Consider the function
$$y = 20x - 2x^2$$
over the interval $[0, 4]$. Let $\lambda = \frac{1}{2}$, so $x' = 2$. In this case,
$$\lambda f(x^A) + (1 - \lambda)f(x^B) = \frac{1}{2}0 + \frac{1}{2}48 = 24$$
and
$$f(\lambda x^A + (1 - \lambda)x^B) = f(2) = 32.$$
For $\lambda = \frac{1}{2}$,
$$f(\lambda x^A + (1 - \lambda)x^B) > \lambda f(x^A) + (1 - \lambda)f(x^B).$$
In fact, this inequality holds for any value of λ between 0 and 1 for this function over the interval $[0, 4]$ or indeed over any interval. Therefore this function is strictly concave.

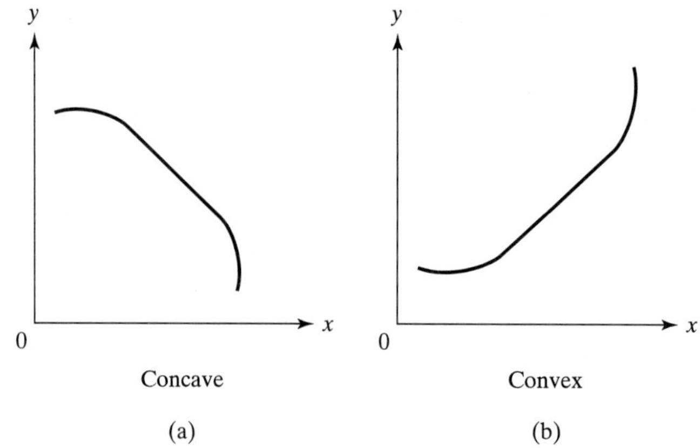

FIGURE 2.11 Concave and Convex Functions

A related pair of definitions for concave and convex functions are given below.

Concave The function $f(x)$ is concave in an interval if, for any two points in that interval x_A and x_B, and for all values of λ in the open interval (0, 1),

$$f(\lambda x_A + (1 - \lambda)x_B) \geq \lambda f(x_A) + (1 - \lambda)f(x_B).$$

Convex The function $f(x)$ is convex in an interval if, for any two points in that interval x_A and x_B, and for all values of λ in the open interval (0, 1),

$$f(\lambda x_A + (1 - \lambda)x_B) \leq \lambda f(x_A) + (1 - \lambda)f(x_B).$$

A function can have a linear segment within an interval and still be concave or convex, as shown in Figures 2.11(a) and 2.11(b), respectively. The functions depicted in these figures fail the requirement of being strictly concave or strictly convex since along the linear segments of the functions

$$f(\lambda x_A + (1 - \lambda)x_B) = \lambda f(x_A) + (1 - \lambda)f(x_B).$$

Alternative definitions of concavity and convexity that draw on the tools of calculus are offered in Chapter 7. In that chapter we show how the concavity of a function is important in a number of areas of economic analysis, including consumption theory and production theory.

Necessary and Sufficient Conditions

An important concept, one that is used repeatedly throughout this book, is that of **necessary and sufficient conditions.** This concept enables us to understand what logical conclusions follow from certain conditions and the relationships among different categories of things. For example, consider a function that we know to be concave. Can we conclude that the function is also strictly concave? The answer, as illustrated by Figure 2.11(a), is "no." If a function is strictly concave, then it is necessarily concave. The fact that a function is concave, however, is not sufficient for concluding that it is also strictly concave.

This concept of necessary and sufficient conditions can be expressed using symbols. The symbol $\Rightarrow$ means "implies," and therefore, the expression

$$P \Rightarrow Q$$

means "if P then Q," "P implies Q," or "P only if Q." The condition P is a **sufficient condition** for Q since if P holds, it follows that Q also holds. Also, this expression shows that the condition Q is a **necessary condition** for P since P cannot hold unless Q also holds.

To illustrate this, consider the relationship between strictly concave and concave functions. The discussion above shows that for the function f,

$$f \text{ strictly concave} \Rightarrow f \text{ concave.}$$

This expression states that strict concavity is a sufficient condition for concavity. Equivalently, this expression states that concavity is a necessary condition for strict concavity.

In the case of the relationship between strictly concave and concave functions, the implication runs in one direction only. In other examples we can have the direction of implication running in each direction, that is,

$$P \Rightarrow Q \quad \text{and} \quad P \Leftarrow Q,$$

which can be written more succinctly as

$$P \Leftrightarrow Q.$$

This is read as "P if and only if Q," "P is equivalent to Q," or "P is a necessary and sufficient condition for Q." In the context of concavity, we can use the necessary and sufficient condition expression to write

$$f \text{ is concave} \Leftrightarrow f(\lambda x^A + (1 - \lambda)x^B) \geq \lambda f(x^A) + (1 - \lambda)f(x^B)$$

for $x^A \neq x^B$ and for any value of λ between 0 and 1.

An example drawn from basic microeconomics further illustrates the relationship between necessary and sufficient conditions. Consider the market for personal computers as depicted by the demand and supply diagrams in Figure 2.12. In this example we consider only two possible exogenous variables, personal income and computer-manufacturing productivity. A decrease in personal income, which we denote as event I, shifts the demand curve for computers to the left. As depicted in Figure 2.12(a), this causes the equilibrium to shift from point a to point b, causing the price of computers to fall and the quantity of computers purchased to decrease. Figure 2.12(b) depicts the supply-side effects of an increase in computer-manufacturing productivity, which we denote as event M, that causes the equilibrium to shift from point g to point h. As shown in this figure, the rightward shift of the supply curve causes the price of computers to fall but, in this case, the quantity of computers purchased rises. If we denote a fall in the price of computers as event F, then we have

$$I \Rightarrow F$$

and

$$M \Rightarrow F.$$

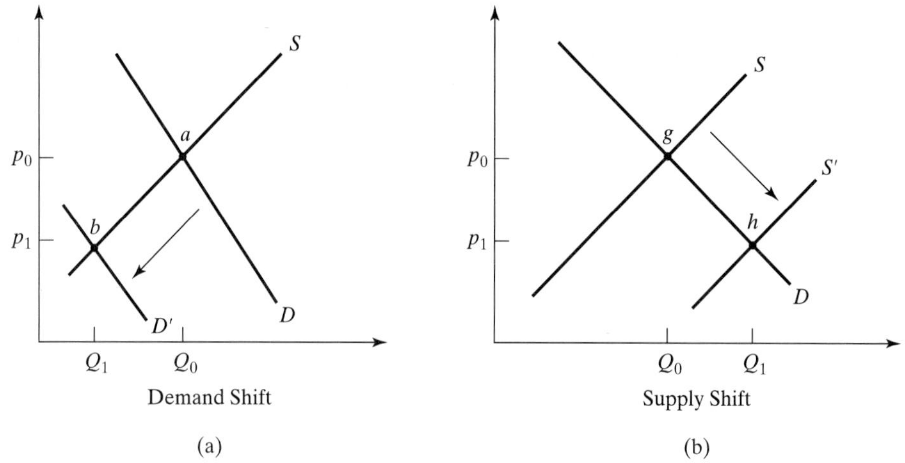

FIGURE 2.12 Demand and Supply for PCs

Thus either I or M is sufficient for F. But I is not necessary for F since the price of computers would also fall if M occurred. So we cannot know, when we observe F, if the cause was M or I.

If we had information on quantity as well as price, then we could distinguish between the two cases. For example, suppose that we observe both an increase in the numbers of computers purchased and a decrease in the price of computers, which we label event S. In the context of this simple example, the demand and supply analysis indicates that

$$M \Leftrightarrow S.$$

On the other hand, if we observe that the price decrease is accompanied by a decrease in the quantity of computers purchased, which we denote as event D, we could conclude that there is a shift in demand since, in this example,

$$I \Leftrightarrow D.$$

Thus evidence on price and quantity in this simple example (that is, knowing S or D instead of merely F) enables us to distinguish between a supply-side shock (M) and a demand-side shock (I).

Exercises 2.2

1. Determine whether the following functions are monotonic, strictly monotonic, or non-monotonic.
   (a) $y = a + bx; b > 0$
   (b) $y = ax^2; a < 0$
   (c) $y = ax + bx^3; a > 0, b > 0$
   (d) $y = a$

2. Which of the following functions are one-to-one?
   (a) a function relating countries to their citizens
   (b) a function relating street addresses to zip codes
   (c) a function relating library call numbers to books
   (d) a function relating a student's identification number to a course grade in a specific class
3. Determine which of the following functions have inverses. Assume their domains are the set of real numbers. Derive the inverse function, $x = f^{-1}(y)$, where applicable. For the functions that do not have inverses, determine if it is possible to restrict the domain x in order to create a one-to-one function that has an inverse.
   (a) $y = 14 + 7x$
   (b) $y = x^2 + 6$
   (c) $y = \sqrt{x}$
   (d) $y = x^3$
4. Prove that the function $y = 10x - 5$ has an inverse. Then prove that both the original function and its inverse are inverse functions of each other by showing that $f(f^{-1}(y)) = y$ and $f^{-1}(f(x)) = x$.
5. Consider the following descriptions of continuous functions with extreme points.
   (a) Can you draw a graph of a function that has only one extreme point that is a local minimum but not a global minimum?
   (b) Can you draw a graph of a function that has two extreme points, each of which are local but not global extreme points?
   (c) If a function has three extreme points, what are its possible number of minima and maxima?
6. Determine the global maximum and global minimum for the function $y = \frac{1}{2}x + 50$ over the domain $[0, 100]$.
7. Sketch the function $y = 4x^2$. Draw secant lines and find the average rates of change for this function over the following intervals for x.
   (a) $[1, 2]$
   (b) $[1, 3]$
   (c) $[-2, -1]$
   (d) $[-2, 2]$
8. Show that the average rate of change of a strictly increasing function is positive and that the average rate of change of a strictly decreasing function is negative.
9. Sketch the function $y = x^2 - 8x + 16$ over the interval $[1, 5]$. Draw a secant line on the function that connects the points $x_A = 1$ and $x_B = 3$.
   (a) If $x' = 2$ is a point on the secant line, determine the value of y' using the equation given in the text.
   (b) What is the slope of the secant line?
   (c) What can you say about this function's concavity or convexity?
10. Sketch the function $y = 8 + 10x - x^2$ over the domain $[0, 7]$.

(a) Assume that $x_A = 1$, $x_B = 4$, and $\lambda = 0.4$. Using the formula $x' = \lambda x_A + (1 - \lambda)x_B$, determine the value of x'. What is the value of $f(x')$?
(b) Calculate the value of y', which is the value of the secant line at x', using the formula $y' = \lambda f(x_A) + (1 - \lambda)f(x_B)$.
(c) Prove that the above function is strictly concave by demonstrating that $f(x') > y'$.

11. For each of the following sets A and B, state whether $A \Rightarrow B, A \Leftarrow B$, or $A \Leftrightarrow B$. Do any of these sets satisfy the necessary and sufficient condition?
    (a) A = even numbered years, B = years in which the Summer Olympic Games are held
    (b) A = a function is monotonic, B = a function is increasing
    (c) A = a function is linear, B = a function is monotonic
    (d) A = a function is one-to-one, B = a function has an inverse function

2.3 A MENU OF FUNCTIONS

Economists use a variety of types of functions. The choice of the function appropriate for a particular model depends upon two factors. First, the mathematical properties of the function should be able to capture the salient economic characteristics of the activity studied. Second, the function should be as simple as possible to address the question at hand. Thus while the simplicity of a linear function makes it an attractive choice for many applications, in other cases it may prove to be too restrictive. For example, a linear function cannot reflect diminishing marginal utility since it is not strictly concave.

In this section we introduce three categories of functions. Some properties of each category are discussed. These functions are used and analyzed more extensively in later chapters.

Power Functions

A **power function** takes the general form

$$f(x) = kx^p, \tag{2.6}$$

where k and p are any constants. The parameter p is the **exponent** of the function.

The use of power functions requires a knowledge of the rules of exponents. Some important rules of exponents and numerical examples of these rules are presented in Table 2.2.

Figures 2.13 to 2.15 present the graphs of the power functions that take the form of (2.6). These graphs vary according to the values of the parameters k and p. Figure 2.13 presents three graphs in which p is a positive, even integer: $f(x) = 2x^2$, $f(x) = -2x^2$, and $f(x) = 2x^4$. These graphs illustrate some particular examples of more general points for any power function of the form of (2.6) when p is a positive even integer.

- $f(0) = 0$.
- If $k > 0$, then $f(x)$ reaches a global minimum at $x = 0$. If $k < 0$, then $f(x)$ reaches a global maximum at $x = 0$.

TABLE 2.2 Rules of Exponents

Rule	Numerical Example
$x^0 = 1$	$4^0 = 1$
$x^1 = x$	$4^1 = 4$
$x^{-p} = \dfrac{1}{x^p}$	$4^{-2} = \dfrac{1}{4^2} = \dfrac{1}{16}$
$x^{m/n} = \sqrt[n]{x^m}$	$4^{3/2} = \sqrt{64} = 8$
$x^a x^b = x^{a+b}$	$4^2 4^1 = (4 \cdot 4) \cdot 4 = 4^3 = 64$
$\dfrac{x^a}{x^b} = x^{a-b}$	$\dfrac{4^3}{4^2} = \dfrac{4 \cdot 4 \cdot 4}{4 \cdot 4} = 4^1 = 4$
$(x^a)^b = x^{ab}$	$(4^2)^3 = (4 \cdot 4)(4 \cdot 4)(4 \cdot 4) = 4^6 = 4096$
$x^a y^a = (xy)^a$	$4^2 3^2 = (4 \cdot 4)(3 \cdot 3) = 12^2 = 144$
$\dfrac{x^a}{y^a} = \left(\dfrac{x}{y}\right)^a$	$\dfrac{4^3}{2^3} = \dfrac{(4 \cdot 4 \cdot 4)}{(2 \cdot 2 \cdot 2)} = \left(\dfrac{4}{2}\right)^3 = 2^3 = 8$

- These functions are symmetric about the vertical axis. They are strictly convex if $k > 0$ or strictly concave if $k < 0$.

The graphs of the power functions $f(x) = x$, $f(x) = x^3$, and $f(x) = -x^3$ are presented in Figure 2.14. This figure illustrates some particular examples of more general points for any power function of the form of (2.6) when p is a positive odd integer.

- If $k > 0$, then the function is monotonic and increasing. If $k < 0$, then the function is monotonic and decreasing.

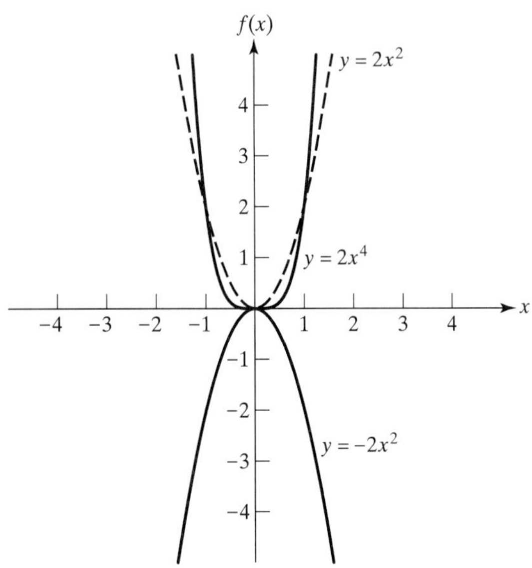

FIGURE 2.13 Power Functions in Which the Exponent Is a Positive Even Number

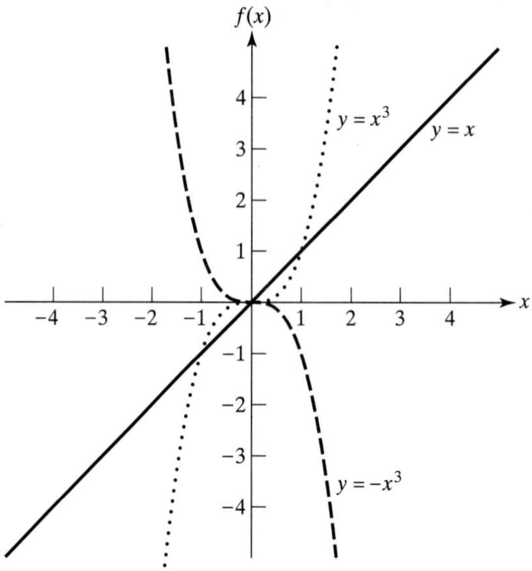

FIGURE 2.14 Power Functions in Which the Exponent Is a Positive Odd Integer

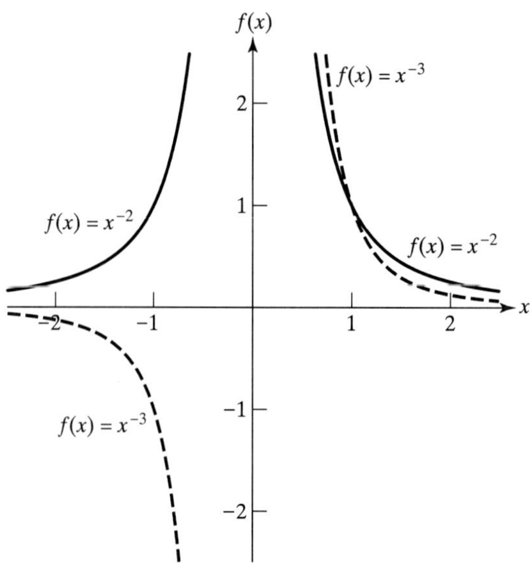

FIGURE 2.15 Power Functions in Which the Exponent Is a Negative Integer

- If $p \neq 1$ and $k > 0$, the function is strictly concave for $x < 0$ and strictly convex for $x > 0$. If $p \neq 1$ and $k < 0$, the function is strictly convex for $x < 0$ and strictly concave for $x < 0$.

Figure 2.15 presents the graphs of the power functions $f(x) = x^{-2}$ and $f(x) = x^{-3}$. This figure illustrates some particular examples of more general points for any power function of the form of (2.6) when p is a negative integer.

- The function is non-monotonic.
- The function is not continuous and has a vertical asymptote at $x = 0$.
- If $k > 0$ and p is a negative even integer, then

$$\lim_{x \to 0^-} kx^p = +\infty \quad \text{and} \quad \lim_{x \to 0^+} kx^p = +\infty.$$

- If $k < 0$ and p is a negative even integer, then

$$\lim_{x \to 0^-} kx^p = -\infty \quad \text{and} \quad \lim_{x \to 0^+} kx^p = -\infty.$$

- If $k > 0$ and p is a negative odd integer, then

$$\lim_{x \to 0^-} kx^p = -\infty \quad \text{and} \quad \lim_{x \to 0^+} kx^p = +\infty.$$

- If $k < 0$ and p is a negative odd integer, then

$$\lim_{x \to 0^-} kx^p = +\infty \quad \text{and} \quad \lim_{x \to 0^+} kx^p = -\infty.$$

- If $k > 0$ and p is a negative even integer, then kx^p is strictly convex for $x > 0$ or for $x < 0$.
- If $k > 0$ and p is a negative odd integer, then kx^p is strictly convex for $x > 0$ and strictly concave for $x < 0$.

Polynomial Functions

A **univariate polynomial function** takes the form

$$y = f(x) = a_0 + a_1x + a_2x^2 + \cdots + a_nx^n, \tag{2.7}$$

where the parameters a_i, $i = 0, 1, 2, \ldots, n$, are real numbers (which may include zero) and the exponents in the polynomial are integers from 1 to n. The **degree** of the polynomial is the value taken by the highest exponent. The polynomial presented here is an nth-degree polynomial or a polynomial of degree n. A linear function like (2.2) presented earlier is a polynomial of degree 1. A polynomial of degree 2 is called a **quadratic function.** A polynomial of degree 3 is called a **cubic function.**

The **roots** of a polynomial are the values of its argument that make the function equal zero. The linear function

$$y = a + bx$$

has the single root

$$x = -\frac{a}{b}$$

since, at this value of x, $y = a + b(-a/b) = 0$.

There are, at most, two distinct roots of any quadratic function. These roots are given by the **quadratic formula.** The roots of a quadratic equation, which are represented by the two values of the argument of the function x_1 and x_2, satisfy the relationship

$$0 = ax^2 + bx + c.$$

To derive the quadratic formula, we first divide each side of this equation by a to get

$$0 = x^2 + \frac{b}{a}x + \frac{c}{a}.$$

Adding $b^2/4a^2 - c/a$ to both sides of this equation gives us

$$\frac{b^2}{4a^2} - \frac{c}{a} = x^2 + \frac{b}{a}x + \frac{b^2}{4a^2}.$$

The right side of this equation is a perfect square; that is,

$$x^2 + \frac{b}{a}x + \frac{b^2}{4a^2} = \left(x + \frac{b}{2a}\right)^2.$$

Therefore the roots of a quadratic function satisfy the relationship

$$\left(x + \frac{b}{2a}\right)^2 = \frac{b^2}{4a^2} - \frac{c}{a}.$$

We isolate x by taking the square root of each side, multiplying the second term on the right by $4a/4a$, subtracting $b/2a$ from each side, and collecting terms to get

$$x_1, x_2 = \frac{-b \pm \sqrt{b^2 - 4ac}}{2a},$$

where the symbol $\pm$ means that one root is found by adding the term in the square root sign and the other is found by subtracting that term. For example, the roots of the quadratic equation

$$y = f(x) = 2x^2 - 2x - 4$$

represented by the graph in Figure 2.3 are

$$x_1, x_2 = \frac{2 \pm \sqrt{4 - (4)(2)(-4)}}{2(2)}$$

$$= -1, 2.$$

The graph of this function, therefore, includes the two points $(-1, 0)$ and $(2, 0)$. It is straightforward to verify that

$$f(-1) = f(2) = 0.$$

There are three different possibilities for the roots of a quadratic equation. When $b^2 - 4ac > 0$, then there are two distinct roots. When $b^2 - 4ac = 0$, then there are two equal roots (also called one multiple root). When $b^2 - 4ac < 0$, then there are two complex roots.[3]

In general, a polynomial of degree n has, at most, n distinct roots. There are no simple formulas for finding the roots of cubic or higher degree polynomial functions. Also, the degree of a polynomial function minus one indicates the largest number of "bends" its graph can have and, therefore, the largest number of local minima and maxima that function can have. A linear function has no bends, a quadratic function has one, a cubic function has at most two, and so on. We return to this point in Chapters 6 and 7.

Exponential Functions

The argument of an **exponential function** appears as an exponent. The general form of the univariate exponential function is

$$y = f(x) = kb^x, \tag{2.8}$$

where k is a constant and b, called the **base,** is a positive number. The rules given in Table 2.2 show that

$$f(0) = kb^0 = k$$

for any base. The sign of the value of this function is the same as the sign of the parameter k for any value of x. When $b > 1$, then b^x monotonically increases with x. In this case,

$$\lim_{x \to -\infty} kb^x = 0.$$

Using the rules given above, we see that

$$\frac{1}{b^x} = \left(\frac{1}{b}\right)^x = b^{-x}.$$

Thus the graph of the function $(1/b)^x$ is a reflection of the function b^x across the y-axis. When $1 > b > 0$, kb^x monotonically decreases with x and

$$\lim_{x \to \infty} kb^x = 0.$$

Figure 2.16 presents four different exponential functions. Function A is $y = 2^x$. Function B, $y = (1/2)^x$, is the reflection of Function A across the y-axis. Function C, $y = 3(2^x)$, looks much like Function A but lies everywhere above it. Function D, $y = 3^x$, has the same intercept as Function A but increases more quickly for positive values of x and decreases more quickly for negative values of x.

---

[3]A complex root is a root is a complex number. A complex number takes the form $a + b\sqrt{-1}$, where a is the real part of the number and $b\sqrt{-1}$ is the imaginary part of the number.

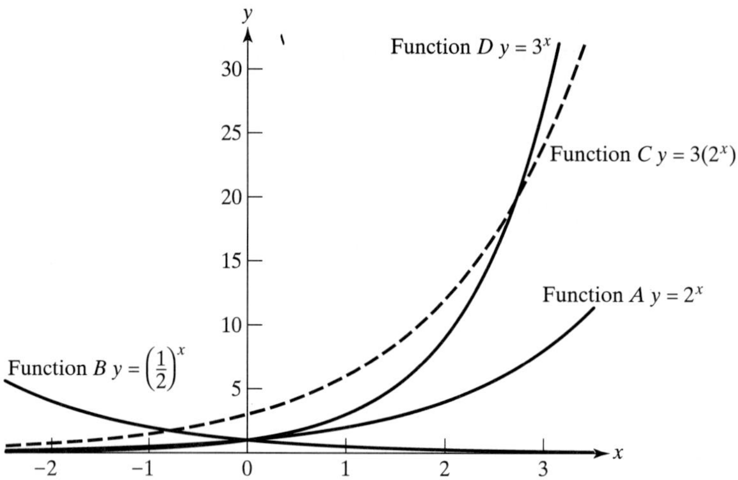

FIGURE 2.16 Some Exponential Functions

Exponential functions are used extensively in economics. The study of these functions and their inverses merits its own chapter. We turn to this study in Chapter 3.

Exercises 2.3

1. Evaluate the following.
   (a) x^2x^{-3}
   (b) x^4y^4
   (c) $(x^4)^5$
   (d) x^3y^2
   (e) $\dfrac{x^{-6}}{y^6}$
2. Condense the following expressions.
   (a) $x^a \cdot x^b \cdot x^c \div x^d$
   (b) $x^{1/2}x^{3/2} \div x^{1/3}$
   (c) $((x^{1/3})^8)^{1/2} \cdot x^2 \div x^{3/4}$
   (d) $x^2y^3 \cdot x^3 \div xy^2 \cdot x^{-2}y$
3. Calculate the following and simplify.
   (a) $16^{3/4}$
   (b) $4^{3/2} \cdot 2^5 \cdot 16$
   (c) $2^{1/2} \cdot 2^{5/2} \div 2^4$
   (d) $\dfrac{x+1}{x+2} \cdot \dfrac{2x^2+7x+3}{x^2+2x+1} \div \dfrac{2x+1}{x+1}$
   (e) $\{(x+1)^4(2x-1) + (x+1)^4(2-x)\}^5$

4. In which quadrant or quadrants does the graph of the power function $y = x^a$ appear when the domain of x is $(-\infty, \infty)$ and
   (a) a is a positive even number.
   (b) a is a positive odd number.
   (c) a is a negative even number.
   (d) a is a negative odd number.
5. Find the roots of the following equations.
   (a) $y = 6 - 5x$
   (b) $y = 6 - 5x - x^2$
   (c) $y = 9 + 6x + x^2$
   (d) $y = x^3 - 2x^2 - x + 2$ (*Hint*: One of the roots is -1.)
6. Find the roots of the function $y = px^2 + 2qx + r$ using the method of completing the square, as presented in the text.
7. Graph the functions $y = 2x^2$ and $y = 2^x$ over the interval $(0, 1]$. How do the values of these functions compare over this interval? What is the y-intercept of each function?
8. Using the functional form and your graph from question 7, now assume that $x_A = 1$ and $x_B = 4$, and plot the functions on the graph. Calculate the average rate of change for each function. Using the formal definitions provided in Section 2.2, determine whether these functions are concave or convex. Consider the specific case of $\lambda = 0.3$.
9. Plot on your graph from question 8 the graph of the exponential functions $y = (1/2)2^x$ and $y = (1/2)4^x$ over the domain $[0, 4]$. Do the two curves share a y-intercept? Why? Now assume for the first function we have $y = (1/4)2^x$. How does this affect the curvature of the graph?
10. How does the graph of the exponential functions from question 9 change when the domain of x is restricted to $(-3, 0]$ for both functions?
11. In applying mathematical methods to economic problems, economists utilize a broad menu of functions for the purpose of accurately specifying the properties of the economic variables in question. Choose the appropriate functional type from the following list of functions for that most accurately specifies the properties of each economic relationship described. (*Hint*: Try sketching a graph of the functions below and see which is appropriate for the relationship described.)
    i. $y = ax + b$; $(a < 0, b > 0)$
    ii. $y = ax^2 + bx + c$; $(a > 0, b < 0, c > 0)$
    iii. $y = \log_a(x - 1)$; $(a > 1)$
    iv. $y = ax^3 + bx^2 + cx$; $(a > 0, b < 0, c > 0)$
    v. $y = A \cdot x^a$; $(a < 0)$
    (a) A production function of one output and one input that exhibits increasing output with an increase in the input but diminishing marginal returns. That is, the rate of change becomes smaller when the input is increased. (*Hint*: This function is concave and monotonic.)

(b) An indifference curve with two goods that exhibits a diminishing marginal rate of substitution (MRS). This means that the more you have of a good, the more you are willing to trade away for the same amount of another good. (*Hint*: This standard indifference curve is convex and monotonic.)

(c) An indifference curve with two goods that are substitutes and that exhibits a constant rate of substitution.

(d) A marginal cost function of one output that exhibits diminishing marginal cost when output is small but increasing marginal cost when output gets larger. (*Hint*: This function is convex but non-monotonic.)

(e) A production function of one output with one input that exhibits increasing returns to scale when output is small and decreasing returns to scale when output is increasing.

12. Consider a function that relates tax revenues R, in billions of dollars, to the average tax rate t such that

$$R = 350t - 500t^2.$$

(a) What tax rate(s) is consistent with raising tax revenues equal to \$60 billion?

(b) What tax rate(s) is consistent with raising tax revenues equal to \$61.25 billion?

Summary

In this chapter you have begun to build up your "tool kit" of skills and concepts. The material presented in this chapter is used throughout the rest of the book. The rules for exponents and for the quadratic formula appear later in a variety of different contexts. The average rate of change of a function and its relationship to the slope of a secant line form the basis of the calculus chapters. Concepts such as concavity are developed more formally in subsequent chapters.

Since subsequent chapters build on the material presented here you should feel comfortable with the concepts, rules, and definitions in this chapter before moving on. As with all other chapters, the best way to do this is by carefully working through the problems offered at the end of each section.

Chapter 3

Exponential and Logarithmic Functions

The growth of variables through time is an important calculation in many branches of economics. The growth rates of variables like national income, wages, the size of the labor force, the value of a currency, and the price of goods and services are common in economics. This chapter will demonstrate that exponential functions, introduced in the previous chapter, have a special role in economic analysis because of their use in calculating the growth of variables over time. Exponential functions also play an important role in a related problem—the calculation of the present value of a future payment. The analysis of the calculation of growth rates presented in Section 3.1 naturally leads to the discussion of a special type of exponential function, presented in Section 3.2, that is instrumental in growth and present value calculations.

Exponential functions are strictly monotonic and, therefore, one-to-one. As discussed in Chapter 2, one-to-one functions have an inverse. The inverse of an exponential function is called a logarithmic function. The properties of logarithmic functions are discussed in Section 3.3. The discussion in that section, along with the accompanying applications, shows how logarithmic functions have a range of uses in economic analysis. These include the transformation of a nonlinear relationship into a linear expression, which is more easily evaluated, and, as is discussed in later chapters, the specification of an economic function with a constant elasticity.

3.1 CALCULATING GROWTH

An issue of central importance in economics is the rate of growth of income. High rates of growth of income can provide dramatic improvements in the standard of living over time, while low rates of income growth lead to stagnant material progress. As shown in Table 3.1, rates of growth of real income per capita varied widely across countries and regions over the period from 1990 to 1999. The average annual rate of growth of per capita income among countries classified as low income was less than one-quarter of the rate among countries classified as high income and just above one-sixth of the rate among countries classified as middle income. There were also striking regional differences in the growth rates of income per capita among low- and middle-income countries. The East Asia and

TABLE 3.1 Average Annual Growth Rate of Income per Capita, 1990–1999

Country Group	Growth Rate
High income countries	1.8%
Middle income countries	2.3%
Low income countries	0.4%
Country or Region (low and middle income countries)	**Growth Rate**
East Asia and Pacific region	6.1%
Latin America and Caribbean region	1.7%
Sub-Saharan Africa	−0.2%
China	9.6%

Pacific region had the most rapid growth while, on average, countries in Sub-Saharan Africa experienced a decline in real income per capita. The country with the highest rate of growth of income per capita during this period was China, with a rate of growth of 9.6%.[1]

While the disparities in growth *rates* are striking, it is not immediately obvious what the implications are for future *levels* of income per capita. To address this question, we begin by determining the general relationship between the growth rate of a variable and its level at different moments in time. As a specific example, suppose per capita income in a country equaled \$1,000 in 1990 and income grew each year at a rate of 5%. Income in 1991 is found by multiplying \$1,000 by 1.05, which gives us \$1,050. We use 1.05 because it represents the original level plus a growth of 5% (that is, $1 + 0.05$). In general terms, defining X_t as the level of income in year t, X_{t+1} as the level of income in year $t + 1$, and r as the growth rate (that is, 0.05), we have

$$X_{t+1} = (1 + r)X_t.$$

What was income in 1992? We use the same method, but in this case, the previous year's income is \$1,050 rather than \$1,000. Income in 1992 was therefore $\$1{,}050 \cdot 1.05 = \$1{,}102.50$. Again, generalizing this, we have

$$X_{t+2} = (1 + r)X_{t+1} = (1 + r)((1 + r)X_t) = (1 + r)^2X_t.$$

The level of income in any year can be determined by repeated application of this calculation. Table 3.2 shows the value of income in different years when there is an initial level of income of \$1,000 and a 5% growth rate. Income in any one year is calculated by multiplying the previous year's income by 1.05. The change in income between one year and the previous year, presented in the third column of Table 3.2, increases with time since income itself grows in each successive year and the change in income between year t and year $t + 1$ equals income in year t times 0.05.

The general result in the final row of Table 3.2 follows from the preceding rows. This general result shows that income in any year can be calculated by multiplying the initial year's income by $(1.05)^n$, where n is the number we add to 1990 to get the

[1]These data are from the World Bank's *World Development Report 2000* (New York: Oxford University Press, 2000), Tables 3 and 11.

TABLE 3.2 Annual Income with a 5% Growth Rate

Year	Y_t	$\Delta Y = Y_t - Y_{t-1}$
1990	$\$1{,}000.00 \times (1.05)^0 = \$1{,}000.00$	
1991	$\$1{,}000.00 \times (1.05)^1 = \$1{,}050.00$	\$50.00
1992	$\$1{,}050 \times 1.05 = \$1{,}000 \times (1.05)^2 = \$1{,}102.50$	\$52.50
1993	$\$1{,}120.50 \times 1.05 = \$1{,}000 \times (1.05)^3 = \$1{,}157.625$	\$55.125
$1990 + n$	$\$1{,}000.00 \times (1.05)^n$	$\$1{,}000((1.05)^n - (1.05)^{n-1})$

desired year. For example, $n = 1$ for 1991, $n = 2$ for 1992, and so on. This generalization even extends to 1990, itself, as well as earlier years. For 1990, $n = 0$ and $1.05^0 = 1$ since any number raised to the zero power equals 1. For 1989, $n = -1$ and $1.05^{-1} = 0.95238$ (approximately), so income in 1989 was approximately \$952.38. Even more generally, the formula for this type of **discrete growth,** that is, growth that occurs through compounding once per period at the end of each period, is as follows.

Growth Formula with Discrete End-of-Period Compounding The relationship between the value of a variable in period t, X_t, and its level in period $t + n$, X_{t+n}, when it grows by the rate r at the end of each period, is

$$X_{t+n} = (1 + r)^n X_t,$$

where r is expressed as a decimal (that is, 5% is expressed as $r = 0.05$) and n can be positive (for periods later than t) or negative (for periods earlier than t).

The growth formula allows us to determine the effect of growth rates on the level of income. For example, per capita income in China was \$370 in 1990. This means that since China's rate of growth was 9.6%, per capita income in 1999 was approximately

$$\$370 \cdot (1.096)^9 = \$370 \cdot 2.28 = \$844.$$

Had China instead grown by the average rate for East Asian and Pacific countries during this period (6.1%), its per capita income in 1999 would have been

$$\$370 \cdot (1.061)^9 = \$370 \cdot 1.70 = \$630.$$

The actual level of income in 1999 is 34% higher than this.[2] The average rate of growth for all low-income countries during this period was 0.4%. If per capita income in China

[2]The **percentage difference** in two variables x and y, using y as a reference, equals

$$\frac{x - y}{y} \cdot 100\%.$$

In this case we have

$$\frac{\$844 - \$630}{\$630} \cdot 100\% = 34\%.$$

Alternatively, the reference level could be the average of x and y. Calculating the difference in this way, we have

$$\frac{x - y}{(1/2)(x + y)} = \frac{\$844 - \$630}{(1/2)(\$630 + \$844)} \cdot 100\% = 29\%.$$

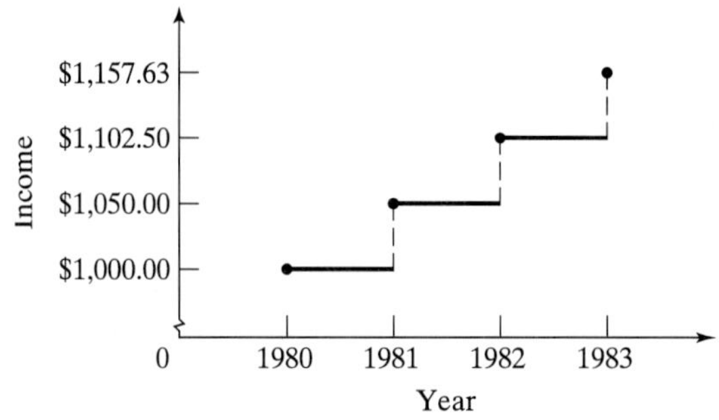

FIGURE 3.1 Income with Compounding at the End of the Year

had grown at this rate, then in 1999 per capita income would have equaled

$$\$370 \cdot (1.004)^9 = \$370 \cdot 1.037 = \$384.$$

Before moving on, it is important to recognize the way in which we are depicting growth in all of these calculations. These calculations assume that the incremental change due to growth occurs only at the end of a period. This type of discrete growth path is reflected in Figure 3.1, which depicts the path of income presented in Table 3.2. The time path of income in this figure is a **step function.** It is usually more natural to think of **continuous growth,** which would be reflected in a smooth evolution over time of variables like income or population. In the next section we will see how to calculate growth that is compounded more often than once at the end of a period, including the limiting (and in many instances more natural) case of continuously growing levels.

Exercises 3.1

1. Assume that $X_t = 100$. What is the value of X_{t+n} for each of the following values of n and r?
   (a) $n = 0, r = 4\%$
   (b) $n = 5, r = 3\%$
   (c) $n = 1, r = 100\%$
   (d) $n = 50, r = 4\%$
2. Now assume that $X_t = 50$. Given the following negative values of n, which indicate time periods that have already passed, and positive values of r, calculate the value of X_{t+n}.
   (a) $n = -4, r = 8\%$
   (b) $n = -4, r = 6\%$
   (c) $n = -1, r = 6\%$
   (d) $n = -10, r = 2\%$
3. Now assume that $X_{t+n} = 25$. Given the following values of n and r, calculate the value of X_t.

(a) $n = 3, r = 4\%$
(b) $n = 3, r = 7\%$
(c) $n = 5, r = 7\%$
(d) $n = 0, r = 100\%$
(e) $n = -5, r = 2\%$

4. Suppose you are a farmer that stores grain in a leaky silo so that you lose 2% of your crop each year as a result of dampness and rot. To obtain the future value of X, you still employ the same formula
$$X_{t+n} = X_t(1 + r)^n.$$
If $r = -2\%$, what is the value of X_{t+n} as n approaches infinity? That is, what is $\lim_{n\to\infty} X_t(1+r)^n$? Will the value of X_{t+n} ever equal zero?

5. Upon graduation, you secure a job with a firm willing to pay you an annual salary of $50,000. Your contract stipulates annual increases equivalent to that year's rate of inflation plus 2%. Assume that $t_0 = 2003$.
   (a) If inflation during your first year is 3%, what will your salary be for 2004?
   (b) If the inflation rate then falls to 2% for each of the next two years, what salary should you expect to earn in 2006?
   (c) In 2006, your firm decides that cost-of-living–based raises are too variable for their budgeting requirements. Instead they offer you a fixed 6% annual increase. What will your salary be in 2012 ($t = 6$)?

6. Assume a firm's net profits are $50 million in 2000 and are expected to grow at a steady rate of 6% per year through the end of the decade. How much would you expect the firm to earn in 2001? In 2003? Now assume that the firm's profits have been growing at 6% since 1997. If a negative value of n can be interpreted as the number of time periods before period t, how much did the company earn in 1998? Graph the path of income growth between 1998 and 2003 and explain why the curve gets steeper over time.

7. Productivity improvements are often considered a primary engine of economic growth. In fact, lagging productivity growth has been named as one of the reasons for stagnant real incomes in the United States in the 1970s and 1980s. Since roughly 1992, however, average annual productivity growth has doubled, mostly through changes in technology, trade, and education. If the expected annual rate of real economic growth in the United States was 2.5% in 1992, but continued productivity enhancements have increased that growth rate to 3.0% per year, how much better off will the United States' economy be in 2010 ($t_0 = 1992$)? If productivity improvements spark a 3.5% growth rate, rather than a 2.5% rate, how much better off will the economy be?

8. Indonesia is one of the most highly populated countries in the world, and it also has one of the fastest growing populations. Its population in 1999 was 207 million. Indonesia's population is expected to grow at a 1.75% average annual rate through 2010. Although China has the world's largest population (1250 million in 1999), its population is expected to grow at an average annual rate of only 1.04% through 2010. Determine what each country's population will be in 2010

if $t_0 = 1999$. Compare the ratio of the two countries' population *levels* in 1999 and 2010 to examine the impact of different population growth *rates.*

9. Write down the formula for the level of the population in Country A at the end of 1995 if the population in 1990 was 100 million and the population grew at the non-compounded rate of 2% per year. If the population had been growing at a 3% rate from 1980 through 1990, what would the population have been in 1985?

3.2 THE EXPONENTIAL

The growth formula discussed in the previous section is an appropriate way to depict a process where the growth of a variable occurs all at once at the end of each period. An example of this may be a savings account in which interest accrues only at the end of each year. This seems somewhat artificial, however, since the value of many assets is recomputed more frequently than once per year. Furthermore, this one-time compounding clearly does not describe a wide range of different types of growth. Population growth, for example, is more or less even over a year: not all babies are born just before midnight on New Year's eve. Likewise, it is more natural to think of a steady growth of national income over a period rather than a spurt of growth at the end of the period.

In this section we will consider alternative compounding frequencies. We begin by analyzing interest compounded a few times per year. We then see how we can extend this to analyze a situation where interest is continuously compounded. Continuous compounding provides a natural way to think about such issues as the growth of a population, the growth in income, or the value of an asset that has very frequent interest accrual. It also turns out that continuous growth can be expressed in a very convenient mathematical form.

Multiple Compounding per Period

Consider the example of \$100 placed in an interest-bearing account on January 1. If this account pays 10% interest, once, at the end of the year, the value of the account on December 31 will be $\$100 \cdot 1.10 = \$110$. This is shown in Panel I of Table 3.3. If the interest is compounded twice during the year, then the account accrues a 5% interest payment at midyear and another 5% interest payment at year's end. At midyear the value of the account is

$$(1.05) \cdot \$100 = \$105.00.$$

At the end of the year the value of the account is

$$(1.05) \cdot \$105.00 = (1.05)^2 \cdot \$100 = \$110.25.$$

The extra \$0.25 accrued in the second period in this case, as compared to the amount that is accrued when interest is paid only at the end of a year, arises because the principal on which the interest is calculated increases over the course of the year. The interest calculated for the period from July 1 to December 31 is based on a principal of \$105.00 rather than \$100. The \$0.25 difference between the twice-per-year interest accrual and the one-time 10% interest payment represents the difference in the

TABLE 3.3 Principal and Interest with Different Frequencies of Compounding

I. Interest Compounded Once per Year					
Date	January 1				December 31
Value of account	\$100.00				\$110.00
Formula	$\$X$				$\$X(1 + r)$
II. Interest Compounded Twice per Year					
Date	January 1		June 30		December 31
Value of account	\$100.00		\$105.00		\$110.25
Formula	$\$X$		$\$X\left(1 + \frac{r}{2}\right)$		$\$X\left(1 + \frac{r}{2}\right)^2$
III. Interest Compounded Four Times per Year					
Date	January 1	March 31	June 30	September 30	December 31
Value of account	\$100.00	\$102.50	\$105.06	\$107.69	\$110.38
Formula	$\$X$	$\$X\left(1 + \frac{r}{4}\right)^1$	$\$X\left(1 + \frac{r}{4}\right)^2$	$\$X\left(1 + \frac{r}{4}\right)^3$	$\$X\left(1 + \frac{r}{4}\right)^4$
IV. Interest Compounded Continuously					
Date	January 1	March 31	June 30	September 30	December 31
Value of account	\$100.00	\$102.53	\$105.13	\$107.79	\$110.52
Formula	$\$X$	$\$Xe^{1/4r}$	$\$Xe^{1/2r}$	$\$Xe^{3/4r}$	$\$Xe^{r}$

midyear principal in the two cases (\$5.00) multiplied by the interest rate for the six-month period from July through December (0.05).

When interest is compounded four times per year, each time at a rate of $\frac{0.10}{4} = 0.025$, the year-end value of the account is

$$(1.025)^4 \cdot \$100 = \$110.38.$$

This exceeds the amount when interest is paid twice a year since the more frequent recomputation of principal means higher interest payments over the course of the year.

More generally, if we divide one period into k equal-sized lengths, the relevant interest rate over any one subperiod is $(1 + r/k)$. Over the entire year, interest will be compounded k times. Therefore we have the following result.

Multiple Compounding in One Period The relationship between the value of a variable at the beginning of period t, X_t, and its value at the beginning of the next period, X_{t+1}, when it grows by the rate r compounded k times during that period, is

$$X_{t+1} = \left(1 + \frac{r}{k}\right)^k X_t.$$

We illustrate the effect of compounding at different frequencies in Figure 3.2. This figure shows the value of a variety of interest-bearing assets that each pay an annual interest rate r but differ according to how often interest compounding occurs. Each of the three assets, labeled A, B, and C, has an initial value of \$100. Interest on Asset A accrues only at the end of a year, so there is one "step" per year. Interest on

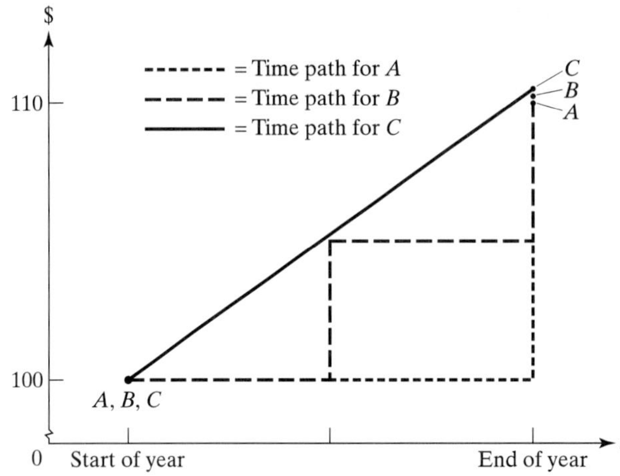

FIGURE 3.2 Compounding at Different Frequencies

Asset B is compounded twice per year, and there are therefore two "steps" per year, one at midyear and one at year's end. Notice that the value of Asset B is above that for Asset A from midyear and thereafter.

In the limit, as the frequency of compounding increases and the duration of the compounding periods decreases, the number of "steps" increases to the point where the value of the asset is approximated by a smooth function. Such a situation is reflected in the graph of the value of Asset C in Figure 3.2. The value of Asset C is greater than the value of the other assets at any moment during the year. Next we turn to the development of a formula for the determination of growth rates with continuous compounding.

Continuous Compounding

The results in Table 3.3 suggest that $(1 + r/k)^k$ increases at a decreasing rate with an increase in k. The difference in the end-of-year value when we double the number of times interest is compounded from one to two is \$0.25. The difference in the end-of-year value when we double the number of times interest is compounded from two to four is only \$0.13. Table 3.4 confirms this pattern by presenting values of $(1 + r/k)$ for a variety of values of k when r equals 0.10 and when $r = 1.00$.

The entry for $k = 1{,}000{,}000$ illustrates a case with very frequent compounding. Note that the difference between the result for $k = 100$ and $k = 1{,}000$ is larger than the difference between the result for $k = 1{,}000$ and $k = 1{,}000{,}000$. This suggests the following limit result.

The Exponential The **exponential, *e*,** is an irrational number where

$$e = \lim_{k \to \infty} \left(1 + \frac{1}{k}\right)^k = 2.71828182845\ldots.$$

TABLE 3.4 Different Frequencies of Compounding

k	$\left(1+\frac{0.10}{k}\right)^k$	$\left(1+\frac{1.00}{k}\right)^k$
1	1.10	2.00
2	1.1025	2.25
10	1.10462	2.59374
100	1.10512	2.70481
1,000	1.105165	2.71692
1,000,000	1.105171	2.71828

This important result shows that, with an annual interest rate of $r = 100$ (that is, 100%), the value of \$100 after one year of continuously compounded interest is \$271.83 since

$$\lim_{k\to\infty}\left(1+\frac{1.00}{k}\right)^k \cdot \$100.00 = \$271.83.$$

An exponential function with the number e as its base is called **the exponential function,** where the definite article "the" distinguishes this function from other exponential functions with other bases. The function e^{ax} can also be written as $\exp(ax)$.

The definition of the exponential must be adapted to make it useful for calculating continuously compounded interest rates other than $r = 1.00$. The expression $(1 + r/k)^k$ can be recast in terms of the exponential function by first noting that

$$\left(1+\frac{r}{k}\right)^k = \left(\left(1+\frac{r}{k}\right)^{k/r}\right)^r = \left(\left(1+\frac{1}{k/r}\right)^{k/r}\right)^r,$$

where the terms before and after the first equal sign are equal using the rules of exponents presented in Chapter 2. As the frequency of compounding (that is, k) goes to infinity, the fraction k/r likewise goes to infinity. Defining $m = k/r$ and using the result for the exponential, we see that

$$\lim_{k/r\to\infty}\left(\left(1+\frac{1}{k/r}\right)^{k/r}\right)^r = \lim_{m\to\infty}\left(\left(1+\frac{1}{m}\right)^{m}\right)^r = e^r = (2.71828182845\ldots)^r.$$

This result allows us to calculate the level at the end of a year of a variable that grows at a continuously compounded rate over the course of the year. Denoting the initial value as $X(t)$, the value at the end of the year as $X(t + 1)$, and the rate of growth as r, we have

$$X(t+1) = e^r \cdot X(t). \tag{3.1}$$

Notice that we depict time periods here in parentheses, following the variable, rather than as subscripts, as was done previously. This follows the convention of using subscripts to denote discrete time periods and parentheses to denote moments measured in continuous time. Discrete time is counted in periods that are identified by integers, while continuous time is counted in moments that are represented by real numbers. Therefore we typically do not have a representation in discrete time such as $X_{0.5}$, but we may have a continuous time moment defined as $X(0.5)$.

We can use (3.1) to confirm the value of the end-of-year value in Panel IV of Table 3.3. Many calculators have an exponent key, which enables you to find e^r (also written as exp (r)) for different values of r. You can verify, with such a calculator, that $e^{0.10} = 1.1052$ (approximately). Therefore the principal and interest from an initial investment of \$100 at a 10% annual interest rate, continuously compounded, equals

$$\$100 \cdot e^{0.10} = \$110.52.$$

There is a straightforward extension of this when the period over which the asset is held differs from one year. The analysis that led to (3.1) on the previous page shows that we can think of a multiyear problem as a series of single-year problems in which the principal changes from one year to the next. For example, the value of \$100 in two years with a 10% interest rate, compounded continuously, can be found by first finding the value of the asset at the end of one year and then calculating another one-year problem. This gives us

$$((\$100 \cdot e^{0.10})e^{0.10}) = \$110.52 \cdot e^{(0.10)} = \$122.14.$$

Using the properties of exponents presented in Chapter 2, we find that this expression can also be evaluated as

$$((\$100 \cdot e^{0.10})e^{0.10}) = \$100 \cdot e^{2(0.10)} = \$100 \cdot e^{0.20} = \$122.14.$$

More generally, we have the following formula for continuous compounding.

Continuous Compounding The value of a variable X at the moment $t + n$ (that is, $X(t + n)$), given its value at the moment t (that is, $X(t)$), when there is a continuously compounded growth (or interest) rate of r per period, is

$$X(t + n) = X(t)e^{r \cdot n}.$$

This results holds for n equal to any real number. For example, when n is a fraction, it reflects the value during some moment within the period. Thus we have the result in Panel IV of Table 3.3 that the initial investment of \$100 made at the beginning of January will yield

$$\$100 \cdot e^{0.10 \cdot 1/2} = \$100 \cdot e^{0.05} = \$105.13$$

at the end of June.

Using this equation to determine per capita income in the Chinese economy in 1999, given its 1990 level and different growth rates, illustrates the difference between continuous compounding and the results presented in Section 3.1, which employ one-time compounding per period. The actual per capita income in 1999, calculated using a growth rate of 9.6%, compounded continuously, and an initial level of per capita income of \$370, is

$$\$370 \cdot e^{0.096 \cdot 9} = \$370 \cdot e^{0.864} = \$878.$$

This is about 4% larger than the level calculated with one-time compounding per period. Calculating per capita income with growth rates of 6.1% and 0.4%, compounded continuously, gives levels of income equal to \$641 and \$384, respectively. The level with 6.1% growth, compounded continuously, differs from its respective value with one-time compounding by about 1.6%. The level with 0.4% growth is virtually the same whether compounding continuously or only at the end of each year. These results show that the proportionate difference in levels, when comparing calculations with continuous or end-of-period compounding, increases with the interest rate itself.

Negative values of n are interpreted as the number of time periods before period t. For example, suppose a country has a population growth rate of 2% per year, and its current population is 50 million people. The population 20 years ago can be calculated as

$$50\text{ million}\cdot e^{0.02\cdot(-20)} = 50\text{ million}\cdot e^{-0.4} = 50\text{ million}\cdot 0.67 = 33.5\text{ million}.$$

When using the continuous compounding formula, it is important to keep in mind the correspondence between the interest rate and the time period. For example, if we define an interest rate as an annual rate (such as 5% per annum, so $r = 0.05$), then the time period must match this definition (that is, n must represent the number of years). We can have any length of time serve as our definition of "one time period," but of course, we need to define the interest rate in a manner that corresponds to this length of time.

Lending periods may be as short as overnight. For example, central banks lend to commercial banks at the end of a business day and are repaid the next morning. The interest rate on these overnight loans is reported as an annual rate. In a particularly striking case, the overnight interest rate offered by the Riksbank, the central bank of Sweden, reached 500% on an annual basis in September 1992, at the time of a crisis in the European Monetary System.[3] The daily interest rate was therefore 500%/365 = 1.37%. Thus a loan of SKr 1,000,000 made at the end of one business day must be repaid with

$$\text{SKr } 1{,}000{,}000\cdot e^{(0.0137)\cdot 1} = \text{SKr } 1{,}013{,}793.$$

the next morning.

Annual and Effective Interest Rates

The difference between the return when interest is continuously compounded and the return when compounding occurs only at the end of a period helps explain signs you might have seen at banks that present both an **annual interest rate** and an **effective interest rate** (sometimes referred to as **yield**). The annual interest rate represents the interest rate used in the continuous compounding calculations. The effective interest rate is the interest rate that would give the same end-of-period return if interest were compounded only once at the end of the period. Defining the annual rate as r_A and the effective rate as r_E, we therefore have, for any initial principal $\$X$,

$$\$X(1 + r_E) = \$X\cdot e^{r_A}.$$

Thus the relationship between the annual rate and the effective rate is

$$r_E = e^{r_A} - 1.$$

[3]See "Swedish interest rate reaches 500%," *Financial Times* (September 17, 1992): 2.

TABLE 3.5 Effective and Annual Interest Rates

Annual Rate (AR)	Effective Rate (ER)	Percentage Difference $\left(\frac{ER - AR}{AR} \times 100\%\right)$
0.02	0.0202	1.0%
0.10	0.1052	5.2%
0.50	0.649	29.7%

For example, a 7% annual rate corresponds to an effective rate of 7.25% since

$$e^{0.07} - 1 = 1.0725 - 1 = 0.0725.$$

The percentage difference between the annual and effective rates increases with the interest rate. This is shown by the results in Table 3.5. The effective interest rate corresponding to the annual interest rate of 2% differs from the annual rate by only 1.0%. This difference grows to 5.2% when the annual rate is 10% and to 29.7% when the annual rate is 50%.

Present Value

Present value represents the amount required today to yield a certain payout at a given time in the future. Present value calculations are used in economic applications that compare values at different moments in time. The method of calculating present value with continuously compounded interest rates follows directly from the analysis above.

To illustrate this, consider the value to you today of a payment of $10,000 made one year from now. If the continuously compounded interest rate available to you in a savings account is 8%, then you would be indifferent to whether you were paid $10,000 at the end of one year or offered some smaller amount today that would be worth $10,000 in one year when invested in a savings account. We can find the amount P that must be offered to you today, in order for you to have $10,000 in one year, by noting that the continuous compounding formula gives

$$\$10{,}000 = P \cdot e^{rt} = P \cdot e^{0.08 \cdot 1} = P \cdot 1.0833.$$

Solving this, we find that

$$P = \frac{\$10{,}000}{1.0833} = \$9{,}231.$$

A calculation of this type is used to find the price of a bond that pays a certain amount at some future date. The calculation given above shows that a bond that pays $10,000 in one year will cost $9,231 today, when the interest rate on comparable assets is 8%. Extending this result, the price P of a bond that pays $10,000 five years from its date of purchase must satisfy the relationship

$$\$10{,}000 = P \cdot e^{rt} = P \cdot e^{0.08 \cdot 5} = P \cdot 1.4918.$$

Thus the current price of the bond is

$$P = \frac{\$10{,}000}{1.4918} = \$6{,}703.$$

This illustrates the general result that the present value of a payment decreases the further into the future the payment is made. These are two examples of the following general formula for calculating present value.

Present Value with Continuous Compounding The present value, $P(t)$, of a payment of $X(t + n)$ that is made n periods in the future, where r is the appropriate continuously compounded interest rate for discounting this payment,

$$P(t) = X(t + n) \cdot e^{-rn}.$$

This formula shows that the price of a bond that pays \$10,000 a year from purchase (that is, the present value of a payment of \$10,000 in one year), when the interest rate on comparable securities is 6%, is

$$\$10{,}000 \cdot e^{-0.06} = \$9{,}417.64.$$

The price of a bond that pays \$10,000 five years from its purchase, when the interest rate is 6%, is

$$\$10{,}000 \cdot e^{-0.30} = \$7{,}408.18.$$

Comparing these present values to those when the interest rate is 8% shows that the present value of a payment increases as the interest rate falls. This inverse relationship between present value and the interest rate demonstrates why bond prices fall when the interest rate increases.

Present value can also be calculated with discrete compounding. Again we want to find the present value needed to provide a future payout. Applying the formula for discrete compounding in the manner we did for continuous compounding gives us the following result.

Present Value with Discrete Compounding The present value, P_t, of a payment of X_{t+n} that is made n periods in the future, when the appropriate interest rate for discounting this payment is r and interest is compounded only at the end of any period, is

$$P_t = X_{t+n} \cdot (1 + r)^{-n}.$$

This result allows us to recalculate the bond-pricing example with once-per-period discrete compounding rather than continuous compounding. With an 8% annual interest rate compounded once at the end of each year, the prices of a one-year and five-year bond, each of which pays \$10,000 at maturity, are

$$\frac{\$10{,}000}{(1.08)^1} = \$9{,}259.26$$

and

$$\frac{\$10{,}000}{(1.08)^5} = \$6{,}805.83,$$

respectively.

Using the results presented in this section, we can determine the relationship between present value computed with continuous compounding and present value computed with discrete compounding with a common interest rate. As shown in the application above, continuous compounding is like having a higher effective interest rate. The present value of a future payment is smaller if the interest rate is larger. Therefore the present value of a future payment is smaller when calculated with continuous compounding than it is when calculated with discrete compounding.

Exercises 3.2

1. Using the formula for multiple compounding in one period, $X_{t+1} = X_t(1+r/k)^k$, calculate the value of X_{t+1} for the following values of r and k. Assume that $X_t = 20$.
   (a) $r = 8\%, k = 4$
   (b) $r = 0.5\%, k = 2$
   (c) $r = 10\%, k = 365$
2. You are given the value of $X_{t+1} = 100$ as the value of X at the end of a period. Negative values of r imply a rate of decline rather than growth. Assuming the following values of r and k, calculate the value of X_t. What can you observe regarding the impact on X_t of relative changes in r and k?
   (a) $r = -5\%, k = 2$
   (b) $r = -5\%, k = 4$
   (c) $r = -3\%, k = 4$
3. You have inherited \$1 million from a wealthy aunt. Her will stipulated that you invest the full amount in a five-year certificate of deposit. The two most competitive banks in your area are offering the following rates: Bank A, 9.0% per annum with annual compounding; Bank B, 8.7% per annum with monthly compounding. With which bank will your inheritance be worth more at the end of five years? how much more?
4. Bank Highrates is offering a deposit-incentive program that pays investors an 8% annual interest rate on any deposit over \$100,000. Calculate the corresponding effective interest rate, or yield.
5. Assuming that $X(t) = 75$, determine the value of $X(t+n)$ for the following combinations of n and r using the continuous compounding formula:
$$X(t+n) = X(t)e^{r \cdot n}.$$
   (a) $n = 3, r = 9\%$
   (b) $n = 0.5, r = 2.5\%$
   (c) $n = -2, r = 11\%$
   (d) $n = 0.25, r = 6\%$
   (e) $n = 0.75, r = -3\%$

6. On January 1 of last year, an investor bought one share of a public utility stock for \$45, which paid a dividend of 3% per annum on a quarterly basis. If there was no change in the stock's market value over the course of the year, what was her return on this investment at year's end? Now assume that the stock's market value increased 10% during the year, on a continuously compounded basis, and each quarter's paid dividend was based on the stock's value on the last day of the quarter. What was the return on this investment at the end of each quarter in dollar terms? What was the investor's total annual percentage return based on the original investment?
7. Using the data for China and Indonesia presented in question 8 of Exercises 3.1 and assuming continuous compounding, calculate the level of each country's population in 2010. What is the ratio of the two countries' populations in 2010? How much bigger, in percentage terms, is this ratio than the answer you got using discrete compounding?
8. While you are a senior in high school, your parents decide to invest in the bond market to help pay for your college tuition. They purchase a bond that will pay \$15,000 in one year plus an interest coupon payment of 7% of the bond's value when the interest rate on comparable assets is also 7%. What is the present value of this bond? If interest rates fall to 5% after the bond purchase, what is the present value of that same investment? What is the present value if interest rates rise to 9.5%?
9. Your financial advisor suggests that zero-coupon U.S. government treasury bonds are an attractive form of long-term savings. Zero-coupon bonds can be purchased at a sizable discount to their face value because they do not pay any interest over the life of the bond. At the time of maturity, the investor receives the bond's face value, which is comprised of the original investment plus the interest accrued over the life of the bond. The bond's return, therefore, is based on the difference between the purchase price and the redemption price. How much should you expect to pay today for a \$25,000 zero-coupon bond that matures in 20 years if the rate of 7.5% is continuously compounded? Use the continuous compounding formula to determine your results.
10. The Cobb-Douglas production function describes the level of output (Y_t) at time t as a function of the amount of labor (L_t), capital (K_t), and the level of productivity (A_t) at that time as

$$Y_t = A_t L_t^{\alpha} K_t^{1-\alpha},$$

where $\alpha = 0.7$. If labor grows at a 3% continuously compounded rate such that

$$L_t = L_0 e^{0.03t}$$

and capital and productivity grow at 2% and 1%, respectively, continuously compounded, devise an equation for total output in year t compared to output in year 0.
11. A person's productivity at a particular job may change with experience. Consider the following model of effective labor input,

$$L(t) = 2 - e^{-0.1t}$$

where L is a measure of the "effective labor input" of a particular worker and t is the worker's tenure (that is, years spent in a particular job).

(a) What is the effective labor input of the worker when she is new and $t = 0$?

(b) What is the worker's labor input if she stays at her job forever? (*Hint*: Take the limit of L as $t \to \infty$.)

(c) Compare the values of L for $t = 0$ and for $t = 1$ as well as the values of L for $t = 10$ and for $t = 11$. Provide a brief economic interpretation in each case of the differences in productivity when tenure increases by 1 year (from 0 to 1 and from 10 to 11).

12. Suppose you have a two-year bond that costs \$1,000. This bond pays interest once per year at the end of each year. The interest rate at the end of the first year is 10%, and the interest rate at the end of the second year is 20%.

(a) What is the value of the bond (principle plus interest) at the end of the second year?

(b) The average of 10% and 20% is 15%. Find the value of a bond that paid 15% at the end of the first year and then 15% again at the end of the second year, and compare this answer to your answer to question 12(a). If the answer differs from the one in part (a), give an explanation concerning the source of the difference.

(c) Now compare the return on two bonds, one of which pays a continuously compounded rate of 10% over the first year and of 20% over the second year, while the other pays a continuously compounded rate of 15% over both of the years. Is there a difference between the value of these bonds? Compare and contrast your answers here to your answers to question 12(b).

3.3 LOGARITHMIC FUNCTIONS

Any exponential function has an inverse since it is strictly monotonic and, therefore, one-to-one. The class of functions that are inverses to exponential functions are **logarithmic functions.** Logarithmic functions are used in many different ways in economics. This section defines these functions and shows some of their useful properties by illustrating their application in economic problems. Later chapters, especially Chapter 7 and Chapter 11, make extensive use of logarithmic functions in a number of other economic applications.

We can begin to learn of some of the properties of logarithmic functions by exploiting the fact that these functions are the inverses of exponential functions. As discussed in Chapter 2, the graph of an inverse of a function is represented by a reflection of that function across the 45° line. Any point (i, j) in the exponential function

$$y = b^x$$

has a corresponding point (j, i) in the logarithmic function

$$y = \log_b(x).$$

Figure 3.3 presents the graph of these two functions. Like the exponential function, the logarithmic function is strictly monotonic and increasing. This figure demonstrates that logarithmic functions are everywhere concave, while exponential functions are everywhere convex. This figure also demonstrates that the arguments of a logarithmic

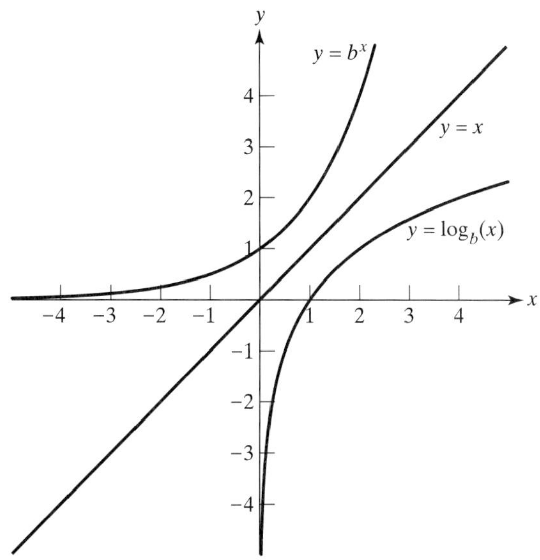

FIGURE 3.3 An Exponential Function and Its Inverse

function are restricted to the set of positive real numbers, while the range of the function is the set of all real numbers, which is the converse of the case for exponential functions. Finally, since all exponential functions of the form $y = b^x$ cross the y-axis at the point (0,1), all logarithmic functions of the form $y = \log_b(x)$ cross the x-axis at the point (1,0).

The definition of a logarithmic function follows.

Logarithmic Function with Base *b* The logarithmic function

$$y = \log_b(x),$$

which is read as "y is the base b logarithm of x," satisfies the relationship

$$b^y = x.$$

This definition of logarithms implies

$$\log_b(b) = 1$$

for any base since $b^1 = b$. By the definition of an inverse function (see Chapter 2), we also have

$$b^{\log_b(x)} = x.$$

The definition of a logarithm enables us to calculate the base 2 logarithms and base 10 logarithms (base 10 logarithms are also called **common logarithms**) in Table 3.6. This table shows that the value of a logarithmic functions is negative for values of its argument that are less than 1. This table also illustrates that the value of a

TABLE 3.6 Base 2 and Base 10 Logarithms

Base 2 Logarithms		Base 10 Logarithms	
$\log_2(0.25) = -2$	because $2^{-2} = \frac{1}{4}$	$\log_{10}(0.01) = -2$	because $10^{-2} = \frac{1}{100}$
$\log_2(0.5) = -1$	because $2^{-1} = \frac{1}{2}$	$\log_{10}(0.1) = -1$	because $10^{-1} = \frac{1}{10}$
$\log_2(1) = 0$	because $2^0 = 1$	$\log_{10}(1) = 0$	because $10^0 = 1$
$\log_2(2) = 1$	because $2^1 = 2$	$\log_{10}(10) = 1$	because $10^1 = 10$
$\log_2(4) = 2$	because $2^2 = 4$	$\log_{10}(100) = 2$	because $10^2 = 100$
$\log_2(8) = 3$	because $2^3 = 8$	$\log_{10}(1000) = 3$	because $10^3 = 1000$

logarithmic functions increases at a decreasing rate. For example, an increase in the value of a base 10 logarithm by 1 means an increase in the argument of the function by a factor of 10.[4]

The comparison between base 2 and common logarithms is also illustrated in Figure 3.4, which plots $\log_2(x)$ and $\log_{10}(x)$ against x. This figure shows that the logarithm of any number greater than 1 is bigger with base 2 than with base 10. For example, $\log_2(2)$ is 1 (since $2^1 = 2$), and $\log_{10}(2)$ is approximately 0.3 (since $10^{0.3}$ is approximately equal to 2). Conversely, the logarithm of any positive number less than 1 is smaller with base 2 than with base 10. For example, $\log_2(0.1) = -3.32$, while $\log_{10}(0.1) = -1$. Both of the functions pass through the point (1,0) since both 2^0 and 10^0 equal 1.

Rules of Logarithms

Economic models often employ a **logarithmic transformation** of the variables of the model. A logarithmic transformation is the conversion of a variable that can take on different real positive values into its logarithm. In this section we demonstrate properties of logarithmic transformations and show why this is such a useful tool for economists.

Economic models frequently include nonlinear relationships. For example, real money balances are represented by the quotient of nominal balances over the price level (M/P), and the real exchange rate equals the product of the nominal exchange rate and the foreign price level divided by the domestic price level (EP^*/P). Nonlinear relationships among variables may be expressed as linear relationships among their logarithms. Multiequation models that include products or quotients are more difficult to solve than models that are linear in the variables of interest. Thus expressing these models in terms of the logarithms of their variables is often a useful strategy for making analysis more straightforward. One caveat, however, is that zero and negative

[4]An interesting application of this property concerns the measurement of the severity of earthquakes. The scale used to measure earthquakes, the Richter scale, is measured in common logarithms. Thus an earthquake that registers 7 on the Richter scale is 10 times as forceful as an earthquake that registers 6 and 100 times as forceful as an earthquake that registers 5.

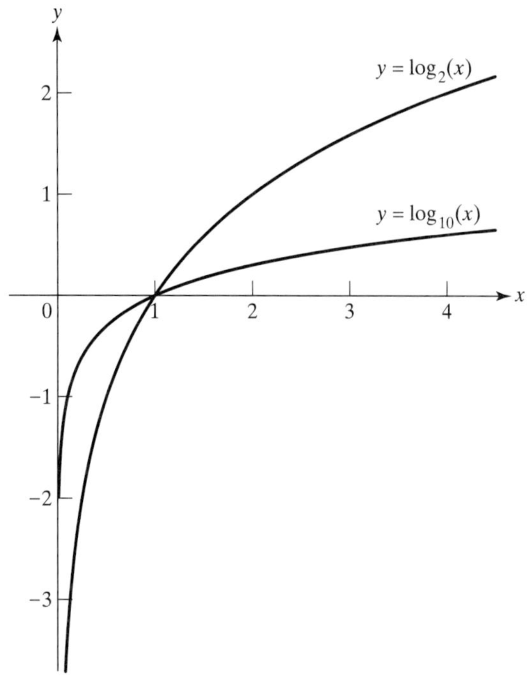

FIGURE 3.4 Base 2 and Base 10 Logarithms

numbers cannot be expressed as logarithms. This limits the set of variables that lend themselves to a logarithmic transformation.[5]

We begin by showing the relationship between the logarithm of two variables and the logarithm of their product. The revenue of a firm, R, is the product of the price of its good, P, and the quantity sold, Q. Define lowercase letters as the logarithms of their uppercase counterparts, so $q = \log_b(Q), p = \log_b(P)$, and $r = \log_b(R)$. By the definitions of logarithms, we then have $Q = b^q$ and $P = b^p$, so

$$R = PQ = b^p b^q = b^{p+q}.$$

The definition of logarithms shows that

$$\log_b(PQ) = p + q.$$

The general rule is as follows.

Logarithmic Transformation of a Product For any two positive variables X and Y,

$$\log_b(XY) = \log_b(X) + \log_b(Y).$$

[5]Another advantage of logarithmic transformations is that they allow the interpretation of coefficients as elasticities. This is shown in Chapter 7.

The rule for the logarithm of a quotient is derived in a similar fashion. To illustrate this rule, we determine the relationship between real money balances, M/P, the logarithm of nominal balances, $m = \log_b(M)$, and the logarithm of prices, $p = \log_b(P)$. Noting that $M = b^m$ and $P = b^p$, we write real money balances as

$$\frac{M}{P} = \frac{b^m}{b^p} = b^{m-p},$$

which shows that $\log(M/P) = m - p$. The general rule follows.

Logarithmic Transformation of a Quotient For any two positive variables X and Y,

$$\log_b\left(\frac{X}{Y}\right) = \log_b(X) - \log_b(Y).$$

Exponents are frequently used in economic modeling. The Cobb-Douglas production function that links output per worker (Q) to capital per worker (K), called the **intensive Cobb-Douglas production function,** is

$$Q = K^{\alpha}.$$

The logarithmic transformation of this relationship can be determined by using the definition of logarithms and other results derived above. Define a variable Z such that it equals the base b logarithm of K^{α}; that is,

$$Z = \log_b(K^{\alpha}).$$

This means that

$$K^{\alpha} = b^Z.$$

We can verify that $Z = \alpha \cdot \log_b(K)$ since

$$K^{\alpha} = b^{\alpha \cdot \log_b(K)} = (b^{\log_b(K)})^{\alpha} = K^{\alpha}.$$

The logarithm of output per worker is $q = \alpha \cdot k$, where $q = \log_b(Q)$ and $k = \log_b(K)$. The general form of this rule is as follows.

Logarithmic Transformation of an Exponent For any positive variable X and any values of λ,

$$\log_b(X^{\lambda}) = \lambda \log_b(X).$$

These three rules can be combined as the need arises. For example, the logarithm of the real exchange rate, $RER = EP^*/P$, is

$$\log_b(RER) = \log_b(E) + \log_b(P^*) - \log_b(P).$$

When output, Y, is related to technology, A, labor, L, and capital, C, by the function

$$Y = AL^{\alpha}C^{\beta},$$

then the logarithm of output is related to the logarithm of technology, labor, and capital by the function

$$\log_b(Y) = \log_b(A) + \alpha \log_b(L) + \beta \log_b(C).$$

Relationship between Logarithms with Different Bases

All of the rules presented so far include logarithms with the same base. We can show the relationship between logarithms with different bases by considering the value of the base J logarithm of a variable H and its base W value, that is, $\log_J H$ and $\log_W H$, respectively. First define some number s such that $H = J^S$. Therefore $s = \log_J H$. The base W value of H, $\log_W H$, can be written as

$$\log_W J^S = s \cdot \log_W J.$$

Substituting for s, we find

$$\log_W H = \log_W J \cdot \log_J H,$$

which can be rewritten as

$$\frac{\log_W H}{\log_J H} = \log_W J.$$

A general property derived from this rule is that if $W < J$,

$$\log_W J > 1,$$

and, therefore,

$$\frac{\log_W H}{\log_J H} \geq 1,$$

and

$$|\log_W H| \geq |\log_J H|,$$

where $|x|$ represents the absolute value of x.[6] This result is illustrated by Table 3.6 and Figure 3.4, which show that $\log_2(x)$ is greater than $\log_{10}(x)$ for all values of x greater than 1 and $\log_2(x)$ is less than $\log_{10}(x)$ for all values of x less than 1.

Natural Logarithms

A **natural logarithm** is a logarithm that takes, as its base, the exponential, e. The natural logarithm of a variable x is written either as $\log_e(x)$ or, more commonly, as $\ln(x)$. The natural logarithm is particularly useful for many applications in economics. In this section we present some of the properties of natural logarithms and show their use in a number of applications.

[6] The relationship between absolute values uses an inequality sign rather than a strict inequality sign to include the case of $H = 1$.

All of the rules for logarithms presented above apply to the natural logarithm since it is just a logarithm with a particular base. Therefore we have the following rules for natural logarithms.

Rules for Natural Logarithms For any variable Z and any positive variables X and Y,

$$\begin{aligned} \ln(e^Z) &= Z, \\ e^{\ln X} &= X, \\ \ln(XY) &= \ln X + \ln Y, \\ \ln\left(\frac{X}{Y}\right) &= \ln X - \ln Y, \quad \text{and} \\ \ln X^Z &= Z \ln X. \end{aligned}$$

The link between the natural logarithm and the exponential, along with the role of the exponential in calculating growth rates, is used in the following application that provides a useful rule of thumb.

Doubling Times and the Rule-of-70

The **Rule-of-70** provides a simple way to calculate the approximate number of years it takes for the level of a variable growing at a constant rate to double. This rule states that the approximate number of years n for a variable growing at the constant growth rate of R percent, to double is

$$n = \frac{70}{R}.$$

For example, a city with an annual population growth rate of 5% will double its population in approximately 14 years. If the growth rate were 7%, it would double its population in approximately 10 years.

A more formal analysis of doubling times reveals some interesting characteristics of growth. First, note that finding doubling times requires us to find the set of values of n and r ($= R/100$) such that the ratio of the future level, $X(t + n)$, to the initial level, $X(t)$, equals 2. Referring back to the formula for continuous compounding and dividing each side of that equation by $X(t)$, we find that finding the doubling times involves finding r and n such that

$$e^{r \cdot n} = \frac{X(t+n)}{X(t)} = 2.$$

The first thing to note is that the initial level of the variable does not affect the number of years it takes for the level to double. Increasing both $X(t + n)$ and $X(t)$ does not alter their ratio. Thus the time it takes for a variable to increase by a certain proportion is not a function of its initial level.

What is the special role of the number 70 in this rule? We can answer this question by taking the natural logarithm of each side of the expression $e^{rn} = 2$. This shows that the relationship between r and n that satisfies the doubling time problem is

$$r \cdot n = \ln(2) = 0.6931\ldots.$$

Remembering that the Rule-of-70 is expressed in percentage growth rates, we have $R \cdot n = 69.31$. Thus any product of R and n that equals (approximately) 70 will show us the combination of a percentage growth rate, compounded continuously, and number of years that leads to the doubling of the level of a variable.

Finally, what are the appropriate numbers for trebling times, quadrupling times, and so on? Following the same procedure, we see that the condition for a variable growing continuously at the constant annual rate r to increase by a factor F in n years is

$$e^{r \cdot n} = F.$$

This means that the relationship between the percentage growth rate, R, and the number of years, n, for a variable to increase by a factor F is

$$R \cdot n = 100 \cdot \ln(F).$$

Since $\ln(3) = 1.099$, the rule of thumb for trebling times is called the "rule-of-110." We can figure out the rule of thumb for quadrupling times without a calculator since

$$\ln(4) = \ln(2^2) = 2 \cdot \ln(2).$$

Therefore, the quadrupling time rule is (approximately) the "rule-of-140." If you can remember that $\ln(5) = 1.6$ and $\ln(7) = 1.95$, then you have rules of thumb for any factor between 2 and 10.

In this application we have used the natural logarithm in conjunction with the equation describing continuously compounded growth to analyze the Rule-of-70. The next application uses properties of natural logarithms and the growth equation in a similar fashion to show how to effectively plot the time path of rapidly growing variables.

Graphing Time Paths of Variables

The dramatic change in the level of a variable when there is rapid growth, or even when there is moderate growth over a long periods, often presents a problem when attempting to graph the path of a variable against time. To illustrate this, consider the case of a country with a constant inflation rate of 30% per year (that is, the growth rate of prices is 0.3). The price level is arbitrarily set to 100 in 1960. The price level in any subsequent year is

$$P(t + 1960) = 100 \cdot e^{0.3 \cdot t},$$

where t is the number of years since 1960. The practical problem with graphing this series is evident if we note that the price level in 1990 equals 810,308. Scaling the vertical axis to allow for numbers this large effectively masks any information in the early part of the sample period.

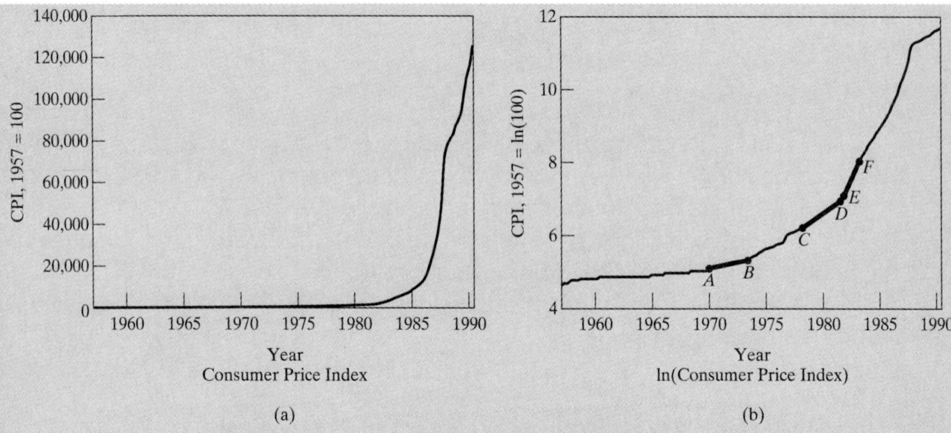

FIGURE 3.5 Consumer Price Index, Mexico, 1957–1990

An alternative strategy is to graph the natural logarithm of prices against time. Taking the natural logarithmic transformation of the above equation gives us

$$\ln(P(t + 1960)) = \ln(100) + \ln(e^{0.3 \cdot t}) = 4.6 + 0.30t,$$

which shows that the graph of the time path of the natural logarithm of prices is a straight line with an intercept of 4.6 and a slope of 0.30. Thus the slope of this line multiplied by 100% gives the percentage rate of growth of prices (that is, the inflation rate).

Actual variables almost never grow at a steady rate, and, therefore, the time path of the natural logarithm of variables will not be straight line. But we can interpret the slope of a line connecting any two points of a graph of the natural logarithm of a variable against time as the average annual rate of change of that variable over the period represented by those two points. This is shown by noting that the slope of the line connecting two points in such a graph, b, equals

$$b = \frac{\ln(X(T + t)) - \ln(X(T))}{t},$$

where T is the base time period and t is the number of periods before or after the base period. Rewriting this expression, we see that

$$\ln(X(T + t)) - \ln(X(T)) = \ln\left(\frac{X(T + t)}{X(T)}\right) = bt.$$

Taking the exponential of each side and rearranging, we find that

$$X(T + t) = X(T)e^{bt},$$

which shows that b, the slope of the line connecting the points, does indeed equal the average annual rate of growth over the time period represented by those points. Multiplying b by 100 gives the percentage rate of growth.

Figure 3.5(a), which presents the consumer price index in Mexico from 1957 to 1990, illustrates the difficulty in reading the graph of a rapidly growing time series.

Over this time span, the price level increased by a factor of over 1500, with an average annual inflation rate of about 22%. The inflation experience was very different during the various periods, but it is very difficult to discern this from Figure 3.5(a).

Figure 3.5(b) offers a more useful depiction of the data by graphing the natural logarithm of consumer prices in Mexico between 1957 and 1990. This figure enables us to discern differences in inflation across time. It shows inflation was in the single digits up until the early 1970s. For example, the slope of the line AB, which connects the points representing the beginning of 1970 and the end of 1972, is 0.07, which translates to an average annual inflation rate of 7% during these two years. Inflation picked up by the end of the 1970s and into the early 1980s. The slope of the line connecting the points representing the beginning of 1978 (C) and the end of 1981 (D) is almost 0.20, indicating an average inflation, over these four years, of almost 20%. Average inflation between the beginning of 1982 (E) and the end of 1983 (F), during which time the debt crisis began, was over 55% per year. By the late 1980s, inflation had slowed to an annual rate of about 21%.

Exercises 3.3

1. Use the rules of logarithms to simplify the following.
   (a) $10^{\log_{10}(100)}$
   (b) $\ln e^x - e^{\ln(x)}$
   (c) $\log_{10}\left(\frac{1}{x^5}\right)$
   (d) $\log_2(a + b)$
   (e) $\ln(e^{a+bx+cz})$
   (f) $\ln(4x)^3$
   (g) $\ln\left(\frac{1}{e^5}[x^\alpha y^{-\beta}]^2\right)$
2. Using the formula for deriving the relationship between logarithms with different bases, $\log_w H = \log_w J \cdot \log_J H$, calculate the following.
   (a) $(\log_2 4)(\log_4 256)$
   (b) $(\log_3 e)(\log_e 27)$
   (c) $(\log_e 10)(\log_{10} 1)$
3. Calculate $\log_2 32$ and $\ln 32$. Using your answers, show that this example illustrates the property that, when $c > d$, $\log_c x$ is less than $\log_d x$, assuming that $x > \log_b b$.
4. On a secretive search through your grandfather's basement you uncover an old, dust-covered stamp collection. You take the collection to a stamp dealer who tells you that it currently is worth \$1,000, but in ten years it will triple its value. Unfortunately, you will have to store the collection in a special warehouse during this time. The storage fee is \$200, compounded continuously at a rate of 5% per year but is not paid until you withdraw your collection from the warehouse. Should you store the stamp collection or sell it immediately and invest the proceeds in the stock market, where you expect to make a 9.5% continuously compounded return over the coming ten years?

5. The theory of consumer behavior is one of the foundations of economic analysis. The linear logarithmic utility function is one of the original functions developed to measure consumer utility and is still widely used by economists. It is written as

$$u = \ln U = \sum_{i=1}^{n} \beta_i \ln q_i,$$

where u is the index of utility, q_i is the quantity of good i, and $0 < \beta_i < 1$. Transform this function back to its original form, where U is utility.

6. There are two ways to calculate the **mean** of a series of data. The **arithmetic mean,** written in the form

$$X_a = \sum_{i=1}^{n} \frac{1}{n} x_i,$$

takes the sum of that series and divides by the number of data points. A **geometric mean,** on the other hand, takes the product of a group of n data points, where each is raised to the exponent $1/n$,

$$X_g = \prod_{i=1}^{n} x^{1/n}.$$

Using a geometric mean and natural logarithms gives less weight to outliers than an arithmetic mean. Using the following per capita income data for several developing countries, calculate the geometric mean by taking the natural logarithm of both sides of the definition. Remember that

$$X_g = e^{\ln(X_g)}.$$

How does your answer compare with the result of the arithmetic mean calculation?

Country	1993 Per-Capita Income ($)
Pakistan	420
Ecuador	1070
Mexico	3470

7. Health care costs in the United States have grown at an average rate of 4.8% between 1990 and 1999, and in 1999 they accounted for 10% of the U.S. Gross Domestic Product (GDP). If health care costs continue to grow at this rate and GDP continues to expand at a 2% average annual rate, what will health care's share of GDP be in 2029 (that is, after 30 years). Is this ratio sustainable over time? What would you expect to happen to the growth of health care expenditures over time?

8. Bank Highrates is still offering the deposit-incentive annual interest rate of 8%. Its upstart competitor, Bank Betterrates, is offering a similar incentive program but will pay an effective rate of 8.25% on an equivalent deposit. Which bank is offering its investors a better deal?

9. The equation in Section 3.1 presents the rule for calculating growth rates with one-time compounding per period. Use the natural logarithmic transformation to show

the general relationship between $1 + r$ and n that must hold for an asset to increase in value from \$15,000 to \$30,000, if the interest on that asset accrues only once at the end of each year. Use a calculator to find exact values of n for each of the following interest rates, and comment on how closely the Rule-of-70 holds.

(a) $r = 0.01$
(b) $r = 0.05$
(c) $r = 0.10$
(d) $r = 0.25$
(e) $r = 1.00$

10. Consider the production function, $Q = 15L^{4/5}K^{1/5}$, where Q is output, L is labor input, and K represents capital input. Using natural logarithms, transform this exponential function into a linear function. Now assume that $L = 10$ and $K = 5$. What is the value of $\ln(Q)$? Remembering that $\exp(\ln(Q)) = Q$, determine the value of Q.
11. You are given \$10,000 as a graduation present, and you want to buy a new car in the near future. Therefore you invest your gift in a conservative money market account paying a continuously compounded 5% per annum. Using the formula
$$X(t + n) = X(t)e^{r \cdot n}$$
and natural logarithms, solve for n to determine how low it will take you to save \$15,000.
12. The housing price index for the United States in 1990 was 144.8, while its value in 1999 was 192.9 (the index is calculated such that it averaged 100 in the 1982–1984 period). What was the average annual continuously compounded inflation rate for housing costs between 1990 and 1999?

Summary

The exponential and logarithmic functions presented in this chapter play an important role in economic analysis. The applications in this chapter point out the use of these functions for growth calculations and present value. We return to the calculation of present value in Chapter 12 when we show how to take the present value of a stream of payments rather than of a one-time payment, as was done here. We also return to the role of the exponential function in describing the growth process in Chapter 14 where we discuss equations in which the rate of change of a variable is a function of its level.

The importance of using logarithmic functions to transform nonlinear relationships into a linear form will become more apparent in the next chapter, where a set of techniques for solving linear functions is presented. Another important property of logarithms is that the coefficient of a linear equation whose variables are natural logarithms can be interpreted as an elasticity. Chapter 7 presents this property and applies it in a number of economic contexts.

Part Two

Matrix Algebra

Chapter 4
Systems of Equations and Matrix Algebra

Chapter 5
Further Topics in Matrix Algebra

This part of the book consists of two chapters that introduce matrix algebra. A **matrix** *is a rectangular array of numbers, variables, or parameters with one or more rows and one or more columns. A matrix offers a compact way to depict a system of equations. Matrix algebra is the set of tools used to characterize and manipulate matrices and, therefore, to analyze systems of linear equations. Economic applications of systems of linear equations include supply and demand analysis, macroeconomic models like the well-known IS/LM model, and dynamic models like those discussed in Part Five of this book. Indeed, virtually all fields of economics involve the analysis of systems of linear equations.*

Chapter 4 begins by reviewing the method for solving a system of equations in the context of some simple economic examples. We next show how matrix algebra is used to represent and solve systems of equations. Chapter 4 presents the solution for a system of two equations. Techniques for finding solutions for systems with more equations are presented in Chapter 5. Chapter 5 also presents a method for transforming a system of equations representing a series of multivariate relationships into an equivalent system of univariate relationships, a technique that will prove useful for analysis of dynamic systems in Chapters 13 and 14.

Matrix algebra is sometimes called **linear algebra** *since it involves the analysis of systems of linear equations like*

$$x_0 = b_0 + b_1x_1 + b_2x_2 + b_3x_3,$$

where the b_i's are parameters and the x_i's are variables. At first this requirement of linearity may strike you as very restrictive. But by simply defining the variables x_0, x_1, x_2, and

x_3 in a variety of ways, the tools presented in this chapter become applicable to a wide set of functions. For example, Chapter 3 shows that the nonlinear equation

$$Y = AX_1^B X_2^C$$

can be rewritten as the linear equation

$$\ln(Y) = \ln(A) + B\ln(X_1) + C\ln(X_2).$$

Thus this nonlinear equation has a linear representation. Also, as discussed in Chapter 7, there are techniques for finding a linear approximation to a nonlinear relationship. Matrix algebra then offers a method for analyzing the system of equations that make up the linear approximation to the original system.

Chapter 4

Systems of Equations and Matrix Algebra

You have probably noted by this stage of your economics education that most graphs used in economics consist of two lines that intersect at one point. The typical microeconomic relationship is depicted by a downward-sloping demand curve and an upward-sloping supply curve that intersect at the equilibrium levels of price and quantity. Most macroeconomic textbooks present the IS curve and the LM curve, which intersect at the equilibrium interest rate and output, or curves representing aggregate demand and aggregate supply, which intersect at the equilibrium price level and output.

While shifting schedules on a graph suggests the qualitative relationship between exogenous and endogenous variables, a more precise quantitative relationship requires an explicit solution of the mathematical model embodied by the schedules. In this chapter we learn how to solve multiequation mathematical models that consist of systems of equations. The chapter begins with a solution technique that uses **repeated substitution** of one equation into another. This technique is straightforward, but it can be cumbersome for models with many equations. Fortunately, a powerful set of tools for handling systems of equations is provided by **matrix algebra** (which is also sometimes called **linear algebra**). In this chapter we present some basic definitions and concepts of matrix algebra. Chapter 5 continues with this subject by presenting more advanced topics.

A **matrix** is a rectangular array of numbers, variables, or parameters with one or more rows and one or more columns. Matrix algebra is the set of tools used to characterize and manipulate matrices. Section 4.2 describes the way in which matrix algebra is used to represent systems of equations. The rules for using matrices are presented in Section 4.3. This section also identifies some special matrices. Section 4.4 discusses the way in which matrix algebra provides a solution to a system of equations. In that section an explicit matrix solution is provided for the case of a system representing two equations with two endogenous variables.

4.1 SOLVING SYSTEMS OF EQUATIONS

Economic models typically consist of a number of equations that represent identities, behavioral relationships, and conditions that constitute an equilibrium. These equations include both **variables,** which are economic quantities that can assume different values, and **parameters,** which are unvarying constants. For example, the equation

$$y = a + b_1x_1 + b_2x_2 + b_3x_3$$

includes the variables y, x_1, x_2, and x_3 and the parameters a, b_1, b_2, and b_3. As discussed in Chapter 1, the variables of a model are classified as either **exogenous** if they are determined outside the context of the model or **endogenous** if they are determined by the model. A **solution** to the model is a representation of the endogenous variables as functions of only the parameters of the model and the exogenous variables.

The simple supply and demand model introduced in Chapter 1 illustrates these concepts. That model concerns the market for the widget. The endogenous variables in the model are the price of a widget, P, the quantity of widgets demanded by consumers, Q^D, and the quantity of widgets supplied by producers, Q^S. The exogenous variables in that model are the price of goods that are potential substitutes for widgets, G, and the price of inputs used in producing widgets, N. The demand equation for widgets is

$$Q^D = \alpha - \beta P + \gamma G, \tag{4.1}$$

and the supply equation is

$$Q^S = \theta + \lambda P - \phi N, \tag{4.2}$$

where the Greek letters in these equations, $\alpha, \beta, \gamma, \theta, \lambda$ and ϕ, represent the parameters of the model. The equilibrium condition is

$$Q^D = Q^S. \tag{4.3}$$

A simultaneous solution of the demand equation, supply equation, and equilibrium condition gives a solution to this model. The value of the endogenous variables in equilibrium are their **equilibrium values.** Denote the equilibrium quantity as Q. In equilibrium,

$$Q = Q^D = Q^S.$$

Therefore to solve for the equilibrium price and quantity, we can begin by setting (4.1) equal to (4.2) to get

$$\alpha - \beta P + \gamma G = \theta + \lambda P - \phi N.$$

Solving for the endogenous variable, P, as a function of the exogenous variables G and N, as well as the parameters of the model, we have

$$P = \frac{\alpha - \theta + \gamma G + \phi N}{\beta + \lambda}. \tag{4.4}$$

This solution shows that the price of widgets increases with an increase in the price of the inputs used in widget production, N, and also increases with an increase in the price of the substitute good, G. We then solve for the equilibrium quantity by substituting this solution for P into either the demand equation (4.1) or the supply equation (4.2), which gives us the equilibrium quantity

$$Q = \frac{\alpha\lambda + \beta\theta + \lambda\gamma G - \beta\phi N}{\beta + \lambda}. \tag{4.5}$$

This solution shows that the equilibrium quantity increases with an increase in the price of the substitute good and decreases with an increase in the price of the input to widget production.

The solution technique used here is called **repeated substitution.** It involves substituting out the endogenous variables such that you get an equation that contains only one endogenous variable. In this case we first obtained an equation that included the endogenous variable P, the exogenous variables G and N, and the parameters. This equation then provides the solution for P, which, in turn, can be used in solving for the other endogenous variable Q. It is important to notice that the order in which the solution for variables is obtained is irrelevant. We would have arrived at the same solution for P and Q if we had first solved for the equilibrium quantity.

Comparative Statics

Economic analysis often considers the effect of a change in an exogenous variable on one or more endogenous variables. For example, we might ask how a change in the price of inputs to widget production affects the price of widgets and the equilibrium quantity of widgets. The answer to this question would represent a **comparative static analysis.** More generally, **comparative statics** compares the value of endogenous variables in one equilibrium to their value in another equilibrium that has resulted from a given change in an exogenous variable. The term "statics" refers to the fact that the analysis is not concerned with the way in which the new equilibrium is reached. Usually comparative static analysis is conducted by varying one exogenous variable at a time in order to isolate the effect of that particular variable. This reflects the effort to look at the effect of a change in a variable, *ceteris paribus*, that is, other things being equal.

The solution to the widget model presented above enables us to analyze the effect of an increase in the price of inputs on the price of widgets and the equilibrium quantity, *ceteris paribus*. We use the capital Greek letter delta, Δ, to denote the change in a variable. We want to solve for ΔP, which is the change in the price of widgets, and ΔQ, which is the change in the equilibrium quantity of widgets, for a given increase in the price of inputs ΔN. Denoting the initial price of inputs as N_0 and the input price after the increase as N_1, the change in the price of inputs is

$$\Delta N = N_1 - N_0.$$

The assumption of *ceteris paribus* is implemented by considering a situation where

$$\Delta G = G_1 - G_0 = 0.$$

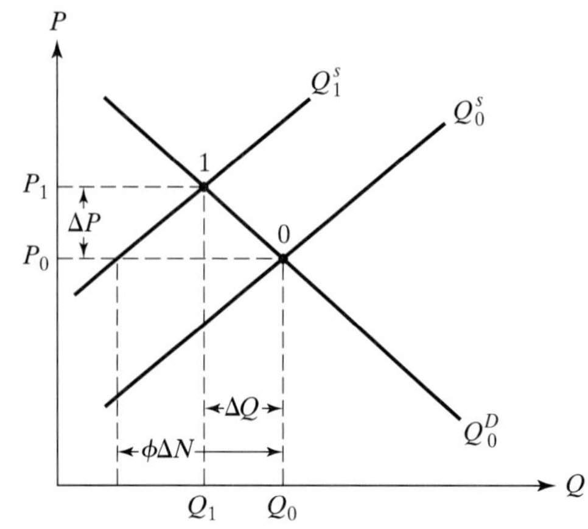

FIGURE 4.1 An Increase in the Price of Inputs

Using the solution for price in (4.4), we find that the change in the price of widgets is

$$\begin{aligned}\Delta P &= P_1 - P_0 \\ &= \frac{\alpha - \theta + \gamma G_1 + \phi N_1}{\beta + \lambda} - \frac{\alpha - \theta + \gamma G_0 + \phi N_0}{\beta + \lambda} \\ &= \frac{\phi}{\beta + \lambda}\,\Delta N.\end{aligned}$$

Using the solution for quantity in (4.5), we find that the change in the equilibrium quantity of widgets is

$$\begin{aligned}\Delta Q &= Q_1 - Q_0 \\ &= \frac{\alpha\lambda + \beta\theta + \lambda\gamma G_1 - \beta\phi N_1}{\beta + \lambda} - \frac{\alpha\lambda + \beta\theta + \lambda\gamma G_0 - \beta\phi N_0}{\beta + \lambda} \\ &= -\frac{\beta\phi}{\beta + \lambda}\,\Delta N.\end{aligned}$$

These results show that an increase in the price of inputs (that is, $\Delta N > 0$) causes an increase in the price of widgets ($\Delta P > 0$) and a decrease in their equilibrium quantity ($\Delta Q < 0$).

Figure 4.1 illustrates the effect of an increase in the price of inputs on the equilibrium price and quantity of widgets using a graph of the demand and supply equations. The initial equilibrium point, where the original supply and demand equations Q_0^S and Q_0^D intersect, is identified as point 0. An increase in the price of inputs by the amount ΔN causes the supply curve to shift horizontally to the left by the amount $\phi\,\Delta N$. The new supply schedule is Q_1^S. The new level of price and quantity, P_1 and Q_1, as well as the change in price and quantity, are identified in the figure.

Repeated substitution is also used to solve the simple **IS/LM** macroeconomic model. This model includes a national income identity

$$Y = C + I + G, \tag{4.6}$$

where Y is national income, C is consumption, I is investment, and G is government purchases, all denominated in millions of dollars. We assume that the consumption function is

$$C = 200 + 0.8Y, \tag{4.7}$$

where in this case the *marginal propensity to consume* equals 0.8. Investment is a function of the interest rate, R (which equals, for example, 0.02 when the interest rate is 2%), and the investment function is assumed to be

$$I = 1000 - 2000R. \tag{4.8}$$

The model also includes a money market equation that describes the demand for real balances, M/P, as a function of the interest rate and income,

$$\frac{M}{P} = -1000R + 0.1Y, \tag{4.9}$$

where M is nominal money balances and P is the price level. The endogenous variables in this model are Y, C, I, and R. The level of government purchases is exogenous. Both the numerator and the denominator of the quotient M/P are assumed exogenous, and, therefore, real money balances are exogenous.

Substituting the consumption equation (4.7) and the investment equation (4.8) into the national income accounting identity (4.6), we have

$$Y = 200 + 0.8Y + 1000 - 2000R + G,$$

or

$$Y = 6000 - 10{,}000R + 5G. \tag{4.10}$$

Rewriting the money market equation (4.9) we have

$$R = 0.0001Y - 0.001\frac{M}{P}. \tag{4.11}$$

Equations (4.10) and (4.11) represent two equations in two unknowns, Y and R. Solving these two equations to obtain Y and R as functions of only G and M/P, we get the solution

$$\begin{aligned} Y &= 3000 + 5\frac{M}{P} + 2.5G \\ R &= 0.3 - 0.0005\frac{M}{P} + 0.00025G. \end{aligned} \tag{4.12}$$

The actual numerical solution for Y and R obviously depends upon our choices of G and M/P. If we choose

$$G = 2000 \quad \text{and} \quad \frac{M}{P} = 1500,$$

then the solution is

$$Y = 15{,}500$$
$$R = 0.05.$$

We could also conduct a comparative static exercise with this model. Expressing the solution (4.12) in changes rather than levels, we have

$$\Delta Y = 5\,\Delta\frac{M}{P} + 2.5\,\Delta G$$
$$\Delta R = -0.0005\,\Delta\frac{M}{P} + 0.00025\,\Delta G. \tag{4.13}$$

Suppose we want to investigate the effect of a \$50 million decrease in government purchases on income and the interest rate, *ceteris paribus*. For the question at hand, $\Delta G = -50$ and $\Delta M/P = 0$. Therefore the comparative static result is

$$\Delta Y = -125$$
$$\Delta R = -0.0125.$$

The Incidence of a Tax

An important question in public finance is the distribution of the burden of a tax. For example, one question of this nature is the extent to which a tax on widgets is borne by the sellers of widgets and the extent to which that tax is borne by the consumers of widgets. As we show, the answer to this question depends upon the relative responsiveness of demand and supply to the price of widgets.

To illustrate this point, we modify the model presented above by distinguishing between the price paid by consumers of widgets, P_C, and the price received by widget producers, P_P. The tax, T, which we assume is a given amount levied on each widget sold, drives a wedge between P_C and P_P as shown by the equation

$$P_C = P_P + T.$$

The distinction between the consumers' price and the producers' price requires a modification of our model. The demand equation (4.1) is now

$$Q^D = \alpha - \beta P_C + \gamma G$$

since the quantity demanded depends upon the price facing consumers. The supply equation (4.2) is now

$$Q^S = \theta + \lambda P_P - \phi N$$

since the quantity supplied is the price facing producers. The equilibrium condition (4.3) remains unchanged. The equilibrium price is found by substituting the tax equation into the demand equation and using the equilibrium condition to obtain

$$\alpha - \beta(P_P + T) + \gamma G = \theta + \lambda P_P - \phi N,$$

or, rewriting this,

$$P_P = \frac{\alpha - \theta - \beta T + \gamma G + \phi N}{\beta + \lambda}.$$

The price facing consumers can then be solved for using this result along with the tax equation to get

$$\begin{aligned} P_C &= \frac{\alpha - \theta + \gamma G + \phi N - \beta T}{\beta + \lambda} + T \\ &= \frac{\alpha - \theta + \gamma G + \phi N + \lambda T}{\beta + \lambda}. \end{aligned}$$

We can investigate the incidence of a tax by examining the effect of a change in the tax, ΔT, on the change in prices facing producers, ΔP_P, and the change in prices facing consumers, ΔP_C, *ceteris paribus*. Using the two solutions above, we find

$$\Delta P_P = -\frac{\beta}{\beta + \lambda}\,\Delta T$$

$$\Delta P_C = \frac{\lambda}{\beta + \lambda}\,\Delta T.$$

These results show that the effects of an increase in the tax are divided between a fall in the price facing producers and an increase in the price facing consumers. A given tax increase has a relatively larger effect on P_P and a relatively smaller effect on P_C when β is relatively larger than λ, that is, when quantity demanded is relatively more price sensitive than quantity supplied. Conversely, when quantity supplied is relatively more price sensitive than quantity demanded and λ is large relative to β, then a given tax increase will cause a relatively big increase in consumers' price and a relatively small decrease in producers' price.

A numerical example illustrates this. Suppose $\beta = 4$ and $\lambda = 1$. In this case a \$1 increase in the price facing consumers decreases the quantity demanded by 4 units, and a \$1 increase in the price received by producers increases the quantity supplied by 1 unit. An increase in the tax rate of \$0.10 per widget lowers producers' price by \$0.08 and raises consumers' price by \$0.02. If, instead, $\beta = 1$ and $\lambda = 1$, then the \$0.10 increase in the tax rate would lower producers' price by \$0.05 and would raise consumers' price by \$0.05.

This result is also illustrated by Figures 4.2(a) and 4.2(b). Each of these two figures has the same supply equation. The price in the supply equation must be consumers' price since this is the variable appearing on the axis. Therefore the supply equations in these two figures are

$$Q^S = \theta + \lambda(P_C - T) - \phi N.$$

The demand equation represented in Figure 4.2(a) has a large value of β relative to the demand equation depicted in Figure 4.2(b). In each figure the initial equilibrium is represented by point 0, with equilibrium price P_0 and equilibrium quantity Q_0.

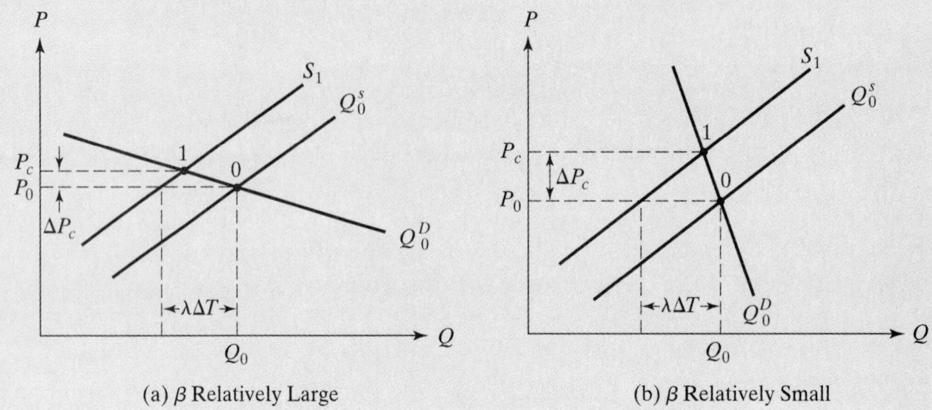

FIGURE 4.2 Incidence of a Tax Increase

An increase in the tax by the amount ΔT causes the supply equation to shift left by the amount $-\lambda \Delta T$. In each figure, the new equilibrium points are identified as point 1. The change in consumers' price, ΔP_C, is much smaller in Figure 4.2(a) than in Figure 4.2(b). The results in these two figures provide another way to demonstrate that a given tax increase has a relatively smaller effect on consumers' price when the sensitivity of quantity demanded to price is relatively large, given the sensitivity of quantity supplied to price. The results in this figure also demonstrate a relatively large effect on producers' price in the case where β is relatively large since the relationship among producers' price, consumers' price, and the tax, expressed in differences, is

$$\Delta P_P = \Delta P_C - \Delta T.$$

This shows that for a given tax increase ΔT, a smaller increase in ΔP_C is associated with a larger decline in producers' price.

Job Creation and Job Destruction

In a dynamic economy, new industries will emerge while older industries fade. For example, there was dramatic growth in high-technology industries in the 1990s while other industries, like textiles, contracted. The reallocation of workers and resources from one industry to another enables the economy as a whole to become more productive and to grow. Workers moving to expanding industries may enjoy higher pay. But reallocation has a costly side as well since, in the wake of job loss, workers could experience a protracted period of unemployment. People who have lost jobs may be forced to move, and their new wages may fall short of their previous compensation.

The total number of new employment positions gained in a particular industry in a particular year is its level of **job creation,** while the total number of new employment positions lost in a particular industry in a particular year is its level of **job destruction.** Job creation and job destruction are called **gross job flows.** The sum of job creation and job destruction is **job reallocation.** The difference between job creation and job destruction is the **net employment change.** If we represent job creation by C, and job destruction by D, then reallocation is $C + D$, while net employment change is $C - D$. It is easy to see that we can have a relatively large amount of job reallocation with little or no job destruction. For example, for all manufacturing industries, the average annual rate of job reallocation between 1973 and 1993 was 19%, while during the same period the average annual net change in overall manufacturing employment was −1.4%.

As discussed by Steven Davis, John Haltiwanger, and Scott Schuh in their book *Job Creation and Job Destruction*,[1] a striking aspect of gross job flows is that there is simultaneous job creation and job destruction within narrowly defined industries. For example, the rates of job creation and job destruction in the industry classified as "Steel Wiredrawing and Steel Nails and Spikes" (which has the Standard Industrial Classification (SIC) number 3315) varied widely between 1989 and 1991. The rates of job creation and job destruction were, respectively, 9.8% and 6.2% in 1989, 6.6% and 6.5% in 1990, and 4.5% and 11.0% in 1991. This means that the reallocation rates were 16.0% in 1989, 13.1% in 1990, and 15.5% in 1991.

Simultaneous job creation and job destruction in an industry reflects heterogeneity among firms within that industry. One possible source of heterogeneity among firms is different degrees of response to changes in the economic environment. These differences, combined with spillover effects from one firm to another, can result in simultaneous job creation and job destruction. This is shown in a model of two firms within an industry, Firm A and Firm B. Each firm has a labor demand schedule that depends upon the wage, W, and the overall demand for goods, Y. We assume the responsiveness of labor demand to overall demand differs across the two firms. Defining the labor demand schedules for the firms as L_A^D and L_B^D, we have

$$L_A^D = -\gamma W + \beta_A Y$$
$$L_B^D = -\gamma W + \beta_B Y,$$

where γ, β_A and β_B are all positive parameters. The use of a common parameter on wages, γ, and different parameters on overall demand, β_A and β_B, allows us to focus on one type of heterogeneity between the firms. The absence of a subscript on Y reflects the assumption that the relevant measure of overall demand is common to both firms. The absence of a subscript on W reflects the assumption that the two firms draw from a common pool of labor and, consequently, pay the same wage. If the number of workers in the common pool of labor is fixed and equal to $\bar{L}$, then

$$\bar{L} = L_A^S + L_B^S,$$

where L_A^S and L_B^S refer to labor supplied to Firms A and B, respectively. Finally, we assume that labor supply equals labor demand for each firm, that is,

$$L_A^D = L_A^S$$
$$L_B^D = L_B^S.$$

[1] Steven Davis, John Haltiwanger, and Scott Schuh, *Job Creation and Job Destruction* (Cambridge, MA: MIT Press, 1996).

Given this condition, we define the equilibrium number of workers hired by the two firms as $L_A = L_A^D = L_A^S$ and $L_B = L_B^D = L_B^S$. Therefore, we can write $\overline{L} = L_A + L_B$.

The key insight from this model is that even though both firms would like to hire more workers in response to an increase in overall demand (shown by the fact that both β_A and β_B are positive), the fixed overall labor supply results in simultaneous job creation and job destruction since one firm will hire more workers while the other will shed workers. To see this, we first solve for the common wage using Firm B's labor demand to get

$$W = \frac{\beta_B Y - L_B}{\gamma}$$

and then substitute out for W in Firm A's labor demand equation to obtain

$$L_A = -\gamma\left(\frac{\beta_B Y - L_B}{\gamma}\right) + \beta_A Y = L_B + (\beta_A - \beta_B)Y.$$

Then rearranging the labor supply equation to read $L_B = \overline{L} - L_A$ and substituting out for L_B in the equation above, we have, after a bit of manipulation,

$$L_A = \left(\frac{\beta_A - \beta_B}{2}\right)Y + \frac{\overline{L}}{2}.$$

We can also express this result in terms of changes rather than levels as

$$\Delta L_A = \left(\frac{\beta_A - \beta_B}{2}\right)\Delta Y$$

since, by assumption, $\Delta\overline{L} = 0$. With $\overline{L}$ constant, we have $\Delta L_B = -\Delta L_A$, and therefore

$$\Delta L_B = -\Delta L_A = \left(\frac{\beta_B - \beta_A}{2}\right)\Delta Y.$$

This result shows that, with an increase in overall demand ($\Delta Y > 0$), there is job creation in Firm A (that is, $\Delta L_A > 0$) and job destruction in Firm B ($\Delta L_B < 0$) if labor demand in Firm A is more responsive to output than labor demand in Firm B (that is, if $\beta_A > \beta_B$). Note that, in this example, there is no net employment change in the industry since, by assumption, $\Delta L_B = -\Delta L_A$. The amount of reallocation in the industry, R, is the sum of the absolute values of ΔL_A and ΔL_B and is equal to

$$R = |\Delta L_A| + |\Delta L_B| = |\beta_B - \beta_A|\,\Delta Y.$$

Thus the amount of reallocation depends both upon the size of the change in the external environment, ΔY, and the extent of heterogeneity, as represented by the size of the difference between β_A and β_B. In this way, heterogeneity within an industry is directly linked to amount of reallocation in that industry.

Exercises 4.1

1. Use repeated substitution to solve for the equilibrium values of $\overline{w}, \overline{x}$, and $\overline{y}$ in each system of equations.
   (a) $y = 10 - 24w$
   $x = 6 - 8w$
   $y = x$
   (b) $y = 36 + 8w$
   $x = 12w - 4$
   $y = \frac{1}{2}x$
   (c) $y = 2w + 8$
   $x = 4w - 6$
   $y = 2x + 2$
   (d) $x = 10w + 3g + b - 4$
   $y = 5w - g - 2h + 2$
   $x = y$
2. Consider the following system of equations where the endogenous variables are z, x, and y and the exogenous variables are h and a:
   $$x = 6z + 3h - 4a + 10$$
   $$y = 4z - h + 6$$
   $$x = y.$$
   (a) Use repeated substitution to solve for the equilibrium values of the endogenous variables, $\overline{z}, \overline{x}$, and $\overline{y}$.
   (b) Using comparative static analysis, determine the impact on $\overline{z}, \overline{x}$, and $\overline{y}$ due to a change in a, *ceteris paribus*.
   (c) Now assume that $\Delta a = 2$. Determine the impact on the above endogenous variables due to this change.
3. Redo question 2, but this time determine the impact on $\overline{z}, \overline{x}$, and $\overline{y}$ due to a change in h, *ceteris paribus*. Assume that $\Delta h = 3$.
4. The following system of equations illustrates the general form of a partial market equilibrium model, which is a model of price determination in a one-good market:
   $$Q_d = Q_s$$
   $$Q_d = a - bP \qquad (a, b > 0)$$
   $$Q_s = c + dP \qquad (c, d > 0).$$
   Using substitution, solve for the equilibrium value of $\overline{P}$ expressed in terms of the parameters a, b, c, and d. Then solve for the equilibrium value of $\overline{Q}$. Graph your results.
5. The simplest Keynesian-style macroeconomic model is the **Keynesian cross.** The equations for a typical Keynesian-cross model include the definition for aggregate

demand

$$AD = C + I,$$

where AD is aggregate demand, C is consumption and I is investment. Consumption is determined by a behavioral equation, which in this problem takes the form

$$C = 3000 + \frac{2}{3}Y,$$

where Y is national income. Investment is exogenous, and, initially, we assume

$$I = 1000.$$

The equilibrium condition requires that aggregate demand equals national income, that is,

$$AD = Y.$$

(a) Determine the equilibrium level of national income and consumption.

(b) Determine the equilibrium level of national income and consumption if $I = 500$.

6. Find a general expression for the relationship between the change in investment and the change in income for the model in question 5.

7. The simple IS/LM macroeconomic model presented in the text resulted in two equations for the two unknowns, Y and R:

$$Y = 3000 + 5\frac{M}{P} + 2.5G$$

$$R = 0.3 - 0.0005\frac{M}{P} + 0.00025G.$$

(a) Solve for the actual values of Y and R, now assuming that

$$G = 3000, \quad M = 400{,}000, \quad \text{and} \quad P = 200.$$

(b) Now conduct a comparative static analysis on the model to determine the impact of a change in M, ΔM, on Y and R, *ceteris paribus*. Assume that $\Delta M = 400$.

8. Use the model in the tax-incidence application to determine the effect of a given change in the tax on widgets, ΔT, on the equilibrium quantity of widgets. How does your answer depend upon the relative size of the parameters β and λ?

9. Solve for the change in the wage, ΔW, for a given change in overall demand, ΔY, using the model developed in the application about job creation and job destruction.

10. Suppose that the labor demand functions of two firms differ in the responsiveness of labor demand to the wage but not in terms of the responsiveness of labor demand to overall demand; that is, for Firms A and B, the respective labor demand functions are

$$L_A^D = -\gamma_A W + \beta Y$$
$$L_B^D = -\gamma_B W + \beta Y.$$

If, as in the discussion of job creation and job destruction, the number of workers in the common pool of labor is fixed and equal to $\overline{L}$ and

$$\overline{L} = L_A^S + L_B^S,$$

find the condition under which Firm A experiences job creation and Firm B experiences job destruction when $\Delta Y > 0$.

4.2 MATRICES AND EQUATIONS

The linear systems of equations presented in the previous section were solved through repeated substitution. This technique was not very cumbersome in those cases, but, in systems with more equations and more variables, we would like a more powerful solution technique. Matrix algebra provides such a technique. In this section we introduce some of the basic elements of matrix algebra, and in the following section we show the way in which matrix algebra can be used to characterize and solve systems of equations.

Before turning to matrices, however, we begin with a discussion of summation notation. This notation will be useful when we move on to matrix algebra.

The Summation Operator

The **summation operator** provides a compact way to write an equation that involves the sum of a number of terms. The summation operator uses the Greek letter sigma (Σ) accompanied by limits that define the range of variables that are to be added. The simplest example of the use of the summation operator is the equation

$$y = x_1 + x_2.$$

This is written as

$$y = \sum_{i=1}^{2} x_i,$$

where i is an index. Only slightly more complicated is the equation

$$y = x_n + x_{n+1} + x_{n+2} + \cdots + x_m$$

which is written as

$$y = \sum_{i=n}^{m} x_i.$$

The equation

$$y = b_1x_1 + b_2x_2 + b_3x_3$$

has both a parameter and a variable in each term. This can be written in summation notation as

$$y = \sum_{i=1}^{3} b_i x_i.$$

Rules for manipulating summations are easily derived by considering the extensive form that the summation represents. For example, consider the sum

$$kx_1 + kx_2 + \cdots + kx_n = \sum_{i=1}^{n} kx_i.$$

Each term in this sum is multiplied by the same constant k. This sum can be rewritten as

$$k(x_1 + x_2 + \cdots + x_n)$$

and then again as

$$k\sum_{i=1}^{3} x_i.$$

Thus, in general, we have

$$\sum_{i=1}^{n} kx_i = k\sum_{i=1}^{n} x_i.$$

It is also easy to show that the sum of a sum can be split up into two separate sums. This property is presented more succinctly by the expression

$$\begin{aligned}\sum_{i=1}^{n}(x_i + y_i) &= x_1 + y_1 + x_2 + y_2 + \cdots + x_n + y_n \\ &= x_1 + x_2 + \cdots + x_n + y_1 + y_2 + \cdots + y_n \\ &= \sum_{i=1}^{n} x_i + \sum_{i=1}^{n} y_i.\end{aligned}$$

Likewise,

$$\sum_{i=1}^{n}(x_i - y_i) = \sum_{i=1}^{n} x_i - \sum_{i=1}^{n} y_i.$$

It is *not* true, however, that the sum of a product can be split up. In terms of the notation,

$$\sum_{i=1}^{n}(x_i \cdot y_i) \neq \left(\sum_{i=1}^{n} x_i\right)\cdot\left(\sum_{i=1}^{n} y_i\right).$$

This can be easily seen through an example. Note that

$$\sum_{i=1}^{2} b_i x_i = b_1 x_1 + b_2 x_2,$$

while

$$\left(\sum_{i=1}^{2} b_i\right)\left(\sum_{i=1}^{2} x_i\right) = (b_1 + b_2)\cdot(x_1 + x_2) = b_1 x_1 + b_2 x_2 + b_1 x_2 + b_2 x_1.$$

Some Matrix Basics

The summation operator provides a compact method for writing linear relationships. Matrix algebra represents an even more compact method. In this section we define the basic units of matrix algebra and present some basic operations.

$$T = \begin{bmatrix} \alpha & \theta & \rho+\chi \\ \gamma & \lambda & \pi \\ \eta & \delta-\mu & \beta \end{bmatrix} \quad f = \begin{bmatrix} 3 \\ 7 \\ 66 \\ 21 \end{bmatrix}$$

$$r = \begin{bmatrix} 2 & \beta & 0 & 1 & 0 \end{bmatrix} \quad S = \begin{bmatrix} 5 & 8 \\ 2 & 6 \\ 7 & 3 \end{bmatrix}$$

FIGURE 4.3 Some Vectors and Matrices

A **matrix** consists of a rectangular array of its **elements,** which may be numbers, variables, or parameters. The **dimension** of a matrix is its number of rows and its number of columns. A special case is a **square matrix,** which has the same number of rows as columns. Another special case is a **vector,** which is a matrix with only one row (a **row vector**) or only one column (a **column vector**). In general, a matrix with m rows and n columns is an $m \times n$ matrix (read as "m by n matrix"). A row vector with k elements therefore has the dimension $1 \times k$, while a column vector with j elements has the dimension $j \times 1$. Figure 4.3 presents the square 3×3 matrix T, the 4×1 column vector f, the 1×5 row vector r, and the 3×2 matrix A (typically matrices are denoted by capital letters and vectors by lowercase letters).

The individual elements of a matrix X are denoted by x_{ij}. The subscript i refers to the row in which that element is found, and the subscript j refers to the column in which it is found. For example, the six elements of the matrix S are

$$s_{11} = 5, \quad s_{12} = 8, \quad s_{21} = 2, \quad s_{22} = 6, \quad s_{31} = 7, \quad \text{and} \quad s_{32} = 3.$$

For any $n \times n$ square matrix X, the n elements x_{ii} are referred to as its **diagonal elements,** while the other $n(n - 1)$ elements x_{ij} for $i \neq j$ are referred to as its **off-diagonal elements.** The diagonal elements of the matrix T are

$$t_{11} = \alpha, \quad t_{22} = \lambda, \quad \text{and} \quad t_{33} = \beta.$$

The **transpose** of an $m \times n$ matrix X, written as X', is an $n \times m$ matrix in which the rows and columns of the original matrix have been interchanged. The first row of the original matrix becomes the first column of the transpose, the second row of the original matrix becomes the second column of the transpose, and so on. In other words, any element x_{ij} in a matrix X represents the element x_{ji} in its transpose X'. For example, the matrix B and its transpose B' are

$$B = \begin{bmatrix} c & d & e & f \\ g & h & i & j \end{bmatrix} \quad \text{and} \quad B' = \begin{bmatrix} c & g \\ d & h \\ e & i \\ f & j \end{bmatrix}.$$

It is straightforward to see that the transpose of a transpose returns the original matrix; that is,

$$(X')' = X.$$

Using Vectors to Depict a Single Linear Equation

A system of equations can be depicted compactly in matrix format. To illustrate this, we begin with a very simple system that consists of one equation and four exogenous variables. This equation is

$$y = a_1x_1 + a_2x_2 + a_3x_3 + a_4x_4.$$

This equation can be expressed using two vectors as

$$y = \begin{bmatrix} a_1 & a_2 & a_3 & a_4 \end{bmatrix} \cdot \begin{bmatrix} x_1 \\ x_2 \\ x_3 \\ x_4 \end{bmatrix}$$

or, more compactly, as

$$y = ax,$$

where a represents the 1×4 row vector and x represents the 4×1 column vector (this notation distinguishes vectors, which lack subscripts, from the elements of vectors, which include subscripts). In this example, the row vector a is **postmultiplied** by the column vector x, or alternatively, the column vector x is **premultiplied** by the row vector a. The system $y = ax$ is represented with summation notation by

$$y = \sum_{i=1}^{4} a_i x_i.$$

This multiplication proceeds by adding the product of the first element of the row vector and the first element of the column vector to the product of the second element of the row vector and the second element of the column vector, and so on. To generalize this rule, for a of dimension $1 \times n$ and x of dimension $n \times 1$, the product is

$$ax = \sum_{i=1}^{n} a_i x_i.$$

The postmultiplication of the $1 \times n$ vector a by the $n \times 1$ vector x yields a **scalar.** A scalar is simply a single number, parameter, or variable. A scalar has dimension 1×1.

This multiplication can proceed only because the vectors are **conformable;** that is, there are as many columns in a as there are rows in x. The term "multiplication" in matrix algebra comes with a prefix of either "pre" or "post" because conformability does not allow for the commutative property that holds with scalars. Thus, for example, while it is true that for two scalars, say 2 and 7, $2 \times 7 = 7 \times 2$, it is not true that for the vectors presented here, ax is the same as xa or, for any two matrices S and T, that ST is the same as TS. In fact, as is shown below, the product xa is not even a scalar but a matrix with dimension 4×4.

Using a Matrix and Vectors to Depict a System of Linear Equations

Next we consider the following system with two equations and six variables

$$y_1 = a_{11}x_1 + a_{12}x_2 + a_{13}x_3 + a_{14}x_4$$
$$y_2 = a_{21}x_1 + a_{22}x_2 + a_{23}x_3 + a_{24}x_4,$$

where the endogenous variables are y_i, $i = 1, 2$; the exogenous variables are x_j, $j = 1, 2, 3, 4$; and the eight a_{ij}'s represent the parameters. Notice that there are now two subscripts for each parameter, the first signifying the equation to which it belongs and the second signifying the variable it multiplies. Using summation notation and the rule for postmultiplying a row vector times a column vector presented previously, we can rewrite this system more compactly in two separate parts:

$$y_1 = \sum_{j=1}^{4} a_{1j}x_j = [a_{11} \quad a_{12} \quad a_{13} \quad a_{14}] \cdot \begin{bmatrix} x_1 \\ x_2 \\ x_3 \\ x_4 \end{bmatrix}$$

$$y_2 = \sum_{j=1}^{4} a_{2j}x_j = [a_{21} \quad a_{22} \quad a_{23} \quad a_{24}] \cdot \begin{bmatrix} x_1 \\ x_2 \\ x_3 \\ x_4 \end{bmatrix}.$$

An even more compact notation defines the 2×1 column vector $y = \begin{bmatrix} y_1 \\ y_2 \end{bmatrix}$, the 2×4 matrix $A = \begin{bmatrix} a_{1j} \\ a_{2j} \end{bmatrix}$, and the 4×1 column vector x as shown above, which gives us

$$y = Ax$$

or, written out fully,

$$\begin{bmatrix} y_1 \\ y_2 \end{bmatrix} = \begin{bmatrix} a_{11} & a_{12} & a_{13} & a_{14} \\ a_{21} & a_{22} & a_{23} & a_{24} \end{bmatrix} \cdot \begin{bmatrix} x_1 \\ x_2 \\ x_3 \\ x_4 \end{bmatrix}.$$

These examples suggest the general rules for matrix multiplication. Following the previous results, in a system $y = Ax$ with m equations and n endogenous variables, the ith row of the system, corresponding to the ith equation in the system, is represented using summation operator notation as

$$y_i = \sum_{j=1}^{n} a_{ij}x_j,$$

where the parameters $a_{1j}, a_{2j}, \ldots, a_{nj}$ represent the n elements in the jth row of the matrix A. Thus the matrix A has n columns and, since there are m equations, m rows. The vector x has n elements, and the vector y has m elements.

The need for the conformability of a matrix system should now be apparent. When a matrix is postmultiplied by a vector, the number of columns in the matrix must equal the number of rows in the vector. A useful device for remembering this is to write a matrix system with the dimensions of the matrix below the matrix and vectors as shown below:

$$\underset{m\times 1}{y} = \underset{m\times n}{A} \cdot \underset{n\times 1}{x}.$$

The second term in the dimension of the matrix (in this case, the n in the $m \times n$) must match the first term in the vector postmultiplying that matrix. The resulting column vector (here, y) will have as many rows as the matrix. Thus the $m \times n$ matrix can be postmultiplied by an $n \times 1$ vector, and the product is a vector of dimension $m \times 1$.

As an exercise, we can write the model of the market for widgets in matrix notation. We first rewrite the three equations (4.1), (4.2), and (4.3) such that the three endogenous variables, Q^S, Q^D, and P, all appear on the left-hand side and the exogenous variables G and N, as well as the intercept parameters α and θ, appear on the right-hand side. This gives us

$$\begin{aligned} Q^D + \beta P &= \alpha + \gamma G \\ Q^S - \lambda P &= \theta - \phi N \\ Q^D - Q^s &= 0. \end{aligned}$$

This system includes a 3×3 matrix of coefficients, which we denote W, postmultiplied by a 3×1 vector of endogenous variables, which we denote v, all of which equals the 3×1 vector of exogenous variables, which we denote g. This system,

$$\begin{bmatrix} 1 & \beta & 0 \\ 0 & -\lambda & 1 \\ 1 & 0 & -1 \end{bmatrix} \cdot \begin{bmatrix} Q^D \\ P \\ Q^S \end{bmatrix} = \begin{bmatrix} \alpha + \gamma G \\ \theta - \phi N \\ 0 \end{bmatrix},$$

is written more compactly as

$$Wv = g.$$

Note that the matrix W has a number of elements equal to zero since not every endogenous variable appears in every equation. Also note that the third element of the vector g is zero since the third equation does not include any exogenous variables.

We can also represent the IS/LM model presented in the previous section in matrix notation. The four equations in that model, (4.6) through (4.9), include the endogenous variables Y, C, I, and R and the exogenous variables G and M/P (where we treat real balances, M/P, as a single exogenous variable). The matrix system corresponding to that model is

$$\begin{bmatrix} 1 & -1 & -1 & 0 \\ -0.8 & 1 & 0 & 0 \\ 0 & 0 & 1 & 2000 \\ 0.1 & 0 & 0 & -1000 \end{bmatrix} \cdot \begin{bmatrix} Y \\ C \\ I \\ R \end{bmatrix} = \begin{bmatrix} G \\ 200 \\ 1000 \\ \dfrac{M}{P} \end{bmatrix}.$$

Matrix Multiplication

The postmultiplication of one matrix by another is just an extension of postmultiplying a matrix by a vector. Consider the two matrices

$$S = \begin{bmatrix} 5 & 8 \\ 2 & 6 \\ 7 & 3 \end{bmatrix} \quad \text{and} \quad B = \begin{bmatrix} c & d & e & f \\ g & h & i & j \end{bmatrix}.$$

The postmultiplication of the matrix S by any of the columns of the matrix B has been shown previously to result in a 3×1 vector. Denoting the ith column of B as $b_{\bullet i}$, we have

$$Sb_{\bullet 1} = \begin{bmatrix} 5c + 8g \\ 2c + 6g \\ 7c + 3g \end{bmatrix}, \quad Sb_{\bullet 2} = \begin{bmatrix} 5d + 8h \\ 2d + 6h \\ 7d + 3h \end{bmatrix}, \quad Sb_{\bullet 3} = \begin{bmatrix} 5e + 8i \\ 2e + 6i \\ 7e + 3i \end{bmatrix}, \quad \text{and} \quad Sb_{\bullet 4} = \begin{bmatrix} 5f + 8j \\ 2f + 6j \\ 7f + 3j \end{bmatrix}.$$

There is one column vector corresponding to each of the four columns of B. The full set of these four column vectors, each of which has three rows, represents the product SB. Thus the matrix $U = SB$ is the 3×4 matrix

$$U = SB = \begin{bmatrix} 5c + 8g & 5d + 8h & 5e + 8i & 5f + 8j \\ 2c + 6g & 2d + 6h & 2e + 6i & 2f + 6j \\ 7c + 3g & 7d + 3h & 7e + 3i & 7e + 3j \end{bmatrix}.$$

We can also present this result using the summation operator. The element u_{ij} of the matrix U is

$$u_{ij} = \sum_{k=1}^{2} s_{ik} b_{kj}.$$

For example,

$$u_{32} = s_{31}b_{12} + s_{32}b_{22} = 7d + 3h.$$

More generally, consider the $m \times n$ matrix A and the $n \times q$ matrix X. Let

$$Y = AX,$$

where Y is an $m \times q$ matrix with the element y_{ij} equal to

$$y_{ij} = \sum_{k=1}^{n} a_{ik} b_{kj}.$$

Thus the ijth element of Y represents the product of the vector representing the ith row of A postmultiplied by the vector representing the jth column of X.

This result shows that the product AX is only defined if the number of columns in A equals the number of rows in X. This generalizes the issue of conformability discussed earlier in the context of a matrix postmultiplied by a vector. In that case we saw that an $m \times n$ matrix must be postmultiplied by an $n \times 1$ vector, and the product is an $m \times 1$ vector. More generally, an $m \times n$ matrix must be postmultiplied by an $n \times q$ matrix, and the product is a matrix with dimension $m \times q$. Thus while SB is a

3×4 matrix, the product BS is not defined since the matrices are not conformable in this way.

One way to remember the demands of conformability is to write the matrices with their dimensions below them. For example,

$$\underset{m \times q}{Y} = \underset{m \times n}{A} \cdot \underset{n \times q}{X}$$

The second term in the dimension of the matrix A, in this case n, must match the first term in the dimension of the matrix X, with the resulting matrix having as many rows as A (which, in this case, is m) and as many columns as X (which, in this case, is q). When $q = 1$, we have a matrix postmultiplied by a column vector. If $m = 1$, then we have a matrix premultiplied by a row vector.

Econometric Specification

Econometrics is the application of statistical techniques to economics in order to analyze data and, in so doing, to empirically test theories. Matrix algebra is used extensively in econometrics since it provides a very compact way to present a lot of information and its techniques provide a powerful way to manipulate equations. This notation is much neater and more accessible than notation using summation operators.

Much of econometrics is concerned with finding the linear relationship that best fits the data being analyzed. For example, in Chapter 8 we will learn about empirical work which uses data from a survey of households to estimate the effect of education and experience on men's earnings. For the ith person in the survey, there is an observation on his earnings, E_i, his years of education, s_i, and his years of workplace experience, x_i. The relationship presented in that application uses a logarithmic transformation of earnings and is linear in years of schooling and quadratic in years of experience. The econometric estimation of this equation involves determining the coefficients β_0, β_1, β_2, and β_3, for the equation

$$\ln(E_i) = \beta_0 + \beta_1 s_i + \beta_2 x_i + \beta_3 x_i^2 + \varepsilon_i,$$

where ε_i represents the "residual" or the difference between the estimated and the actual relationship for the ith individual. Econometrics provides a way to find values of the coefficients such that this equation best "fits" the data.

A survey consisting of n respondents will provide an $n \times 1$ vector of earnings, an $n \times 1$ vector of years of schooling, and an $n \times 1$ vector of years of experience. In matrix format, the n observations from this survey can be represented as

$$e = Y\beta + \varepsilon,$$

where e is the $n \times 1$ vector of the natural logarithm of earnings, β is the 4×1 vector of estimated coefficients, ε is the $n \times 1$ vector of residuals, and Y is the $n \times 4$ matrix of data on the individuals in the survey. Each of the elements in the first column of Y is 1. The second column of Y is the observation of education for each of the n individuals. The third column is the set of observations for each individual of his years of experience, and the fourth column is this number squared. The simplicity of the matrix notation for this system demonstrates an advantage of using matrix algebra.

Exercises 4.2

1. Expand each summation expression.

   (a) $\sum_{i=1}^{5} ax_i$

   (b) $\sum_{i=1}^{n} b_i x^i$

   (c) $\left(\sum_{i=2}^{3} x_{i+1}\right)\left(\sum_{i=2}^{3} y_{i-1}\right)$

   (d) $\sum_{i=1}^{3} ix_i(x_i + 2)$

   (e) $\sum_{i=-1}^{-4} x^i$

2. Indicate the dimensions of each matrix.

   (a) $A = \begin{bmatrix} a & b \\ c & d \end{bmatrix}$

   (b) $b = \begin{bmatrix} x & y & z \end{bmatrix}$

   (c) $c = \begin{bmatrix} \alpha \\ \lambda \\ \phi \end{bmatrix}$

   (d) $D = \begin{bmatrix} 1 & 2 & 3 \\ 4 & 5 & 6 \end{bmatrix}$

3. For each matrix, determine which element occupies the requested matrix position.

   (a) $A = \begin{bmatrix} 70 & 25 \\ 40 & -100 \end{bmatrix}; a_{22} = ?$

   (b) $B = \begin{bmatrix} a & h & m \\ f & j & n \end{bmatrix}; b_{13} = ?$

   (c) $C = \begin{bmatrix} \frac{1}{2} & \frac{1}{3} \\ -1 & \frac{1}{5} \\ -5 & 4 \\ 20 & -10 \end{bmatrix}; c_{21} = ?$

   (d) $D = \begin{bmatrix} \beta & \mu & \phi \\ \gamma & \alpha & \theta \\ \delta & \varepsilon & \lambda \end{bmatrix}; d_{23} = ?$

4. Let

$$B = \begin{bmatrix} z & a & 1 & 4 \\ y & b & 2 & 3 \\ x & c & 3 & 2 \\ w & d & 4 & 1 \end{bmatrix}.$$

(a) Identify the diagonal and off-diagonal elements of B.
(b) Find the transpose B'.
(c) Show that the transpose of B' equals B, that is,

$$(B')' = B.$$

(d) Which elements occupy the positions b_{21}, b_{32}, and b_{44} in the original matrix? What is their position in B'? What effect does the transposition of matrix B have on the placement of the diagonal and off-diagonal elements?

5. Determine if the following are conformable for matrix multiplication, and if so, indicate the dimension of the resulting product.

(a) $\begin{bmatrix} 2 & 4 & 6 & 8 \\ 1 & 3 & 5 & 7 \end{bmatrix} \cdot \begin{bmatrix} 2 & 4 \\ 1 & 3 \end{bmatrix}$

(b) $\begin{bmatrix} a & b & c \end{bmatrix} \cdot \begin{bmatrix} a \\ b \\ c \end{bmatrix}$

(c) $\begin{bmatrix} m & p \\ n & q \\ o & r \end{bmatrix} \cdot \begin{bmatrix} s & v \\ t & w \\ u & x \end{bmatrix}$

(d) A row vector of dimension $1 \times k$ and a matrix of dimension $k \times l$

6. Consider the system of equations that is illustrated using the summation operator below, where y_i represents the endogenous variables, c_j represents the exogenous variables, and b_{ij} represents the parameters:

$$y_1 = \sum_{j=1}^{3} b_{1j} c_j$$

$$y_2 = \sum_{j=1}^{3} b_{2j} c_j.$$

(a) Illustrate this system in expanded matrix format.
(b) What is the compact matrix notation for this system?
(c) What is the dimension of the matrix of parameters? the vector of exogenous variables? Is this system conformable for multiplication?
(d) Using summation operator notation, give an expression for the ith equation in the system.

7. In the following examples, assume that matrix S is the solution matrix such that $S = UV$, where S, U, and V can be either vectors or matrices. Perform matrix

multiplication for each of the following examples to determine S.

(a) $U = \begin{bmatrix} 7 \\ 9 \\ 4 \end{bmatrix}, V = \begin{bmatrix} a & b & c & d \end{bmatrix}$

(b) $U = \begin{bmatrix} 0 & \frac{1}{3} \\ \frac{2}{3} & 1 \end{bmatrix}, V = \begin{bmatrix} 0 & \frac{3}{2} & 6 \\ 3 & 6 & 12 \end{bmatrix}$

(c) $U = \begin{bmatrix} 7 & 5 & 4 & 2 \end{bmatrix}, V = \begin{bmatrix} 1 & 0 & 0 & 0 \\ 0 & 1 & 0 & 0 \\ 0 & 0 & 1 & 0 \\ 0 & 0 & 0 & 1 \end{bmatrix}$

(d) $U = \begin{bmatrix} a & g & h \\ x & w & p \\ b & c & d \end{bmatrix}, V = \begin{bmatrix} 1 & 0 \\ -1 & 4 \\ 7 & 2 \end{bmatrix}$

8. Consider the matrices

$$A = \begin{bmatrix} 2 & 4 \\ 1 & 5 \\ 7 & 6 \end{bmatrix} \quad \text{and} \quad B = \begin{bmatrix} \frac{1}{2} \\ \frac{1}{3} \end{bmatrix}.$$

(a) Is the product AB defined? Is the product BA defined?

(b) What is the dimension of AB (if it exists) and the dimension of BA (if it exists)?

(c) What is the transpose of matrix A?

(d) Can you postmultiply matrix A' by vector B? If so, find $A'B$.

9. The following matrix system, written compactly as $Wv = g$, corresponds to a Keynesian macroeconomic model, where AD is aggregate demand, C is consumption, I is investment, Y is national income, and r is the interest rate,

$$\begin{bmatrix} 1 & -1 & -1 & 0 \\ 0 & 1 & 0 & -\frac{3}{4} \\ 0 & 0 & 1 & 0 \\ 1 & 0 & 0 & -1 \end{bmatrix} \cdot \begin{bmatrix} AD \\ C \\ I \\ Y \end{bmatrix} = \begin{bmatrix} 0 \\ 2000 \\ 500 - 1000r \\ 0 \end{bmatrix}.$$

Use matrix multiplication to determine the equations that comprise the model.

10. The following equations model the determinants of exports and imports in an economy:

$$X = 1000 - 20E + 0.2Y_F$$
$$M = 450 + 10E + 0.15Y_D,$$

where the exports (X), imports (M), and the real exchange rate (E) are endogenous variables. Foreign and domestic income, X_F and Y_D, respectively, are the exogenous variables. Suppose that we wish to investigate the long-run properties of the real exchange rate. We assume that, in the long run, exports must equal imports.

(a) Write this model as a matrix system.

(b) Using repeated substitution, solve for the real exchange rate and the equilibrium level of either exports or imports as a function of foreign and domestic income.

(c) Determine the relationship between ΔE and ΔY_F. Also determine the relationship between ΔE and ΔY_D.

(d) Suppose that, over the long run, ΔY_F increases by 100 and ΔY_D increases by 90. What is ΔE?

4.3 MATRIX OPERATIONS

As shown in the previous section, matrix algebra defines systems of equations using a very compact and simple notation. Manipulating systems of equations is also facilitated by matrix algebra. In this section we present some rules for matrix operations, including matrix addition, matrix subtraction, and matrix multiplication.

Matrix Addition and Subtraction

Matrices that are of the same dimension can be added to and subtracted from each other. Matrix addition involves adding each of the elements of one matrix to the respective element of another matrix. For example, consider the 2×2 matrices

$$G = \begin{bmatrix} 3 & 6 \\ 1 & 4 \end{bmatrix} \quad \text{and} \quad H = \begin{bmatrix} 0 & -2 \\ 5 & 3 \end{bmatrix}.$$

Their sum is

$$G + H = \begin{bmatrix} 3 & 4 \\ 6 & 7 \end{bmatrix}.$$

Since addition of matrices just involves the addition of each of the respective elements, it is easy to see that the **commutative law of addition** holds for matrices. Thus

$$G + H = H + G.$$

Also, the **associative law of addition** holds for matrix addition since the order of addition does not matter. That is, for any three matrices of the same dimension,

$$(A + B) + C = A + (B + C).$$

The sum of any matrix A and a **zero matrix,** that is, a matrix of the same dimension consisting of all zeros, is the matrix A.

Matrix subtraction, likewise, is defined only between two matrices that are of the same dimension. One matrix is subtracted from another by subtracting each element of one matrix from the respective element of the other. Thus the ijth element of the matrix $C = A - B$, where A and B are two matrices of the same dimension, is

$c_{ij} = a_{ij} - b_{ij}$. Using the matrices G and H defined previously, we have

$$G - H = \begin{bmatrix} 3 & 8 \\ -4 & 1 \end{bmatrix} \quad \text{and} \quad H - G = \begin{bmatrix} -3 & -8 \\ 4 & -1 \end{bmatrix}.$$

Rules for Matrix Multiplication

Section 4.2 shows how systems of equations are represented through matrix multiplication. In this section we discuss some rules for manipulating the products of two or more matrices.

As discussed above, a basic rule for multiplying scalars is the **commutative law of multiplication.** That is, for any two scalars x and y, $xy = yx$. This law does not extend to matrices. This can be seen immediately by the requirement of conformability discussed earlier. For example, if the matrix A has dimension $m \times n$ and the matrix B has dimension $n \times p$, the product AB is defined, but the product BA is not. Even when both AB and BA are defined, however, these two products are typically not equal. For example, if B is $n \times m$, then both AB and BA are defined, but these products must differ since AB is $m \times m$ and BA is $n \times n$.

The product of two square matrices is another square matrix with the same dimension as each of the original matrices. Even in this case, however, the commutative law does not hold. For example, consider the 2×2 matrices G and H defined earlier. The two products GH and HG are

$$GH = \begin{bmatrix} 30 & 12 \\ 20 & 10 \end{bmatrix} \quad \text{and} \quad HG = \begin{bmatrix} -2 & -8 \\ 18 & 42 \end{bmatrix}.$$

Another multiplication law with respect to scalars that you are familiar with is the **associative law of multiplication.** This law states that, for any three scalars, the order of multiplication does not matter. For example,

$$x \cdot (y \cdot z) = (x \cdot y) \cdot z.$$

The matrix version of this law does hold. For any three matrices that meet the requirements of conformability,

$$(XY)Z = X(YZ).$$

For example, defining the 2×3 matrix J as

$$J = \begin{bmatrix} 3 & 0 & 2 \\ 0 & -1 & 1 \end{bmatrix}$$

and the matrices G and H as we did earlier, it is straightforward to show that

$$(GH)J = G(HJ) = \begin{bmatrix} 90 & -12 & 72 \\ 60 & -10 & 50 \end{bmatrix}.$$

The rule concerning the **transpose of a product** can be determined by considering a representative element of a product matrix. Consider the $p \times q$ matrix $C = AB$, where the matrix A is $p \times n$ and the matrix B is $n \times q$. The ijth element of this matrix,

c_{ij}, is the sum of the products of the elements in the ith row of A and the elements in the jth column of B. That is,

$$c_{ij} = \sum_{k=1}^{n} a_{ik} b_{kj}.$$

By the definition of a transpose, the jith element of C' is also c_{ij}, which is the sum of the product of the elements of the jth row of B' and the elements of the ith column of A'. That is,

$$c'_{ji} = \sum_{k=1}^{n} b'_{jk}\, a'_{ki}.$$

For the matrix as a whole, C' is obtained by postmultiplying B' by A'. Thus the rule for the transpose of a product is

$$(AB)' = B'A'.$$

As an example of this, consider the transposes of the matrices G and H defined earlier. The transpose of the product of G postmultiplied by H is

$$(GH)' = H'G' = \begin{bmatrix} 0 & 5 \\ -2 & 3 \end{bmatrix} \cdot \begin{bmatrix} 3 & 1 \\ 6 & 4 \end{bmatrix} = \begin{bmatrix} 30 & 20 \\ 12 & 10 \end{bmatrix}.$$

It is readily seen that this product equals $(GH)'$ by referring to the previous result for GH.

Matrices and vectors can also be **multiplied by a scalar.** This involves simply multiplying each element of the matrix or the vector by the scalar. For example, consider the $m \times n$ matrix R with elements r_{ij}. The product of this matrix and the scalar k is the $m \times n$ matrix $S = kR$, where the ijth element of S, s_{ij}, is equal to $k \cdot r_{ij}$. Multiplying the matrix G by the scalar 3 results in

$$3 \cdot G = \begin{bmatrix} 9 & 18 \\ 3 & 12 \end{bmatrix}.$$

An important type of matrix is the **identity matrix.** The identity matrix plays a similar role in matrix algebra as the number 1 plays in the multiplication and division of scalars. An identity matrix is a square matrix with the special property that the product of any matrix X and a conformable identity matrix I is the matrix X. That is, $XI = X$ and $IX = X$ for any X (though note that if X is not square, the identity matrix that premultiplies it has a different dimension than the identity matrix that postmultiplies it). Also, as is discussed below, the product of a matrix and its inverse is the identity matrix, just as the product of a number and its inverse is 1.

The need for an identity matrix to be square can be seen by considering the requirement of conformability and the rule for the dimension of the product of two matrices. An $m \times n$ matrix X must be postmultiplied by a matrix I with n rows, and if the product XI is also to be $m \times n$, the matrix I must have n columns. The identity matrix that premultiplies the $m \times n$ matrix X must have m columns, and the product IX is $m \times n$ only if I has m rows.

Each of the diagonal elements of any identity matrix equals 1, and each of its off-diagonal elements equals 0. For example, a 3×3 identity matrix is

$$I = \begin{bmatrix} 1 & 0 & 0 \\ 0 & 1 & 0 \\ 0 & 0 & 1 \end{bmatrix}.$$

The product JI of the 2×3 matrix J presented earlier and a 3×3 identity matrix can readily be seen to be equal to the original matrix J since

$$JI = \begin{bmatrix} (3\cdot1+0\cdot0+2\cdot0) & (3\cdot0+0\cdot1+2\cdot0) & (3\cdot0+0\cdot0+2\cdot1) \\ (0\cdot1-1\cdot0+1\cdot0) & (0\cdot0-1\cdot1+1\cdot0) & (0\cdot0-1\cdot0+1\cdot1) \end{bmatrix} = J.$$

Postmultiplying J by an identity matrix to obtain JI also gives the product J, but in this case the identity matrix must be 2×2.

Exercises 4.3

1. Perform addition or subtraction on the following sets of matrices.
   (a) $\begin{bmatrix} \frac{1}{2} & 1 \\ 0 & -\frac{1}{2} \end{bmatrix} + \begin{bmatrix} \frac{1}{2} & -1 \\ 0 & \frac{3}{2} \end{bmatrix}$
   (b) $\begin{bmatrix} 2 \\ 1 \end{bmatrix} - \begin{bmatrix} a \\ b \end{bmatrix}$
   (c) $[7 \quad 4 \quad 5 \quad 6] - [10 \quad -5 \quad -20 \quad 1]$
2. Consider the matrices

$$A = \begin{bmatrix} 15 & 8 & 12 \\ -7 & 0 & 1 \\ 2 & 3 & -4 \end{bmatrix} \quad \text{and} \quad B = \begin{bmatrix} -10 & 0 & 2 \\ 6 & -\frac{2}{3} & -1 \\ 5 & 5 & 4 \end{bmatrix}.$$

   (a) Show that $A + B = B + A$.
   (b) What is the value of $A - B$?
   (c) Using scalar multiplication, show that $-B + A = A - B$.
3. Consider the matrices

$$K = \begin{bmatrix} \alpha & \phi & \theta & \beta \\ \delta & \mu & \beta & \alpha \end{bmatrix}, \quad L = \begin{bmatrix} 1 & 2 \\ 3 & 4 \\ 5 & 6 \end{bmatrix}, \quad \text{and} \quad M = [1 \quad 0 \quad 1].$$

   (a) Arrange these three matrices so they are conformable for matrix multiplication.
   (b) Show that the associative law of multiplication holds in this example.
4. Consider the matrix

$$A = \begin{bmatrix} 2 & 4 & 5 & 7 \\ 0 & 0 & -1 & 6 \\ -5 & 8 & 9 & 2 \end{bmatrix}.$$

(a) What are the dimensions of the identity matrix in the product AI? What are the dimensions of the identity matrix in the product IA?

(b) Find AI.

(c) Find IA.

5. The matrices X and Y are

$$X = \begin{bmatrix} 4 & 6 \\ 1 & 2 \end{bmatrix} \quad \text{and} \quad Y = \begin{bmatrix} -3 & 5 & 0 & 1 \\ 7 & 2 & -4 & 3 \end{bmatrix}.$$

(a) Determine the transpose of each matrix, X' and Y'.

(b) Show that $(XY)' = Y'X'$.

4.4 THE SOLUTIONS TO MATRIX SYSTEMS

The solution of a system of equations solves for the endogenous variables as a function of the parameters of the model and the exogenous variables. For example, the solution to the widget example presented in Section 4.1 shows how the price and equilibrium quantity of widgets depend upon the parameters of the model, as well as the price of competing goods and the price of inputs. This system is represented in matrix notation as

$$Wv = g,$$

where g is the vector of exogenous variables and v is the vector of endogenous variables. The solution requires pre-multiplying both the right-hand side and left-hand side of the original system by a matrix such that the vector v is isolated. Suppose there is a matrix A that, when postmultiplied by W, yields an identity matrix. That is,

$$AW = I.$$

The matrix A is called the **inverse** of the matrix W.[2] The inverse allows us to solve a system of equations since premultiplying the left-hand side of the original system by A yields

$$AWv = Iv = v.$$

Therefore the solution to the system is

$$v = Ag.$$

If a matrix has an inverse, it is called **nonsingular** or **invertible.** Typically the inverse to a matrix A is denoted A^{-1}.[3] Employing this notation, we have

$$A^{-1}A = AA^{-1} = I. \tag{4.14}$$

---

[2] Only square matrices have inverses. The remainder of this chapter deals with square matrices exclusively, and the adjective "square" is implied whenever we use the word "matrix" for the rest of the chapter.

[3] It is important to note that the notation does *not* mean that each element of A^{-1} is equal to 1 divided by the respective element of the matrix A.

For example, consider the 2×2 matrix

$$M = \begin{bmatrix} 1 & 1 \\ 3 & 4 \end{bmatrix}.$$

We can confirm that the inverse to this matrix, M^{-1}, is

$$M^{-1} = \begin{bmatrix} 4 & -1 \\ -3 & 1 \end{bmatrix}$$

since the product $M^{-1}M$ is

$$M^{-1}M = \begin{bmatrix} (4\cdot 1)+(-1\cdot 3) & (4\cdot 1)+(-1\cdot 4) \\ (-3\cdot 1)+(1\cdot 3) & (-3\cdot 1)+(1\cdot 4) \end{bmatrix} = \begin{bmatrix} 1 & 0 \\ 0 & 1 \end{bmatrix}.$$

As an exercise, you should check that MM^{-1} also equals the 2×2identity matrix.

As we show in Chapter 5, the inverse for the matrix W in the widget example given above is

$$W^{-1} = \begin{bmatrix} \frac{\lambda}{\beta+\lambda} & \frac{\beta}{\beta+\lambda} & \frac{\beta}{\beta+\lambda} \\ \frac{1}{\beta+\lambda} & \frac{-1}{\beta+\lambda} & \frac{\lambda}{\beta+\lambda} \\ \frac{\lambda}{\beta+\lambda} & \frac{\beta}{\beta+\lambda} & \frac{-\lambda}{\beta+\lambda} \end{bmatrix}.$$

You can confirm that this matrix is the inverse of W by showing that

$$W^{-1}W = WW^{-1} = I.$$

Therefore the solution to this system is

$$v = W^{-1}g,$$

which is

$$\begin{bmatrix} Q^D \\ P \\ Q^S \end{bmatrix} = \begin{bmatrix} \frac{\lambda}{\beta+\lambda} & \frac{\beta}{\beta+\lambda} & \frac{\beta}{\beta+\lambda} \\ \frac{1}{\beta+\lambda} & \frac{-1}{\beta+\lambda} & \frac{-1}{\beta+\lambda} \\ \frac{\lambda}{\beta+\lambda} & \frac{\beta}{\beta+\lambda} & \frac{-\lambda}{\beta+\lambda} \end{bmatrix} \cdot \begin{bmatrix} \alpha+\gamma G \\ \theta-\phi N \\ 0 \end{bmatrix}.$$

Properties of the Inverse of a Matrix

We derive here properties of the inverse of a nonsingular matrix using the rules of matrix multiplication presented earlier.

Property 1 For any nonsingular matrix A,

$$(A^{-1})^{-1} = A.$$

We can prove this rule by premultiplying each side of the above expression by A^{-1}. The right-hand side equals the identity matrix, and so we have

$$A^{-1}[(A^{-1})^{-1}] = I.$$

By the definition of the inverse, it must be true that the expression in square brackets equals A.

Property 2 The inverse of a matrix A is unique.

To prove this, first suppose that the matrix A has two inverses, B and C. We want to check to see whether B and C are the same. If both B and C are inverses to A, then by (4.14) we have

$$AC = I \quad \text{and} \quad BA = I.$$

This implies that

$$B = BI = B(AC) = (BA)C = IC = C,$$

where we have made use of the associative law of multiplication. Thus $B = C$, and, in fact, there is only one inverse to A.

Property 3 For any nonsingular matrix A,

$$(A')^{-1} = (A^{-1})'$$

This property can be shown by considering a matrix A and its inverse B. By (4.14),

$$AB = BA = I.$$

Taking the transpose of both AB and BA and noting that for any identity matrix, $I' = I$, we have

$$(AB)' = (BA)'.$$

By the rule for the transpose of a product, this expression can be rewritten as

$$B'A' = A'B'.$$

Premultiply both sides by $(A')^{-1}$. The right-hand side equals

$$(A')^{-1}A'B' = IB' = B'.$$

Note that $B' = (A^{-1})'$. The left-hand side equals

$$(A')^{-1}B'A' = (A')^{-1}(AB)' = (A')^{-1}I' = (A')^{-1}.$$

Thus

$$(A')^{-1} = B' = (A^{-1})'.$$

Property 4 If A and B are nonsingular and of the same dimension, then AB is nonsingular and

$$(AB)^{-1} = B^{-1}A^{-1}.$$

The inverses of A and B are A^{-1} and B^{-1}, respectively. The product of the matrices, AB, can be postmultiplied by the product of the inverses, $B^{-1}A^{-1}$. By the associative law, we have

$$AB(B^{-1}A^{-1}) = A(BB^{-1})A^{-1} = (AI)A^{-1} = AA^{-1} = I.$$

Thus AB is nonsingular, and it has the inverse $B^{-1}A^{-1}$

The Existence of an Inverse

A sufficient condition for there to be a unique solution to a system of equations

$$Ax = y,$$

where x is a vector of endogenous variables and y is a vector of exogenous variables, is that the inverse of the matrix A exists. The number of equations in this system equals the number of rows in A, and the number of endogenous variables equals the number of columns in A. We will focus on square matrices, where there are the same number of equations as "unknowns" (that is, endogenous variables). Not all square matrices have inverses. If two equations of a system are redundant, then the system does not contain enough information to provide a unique solution. The system also does not have a solution if two equations of the system are mutually inconsistent.

A simple example of a system with a redundant equation is

$$2x_1 + 3x_2 = 4$$
$$4x_1 + 6x_2 = 8$$

since, in this case, the second equation is just twice the first equation. Therefore the second equation contains no information that is not already evident from the first equation. In this case there are an infinite number of combinations of x_1 and x_2 consistent with these two equations.

An example of a system with two mutually inconsistent equations is

$$2x_1 + 3x_2 = 4$$
$$4x_1 + 6x_2 = 4$$

since the left side of the second equation equals twice the left side of the first equation, but the right side of each equation is the same. In this case no combination of x_1 and x_2 solves this system.

The failure of these two systems to provide a unique solution shows that the simple counting rule of having the number of equations equal to the number of unknowns is not sufficient. In these simple cases, the shortcomings of the system are somewhat transparent. How do we detect whether other systems have unique solutions? It follows from the above discussion that this question is identical to the question of whether the square matrix A in the system $Ax = y$ is invertible.

The question of whether or not a matrix is nonsingular is linked to the value of its **determinant.** The determinant of a square matrix A, written $|A|$, is a scalar associated with that matrix. In this section we present the determinant of a 2×2 matrix. The next chapter presents the method for finding the determinant of a higher-order matrix and rules concerning determinants.

The generic 2×2 matrix A, which consists of the elements a_{11}, a_{12}, a_{21} and a_{22}, is written

$$A = \begin{bmatrix} a_{11} & a_{12} \\ a_{21} & a_{22} \end{bmatrix}$$

and has the determinant

$$|A| = a_{11}a_{22} - a_{12}a_{21}.$$

For example, the determinant of the matrix

$$Q = \begin{bmatrix} 4 & 3 \\ 1 & 5 \end{bmatrix}$$

is $|Q| = 4 \cdot 5 - 3 \cdot 1 = 17$. The determinant of the 2×2 matrix in the widget model,

$$\begin{bmatrix} 1 & \beta \\ 1 & -\lambda \end{bmatrix},$$

is $-\beta - \lambda$.

Using this rule for a 2×2 matrix, it is straightforward to show that, for any matrix of this dimension, its determinant equals the determinant of its transpose; that is,

$$|A| = |A'|.$$

It is also easy to show that switching the columns or rows of the matrix does not affect the value of its determinant. In fact, as shown in the next chapter, these results are more general and apply to the determinant of a matrix of any dimension.

The value of the determinant provides a necessary and sufficient test for whether or not a matrix has an inverse. If the matrix A is nonsingular (that is, if A^{-1} exists), then $|A| \neq 0$, and if $|A| \neq 0$, then A is nonsingular. If, on the other hand, $|A| = 0$, then A is singular (that is, A^{-1} does not exist), and if A is singular, then $|A| = 0$. Using the notation introduced in Chapter 2,

$$|A| \neq 0 \Leftrightarrow A^{-1} \text{ exists},$$

or, equivalently,

$$|A| = 0 \Leftrightarrow A^{-1} \text{ does not exist}.$$

The matrices G and H presented above are each nonsingular. The determinants are

$$|G| = 3 \cdot 4 - 6 \cdot 1 = 6$$

and

$$|H| = 0 \cdot 3 - (-2) \cdot 5 = 10.$$

The nonzero determinants show that neither matrix has one row that is a multiple of another nor has one column that is a multiple of another.

As an example of a singular matrix, consider the system of two equations described earlier in which the second equation is a multiple of the first equation. This system can be written in matrix notation as

$$\begin{bmatrix} 2 & 3 \\ 4 & 6 \end{bmatrix} \cdot \begin{bmatrix} x_1 \\ x_2 \end{bmatrix} = \begin{bmatrix} 4 \\ 8 \end{bmatrix}.$$

The determinant of the matrix of this system is $2 \cdot 6 - 3 \cdot 4 = 0$. The system described earlier in which the two equations are mutually inconsistent shares the same matrix as this system, and therefore, the determinant of the matrix of that system is also zero.

A matrix is singular if one row is a multiple of another. This is easy to show in the 2×2 case. Consider the matrix V in which the second row is k times the first row (so $v_{21} = k \cdot v_{11}$ and $v_{22} = k \cdot v_{12}$):

$$V = \begin{bmatrix} v_{11} & v_{12} \\ k \cdot v_{11} & k \cdot v_{12} \end{bmatrix}.$$

The determinant of this matrix is

$$|V| = v_{11} \cdot k \cdot v_{12} - v_{12} \cdot k \cdot v_{11} = 0.$$

A matrix is also singular if one of its columns is a multiple of any other of its columns. Again, in the 2×2 case, we can show this explicitly by defining a matrix U in which the second column is k times the first column:

$$U = \begin{bmatrix} u_{11} & k \cdot u_{11} \\ u_{21} & k \cdot u_{21} \end{bmatrix}.$$

In this case the determinant is

$$|U| = u_{11} \cdot k \cdot u_{21} - u_{21} \cdot k \cdot u_{11} = 0.$$

These results are shown in the more general $n \times n$ case in the next chapter.

The Inverse of a 2 × 2 Matrix

To conclude this chapter, we present the inverse of a generic 2×2 matrix. We use this result to provide a solution for a two-equation matrix representation of the widget model. An application that closes this section also uses this result to discuss a model that provides a possible theoretical reason for the increasing disparity between the wages to skilled and unskilled workers. In the next chapter we present a method for finding the inverse of a higher-dimension matrix.

Again, consider a generic 2×2 matrix

$$A = \begin{bmatrix} a_{11} & a_{12} \\ a_{21} & a_{22} \end{bmatrix}.$$

The inverse of this matrix, A^{-1}, is another 2×2 matrix, which has the property that

$$A^{-1}A = AA^{-1} = I.$$

It is straightforward to show that the inverse of A is

$$A^{-1} = \frac{1}{|A|}\begin{bmatrix} a_{22} & -a_{12} \\ -a_{21} & a_{11} \end{bmatrix} = \begin{bmatrix} \dfrac{a_{22}}{a_{11}a_{22} - a_{12}a_{21}} & \dfrac{-a_{12}}{a_{11}a_{22} - a_{12}a_{21}} \\ \dfrac{-a_{21}}{a_{11}a_{22} - a_{12}a_{21}} & \dfrac{a_{11}}{a_{11}a_{22} - a_{12}a_{21}} \end{bmatrix},$$

where the fraction $1/|A|$ is a scalar. We can check that this is, in fact, the inverse of A by multiplying AA^{-1} and noting that this product is the 2×2 identity matrix. Also, by Property 2 of inverses discussed earlier, this is the only inverse of A since the inverse of a matrix is unique.

Note that each element of A^{-1} is a fraction with the denominator equal to the determinant of A. The matrix

$$\begin{bmatrix} a_{22} & -a_{12} \\ -a_{21} & a_{11} \end{bmatrix}$$

is called **the adjoint of A,** which is also written as **adj A.** The adjoint of a matrix is another matrix of the same dimension. The general rule for finding adjoints of higher-dimension matrices is presented in Chapter 5.

We can rewrite the inverse of this 2×2 matrix, or indeed of a nonsingular matrix of any dimension, as

$$A^{-1} = \frac{1}{|A|}(\text{adj } A). \tag{4.15}$$

For the 2×2 case presented here, a useful mnemonic for remembering the adjoint is that the diagonal terms switch position and the off-diagonal terms switch sign. For example, the adjoints of the matrices G and H that we defined earlier are

$$\text{adj } G = \begin{bmatrix} 4 & -6 \\ -1 & 3 \end{bmatrix} \quad \text{and} \quad \text{adj } H = \begin{bmatrix} 3 & 2 \\ -5 & 0 \end{bmatrix}.$$

As shown earlier, the determinants of these matrices are $|G| = 6$ and $|H| = 10$. Thus the inverses are

$$G^{-1} = \begin{bmatrix} \frac{2}{3} & -1 \\ -\frac{1}{6} & \frac{1}{2} \end{bmatrix} \quad \text{and} \quad H^{-1} = \begin{bmatrix} \frac{3}{10} & \frac{1}{5} \\ -\frac{1}{2} & 0 \end{bmatrix}.$$

You can use the rules of matrix multiplication to confirm that $GG^{-1} = G^{-1}G = I$ and $HH^{-1} = H^{-1}H = I$.

We can use the equilibrium condition (4.3) to write the model for the market for widgets as a system with two equations and two endogenous variables, P and Q. In this case, the equations of the model are

$$Q + \beta P = \alpha + \gamma G$$
$$Q - \lambda P = \theta - \phi N,$$

which can be written in matrix form as

$$\begin{bmatrix} 1 & \beta \\ 1 & -\lambda \end{bmatrix} \cdot \begin{bmatrix} Q \\ P \end{bmatrix} = \begin{bmatrix} \alpha + \gamma G \\ \theta - \phi N \end{bmatrix}.$$

As discussed above, the determinant of the 2×2 matrix of this system is $-\lambda - \beta$. The adjoint of this matrix is

$$\begin{bmatrix} -\lambda & -\beta \\ -1 & 1 \end{bmatrix},$$

and the inverse is

$$\begin{bmatrix} \dfrac{\lambda}{\beta + \lambda} & \dfrac{\beta}{\beta + \lambda} \\ \dfrac{1}{\beta + \lambda} & \dfrac{-1}{\beta + \lambda} \end{bmatrix}.$$

Therefore the solution to this system is

$$\begin{bmatrix} Q \\ P \end{bmatrix} = \begin{bmatrix} \dfrac{\lambda}{\beta + \lambda} & \dfrac{\beta}{\beta + \lambda} \\ \dfrac{1}{\beta + \lambda} & \dfrac{-1}{\beta + \lambda} \end{bmatrix} \begin{bmatrix} \alpha + \gamma G \\ \theta - \phi N \end{bmatrix}.$$

It is straightforward to confirm that the solutions for P and $Q = Q^D = Q^S$ in this two-equation system match those in the three-equation system.

Wage Gaps and International Trade

The wage gap between more educated, more highly skilled workers and relatively less skilled workers in the United States widened over the 1980s. At the same time, trade with developing countries became a much bigger part of overall U.S. imports. Is greater international competition a possible culprit behind widening wage disparities? A possible link between these two trends is suggested by a result from international trade theory known as the **Stolper-Samuelson effect.**[4]

We consider a simple example of a trade model where there are two factors of production in a country, skilled labor (S) and unskilled labor (U). This country produces two goods, textiles (T) and computers (C). Production is described by the *technical coefficients* a_{ij}, each of which represents the amount of input i (either S or U)

[4]The original reference is Wolfgang Stolper and Paul Samuelson, "Protection and real wages," *Review of Economic Studies* 9 (1941): 58–73.

required to produce good j (either T or C). That is,

$$a_{UT} = \frac{U_T}{T} = \frac{\text{unskilled labor in textiles}}{\text{output of textiles}}$$

$$a_{ST} = \frac{S_T}{T} = \frac{\text{skilled labor in textiles}}{\text{output of textiles}}$$

$$a_{UC} = \frac{U_C}{C} = \frac{\text{unskilled labor in computers}}{\text{output of computers}}$$

$$a_{SC} = \frac{S_C}{C} = \frac{\text{skilled labor in computers}}{\text{output of computers}},$$

where U_C and S_C are the number of unskilled and skilled workers, respectively, in the computer industry and U_T and S_T are the number of unskilled and skilled workers in the textile industry. In this application we assume that these coefficients are constant, although the results of the analysis are the same when the coefficients can vary by assuming a more flexible production technology.

We assume perfect competition, which implies zero profits. Thus the total wage bill equals total revenues. Denoting the wage to unskilled labor w and the salary to skilled labor as s, the zero-profit condition for the two industries is

$$U_C w + S_C s = p_C C \quad \text{and} \quad U_T w + S_T s = p_T T,$$

whereP_C and P_T represent the price of computers and textiles, respectively.

The zero-profit conditions can be divided by total output in each industry (either C or T) to obtain

$$\frac{U_C}{C} w + \frac{S_C}{C} s = p_C \quad \text{and} \quad \frac{U_T}{T} w + \frac{S_T}{T} s = p_T.$$

Note that these fractions equal the technical coefficients. This system can be expressed as $Aw = p$, where A is the matrix of technical coefficients, w is the vector of payments to labor (that is, wages and salaries), and p is the vector of prices, as shown by

$$\begin{bmatrix} a_{UT} & a_{ST} \\ a_{UC} & a_{SC} \end{bmatrix} \cdot \begin{bmatrix} w \\ s \end{bmatrix} = \begin{bmatrix} p_T \\ p_C \end{bmatrix}.$$

The determinant of the matrix of technical coefficients is $|A| = a_{UT} \cdot a_{SC} - a_{UC} \cdot a_{ST}$. This determinant is positive if textile production uses unskilled labor relatively more intensively than does computer production (that is, $a_{UT}/a_{ST} > a_{UC}/a_{SC}$), an assumption we make. Note that if these relative intensities are the same, then the determinant is zero. In that case the two industries are basically the same, and the two equations are either redundant (if $p_T = p_C$) or mutually inconsistent (if $p_T \neq p_C$).

Changes in the prices of computers or textiles affect the wages of both skilled and unskilled workers. The solution of this system of equations, $w = A^{-1}p$, shows this explicitly. Using the results above to find A^{-1}, we have

$$\frac{1}{|A|} \begin{bmatrix} a_{SC} & -a_{ST} \\ -a_{UC} & a_{UT} \end{bmatrix} \cdot \begin{bmatrix} p_T \\ p_C \end{bmatrix} = \begin{bmatrix} w \\ s \end{bmatrix}.$$

In this model the effect of greater trade with developing countries is to lower the relative price of textiles. Considering the comparative static experiment of a decrease in P_T and no change in P_C and rewriting the solution in terms of changes, we have

$$\frac{1}{|A|}\begin{bmatrix} a_{SC} & -a_{ST} \\ -a_{UC} & a_{UT} \end{bmatrix} \cdot \begin{bmatrix} \Delta p_T \\ 0 \end{bmatrix} = \begin{bmatrix} \Delta w \\ \Delta s \end{bmatrix}.$$

The solution shows that $\Delta w = a_{SC}/|A|\Delta p_T$ and $\Delta s = -a_{UC}/|A|\Delta p_T$. Since Δp_T is negative, this result shows that wages to the unskilled fall and wages to the skilled rise. So there is a theoretical possibility of a link between increased trade with developing countries and an increase in the wage gap between skilled and unskilled workers in the United States. The actual extent to which the increasing wage gap in the United States is attributable to increasing international competition, however, is a matter of continuing debate.[5]

Exercises 4.4

1. Determine which of the following matrices are nonsingular.

   (a) $G = \begin{bmatrix} 12 & -3 \\ 1 & 4 \end{bmatrix}$

   (b) $H = \begin{bmatrix} \frac{1}{2} & 2 \\ \frac{1}{6} & \frac{2}{3} \end{bmatrix}$

   (c) $J = \begin{bmatrix} 2 & 5 \\ 4 & 9 \end{bmatrix}$

   (d) $K = \begin{bmatrix} 4 & -4 \\ 1 & 1 \end{bmatrix}$

2. Consider the matrix

$$A = \begin{bmatrix} \phi a & \beta b \\ c & d \end{bmatrix}.$$

   (a) What value of ϕ, as a function of a, b, c, d, and β, makes this matrix nonsingular?

   (b) What value of β makes this matrix nonsingular?

   (c) If $\phi = \beta$ what value of a makes this matrix singular?

3. Consider each of the following systems of equations of the general form $Ax = y$. For a solution to exist for each system, the inverse of matrix A must also exist. Without calculating the answer, determine which of these systems can be solved.

   (a) $4x_1 - 5x_2 = 10$ and $8x_1 = 16$

   (b) $2x_1 + 4x_2 = 7$ and $3x_1 + 6x_2 = 14$

   (c) $9x_1 - 6x_2 = 0$ and $6x_1 - 4x_2 = 1$

[5] In an overview of research on this topic, Richard Freeman concludes, "... trade matters, but it is neither all that matters nor the primary cause of observed changes [in the relative decline of wages of the less-skilled]." See "Are your wages set in Beijing?" *Journal of Economic Perspectives* 9, no. 3, (Summer 1995): 15–32. This quote is found on page 30.

4. Find the determinant for each matrix. Indicate whether each matrix is nonsingular.

(a) $\begin{bmatrix} 2 & -4 \\ 6 & 10 \end{bmatrix}$

(b) $\begin{bmatrix} 1 & 1 \\ -1 & 0 \end{bmatrix}$

(c) $\begin{bmatrix} 4 & -6 \\ -2 & 3 \end{bmatrix}$

(d) $\begin{bmatrix} 1-\beta & \beta \\ 1 & \beta \end{bmatrix}$

(e) $\begin{bmatrix} \frac{1}{2} & -8 \\ -\frac{1}{4} & 4 \end{bmatrix}$

(f) $\begin{bmatrix} a-\lambda & b \\ c & d-\lambda \end{bmatrix}$

5. Find the adjoint for each nonsingular matrix.

(a) $\begin{bmatrix} 2 & 3 \\ 4 & 7 \end{bmatrix}$

(b) $\begin{bmatrix} -1 & 3 \\ 9 & -4 \end{bmatrix}$

(c) $\begin{bmatrix} 0 & 2 \\ -2 & 1 \end{bmatrix}$

(d) $\begin{bmatrix} \frac{1}{2} & 6 \\ -3 & 4 \end{bmatrix}$

6. Determine the inverse of the matrix A

$$A = \begin{bmatrix} 6 & -2 \\ 3 & 5 \end{bmatrix}$$

by first finding its determinant, $|A|$, and then its adjoint, adj A. Show that $AA^{-1} = A^{-1}A = I$.

7. Find the inverse for each nonsingular matrix in questions 4 and 5.

8. Consider the simplified, two-equation, national income model

$$Y = C+I+G$$
$$C = a+bY,$$

where national income (Y) and consumption (C) are endogenous variables and investment (I) and government spending (G) are exogenous variables. The parameters in the consumption function, a and b, represent the autonomous consumption expenditure and the marginal propensity to consume, respectively.

(a) Set up this model with a 2×2 matrix of coefficients, a 2×1 vector of endogenous variables, and a 2×1 vector of constants (consider $I + G$ to be one constant).

(b) This model can be expressed as $Ax = y$, where A is the coefficient matrix, x is the vector of endogenous variables, and y is the vector of constants. Remembering that $x = A^{-1}y$, find the solution to this system of equations.

9. The profit functions of two airplane manufacturers, the European firm Airbus and the American firm Boeing, are

$$A = -\frac{1}{2}B + F$$

$$B = -\frac{1}{2}A + G,$$

where A is the profits of Airbus, B is the profits of Boeing, F is a subsidy from the governments of Europe to Airbus, and G is a subsidy from the U.S. government to Boeing.

(a) Express these two equations as a matrix system with A and B as the endogenous variables and F and G as the exogenous variables.

(b) Determine the solution if each government provides a subsidy of \$100 million.

(c) What happens to the profits of each firm if the European governments increase their subsidy to \$200 million, while the U.S. government keeps its subsidy equal to \$100 million?

10. Consider an example of a country which produces two goods, wheat (W) and steel (S), using two factors of production, labor (L) and land (K). The technical coefficients of production a_{ij} are

$$a_{LS} = 12$$
$$a_{KS} = 4$$
$$a_{LW} = 2$$
$$a_{KW} = 6,$$

where i represents the amount of input required to produce good j. The zero-profit condition for these two industries, divided by total output, is

$$\frac{L}{S}w + \frac{K}{S}r = p_s \quad \text{and} \quad \frac{L}{W}w + \frac{K}{W}r = p_w,$$

where w is the wage paid to labor and r is the rent paid to capital. This system can be expressed in matrix format as $Aw = p$, where A is the matrix of technical coefficients, w is the return paid to the factors of production, and p is the vector of prices.

(a) Set up this system of equations in matrix format.

(b) What is the determinant of the matrix of technical coefficients? What does the sign of the determinant indicate about the relative intensity of labor usage in the production processes of both goods?

(c) Find the solution of this system of equations, $w = A^{-1}p$.

(d) Now assume that the price of steel $P_s = 128$ and the price of wheat $P_W = 48$. What are the resulting values of w and r?

(e) What is the impact on w and r if P_W rises to 64 ($\Delta P_W = 16$)? Can you provide an intuition for your result?

Summary

Systems of equations from simple demand and supply systems to more complicated econometric modeling show up often in economic analysis. Matrix algebra provides a powerful set of tools for analyzing linear systems of equations. This chapter introduces some important concepts in matrix algebra. The chapter also provides the solution for a 2×2 system and applies this to an international trade model. Chapter 5 continues with the presentation of matrix algebra by showing how to find the determinant and inverse of higher-dimension matrices as well as with other properties of matrices that are used in economic analysis.

Chapter 5

Further Topics in Matrix Algebra

Matrix algebra provides a set of powerful techniques for representing and solving systems of equations. Chapter 4 introduces matrix algebra and presents a number of its basic results, such as the relationship between the value of the determinant of a matrix and the existence of its inverse and the use of the inverse to solve a system of equations. The actual implementation of some of these results, however, was limited in the discussion of Chapter 4. In particular, the formulas for evaluating the determinant and calculating the inverse of a 2×2 matrix are presented, but more general rules for finding the determinants and the inverses of matrices of higher dimension are not developed. In the first two sections of this chapter, we generalize some of the formulas presented in Chapter 4 by presenting methods for evaluating determinants and calculating inverses for square matrices of any dimension.

The determinant of a square matrix of any dimension can be evaluated using the technique presented in Section 5.1. In Section 5.2 we demonstrate how to calculate the inverse of a nonsingular matrix of any dimension. This section also presents a method called **Cramer's rule** for solving for a subset of the endogenous variables of a system. This technique requires fewer calculations than does full matrix inversion. The technique presented in Section 5.2 will enable you to analyze and solve higher-dimension economic models. We illustrate the methods presented in these two sections with the model of the market for widgets and the IS/LM model introduced in Chapter 4.

The third section of this chapter presents a method for converting a square matrix into a diagonal matrix through the creation of new variables that are combinations of the variables of the original system of equations. This technique helps reduce complicated systems of equations to a series of univariate relationships, which can be more easily solved. A component of this technique is the calculation of a set of scalars associated with a matrix called the **characteristic roots** or **eigenvalues.** These scalars are important for characterizing dynamic models like those found in macroeconomics or finance. We draw on these techniques in the analysis of dynamic models in Chapters 13 and 14.

5.1 EVALUATING DETERMINANTS

The determinant is a scalar associated with a square matrix. As discussed in Chapter 4, the determinant of a singular matrix equals zero, while a nonsingular matrix has a determinant that differs from zero. The determinant is also used in the calculation of the inverse of a matrix as shown by (4.15). In Chapter 4 we presented the formula for the determinant of a 2×2 matrix. In this section we show how to evaluate the determinant of a matrix of any dimension.

We begin our presentation of the technique for evaluating the determinants of any square matrix by presenting the determinants for a general 2×2 matrix and a general 3×3 matrix. Recall from Chapter 4 that the determinant of the 2×2 matrix

$$A = \begin{bmatrix} a_{11} & a_{12} \\ a_{21} & a_{22} \end{bmatrix}$$

consists of two terms, each of which is the product of two elements of the matrix. The determinant of this matrix, denoted $|A|$, is

$$|A| = a_{11}a_{22} - a_{12}a_{21}.$$

The determinant of the general 3×3 matrix

$$B = \begin{bmatrix} b_{11} & b_{12} & b_{13} \\ b_{21} & b_{22} & b_{23} \\ b_{31} & b_{32} & b_{33} \end{bmatrix}$$

consists of six terms, each of which is the product of three elements of the matrix. This determinant is

$$|B| = b_{11}b_{22}b_{33} - b_{11}b_{23}b_{32} - b_{12}b_{21}b_{33} + b_{12}b_{31}b_{23} + b_{13}b_{21}b_{32} - b_{13}b_{31}b_{22}.$$

For example, the determinant of

$$W = \begin{bmatrix} 1 & \beta & 0 \\ 0 & -\lambda & 1 \\ 1 & 0 & -1 \end{bmatrix},$$

the matrix associated with the three-equation widgets model presented in the previous chapter, is

$$\begin{aligned} |W| &= (1 \cdot (-\lambda) \cdot (-1)) - (1 \cdot 1 \cdot 0) - (\beta \cdot 0 \cdot (-1)) \\ &\qquad + (\beta \cdot 1 \cdot 1) + (0 \cdot 0 \cdot 0) - (0 \cdot 1 \cdot (-\lambda)) \\ &= \lambda + \beta. \end{aligned}$$

Examining the determinants $|A|$ and $|B|$ reveals some common properties. Each of the two terms in $|A|$ has one element from one row and column and another element from a different row and column. That is, each term consists of $a_{ij}a_{mn}$, where $i \neq m$ and $j \neq n$, though i may equal j and m may equal n. In a similar fashion, each of the six separate products that constitute the determinant $|B|$ draws one element from one row and column, a second element from a different row and column, and a third element from yet a different row and column. That is, each term $b_{ij}b_{mn}b_{xy}$ has one and only one element from each row, so $i \neq m, i \neq x$, and $m \neq x$, and one and only one element from each column, so $j \neq n, j \neq y$ and $n \neq y$.

Another common property of the two determinants $|A|$ and $|B|$ is that each consists of the sum of all possible products that draw one and only one element from each row and one and only one element from each column. The two terms $a_{11}a_{22}$ and $a_{12}a_{21}$ are the only ones that draw one element from one row and column and another element from another row and column. There are six possible combinations of the elements of B that have one and only one element from each row and each column. These combinations are represented by the six terms in $|B|$ given previously. More generally, an $n \times n$ matrix has

$$n! = n \times (n-1) \times (n-2) \times \cdots \times 2 \times 1$$

terms that draw one and only one element from each row and each column ($n!$ is read as "n factorial"). Thus the determinant of a 2×2 matrix has 2 terms, the determinant of a 3×3 matrix has 6 terms, and the determinant of a 4×4 matrix has 24 terms.

A method for evaluating the determinant that provides a systematic way to obtain all products that draw one and only one element from each row and column and also properly assigns a sign to each product is called **Laplace expansion.** This method involves evaluating determinants of matrices that consist of a subset of the elements of the original matrix. To demonstrate this method, consider the determinant of the 3×3 matrix B presented earlier. We first rewrite this determinant as

$$|B| = b_{11}(b_{22}b_{33} - b_{23}b_{32}) - b_{12}(b_{21}b_{33} - b_{31}b_{23}) + b_{13}(b_{21}b_{32} - b_{31}b_{22}).$$

Consider the first term,

$$b_{11}(b_{22}b_{33} - b_{23}b_{32}).$$

This term is the product of b_{11} and the determinant of the submatrix of B obtained by eliminating the row and column in which b_{11} appears, that is,

$$\begin{vmatrix} b_{22} & b_{23} \\ b_{32} & b_{33} \end{vmatrix}.$$

The second term,

$$-b_{12}(b_{21}b_{33} - b_{31}b_{23}),$$

equals -1 times the product of b_{12} and the determinant of the 2×2 submatrix of B obtained by eliminating its first row and second column,

$$\begin{vmatrix} b_{21} & b_{23} \\ b_{31} & b_{33} \end{vmatrix}.$$

Likewise, the third term is the product of b_{13} and the determinant of the 2×2 matrix left when the first row and the third column of B is eliminated,

$$\begin{vmatrix} b_{21} & b_{22} \\ b_{31} & b_{32} \end{vmatrix}.$$

This is a Laplace expansion of the matrix B along its first row.

The determinant of a matrix can be evaluated with a Laplace expansion along any one of its rows or any one of its columns. For example, rewriting $|B|$ by factoring out the terms in its third column gives us

$$|B| = b_{13}(b_{21}b_{32} - b_{31}b_{22}) - b_{23}(b_{11}b_{32} - b_{31}b_{12}) + b_{33}(b_{11}b_{22} - b_{21}b_{12}).$$

Each term in parentheses represents the determinant of the 2×2 submatrix of B obtained when the row and the column represented by the element multiplying that term is eliminated.

The Laplace expansion method, discussed here in the context of a 3×3 matrix, can be expressed in another way that enables us to generalize this method to matrices of higher dimensions. We first offer the following two definitions.

Minor Let A be an $n \times n$ matrix. Let M_{ij} be the $(n-1) \times (n-1)$ matrix obtained by deleting the ith row and the jth column of A. The determinant of that matrix, denoted $|M_{ij}|$, is called the **minor** of a_{ij}.

Cofactor Let A be an $n \times n$ matrix. The cofactor C_{ij} is a minor multiplied by either 1, if $(i + j)$ is an even integer, or -1, if $(i + j)$ is an odd integer. That is,

$$C_{ij} = (-1)^{i+j}|M_{ij}|.$$

Laplace expansion can be expressed in a compact way using cofactors. For example, the evaluation of the determinant of B through a Laplace expansion along its first row can be written as

$$|B| = \sum_{j=1}^{3} b_{1j}C_{1j}.$$

The Laplace expansion of B along its third column can be written as

$$|B| = \sum_{i=1}^{3} b_{i3}C_{i3}.$$

The determinant of the matrix

$$W = \begin{bmatrix} 1 & \beta & 0 \\ 0 & -\lambda & 1 \\ 1 & 0 & -1 \end{bmatrix}$$

can be evaluated through a Laplace expansion along its first row. This gives us

$$\begin{aligned} |W| &= 1 \cdot (-1)^2 \cdot \begin{vmatrix} -\lambda & 1 \\ 0 & -1 \end{vmatrix} + \beta \cdot (-1)^3 \cdot \begin{vmatrix} 0 & 1 \\ 1 & -1 \end{vmatrix} + 0 \cdot (-1)^4 \cdot \begin{vmatrix} 0 & -\lambda \\ 1 & 0 \end{vmatrix} \\ &= \lambda + \beta, \end{aligned}$$

where the minors are the 2×2 determinants and the cofactors are the minors multiplied by -1 raised to the appropriate power.

More generally, the determinant of the $n \times n$ matrix can be evaluated by a Laplace expansion along its ith row or along its jth column. The general rule for finding the determinant of an $n \times n$ matrix A, with the representative element a_{ij} and the set of cofactors C_{ij}, through a Laplace expansion along its ith row, is

$$|A| = \sum_{j=1}^{n} a_{ij}C_{ij}.$$

The same determinant can be evaluated by a Laplace expansion along the jth column of the matrix, which gives us

$$|A| = \sum_{i=1}^{n} a_{ij}C_{ij}.$$

These expressions illustrate why Laplace expansion is also referred to as **cofactor expansion.** Note that the formula for the determinant of a 2×2 matrix conforms to this rule if any minor is interpreted as the element left over by the elimination of a row and a column.

The determinants of matrices of higher dimension can be evaluated through a repeated application of Laplace expansion. The determinant of an $n \times n$ matrix can be found by first reducing the problem to one of evaluating the determinant of an $(n-1) \times (n-1)$ matrix and then repeating this technique until the evaluation of a 2×2 matrix remains. The number of calculations required to evaluate a determinant can be reduced by choosing to conduct the Laplace expansion along the row or column of the matrix that has the most number of elements equal to zero.

As an illustration of the evaluation of a determinant using a Laplace expansion, consider the matrix of the IS/LM model presented in Chapter 4. That matrix, which we call H, is

$$H = \begin{bmatrix} 1 & -1 & -1 & 0 \\ -0.8 & 1 & 0 & 0 \\ 0 & 0 & 1 & 2000 \\ 0.1 & 0 & 0 & -1000 \end{bmatrix}.$$

A Laplace expansion along the second, third, or fourth rows, or along the second, third, or fourth columns, would involve two terms that are multiplied by zero. We evaluate $|H|$ here through a Laplace expansion along the fourth column. This gives us

$$|H| = 2000 \cdot (-1)^7 \begin{vmatrix} 1 & -1 & -1 \\ -0.8 & 1 & 0 \\ 0.1 & 0 & 0 \end{vmatrix} + (-1000) \cdot (-1)^8 \begin{vmatrix} 1 & -1 & -1 \\ -0.8 & 1 & 0 \\ 0 & 0 & 1 \end{vmatrix},$$

where the two terms multiplied by zero are not explicitly included in this expression. Each of the two determinants of the 3×3 matrices in this expression can be evaluated by a Laplace expansion. Evaluating each of these determinants by a Laplace expansion along the third row, we have

$$\begin{vmatrix} 1 & -1 & -1 \\ -0.8 & 1 & 0 \\ 0.1 & 0 & 0 \end{vmatrix} = 0.1 \cdot (-1)^4 \cdot \begin{vmatrix} -1 & -1 \\ 1 & 0 \end{vmatrix} = 0.1$$

and

$$\begin{vmatrix} 1 & -1 & -1 \\ -0.8 & 1 & 0 \\ 0 & 0 & 1 \end{vmatrix} = 1 \cdot (-1)^6 \cdot \begin{vmatrix} 1 & -1 \\ -0.8 & 1 \end{vmatrix} = 0.2.$$

Therefore

$$\begin{aligned} |H| &= 2000 \cdot (-1)^7 (0.1) + (-1000) \cdot (-1)^8 (0.2) \\ &= -400. \end{aligned}$$

The Laplace expansion technique can be used to obtain some general results concerning a **diagonal matrix.** All the elements of a diagonal matrix, a_{ij} for $i \neq j$, are zero, while the elements of this matrix that make up its diagonal, a_{ij} for $i \neq j$, are either nonzero or zero. Consider the general form of a 3×3 diagonal matrix D,

$$D = \begin{bmatrix} d_{11} & 0 & 0 \\ 0 & d_{22} & 0 \\ 0 & 0 & d_{33} \end{bmatrix}.$$

Expanding along the first row results in the term $d_{11}C_{11}$ and two other terms that are multiplied by zero. The cofactor is

$$C_{11} = (-1)^2 (d_{22} \cdot d_{33}),$$

and, therefore,

$$|D| = d_{11} \cdot d_{22} \cdot d_{33}.$$

In a similar fashion, we can find the determinant of the general form of a 4×4 diagonal matrix

$$D = \begin{bmatrix} d_{11} & 0 & 0 & 0 \\ 0 & d_{22} & 0 & 0 \\ 0 & 0 & d_{33} & 0 \\ 0 & 0 & 0 & d_{44} \end{bmatrix}$$

by a Laplace expansion along its first row. This gives us three terms that are multiplied by zero and the term $d_{11}C_{11}$. We know from the 3×3 case that

$$C_{11} = (-1)^2(d_{22} \cdot d_{33} \cdot d_{44}),$$

and therefore, for a 4×4 diagonal matrix D with diagonal elements d_{ii},

$$|D| = d_{11}d_{22}d_{33}d_{44}.$$

In general, the determinant of any diagonal matrix is the product of its diagonal elements. Thus a diagonal matrix is nonsingular if and only if all its diagonal elements are nonzero.

An exercise at the end of this section asks you to use a procedure like this to show that the determinant of any **triangular matrix** is also the product of its diagonal elements. A triangular matrix is one in which all the elements below the diagonal are zero (a **lower triangular matrix**) or all the elements above the diagonal are zero (an

upper triangular matrix). Thus any triangular matrix is nonsingular if and only if all its diagonal elements are nonzero.

Exercises 5.1

1. Find the determinant of each 3×3 matrix where

$$|B| = b_{11}b_{22}b_{33} - b_{11}b_{23}b_{32} - b_{12}b_{21}b_{33} + b_{12}b_{31}b_{23} + b_{13}b_{21}b_{32} - b_{13}b_{31}b_{22}.$$

(a) $B = \begin{bmatrix} 5 & 0 & 4 \\ 0 & 3 & 1 \\ 2 & 6 & 0 \end{bmatrix}$

(b) $B = \begin{bmatrix} \frac{1}{2} & -1 & 0 \\ 1 & -2 & 0 \\ 2 & -4 & 0 \end{bmatrix}$

(c) $B = \begin{bmatrix} 1 & \lambda & -1 \\ 0 & \phi & 1 \\ -1 & 0 & 1 \end{bmatrix}$

2. Find the minor and cofactor of each 3×3 matrix along the second column.

(a) $A = \begin{bmatrix} 9 & 8 & 7 \\ 6 & 5 & 4 \\ 3 & 2 & 1 \end{bmatrix}$

(b) $A = \begin{bmatrix} 8 & 1 & 4 \\ -3 & \frac{1}{2} & 2 \\ -5 & 0 & 1 \end{bmatrix}$

(c) $A = \begin{bmatrix} a & b & c \\ b & c & a \\ c & a & b \end{bmatrix}$

3. Evaluate the determinants of the matrices in question 1 using the Laplace expansion method along the third row.
4. Consider the following system of equations:

$$\begin{aligned} 6x_1 + 2x_2 - 3x_3 &= 10 \\ 2x_1 + 4x_2 + x_3 &= 0 \\ x_1 - x_3 &= 2. \end{aligned}$$

Find the determinant of matrix A, which is the matrix of parameters.

5. Evaluate each determinant.

(a) $A = \begin{bmatrix} 1 & 0.5 & 0.5 & 2 \\ 0 & 1 & 2 & 0 \\ -1 & 1 & 10 & 0 \\ 0 & 5 & 1 & -1 \end{bmatrix}$

(b) $A = \begin{bmatrix} 2 & 7 & 0 & 1 \\ 0 & 0 & 9 & 0 \\ 5 & 7 & 4 & 6 \\ 1 & -2 & -1 & 0 \end{bmatrix}$

(c) $A = \begin{bmatrix} 4 & -4 & 0 & 0 \\ 2 & 2 & -1 & 1 \\ 3 & 0 & 1 & 0 \\ 7 & 5 & 2 & 1 \end{bmatrix}$

6. A standard IS/LM model can be expressed as the 4×4 matrix system H,

$$\begin{bmatrix} 0 & 1 & 0 & d \\ -1 & -1 & 1 & 0 \\ 1 & 0 & -b & 0 \\ 0 & 0 & k & -j \end{bmatrix} \cdot \begin{bmatrix} C \\ I \\ Y \\ R \end{bmatrix} = \begin{bmatrix} e \\ G \\ a \\ \frac{M}{P} \end{bmatrix},$$

where lowercase letters represent parameters and uppercase letters represent variables. The variables in the 4×1 vector v, consumption (C), investment (I), income (Y), and interest rates (R), are endogenous. The variables in the 4×1 vector p are exogenous and represent government spending (G) and the real money supply (M/P). The first row of H represents the investment equation, the second row represents the national income accounting identity, the third row represents the consumption equation, and the fourth row represents money demand. Find the determinant of this system.

7. Use Laplace expansion to demonstrate that the determinant of the lower triangular matrix

$$T = \begin{bmatrix} t_{11} & t_{12} & t_{13} & t_{14} & t_{15} \\ 0 & t_{22} & t_{23} & t_{24} & t_{25} \\ 0 & 0 & t_{33} & t_{34} & t_{35} \\ 0 & 0 & 0 & t_{44} & t_{45} \\ 0 & 0 & 0 & 0 & t_{55} \end{bmatrix}$$

is the product of its diagonal elements.

8. Use a Laplace expansion to find the determinant of the matrix

$$\begin{bmatrix} a & b & c \\ d & e & f \\ a + kd & b + ke & c + kf \end{bmatrix}.$$

Can you provide a reason for the result you find?

5.2 SOLVING SYSTEMS OF EQUATIONS

As discussed in Chapter 4, the solution to a system of equations

$$Ax = y,$$

where A is an $n \times n$ matrix of parameters, x is an $n \times 1$ vector of endogenous variables, and y is an $n \times 1$ vector of exogenous variables, is

$$x = A^{-1}y,$$

where A^{-1} is the inverse of the matrix A. The existence of a unique solution requires that the matrix A be nonsingular. If A is nonsingular, then $|A| \neq 0$. As discussed in Chapter 4, the determinant is also instrumental in calculating an inverse since, as shown by (4.15), the inverse of any nonsingular matrix A is

$$A^{-1} = \frac{1}{|A|} \operatorname{adj}(A),$$

where **adj (*A*)** is the **adjoint matrix** of A. In this section we show how to calculate the inverse of a nonsingular matrix of any dimension.

Since the previous section demonstrates how to evaluate the determinant of a matrix, we now turn our attention to evaluating the adjoint matrix.

Adjoint Matrix Let A be an $n \times n$ matrix A. Define the $n \times n$ matrix in which the (i, j)th element is the cofactor C_{ij} of A as the matrix of cofactors. The adjoint matrix is an $n \times n$ matrix that is the transpose of the matrix of cofactors.

The simplest example of this is a 2×2 matrix. Consider the 2×2 matrix

$$A = \begin{bmatrix} a_{11} & a_{12} \\ a_{21} & a_{22} \end{bmatrix}.$$

As discussed above, each of the four minors $|M_{ij}|$ of this matrix is the element of the matrix left when the ith row and the jth column are eliminated. Assigning the proper signs to these minors, we have the matrix of cofactors C, where

$$C = \begin{bmatrix} a_{22} & -a_{21} \\ -a_{12} & a_{11} \end{bmatrix}.$$

The adjoint matrix is the transpose of the matrix of cofactors, and it equals

$$\operatorname{adj}(A) = C' = \begin{bmatrix} a_{22} & -a_{12} \\ -a_{21} & a_{11} \end{bmatrix}.$$

The inverse divides each element of this adjoint matrix by the determinant. Therefore, as shown in the previous chapter,

$$A^{-1} = \frac{1}{|A|} \operatorname{adj}(A) = \begin{bmatrix} \dfrac{a_{22}}{a_{11}a_{22}-a_{12}a_{21}} & \dfrac{-a_{12}}{a_{11}a_{22}-a_{12}a_{21}} \\ \dfrac{-a_{21}}{a_{11}a_{22}-a_{12}a_{21}} & \dfrac{a_{11}}{a_{11}a_{22}-a_{12}a_{21}} \end{bmatrix}.$$

As an example of a 3 × 3 system, consider the widget model

$$Wv = g$$

presented earlier, where

$$W = \begin{bmatrix} 1 & \beta & 0 \\ 0 & -\lambda & 1 \\ 1 & 0 & -1 \end{bmatrix}, \quad v = \begin{bmatrix} Q^D \\ P \\ Q^S \end{bmatrix}, \quad \text{and} \quad g = \begin{bmatrix} \alpha + \gamma G \\ \theta - \phi N \\ 0 \end{bmatrix}.$$

The solution to this model is

$$v = W^{-1}g.$$

This solution requires evaluating the inverse of W. Each of the minors of W is the determinant of a 2 × 2 matrix. The matrix of cofactors of W is

$$\begin{bmatrix} \lambda & 1 & \lambda \\ \beta & -1 & \beta \\ \beta & -1 & -\lambda \end{bmatrix}.$$

Therefore the adjoint of W is

$$\text{adj}\,(W) = \begin{bmatrix} \lambda & \beta & \beta \\ 1 & -1 & -1 \\ \lambda & \beta & -\lambda \end{bmatrix},$$

and the inverse is

$$W^{-1} = \begin{bmatrix} \dfrac{\lambda}{\beta+\lambda} & \dfrac{\beta}{\beta+\lambda} & \dfrac{\beta}{\beta+\lambda} \\ \dfrac{1}{\beta+\lambda} & \dfrac{-1}{\beta+\lambda} & \dfrac{-1}{\beta+\lambda} \\ \dfrac{\lambda}{\beta+\lambda} & \dfrac{\beta}{\beta+\lambda} & \dfrac{-\lambda}{\beta+\lambda} \end{bmatrix}.$$

The solution to this model, $v = W^{-1}g$, can be written out explicitly as

$$\begin{bmatrix} Q^D \\ P \\ Q^S \end{bmatrix} = \begin{bmatrix} \dfrac{\lambda}{\beta+\lambda} & \dfrac{\beta}{\beta+\lambda} & \dfrac{\beta}{\beta+\lambda} \\ \dfrac{1}{\beta+\lambda} & \dfrac{-1}{\beta+\lambda} & \dfrac{-1}{\beta+\lambda} \\ \dfrac{\lambda}{\beta+\lambda} & \dfrac{\beta}{\beta+\lambda} & \dfrac{-\lambda}{\beta+\lambda} \end{bmatrix} \begin{bmatrix} \alpha + \gamma G \\ \theta - \phi N \\ 0 \end{bmatrix}.$$

This solution expresses the values of the endogenous variables that make up the elements of the vector v as functions of the exogenous variables that make up the elements of the vector g.

We can use this solution to conduct comparative static experiments, like those presented in Chapter 4, by noting that the system can be written in terms of the change in variables:

$$\Delta v = W^{-1}\,\Delta g,$$

where Δv represents the vector of the change in the endogenous variables and Δg represents the vector of the change in the exogenous variables. Writing this out explicitly, we have

$$\begin{bmatrix} \Delta Q^D \\ \Delta P \\ \Delta Q^S \end{bmatrix} = \begin{bmatrix} \dfrac{\lambda}{\beta+\lambda} & \dfrac{\beta}{\beta+\lambda} & \dfrac{\beta}{\beta+\lambda} \\ \dfrac{1}{\beta+\lambda} & \dfrac{-1}{\beta+\lambda} & \dfrac{-1}{\beta+\lambda} \\ \dfrac{\lambda}{\beta+\lambda} & \dfrac{\beta}{\beta+\lambda} & \dfrac{-\lambda}{\beta+\lambda} \end{bmatrix} \begin{bmatrix} \gamma \cdot \Delta G \\ -\phi \cdot \Delta N \\ 0 \end{bmatrix},$$

where $\Delta\alpha = 0$ and $\Delta\theta = 0$ since the parameters do not change. This solution can be used to determine the effect of a \$1 increase in the price of substitute goods, *ceteris paribus.* Setting $\Delta G = 1$ and $\Delta N = 0$, we find

$$\Delta Q^D = \Delta Q^S = \frac{\lambda\gamma}{\beta+\lambda}$$

$$\Delta P = \frac{\gamma}{\beta+\lambda}.$$

This solution can also be used to determine the effect of a \$1 increase in the price of inputs, *ceteris paribus.* Setting $\Delta N = 1$ and $\Delta G = 0$, we find

$$\Delta Q^D = \Delta Q^S = \frac{-\phi\beta}{\beta+\lambda}$$

$$\Delta P = \frac{\phi}{\beta+\lambda}.$$

Thus an increase in the price of the input reduces equilibrium quantity and increases equilibrium price.

Cramer's rule

The evaluation of an inverse provides the key ingredient for the solution to an entire system of equations. An alternative method for finding the solution of a subset of the endogenous variables is a technique known as **Cramer's rule.** Cramer's rule is especially useful for comparative static questions that require calculating the response of a subset of the endogenous variables to a change in one or more exogenous variables.

The derivation of Cramer's rule begins with the formula for the solution of a matrix system. For example, consider $Ax = y$, where A is a 4×4 matrix. The discussion above shows that

$$A^{-1} = \frac{1}{|A|} \operatorname{adj}(A) = \frac{1}{|A|} \begin{bmatrix} C_{11} & C_{21} & C_{31} & C_{41} \\ C_{12} & C_{22} & C_{32} & C_{42} \\ C_{13} & C_{23} & C_{33} & C_{43} \\ C_{14} & C_{24} & C_{34} & C_{44} \end{bmatrix},$$

where C_{ij} is the cofactor associated with element a_{ij} of the matrix A. Therefore the solution to this system is

$$x = A^{-1}y,$$

which, when written out explicitly, is

$$\begin{bmatrix} x_1 \\ x_2 \\ x_3 \\ x_4 \end{bmatrix} = \frac{1}{|A|} \begin{bmatrix} C_{11} & C_{21} & C_{31} & C_{41} \\ C_{12} & C_{22} & C_{32} & C_{42} \\ C_{13} & C_{23} & C_{33} & C_{43} \\ C_{14} & C_{24} & C_{34} & C_{44} \end{bmatrix} \cdot \begin{bmatrix} y_1 \\ y_2 \\ y_3 \\ y_4 \end{bmatrix}.$$

The solution for any particular endogenous variable, say x_1, equals

$$x_1 = \frac{1}{|A|} \sum_{j=1}^{4} C_{j1} \cdot y_j.$$

The term

$$\sum_{j=1}^{4} C_{j1} \cdot y_j$$

has an interesting interpretation. First take the original matrix A, and replace its first column with the vector y. We call this matrix A_1, where the subscript refers to the column replaced by the vector y. This matrix is

$$A_1 = \begin{bmatrix} y_1 & a_{12} & a_{13} & a_{14} \\ y_2 & a_{22} & a_{23} & a_{24} \\ y_3 & a_{32} & a_{33} & a_{34} \\ y_4 & a_{42} & a_{43} & a_{44} \end{bmatrix}.$$

We can find the determinant of the matrix A_1 through a Laplace expansion along its first column. Therefore

$$|A_1| = \sum_{j=1}^{4} C_{ji} y_j.$$

This expansion appears in the solution for the endogenous variable x_1 given above. Thus

$$x_1 = \frac{|A_1|}{|A|}.$$

We can evaluate the determinant $|A_1|$ by the Laplace expansion along the first column or, if more convenient, by any other Laplace expansion as well.

More generally, we have the following.

Cramer's rule For the system of equations $Ax = y$, where A is an $n \times n$ nonsingular matrix, the solution for the ith endogenous variable, x_i is

$$x_i = \frac{|A_i|}{|A|},$$

where the matrix A_i represents a matrix that is identical to the matrix A but for the replacement of its ith column with the $n \times 1$ vector y.

As an example of Cramer's rule, consider the three-equation system

$$\begin{aligned} x_1 + 2x_2 - 2x_3 &= 1 \\ 2x_2 + x_3 &= 4 \\ x_1 + x_3 &= 8, \end{aligned}$$

which can be expressed in matrix form $Ax = y$ or, more explicitly, as

$$\begin{bmatrix} 1 & 2 & -2 \\ 0 & 2 & 1 \\ 1 & 0 & 1 \end{bmatrix} \cdot \begin{bmatrix} x_1 \\ x_2 \\ x_3 \end{bmatrix} = \begin{bmatrix} 1 \\ 4 \\ 8 \end{bmatrix}.$$

We find that $|A| = 8$. Replacing the first column of A with the vector y gives us the matrix

$$A_1 = \begin{bmatrix} 1 & 2 & -2 \\ 4 & 2 & 1 \\ 8 & 0 & 1 \end{bmatrix},$$

which has the determinant 42. Thus $x_1 = \frac{42}{8}$. In a similar fashion, we find $|A_2| = 5$, so $x_2 = \frac{5}{8}$; and $|A_3| = 22$, so $x_3 = \frac{22}{8}$.

We can also use Cramer's rule to study comparative statics in the IS/LM model in Chapter 4. That model, represented in matrix format and in changes rather than levels, is

$$H \cdot \Delta x = \Delta y,$$

or, more explicitly,

$$\begin{bmatrix} 1 & -1 & -1 & 0 \\ -0.8 & 1 & 0 & 0 \\ 0 & 0 & 1 & 2000 \\ 0.1 & 0 & 0 & -1000 \end{bmatrix} \cdot \begin{bmatrix} \Delta Y \\ \Delta C \\ \Delta I \\ \Delta R \end{bmatrix} = \begin{bmatrix} \Delta G \\ 0 \\ 0 \\ \Delta \frac{M}{P} \end{bmatrix},$$

where the changes in consumption (ΔC), investment (ΔI), income (ΔY), and interest rates (ΔR) are endogenous, while the changes in government spending (ΔG) and the real money supply ($\Delta M/P$) are exogenous. The first row H represents the national income accounting identity, the second row represents the consumption equation, the third row represents the investment demand equation, and the fourth row represents the money market equilibrium equation.

We can use Cramer's rule to determine the effect of an expansion of government spending by \$100 on income, *ceteris paribus.* Replacing the first column of H as appropriate for this question, we have

$$H_1 = \begin{bmatrix} 100 & -1 & -1 & 0 \\ 0 & 1 & 0 & 0 \\ 0 & 0 & 1 & 2000 \\ 0 & 0 & 0 & -1000 \end{bmatrix},$$

and, expanding along the first column, we find

$$\begin{aligned} |H_1| &= 100(-1)^2 \cdot \begin{vmatrix} 1 & 0 & 0 \\ 0 & 1 & 2000 \\ 0 & 0 & -1000 \end{vmatrix} \\ &= 100 \cdot 1 \cdot (-1000 \cdot 1 - (2000) \cdot 0) = -100{,}000, \end{aligned}$$

where the term in parentheses in the second line is the Laplace expansion of the 3×3 matrix in the previous line along the first row.[1] As shown in Section 5.1, $|H| = -400$, and, therefore,

$$\Delta Y = \frac{|H_1|}{|H|} = \frac{-100{,}000}{-400} = 250.$$

This result shows that an increase in government spending by \$100 results in an overall increase in income by \$250, and, therefore, the multiplier in this model is 2.5. This calculation is simpler than calculating the full inverse H^{-1} since H_1 includes a column in which all elements but one are zero. More generally, Cramer's rule is especially useful for comparative static analysis where only one exogenous variable changes since it involves fewer calculations than would be required by full matrix inversion.

Sources of Comparative Advantage

Countries differ in their relative supplies of factors of production. A country like the United States has a relative abundance of skilled labor and capital, while a country like India has a relative abundance of unskilled labor. One of the central theories of international trade, the Heckscher-Ohlin theory, focuses on differences in relative factor supplies as the source of comparative advantage and, therefore, as the determinant of the pattern of production across countries. The pattern of production across countries, in turn, serves as the principal determinant of the pattern of international trade.

A model very similar to the one described in the application about wage gaps and international trade in Chapter 4 shows how relative factor supplies affect the pattern of production. As in that model, we assume that there are two factors of production. In this case, we call these two factors labor, L, and capital, K. These factors are used to produce two goods: manufactured goods, M, and food, F. We define the amount

[1] Alternatively, noticing that H_1 is a lower triangular matrix, we could have used the result presented at the end of the last section, which indicates that $|H_1|$ is the product of the diagonal elements of H_1.

of labor devoted to the production of manufactured goods as L_M and the remaining labor in the economy, which is devoted to the production of food, as L_F. Likewise, K_M and K_F represent the amount of capital devoted to the production of manufactured goods and food, respectively. Thus, $L = L_M + L_F$ and $K = K_M + K_F$. We divide and multiply the terms in these two equations by either the total output of manufactured goods or the total output of food to obtain

$$\frac{K_M}{M}M + \frac{K_F}{F}F = K$$
$$\frac{L_M}{M}M + \frac{L_F}{F}F = L.$$

As in the discussion of wage gaps and international trade, we define the technical coefficient a_{ij} as the amount of input i needed to produce one unit of good j (so, for example, $a_{KM} = K_M/M$, $a_{LF} = L_F/F$, and so on). Then the two equations given above can be rewritten in the matrix form

$$\begin{bmatrix} a_{KM} & a_{KF} \\ a_{LM} & a_{LF} \end{bmatrix} \cdot \begin{bmatrix} M \\ F \end{bmatrix} = \begin{bmatrix} K \\ L \end{bmatrix}.$$

We assume that the determinant of the matrix of technical coefficients, $|A| = a_{KM}a_{LF} - a_{LM}a_{KF}$, is positive. This reflects the assumption that the production of manufactured goods uses capital more intensively than does the production of food and therefore, $(a_{KM}/a_{LM}) > (a_{KF}/a_{LF})$.

Theories of international trade suggest that a country exports goods that it produces in relative abundance and imports goods that would be relatively scarce if supplied only by domestic producers. The Heckscher-Ohlin theory focuses on relative factor supplies as the source of varying international patterns of production as opposed to, say, international differences in technology. The two-equation system presented above shows the link between factor supplies and the pattern of production. This is particularly evident if we use Cramer's rule to determine the effect of an increase in the amount of capital in one country on its pattern of production. First, note that we can rewrite the two-equation system in terms of the changes in factors and goods as

$$\begin{bmatrix} a_{KM} & a_{KF} \\ a_{LM} & a_{LF} \end{bmatrix} \cdot \begin{bmatrix} \Delta M \\ \Delta F \end{bmatrix} = \begin{bmatrix} \Delta K \\ \Delta L \end{bmatrix}.$$

We consider the case where $\Delta K > 0$ and $\Delta L = 0$. Then, using Cramer's rule, we have the change in the output of manufactured goods as

$$\Delta M = \frac{\begin{vmatrix} \Delta K & a_{KF} \\ 0 & a_{LF} \end{vmatrix}}{|A|} = \frac{a_{LF}}{a_{KM}a_{LF} - a_{LM}a_{KF}}\Delta K > 0$$

and the change in the output of food as

$$\Delta F = \frac{\begin{vmatrix} a_{KM} & \Delta K \\ a_{LM} & 0 \end{vmatrix}}{|A|} = -\frac{a_{LM}}{a_{KM}a_{LF} - a_{LM}a_{KF}}\Delta K < 0.$$

It is striking that the output of food *decreases* with the increase in the amount of capital in the economy. The reason for this is that the new capital goes disproportionately to the sector that uses it relatively intensively and, in so doing, draws resources away from the production of food. The result that an increase in the supply of one factor leads to an increase in the production of the good that uses it intensively and a decrease in the production of other good is known as the **Rybczynski theorem.**[2]

The empirical relevance of this model is limited by its assumption of only two factors and two goods. However, in a more general model, with more factors and more goods, the result that the output of any good decreases with an increase in the supply of at least one particular factor continues to hold. This result is used by James Harrigan to test whether the supplies of three factors, skilled labor (S), unskilled labor (U), and capital (K), contribute to, or detract from, the output of particular categories of goods among Organization for Economic Cooperation and Development (OECD) countries.[3] Two of the results he obtains in a series of industry-by-industry cross-country estimations are

$$\begin{aligned} Y_{I\&S} &= 0.824K - 2.311S - 0.590U \\ Y_{P\&P} &= 0.570K + 1.089S - 0.529U, \end{aligned}$$

where $Y_{I\&S}$ is the output of the iron and steel industry and $Y_{P\&P}$ is the output of the printing and publishing industry. These results suggest that the supply of capital contributes to the comparative advantage of a country's iron and steel industry while both the supplies of skilled and unskilled labor contribute to, as Harrigan puts it, a country's comparative disadvantage in that industry. Also, these results suggest that the supplies of capital and skilled labor contribute to the comparative advantage of a country's printing and publishing industry while the supply of unskilled labor contributes to its comparative disadvantage in that industry.

Exercises 5.2

1. Find the adjoint matrix, adj(A), for each matrix.

(a) $A = \begin{bmatrix} 3 & -3 & 2 \\ 4 & 7 & 1 \\ 0 & 10 & 5 \end{bmatrix}$

(b) $A = \begin{bmatrix} a & b & c \\ c & b & a \\ b & a & c \end{bmatrix}$

[2] The original article is T. M. Rybczynski, "Factor endowments and relative commodity prices," *Economica* 22(1955): 336–341. A more general formulation of the Rybczynski theorem than the one presented here allows for varying values of the technical coefficients. The Rybczynski theorem assumes that relative factor prices do not change with a change in relative factor supplies.

[3] James Harrigan, "Factor endowments and the international location of production: Econometric evidence for the OECD, 1970–1985," *Journal of International Economics* 39, no. 1/2 (August 1995): 123–141.

(c) $A = \begin{bmatrix} 1 & 2 & 4 & 0 \\ -5 & 1 & 0 & 0 \\ 10 & 8 & 6 & 4 \\ -3 & 7 & 0 & 1 \end{bmatrix}$

(d) $A = \begin{bmatrix} 0 & 2 & 6 & 8 \\ -5 & 7 & 1 & 0 \\ 0 & 0 & 3 & 4 \\ 7 & 1 & 1 & 2 \end{bmatrix}$

2. Calculate the inverse of each matrix in question 1.
3. Consider the following simple Keynesian macroeconomic model

$$\begin{aligned} Y &= C + I + G \\ C &= 200 + 0.8Y \\ I &= 1000 - 2000R, \end{aligned}$$

where the endogenous variables include national income (Y), consumption (C), and investment (I), and the exogenous variables include government spending (G) and the interest rate (R).

(a) Set up this model with a 3×3 matrix of parameters, a 3×1 vector of endogenous variables, and a conformable vector of exogenous variables.

(b) Find the inverse of the 3×3 matrix of parameters.

(c) Evaluate the effect of a \$50 billion decrease in government spending on income. Compare this result to the one obtained in Section 4.1. Does your answer here differ, and if so, can you provide an economic rationale for this difference?

4. Consider the export/import model

$$\begin{aligned} X &= 1000 - 20E + 0.2Y_F \\ M &= 450 + 10E + 0.15Y_D \\ X &= M, \end{aligned}$$

where X represents exports, M represents imports, E represents the exchange rate, Y_F represents foreign income, and Y_D represents domestic income. The exogenous variables include Y_F and Y_D, and the endogenous variables are X, M, and E.

(a) Set this up as a system of equations, and solve this system by finding the inverse of the matrix of parameters.

(b) Determine the impact on exports of a \$100 increase in foreign income, *ceteris paribus.*

5. Find the solution to each system of equations using Cramer's rule.

(a) $5x + 4y = 20$
$3x - 2y = 12$

(b) $\frac{1}{2}x + 4y = 16$
$3x - 10y = 40$

(c) $10x + y - 2z = 30$

$x - y = 1$

$3x - 4y + z = 15$

(d) $4x - \frac{1}{3}y + 3z = 12$

$y + z = 6$

$6x - 2z = 3$

6. Consider a Keynesian-style macroeconomic model that is identical to the one presented in question 3 except that consumption depends upon the interest rate as well as income. That is,

$$C = 200 + 0.8Y - 1000R.$$

   (a) Set up this model in a matrix framework.
   (b) Use Cramer's rule to solve for national income in this model. Compare this result to the one obtained in question 3. Can you give an economic rationale for the difference between the two models?

7. A homogeneous equation system is one that takes the form $Ax = 0$, where 0 represents an $n \times 1$ vector in which each element equals zero. Use Cramer's rule to show that when A is nonsingular, the only solution to this system is that each element of the $n \times 1$ vector x equals zero.

8. Using the model in the application about sources of comparative advantage, determine the effect of an increase in labor, *ceteris paribus,* on the amount of manufactured goods and the amount of food produced in an economy. Use Cramer's rule to obtain your answer.

5.3 CHARACTERISTIC ROOTS AND DIAGONAL SYSTEMS

In Part Five of this book, we study dynamic relationships where the value of a variable today depends upon its level at other times (Chapter 13) or where the rate of change of a variable is a function of its level (Chapter 14). In each of these chapters, we first develop solutions for univariate dynamic functions. Solutions to systems of dynamic functions are more complicated to obtain. One strategy is to transform a system of multivariate equations into an equivalent system of univariate equations. In this section we show how to transform a system of multivariate linear equations into an equivalent system of univariate equations through a linear transformation of the original system.

More concretely, consider a system of multivariate linear equations

$$Ax = y,$$

where A is a nonsingular, nondiagonal square matrix and x and y are conformable vectors. Under certain conditions, we can diagonalize this system, that is, we can find a matrix such that by premultiplying both Ax and y by that matrix, we have

$$\Lambda u = v,$$

where Λ is a diagonal matrix of the same dimension as A and the vectors u and v are vectors of the same dimension as x and y. In this section we discuss the conditions required for diagonalizing the matrix A. We also show how to calculate a matrix which enables us to diagonalize A. Diagonalization involves the calculation of **characteristic roots** (also called **eigenvalues**) of a matrix. Each characteristic root of a matrix will have an associated **characteristic vector** (also called **eigenvector**). We illustrate the calculation of characteristic roots and characteristic vectors with reference to a 2×2 example.

Characteristic Roots

A characteristic root of a square matrix is a scalar that, when subtracted from each of the diagonal elements of that matrix, results in a singular matrix. Using matrix notation to formulate this condition, a characteristic root of the matrix A, denoted λ, must make the matrix

$$A - \lambda I$$

singular. The material presented in the previous chapter shows that each of the diagonal elements of the matrix λI equals λ and every off-diagonal element equals zero. It is immediately apparent that at least one of the characteristic roots of a singular matrix equals zero because the determinant

$$|A - 0I| = |A|$$

must equal zero. By the same reasoning, none of the characteristic roots of a nonsingular matrix equals zero.

Characteristic roots can be calculated by finding the values of λ, such that

$$|A - \lambda I| = 0.$$

For example, the characteristic roots of the 2×2 matrix

$$A = \begin{bmatrix} 2 & 2 \\ 1 & 3 \end{bmatrix} \tag{5.1}$$

can be found by evaluating the determinant

$$|A - \lambda I| = \begin{vmatrix} 2 - \lambda & 2 \\ 1 & 3 - \lambda \end{vmatrix}.$$

This determinant equals

$$|A - \lambda I| = \lambda^2 - 5\lambda + 4,$$

and thus the roots of this equation provide the values of λ that make $(A - \lambda I)$ singular. This equation is called the **characteristic polynomial.** Using the quadratic formula (see Chapter 2), we find that the roots of this particular equation are $\lambda = 4$ and $\lambda = 1$. Checking this, we find that

$$\begin{vmatrix} -2 & 2 \\ 1 & -1 \end{vmatrix} = 0 \quad \text{and} \quad \begin{vmatrix} 1 & 2 \\ 1 & 2 \end{vmatrix} = 0.$$

The **characteristic equation** for a 2×2 matrix with elements a_{ij} is

$$\lambda^2 - (a_{11} + a_{22})\lambda + (a_{11}a_{22} - a_{12}a_{21}) = 0.$$

Note that the last term in parentheses is the determinant of the original matrix A. The term $(a_{11} + a_{22})$ is the **trace** of the matrix A, which we write **tr (A).** The trace of a square matrix is the sum of the diagonal elements of the matrix. The quadratic formula shows that the two roots of this equation are

$$\lambda_1, \lambda_2 = \frac{\operatorname{tr}(A) \pm \sqrt{\operatorname{tr}(A)^2 - 4|A|}}{2}.$$

In general, an $n \times n$ matrix has a characteristic polynomial of degree n, and, therefore, it has at most n distinct characteristic roots. The values of the characteristic roots of a matrix are used in the following result concerning whether a matrix A is **diagonalizable;** that is, whether there exists a nonsingular matrix of the same dimension, P, and a diagonal matrix of the same dimension, D, such that

$$P^{-1}AP = D.$$

Note that the following result provides a sufficient, though not necessary, condition concerning whether a matrix is diagonalizable.

Diagonalizable Matrix (Sufficient Condition) A sufficient condition for an $n \times n$ matrix to be diagonalizable is that all of its n characteristic roots, $\lambda_1, \lambda_2, \ldots, \lambda_n$, are real and also that all of its n characteristic roots are distinct (that is, $\lambda_i \neq \lambda_j$ for any i, j where $i \neq j$).

Thus the 2×2 matrix A is diagonalizable if it meets the two conditions that

$$\operatorname{tr}(A)^2 \geq 4|A|,$$

since this means that its two characteristic roots are real, and

$$\operatorname{tr}(A)^2 \neq 4|A|,$$

since this means that its two characteristic roots are distinct and $\lambda_1 \neq \lambda_2$.[4] If

$$4|A| > \operatorname{tr}(A)^2,$$

then the characteristic roots will be **complex numbers.** A typical complex number takes the form $a + bi$, where a and b are real numbers and $i^2 = -1$. The real number a is called the real part of $a + bi$, while b is called the imaginary part.[5]

[4] To see that this condition is not necessary, consider a 2×2 diagonal matrix T that has 2 as each of its diagonal elements. The repeated characteristic root of this matrix is 2. But even though there are not two distinct characteristic roots, this matrix is diagonalizable since, for any diagonal matrix D, the product $D^{-1}TD$ is diagonal. In fact, there is no simple necessary and sufficient condition concerning characteristic roots alone that indicates whether a matrix is diagonalizable.

[5] While we do not study complex numbers in this book, there is some discussion of the dynamics of systems with complex roots in Chapter 13 and Chapter 14. For a discussion of complex numbers see Carl Simon and Lawrence Bloom, *Mathematics for Economists* (New York: W. W. Norton, 1994), Appendix A3.

We can use the solution for the characteristic roots to show that the sum of the two characteristic roots of a 2×2 matrix equals the trace of this matrix. Adding the two characteristic roots, we have

$$\lambda_1 + \lambda_2 = \frac{\mathrm{tr}(A) + \sqrt{\mathrm{tr}(A)^2 - 4|A|}}{2} + \frac{\mathrm{tr}(A) - \sqrt{\mathrm{tr}(A)^2 - 4|A|}}{2} = \mathrm{tr}(A).$$

We also note that the product of the two characteristic roots of a 2×2 matrix equals the determinant of the matrix. That is,

$$\lambda_1\lambda_2 = \frac{\mathrm{tr}(A) + \sqrt{\mathrm{tr}(A)^2 - 4|A|}}{2} \cdot \frac{\mathrm{tr}(A) - \sqrt{\mathrm{tr}(A)^2 - 4|A|}}{2} = |A|.$$

These results for the sum and product of characteristic roots allow us to easily characterize the signs of the two characteristic roots of a 2×2 matrix when these roots are real.[6]

Signs of the Characteristic Roots of a 2 × 2 Matrix Let A be a 2×2 matrix with the two real characteristic roots λ_1 and λ_2. Then,

$$\begin{aligned}
&\lambda_1 > 0 \quad \text{and} \quad \lambda_2 > 0 \quad \text{if} \quad \mathrm{tr}(A) > 0 \quad \text{and} \quad |A| > 0,\\
&\lambda_1 < 0 \quad \text{and} \quad \lambda_2 < 0 \quad \text{if} \quad \mathrm{tr}(A) < 0 \quad \text{and} \quad |A| > 0, \quad \text{and}\\
&\lambda_1 > 0 \quad \text{and} \quad \lambda_2 < 0 \quad (\text{or, equivalently, } \lambda_1 < 0 \quad \text{and} \quad \lambda_2 > 0) \quad \text{if} \quad |A| < 0.
\end{aligned}$$

This result works, of course, because the product of two roots (which is the determinant of the matrix) is positive if the roots are of the same sign and negative if the roots are of different signs. Also, if the roots are of the same sign, their sum (which is the trace of the matrix) is negative if both roots are negative and positive if both roots are positive.

We also note that the characteristic equation can be written as

$$\lambda^2 - (a_{11} + a_{22})\lambda + a_{11}a_{22} = a_{12}a_{21},$$

where

$$\lambda^2 - (a_{11} + a_{22})\lambda + a_{11}a_{22} = (\lambda - a_{11})(\lambda - a_{22}).$$

Therefore for both of the two characteristic roots, λ_i for $i = 1, 2$,

$$\frac{(\lambda_i - a_{22})}{a_{21}} = \frac{a_{12}}{(\lambda_i - a_{11})}.$$

These results will prove useful when characterizing a multiequation system of dynamic equations like those discussed in Chapters 13 and 14.

Characteristic Vectors

Each of the characteristic roots of a matrix is associated with a **characteristic vector** (also called an **eigenvector**) p. The characteristic vector p_i associated with the characteristic

[6] In the case of complex roots, these conditions can be used to find the signs of the real parts of the characteristic roots.

root λ_i has the property that

$$Ap_i = p_i\lambda_i, \tag{5.2}$$

where $p_i\lambda_i$ is an $n \times 1$ vector in which each of the n elements of p_i are multiplied by the characteristic root λ_i. For example, referring to the matrix in the two-equation system discussed earlier,

$$A = \begin{bmatrix} 2 & 2 \\ 1 & 3 \end{bmatrix},$$

the characteristic vector associated with the characteristic root 4 consists of two elements p_1 and p_2, such that

$$\begin{bmatrix} 2 & 2 \\ 1 & 3 \end{bmatrix} \cdot \begin{bmatrix} p_1 \\ p_2 \end{bmatrix} = \begin{bmatrix} 4p_1 \\ 4p_2 \end{bmatrix}.$$

Writing out this system, we have

$$\begin{aligned} 2p_1 + 2p_2 &= 4p_1 \\ p_1 + 3p_2 &= 4p_2, \end{aligned}$$

which can be solved to obtain

$$\begin{aligned} p_1 &= 1 \\ p_2 &= 1. \end{aligned}$$

Note, however, that any pair p_1 and p_2, where $p_1 = p_2$, also solves these two equations. Thus characteristic vectors are only defined up to a multiplicative constant. For example, $p_1 = p_2 = 3$ also solves this system. Likewise, the characteristic vector associated with the characteristic root 1 consists of two elements p_1 and p_2, such that

$$\begin{bmatrix} 2 & 2 \\ 1 & 3 \end{bmatrix} \cdot \begin{bmatrix} p_1 \\ p_2 \end{bmatrix} = \begin{bmatrix} p_1 \\ p_2 \end{bmatrix}.$$

Writing out this system, we have

$$\begin{aligned} 2p_1 + 2p_2 &= p_1 \\ p_1 + 3p_2 &= p_2, \end{aligned}$$

which can be solved to obtain

$$\begin{aligned} p_1 &= -2 \\ p_2 &= 1. \end{aligned}$$

Again, the elements of this vector are only defined up to a multiplicative constant since, for example, $p_1 = -4$ and $p_2 = 2$ also solves this system.

We denote the $n \times n$ matrix consisting of the n column vectors $[p_1, p_2, \ldots, p_n]$ as P. For example, a matrix of characteristic vectors associated with the 2×2 matrix A in (5.1) is

$$P = [p_1 p_2] = \begin{bmatrix} 1 & -2 \\ 1 & 1 \end{bmatrix}.$$

A necessary and sufficient condition for the $n \times n$ matrix P to be nonsingular is that its columns are linearly independent. This means that it is not possible to obtain any characteristic vector that constitutes one of the columns of P through a linear combination of one or more of the other columns of P (for example, P would not be nonsingular if there were a relationship among the characteristic vectors that constitute its columns $p_5 = 2p_7$ or if $p_2 = p_1 + 5p_3$). A necessary and sufficient condition for an $n \times n$ matrix A to be diagonalizable is that it is possible to obtain an $n \times n$ nonsingular matrix P of its characteristic vectors. There is no simple necessary and sufficient condition, however, that dictates when it is possible to find a nonsingular matrix P.

Extending (5.2), which includes a particular characteristic root and its associated characteristic vector, to each of the characteristic roots and associated characteristic vectors of a matrix, we have

$$AP = P\Lambda,$$

where the $n \times n$ matrix AP consists of the n column vectors $Ap_1, Ap_2, \ldots, Ap_n$ and the $n \times n$ matrix $P\Lambda$ consists of the set of column vectors $p_1\lambda_1, p_2\lambda_2, \ldots, p_n\lambda_n$. Thus, for the matrix

$$A = \begin{bmatrix} 2 & 2 \\ 1 & 3 \end{bmatrix},$$

we have $AP = P\Lambda$ as

$$\begin{bmatrix} 2 & 2 \\ 1 & 3 \end{bmatrix} \cdot \begin{bmatrix} 1 & -2 \\ 1 & 1 \end{bmatrix} = \begin{bmatrix} 1 & -2 \\ 1 & 1 \end{bmatrix} \cdot \begin{bmatrix} 4 & 0 \\ 0 & 1 \end{bmatrix}.$$

If there are n distinct roots of the matrix A and the matrix P has an inverse P^{-1}, then we can premultiply each side of the above expression to get

$$P^{-1}AP = \Lambda,$$

where Λ is a diagonal matrix with its nonzero elements equal to the n characteristic roots of A. Continuing with (5.1) to illustrate this, we have

$$P^{-1} = \begin{bmatrix} \frac{1}{3} & \frac{2}{3} \\ -\frac{1}{3} & \frac{1}{3} \end{bmatrix},$$

and therefore,

$$P^{-1}AP = \begin{bmatrix} \frac{1}{3} & \frac{2}{3} \\ -\frac{1}{3} & \frac{1}{3} \end{bmatrix} \cdot \begin{bmatrix} 2 & 2 \\ 1 & 3 \end{bmatrix} \cdot \begin{bmatrix} 1 & -2 \\ 1 & 1 \end{bmatrix} = \begin{bmatrix} 4 & 0 \\ 0 & 1 \end{bmatrix} = \Lambda.$$

Transforming a System of Equations

The characteristic roots and characteristic vectors of a matrix can be used to transform a system of equations into a diagonal system. Each of the variables in this diagonal system are a linear combination of the variables in the original system. For example, consider the system

$$Ax = y,$$

where A is the 2×2 matrix defined in (5.1) and

$$x = \begin{bmatrix} x_1 \\ x_2 \end{bmatrix} \quad \text{and} \quad y = \begin{bmatrix} 3 \\ 9 \end{bmatrix}.$$

To transform this into a diagonal system, we first note that

$$Ax = AIx = APP^{-1}x$$

and that

$$y = Iy = PP^{-1}y.$$

Define the vectors

$$u = P^{-1}x = \begin{bmatrix} \frac{1}{3} & \frac{2}{3} \\ -\frac{1}{3} & \frac{1}{3} \end{bmatrix} \cdot \begin{bmatrix} x_1 \\ x_2 \end{bmatrix} = \begin{bmatrix} \frac{1}{3}x_1 + \frac{2}{3}x_2 \\ -\frac{1}{3}x_1 + \frac{1}{3}x_2 \end{bmatrix}$$

and

$$v = P^{-1}y = \begin{bmatrix} \frac{1}{3} & \frac{2}{3} \\ -\frac{1}{3} & \frac{1}{3} \end{bmatrix} \cdot \begin{bmatrix} 3 \\ 9 \end{bmatrix} = \begin{bmatrix} 7 \\ 2 \end{bmatrix}.$$

The elements of the vectors u and v represent linear combinations of the elements of x and y. The system

$$Ax = y$$

is equivalent to the system

$$APu = Pv.$$

Multiplying each side of this by the matrix P^{-1}, we obtain the transformed system

$$\Lambda u = v,$$

where we have used the result that

$$P^{-1}AP = \Lambda.$$

In this case the system $\Lambda u = v$ is

$$\begin{bmatrix} 4 & 0 \\ 0 & 1 \end{bmatrix} \cdot \begin{bmatrix} u_1 \\ u_2 \end{bmatrix} = \begin{bmatrix} 7 \\ 2 \end{bmatrix}.$$

In the more general case where A is a nonsingular $n \times n$ matrix with the n distinct characteristic roots $\lambda_1, \lambda_2, \ldots, \lambda_n$, the system $\Lambda u = v$ represents n univariate relationships:

$$\lambda_1 u_1 = v_1, \quad \lambda_2 u_2 = v_2, \quad \ldots, \quad \lambda_n u_n = v_n.$$

These univariate relationships may be easier to solve than the original system of equations.

In the 2×2 case we are using here to illustrate this technique, the solution to the univariate relationship $4u_1 = v_1$ is $u_1 = 1/4v_1$, and the solution to the univariate relationship $u_2 = v_2$ is immediately apparent. Therefore a solution to this system is

$$\begin{bmatrix} u_1 \\ u_2 \end{bmatrix} = \begin{bmatrix} \frac{1}{4} & 0 \\ 0 & 1 \end{bmatrix} \cdot \begin{bmatrix} 7 \\ 2 \end{bmatrix} = \begin{bmatrix} \frac{7}{4} \\ 2 \end{bmatrix}.$$

Once the system of univariate relationships is solved, we can transform back to the original system by premultiplying u and v by P since

$$Pu = PP^{-1}x = x$$

and

$$Pv = PP^{-1}y = y.$$

Finishing the example presented here, we have

$$\begin{bmatrix} 1 & -2 \\ 1 & 1 \end{bmatrix} \cdot \begin{bmatrix} \frac{7}{4} \\ 2 \end{bmatrix} = \begin{bmatrix} -\frac{9}{4} \\ \frac{15}{4} \end{bmatrix} = \begin{bmatrix} x_1 \\ x_2 \end{bmatrix}.$$

Of course we have taken a very roundabout route to solve this simple system of two equations in two unknowns. But the technique of finding a solution by first diagonalizing a system will prove very useful in Chapters 13 and 14 in which we have straightforward solutions to univariate problems but not to multivariate problems.

Exercises 5.3

1. Find the characteristic roots of each 2×2 matrix. Confirm that the product of the characteristic roots equals the determinant of each matrix.
   (a) $A = \begin{bmatrix} 4 & -1 \\ -3 & 2 \end{bmatrix}$
   (b) $A = \begin{bmatrix} -1 & 0 \\ 2 & -3 \end{bmatrix}$
   (c) $A = \begin{bmatrix} 5 & 6 \\ -1 & -2 \end{bmatrix}$
2. For each matrix presented in question 1 and its corresponding characteristic roots, find the following results.
   (a) Determine the value of the matrix P, which is the matrix of characteristic vectors associated with the given matrix.
   (b) Calculate the inverse of P, and show that $P^{-1}AP = \Lambda$ for the given matrix.
3. Consider the following system of two equations with two unknowns:

$$\begin{aligned} 2x_1 + 6x_2 &= 20 \\ x_1 - 3x_2 &= 4. \end{aligned}$$

   (a) Set this system up in matrix format with A, the matrix of coefficients, x, the vector of endogenous variables, and y, the vector of constants.

(b) Find the characteristic roots for the above system of equations.

(c) Determine the elements of the matrix P, which is the matrix of characteristic vectors.

(d) Take the inverse of matrix P, and show that $P^{-1}AP = \Lambda$, where Λ is a diagonal matrix with its nonzero elements equal to the two characteristic roots of matrix A.

4. Transform the system of equations in question 3 into a diagonal system. Remember that

$$Ax = APP^{-1}x \quad \text{and} \quad y = PP^{-1}y.$$

(a) Define the vector u, which equals $P^{-1}x$. Define the vector v, which equals $P^{-1}y$.

(b) Show that $APu = Pv$.

(c) Remembering that $P^{-1}AP = \Lambda$, multiply each side of the equation in part (b) above by P^{-1}. Show that $\Lambda u = v$.

(d) Solve the system of univariate relationships.

(e) Transform this system back to its original form by premultiplying u and v by P, such that $Pu = PP^{-1}x = x$ and $Pv = PP^{-1}y = y$.

(f) What are the values of x and y that solve the original system?

5. A univariate linear difference equation takes the form

$$x_t = ax_{t-1} + c,$$

where the subscripts are integers that refer to time periods and a and c are parameters ($a \neq 1$). If x_t does not equal its steady state value $\bar{x}$, where

$$\bar{x} = \frac{c}{1-a},$$

then, over time, x_t approaches $\bar{x}$ if $-1 < a < 1$, and the difference equation is *stable*. If $a > 1$ or $a < -1$ and $x_t \neq \bar{x}$, then, over time, x_t diverges further and further from $\bar{x}$, and the equation is *unstable*. A *system* of linear difference equations,

$$\begin{bmatrix} x_t \\ y_t \end{bmatrix} = \begin{bmatrix} a & b \\ c & d \end{bmatrix} \cdot \begin{bmatrix} x_{t-1} \\ y_{t-1} \end{bmatrix},$$

is stable if a transformation of this system in which the variables are linear combinations of x and y is also stable. One such transformation results in a diagonal 2×2 matrix with its elements equal to the characteristic roots of the original matrix. Thus we need only check to see that the two characteristic roots of the matrix are each between -1 and 1 to ensure that this system is stable. Use this result to determine whether each of the following systems of equations are stable or unstable.

(a) $\begin{bmatrix} x_t \\ y_t \end{bmatrix} = \begin{bmatrix} 0.40 & 0.35 \\ 0.05 & 0.10 \end{bmatrix} \cdot \begin{bmatrix} x_{t-1} \\ y_{t-1} \end{bmatrix}$

(b) $\begin{bmatrix} x_t \\ y_t \end{bmatrix} = \begin{bmatrix} 1.00 & 0.25 \\ 1.25 & 0.00 \end{bmatrix} \cdot \begin{bmatrix} x_{t-1} \\ y_{t-1} \end{bmatrix}$

(c) $\begin{bmatrix} x_t \\ y_t \end{bmatrix} = \begin{bmatrix} 0.75 & 0.50 \\ 0.50 & 0.75 \end{bmatrix} \cdot \begin{bmatrix} x_{t-1} \\ y_{t-1} \end{bmatrix}$

6. Use the characteristic polynomial to find the characteristic roots of the diagonal matrix

$$\begin{bmatrix} a & 0 \\ 0 & b \end{bmatrix}.$$

Then generalize this result by determining the n characteristic roots of the $n \times n$ diagonal matrix D which has the nonzero diagonal elements $d_{11}, d_{22}, \ldots, d_{nn}$, all of which are real numbers. (*Hint*: use the result from Section 5.1 concerning the determinant of a diagonal matrix.)

Summary

This chapter allows you to implement the results presented in the previous chapter for systems of more than two equations. The Laplace expansion technique presented in Section 5.1 provides a useful method for evaluating the determinant of an $n \times n$ matrix by finding the determinants of a series of smaller submatrices. The material in Section 5.2 shows how to calculate the inverse of a matrix using the determinant and the adjoint. Cramer's rule provides a way to calculate the solution for a subset of the endogenous variables without calculating the full inverse. The techniques presented in these two sections are useful for a range of areas in economics such as macroeconomics and international trade, in which you need to solve multiequation systems.

Section 5.3 presents some new techniques from matrix algebra. These techniques show how to reformulate a multivariate system of equations into a similar system consisting of univariate relationships. Part of this technique requires the calculation of the characteristic roots of the matrix of the system. This technique is used extensively in economics when the model includes multivariate systems of dynamic equations. These types of models frequently arise in macroeconomics, international finance, and growth theory. We return to the calculation of characteristic roots and the diagonalization of systems of equations in Chapters 13 and 14.

Part Three

Differential Calculus

Chapter 6
An Introduction to Differential Calculus

Chapter 7
Univariate Calculus

Chapter 8
Multivariate Calculus

Mathematical models of economic behavior involve functions that describe the relationship among variables. In Part Two of this book, we learned methods for solving and analyzing models that consist of linear equations. Many economic relationships, however, are best modeled as nonlinear relationships. Economic properties, such as diminishing marginal utility or decreasing returns to scale, demand a nonlinear representation. The three chapters constituting Part Three of this book, Chapters 6, 7 and 8, present methods for analyzing linear as well as nonlinear functions using differential calculus.

In these chapters the central question of differential calculus that we ask is how the value of a function is altered by a change in one or more arguments of that function. There is a natural link between this question and the comparative static analysis introduced in Chapter 4, though, in these chapters, we generalize this type of analysis to include nonlinear functions. As we show in these chapters, differential calculus offers a direct mathematical context for many economic concepts.

This part begins with Chapter 6, which develops your intuition for understanding calculus of functions with only one argument. An important part of this intuition involves the use of limits, which are introduced in Chapter 2. Applications in this chapter illustrate the manner in which differential calculus offers a mathematical technique for addressing questions that arise in economic analysis.

Chapter 7 presents rules that enable you to apply differential calculus to a wide range of functions. The discussion in this chapter reinforces the concept presented in Chapter 6 that differential calculus corresponds to the practice, in economic analysis, of studying the effects of changes "at the margin." Material in this chapter also offers a mathematical technique that corresponds to logical "chains of reasoning" in complex economic relationships.

Chapter 8 extends our study of differential calculus to multivariate functions, that is, functions with more than one variable as arguments. The discussion in Chapter 8 shows how differential calculus of functions of several variables corresponds directly to the economic concept of ceteris paribus, *that is, one of holding "everything else equal." Multivariate calculus is used in virtually all fields of economics. Applications in Chapter 8 show some of these uses in microeconomics, macroeconomics, the economics of growth, and labor economics.*

Chapter 6

An Introduction to Differential Calculus

Economic models provide a framework for understanding the responsiveness of an endogenous variable to a change in an exogenous variable. Models allow economists to pose questions such as What is the effect of an increase in the money supply of \$1 billion on national income? How many fewer teenagers will begin smoking each year if an additional tax of \$0.25 is imposed on each pack of cigarettes? What tariff revenues will be received when a 10% duty is charged on all imported cars? The answers to these types of questions involve a **comparative static analysis,** which compares the response of endogenous variables to changes in exogenous variables. In Chapters 4 and 5 we learned methods for conducting comparative static analysis on linear multiequation models. In this chapter we begin our study of methods for conducting comparative static analysis with nonlinear functions.

An important set of tools for conducting comparative static analysis, as well as other types of economic analysis, is provided by **differential calculus.** Differential calculus shows how the value of a function varies with respect to changes in one or more of its arguments. Differential calculus thus provides a method for analyzing economic functions and understanding how changes in exogenous variables affect endogenous variables in economic models.

In this chapter we introduce differential calculus. We begin with an example of the effect of a change in tax rates on tax revenues to illustrate the kinds of questions differential calculus can address. A very general method for looking at this question considers the value of the function for two different values of its argument. This method provides an exact answer to the question of how much the value of a function changes with a change in its argument, but it can be cumbersome to implement in many cases. A more convenient method, which looks at the change in the value of a function for very small changes in its argument, is presented. This method is at the heart of differential calculus. As we discuss, very small changes in the argument of a function correspond to the important economic notion of changes at the margin.

6.1 FUNCTIONS AND RATES OF CHANGE

Predictions of the effects of changing economic policies are often based upon simple extrapolation. For example, the prediction of the revenue effects of a change in the tax rate on a certain economic activity may simply assume that the change in the tax rate does not affect the level of that activity. Economic theory suggests, however, that people respond to changing conditions. Thus tax revenues are affected both directly by a change in the tax rate and indirectly through changes in the tax base.

We can illustrate this point with the following simple example. Consider the revenues collected from a sales tax on widgets. The amount of tax revenues, R, equals the product of the tax rate, t, and the amount of widgets sold, Q. That is,

$$R = t \cdot Q.$$

If the amount of widgets sold does not depend upon the sales tax rate, then tax revenues are a simple linear function of the sales tax rate. This relationship is represented by the straight line $0L$ in Figure 6.1. We may expect, however, that an increase in the sales tax on widgets lowers widget sales, thereby reducing the tax base on which revenues are raised.[1] The tax revenue schedule $0C$ in Figure 6.1 captures this effect. Comparing $0C$ with $0L$ shows that revenues are lower when sales are affected by the tax rate than when sales are invariant to the tax rate. This is shown in Figure 6.1 by the fact that $0L$ is everywhere above $0C$.

Figure 6.1 also illustrates that the response of tax revenues to a change in the tax rate depends upon whether sales are affected by the tax rate. The ratio of the change in tax revenues to the change in the tax rate is represented by the quotient

$$\frac{\Delta R}{\Delta t},$$

where the Greek letter, capital delta (Δ), represents the change in a variable, so, for example, ΔR represents the change in revenues. You may recognize from the discussion in Chapter 2 that this quotient represents the slope of a secant line connecting the point on the revenue function that corresponds to the initial tax rate and the point that corresponds to the subsequent tax rate. When Q is independent of t (as in the case represented by $0L$ in Figure 6.1), the slope $\Delta R/\Delta t$ is constant since any segment of a straight line has the same slope as any other segment of that line. In contrast, the relationship between the change in tax revenues and the change in tax rates when sales are affected by taxes is not constant. In this case $\Delta R/\Delta t$ is represented by the slope of a secant line connecting two points on schedule $0C$. We see that the slopes of the secant lines EF, FG, and EG are all different.

The slope of any secant line connecting two points on the schedule $0C$ depends upon two factors: the initial tax rate and the size of the change in tax rates. This is evident from the slopes of the secant lines in the figure. The secant line EF is steeper than the secant line FG, reflecting the fact that ΔR, and thus $\Delta R/\Delta t$, is larger when the tax

[1] Recall the application of the incidence of a tax in Chapter 4. A tax levied on each widget was shown to increase the price of widgets to consumers, decrease the price of widgets received by producers, and lower the quantity of widgets bought and sold.

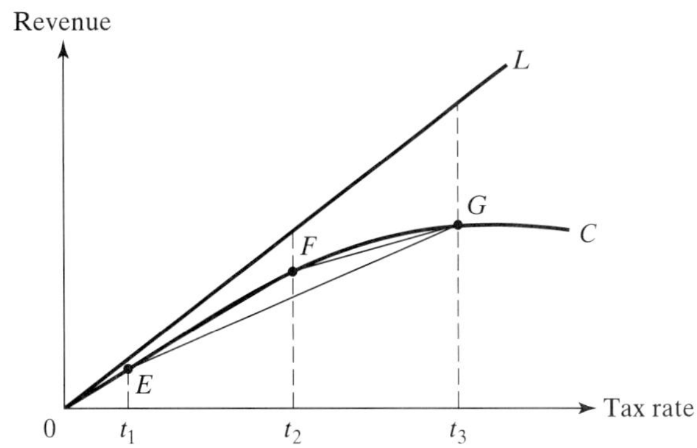

FIGURE 6.1 Tax Revenues and Tax Rates

rate rises from t_1 to t_2 than when the tax rate rises by an equivalent amount from t_2 to t_3. Also, the secant line EF has a steeper slope than the secant line EG, demonstrating that $\Delta R/\Delta t$ is larger when the tax rate rises from t_1 to t_2 than when the tax rate rises from t_1 to t_3.

This example points out the shortcomings of determining the effect of a policy change with simple extrapolation, whether assuming other factors will not change or assuming past experience serves as a good guide for the future. In this example the effect on revenues of a change in the tax rate from t_2 to t_3, along the schedule $0C$, is different from the effect if Q does not change (as in $0L$). Even taking into account the response of Q to t, the effect on revenues of a tax increase from t_1 to t_2 differs from that of an equally large tax increase from t_2 to t_3.

6.2 THE DIFFERENCE QUOTIENT

The example presented above focuses on the responsiveness of tax revenues to tax rates, as represented by the slope of the secant lines in Figure 6.1. This quotient, $\Delta R/\Delta t$, is the **difference quotient** for the function relating tax revenues to tax rates. The difference quotient shows how the value of a function changes with respect to a change in its argument. In this section we introduce the device of the difference quotient by finding its explicit value for two different specifications of the tax revenue function.

In order to explicitly determine $\Delta R/\Delta t$, we must have an explicit relationship between R and t. By definition, tax revenue equals the product of the tax rate and the quantity sold; that is, $R = tQ$. The simplest case is the linear relationship

$$R_i = t_i \cdot \overline{Q}, \tag{6.1}$$

where $\overline{Q}$ is constant and subscripts on revenue and the tax rate refer to different values of these variables. As discussed above, $\Delta R/\Delta t$ is constant in this case. This equation is represented by $0L$ in Figure 6.1.

We can show more explicitly that $\Delta R/\Delta t = \overline{Q}$ for the model represented by (6.1), regardless of the initial value of the tax rate or of the size of the change in taxes. Consider the case where the tax rate changes from t_i to t_j, that is, where $\Delta t = t_j - t_i$. The original level of revenue, R_i, is

$$R_i = t_i \cdot \overline{Q}.$$

The revenue corresponding to the new tax rate, R_j, is

$$R_j = t_j \cdot \overline{Q} = t_i \cdot \overline{Q} + \Delta t \cdot \overline{Q},$$

where the change in the tax rate is $\Delta t = t_j - t_i$, so $t_j = t_i + \Delta t$. The term Δt just represents some number, and it can be added, subtracted, multiplied, or divided like any other number. The difference in revenues, $\Delta R = R_j - R_i$, is found by subtracting the right-hand side of the equation for R_i from the right-hand side of the equation for R_j to obtain

$$\Delta R = (t_i \cdot \overline{Q} + \Delta t \cdot \overline{Q}) - (t_i \cdot \overline{Q}) = \Delta t \cdot \overline{Q}.$$

In this case the difference quotient, for any arbitrary starting tax rate, t_i, and any arbitrary change in tax rates, Δt, is found by dividing each side of the above equation by Δt. This difference quotient is

$$\frac{\Delta R}{\Delta t} = \frac{\Delta t \cdot \overline{Q}}{\Delta t} = \overline{Q}.$$

The ratio of the change in tax revenues to a change in tax rates is constant since we are assuming here that $\overline{Q}$ does not vary with the tax rate. In terms of Figure 6.1, the slope of the schedule $0L$, which equals $\Delta R/\Delta t$, is constant and equal to $\overline{Q}$.

We can consider a case similar to the schedule $0C$ in Figure 6.1 by assuming that there is a negative relationship between Q and t,

$$Q = \alpha - \beta t,$$

where α and β represent positive numbers. This relationship shows that higher tax rates lead to a fall in widget consumption. Substituting this relationship into the identity for tax revenue, $R = tQ$, we have

$$R = \alpha t - \beta t^2. \tag{6.2}$$

We derive an explicit relationship for the difference quotient $\Delta R/\Delta t$ for the quadratic revenue function (6.2) by following the same procedure as in the case of the linear function (6.1). Again consider any arbitrary starting value of the tax rate, t_i. The initial level of revenue is

$$R_i = \alpha t_i - \beta t_i^2.$$

The level of revenues after a change in the tax rate, R_j, can be written as a function of the initial tax rate, t_i, and the change in the tax rate, Δt, since $t_j = t_i + \Delta t$. This gives us

$$\begin{aligned} R_j &= \alpha(t_i + \Delta t) - \beta(t_i + \Delta t)^2 \\ &= \alpha(t_i + \Delta t) - \beta(t_i^2 + 2t_i \Delta t + \Delta t^2). \end{aligned}$$

The change in revenues for a given change in tax rates, $\Delta R/\Delta t$, is found by subtracting R_i from R_j and dividing by Δt. This gives us

$$\frac{\Delta R}{\Delta t} = \frac{\alpha(t_i + \Delta t) - \beta(t_i^2 + 2t_i \Delta t + \Delta t^2) - (\alpha t_i - \beta t_i^2)}{\Delta t}$$

or

$$\frac{\Delta R}{\Delta t} = \frac{\alpha\,\Delta t - 2\beta t_i\,\Delta t - \beta\,\Delta t^2}{\Delta t}$$

or

$$\frac{\Delta R}{\Delta t} = \alpha - 2\beta t_i - \beta\,\Delta t. \tag{6.3}$$

This result demonstrates that the change in tax revenues due to a change in tax rates depends upon both the initial value of the tax rate, t_i, and the size of the change in the tax rate, Δt, when the relationship between the tax revenues and the tax rate is as given in (6.2). In particular, for any size increase in the tax rate, the difference quotient decreases as the initial tax rate, t_i, rises since t_i is multiplied by the negative number -2β. Also, for any initial value of the tax rate, the difference quotient decreases with a bigger change in the tax rate since the coefficient on Δt is $-\beta$.

These results are apparent from an inspection of Figure 6.1. The difference quotient $\Delta R/\Delta t$ represents the slope of the secant line connecting the points on $0C$ corresponding to the initial and the subsequent tax rates. Notice that the slope of the secant line connecting the points on $0C$ that correspond to the tax rates t_1 and t_2 is steeper than the slope of the secant line connecting the points on $0C$ that correspond to t_2 and t_3. This comparison is one in which Δt is held constant since the distance between t_1 and t_2 is the same as that between t_2 and t_3. We also see that the size of Δt, holding t_1 constant, affects the difference quotient. The slope of the secant line connecting the points on $0C$ that correspond to t_1 and t_2 is steeper than the slope of the secant line connecting the points that correspond to t_1 and t_3.

A numerical exercise also helps illustrate how the difference quotient varies in the linear and quadratic cases. Table 6.1 reports the tax revenues and difference quotients for the linear revenue function

$$R = 200t$$

and the quadratic revenue function

$$R = 200t - 200t^2.$$

TABLE 6.1 Difference Quotients for Different Tax Revenue Specifications

	$R = 200t$		$R = 200t - 200t^2$	
Tax rate	R	$\frac{\Delta R}{\Delta t}$	R	$\frac{\Delta R}{\Delta t}$
0.10	20		18	
		200		150
0.15	30		25.5	
		200		130
0.20	40		32	

The numbers in the table demonstrate that the linear function has a constant value of $\Delta R/\Delta t$ equal to 200. This, of course, corresponds to the result we found for the general linear revenue function $R = t\overline{Q}$. In the quadratic case, the difference quotient varies. The value of $\Delta R/\Delta t$ decreases with larger values of the initial tax rate, holding constant the size of the change in tax rates. This is what we expect from (6.3) since the initial tax rate is multiplied by -2β.

This table also demonstrates that the size of the change in the tax rate, given its initial value, affects the difference quotient in the quadratic case though not in the linear case. The difference quotient calculated for a change in the tax rate from 0.10 to 0.20 yields a value of

$$\frac{\Delta R}{\Delta t} = \frac{40 - 20}{0.10} = 200$$

in the linear case, which is the same as the difference quotient for a smaller change in the tax rate with the same initial value. In the quadratic case, a change in the tax rate from 0.10 to 0.20 yields the difference quotient

$$\frac{\Delta R}{\Delta t} = \frac{32 - 18}{0.10} = 140,$$

which is smaller than the value of 150 for a change in the tax rate from 0.10 to 0.15. The result for the difference quotient of the quadratic revenue function in (6.3) shows that a bigger value of Δt corresponds to a smaller value of $\Delta R/\Delta t$, given the initial tax rate, since Δt appears with the negative coefficient $-\beta$.

The General Form of the Difference Quotient

We can generalize the procedure of the previous subsection so that it applies to any function by using the following formula for the difference quotient.

Difference Quotient The difference quotient for the function $y = f(x)$ for an initial value x_0 and a change in x equal to Δx is

$$\frac{\Delta y}{\Delta x} = \frac{f(x_0 + \Delta x) - f(x_0)}{\Delta x},$$

where the terms $f(x_0)$ and $f(x_0 + \Delta x)$ represent the function evaluated at the values of the argument x_0 and $x_0 + \Delta x$, respectively.

As discussed in Chapter 2, the notation $f(\bullet)$ means that the function f takes whatever term is in parentheses as its argument. For example, for the function

$$f(x) = 4x^2 + \ln(x),$$

when $x = 1$,

$$f(1) = 4(1^2) + \ln(1) = 4.$$

When $x = x_0 + \Delta x$, then

$$f(x_0 + \Delta x) = 4((x_0 + \Delta x)^2) + \ln(x_0 + \Delta x).$$

It is important to see that it is, generally, *not* true that

$$f(x_0 + \Delta x) = f(x_0) + f(\Delta x).$$

For example, for this function, when $x_0 = 1$ and $\Delta x = 1$,

$$f(x_0 + \Delta x) = f(2) = 16.7,$$

which does not equal

$$f(x_0) + f(\Delta x) = f(1) + f(1) = 8.$$

The results presented for the tax revenue functions are specific examples of the general results for any linear function and any quadratic function. The difference quotient for any linear function

$$y = a + bx$$

is

$$\frac{\Delta y}{\Delta x} = \frac{f(x_0 + \Delta x) - f(x_0)}{\Delta x} = \frac{(a + bx_0 + b\Delta x) - (a + bx_0)}{\Delta x} = b. \tag{6.4}$$

The value of this difference quotient depends solely on the parameter b. The difference quotient for any quadratic function

$$y = a + bx + cx^2$$

is

$$\begin{aligned}\frac{\Delta y}{\Delta x} &= \frac{f(x_0 + \Delta x) - f(x_0)}{\Delta x}\\ &= \frac{(a + bx_0 + b\Delta x + c(x_0 + \Delta x)^2) - (a + bx_0 + cx_0^2)}{\Delta x}\\ &= b + 2cx_0 + c\Delta x.\end{aligned} \tag{6.5}$$

The value of this difference quotient depends upon both x_0 and Δx.

It is important to note here that the difference quotient of a function is itself a function of both the parameters of the original equation and the level of and change in the variables of the function. For example, the difference quotient of the general quadratic function given in (6.5) depends upon the parameters b and c, the initial level of the argument, x_0, and the change in the argument, Δx. In the next section we examine a method for "holding constant" the effect on the difference quotient of the size of the change in Δx.

Exercises 6.2

1. Find the difference quotient for each linear or quadratic function as a function of x_0 and Δx.
   (a) $y = 5x$
   (b) $y = 30 - 15x$
   (c) $y = 6x^2 + 2x + 9$
   (d) $y = 1 - x^2$

2. Solve for the difference quotient $(\Delta y/\Delta x)$ for each of the four functions in question 1. Assume that $x_0 = 2$ and $\Delta x = 4$. How do each of your answers vary if $\Delta x = 2$?
3. Find the difference quotient for each cubic function.
   (a) $z = gx^3$
   (b) $w = a + bx + cx^2 + gx^3$
4. Define a function $y = w - z$, where w and z are the functions identified in question 3.
   (a) Using the results you obtained for the difference quotients for w and z, determine the difference quotient for y, $\Delta y/\Delta x$.
   (b) Based on your answer to part (a), determine the difference quotient for a polynomial of degree 4 that has the general form

$$h = a + bx + cx^2 + gx^3 + dx^4.$$

5. Assuming that $x_0 = 1$ and $\Delta x = 1$, find the value of the difference quotient for each of the following functions. Now calculate each value assuming that $x_0 = 2$. Finally, assuming that $\Delta x = 2$, determine the value of each difference quotient. What is the relative impact, on each function's difference quotient, of doubling the value of x_0? Of doubling the value of Δx?
   (a) $y = 10x - 4$
   (b) $y = 3x^2 + 6x - 5$
   (c) $y = x^3 + 4x^2 - 6x + 12$
6. The following wage function presents the relationship between the age of an employee and his wages:

$$Wage = 10 + 60\,age - 0.25\,age^2.$$

   Using the difference quotient, find the change in wages at the beginning of each of the following decades: $age = 20$, $age = 30$, $age = 40$, and $age = 50$. Consider the case of $\Delta\,age = 1$. What happens to this employee's earnings as he gets older?
7. Total revenue is defined as price times quantity, or

$$TR = P \cdot Q,$$

   where $P = 10 - 0.5Q$.
   (a) Derive the equation for the total revenue function where Q is the only argument.
   (b) Apply the difference quotient $\Delta TR/\Delta Q$, and determine the impact of a change in Q on total revenue. If $Q_0 = 5$, what is the impact of a one unit change in Q on total revenue?
   (c) How does the impact on total revenue change if $Q_0 = 3$ and $\Delta Q = 1$?
   (d) Now hold $Q_0 = 3$, but consider the impact on total revenue when $\Delta Q = 2$.
8. Calculate the difference quotient for the function

$$y = 4x^2 - 2x + 7,$$

   where $x_0 = 3$ and $\Delta x = 3$.
   (a) Holding x_0 constant, determine the impact on the difference quotient when $\Delta x = 1.5$ and $\Delta x = 0.5$.

(b) Based on your answers, what would the value of the limit of the difference quotient be as Δx approaches zero; that is, what is $\lim_{\Delta x \to 0} \Delta y/\Delta x$?

6.3 CHANGES AT THE MARGIN AND THE DERIVATIVE

The analytical results presented above demonstrate that, in general, the difference quotient of a function $y = f(x)$ depends upon the parameters of the original function, as well as the argument of the function, x, and the change in the argument of the function, Δx. We can, in a sense, standardize the difference quotient by specifying a common Δx to be used in the calculation of all difference quotients. In calculus, we consider the limit of the difference quotient as Δx approaches zero. We call the difference quotient as Δx approaches zero the **derivative.**

Derivative The derivative of the function $y = f(x)$, which is written as dy/dx, is

$$\frac{dy}{dx} = \lim_{\Delta x \to 0} \frac{f(x_0+\Delta x)-f(x_0)}{\Delta x},$$

provided that the limit exists.

The notation used for the derivative is very similar to the notation for the difference quotient, especially when you consider that the English letter that most closely corresponds to the Greek letter Δ is d. Another way of denoting a derivative is by $f'(x)$, which is read as "f prime of x" or "f prime x." This notation highlights the fact that the derivative is itself a function.

The requirement, in this definition, that the limit exists is discussed in more detail later in this chapter. Chapter 2 discusses the concept of limits and rules for finding the limiting value of functions. It might strike you, at first, as odd to think about evaluating a difference quotient as Δx approaches zero. You may reason that if Δx approaches zero and y is a function of x, then Δy should approach zero as well. While this may be true, it does not follow that the quotient $\Delta y/\Delta x$ approaches zero as Δx approaches zero.

The easiest way to see this is to determine the derivatives for the general forms of the linear and quadratic functions. Equation (6.4) shows that the difference quotient for the linear function evaluated at x_0,

$$y_0 = a + bx_0,$$

is

$$\frac{f(x_0 + \Delta x) - f(x_0)}{\Delta x} = b.$$

The term Δx is not part of this difference quotient, so the derivative is identical to the difference quotient for a linear function. Therefore, for this function,

$$\frac{dy}{dx} = \lim_{\Delta x \to 0} \frac{f(x_0+\Delta x)-f(x_0)}{\Delta x} = b.$$

The difference quotient of a quadratic function, given in (6.5), does include the term Δx. Therefore its derivative is not the same as its difference quotient. The derivative of the quadratic function evaluated at x_0,

$$y = a + bx_0 + cx_0^2,$$

is found by simply taking the limit of the difference quotient (6.5) as Δx approaches zero, which gives us

$$\begin{aligned} \frac{dy}{dx} &= \lim_{\Delta x \to 0} \frac{f(x_0 + \Delta x) - f(x_0)}{\Delta x} \\ &= \lim_{\Delta x \to 0} (b + 2cx_0 + c\Delta x) \\ &= b + 2cx_0. \end{aligned} \tag{6.6}$$

The value of the derivative of a quadratic function depends upon the point at which it is evaluated. In particular, the derivative of a quadratic function is a linear function with x_0 as its argument.

Like the difference quotient, the derivative may also be thought of as the rate of change of a function. Since the derivative is defined for very small changes in x, it is sometimes referred to as the **instantaneous rate of change** of the function. The adjective "instantaneous" draws from the original use of the derivative in physics to analyze functions that described the motion of objects (including, apocryphally, an apple falling onto the head of Isaac Newton as he sat under a tree) that have time as their argument.

The mathematical concept of the derivative has a direct correspondence to the economic concept of looking at relationships "at the margin." Economic analysis typically focuses on the effects of very small or "marginal" changes. This is reflected by many terms in economics, such as *marginal revenue*, *marginal productivity*, and *marginal propensity to consume.* The derivative, which looks at the responsiveness of a function for a very small change in its argument, thus provides an important tool for conducting economic analysis.

The Geometry of Derivatives

In the discussion of the effect of the tax rate on tax revenue, the difference quotient $\Delta R/\Delta t$ was also referred to as the slope of a secant line. There is a similar geometric interpretation of the derivative. The derivative of a function at a given value represents the slope of a line tangent to that function at that value.

Figure 6.2 illustrates this geometric interpretation. The slope of the secant line AB represents the value of the difference quotient $\Delta y/\Delta x$ for an initial value of x equal to x_A and $\Delta x = x_B - x_A$. The slope of the secant line AC represents the value of the difference quotient for the same initial value of x and the smaller change in x, $\Delta x = x_C - x_A$. In the limit as Δx approaches zero, the secant line becomes identical to the line that is tangent to the function at point A, which is depicted as the line TAT in Figure 6.2. Thus the value of the derivative of the function at the point x_A, that is, dy/dx evaluated at x_A, is the slope of the line tangent to the function at that point. Note that the value of the derivative varies with the point at which it is evaluated. The slope of a line tangent to the function in Figure 6.2 is different at each point on the function.

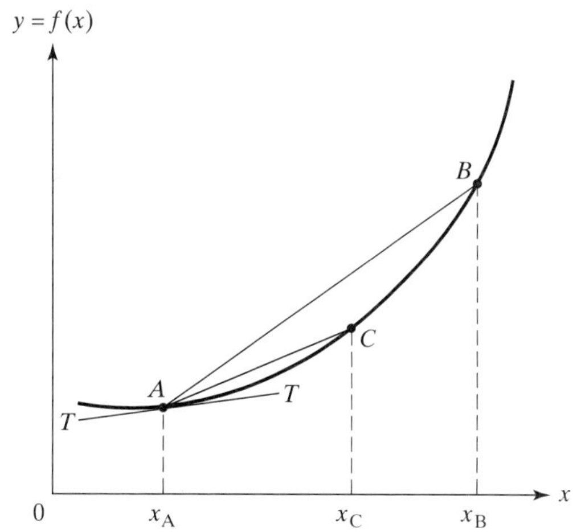

FIGURE 6.2 Secant Lines and a Tangent Line

Another diagram emphasizes that the derivative is itself a function. The upper panel of Figure 6.3 presents the quadratic tax revenue function

$$R(t) = 200t - 200t^2,$$

and the lower panel presents its derivative. The derivative is

$$R'(t) = 200 - 400t \tag{6.7}$$

since the revenue function is a specific example of the general quadratic function with $a = 0, b = 200$, and $c = -200$. The lower panel of this figure demonstrates that the marginal tax revenue at any tax rate represents the slope of a line tangent to the total tax revenue function at that tax rate. The tangent lines to the total tax revenue function have positive slopes for tax rates less than t_M since $R(t)$ increases with higher tax rates for $t < t_M$. In this range, the derivative $R'(t)$ is positive. For example, the slope of the line AA, which is tangent to the total tax revenue line at $f(t_A)$, is equal to G. Tax rates greater than t_M correspond to negative values of the derivative $R'(t)$ since $R(t)$ decreases with larger values of t for $t > t_M$. The slope of the line CC, which is tangent to the total tax revenue function at $f(t_C)$, is $-H$. The tangent line is horizontal at the tax rate t_M, a point where $R'(t) = 0$.

We can identify the actual value of the slope of the tangent line evaluated at various points by simply evaluating the function in (6.7) at those points. For example, if $t_A = 0.25$, then $G = 100$. If $t_C = 0.80$, then $-H = -120$. We can also find the tax rate that corresponds to maximum revenue by finding the value of t that makes the derivative zero. Setting $R'(t) = 0$ and solving for t, we find that revenues reach their peak at $t_M = 0.50$. Any further increase in the tax rate beyond 0.50 would decrease tax revenue since the effect of the lower sales of widgets on tax revenue more than offsets the effect of a higher tax rate.

Like Figure 6.3, Figure 6.4 also consists of two graphs where the lower graph is the derivative of the function in the upper graph. We can sketch the derivative of the

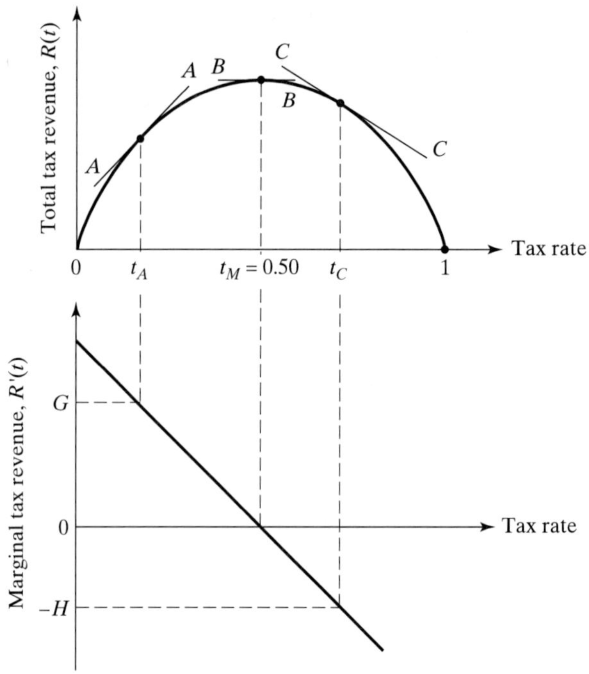

FIGURE 6.3 A Total Tax Revenue Function and Its Marginal Tax Revenue Function

function $g(x)$ in Figure 6.4, even though its form is not explicitly presented, by keeping in mind some general results concerning the derivative.

1. The derivative $g'(x)$ is positive when the slope of a line tangent to $g(x)$ is positive, regardless of whether $g(x)$ itself is negative or positive. For example, in the range x_a to x_b, the function $g(x)$ is strictly increasing, and the derivative $g'(x)$ is positive. Likewise, $g'(x)$ is negative when the slope of a line tangent to $g(x)$ is negative, as in the range x_b to x_c.

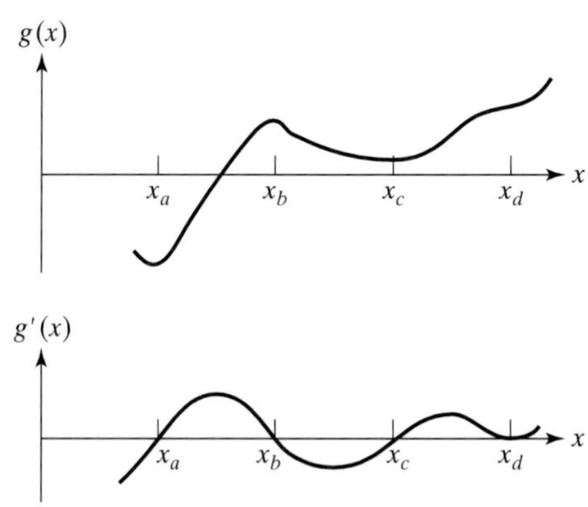

FIGURE 6.4 A Function and Its Derivative

2. The derivative $g'(x)$ equals zero when the slope of a line tangent to $g(x)$ is zero.
3. The derivative of the function equals zero at any local or global extreme point (see Chapter 2 for a definition of extreme points). The three extreme points in Figure 6.4 are $g(x_a)$, $g(x_b)$, and $g(x_c)$.
4. The derivative also equals zero at $g(x_d)$ since the slope of a line tangent to the function is zero at that point, even though this is not an extreme point.

This discussion of Figures 6.3 and 6.4 demonstrates some important points that we return to in Chapter 9 in our discussion of identifying and characterizing extreme points of a function.

The International Pattern of Women's Work

The rate at which women participate in the labor force of a country reflects a number of important factors, not least of which is their social standing. But women's rate of participation in the labor force also demonstrates the **substitution effect** and the **income effect** of higher wages on labor supply. Through the substitution effect, a higher wage makes work more attractive, and therefore, higher wages may tend to be associated with increased labor-force participation. On the other hand, there is a tendency for labor supply to decrease as wages rise since, with higher income, people may choose to spend more time in activities that do not provide pay, such as child-rearing and leisure.

These substitution and income effects, working in opposing directions, lead to a U-shaped relationship between the rate of participation of women in the labor force and income per capita across countries. In low-income countries, economic development often takes the form of the emergence of manufacturing sectors that primarily hire men. Thus, as countries develop and income per capita rises, women's participation in the labor force tends to decline as a consequence of both an increase in family income and the reduction in opportunities for work on family farms due to urbanization. After a certain level of economic development, women may find more opportunities in service-sector jobs. Also, there is a marked increase in the education levels of girls as income per capita rises, which increases the employment opportunities of women in richer countries. Claudia Goldin finds that the downward-sloping part of the U-shaped female-participation-rate relationship reflects the experience of African and south Asian countries, the bottom of the U characterizes the data for South and Central American countries while countries of southern Europe and east Asia and industrial countries make up the upward-sloping part of the U.[2]

Kristin Mammen and Christina Paxson estimate the relationship between income per capita and the rate of participation of women in the labor force using a data set that includes observations for four different time periods for each of 90 countries.[3] In one of their specifications, they find the relationship between the rate of participation in the labor force of women between the ages of 45 and 59, P; the logarithm of national

[2] Claudia Goldin, "The U-Shaped Female Labor Force Function in Economic Development and Economic History," in T. Paul Schultz, ed., *Investment in Women's Human Capital* (Chicago: University of Chicago Press, 1995).

[3] Kristin Mammen and Christina Paxson, "Women's work and economic development," *Journal of Economic Perspective* 14, no. 4 (Fall 2000): 141–164. The result presented here, corresponding to the ordinary least squares curve in Figure 2 of the article, was kindly provided by the authors.

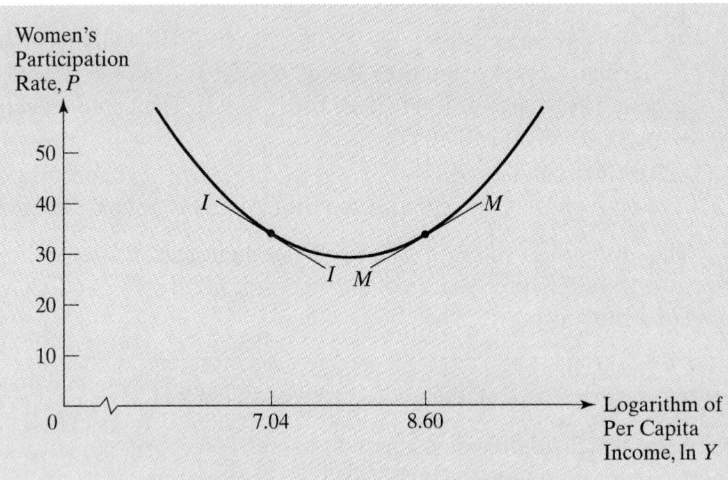

FIGURE 6.5 Women's Labor-Force Participation Rates and the Logarithm of Income per Capita

income per capita (in constant 1985 dollars), $\ln Y$; and the square of the logarithm of national income per capita, $(\ln Y)^2$, to be

$$P = 501.42 - 120.43 \ln Y + 7.68(\ln Y)^2.$$

We can show that this equation exhibits a U-shaped relationship using the results derived in this chapter concerning the derivative of a quadratic function. Applying the result in (6.6), we find that the derivative of P with respect to $\ln Y$ is

$$\frac{dP}{d \ln Y} = -120.43 + 15.36 \ln Y.$$

This derivative is negative for any value of $\ln Y$ less than 7.84, and therefore, the participation-rate function is decreasing in the range 0 to 7.84. The derivative is equal to zero at the value of $\ln Y = 7.84$, which corresponds to a level of income of \$2,540 (since $e^{7.84} = \$2{,}540$), and the line tangent to the function at this point is flat. The function is increasing for values of $\ln Y$ greater than 7.84 since the derivative $dP/d \ln Y$ is positive in this range. The labor-participation rate function is plotted in Figure 6.5.

We can also use the derivative to estimate, at different levels of income, how a small change in income is associated with a change in the participation rate of women in the labor force. For example, the per capita income in India in 1985 was \$1,140, and since $\ln(1140) = 7.04$, the estimated participation rate was

$$501.42 - 120.43 \times 7.04 + 7.68 \times (7.04)^2 = 34.23\%,$$

which is a bit above the actual value of 33.42%. The estimated derivative for a country with a per capita income of \$1,140 is

$$\frac{dP}{d \ln Y} = -120.43 + 15.36 \times 7.04 = -12.30.$$

The line tangent to the function at the value $\ln Y = 7.04$, which has the slope -12.30, is represented by the line II in Figure 6.5. This derivative suggests that a small increase in income per capita in India would tend to decrease the participation rate of women in the labor force. For example, an increase in $\ln Y$ from 7.04 to 7.05, corresponding to an increase in Y from \$1,140.00 to \$1,151.40 (an increase of 1%) is estimated to decrease the participation rate by $-12.30 \times 0.01 = -0.123\%$. As another example, the per capita income in Mexico in 1985, at \$5,416.00, was higher than that of India, but the estimated participation rate of women in the labor force for a country at this level of income, 33.08% is close to that of a country with an income of \$1,140.00. In this case, however, the derivative is positive since

$$\frac{dP}{d\ln Y} = -120.43 + 15.36\ln(5416) = -120.43 + 15.36 \times 8.60 = 11.67$$

and an increase in income in Mexico is estimated to raise the participation rate of women in the labor force. The line tangent to the function at the value $\ln Y = \ln(5416) = 8.60$ is labelled MM in Figure 6.5. The slope of this line is 11.67, suggesting that an increase in $\ln Y$ from 8.60 to 8.61 (corresponding to a 1% increase in income from \$5,416 to \$5,470) leads to an increase in the participation rate of women of $11.67 \times 0.01 = 0.1167\%$.

Differentiability and the Existence of a Derivative

The derivative of a function provides one way to characterize certain aspects of that function. We have not yet discussed, however, whether a function has a derivative over its entire range. In this section we discuss what is required for a derivative to exist. We also provide some economic examples where derivatives do not exist.

A function is **differentiable** over a certain interval if a derivative exists for each point in that interval. Not all functions are differentiable in their entire domain. The geometric interpretation of the derivative provides some insight as to whether a particular function is differentiable. The derivative can be thought of as the slope of a line tangent to the original function. If there is no unique tangent line at a certain value of a function, then a derivative does not exist for that value. For example, Figure 6.6 presents two functions that do not have derivatives at point x_N. The function in Figure 6.6(a) has a "corner point" at x_N. Many different straight lines, each with different slopes, can

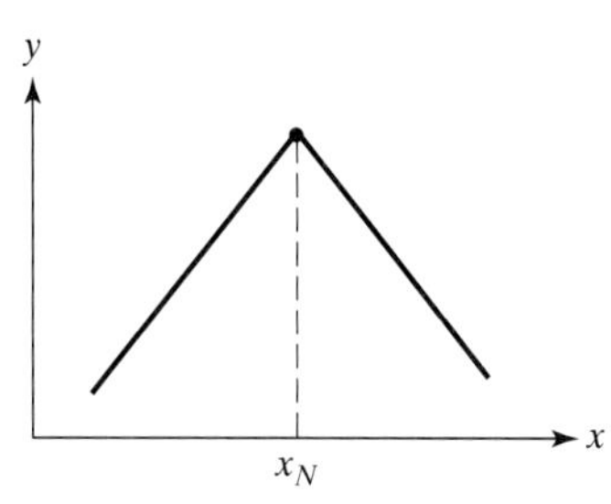

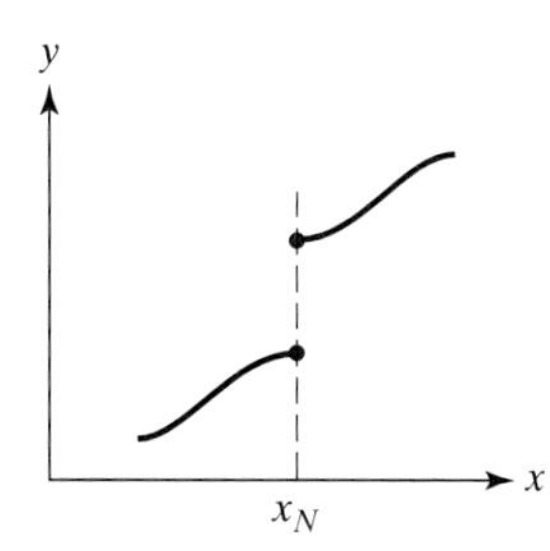

FIGURE 6.6 Functions Not Everywhere Differentiable

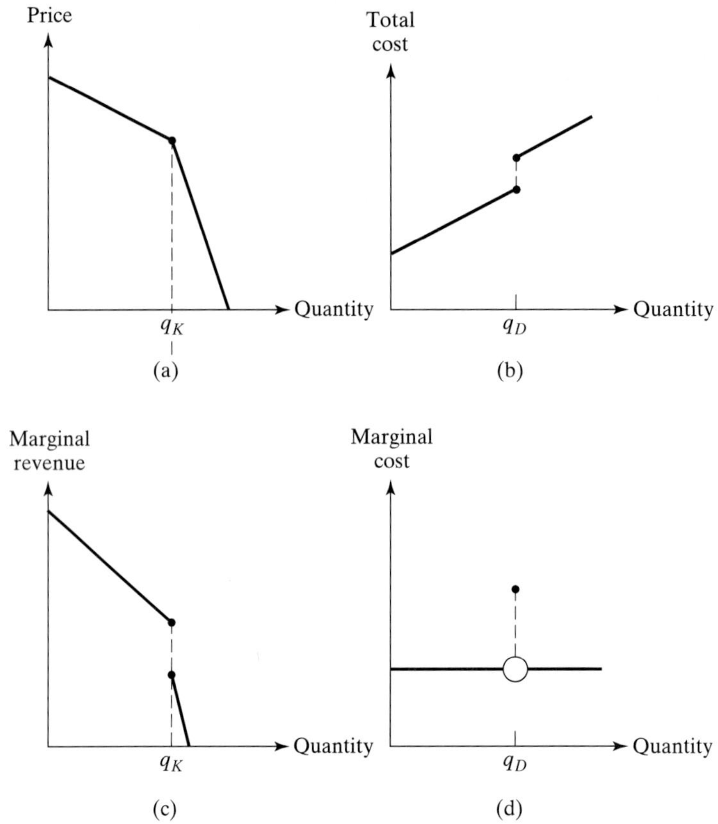

FIGURE 6.7 Oligopolistic Demand and Cost Functions

intersect this function at this corner point. The function in Figure 6.6(b) "jumps" at x_N. At this point, there is not a well-defined tangent line.

These geometric examples suggest that a function is differentiable over a certain interval if each point in that interval is associated with a unique tangent line. This requires, in turn, that, in this interval, the function be *continuous* and *smooth*. The conditions for a function to be continuous are discussed in Chapter 2. A function is smooth if it has no "corner points," that is, no points where it is possible to draw more than one tangent line.

A function is not differentiable at a point where it is not smooth or not continuous. The following examples from microeconomics illustrate functions that are not differentiable at certain points. The kinked oligopolistic demand curve is presented in Figure 6.7(a). The kink occurs at the quantity q_K. The associated marginal revenue curve in Figure 6.7(c) is not defined at q_K. The total cost curve in Figure 6.7(b) is discontinuous at the quantity q_D since a purchase of additional capital (like a new factory or new equipment) is required to increase output above that amount. This discontinuity means that the associated marginal cost function in Figure 6.7(d) is not defined at that quantity.

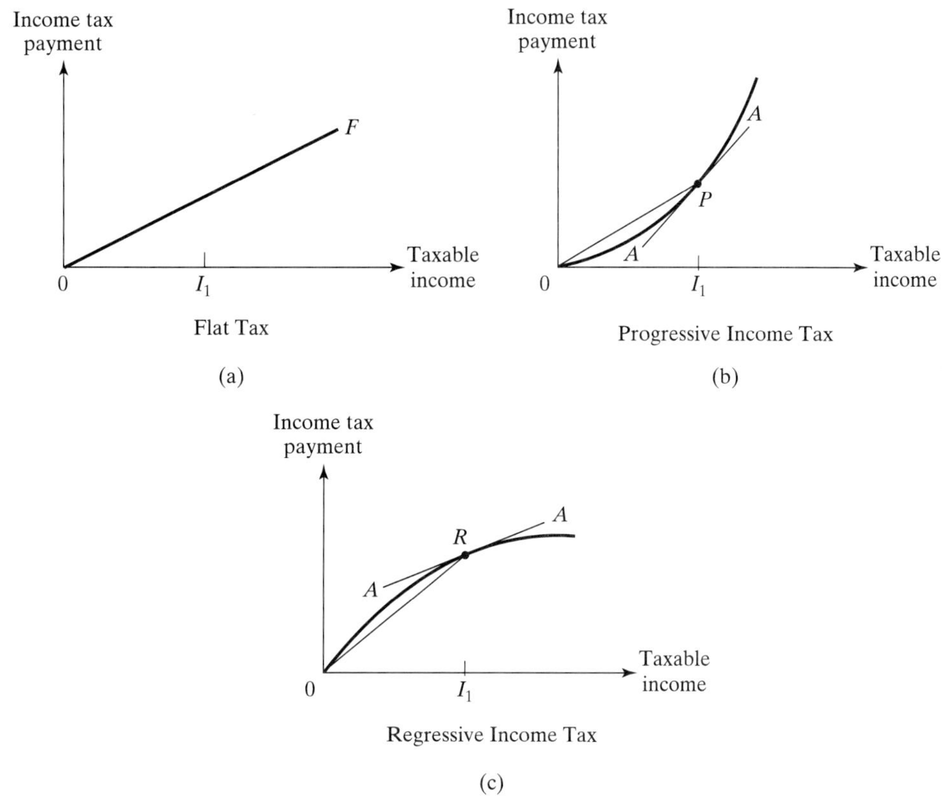

FIGURE 6.8 Tax Payments and Taxable Income

A Digression on Average versus Marginal Values

In economics we often are interested in both marginal and average values. For example, in the microeconomic analysis of labor markets, there is consideration of both the marginal productivity of labor and the average productivity of labor; public finance looks at both marginal tax rates and average tax rates.

There is a particular geometric interpretation of marginal and average values based upon tangent lines and secant lines. We illustrate this with the example of the progressivity of a tax system. The relationship between total tax payments due to the government and the taxable income reported to the government may differ in the three ways depicted in the graphs in Figure 6.8. Each graph plots income tax payments along the vertical axis as a function of taxable income along the horizontal axis. Figure 6.8(a) shows the relationship between tax payments and income if there is a flat tax, where the tax rate does not depend upon the level of income. Figure 6.8(b) depicts a progressive income tax, where the tax rate on the last dollar earned rises with total income. Figure 6.8(c) depicts a regressive income tax, where the tax rate on the last dollar earned decreases with total income.

The marginal tax rate is the tax paid on the last dollar of income earned. In the figures, the marginal tax rate at any level of income is represented by the slope of a line tangent to the tax payments schedule at that level of income. In Figure 6.8(b), the slope of the tangent line APA is the marginal tax rate in the progressive tax system at income level I_1. The marginal tax rate in the regressive tax system at this income level is given by the slope of the line ARA in Figure 6.8(c). There is a constant marginal tax rate in the flat tax system. Geometrically, this is reflected by the fact that there is a constant slope along the line $0F$. As drawn in Figure 6.8, at the income level I_1, the marginal tax rate is highest for the progressive tax system and lowest for the regressive tax system.

The average tax rate at a particular level of income, say I_1, equals

$$\frac{T_1}{I_1},$$

where T_1 represents tax payments due when income equals I_1. This average tax revenue can be represented in each figure by the slope of a secant line from the origin to the point on the income tax payment schedule corresponding to the level of income I_1. For example, at the level of income I_1, the average tax rate equals the slope of the line $0P$ in the progressive tax system, the slope of the line $0R$ in the regressive tax system, and the slope of the line $0F$ in the flat tax system.

The average tax rate in the flat tax system is constant since the marginal tax rate is constant and, therefore, equal to the average tax rate. The average tax rate changes if the slope of the tangent line does not equal the slope of the secant line at any given point. The marginal tax rate does not equal the average tax rate at any point where the slopes of the tangent and secant lines are not equal. For example, in the progressive tax system, the marginal tax rate is always greater than the average tax rate. Therefore the average tax rate rises with higher personal income. The opposite holds for the regressive tax system. In that case the marginal tax rate is always lower than the average tax rate, and, therefore, the average tax rate falls with higher levels of personal income.

The simple geometry of the relationship between marginal and average compares the slope of a ray from the origin to the value of the derivative of a function (which represents the slope of the tangent line) as we move out along a function. The slope of the ray from the origin will increase as we move out along the function as long as the derivative of the function is greater than the slope of the ray from the origin. The slope of the ray from the origin will decrease as we move out along the function as long as the derivative is less than the slope of that ray. A linear function has a constant slope, a constant derivative, and, therefore, an unvarying average value.

In algebraic terms, the slope of a ray from the origin to any point (x_0, y_0) on a function $f(x)$ is its average value

$$\frac{f(x_0)}{x_0},$$

while the slope of a tangent line at that point is its marginal value $f'(x_0)$. If the slope of the ray from the origin to the function at x_0 (that is, the average value of the function at that point) is less than the slope of the tangent line (that is, its marginal value at that point), then

$$f'(x_0) > \frac{f(x_0)}{x_0}.$$

In this case, for a small increase in the argument of the function from x_0 to $x_0 + \Delta x$, the average increases. That is,

$$\frac{f(x_0 + \Delta x)}{x_0 + \Delta x} > \frac{f(x_0)}{x_0}. \tag{6.8}$$

This result can be shown by considering the difference quotient for small values of Δx as an approximation of the derivative. In this case the condition that the marginal value is greater than the average value requires

$$\frac{f(x_0 + \Delta x) - f(x_0)}{\Delta x} > \frac{f(x_0)}{x_0},$$

which just requires that the slope of a secant line joining the points $f(x_0)$ and $f(x_0 + \Delta x)$ is greater than the slope of a ray from the origin to the point $f(x_0)$. This condition is equivalent to

$$\frac{f(x_0 + \Delta x)}{\Delta x} > \frac{f(x_0)}{x_0} + \frac{f(x_0)}{\Delta x}$$

or

$$\frac{f(x_0 + \Delta x)}{\Delta x} > \frac{(x_0 + \Delta x) \cdot f(x_0)}{x_0 \cdot \Delta x}.$$

Multiplying each side of this by $\Delta x/(x_0 + \Delta x)$ gives us the expression in (6.8). Analogously, if the average value of the function at x_0 is greater than its marginal value at that point and, therefore,

$$f'(x_0) < \frac{f(x_0)}{x_0},$$

then for a small positive value of Δx,

$$\frac{f(x_0 + \Delta x)}{x_0 + \Delta x} < \frac{f(x_0)}{x_0}.$$

Exercises 6.3

1. Using the general form for linear and quadratic functions, determine the derivative of each function.
   (a) $y = 30x + 10$
   (b) $y = 8x^2 - 6x + 12$
   (c) $y = 6$
   (d) $y = \sqrt{3} - 2x^2$
2. Evaluate the derivatives you obtained in question 1 for $x_0 = 3$ and $x_0 = 6$.
3. "Sin" taxes, or those taxes levied on such items as cigarettes and liquor, often serve a dual purpose. While they increase tax revenues to the government, they also may act to discourage consumption. Assume that the total sin tax revenue function is

$$R(t) = 50 + 25t - 75t^2.$$

Using the general result for quadratic functions obtained in (6.6), derive the marginal sin tax revenue function. Solve for t_m to determine the maximum sin tax rate that should be levied in order to maximize tax revenue. How would revenues be affected if taxes were set higher than t_m?

4. A function is differentiable over a certain range if there exists a unique tangent line at each point in that range. In this range, the function must be continuous and smooth. Determine whether the following functions are differentiable, and if not, explain why. Assume that the range is the set of real numbers unless otherwise indicated.
   (a) $y = 3x^2 + 11x + 10$
   (b) $y = 5x^3 - 2\ln x;\ x > 0$
   (c) $y = |2x - 4| + 3$
   (d) $y = \sqrt{(x^4 - 1)};\ x \geq 1$
   (e) $y = \dfrac{x^2 - 2x + 1}{(1 - x)^2}, -2 \leq x \leq 2$
5. Drawing on the example of the three tax systems in the text (constant, progressive, and regressive), graph an example of three tax systems where, at a level of income I_a, the average tax rates are equal but the marginal rates are not. Draw a second graph where, at a level of income I_m, the marginal tax rates are the same but the average tax rates are different.
6. Calculate the average change and the marginal change for each function over the specified values of x, where the marginal change is obtained by evaluating the derivative at each value of x. What is the relationship between the average rate of change of a function and the average of a function's marginal change?
   (a) $y = x^2 + 2x - 3;\ [2, 3]$
   (b) $y = \dfrac{1}{4}x^2;\ [2, 6]$
   (c) $y = 4 - 3x - x^2;\ [-5, -1]$
   (d) $y = x^{1/2}$
7. Consider a total cost function where q is the single argument such that
$$TC(q) = 10 + 2q^2$$
   and $q \geq 0$. Do you expect the slope of the marginal cost curve at any given point to be greater than or less than the slope of the average cost curve? What impact will an increase in output have on the slope of the average cost curve?
8. You own an apparel-producing company whose total revenue function is
$$TR = 8Q - 0.5Q^2.$$
   (a) Graph this function over the range $0 \leq Q \leq 6$ to obtain an indication of the curvature of the function.
   (b) Find the derivative of this function (dTR/dQ), which represents marginal revenue.
   (c) Find the average revenue function, $TR(Q)/Q$.
   (d) Which is greater, the slope of the marginal revenue curve or the average revenue curve?
   (e) What is the impact of an increase in Q on the slope of the average revenue curve?

9. Sketch a graph of the quadratic function

$$y = 4x^2 - 8x + 3$$

by first setting the function equal to zero and finding the roots using the quadratic formula. Plot several points over the range $[0, 2]$.

   (a) Determine the derivative of the function, $f'(x)$, and calculate the value of x when $f'(x) = 0$. This will indicate the quadratic function's extreme value, where the slope of a tangent drawn to this point equals zero. Characterize the extreme value as either a global or local maximum or minimum.

   (b) Sketch a graph of the derivative.

10. Now sketch a graph of the cubic function

$$y = x^3 - x^2 - 9x + 9,$$

where one of the roots is $x = 1$. Plot several points over the range $(-5, 5)$.

   (a) By following the general form of the derivative of a quadratic function and remembering that the derivative is the difference quotient in the limit as the Δx approaches zero, determine the derivative of the cubic function.

   (b) Calculate the values of x when $f'(x) = 0$ by finding the roots of the derivative equation. This result will indicate the cubic function's two extreme values, where the derivative equals zero and the slope of a line drawn at each of these points equals zero.

   (c) Sketch a graph of the derivative of the cubic function. Is the derivative function concave or convex?

11. In another estimate, using a slightly different method, Mammen and Paxson find the relationship between the participation rate of women in the labor force (P), the logarithm of national income ($\ln Y$), and the square of the logarithm of national income $(\ln Y)^2$ to be

$$P = 220.7 - 58.2 \ln Y + 3.9 (\ln Y)^2.$$

   (a) At what point is the derivative of this function equal to zero?

   (b) Compare the derivative of this function, evaluated at the value of the logarithm of income for India in 1985 ($\ln(1140) = 7.40$) and at the value of the logarithm of income for Mexico in 1985 ($\ln(5416) = 8.60$) to the derivatives for these values presented in the discussion of the pattern of women's work. If you were to sketch this function, would you expect it to be "flatter" or "steeper" than the function presented in the application?

6.4 DERIVATIVES AND DIFFERENTIALS

The derivative of a function used in economic analysis enables us to calculate the marginal rate of change of that function. For example, the derivative of the tax revenue function presented in the previous section represents the change in tax revenues corresponding to a very small change in tax rates. A distinct though related question concerns the overall change in tax revenues that would arise in response to a given change in the tax rate. One way to estimate this is through the use of the **differential.** In this section we show the relationship between the differential and the derivative. We also demonstrate the use of the differential to estimate the change in the value of a function given a change in its argument.

The link between a differential and a derivative can be understood by first considering discrete changes in the variables x and y when these two variables are related through the function $y = f(x)$. The discrete change $\Delta y = y_1 - y_0$ due to a change in x from x_0 to x_1 equals $f(x_1) - f(x_0)$. Substituting $x_1 = \Delta x + x_0$, we get

$$\Delta y = f(x_0 + \Delta x) - f(x_0).$$

Multiplying and dividing the last term by Δx gives us

$$\Delta y = \left(\frac{f(x_0 + \Delta x) - f(x_0)}{\Delta x}\right) \Delta x.$$

The term in parentheses is just the difference quotient. This expression shows that the change in y exactly equals the difference quotient times the change in x.

The difference quotient, while providing an exact relationship between Δx and Δy, may often be more cumbersome to evaluate than the derivative. We can use the derivative to obtain an estimate of the relationship between Δx and Δy. This estimate is called the differential.

The Differential Define dx as an arbitrary change in x from its initial value x_0 and dy as the resulting change in y along the tangent line from the initial value of the function $y_0 = f(x_0)$. The differential of $y = f(x)$, dy, evaluated at x_0, is

$$dy = f'(x_0) \cdot dx.$$

A geometric interpretation of the differential draws on the interpretation of the derivative at a certain point as the slope of a line tangent to a function at that point. Figure 6.9 offers a geometric presentation of the differential. The differential, dy, shows the estimated change in y due to a change in x from x_0 to $x_0 + dx$, along a line tangent to the function at the point x_0. This estimated change in y equals the product of dx and the slope of the line tangent to the function at x_0, $f'(x_0)$. In Figure 6.9, $dy = y_D - y_0$. The actual change in the value of the function, Δy, corresponding to this change in the argument of the function from x_0 to $x_0 + dx$ is

$$\Delta y = f(x_0 + dx) - f(x_0).$$

The actual change in the value of the function is depicted in the figure as the distance $y_A - y_0$. The differential dy is not exactly equal to the actual change in the value of the function, Δy, though it does provide an approximation of the actual change.

An economic example illustrates the use of the differential to find an approximate change in the value of a function when its argument changes by a discrete amount. Consider the relationship between import levels, m, and tariff rates, t. Suppose that these two variables are linked by the function $m = g(t)$ where

$$m = g(t) = 1000 - 200t + 250t^2.$$

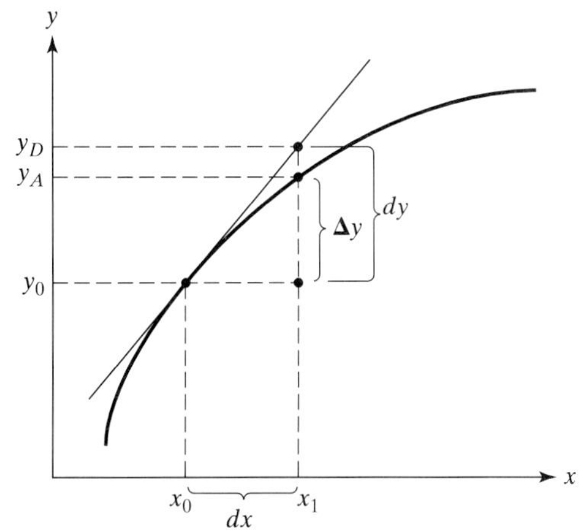

FIGURE 6.9 Differential Approximation and Actual Change of a Function

Suppose the initial tariff rate is 0.2 and it is scheduled to rise to 0.25. The actual change in imports is

$$\begin{aligned} \Delta m &= g(0.25) - g(0.20) \\ &= 965.6 - 970.0 \\ &= -4.4. \end{aligned}$$

Alternatively, we can use the differential approximation, evaluating the derivative at the initial level of the tariff. Following the rule for the derivative of a quadratic function given in (6.6), we find that the derivative of the import function is

$$g'(t) = -200t + 500t.$$

The estimated value of the change in imports using the differential is

$$\begin{aligned} dm &= g'(t) \cdot dt \\ &= (-200 + 500t) \cdot dt \\ &= (-200 + 500(0.20)) \cdot 0.05 \\ &= -5. \end{aligned}$$

The extent to which the differential serves as a good approximation to the actual change of the value of a function for discrete changes in its argument depends upon the size of the change of the argument. Table 6.2 illustrates the relationship between dm and Δm for different values of Δt. The last column of this table presents the percentage difference between the differential approximation, dm, and the actual change in the function, Δm. This column shows that the differential approximation works better, the smaller the change in tariff rates. This is as expected since the derivative is calculated for very small changes and the larger the change in Δt, the less appropriate the minute approximation. This is also shown in Figure 6.10. In this figure, the difference

TABLE 6.2 Actual and Approximate Changes in Imports

t	m	Δm (actual)	dm (estimated)	Difference (%)
0.2	970.0	0.0	0.0	0
0.25	965.6	−4.4	−5.0	14
0.3	962.5	−7.5	−10.0	33
0.4	960.0	−10.0	−20.0	100

between the line tangent to the import function and the function itself increases as the tariff rate rises beyond 0.20. At $t = 0.25$, this difference equals −0.6, while at $t = 0.30$, this difference equals −2.5.

The extent to which the differential serves as a good approximation to the actual change of the value of a function also depends upon the function itself. The differential approximation holds more closely for functions that are closer to being linear. This is illustrated by considering the differential approximation for the function

$$y = 100 + 200x - \beta x^2$$

for different values of β. When $\beta = 0$, this function is linear, and as the absolute value of β increases, the quadratic term has a larger effect on the value of the function. The differential approximation of this function for a given change in its argument dx is

$$dy = (200 - 2\beta x_0)\, dx,$$

while the actual change in the value of the function for the change dx is

$$\Delta y = (200 - 2\beta x_0 - \beta\, dx)\, dx.$$

Table 6.3 presents the differential approximation, dy, and the actual change in the function, Δy, for different values of β when $x_0 = 10$ and $dx = 1$. In the linear case

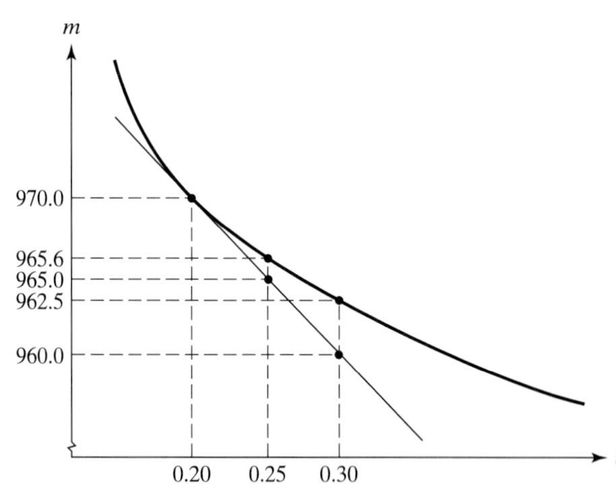

FIGURE 6.10 Actual and Approximate Changes in Imports

TABLE 6.3 Actual and Approximate Changes with Varying Nonlinearity ($x_0 = 10$, $dx = 1$)

β	Δy (actual)	dy (estimated)	Difference (%)
0	200	200	0
2	158	160	1.3
4	116	120	3.5
6	74	80	8.1
8	32	40	25

where $\beta = 0$, the differential equals the function, and $dy = \Delta x$. As β increases in value, there is an increasing divergence between Δy and dy. This is also illustrated in Figure 6.11, which presents segments of the function $y = 100 + 200x - \beta x^2$ and the differential $dy = (200 - 2\beta x_0)\,dx$ for $x_0 = 10$ and $dx = 1$. These segments are presented in Figure 6.11 (a), (b), and (c) for values of β equal to 0, 2, and 8, respectively. This figure illustrates that with larger values of β, the differential less closely approximates the actual change in the value of the function for a given change in its argument.

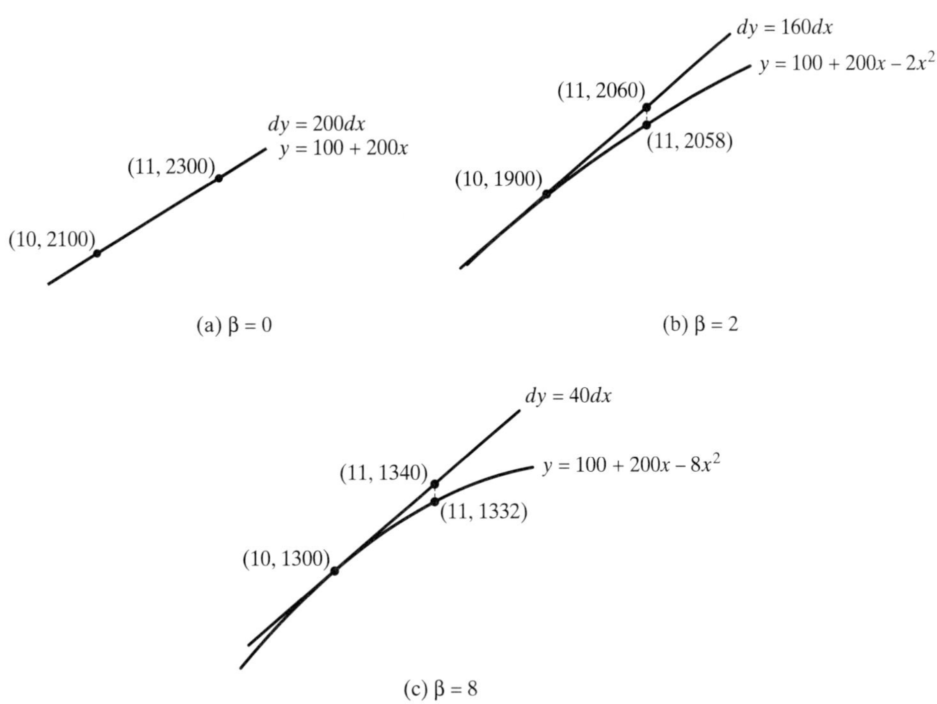

FIGURE 6.11 Differential Approximation for Beta with Different Functions

Exercises 6.4

1. Find the differential dy for a given change in x, dx, for each function.
   (a) $y = 7x^2 - 3x + 5$
   (b) $y = 10x - \frac{1}{4}x^2$
   (c) $y = -x^2$
   (d) $y = x^3 + 3x - 6$
2. For the functions given in question 1, use the differential to approximate Δy due to a discrete change in x from 10 to 10.1. (*Hint:* $\Delta y \approx f'(x) \cdot \Delta x$)
3. For each function, use the differential to evaluate Δy due to the given changes in x. Assume that $x_0 = 2$ for all of the examples.
   (a) $y = 3x^2 + \frac{1}{3}x - 4$; $\Delta x = 0.5$, $\Delta x = 2$
   (b) $y = \frac{1}{2}x^2 - 14$; $\Delta x = \frac{1}{4}$; $\Delta x = 10$
   (c) $y = 16 - 4x + x^3$; $\Delta x = 8$, $\Delta x = 0.2$
4. For the functions given in question 3, calculate the actual values of y, and compare your answers to those obtained using the differential approximation. What is the percentage difference between the actual and estimated results for each set of changes in x?
5. In a simple model of national income determination, income equals expenditures, and in its most basic form, consumption is a function of income alone such that

$$C(Y) = C_0 + \beta Y,$$

   where C_0 is an exogenous variable representing autonomous consumption and β is a parameter. Assume that $C_0 = 1{,}000$, $\beta = 0.8$, and $Y = 10{,}000$.
   (a) Find the derivative of the consumption function, and provide an interpretation of its economic meaning.
   (b) Use the differential to approximate the effect on consumption of a \$1,000 increase in Y. Now calculate the actual difference in consumption due to ΔY. Explain your results.
6. The quantity of investment (I) in an economy depends, in part, on the real interest rate (r) since the interest rate measures the cost of borrowing. This relationship can be illustrated by the function $I = f(r)$. To find ΔI for a finite Δr, consider the function

$$I = f(r) = 600 - 150r + 400r^2.$$

   (a) Use the differential approximation $\Delta I = f'(r) \cdot \Delta r$ to calculate ΔI for the following Δr. Assume that $r_0 = 2.0\%$ (that is, $r_0 = 0.02$) and

$$\Delta r_1 = 0.5\% \quad \text{and}$$
$$\Delta r_2 = 1.0\%.$$

(b) Alternatively, calculate the actual value of ΔI by first finding its initial level when $r = 2.0\%$ and then plugging each additional interest rate assumption into the original function.

(c) How well does the differential calculation approximate the actual ΔI?

(d) For which change in real interest rates, Δr_1 or Δr_2, does it provide a more accurate result?

7. Graph the function $y = 11 + 10x - x^2$ by first finding its roots when the value of the function equals zero. Using the derivative of the function, create an expression for the differential, which is the equation for the line tangent to this function at any given point. Assuming that $x_0 = 1$, plot the line tangent to the original function. Consider the following values of Δx:

$$\Delta x = 0.5, \quad \Delta x = 1.0, \quad \Delta x = 1.75, \quad \text{and} \quad \Delta x = 3.0.$$

Show that for increasingly larger values of Δx, the differential approximation becomes a less accurate approximation for the actual value of Δy.

8. Using the quadratic function presented in the application about the international pattern of women's work, find the differentials for labor-force participation rates, dP, for the following changes in the logarithm of national income, $d\ln Y$, evaluated at the given values.

(a) A change in income of 10% ($d\ln Y = 0.1$) for Mozambique, which had a level of income equal to \$763 in 1985 ($\ln(763) = 6.64$).

(b) A change in income of 25% ($d\ln Y = 0.25$) for Mozambique in 1985.

(c) A change in income of 10% ($d\ln Y = 0.1$) for Israel, which had a level of income equal to \$8,788 in 1985 ($\ln(8788) = 9.08$).

(d) A change in income of 25% ($d\ln Y = 0.25$) for Israel in 1985.

Summary

This chapter introduces the concept of the derivative. The derivative shows how the value of a function changes in response to very small changes in its argument. In economics, this has a natural correspondence to the notion of making decisions "at the margin." This close correspondence makes the derivative one of the most frequently used mathematical tools in economics.

A good command of the material presented in this chapter is important since the concepts introduced here are drawn on throughout the rest of Part Three. In the next chapter, rules for differentiating a wide range of functions are presented. Chapter 8 extends the analysis of derivatives to functions with more than one argument. The derivative is also used extensively in Part Four, where the link between the derivative and extreme points discussed in this chapter is developed more fully. Chapters 12, 14, and 15 in Part Five also use the derivative extensively in their presentation of dynamic analysis.

Chapter 7

Univariate Calculus

There are 29 entries that begin with the word "marginal" in *The MIT Dictionary of Modern Economics*, including *marginal cost*, *marginal revenue*, *marginal product*, *marginal utility,* and *marginal disutility.*[1] There is a direct correspondence between the mathematical concept of the derivative and the economic concept of considering decisions made "at the margin," the point where the last unit is produced or consumed. This correspondence makes differentiation, which is the evaluation of a derivative, one of the core mathematical techniques in economics.

In Chapter 6, derivatives of linear and quadratic functions are calculated by finding the limits of the difference quotients as the change in the arguments of those functions approaches zero. In this chapter we present rules for differentiating a wider class of functions. Differentiation would be tedious and difficult if finding the derivative of any function required a fresh application of the difference quotient. Alternatively, differentiation would be unwieldy if it involved looking up derivatives from an exhaustive list of functions. Fortunately, the few rules presented in this chapter encompass almost all the functions you are likely to come across in economics.

The chapter begins with a section presenting rules of differentiation for functions that are themselves sums, differences, or products of other functions. This section also presents the rules of differentiation for constant-valued functions, power functions, and exponential functions. Section 7.2 presents an important rule called the chain rule. The chain rule enables us to generalize the rules presented in Section 7.1, as well as to develop rules for quotients and logarithmic functions. Section 7.3 concludes the chapter with a discussion of the general concept of the second derivative. Included in this section is a discussion of the use of the derivative and the second derivative for finding linear approximations for nonlinear functions.

---

[1] David W. Pearce, ed., *The MIT Dictionary of Modern Economics*. 4th ed. (Cambridge, MA: MIT Press, 1992.)

7.1 RULES OF DIFFERENTIATION

In the last chapter, we defined the derivative of a univariate function $y = f(x)$ evaluated at x_0 as

$$\frac{dy}{dx} = \lim_{\Delta x \to 0} \frac{f(x_0 + \Delta x) - f(x_0)}{\Delta x}.$$

We used this definition to determine the rules of differentiation for the general linear and quadratic functions. In this section we derive the general rules for the sum, difference, and product of functions using the value of the limit of the difference quotient as Δx approaches zero. The rules of differentiation for two specific types of functions, power functions and exponential functions, are then presented. As in the previous chapter, the derivative of a function such as $z = g(x)$ is written as either dz/dx or as $g'(x)$.

Sum-Difference Rule For any two functions $f(x)$ and $g(x)$,

$$\frac{d(f(x) \pm g(x))}{dx} = f'(x) \pm g'(x),$$

where the symbol $\pm$ means "either addition or subtraction." ■

To prove the sum-difference rule, first define the function $h(x)$ as the sum or difference of the two functions $f(x)$and $g(x)$; that is, $h(x) = f(x) \pm g(x)$. The derivative of $h(x)$ equals

$$\begin{aligned} h'(x) &= \lim_{\Delta x \to 0} \frac{h(x + \Delta x) - h(x)}{\Delta x} \\ &= \lim_{\Delta x \to 0} \frac{(f(x + \Delta x) \pm g(x + \Delta x)) - (f(x) \pm g(x))}{\Delta x} \\ &= \lim_{\Delta x \to 0} \frac{f(x + \Delta x) - f(x)}{\Delta x} \pm \lim_{\Delta x \to 0} \frac{g(x + \Delta x) - g(x)}{\Delta x} \\ &= f'(x) \pm g'(x). \end{aligned}$$

This rule extends to the sum or difference of any number of functions. As an example of this rule, the derivative of the function

$$h(x) = (4 + 2x) + (x^2 - 5x - 5)$$

is the sum of the derivatives of the two terms in parentheses; that is,

$$h'(x) = 2 + (2x - 5) = 2x - 3.$$

Of course, we also obtain this result by simply adding the terms in parentheses in the original function and then using the rule for the derivative of a quadratic function.

Scalar Rule Let $g(x) = k \cdot f(x)$ where k is a real number. Then

$$g'(x) = k \cdot f'(x).$$

To prove this rule, note that the derivative for the function $k \cdot f(x)$ is

$$\begin{aligned} g'(x) &= \lim_{\Delta x \to 0} \frac{k \cdot f(x + \Delta x) - k \cdot f(x)}{\Delta x} \\ &= k \cdot \lim_{\Delta x \to 0} \frac{f(x + \Delta x) - f(x)}{\Delta x} \\ &= k \cdot f'(x). \end{aligned}$$

Product Rule For $f(x) = g(x) \cdot h(x)$,

$$f'(x) = g'(x) \cdot h(x) + h'(x) \cdot g(x).$$

The proof of this rule is a bit more involved than the previous two. First we note that

$$\begin{aligned} f'(x) &= \lim_{\Delta x \to 0} \frac{f(x + \Delta x) - f(x)}{\Delta x} \\ &= \lim_{\Delta x \to 0} \frac{g(x + \Delta x) \cdot h(x + \Delta x) - g(x) \cdot h(x)}{\Delta x}. \end{aligned}$$

Adding and subtracting $h(x) \cdot g(x + \Delta x)/\Delta x$ to the last expression, rearranging terms, and factoring, we get

$$f'(x) = \lim_{\Delta x \to 0} h(x) \cdot \left[\frac{g(x + \Delta x) - g(x)}{\Delta x} \right] + \lim_{\Delta x \to 0} g(x + \Delta x) \cdot \left[\frac{h(x + \Delta x) - h(x)}{\Delta x} \right].$$

When we take the limit of this expression as $\Delta x \to 0$, the expressions in the first and second square brackets become $g'(x)$ and $h'(x)$, respectively, and the expression $g(x + \Delta x)$ becomes $g(x)$. This gives us the product rule.

As an example of the product rule, consider the function

$$w(z) = u(z) \cdot v(z),$$

where

$$u(z) = (2z + 1) \quad \text{and} \quad v(z) = (5z + 7).$$

The derivatives of $u(z)$ and $v(z)$ are

$$u'(z) = 2 \quad \text{and} \quad v'(z) = 5.$$

Therefore

$$w'(z) = 2(5z + 7) + 5(2z + 1) = 20z + 19.$$

We can check this result by multiplying $u(z)$ by $v(z)$ and then using the rule for the derivative of quadratic functions since

$$w(z) = 10z^2 + 19z + 7.$$

A straightforward extension of the product rule shows how to take the derivative of the product of any number of functions. For example, consider the function

$$f(x) = m(x) \cdot n(x) \cdot h(x).$$

To find the derivative $f'(x)$ using the product rule, first define

$$g(x) = m(x) \cdot n(x).$$

The product rule shows that

$$g'(x) = m'(x) \cdot n(x) + n'(x) \cdot m(x).$$

Substituting this result into the product rule, we get

$$\begin{aligned} f'(x) &= [m'(x) \cdot n(x) + n'(x) \cdot m(x)]h(x) + h'(x) \cdot m(x) \cdot n(x) \\ &= m'(x) \cdot n(x) \cdot h(x) + n'(x) \cdot m(x) \cdot h(x) + h'(x) \cdot m(x) \cdot n(x). \end{aligned}$$

Power Rule The derivative of the function $f(x) = k \cdot x^n$ is

$$f'(x) = n \cdot k \cdot x^{n-1}.$$

An argument to support this result considers the pattern of the relationship between a class of functions and their derivatives. For example, we have seen that the simple linear function $f(x) = k \cdot x$, which fits the function described in the power rule for the case $n = 1$, has the derivative $f'(x) = k$. The function $f(x) = k \cdot x^2$ has the derivative $f'(x) = 2kx$. If you completed the problems in Chapter 6, you found that the cubic function $f(x) = k \cdot x^3$ has the derivative $3kx^2$. The pattern that emerges is consistent with the power rule.

The power rule admits any value of n. For $n = 0$, we see that we have the **constant-valued function rule,** which states that for the function $y = k$,

$$\frac{dy}{dx} = 0.$$

The power rule also shows that for functions of the form $y = 1/x^n = x^{-n}$,

$$\frac{dy}{dx} = -n \cdot x^{-n-1}.$$

The power rule can be applied to find the derivatives of the following three specific functions. The derivative of the function

$$f(x) = 2x^4$$

is

$$f'(x) = 8x^3.$$

The derivative of

$$r = 6\sqrt{t} = 6t^{0.5}$$

is

$$\frac{dr}{dt} = 3t^{-0.5} = \frac{3}{\sqrt{t}}.$$

The derivative of

$$v = \frac{5}{w^3} = 5w^{-3}$$

is

$$\frac{dv}{dw} = -15w^{-4} = -\frac{15}{w^4}.$$

Another rule of differentiation that is frequently used in economics concerns exponential functions.

Exponential Function Rule The derivative of the exponential function $f(x) = e^{kx}$ is

$$f'(x) = k \cdot e^{kx}.$$

The following argument supports this rule. Note that the difference quotient for the exponential function $f(x) = e^{kx}$ is

$$\begin{aligned} f'(x) &= \lim_{\Delta x \to 0} \frac{e^{kx + k\Delta x} - e^{kx}}{\Delta x} \\ &= \lim_{\Delta x \to 0} e^{kx}\left[\frac{e^{k\Delta x} - 1}{\Delta x}\right]. \end{aligned}$$

Since e^{kx} does not vary with Δx, this expression can be written as

$$f'(x) = e^{kx} \lim_{\Delta x \to 0}\left[\frac{e^{k\Delta x} - 1}{\Delta x}\right].$$

The exponential function rule, therefore, implies that the limit of the expression in the square brackets as Δx approaches zero equals k. To show the plausibility of this result, consider the case where Δx is very small so that, approximately,

$$k = \frac{e^{k\Delta x} - 1}{\Delta x}.$$

We can rearrange this relationship to get

$$1 + k \cdot \Delta x = e^{k\Delta x}$$

or

$$e = (1 + k \cdot \Delta x)^{1/k\Delta x}.$$

In Chapter 3 it is shown that

$$e = \lim_{h \to 0}(1 + h)^{1/h}.$$

Since $k \cdot \Delta x \to 0$ as $\Delta x \to 0$, it follows that

$$e = \lim_{\Delta x \to 0} (1 + k \cdot \Delta x)^{1/k\Delta x},$$

and, therefore, the conjecture that $k \approx (e^{(k\Delta x)} - 1)/\Delta x$ (where $\approx$ means "approximately equal to") is confirmed.

We close this section with an application that uses the exponential function rule.

Growth Rates

In Chapter 3 we learned that the value at time t of a variable x growing at a constant rate r equals

$$x(t) = x(0) \cdot e^{rt},$$

where $x(0)$ is the value of x at some initial time period. In that chapter, the parameter r was defined as the **growth rate.** Using the rule for the derivative of an exponential function, we can now show this result by first taking the derivative of $x(t)$ with respect to time,

$$\frac{dx(t)}{dt} = x(0) \cdot e^{rt} \cdot r.$$

Dividing the left-hand side of this expression by $x(t)$ and the right-hand side by the equivalent value $x(0) \cdot e^{rt}$, we obtain

$$\frac{dx(t)}{dt} \cdot \frac{1}{x(t)} = r.$$

The expression $dx(t)/dt \cdot 1/x(t)$ represents the growth rate of the variable $x(t)$. This is sometimes called the **instantaneous growth rate** since it is the growth rate over a very small unit of time. This is closely linked to the **proportional change** of a variable between time $t - 1$ and time t, which is

$$\frac{x_t - x_{t-1}}{x_{t-1}},$$

and the **percentage change,** which is

$$\frac{x_t - x_{t-1}}{x_{t-1}} \times 100\%.$$

An instantaneous growth rate, a proportional change, and a percentage change are all unit free; that is, their values do not depend upon the units used to measure the variable. For example, the growth rate and the proportional or percentage change of a monetary amount do not change whether the units are cents, dollars, or millions of dollars. This is a result of dividing $x_t - x_{t-1}$ by x_{t-1}, in the case of proportional and percentage changes and dividing $dx(t)/dt$ by $x(t)$, in the case of the instantaneous growth rate.

Exercises 7.1

1. Find the derivative of each function.
   (a) $y = \sqrt{x^3}$
   (b) $y = 25$
   (c) $y = \dfrac{7}{4x^4}$
   (d) $y = 8x^2 + 3\sqrt{x} - 14$
   (e) $y = \dfrac{1}{3}x^{-2} - 2x$
2. Find $g'(1)$ and $g'(4)$ for each function.
   (a) $y = g(x) = 12x^2$
   (b) $y = g(x) = ax^{-2}$
   (c) $y = g(x) = 4x^{1/2}$
   (d) $y = g(x) = e^{2x}$
3. Explain the difference between $f'(x) = 0$ and $f'(x_0) = 0$.
4. Using the product rule, differentiate each function.
   (a) $y = (4x - 7)(3x + 5)$
   (b) $y = (3x + 4)(5x^2 + 10x + 6)$
   (c) $y = (5x + 2)(x + 4)(x^2)$
   (d) $y = (x^3 - 10)x^2$
   (e) $y = (x^{-2} - 4)6x$
5. In economic analysis, functions are often given in general rather than specific form, meaning that there is no numerical specification. If average revenue, AR, is a function of Q, that is, $AR = f(Q)$, and $TR = AR \cdot Q$, where TR is total revenue, find the derivative of the total revenue function (that is, marginal revenue).
6. Differentiate each exponential function.
   (a) $y = xe^x$
   (b) $y = 10e^{-x/5}$
   (c) $y = axe^{bx}$
   (d) $y = 2xe^{x^2+4}$
   (e) $y = e^{3x^3 - x^2 + 5x - 6}$
7. Determine the derivative of each function, and evaluate it over the given interval. Assess whether the derivative is increasing or decreasing over the interval.
   (a) $y = 4 + 20x - 4x^2$; $[-1, 1]$
   (b) $y = e^{2x}$; $[0, 2]$
   (c) $y = 3 \ln x$; $[4, 6]$
   (d) $y = 2(x + 1)^2$; $[-5, 1]$
8. The assumption of profit maximization, where profit is equal to the difference between revenue and cost, is frequently used in microeconomics. To maximize profit, or achieve the greatest difference between revenue and cost, the firm selects that

output at which marginal revenue equals marginal cost. Given the demand function

$$P = 70 - 10Q,$$

determine total revenue. (*Hint*: $TR = P \cdot Q$.) Find the associated marginal revenue function, and obtain the marginal cost function from the total cost function

$$TC(Q) = 175 - 50Q + 20Q^2.$$

At what quantity of output is profit maximized?

9. Consider the equation for money demand

$$\frac{M}{P} = e^{-\lambda i},$$

where the ratio M/P equals the nominal money supply divided by the price level, i is the nominal interest rate, and λ is a positive constant. What is the derivative of money demand with respect to small changes in the interest rate? What does this derivative imply about the relationship between money demand and interest rates?

10. Determine the instantaneous growth rate of y for each equation.
    (a) $y = e^{.05t}$
    (b) $y = \frac{1}{2}e^{.045t}$
    (c) $y = e^{t}$

7.2 THE CHAIN RULE AND COMPOSITE FUNCTIONS

Many economic situations involve a chain of relationships that link an ultimate outcome to its original cause. For example, in a simple Keynesian model, a change in the money supply affects the interest rate, which affects investment demand, which affects output. In this section we present the **chain rule,** which shows how to evaluate a derivative when a variable's effect works through one function embedded in another. The chain rule shows how to evaluate the derivative of output with respect to the money supply given separate functions linking interest rates to money supply, investment demand to interest rates, and output to investment demand. The chain rule is also useful for deriving more general forms of the rules presented in Section 7.1, as well as for deriving rules for some other types of functions.

The chain rule shows how to differentiate **composite functions,** that is, functions in which the arguments are themselves functions. Given the functions

$$y = g(u)$$

and

$$u = h(x),$$

the composite function $f(x)$ is

$$y = g(h(x)) = f(x).$$

This notation means that the value of $f(x)$ for any particular value of x is found by first finding the value of $h(x)$ for that value and then using this as the argument in the function $g(x)$. We can refer to the function $h(x)$ as the **inside function** and the function $g(x)$ as the **outside function.**

It is important to note that, in general, switching the inside and outside functions gives an altogether different composite function. Thus, in general,

$$g(h(x)) \neq h(g(x)).$$

An example illustrates this. Consider the inside function $h(x) = e^x$ and the outside function $g(h(x)) = 2 \cdot h(x)$. Then for $x = 1$,

$$g(h(1)) = 2 \cdot e^1 = 5.44.$$

Switching the inside and the outside functions gives a different result. In this case

$$h(g(1)) = e^{(2 \cdot 1)} = 7.39.$$

Composite functions can be differentiated using the rules presented in the previous section along with a rule that shows how to account for the interaction of the functions. This latter rule is called the chain rule.

Chain Rule The derivative of the composite function

$$y = f(x) = g(h(x)),$$

where

$$u = h(x),$$
$$g(h(x)) \equiv g(u)$$

and both $h(x)$ and $g(u)$ are differentiable functions, is

$$\frac{df(x)}{dx} = g'(h(x)) \cdot h'(x)$$

or, written differently,

$$\frac{dy}{dx} = \frac{dy}{du} \cdot \frac{du}{dx}.$$

Intuitively, the chain rule accounts for the change in the value of a composite function by first calculating the change in the value of the inside function and then using this result to calculate the change in the value of the outside function. The name "chain rule" comes from the fact that this rule links the separate parts of the composite function in a chain.

As we have shown, in general,

$$g(h(x)) \neq h(g(x)).$$

Thus it is not surprising that the chain rule shows us that the derivative of $g(h(x))$ is generally not the same as the derivative of $h(g(x))$. Taking a simple example, the derivative of

$$g(h(x)) = 2(e^x)$$

is

$$g'(h(x)) \cdot h'(x) = 2e^x,$$

while the derivative of

$$h(g(x)) = e^{2x}$$

is

$$h'(g(x)) \cdot g'(x) = 2e^{2x}.$$

There are many cases where the chain rule serves as a formal statement of economic reasoning. For example, consider a simple Keynesian model. Denote the function that links interest rates to money as

$$r = \lambda(m),$$

the function that links investment demand to interest rates as

$$i = \eta(r),$$

and the function that links output to investment as

$$y = \kappa(i).$$

The composite function linking output to money is

$$y = \kappa(\eta(\lambda(m))) = \Lambda(m).$$

The chain rule shows that the derivative of output with respect to money depends upon all the links in the chain of causation. Using the previous notation, we have

$$\frac{dy}{dm} = \frac{dy}{di} \cdot \frac{di}{dr} \cdot \frac{dr}{dm}.$$

The chain rule can be used in conjunction with any of the rules of differentiation presented in the previous section. For example, consider the function $f(x) = g(h(x))$, where $g(x) = x^3$ and $h(x) = x^2$. Using the chain rule and the power rule, we have

$$f'(x) = 3 \cdot (h(x))^2 \cdot h'(x) = 3 \cdot (x^2)^2 \cdot 2x = 6x^5.$$

You may have noticed that this is a somewhat trivial example of the use of the chain rule since

$$f(x) = (x^2)^3 = x^6.$$

The simpler specification of the power rule provides a more direct evaluation of $f'(x) = 6x^5$. But, in many cases, the chain rule provides a simpler method for finding a derivative than does the power rule. For example, consider the function

$$y = (2 + 3x^2)^{20}.$$

It would be extremely tedious to multiply out this function and then use the power rule. Instead, it is much easier to use the general form of the power function, where $h(x) = (2 + 3x^2)$ and $g(x) = x^{20}$, to get

$$y = 20 \cdot (2 + 3x^2)^{19} \cdot 6x = 120x \cdot (2 + 3x^2)^{19}.$$

The Chain Rule and General Rules of Differentiation

The chain rule provides a powerful way to obtain more general forms of the rules presented in the previous section. We present some of these rules here.

General Power Rule For the function $f(x) = k[h(x)]^n$,

$$f'(x) = k \cdot n \cdot [h(x)]^{n-1} \cdot h'(x).$$

This rule combines the chain rule, where $h(x)$ is the inside function and $k[x]^n$ is the outside function, with the power rule presented in the previous section. In a similar fashion, combining the chain rule with the rule for the derivative of exponential functions gives us the general rule for exponential functions.

General Exponential Function Rule For the function $f(x) = e^{h(x)}$,

$$f'(x) = e^{h(x)} \cdot h'(x).$$

Some examples demonstrate the use of these general rules of differentiation. The derivative of

$$f(x) = [g(x) \cdot h(x)]^n$$

is

$$f'(x) = n[g(x) \cdot h(x)]^{n-1}[g'(x) \cdot h(x) + h'(x) \cdot g(x)].$$

The derivative of

$$f(x) = e^{x^2}$$

is

$$f'(x) = 2x \cdot e^{x^2}.$$

The derivative of

$$f(x) = (e^x)^2$$

is

$$f'(x) = 2e^x \cdot e^x = 2(e^x)^2.$$

Note that the third example switches the inside and outside functions from the second example and that the derivatives in these two examples differ.

Other Rules of Differentiation

The chain rule can also be used in conjunction with the rules presented earlier to evaluate the derivatives of other types of functions. The chain rule, the power function rule, and the product rule can be used to derive the rule for the derivative of a quotient.

Quotient Rule The derivative of $f(x) = \dfrac{g(x)}{h(x)}$ is

$$f'(x) = \frac{g'(x)\cdot h(x) - h'(x)\cdot g(x)}{[h(x)]^2}.$$

To prove this, define the function $j(x) = [h(x)]^{-1}$. From the general power rule, we have

$$\frac{d(j(x))}{dx} = -1\cdot[h(x)]^{-2}\cdot h'(x).$$

From the product rule, we have

$$\frac{d(f(x))}{dx} = g'(x)\cdot j(x) + j'(x)\cdot g(x).$$

Substituting the derivative $j'(x)$ into the result from the product rule gives us the quotient rule. An example of the quotient rule is that the derivative of the function

$$r(x) = \frac{(x+1)^2}{(x-1)^2}$$

is

$$r'(x) = \frac{2(x+1)\cdot(x-1)^2 - 2(x-1)\cdot(x+1)^2}{(x-1)^4}$$
$$= \frac{2(x+1)(x-1) - (x+1)^2}{(x-1)^3}.$$

The following application makes use of the quotient rule.

The Money Multiplier and the Great Depression

The money supply is a key macroeconomic policy variable. Central banks, charged with the control of the money supply, actually control only the stock of currency in circulation, so-called **high-powered money.** The supply of money that is more directly linked to the determination of macroeconomic aggregates, like unemployment and inflation, is a multiple of the stock of currency in circulation and includes bank deposits as well as currency in circulation. With fractional reserve banking, whereby banks do not need to back fully their liabilities with reserves, the money supply is larger than the amount of currency in circulation. The **money multiplier,** which represents the relationship between the stock of currency in circulation and the money supply, is itself influenced by the reserves held by banks as well as by people's choices concerning the relative amount of liquid assets they wish to hold as currency rather than as checkable deposits.

At times, the money multiplier can change dramatically. These swings in the value of the money multiplier alter the money supply. For example, the onset of the Great Depression of the 1930s was marked by a large contraction in the money supply as a result of a decrease in the money multiplier. Milton Friedman and Anna Schwartz, in their classic study *A Monetary History of the United States, 1867–1960,* argue that this monetary contraction was the primary cause of the Great Depression.[2]

Friedman and Schwartz link the decrease in the money multiplier to two responses to widespread bank failures in the early 1930s: an increase in the public's desired holdings of currency as compared to checkable deposits and an increase in the reserves held by banks. The consequences for the money multiplier can be understood by analyzing how the stock of currency in circulation is translated to a larger money supply through fractional reserve banking. Under fractional reserve banking, a bank that receives \$10,000 of currency in the form of a deposit retains a portion, say \$1,000, as reserves and lends out the rest. This lending takes the form of checkable deposits that borrowers can then draw down. The money supply held by the public, M, is the sum of the stock of currency they hold, C, and the value of their checkable deposits at commercial banks, D, such that

$$M = C + D.$$

The currency in circulation, denoted as H to represent high-powered money, is the sum of currency held by the public, C, and the reserves held by banks, R, such that

$$H = C + R.$$

These two relationships can be combined to show that

$$\frac{M}{H} = \frac{C + D}{C + R}.$$

This can be rewritten to show the relationship between the money supply and the stock of high-powered money as

$$M = \left(\frac{C + D}{C + R}\right)H.$$

The term in parentheses can be rewritten by dividing both the numerator and the denominator by D to give us

$$M = \left(\frac{c + 1}{c + r}\right)H = \theta H,$$

[2]See Milton Friedman and Anna Schwartz, *A Monetary History of the United States*, 1867–1960 (Princeton, NJ: Princeton University Press for National Bureau of Economic Research, 1963).

where $c = C/R$ is the **currency-deposit ratio** $(c > 0)$, $r = R/D$ is the **reserve ratio** $(0 < r < 1)$, and the money multiplier is $\theta = c + 1/c + r$. The currency-deposit ratio reflects the public's relative desire for holding its liquid assets in the form of currency rather than as checkable deposits, while the reserve ratio reflects both legal requirements facing banks as well as banks' goal of meeting depositors' demands for withdrawals.

It is clear that the money multiplier, θ, decreases with an increase in the reserve ratio, r. Thus, for any stock of high-powered money, the money supply falls with an increase in the reserve ratio. It is less clear how an increase in the currency-deposit ratio affects the money multiplier, however, since c appears in both the numerator and the denominator of the money multiplier. We can use the quotient rule to see how a change in c affects θ. First define $g(c) = (c + 1)$ and $h(c) = (c + r)$, and note that $g'(c) = 1$ and $h'(c) = 1$. Then, using the quotient rule, we have

$$\begin{aligned}\frac{d\theta}{dc} &= \frac{g'(c)\,h(c) - h'(c)\,g(c)}{(h'(c))^2}\\ &= \frac{(c + r) - (c + 1)}{(c + r)^2}\\ &= \frac{r - 1}{(c + r)^2} < 0\end{aligned}$$

since, as noted above, the reserve ratio is less than 1. This result shows that an increase in the currency-deposit ratio reduces the money multiplier and, for any stock of high-powered money, reduces the money supply.

Friedman and Schwartz show that the stock of high-powered money increased by $17\frac{1}{2}\%$ between August 1929 and March 1933. However, the combined effects of an increase in the currency-deposit ratio and an increase in the reserve ratio led to an overall decline of the money supply of 35%. Thus, the perception of monetary ease as a result of the increase in the stock of high-powered money was belied by the fact of monetary tightness as a result of the collapse of the money multiplier. The consequences of this mistake were, in the words of Friedman and Schwartz, tragic.

Another application of the chain rule, along with the general rule concerning the derivative of an exponential function, provides the rule for taking the derivative of logarithmic functions. We begin with the special case of $f(x) = \ln(x)$.

Natural Logarithmic Function Rule The derivative of $f(x) = \ln(x)$, is

$$f'(x) = \frac{d\ln x}{dx} = \frac{1}{x}.$$

This rule can be proved by considering the composite function

$$h(x) = e^{\ln(x)},$$

where the exponential function is the outside function and the logarithmic function is the inside function. Of course this is just the function $h(x) = x$ with derivative $h'(x) = 1$.

But, by the chain rule, we see that this is also equal to

$$h'(x) = \frac{d\ln(x)}{dx} \cdot e^{\ln(x)} = \frac{d\ln(x)}{dx} \cdot x.$$

Since we also have $h'(x) = 1$, setting these two expressions for the derivative equal to each other and rearranging, we obtain the rule given previously.

It is straightforward to apply this rule to the derivatives of logarithms with bases other than *e*. Recall from the discussion in Chapter 3 that

$$\log_b(x) = \frac{\ln(x)}{\ln(b)}.$$

The general rule for logarithms with other bases follows directly.

Logarithmic Function Rule The derivative of $f(x) = \log_b(x)$ is

$$\frac{d\log_b(x)}{dx} = \frac{1}{x} \cdot \frac{1}{\ln(b)}.$$

A more general rule concerning the derivatives of natural logarithmic functions of the form $\ln(h(x))$ can be derived by using the chain rule and the rule for the derivative of a natural logarithmic function.

General Natural Logarithmic Function Rule The derivative of $f(x) = \ln(h(x))$ is

$$f'(x) = \frac{d(\ln(h(x))}{dx} = \frac{h'(x)}{h(x)}.$$

An application of the rule for the derivative of a logarithmic function is that the derivative of

$$f(x) = \ln(x^n)$$

is

$$f'(x) = \frac{nx^{n-1}}{x^n} = \frac{n}{x}.$$

Applying the logarithmic function rule and the quotient rule, we find that the derivative of

$$f(x) = \ln\left(\frac{g(x)}{h(x)}\right)$$

is

$$f'(x) = \left[\frac{g'(x)}{h(x)} - \frac{h'(x) \cdot g(x)}{[h(x)]^2}\right] \div \left[\frac{g(x)}{h(x)}\right] = \left[\frac{g'(x)}{g(x)} - \frac{h'(x)}{h(x)}\right].$$

Alternatively, we could have derived this rule by noting that

$$f(x) = \ln\left(\frac{g(x)}{h(x)}\right) = \ln(g(x)) - \ln(h(x)),$$

and, by the logarithmic function rule, we obtain the same solution for $f'(x)$.

Sustainability of Deficits

An important fiscal policy issue is whether budget deficits are sustainable. Budget deficits can be sustained in the long run if the debt-to-GDP ratio is not increasing. The government's debt represents its accumulated budget deficits. The government's debt increases when there is a budget deficit and decreases when there is a budget surplus. As we will see, however, it is not necessary to have a budget surplus to have a declining debt-to-GDP ratio.

Define the debt-to-GDP ratio at time t as $Q(t)$, the value of the government debt as $B(t)$, and national income as $Y(t)$, So

$$Q(t) = \frac{B(t)}{Y(t)}.$$

The government's deficit at any moment equals the change in the level of its debt, that is, $dB(t)/dt$. When the government has a balanced budget, $dB(t)/dt = 0$; when it runs a budget deficit, $dB(t)/dt > 0$; and when it runs a budget surplus, $dB(t)/dt < 0$.

A sustainable fiscal policy is one where $Q(t)$ is either constant or declining over time; that is, $dQ(t)/dt$ is either zero or negative. Conditions consistent with a constant value of $dQ(t)/dt$ can be found through the use of either the quotient rule or the logarithmic rule. Using the quotient rule, we find that the derivative of $B(t)/Y(t)$ with respect to time is

$$\frac{dQ(t)}{dt} = \frac{dB(t)}{dt} \cdot \frac{1}{Y(t)} - B(t) \cdot \frac{dY(t)}{dt} \cdot \frac{1}{(Y(t))^2}.$$

It is easy to see that it is not necessary for $dB(t)/dt$ to equal zero for $dQ(t)/dt$ to equal zero. Instead, the condition for $dQ(t)/dt$ to equal zero is

$$\frac{dQ(t)}{dt} = 0 \quad \text{if} \quad \frac{dB(t)}{dt} \cdot \frac{1}{Y(t)} = B(t) \cdot \frac{dY(t)}{dt} \cdot \frac{1}{(Y(t))^2}$$

or

$$\frac{dQ(t)}{dt} = 0 \quad \text{if} \quad \frac{dB(t)}{dt} \cdot \frac{1}{B(t)} = \frac{dY(t)}{dt} \cdot \frac{1}{Y(t)}.$$

You may recognize the variables expressed in this manner as instantaneous growth rates. This last condition shows that a fiscal policy is sustainable (that is, the instantaneous growth rate of the debt-to-GDP ratio is zero or negative), even if there is a budget deficit ($dB/dt > 0$), as long as the growth rate of the economy is at least equal to the growth rate of the debt.

Using the rule for the derivative of natural logarithms, we can obtain the same result. The natural logarithm of the debt-to-GDP ratio is

$$\ln(Q(t)) = \ln\left(\frac{B(t)}{Y(t)}\right) = \ln(B(t)) - \ln(Y(t)).$$

A straightforward application of the rule concerning the derivative of natural logarithms gives us the following derivative of this expression with respect to time:

$$\frac{dQ(t)}{dt} \cdot \frac{1}{Q(t)} = \frac{dB(t)}{dt} \cdot \frac{1}{B(t)} - \frac{dY(t)}{dt} \cdot \frac{1}{Y(t)}.$$

This shows the link between the instantaneous rate of change of the debt-to-GDP ratio and the instantaneous growth rates of the government debt and of real GDP.

The general form of the result in this application is widely used in economics. For any two variables that vary over time, the growth rate of the quotient of these two variables equals the growth rate of the variable that is the numerator minus the growth rate of the variable that is the denominator. For example, real money balances are defined as the ratio of nominal balances, $M(t)$, to the price level, $P(t)$. The instantaneous rate of change of real money balances equals

$$\frac{d(M(t)/P(t))}{dt} \cdot \frac{1}{(M(t)/P(t))} = \frac{dM(t)}{dt} \cdot \frac{1}{M(t)} - \frac{dP(t)}{dt} \cdot \frac{1}{P(t)}.$$

The first term on the right-hand side is the growth rate of the money supply, and the second term is the instantaneous rate of inflation (that is, the growth rate of prices).

Elasticities

An **elasticity** measures a specific form of responsiveness: the percentage change in one variable that accompanies a 1% change in another. An elasticity is not affected by the units used to measure variables since, as discussed previously, percentage changes are unit free. This is one reason why economic analysis includes many forms of elasticities, including price elasticity, supply elasticity, demand elasticity, and import elasticity. Also, economic functions are sometimes presented in a form where there is a constant elasticity. An application in this section offers an example where a constant-elasticity function better characterizes an empirical relationship than does a function with a changing elasticity.

The elasticity between two variables, $\epsilon_{y,x}$, is the ratio of percentage changes (which is also equal to the ratio of proportionate changes since the factors, 100%, cancel). Formally, an **arc elasticity** between y and x is

$$\epsilon_{y,x} = \frac{\Delta y/y}{\Delta x/x} = \frac{\Delta y}{\Delta x} \cdot \frac{x}{y},$$

where Δy and Δx represent discrete changes in y and x, respectively. A **point elasticity** represents an elasticity for very small changes in variables and is defined as

$$\epsilon_{y,x} = \frac{dy/y}{dx/x} = \frac{dy}{dx} \cdot \frac{x}{y}.$$

Using the rules of differentiation, we can determine the point elasticity of a function. For example, consider the general form of a linear demand function,

$$q = \alpha - \beta p.$$

The elasticity of this function is its derivative of quantity q with respect to price p times the ratio p/q. That is,

$$\epsilon_{q,p} = \frac{dq}{dp} \cdot \frac{p}{q} = -\beta \frac{p}{q}.$$

The terms **elastic, unit elastic,** and **inelastic** represent elasticities that are, in absolute value, greater than 1, equal to 1, and less than 1, respectively. As shown in Figure 7.1, the elasticity of the linear demand curve changes along the curve since p and q appear in the elasticity. Substituting the value $\alpha/\beta - q/\beta$ for p in the elasticity formula, we find that this linear demand curve has unit elasticity (that is, $\epsilon_{q,p} = -1$) at the value $q = \alpha/2$, which corresponds to $p = \alpha/2\beta$. For prices above $\alpha/2\beta$, the demand curve is elastic (that is, $\epsilon_{q,p} < -1$ or $|\epsilon_{q,p}| > 1$), and at lower prices, the demand curve is inelastic (that is, $\epsilon_{q,p} > -1$ or $|\epsilon_{q,p}| < 1$).

The demand function

$$Q = \alpha P^{-\beta}$$

has constant elasticity since

$$\begin{aligned}
\epsilon_{Q,P} &= \frac{dQ}{dP} \cdot \frac{P}{Q} \\
&= -\alpha \beta P^{-\beta-1} \cdot \frac{P}{Q} \\
&= -\alpha \beta P^{-\beta-1} \cdot \frac{P}{\alpha P^{-\beta}} \\
&= -\beta.
\end{aligned}$$

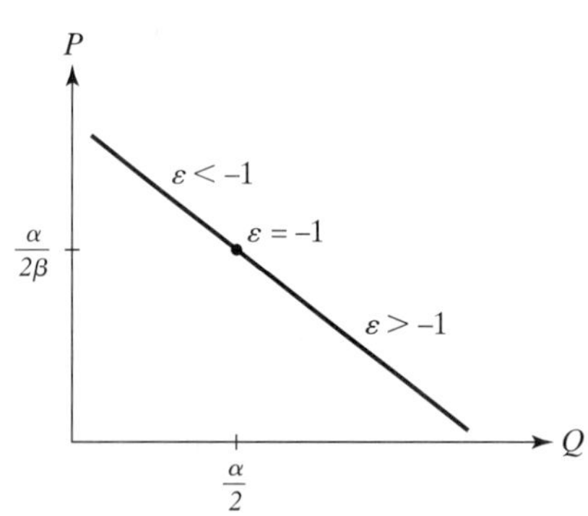

FIGURE 7.1 Elasticities of a Linear Demand Function

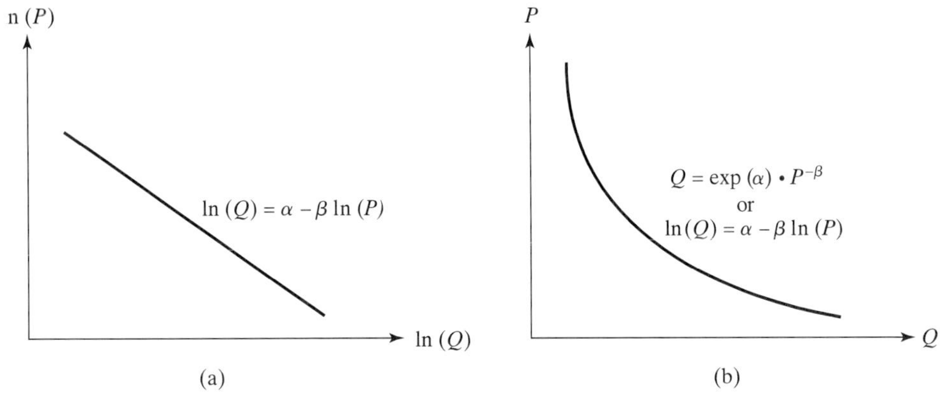

FIGURE 7.2 A Log-Line ar Demand Function

The monotonic transformation of this demand function,

$$\ln(Q) = \ln(\alpha) - \beta \ln(P),$$

also exhibits constant elasticity. This is a **log-linear** function since it links the logarithms of variables through a linear relationship. This downward-sloping demand function is presented in Figure 7.2(a) and (b). The axes of Figure 7.2(a) represent the logarithms of price and quantity. Therefore this demand function is a straight line with slope $-\beta$ in this plane. In Figure 7.2(b), the axes represent P and Q. In this plane, the demand curve is represented by a curve that is convex. The slope of this line (that is, dQ/dP) is not constant; but, along the line, proportionate change (that is, $(dQ/Q)/(dP/P)$) is constant, and therefore, this function exhibits constant elasticity.

The differential of this log-linear demand equation,

$$\frac{d\ln(Q)}{dQ}\,dQ = -\beta\,\frac{d\ln(P)}{dP}\,dP,$$

can be manipulated to show that the equation exhibits constant elasticity. The rules for differentiating a logarithmic function indicate that this expression can be rewritten as

$$\frac{1}{Q}\,dQ = -\beta\,\frac{1}{P}\,dP.$$

Rearranging terms, we have

$$\frac{dQ/Q}{dP/P} = -\beta,$$

which shows that this function has constant elasticity. More generally, we have

$$\epsilon_{y,x} = \frac{dy}{dx} \cdot \frac{x}{y} = \frac{dy/y}{dx/x} = \frac{d\ln(y)}{d\ln(x)}.$$

Infant Mortality and Income per Capita

Cross-country data for over three hundred countries presented in Figure 7.3(a) demonstrates wide variation in infant mortality rates and income per capita.[3] The relationship between infant mortality and income per capita revealed by this scatter plot, however, is not very informative. This figure only shows that there is a range of infant mortality rates at low income levels and there is also a range of income levels at which there is low infant mortality.

A clearer link between infant mortality and income per capita is provided in Figure 7.3(b). This figure plots the logarithm of infant mortality against the logarithm of income per capita. The data in this figure exhibit a clear linear relationship. Using the statistical tool of ordinary least squares, it is found that the line that best fits this relationship is

$$\ln(INF) = 7.52 - 0.55\ln(INC),$$

where INF is infant mortality and INC is income per capita. Thus the elasticity of infant mortality with respect to income per capita is -0.55. A 10% increase in income per capita is associated with a 5.5% drop in infant mortality rates in these data. This relationship is highly statistically significant.[4]

The branch of economics called **econometrics** uses statistical analysis to find the relationship among variables. Econometric analysis requires the specification of a functional form, that is, whether the line is to be fit to a simple linear combination, a quadratic combination, or a log-linear combination of the data, or to some other form. This example illustrates that the choice of the functional form is an important aspect of econometric analysis.

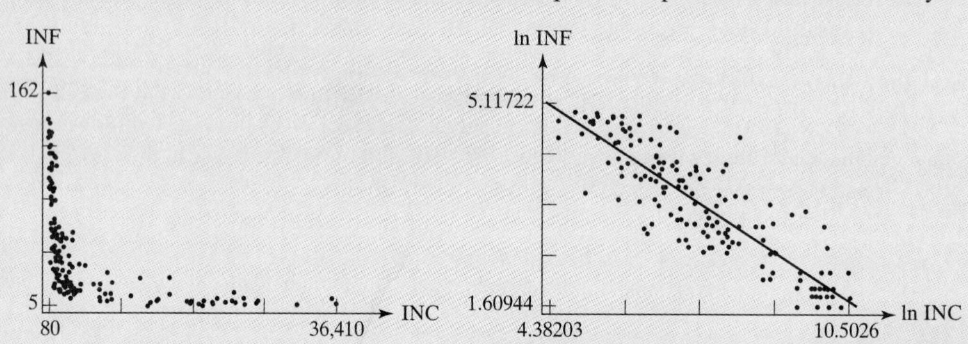

Infant Mortality and GNP/ Capita

(a)

Logarithms of Infant Mortality and Income/Capita

(b)

FIGURE 7.3 Infant Mortality and Income per Capita

The Incidence of a Tax Once Again

In Chapter 4 we use a linear model of demand and supply to investigate the incidence of a tax, that is, the distribution of the burden of the tax on consumers and producers. A more general form of the solution presented in that application can be obtained using elasticities and the techniques presented in this chapter.

---

[3] These data are in *The World Bank Atlas* 1995 (Washington DC: The World Bank, 1995).

[4] The t-statistic on the income coefficient is -31.3. The R^2 of the regression is 0.76.

As with the application in Chapter 4, we again consider the market for widgets. The quantity of widgets demanded by consumers is given by the general function $Q^D(P_C)$, where P_C is the price consumers face and we assume

$$\frac{dQ^D}{dP_C} < 0.$$

The quantity of widgets offered by producers is given by the general function $Q^S(P_P)$, where P_P is the price obtained by producers and we assume

$$\frac{dQ^S}{dP_P} > 0.$$

As in the application in Chapter 4, the difference between P_C and P_P is the tax levied on each widget. So

$$P_C = P_P + T.$$

We solve for the changes in prices due to a small increase in the tax from an initial tax of zero. As a comparative static analysis, we study the change from one equilibrium to another. In equilibrium,

$$Q^D(P_C) = Q^S(P_P).$$

We can take the differential of each side of this equilibrium relationship (see Chapter 6) to obtain

$$\frac{dQ^D}{dP_C} dP_C = \frac{dQ^S}{dP_P} dP_P,$$

where dP_C and dP_P are arbitrary changes in the price facing consumers and the price facing producers, respectively, from their initial values. Taking the differential of the relationship among prices and the tax, we have

$$dP_C = dP_P + dT.$$

Substituting this equation into the previous one, we get

$$\frac{dQ^D}{dP_C}(dP_P + dT) = \frac{dQ^S}{dP_P} dP_P$$

or

$$\left(\frac{dQ^D}{dP_C} - \frac{dQ^S}{dP_P}\right) dP_P = -\frac{dQ^D}{dP_C} dT.$$

At the initial tax rate of zero, we have $P_P = P_C = P$. We also have, at the initial equilibrium, $Q^D = Q^S = Q$. Multiplying each side of the above expression by P/Q gives us

$$\left(\frac{dQ^D}{dP_C} \cdot \frac{P}{Q} - \frac{dQ^S}{dP_P} \cdot \frac{P}{Q}\right) dP_P = -\frac{dQ^D}{dP_C} \cdot \frac{P}{Q} dT.$$

Defining the following elasticities of demand and supply evaluated at the original price and quantity P and Q as

$$\frac{dQ^D}{dP_C} \cdot \frac{P}{Q} = \epsilon^D < 0$$

$$\frac{dQ^S}{dP_P} \cdot \frac{P}{Q} = \epsilon^S > 0,$$

we have

$$(\epsilon^D - \epsilon^S)\, dP_P = -\epsilon^D\, dT.$$

Therefore we have

$$\frac{dP_P}{dT} = -\frac{\epsilon^D}{\epsilon^D - \epsilon^S} = -\frac{1}{1 - \epsilon^S/\epsilon^D}.$$

Since ϵ^D is negative and ϵ^S is positive, we see that

$$-1 < \frac{dP_P}{dT} < 0.$$

The price facing producers decreases by more for a given increase in the tax if the supply elasticity is small relative to the demand elasticity, and conversely, it decreases by less if the supply elasticity is large relative to the demand elasticity.

The change in the price facing consumers can easily be obtained by noting that

$$\frac{dP_C}{dT} = \frac{dP_P}{dT} + 1.$$

So

$$\begin{aligned}\frac{dP_C}{dT} &= 1 - \frac{\epsilon^D}{\epsilon^D - \epsilon^S}\\ &= -\frac{\epsilon^S}{\epsilon^D - \epsilon^S}\\ &= \frac{1}{1 - \epsilon^D/\epsilon^S}\end{aligned}$$

and

$$0 < \frac{dP_C}{dT} < 1.$$

The price facing consumers increases by more for a given increase in the tax if the demand elasticity is small relative to the supply elasticity, and conversely, it increases by less if the demand elasticity is large relative to the supply elasticity.

You can compare these results to those in the application in Chapter 4. In that application, we found that a given tax increase has a relatively larger effect on the price facing producers and a relatively smaller effect on the price facing consumers if quantity demanded is relatively more price sensitive than quantity supplied. Conversely, if quantity supplied is relatively more price sensitive than quantity demand, then a given tax increase causes a relatively big increase in consumers' price and a relatively small decrease in producers' price.

Exercises 7.2

1. Use the chain rule to find the derivative, $f'(x)$, of each function.
   (a) $f(x) = (x + 1)^3 + (x^2 - 2x)^2 - 5$
   (b) $f(x) = (2x + 4)^{99}$
   (c) $f(x) = (5x^2 + 10x + 3)^{20}$
   (d) $f(x) = [e^x]^{ab}$
   (e) $f(x) = [e^{x^a}]^b$
   (f) $f(x) = (e^{a+bx+cx^2})^{10}$
2. Use the quotient rule to differentiate each function.
   (a) $f(x) = \dfrac{(2x + 7)}{(x^2 - 1)}$
   (b) $f(x) = \dfrac{(bx^3 + cx^2 + x - 4)}{x}$
   (c) $f(x) = \dfrac{e^{2x}}{x^2}$
   (d) $f(x) = \dfrac{(3x + 2)^2}{x}$
3. Consider a total cost function $f(x)$ and its average cost function $A(x) = f(x)/x$.
   (a) Using the quotient rule, take the derivative of the average cost function $A'(x)$ to obtain a relationship between average cost and marginal cost, $f'(x)$.
   (b) When $A'(x) < 0$, is marginal cost greater or less than average cost? Is the average cost function decreasing or increasing in this scenario?
   (c) When $A'(x) > 0$, is marginal cost greater or less than average cost? How does this affect the slope of the average cost function?
   (d) If marginal cost equals average cost, what does this suggest about the slope of $A'(x)$?
4. Use the rules for differentiating logarithms to find the derivative of each function.
   (a) $f(x) = x^{-4} + \ln ax$
   (b) $f(x) = 4x^3 \ln x^2$
   (c) $f(x) = \ln x - \ln(1 + x)$
   (d) $f(x) = \ln\left(\dfrac{2x^2}{5x}\right)$
   (e) $f(x) = \log_2(6x)$
5. Nations are becoming increasingly interdependent, and so domestic economic events and policies can have a significant effect on other countries' economies. For

example, a change in the budget deficit (*def*) of Country *A* may affect domestic interest rates (i_d). A change in domestic rates may affect capital flows from abroad (k_f), which may have an impact on the international value of the domestic currency (e_d). A change in the value of the exchange rate usually has an impact on a country's trade balance (*tb*), so that a decrease in the exchange rate (measured in units of domestic currency) stimulates imports and depresses exports. The changing trade balance for Country *B*, which is simply the mirror image of the change to Country *A*'s trade balance, may lead to a change in economic activity in Country $B\,(y_f)$.

(a) Using the chain rule, express each of the given relationships as a derivative to create a chain that links Country *A*'s budget deficit and Country *B*'s economic activity ($dY/dDef$).

(b) Determine the direction of the impact (positive or negative) of each factor in the chain.

(c) What is the ultimate effect of an increase in Country *A*'s budget deficit on Country *B*'s economic activity?

6. The rule for the derivative of logarithms with bases other than *e* is

$$\frac{d\log_b(x)}{dx} = \frac{1}{x} \cdot \frac{1}{\ln_b},$$

as stated previously. Remembering that the general form of the derivative of a natural logarithmic function is

$$\frac{d(\ln(h(x)))}{dx} = \frac{h'(x)}{h(x)},$$

determine the general form of this rule.

7. Using the general form of the rule developed in question 6, find the derivative of each common logarithmic function

(a) $y = \log_2(2x + 3)$

(b) $y = \log_4 8x^2$

(c) $y = x^3 \log_2 x$

(d) $y = \dfrac{\log_3 x}{2x}$

8. A standard tool of economic analysis is the Cobb-Douglas production function. This function shows how much output (Q) is produced with a given amount of labor (L) and capital (K) as follows: $Q = AK^{\alpha}L^{1-\alpha}$. The parameter A represents the efficiency of the economy, so A increases with technological change. Suppose that, over time, efficiency, capital, and labor each grow at the rates

$$A(t) = A_0 e^{ct}, \quad K(t) = K_0 e^{ft}, \quad \text{and} \quad L(t) = L_0 e^{gt},$$

where A_0, K_0, and L_0 are initial values for technology, capital, and labor, respectively, and c, f, and g are their respective rates of growth. What is the percentage growth rate of output in terms of the production parameters and the growth parameters c, f, and g? (*Hint*: Recall that the derivative of a natural logarithm is close to a percentage change.)

9. Using the formula $\epsilon_{y,x} = (dy/dx) \cdot (x/y)$, determine the point elasticity of each function. Specify whether these elasticities are elastic, unit elastic, or inelastic. Assess whether the elasticities change given different values of x and y.
   (a) $y = 100 - 20x$, where $x = 4$
   (b) $y = 16 - 8x + x^2$, where $x = 1.5$
   (c) $\ln(y) = 6 - 0.5\ln(x)$, where $x = 3$
   (d) $y = 50x^{-2}$, where $x = 2$
10. In one of the applications in this section, it was found that a log-linear functional form provided a better estimate of the statistical relationship between infant mortality and income per capita than did a linear specification. Two other alternative functional forms that might be applied to estimate this link are the quadratic form and the simple linear form:

$$\text{Quadratic estimate: } INF = 88 - 0.011 \cdot INC - 0.35 \cdot INC^2$$

$$\text{Linear estimate: } INF = 77 - 4 \cdot INC$$

Using the following set of dollar-denominated, per capita income levels, determine the point elasticities at each level of income for both functional forms.

Country	1994 Per Capita Income
Sri Lanka	540
Venezuela	2,910
Sweden	27,010

11. Assume that Country *X* has no domestic production of widgets. Its demand for widgets, therefore, is based exclusively on imports. Consider the import demand function

$$Q_M = 20 - 0.5P_M,$$

where P_M is the price of imports.
   (a) At what quantity does this import demand curve exhibit unit elasticity, that is, $\epsilon_{q,p} = -1$ (or $|\epsilon_{q,p}| = 1$)? If $Q_M = 8$, is import demand elastic or inelastic? what if the quantity demanded rises to 11?
   (b) Now assume that the import demand function is written as a log-linear specification, $\ln(Q) = 20 - 0.5\ln(P)$. What is the elasticity of this function, and how would you characterize it (that is, elastic, inelastic, unit elastic)? What happens to the elasticity if the quantity demanded changes?
12. Consider again the market for widgets and the incidence of a tax on consumers' and producers' prices. The quantity of widgets demanded by consumers is

$$Q^D = 24 - 3P_C,$$

and the quantity of widgets offered by suppliers is given by the function

$$Q^S = 15 + 6P_P,$$

where Q^D and Q^S are the quantity of widgets demanded and supplied, respectively, and P_C and P_S are the consumers' and producers' prices. The relationship between consumers' and producers' prices can be defined by the function $P_C = P_P + T$.

(a) Assume, initially, that there is no tax so that $P_P = P_C = P$. What is the equilibrium price and quantity in the widget market?

(b) Assuming that $\epsilon^D < 0$, determine the elasticity of demand at the original equilibrium price and quantity.

(c) Assuming that $\epsilon^S > 0$, determine the elasticity of supply at the original equilibrium price and quantity.

(d) Now assume that a tax of 0.3 ($T = 0.3$) has been levied on widget production. Determine the impact that a change in T has on producers' prices with the formula

$$\frac{dP_P}{dT} = \frac{1}{1 - \epsilon^S/\epsilon^D}.$$

Determine the impact on consumers' prices with the formula

$$\frac{dP_C}{dT} = \frac{1}{1 - \epsilon^D/\epsilon^S}.$$

(e) Which price, P_C or P_P, responds more to the increase in T? Why? Calculate the new equilibrium quantity, consumers' price, and producers' price.

13. Assume now that the demand and supply of widgets are log-linear functions of the form

$$\ln(Q^D) = 10 - 2\ln(P) \quad \text{and} \quad \ln(Q^S) = 5 + 0.5\ln(P).$$

Repeat question 12, but assume that $T = 1.0$ in part (d). Recall that the original forms of the log-linear functions are

$$Q^D = e^{\alpha} p^{-\beta} \quad \text{and} \quad Q^S = e^{\theta} p^{\gamma}.$$

14. A person's productivity at a particular job may change with experience. Consider the following model of effective labor input, L,

$$L = 10(1 - e^{-0.1t}) + 2,$$

where L is a measure of the "effective labor input" of a particular worker and t is the worker's tenure (that is, years spent in a particular job). Use differentiation to determine the marginal change in the effective labor input with respect to time on the job, t. Provide a brief economic interpretation of the differences in these values of dL/dt.

7.3 THE SECOND DERIVATIVE

Several concepts in economics concern changes in the marginal contribution of a variable. For example, utility functions are assumed to exhibit diminishing marginal utility, and cost functions may have increasing marginal costs or decreasing marginal costs. We have seen that the economic concept of "the margin" corresponds to the mathematical concept of the derivative. Therefore changing marginal utility or changing marginal cost is reflected in a changing value of the derivative of a utility function or a changing value of the derivative of a cost function, respectively.

The derivative of a function is itself a function. The derivative of the derivative of a function is that function's **second derivative.** Alternatively, the second derivative can be thought of as representing the rate of change of the rate of change of the original function. More formally, we have the following definition.

Second Derivative The second derivative of a function

$$y = f(x),$$

denoted as $f''(x)$ or d^2y/dx^2, is the derivative of its first derivative. That is,

$$\frac{d^2y}{dx^2} = \frac{d}{dx}\left(\frac{dy}{dx}\right).$$

If the wording "derivative of the derivative" or "rate of change of the rate of change" seems convoluted, you might want to consider a simple example from physics that provides a natural interpretation of the second derivative. Consider a function that describes the position of an object at any moment in time. The derivative of that function with respect to time describes the object's velocity. The second derivative describes the change in velocity over time, that is, the object's acceleration.

An economic example of the interpretation of the first and second derivatives concerns prices, inflation, and the rate of change of inflation. Consider a function that describes the natural logarithm of the price level of an economy at any moment in time. The derivative of that function with respect to time represents the instantaneous inflation rate. The second derivative with respect to time represents the rate of change of inflation. To illustrate further, consider what happens during a hyperinflation when prices are rising rapidly at an increasing rate. The first derivative of the price function is positive since prices are rising. The second derivative is also positive since inflation is rising.

The second derivative of a function is found by simply applying the rules of differentiation to the first derivative. An example illustrates this. The quadratic tax revenue function from Chapter 6,

$$R(t) = 200t - 200t^2,$$

has the derivative

$$R'(t) = 200 - 400t.$$

The second derivative of the revenue function is simply the derivative of the first derivative:

$$R''(t) = \frac{dR'(t)}{dt} = \frac{d(200 - 400t)}{dt} = -400.$$

The first derivative of this function shows its rate of change. The function is increasing for tax rates less than 0.5 since $R'(t) > 0$ in this interval. The function is decreasing for tax rates greater than 0.5 since $R'(t) < 0$ in this range. The tangent line to the function has a slope of zero for $t = 0.5$ since this gives us $R'(t) = 0$.

The second derivative shows how the rate of change of the original function changes with the argument of the function. Any quadratic equation has a constant second derivative. This particular quadratic function has a negative second derivative, demonstrating that the slope of the function is decreasing with larger values of its argument.

Two Utility Functions

Standard microeconomic analysis is based upon certain assumptions concerning behavior. One assumption is that more of a good is preferred to less of a good **(nonsatiation).** In addition, sometimes the assumption is made that the extra benefit from consuming an additional unit of a good is greater when overall consumption of the good is lower than when it is higher **(diminishing marginal utility).**

An example of a utility function that exhibits both nonsatiation and diminishing returns is a **square root utility function.** This function specifies that the utility from consuming a certain amount of good c, $U(c)$, equals some parameter times the square root of the level of the good consumed as shown by

$$U(c) = \alpha\sqrt{c},$$

where α is a positive parameter and $c \geq 0$. The marginal utility function associated with this utility function is

$$U'(c) = \frac{1}{2} \cdot \frac{\alpha}{\sqrt{c}}.$$

This utility function exhibits nonsatiation since the marginal utility of consumption is always positive and, therefore, more of the good results in higher utility. This utility function also exhibits diminishing marginal utility since marginal utility decreases as the level of the consumption of the good rises. This is reflected by the fact that the second derivative of the utility function,

$$U''(c) = \frac{dU'(c)}{dc} = -\frac{\alpha}{4} \cdot c^{-3/2},$$

is negative for all positive values of c.

Another common specification for a utility function is the **logarithmic utility function**

$$U(c) = \beta \ln(c),$$

where β is a positive parameter and $c \geq 0$. This utility function also exhibits nonsatiation since the first derivative, representing marginal utility, is always positive. Using the rule for the derivative of natural logarithms, we find that marginal utility is

$$U'(c) = \frac{\beta}{c},$$

which is positive for all positive values of c. The utility function exhibits diminishing marginal utility since its second derivative,

$$U''(c) = -\frac{\beta}{c^2},$$

is negative for any positive value of c. Thus the logarithmic utility function, like the square root utility function, exhibits both nonsatiation and diminishing marginal utility.

Figures 7.4 and 7.5 illustrate the properties of these utility functions. The top panels of the figures feature the square root utility function and the logarithmic utility function. These panels show that higher levels of consumption lead to higher levels of utility. This is also reflected in the middle panels in each figure, which feature marginal utility for each utility function. Marginal utility is positive for all positive levels of consumption. The third panels in the figures give the second derivatives of the utility functions. These second derivatives are negative for all values of c, which reflects diminishing marginal utility.

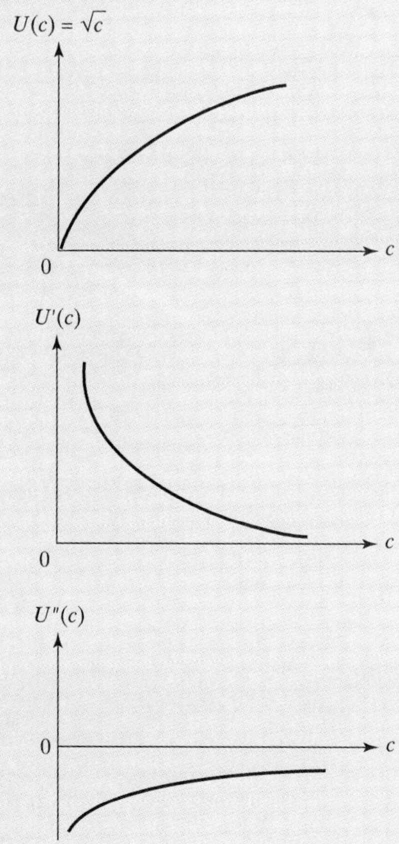

FIGURE 7.4 Square Root Utility Function

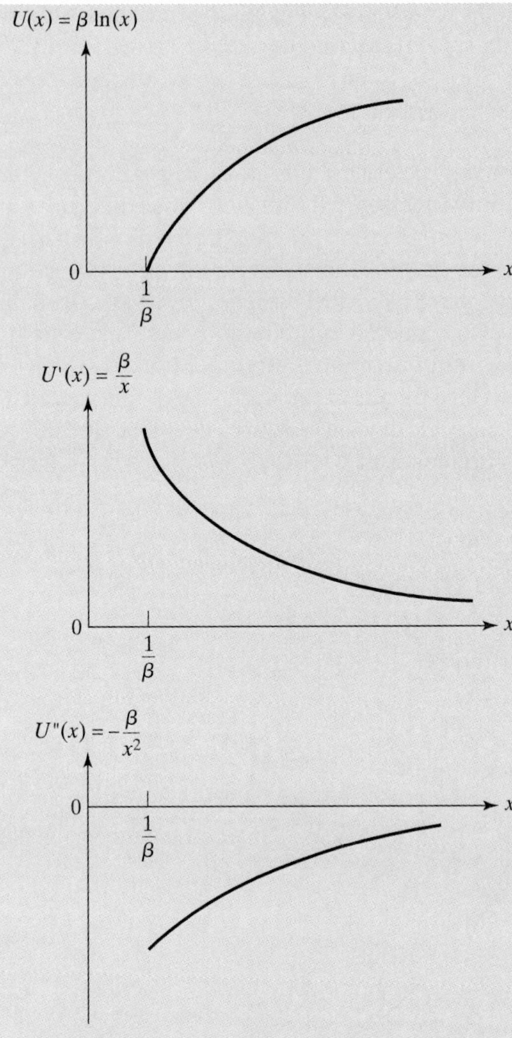

FIGURE 7.5 Logarithmic Utility Function

Concavity

The concavity of a function used in economics often corresponds to an important economic concept. For example, as shown previously, the concavity of a utility function, which illustrates how marginal utility changes with consumption, reflects the concept of diminishing marginal utility. Likewise, the concavity of a production function, which shows how marginal product declines with the increased use of an input, is the mathematical counterpart to the economic concept of diminishing returns to inputs.

The concavity of a function reflects its curvature. In Chapter 2 we define concavity with respect to the relationship between the value of a function over an interval and the secant line connecting the endpoints of that interval. A function is strictly convex over an interval if a secant line connecting any two points in that interval lies wholly above the graph of that function. A function is strictly concave over an interval if a secant line connecting any two points in that interval lies wholly below the graph of that function.

The sign of the second derivative of a function provides information on its curvature. Figure 7.6(a) and (b) exhibits functions with second derivatives that are negative everywhere. These functions are strictly concave. Figure 7.6(c) and (d) exhibits functions with second derivatives that are positive everywhere. These functions are strictly convex. The second derivative rules for concavity are as follows.

Strictly Concave A function $f(x)$ is strictly concave over an interval if $f''(x) < 0$ for all values of x in that interval.

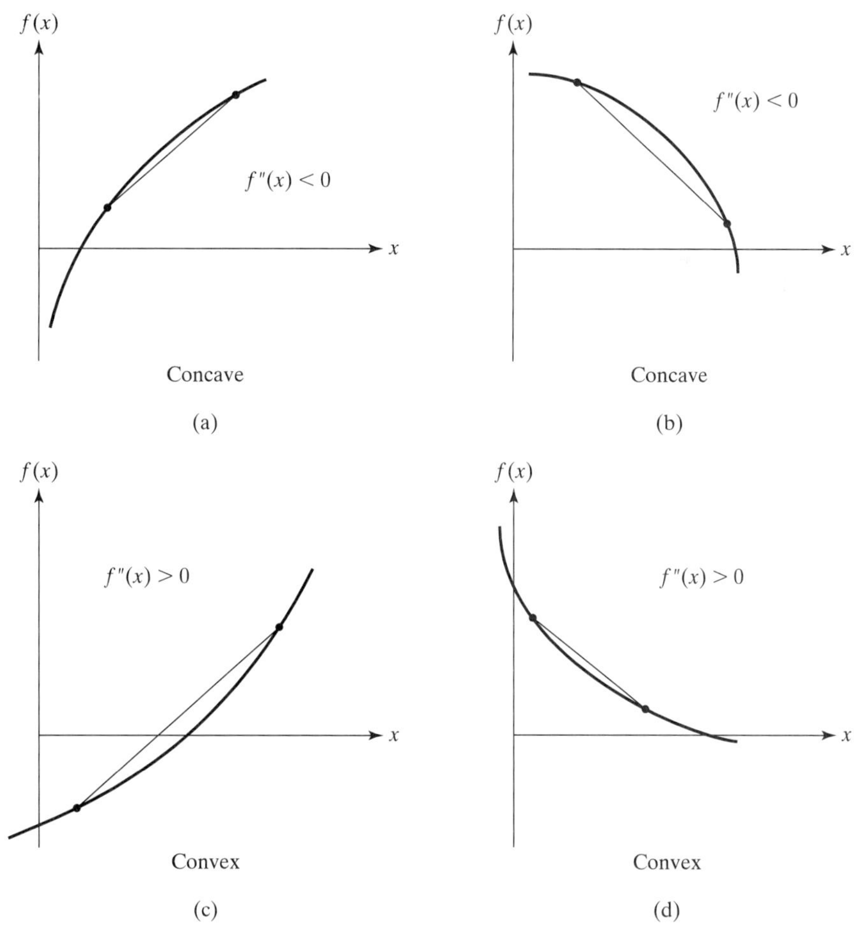

FIGURE 7.6 Concave and Convex Functions

Strictly Convex A function is strictly convex over an interval if $f''(x) > 0$ for all values of x in that interval.

Just as with the definitions of concave and convex functions in Chapter 2, a modified version of these definitions includes weak inequalities (that is, $\leq$ rather than $<$ and $\geq$ rather than $>$).

Concave A function $f(x)$ is concave over an interval if $f''(x) \leq 0$ for all values of x in that interval.

Convex A function is convex over an interval if $f''(x) \geq 0$ for all values of x in that interval.

Note that the second derivative conditions are sufficient but not necessary. For example, the second derivative of a function may equal zero when evaluated at some point within an interval in which the function is strictly convex. This is the case with the function

$$f(x) = 100 - x^4.$$

The second derivative of this function is

$$f''(x) = -12x^2.$$

This function is strictly concave over its entire domain even though $f''(0) = 0$.

Utility Functions and Risk Aversion

The curvature of a utility function is related to its implicit modeling of risk aversion. Consider the following situation. Suppose you could either receive a dozen cookies or, alternatively, play a game where you flip a coin and receive 18 cookies if the coin comes up heads and 6 cookies if it comes up tails. Which would you prefer?

The expected outcome from the coin-flip option weighs each outcome by its probability of occurring. The expected outcome from the coin-flip option,

$$\left(\frac{1}{2} \cdot 18 + \frac{1}{2} \cdot 6\right) = 12,$$

is the same as the expected outcome of getting a dozen cookies with certainty. Your choice of picking the gamble versus the certain outcome depends upon your attitude toward risk.

If you are risk-averse, then you prefer the certain outcome to the coin flip. The utility function in Figure 7.7(a) reflects this. Mathematically, the utility from the coin flip can be expressed as the utility from each outcome, weighted by the likelihood of that outcome. With this function, the utility from the certain outcome, $U(12)$, exceeds the expected utility of the outcomes under the coin-flip option,

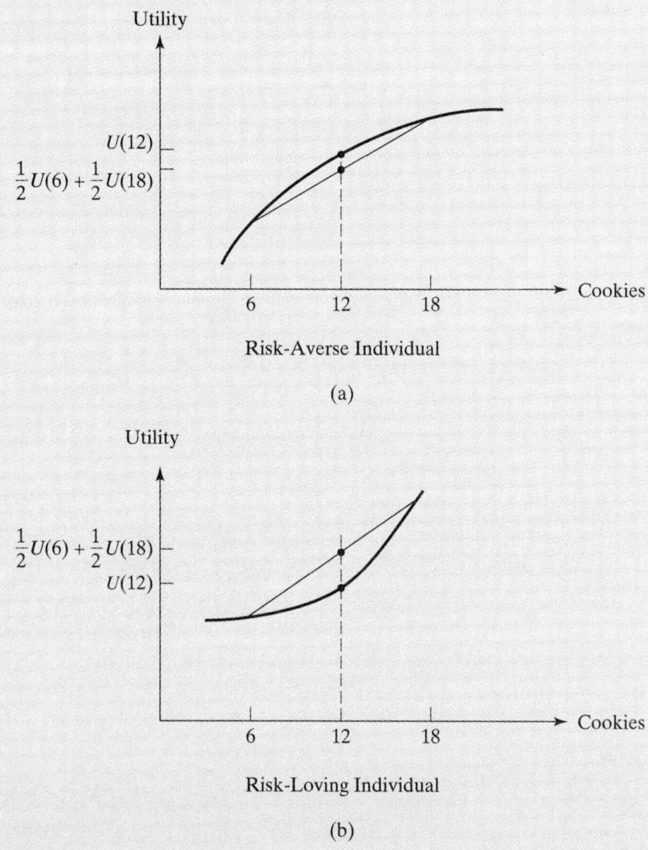

FIGURE 7.7 Utility Functions for Risk-Averse and Risk-Loving Individuals

$$\frac{1}{2} \cdot U(6) + \frac{1}{2} \cdot U(18).$$

If you are risk-loving, then your Utility function would be that in Figure 7.7(b). In this case the expected utility from the coin-flip option exceeds the certain utility from receiving a dozen cookies since, in this case,

$$\frac{1}{2} \cdot U(6) + \frac{1}{2} \cdot U(18) > U(12).$$

A utility function reflects risk aversion over an interval where it is concave. The square root and logarithmic functions discussed in this chapter imply risk aversion over their entire ranges. A utility function implies risk loving over an interval where it is convex. It is plausible to think of people exhibiting risk-loving behavior, at least over some ranges, since people gamble at casinos and buy lottery tickets even though the expected value of these activities is negative.

Concave utility functions that are more bowed reflect a higher degree of risk aversion. One specific way to measure the risk aversion associated with a utility function is to determine its **coefficient of relative risk aversion.** The coefficient of relative risk aversion, which we will call γ, is defined as

$$\gamma = -\frac{U''(c)\cdot c}{U'(c)}.$$

Using this formula, it is straightforward to show that the coefficient of relative risk aversion for the logarithmic utility function is constant and equals 1, while the coefficient of relative risk aversion for the square root utility function is constant and equals 1/2. Thus the logarithmic utility function, which is more bowed than the square root utility function, implies more relative risk aversion than the square root utility function.

Linearization of Functions and Taylor Series

It is often useful to be able to express a function in a linear form. For example, the tools of matrix algebra can be used with systems of linear equations. Standard econometric specifications require linearity. In this section we show how the tools of calculus can be used to find a linear approximation to a nonlinear equation.

Consider a general nonlinear function

$$y = f(x),$$

which is depicted in Figure 7.8. We want to find a linear function that serves as an approximation for this function around the point $x = a$. The simplest approximation is the function

$$g(x) = a.$$

Of course this constant-valued function does not work well once we move from the point $f(a)$. A better approximation is given by a linear function of the form

$$h(x) = f(a) + b \cdot (x - a).$$

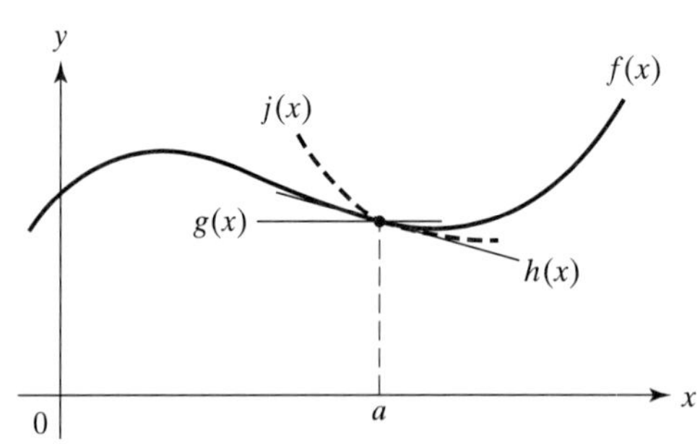

FIGURE 7.8 Taylor Series Approximations

What value of b is best? As discussed in Chapter 6, the differential is the equation for the tangent line to the function at the point $x = a$. Therefore the best linear approximation to the function around the point $x = a$ is

$$h(x) = f(a) + f'(a) \cdot (x - a),$$

where $f'(a)$ is the derivative of the function evaluated at $x = a$.

A better approximation of this function allows for some curvature. The general form of a quadratic approximation to this function is

$$j(x) = f(a) + f'(a) \cdot (x - a) + c(x - a)^2.$$

What is the best value for c? Just as we want the slope of the linear approximation to be the same as the slope of a line tangent to the function around $x = a$, we want the rate of change of the slope of the quadratic approximation to be equal to the rate of change of the rate of change of the function around that point. This means that we want to pick c such that

$$j''(x) = f''(x).$$

The second derivative of $j(x)$ is $j''(x) = 2c$. For $j''(x)$ to equal $f''(x)$ at $x = a$, we need

$$c = \frac{1}{2} f''(a).$$

Thus the quadratic approximation to the function around the point $x = a$ is

$$j(x) = f(a) + f'(a) \cdot (x - a) + \frac{1}{2} f''(a) \cdot (x - a)^2.$$

If we continued this for cubic or higher-degree approximations, we would find that the nth-degree approximation to the function $f(x)$, which we call $m(x)$, around the point $x = a$ is

$$m(x) = \frac{f(a)}{0!} + \frac{f'(a)}{1!} \cdot (x - a) + \frac{f''(a)}{2!} \cdot (x - a)^2 + \cdots + \frac{f^{(n)}(a)}{n!} \cdot (x - a)^n,$$

where $f^{(n)}(a)$ is the nth derivative of $f(x)$ evaluated at $x = a$ and, as discussed in Chapter 5,

$$n! = n \times (n - 1) \times (n - 2) \times \cdots \times 3 \times 2 \times 1,$$

where $n!$ is read as "n factorial." By definition, $0! = 1$ and also we have $1! = 1$. The function $m(x)$ is called the ***n*th-degree Taylor series expansion** of $f(x)$ around the point $x = a$.

For example, consider the function

$$y = e^{x/2} - e^{-x/2}$$

expanded around the point $x = 2$. The linear approximation to this function is

$$h(x) = [e^1 - e^{-1}] + \left(\frac{1}{2}[e^1 + e^{-1}]\right) \cdot (x - 2).$$

TABLE 7.1 Percentage Deviation of Taylor Series Expansions from Original Function

	Percentage Deviation of Original function, $f(x)$, from	
	Linear Approximation, $h(x)$	Quadratic Approximation, $j(x)$
x	$\left(\frac{h(x) - f(x)}{f(x)} \times 100\%\right)$	$\left(\frac{j(x) - f(x)}{f(x)} \times 100\%\right)$
1.4	−6.1	0.9
1.7	−1.3	0.09
1.9	−0.13	0.003
2.0	0	0
2.1	−0.12	−0.003
2.3	−1.0	−0.06
2.6	−3.5	−0.43

The quadratic approximation, $j(x)$, is

$$j(x) = [e^1 - e^{-1}] + \left(\frac{1}{2}[e^1 - e^{-1}]\right) \cdot (x - 2) + \left(\frac{1}{8}[e^1 - e^{-1}]\right) \cdot (x - 2)^2.$$

Table 7.1 presents the percentage deviation of the linear approximation ($h(x)$) and the quadratic approximation ($j(x)$) of this function from its actual value. Note that the quadratic Taylor series expansion, $j(x)$, more closely approximates the original function than does the linear Taylor series expansion, $h(x)$. Note also that the difference between either approximation and the original function increases with the distance from 2, the value of x around which each approximation is calculated.

Exercises 7.3

1. Find the second derivative of each function.
   (a) $y = 9 - 3x + 7x^2 - x^3$
   (b) $y = \dfrac{4x+5}{x}$
   (c) $y = \ln 4x$
   (d) $y = x^2e^x$
   (e) $y = (x^{-6})^4$
2. Differentiate $f(x) = 3x^{8/3}$ three times. Show that the third derivative of this function cannot be evaluated at $x = 0$.
3. Determine whether each function is convex or concave. Do any of the functions exhibit both convexity and concavity? What does this imply about the second derivative? Assume that the interval is the set of real numbers unless otherwise indicated.
   (a) $y = 4 - 4x + x^2$

(b) $y = 6x^{1/2}, 0 < x < \infty$

(c) $y = 18 + 12x - 6x^2 + x^3$

(d) $y = \ln 3x^3, 0 < x < \infty$

4. Consider the function $y = 1/3x^3 - 4x^2 + 6x + 8$ over the interval [0, 4]. Use the second derivative to determine whether the function is concave or convex. Confirm your results with the definitions for concavity and convexity found in Chapter 2, where a function is

$$\text{Concave: if } f(\lambda x^A + (1-\lambda)x^B) \geq \lambda f(x^A) + (1-\lambda)f(x^B) \quad \text{and}$$
$$\text{Convex: if } f(\lambda x^A + (1-\lambda)x^B) \leq \lambda f(x^A) + (1-\lambda)f(x^B).$$

Assume that $\lambda = 0.4, x^A = 0$, and $x^B = 4$.

5. Consider the function $f(x) = x^6 + 8x$. Find the second derivative of this function, and evaluate it over the interval $-2 < x < 2$. Is this function concave or convex? Can you use the term "strictly" to qualify the curvature of this function?

6. The law of diminishing marginal returns states that the incremental output obtained from additional units of a variable input, if all other inputs are held constant, decreases as more of the variable input is added. Geometrically, this means that the slope of the total product curve is decreasing and the slope of the marginal product curve is negative. This can be determined by taking the derivative of the marginal product function, which is the same as taking the second derivative of the total product function. Consider the following short-run production function in which capital is held constant and labor is the variable input:

$$Q = f(K_0, L) = 50K^{1/3}L^{2/3}.$$

Assume that capital is held constant at $K = 27$. Calculate the total product and the marginal product of labor. Can you determine if this production function exhibits diminishing marginal returns to labor?

7. The Stone-Geary utility function is written as

$$u = \ln U = \sum_{i=1}^{n} \beta_i \ln (q_i - \gamma_i),$$

where u is the utility index; q_i is commodity i, $0 < \beta_i < 1$, $\gamma_i > 0$; and $q_i - \gamma_i > 0$. Find the marginal utility of this function with respect to q_i. What is the significance of a positive marginal utility? Find the second derivative of this function. Does the function exhibit diminishing marginal utility? What does the second derivative suggest about the curvature of the original utility function?

8. Suppose each equation below is a utility function for the consumption of cookies, c. What restrictions on the parameters (for example, positive, negative, less than 1, and so forth) are required for the utility function to reflect that utility rises at a decreasing rate with the number of cookies consumed? (Assume that $c > 0$.)

(a) $U(c) = \Psi + ae^{\beta c}$, where the parameters are a, β and Ψ

(b) $U(c) = \theta\, c^{\lambda}$, where the parameters are θ and λ

9. Consider the following function, which links the level of consumption of a good, x, to the utility it provides:

$$U(x) = -\left(\frac{1}{\alpha}\right)e^{-\alpha x}.$$

Find the coefficient of relative risk aversion

$$\gamma = -\frac{U''(x) \cdot x}{U'(x)},$$

which determines the function's degree of risk aversion. Find the coefficient of absolute risk aversion

$$\theta = -\frac{U''(x)}{U'(x)}$$

for this utility function.

10. Find the coefficient of absolute risk aversion

$$\theta = -\frac{U''(c)}{U'(c)}$$

for the square root function $U(c) = a\sqrt{c}$ and the logarithmic function $U(c) = \beta \ln(c)$.

11. Using the Taylor series expansion formula, find the linear and quadratic approximations to each function, expanded around the point $x = 2$. Evaluate the Taylor series expansions at $\Delta x = 0.1$, and determine the deviation of the approximations from each function's actual value.
    (a) $f(x) = 3x^2 - 5x + 1$
    (b) $f(x) = \ln(2x)$
    (c) $f(x) = e^{3x}$
12. Find the nth-degree Taylor approximation for $f(x) = e^x$ around the point $x = 0$.

Summary

This chapter puts into practice the intuition developed in Chapter 6 by showing how to differentiate a wide range of functions. Many types of functions you will encounter in economics can be differentiated by a straightforward application of the rules presented in Section 7.1. Other functions may be differentiated by the use of these rules along with the chain rule.

Chapter 8 extends the analysis here by looking at functions that have more than one argument. As is shown in that chapter, the differentiation of these types of functions does not require a new set of tools. Instead, the rules learned in this chapter, appropriately applied and interpreted, can be used for functions with more than one argument.

The rules presented in this chapter are used extensively in economics. A particularly important set of applications of these rules concerns optimization and extreme values. We turn to this topic in Chapters 9, 10, and 11.

Chapter 8

Multivariate Calculus

Economic analysis often proceeds by considering the consequences of a certain event, *ceteris paribus,* that is, holding "everything else equal." For example, economists typically analyze the effects of an expansionary monetary policy while holding constant such other exogenous factors as fiscal policy, oil prices, or productivity advances. The advantage of this approach is that it identifies the exclusive impact of the variable under study rather than confounding its effect with the effect of other variables.

Of course the real world seldom offers a situation where one and only one variable changes at a time. The tendency for economists to hedge their predictions based upon the possibility of unforeseen changes in other factors led President Harry Truman to state in frustration that he would prefer to be served by a "one-armed economist" who was precluded from saying "...while on the other hand ...".

Economic models typically include several exogenous variables since the real world seldom offers simple *uni*variate economic relationships between one exogenous variable and an endogenous variable. A *multi*variate function has more than one variable as an argument. An analysis of these functions requires a set of mathematical tools like the derivative. The discussion of the derivative in the previous two chapters, however, was in the context of univariate functions. In this chapter we extend the rules of differentiation to include multivariate functions.

There is a close link between the material presented in this chapter and the discussion of derivatives and the rules of differentiation in a univariate setting. As in the univariate case, the derivative of a multivariate function with respect to one of its arguments represents the rate of change in the value of that function due to a very small change in that argument. In fact you do not need to learn a new multivariate version of the set of rules for differentiation. Instead, you need to keep in mind the concept that the derivative in the multivariate case explicitly holds constant the effects of all other variables. This fits in naturally with your training in other economic courses in which you learn to consider effects of changes in variables, *ceteris paribus.*

The concept of *ceteris paribus* is introduced in this text in Chapter 4. There, in the context of a discussion of comparative statics, *ceteris paribus* refers to changing the value of one exogenous variable in a system of linear equations. In this chapter we learn how to extend this method to differentiation of nonlinear equations.

To introduce the concept of the effect of a change in one variable, *ceteris paribus,* we present, in the next section, an example showing how wage differences between men and women may reflect a variety of factors. This example focuses on a qualitative difference between two groups. As we learned in the previous chapters, the derivative reflects the effect of very small changes in the argument of a function. The difference in gender is not incremental, however, so, in the following section, we discuss wage determination as a function of a variable that can vary by small amounts. The examples in the next sections demonstrate the relationship between the derivative of a multivariate function with respect to one of its arguments and the derivative of a univariate function. The multivariate counterparts to other concepts taught in the previous two chapters, the differential and the derivative of composite functions, are also presented in this chapter.

8.1 *CETERIS PARIBUS* AND MULTIVARIATE FUNCTIONS

Often we wish to consider the effect of a change in one and only one of the arguments of a multivariate function to isolate the influence of that factor. To illustrate this, we discuss, in this section, a simplified version of how economists look at wage determination among a group of individuals, with a particular focus on the presence of discrimination. More broadly, the examples in this section illustrate the use of the intellectual device of *ceteris paribus.*

Data from surveys of large numbers of individuals enable economists to examine the possible determinants of wages across individuals. Labor economics suggests that an individual's wage depends upon a number of factors, including education, training, and years on the job. Economists look for evidence of discrimination by determining if factors such as gender or race also significantly affect wages, with the effect of other factors held constant.

As a simple example of this, suppose a survey finds that the average wage paid to women is \$10.00 per hour and the average wage paid to men is \$14.00 per hour. This survey also finds that the average number of years a person works for a particular firm (which is called tenure) is four years for women and six years for men. One possible explanation for this difference is that there is a univariate relationship between hourly wages, W, and tenure, T, and it is

$$W = 2 + 2T.$$

This relationship implies that groups with less tenure have lower wages. This difference across groups, however, would not be viewed as discrimination by many economists since the determinant of the wage of any individual is independent of his or her affiliation with a particular group. Thus evidence showing that women are paid, on average, lower hourly wages than men may just reflect the fact that women tend to have, on average, less tenure than men. This is illustrated in Figure 8.1(a).

Finding evidence of discrimination requires identifying differences in wages associated with gender, while holding constant other factors that affect wages, such as age, experience, and education. In such a case, women and men would face different returns in the labor market based solely on gender. Suppose that the slope of the wage-age

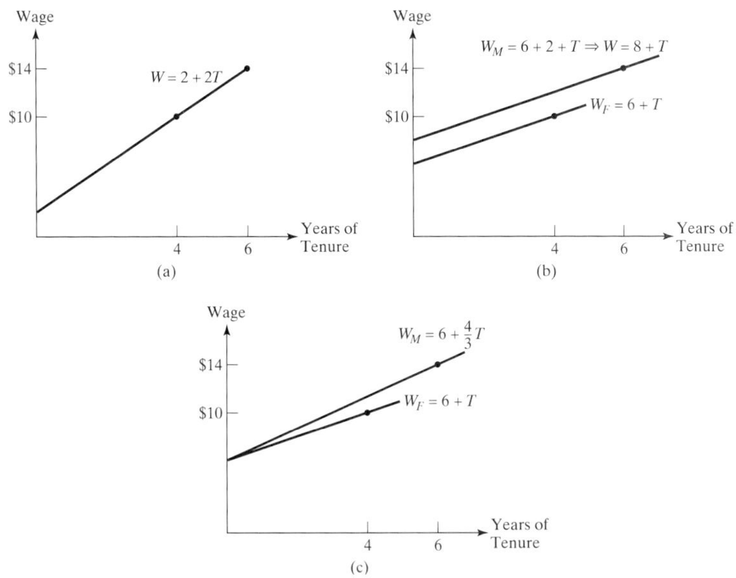

FIGURE 8.1 Influence of Tenure and Gender on Wages of Men and Women

relationship is the same for men and women but the intercepts differ. This is the situation depicted in Figure 8.1(b), which plots the multivariate wage function

$$W = 6 + 2M + T,$$

where M is a variable that takes the value 0 for women and 1 for men. (In econometrics, a variable that identifies a qualitative difference and takes a value of either 0 or 1 is called a dummy variable.) In this case women are paid lower wages than men even if the effect of tenure is held constant. As shown in Figure 8.1(b), this relationship is also consistent with the findings in the survey. Women, who average four years of tenure, are paid an average wage of \$10.00 per hour, while men, who average six years of tenure, are paid an average of \$14.00 per hour. Unlike the first equation, however, this equation shows evidence of discrimination since the wages paid to two workers differ even though these workers are equivalent in all relevant regards (in this case, just tenure) except gender. For example, a woman with five years of tenure would earn \$11.00 per hour, while a man with the same amount of tenure would earn \$13.00 per hour.

The extra amount earned by a man solely by virtue of gender can be found by taking the difference between the wage for men, W_M, and the wage for women, W_F, at any level of tenure. The difference $W_M - W_F$ can be thought of as the difference quotient $\Delta W/\Delta M$ since the variable M represents the "change in gender" and, by definition of this variable, $\Delta M = 1$. The difference quotient is

$$\frac{\Delta W}{\Delta M} = \frac{W_M - W_F}{1} = [6 + 2 \cdot (1) + T] - [6 + 2 \cdot (0) + T] = 2.$$

This result shows that if the effect of tenure is held constant, there is a \$2.00 premium paid to men. This means that the \$4.00 difference in average wages between men and women is composed of \$2.00 that is attributable to the difference in average tenure and \$2.00 that is attributable to gender. Thus the coefficient of 2 in the wage equation shows the effect of gender, *ceteris paribus.*

Alternatively, we may think that differences in wages between men and women occur in the growth of their wages over the time spent at a firm. A simple wage equation that reflects this has the dummy variable M enter interactively with the tenure variable as shown in the equation

$$W = 6 + T + \frac{MT}{3}.$$

This equation is represented in Figure 8.1(c). The steeper schedule represents the relationship between wages and tenure for men, while the flatter schedule represents this relationship for women. In this case we can separate the \$4.00 difference between the average wages of men and women into an amount due to discrimination and an amount due to differences in tenure by calculating the difference between men's and women's wages. This difference quotient is

$$\frac{\Delta W}{\Delta M} = \frac{W_M - W_F}{1} = \left[6 + T + \frac{1}{3}(1)T\right] - \left[6 + T + \frac{1}{3}(0)T\right] = \frac{1}{3}T.$$

This shows that the difference between the wages of men and those of women grows with tenure. For example, the difference between the average wages of men and women with three years of tenure is \$1.00, while the difference between the average wages of men and women with six years of tenure is \$2.00.

The key point in these last two examples is that wages are determined by a multivariate function with two arguments, tenure and gender. Differences in wages across groups reflect differences in both variables. To isolate the effect of gender, it is necessary to hold constant the effect of tenure. The effect of gender might then be constant for different levels of tenure, as it was in the first example, or it might vary with tenure, as in the second example.

8.2 PARTIAL DERIVATIVES

The multivariate functions presented in the previous section illustrate how one variable, gender, may affect wage determination, *ceteris paribus.* The difference in wages between men and women is calculated by finding the difference quotient $\Delta W/\Delta M$. Unlike the difference quotients presented in Chapter 6, however, the difference quotient $\Delta W/\Delta M$ cannot be considered for very small changes in the variable M since this variable takes the value of either 0 or 1 and does not allow for incremental differences in gender.

In this section we consider the change in the values of multivariate functions with respect to arguments that are continuous in order to find the **partial derivative.** A partial derivative of a multivariate function with respect to any one of its arguments represents the rate of change of the value of that function due to a very small change in that argument *while all the other variables that are also arguments of this function are held constant.* The difference quotients presented in the previous section have already introduced us to the *ceteris paribus* characteristic of a partial derivative.

The definition of a partial derivative closely parallels that of the derivative presented in Chapter 6.

Partial Derivative The partial derivative of the function $y = f(x_1, x_2, \ldots, x_n)$ with respect to its argument x_i, written as $\partial y/\partial x_i$, is

$$\frac{\partial y}{\partial x_i} = \lim_{\Delta x_i \to 0} \frac{f(x_1, \ldots, x_i + \Delta x_i, \ldots, x_n) - f(x_1, \ldots, x_i, \ldots, x_n)}{\Delta x_i},$$

provided that the limit exists.

Note that, as with the derivative, this definition requires that the limit exists. The conditions required for the limit to exist are analogous to those discussed for a univariate function in Chapter 6. For example, the wage equation presented in Section 8.1 has no partial derivative with respect to the variable M since the function is not continuous with respect to M.

The notation for the partial derivative reflects both its link to the derivative of a univariate function and the way in which it is distinct. In

$$\frac{\partial y}{\partial x_i}$$

or, alternatively,

$$\frac{\partial}{\partial x_i} f(x_1, x_2, \ldots, x_n),$$

the symbol ∂ replaces the d used in the derivative of a univariate function. Another way to denote this partial derivative is

$$f_i(x_1, x_2, \ldots, x_n)$$

or, more compactly, f_i. For a function in which the variables are denoted by different letters rather than subscripts, such as

$$f(x, z),$$

the partial derivative with respect to one of the arguments (say, x) is denoted by

$$f_x(x, z)$$

or, more compactly, f_x. This notation is the partial derivative analogue to the notation for the derivative of a univariate function, $f'(x)$. The "prime" notation used for a univariate function would obviously be ambiguous in the case of a multivariate function.

For partial differentiation, it is not necessary to learn a new set of rules distinct from those presented in Chapter 7. Instead, we have the following rule.

Evaluating Partial Derivatives The partial derivative of a multivariate function with respect to one of its arguments is found by applying the rules for univariate differentiation and treating all the other arguments of the function as constant.

As an example of this rule, consider again the multivariate wage function

$$W = 6 + 2M + T.$$

We can find the partial derivative of W with respect to T since it is possible to consider very small changes in tenure. This partial derivative, written, $\partial W/\partial T$, is calculated by using the rules for differentiation presented in the previous chapter and treating $6 + 2 \cdot M$ as a constant. Thus we have

$$\frac{\partial W}{\partial T} = 1.$$

Some other examples further illustrate the calculation of partial derivatives. The function

$$y = 2x^2z^3$$

has the two partial derivatives,

$$\frac{\partial y}{\partial x} = 4xz^3 \quad \text{and} \quad \frac{\partial y}{\partial z} = 6x^2z^2.$$

The function

$$f(x_1, x_2) = \sqrt{x_1 + 3x_2^2}$$

has the two partial derivatives,

$$f_1(x_1, x_2) = \frac{1}{2\sqrt{x_1 + 3x_2^2}} \quad \text{and} \quad f_2(x_1, x_2) = \frac{3x_2}{\sqrt{x_1 + 3x_2^2}}.$$

The function

$$h(x, y, z) = \ln(5x + 2y - 3z)$$

has the three partial derivatives,

$$h_x(x, y, z) = \frac{5}{5x + 2y - 3z},$$

$$h_y(x, y, z) = \frac{2}{5x + 2y - 3z}, \quad \text{and}$$

$$h_z(x, y, z) = \frac{-3}{5x + 2y - 3z}.$$

The following application illustrates the use of partial differentiation in the context of the interpretation of empirical results from a study of wage determination.

The Financial Returns to Education

The wage equation presented earlier is a simplification of the type of equation economists actually estimate in order to examine issues like the economic return to schooling. A pioneer in this field is Jacob Mincer. In his book *Schooling, Experience and Earnings,* Mincer provides a number of results that show the link between annual earnings, E;

years of school completed, S; and years of workplace experience, X.[1] For example, in one specification, he finds that the natural logarithm of the annual earnings of white males who did not work on farms was related to schooling and experience as follows:

$$\ln E = 6.2 + 0.21S + 0.08X - 0.001X^2.$$

Mincer chose a **semi-log specification** for this equation, where the dependent variable is expressed as a logarithm, while the independent variables are expressed as natural numbers. This specification relates changes in the levels of the independent variables to percentage changes in the dependent variable. For example, the partial derivative of annual earnings with respect to years of school completed is

$$\frac{\partial \ln E}{\partial S} = \frac{\partial E}{\partial S}\frac{1}{E} = 0.21.$$

This result indicates that an increase in schooling by one year increases annual earnings by 21% if the effect of experience is held constant. This derivative can also be evaluated by noting that the earnings equation can be written as

$$e^{\ln E} = E = e^{(6.2 + 0.21S + 0.08X - 0.001X^2)}.$$

By the rules for differentiating an exponential function,

$$\frac{\partial E}{\partial S} = 0.21e^{(6.2 + 0.21S + 0.08X - 0.001X^2)} = 0.21E.$$

This specification suggests that the effect of experience on annual earnings varies with the number of years in the workforce since

$$\frac{\partial \ln E}{\partial X} = \frac{\partial E}{\partial X}\frac{1}{E} = 0.08 - 0.002X.$$

For example, for an average man in the sample with a given amount of schooling, the increase in his annual earnings in his tenth year in the workforce is 6%, while the increase in his earnings in his twentieth year is 4%.

In another specification, Mincer finds

$$\ln E = 4.9 + 0.26S - 0.003S^2 - 0.004XS + 0.15X - 0.002X^2.$$

The partial derivative of earnings with respect to schooling, in this case, is

$$\frac{\partial \ln E}{\partial S} = \frac{\partial E}{\partial S}\frac{1}{E} = (0.26 - 0.006S - 0.004X).$$

This result implies that the marginal return to schooling declines with years of schooling. For example, looking at the average man in the sample who has 8 years of experience, we see that the estimated marginal benefit of another year of schooling is 18% if he has 8 years of education $(0.26 - 0.006 \cdot (8) - 0.004 \cdot (8))$, while the estimated marginal benefit of another year of schooling is 15.6% if he has 12 years of education and 13.2% if he has 16 years of education.

[1] Jacob Mincer, *Schooling, Experience and Earnings* (New York: Columbia University Press, 1974).

Another application of the partial derivative sheds light on one source of aggregate differences in real wages (that is, the wage relative to the price level) across countries. In neoclassical theory, wages are equal to the marginal product of labor. We consider the marginal product of labor for the Cobb-Douglas production function, which takes the form

$$Q = AK^{1-\alpha}L^{\alpha},$$

where $0 < \alpha < 1$, K is the amount of capital, L is the amount of labor, and A is a measure of productivity.

The marginal product of labor is found by taking the partial derivative of output with respect to labor. This partial derivative is calculated by using the rules for differentiation presented in the previous chapter and treating capital as a constant. Thus the marginal product of labor is

$$\frac{\partial Q}{\partial L} = \alpha AK^{1-\alpha}L^{\alpha-1} = \alpha A\left(\frac{K}{L}\right)^{1-\alpha}.$$

In neoclassical theory, the real wage is equated with the marginal product of labor. The partial derivative shows that the real wage depends upon both the amount of labor in the economy and the amount of capital. The term $(K/L)^{1-\alpha}$ increases with either an increase in K or a decrease in L. Thus the marginal product of labor and the real wage increase with a larger capital stock. This model therefore predicts that countries with larger capital stocks have higher real wages, *ceteris paribus*.

In a manner completely analogous to the market for labor, neoclassical theory predicts that the real return to capital, r, is equated to the marginal product of capital, $\partial Q/\partial K$. In a Cobb-Douglas production function, the marginal product of capital is

$$\frac{\partial Q}{\partial K} = (1 - \alpha)AK^{-\alpha}L^{\alpha} = (1 - \alpha)A\left(\frac{L}{K}\right)^{\alpha}.$$

This suggests that the rate of return to capital is relatively high in countries that have a relatively large labor-capital ratio. These high rates of return should prompt capital inflows into capital-scarce countries. A puzzle, however, concerns why so little capital seems to flow from rich to poor countries. This puzzle is addressed in the following application.

Why Doesn't Capital Flow to Poor Countries?

In an article published in 1990, Robert Lucas of the University of Chicago calculates the size of the relative returns to capital in India and the United States with some simple statistics and the relative marginal products of capital.[2] To follow Lucas's argument, we multiply and divide the partial derivative of output with respect to capital

[2] Robert E. Lucas, Jr., "Why doesn't capital flow from rich to poor countries?" *American Economic Review* 80, no. 2 (May 1990): 92–96.

given previously by $Q^{-\alpha/(1-\alpha)}$ in order to have the marginal product expressed as a function of output per worker, Q/L. This gives us

$$r = \frac{\partial Q}{\partial K} = (1 - \alpha) \cdot A^{1/(1-\alpha)} \cdot \left(\frac{Q}{L}\right)^{-\alpha/(1-\alpha)}.$$

Lucas considers a value of α of 0.6, which is an average of estimated values of this parameter for India and the United States. Noting that output per capita in the United States is 15 times larger than output per capita in India and assuming that the parameter A is the same across countries, we find that the ratio of the real return on capital in the United States and India is

$$\frac{r_{\text{India}}}{r_{\text{U.S.}}} = \left(\frac{1}{15}\right)^{-0.6/0.4} = 15^{1.5} \approx 58.$$

That is, the return on capital should be about 58 times as large in India as in the United States! Lucas states that " . . . in the face of return differentials of this magnitude, investment goods would flow rapidly from the United States and other wealthy countries to India and other poor countries. Indeed, one would expect *no* investment to occur in the wealthy countries in the face of return differentials of this magnitude."

Of course, investment does take place in wealthy countries, and there is a relatively small amount of capital flow from rich to poor countries. Lucas addresses this paradox by reconsidering his calculations. He first notes that workers in the United States have greater skills (which economists call **human capital**) than workers in India. The appropriate measure of Q/L is then output per *effective worker* rather than actual output per worker. Lucas uses an estimate that the average American worker is five times as productive as the average Indian worker. In this case the ratio of output per effective worker in the two countries is 3, and the ratio of returns is $(1/3)^{-0.6/0.4} \approx 5$. While this revised estimate partially addresses the puzzle, the ratio still seems high given the lack of substantial capital flows.

Lucas next considers an alternative production function that incorporates external effects, whereby an increase in human capital per worker, h, has the additional effect of increasing overall productivity. A production function that captures this effect is

$$Q = AK^{1-\alpha}L^{\alpha}h^{\gamma}.$$

The marginal product of capital in this case is

$$\frac{\partial Q}{\partial K} = (1 - \alpha) \cdot A^{1/(1-\alpha)} \cdot \left(\frac{Q}{L}\right)^{-\alpha/(1-\alpha)} h^{\gamma/(1-\alpha)},$$

where again we multiply and divide the partial derivative of output with respect to capital by $Q^{-\alpha/(1-\alpha)}$ in order to have the marginal product expressed as a function of output per worker. With the estimate of human capital in the United States as five times that in India, using output per effective worker, and employing an estimate of

$\gamma = 0.4$, we find that the ratio of returns in India to those in the United States is[3]

$$\frac{r_{India}}{r_{U.S.}} = \left(\frac{1}{3}\right)^{-0.6/0.4}\left(\frac{1}{5}\right)^{0.4/0.4} \approx 1.04.$$

According to this estimate, then, there is little difference in the rate of return in the two countries. Thus the differences in skills across countries, along with the impact of these skill differences on overall productivity, provide one potential reason why capital does not flow from rich to poor countries.[4]

A Geometric Interpretation of Partial Derivatives

In the previous chapter, the derivative of a univariate function is illustrated with a two-dimensional graph. There it is shown that the derivative of a function at a certain value of its argument can be interpreted as the slope of a line tangent to the function at that value of its argument. There is a similar geometric interpretation of the partial derivative.

As an example, consider the Cobb-Douglas production function discussed earlier. We can depict this as a three-dimensional graph linking the two inputs to the level of output. Figure 8.2(a) depicts this relationship, with the amount of labor measured along one axis, the amount of capital measured along another axis, and the resulting level of output measured by the height of the surface above the labor-capital plane.

The depiction of the partial derivative of output with respect to labor is somewhat complicated by the difficulty in depicting three dimensions on a two-dimensional piece of paper. We can get around this complication by considering the partial derivative as the tangent of a "slice" of the three-dimensional graph. These slices hold constant one factor while varying the level of the other factor. For example, Figure 8.2(b) presents the slice of the production function for the level of capital K_0, and Figure 8.2(c) presents the slice of the production function for the higher level of capital K_1. The marginal product of labor at any level of labor and capital is represented by the slope of the line tangent to the production function at that level of labor for the slice taken at that level of capital.

Figures 8.2(b) and 8.2(c) demonstrate the manner in which the marginal product of labor changes with the amount of labor, with capital held constant. In both diagrams, the tangent line at the level of labor L_0 is steeper than the tangent line at the level of labor L_1. This shows that, with the level of capital held constant, the marginal product of labor decreases with higher levels of labor. These diagrams also demonstrate that, with the level of labor held constant, the marginal product of labor increases with the amount of capital. This is shown by comparing the slopes of the tangents at a common level of labor in each diagram. At both L_0 and L_1, the tangent line is steeper in Figure 8.2(c) than in Figure 8.2(b) because the level of capital is higher in Figure 8.2(c).

[3] Lucas uses the estimate $\gamma = 0.4$ based upon some calculations that draw from empirical research on growth in the United States, though he acknowledges that he cannot verify the accuracy of the assumptions used to derive this estimate.

[4] Another possible explanation is that there is a paucity of capital flows, despite a large interest rate differential, because the interest differential compensates investors for the riskiness of factors such as the higher likelihood of expropriation in developing countries.

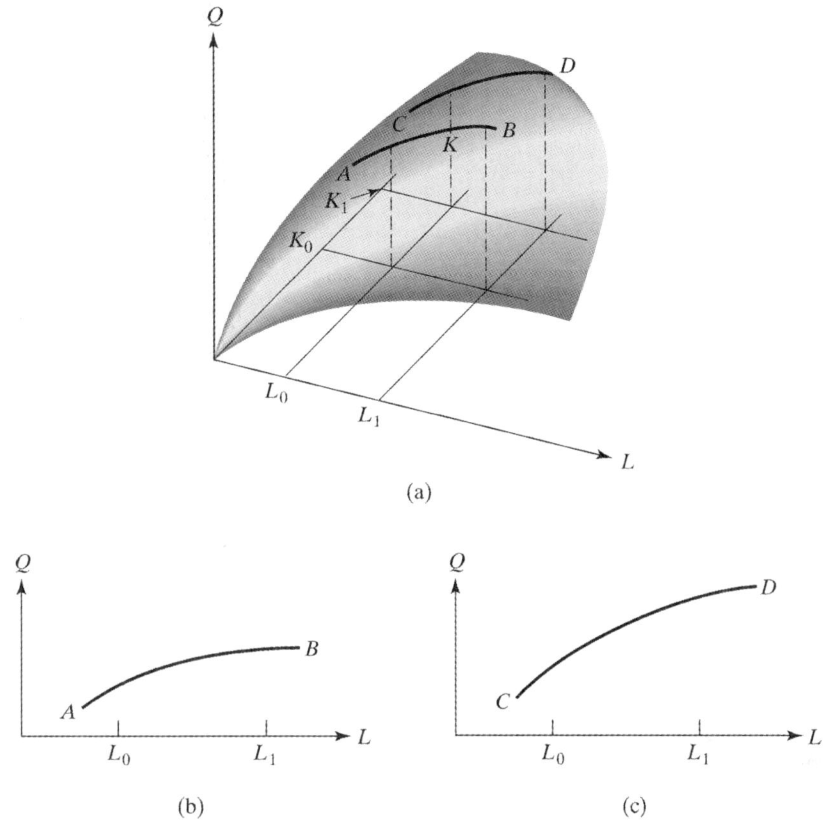

FIGURE 8.2 A Production Function and Its "Slices"

Second Partial Derivatives and Cross Partial Derivatives

In Chapter 7 we discuss the second derivative of a univariate function. The second derivative, which is the derivative of the first derivative, shows how the first derivative itself varies with small changes in the argument of the function. The multivariate analogue to this is the set of second partial derivatives and cross partial derivatives. A **second partial derivative** is a measure of how a partial derivative with respect to one argument of a multivariate function changes with a very small change in that argument. A **cross partial derivative** is a measure of how a partial derivative taken with respect to one of the arguments of the multivariate function varies with a very small change in another argument of that function.

The notation for second partial derivatives and cross partial derivatives is a natural extension of the notation for partial derivatives and for second derivatives. Consider the function

$$y = f(x_1, x_2)$$

with the two partial derivatives

$$f_1(x_1, x_2) \quad \text{and} \quad f_2(x_1, x_2),$$

which can also be written as

$$\frac{\partial y}{\partial x_1} \quad \text{and} \quad \frac{\partial y}{\partial x_2},$$

respectively. The second partial derivative of $f(x_1, x_2)$ with respect to x_1 is denoted as

$$f_{11}(x_1, x_2) \quad \text{or} \quad \frac{\partial^2 y}{\partial x_1^2}.$$

Likewise, the second partial derivative with respect to x_2, is denoted as

$$f_{22}(x_1, x_2) \quad \text{or} \quad \frac{\partial^2 y}{\partial x_2^2}.$$

The cross partial derivative representing the partial derivative of $f_1(x_1, x_2)$ taken with respect to x_2 is denoted as

$$f_{12}(x_1, x_2) \quad \text{or} \quad \frac{\partial^2 y}{\partial x_1 \, \partial x_2}.$$

The cross partial derivative of $f_2(x_1, x_2)$ taken with respect to x_1 is denoted as

$$f_{21}(x_1, x_2) \quad \text{or} \quad \frac{\partial^2 y}{\partial x_2 \, \partial x_1}.$$

Using three functions presented earlier, we illustrate the calculation of second partial derivatives and cross partial derivatives. The function

$$y = 2x^2z^3$$

has the two second partial derivatives

$$\frac{\partial^2 y}{\partial x^2} = 4z^3 \quad \text{and} \quad \frac{\partial^2 y}{\partial z^2} = 12x^2z$$

and the cross partial derivative

$$\frac{\partial^2 y}{\partial x \, \partial z} = \frac{\partial^2 y}{\partial z \, \partial x} = 12xz^2.$$

The function

$$f(x_1, x_2) = \sqrt{x_1 + 3x_2^2}$$

has the two second partial derivatives

$$f_{11}(x_1, x_2) = -\frac{1}{4(x_1 + 3x_2^2)^{3/2}}$$

$$f_{22}(x_1, x_2) = -\frac{9x_2^2}{(x_1 + 3x_2^2)^{3/2}} + \frac{3}{(x_1 + 3x_2^2)^{1/2}}$$

and the cross partial derivative

$$f_{12}(x_1, x_2) = f_{21}(x_1, x_2) = -\frac{3x_2}{2(x_1 + 3x_2^2)^{3/2}}.$$

The function

$$h(x, y, z) = \ln(5x + 2y - 3z)$$

has the three second partial derivatives

$$h_{xx}(x, y, z) = -\frac{25}{(5x + 2y - 3z)^2},$$
$$h_{yy}(x, y, z) = -\frac{4}{(5x + 2y - 3z)^2}, \quad \text{and}$$
$$h_{zz}(x, y, z) = -\frac{9}{(5x + 2y - 3z)^2}$$

and the three cross partial derivatives

$$h_{xy}(x, y, z) = h_{yx}(x, y, z) = -\frac{10}{(5x + 2y - 3z)^2},$$
$$h_{xz}(x, y, z) = h_{zx}(x, y, z) = \frac{15}{(5x + 2y - 3z)^2}, \quad \text{and}$$
$$h_{yz}(x, y, z) = h_{zy}(x, y, z) = \frac{6}{(5x + 2y - 3z)^2}.$$

Notice that, in the first two examples, there is only one distinct cross partial derivative since

$$\frac{\partial^2 y}{\partial x\, \partial z} = \frac{\partial^2 y}{\partial z\, \partial x} \quad \text{and} \quad f_{12} = f_{21},$$

respectively. In the third example, there are three distinct cross partial derivatives since

$$h_{xy} = h_{yx}, \quad h_{xz} = h_{zx}, \quad \text{and} \quad h_{yz} = h_{zy}.$$

These results suggest that the order of differentiation for a cross partial derivative does not matter and, in general, $f_{ij} = f_{ji}$ as long as each partial derivative is itself differentiable. This is, in fact, generally true, and this result is known as **Young's Theorem.**

Young's Theorem If all the partial derivatives of the function

$$f(x_1, x_2, \ldots, x_n)$$

exist and are themselves differentiable with continuous derivatives, then

$$\frac{\partial}{\partial x_i} \cdot \frac{\partial f(x_1, x_2, \ldots, x_n)}{\partial x_j} = \frac{\partial}{\partial x_j} \cdot \frac{\partial f(x_1, x_2, \ldots, x_n)}{\partial x_i}$$

or, written differently,

$$f_{ji}(x_1, x_2, \ldots, x_n) = f_{ij}(x_1, x_2, \ldots, x_n)$$

for any i and j from 1 to n.

Young's Theorem shows that a multivariate function that is fully differentiable with respect to all of its n arguments has, at most, n distinct partial derivatives, n distinct second partial derivatives, and $(n^2 - n)/2$ (rather than $n^2 - n$) distinct cross partial derivatives.

For economic examples of second partial derivatives and a cross partial derivative, we turn again to the Cobb-Douglas production function. The second partial derivative of this production function with respect to labor is found by taking the partial derivative with respect to labor of the function

$$\frac{\partial Q}{\partial L} = \alpha A K^{1-\alpha} L^{\alpha-1}.$$

The second partial derivative is

$$\frac{\partial^2 Q}{\partial L^2} = -(1 - \alpha)\alpha A K^{1-\alpha} L^{\alpha-2}.$$

This second partial derivative shows how the marginal product of labor changes with small changes in the amount of labor. The second partial derivative with respect to capital is found in a similar manner and is

$$\frac{\partial^2 Q}{\partial K^2} = -(1 - \alpha)\alpha A K^{-\alpha-1} L^{\alpha}.$$

This second partial derivative shows how the marginal product of capital changes with small changes in the amount of capital. Each of these second partial derivatives is negative. This reflects the economic concept of **diminishing marginal productivity,** which means that the marginal product of an input decreases as more of that input is used.

The single cross partial derivative of the Cobb-Douglas production function is

$$\frac{\partial^2 Q}{\partial K \partial L} = \frac{\partial^2 Q}{\partial L \partial K} = (1 - \alpha)\alpha A K^{-\alpha} L^{\alpha-1}.$$

This is a positive number since K and L are positive. The economic interpretation is that the marginal product of either input rises as more of the other input is used.

The second partial derivatives and cross partial derivative are used to derive the graph of the neoclassical demand for labor. In neoclassical theory, firms hire workers to the point where the real wage, w, equals the marginal product of labor, MPL. Using the results presented earlier in the chapter, we find that this condition is satisfied when

$$W = \alpha A \left(\frac{K}{L}\right)^{1-a}.$$

The labor demand schedule L_0L_0 in Figure 8.3 traces out the demand for labor as the wage varies when the capital stock is K_0. A lower real wage leads to an increase in

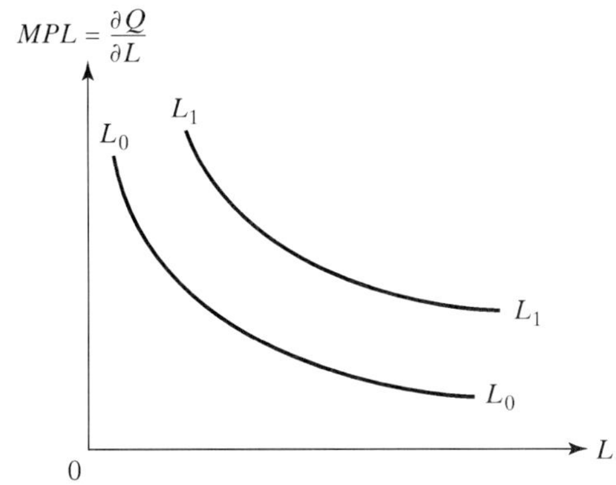

FIGURE 8.3 Labor Demand at Different Levels of Capital

the demand for labor since the right-hand side of the previous expression decreases with an increase in L. The slope of the labor demand schedule at any level of labor can be found explicitly by taking the partial derivative of the right-hand side, which, of course, is the second partial derivative of the production function with respect to labor, $\partial^2 Q/\partial L^2$. As shown above, this is negative.

The labor demand schedule shifts with the amount of capital in an economy. An increase in the amount of capital, say from K_0 to K_1, increases the productivity of labor and, thus, increases labor demand at any real wage. This is represented by an outward shift in the labor demand schedule from L_0L_0 to L_1L_1. The exact relationship between a small change in capital and the demand for labor is given by the cross partial derivative, $\partial^2 Q/\partial L\, \partial K$, which, as shown earlier, is positive for the Cobb-Douglas production function.

We close this section with an application that uses the second derivative to compare two different statistics that measure central tendency.

Means and Outliers

One statistic used to measure the central tendency of a set of observations is the **mean** or **average.** But there are a number of different ways to calculate the mean of a set of observations. The most common method involves the calculation of the **arithmetic mean.** The arithmetic mean of a set of n observations $x_1, x_2 \ldots, x_n$, which we denote as $\bar{x}_A$, is

$$\bar{x}_A = \frac{1}{n}(x_1 + x_2 + \cdots + x_n) = \sum_{i=1}^{n} x_i$$

(see Section 4.2 of Chapter 4 for a definition of the summation operator, Σ). Another measure of the central tendency of a set of observations is the **geometric mean.** The geometric mean of a set of n observations $x_1, x_2, \ldots, x_n$, which we denote as $\bar{x}_G$, is

$$\bar{x}_G = x_1^{1/n} x_2^{1/n} \ldots x_n^{1/n} = \prod_{i=1}^{n} x_i^{1/n}$$

where $\prod$ is a product operator representing the multiplication of the n observations x_1 to x_n. For example, the arithmetic mean of the three numbers 8, 8, and 64 is $\frac{80}{3} = 26\frac{2}{3}$, while the geometric mean of these three numbers is $8^{1/3}8^{1/3}64^{1/3} = 2 \times 2 \times 4 = 16$.

The fact that the geometric mean of these three numbers is less than the arithmetic mean reflects an important result; namely, the geometric mean gives less weight to **outliers,** or observations with unusually large or small values, than does the arithmetic mean. In the case of the three numbers 8, 8, and 64, the outlier is 64. The arithmetic mean is more affected by the presence of this outlier than is the geometric mean and, consequently, is larger than the geometric mean.

We can use the second partial derivative to show that, in general, outliers affect an arithmetic mean more than a geometric mean.[5] The partial derivative of the arithmetic mean with respect to the ith observation used to calculate it, x_i, is

$$\frac{\partial \bar{x}_A}{\partial x_i} = \frac{1}{n},$$

and the second partial derivative, $\partial^2 \bar{x}_A / \partial x_i^2$, is zero. Therefore, the arithmetic mean increases at a constant rate with an increase in its ith observation. The partial derivative of the geometric mean with respect to its ith observation is

$$\frac{\partial \bar{x}_G}{\partial x_i} = \frac{1}{n}\left(x_1^{1/n} x_2^{1/n} \ldots x_i^{1/n-1} \ldots x_n^{1/n}\right),$$

while the second partial derivative is

$$\frac{\partial^2 \bar{x}_G}{\partial x_i^2} = \left(\frac{1}{n} - 1\right)\frac{1}{n}\left(x_1^{1/n} x_2^{1/n} \ldots x_i^{1/n-2} \ldots x_n^{1/n}\right),$$

which is negative since $1/n$ is necessarily less than 1 for any $n > 1$. We can interpret this second partial derivative to mean that an increase in the ith observation increases the value of the geometric mean (since the first derivative is positive) but at a decreasing rate (since the second derivative is negative). On the other hand, the same increase in the ith observation increases the value of the arithmetic mean at a constant rate. Thus starting with a set of observations, an increase in one observation raises the geometric mean at a lower rate than the arithmetic mean, or conversely, a decrease in one of the observations reduces the geometric mean at a lower rate than the arithmetic mean.

A numerical example illustrates this point. Consider the three pairs of numbers denoted I, II, and III where $I = (4, 4)$, $II = (4, 9)$, and $III = (4, 16)$. The arithmetic averages of these three pairs are 4, $6\frac{1}{2}$, and 10, respectively, while the geometric averages are 4, 6, and 8, respectively. We define the rate of change of the average between pairs I and II, $\bar{x}_I$ and $\bar{x}_{II}$, as

$$\Delta_{II} = \frac{\bar{x}_{II} - \bar{x}_I}{5}$$

[5] You may recall that question 6 at the end of Section 3.3 of Chapter 3 asks you to calculate the arithmetic and geometric means of three numbers in order to see the relative effect of an outlier.

since the difference in the two pairs of numbers I and II is only that II includes 9 rather than 4. Likewise, we define the rate of change of the average between pairs I and III, $\bar{x}_I$ and $\bar{x}_{III}$, as

$$\Delta_{III} = \frac{\bar{x}_{III} - \bar{x}_I}{12}.$$

Then, for the arithmetic average, $\Delta_{II} = \frac{1}{2}$ and $\Delta_{III} = \frac{1}{2}$. Thus the rate of change of the arithmetic average does not change between one set of numbers and another. In contrast, the rate of change of the geometric average declines, from $\Delta_{II} = \frac{2}{5}$ to $\Delta_{III} = \frac{1}{3}$, as we move from a comparison of a pair of numbers with a smaller outlier to a comparison of a pair of numbers with a larger outlier.

Exercises 8.2

1. Find the partial derivatives of each function.
   (a) $y = f(x_1, x_2) = 12x_1^4 - 6x_1^2x_2 + 4x_2^3$
   (b) $y = f(x_1, x_2) = (3x_1^2 + 5x_1 + 1)\cdot(x_2 + 4)$
   (c) $y = f(x_1, x_2) = \dfrac{(7x_1 - x_1x_2^2)}{(x_1 - 2)}$
   (d) $y = f(x_1, x_2) = (2e^{x_1})\cdot(e^{2x_1}\cdot x_2^2)$
   (e) $y = f(x_1, x_2) = 2\ln 3x_1 - 4\ln 2x_1x_2$
   (f) $y = f(x_1, x_2) = x_1^2 + 2x_1x_2^{1/2} - 4x_2$
2. For each function in question 1, find the two second partial derivatives and the single cross partial derivative.
3. Find the value of each partial derivative in question 1 when $x_1 = 1$ and $x_2 = 4$.
4. If

$$u = \ln(v^4 + x^4 + y^4 + z^4 - 4vxyz),$$

   show that

$$v\frac{\partial u}{\partial v} + x\frac{\partial u}{\partial x} + y\frac{\partial u}{\partial y} + z\frac{\partial u}{\partial z} = 4.$$

5. Consider the function

$$f(w,x,y,z) = \alpha w^\gamma + \frac{\beta x}{\theta y}\cdot\ln(\phi z).$$

   (a) Find the four partial derivatives and the four second partial derivatives of this function.
   (b) Determine the cross partial derivatives $f_{xz}(w, x, y, z)$ and $f_{wy}(w, x, y, z)$.
   (c) According to Young's Theorem, how many unique cross partial derivatives can be obtained from the original function?

6. Assume that demand for sugar is a function of income (Y), the price of sugar (P_S), and the price of saccharine (P_C), a sugar substitute, as follows:

$$Q_d = f(Y, P_C, P_S) = 0.05Y + 10P_C - 5P_S^2.$$

   (a) Find the partial derivatives of this demand function.

   (b) The elasticity of demand with respect to income is defined as

$$\frac{\partial Q_d}{\partial Y} \cdot \frac{Y}{Q_d}.$$

   Find the elasticity of demand with respect to income when $Y = 10{,}000$, $P_S = 5$, and $P_C = 7$.

   (c) The own-price elasticity of demand in this example is

$$\frac{\partial Q_d}{\partial P_S} \cdot \frac{P_S}{Q_d}.$$

   Find the own-price elasticity of demand when $Y = 10{,}000$, $P_S = 5$, and $P_C = 7$.

   (d) The cross-price elasticity of demand refers to the percentage change in the quantity demanded for a good due to a 1% change in the price of another good. In this example, the cross-price elasticity of sugar with respect to saccharine is

$$\frac{\partial Q_d}{\partial P_C} \cdot \frac{P_C}{Q_d}.$$

   Find the cross-price elasticity of demand when $Y = 10{,}000$, $P_S = 5$, and $P_C = 7$.

7. An application in Chapter 7 introduced the money multiplier,

$$\theta = \frac{1 + c}{c + r}.$$

   We showed that $d\theta/dc < 0$. More generally, for the function

$$f(x, y, z) = \frac{y + x}{z + x},$$

   where x, y, and z are each positive, show the conditions under which $f_x(x, y, z) < 0$.

8. In the application presented in this section, one of Jacob Mincer's specifications relating earnings to schooling and workplace experience is

$$\ln E = 4.9 + 0.26S - 0.003S^2 - 0.004XS + 0.15X - 0.002X^2.$$

   (a) What is the partial derivative of the logarithm of earnings with respect to experience, $\partial \ln E/\partial X$?

   (b) What is the percentage impact on earnings due to a one year increase in experience if $S = 20$ and $X = 5$?

   (c) What is the impact on the dollar value of earnings due to a one year increase in experience if $S = 20$ and $X = 5$?

   (d) What is the percentage impact on earnings due to an increase in experience of 1% if $S = 20$ and $X = 5$?

(e) Does this specification exhibit diminishing marginal returns to earnings with regard to experience?

9. Consider the application on Robert Lucas's study of the international differences in the return to capital. Assume that A, a measure of productivity, is allowed to vary across countries. Use the original specification of marginal product expressed as a function of output per worker,

$$r = \frac{\partial Q}{\partial K} = (1 - \alpha) \cdot A^{1/(1-\alpha)} \cdot \left(\frac{Q}{L}\right)^{-\alpha/(1-\alpha)},$$

for the following problems.

(a) Calculate the ratio of the real return on capital. Assume that $A = 3$ for the United States and $A = 2$ for India. Recall that output per capita in the United States is 15 times larger than that in India and $\alpha = 0.6$.

(b) Assuming that A_i is allowed to vary, where $i = (India, U.S.)$, determine the general formula for calculating the ratio of the real return on capital by taking the partial derivative

$$\frac{\partial(r_{India}/r_{U.S.})}{\partial(A_{India}/A_{U.S.})}.$$

10. Consider a production function that takes the form

$$y = 10L^{1/2}K^{1/2},$$

and assume that capital is constant at $K_0 = 64$.

(a) If the real wage is equivalent to the marginal product of labor such that

$$w = \alpha A\left(\frac{K}{L}\right)^{1-\alpha} = 10,$$

how much labor will be demanded? What happens to the demand for labor when the real wage declines to $w = 8$? Assuming that capital is K_0, trace out the graph of the demand for labor.

(b) Now assume that the capital used in the production process is allowed to vary and increases to $K = 100$. Holding the real wage constant at $w = 8$, how much labor will be demanded? How does the increase in capital affect the graph of the demand for labor?

(c) Determine the cross partial derivative of this production function, $\partial^2 y/\partial K\, \partial L$, and provide an intuition for the sign on your result.

11. The demand for hamburgers at the Ye Olde College Diner is a function of both the price of the hamburgers and the number of months since the begining of the school year, as shown by the function

$$Q_D = e^4 P^{-0.25} e^{-0.125t},$$

where Q_D is quantity demanded, P is the price of hamburgers, t is the number of months since September (so $t = 0$ in September, $t = 1$ in October, and so forth).

(a) Show how the demand for hamburgers varies with their price in September, January, and May.

(b) Show how the demand for hamburgers varies with the number of months since September, for a given price of hamburgers.

12. A **weighted arithmetic mean** of n observations, $x_1, x_2, \ldots, x_n$, is

$$\bar{x}_A = \omega_1 x_1 + \omega_2 x_2 + \cdots + \omega_n x_n = \sum_{i=1}^{n} \omega_i x_i,$$

where each of the n weights, $\omega_1, \omega_2, \ldots, \omega_n$ is less than 1 and the sum of the weights equals 1; that is,

$$\sum_{i=1}^{n} \omega_i = 1.$$

A **weighted geometric mean** of n observations, $x_1, x_2, \ldots, x_n$, is

$$\bar{x}_A = x_1^{\omega_1} x_2^{\omega_2} \cdots x_n^{\omega_n} = \prod_{i=1}^{n} x_i^{\omega_i}.$$

Find the first and second partial derivatives of both the weighted arithmetic mean and the weighted geometric mean with respect to the ith observation, x_i. Are the results with respect to outliers for the weighted means consistent with those described in the application about means and outliers?

8.3 COMPOSITE FUNCTIONS AND THE CHAIN RULE

Often, in economics, the arguments of multivariate functions are themselves functions of other variables. For example, investment may depend upon the real interest rate and disposable income, which each vary with the level of government spending. In this case the investment function is a multivariate **composite function** since its arguments are each functions of another variable. The chain rule, presented in a univariate context in Chapter 7, indicates how to take the derivative of a composite function. In that section it is shown that the derivative of the univariate composite function

$$y = f(x) = g(h(x))$$

is

$$\frac{dy}{dx} = g'(h(x)) \cdot h'(x).$$

A multivariate form of the chain rule can be used with multivariate composite functions. The first form of this rule that we present concerns cases where the arguments of the outside function are themselves univariate functions of another variable.

Multivariate Chain Rule (I) If the arguments of the differentiable function

$$y = f(x_1, x_2, \ldots, x_n)$$

are themselves differentiable functions of the variable t such that

$$x_1 = g^1(t), \quad x_2 = g^2(t), \quad \ldots, \quad x_n = g^n(t),$$

where $g^i(t)$ is the ith univariate function, then

$$\frac{dy}{dt} = f_1 \cdot \frac{dx_1}{dt} + f_2 \cdot \frac{dx_2}{dt} + \cdots + f_n \cdot \frac{dx_n}{dt},$$

where

$$f_i = \frac{\partial y}{\partial x_i}.$$

As an example of the chain rule, consider the function

$$y = f(x_1, x_2) = x_1^2 x_2,$$

where

$$x_1 = t^2 \quad \text{and} \quad x_2 = 3t - 1.$$

Then

$$\frac{dx_1}{dt} = 2t \quad \text{and} \quad \frac{dx_2}{dt} = 3,$$

and

$$f_1 = 2x_1x_2 \quad \text{and} \quad f_2 = x_1^2.$$

Using the chain rule, we find that

$$\begin{aligned}\frac{dy}{dt} &= (2x_1x_2)2t + 3x_1^2 \\ &= 4t(t^2(3t - 1)) + 3((t^2)^2) \\ &= 15t^4 - 4t^3.\end{aligned}$$

Of course, we would have also obtained this answer if we first expressed y as a function of t,

$$y = (t^2)^2(3t - 1) = 3t^5 - t^4,$$

and then simply taken the derivative of this function with respect to t.

To illustrate the chain rule in its general form, we consider a simple model of presidential elections. It is well established by political scientists that economic factors affect the popularity of an incumbent. An incumbent's chance of reelection may thus depend upon variables such as the unemployment rate, U, and the inflation rate, π, in the year of the election. A simple function that captures this relationship relates the ratio of the votes going to an incumbent relative to those going to the challenger, V, as a function of the unemployment rate and the inflation rate:

$$V = f(U, \pi).$$

The partial derivatives of the voting function are

$$f_U(U,\pi) < 0 \quad \text{and} \quad f_\pi(U,\pi) < 0,$$

reflecting our assumption that higher unemployment or higher inflation lowers the proportion of votes going to the incumbent. We also model unemployment and inflation as a function of monetary policy, as shown by

$$U = w(M) \quad \text{and} \quad \pi = p(M).$$

We assume that

$$\frac{dU}{dM} < 0 \quad \text{and} \quad \frac{d\pi}{dM} > 0,$$

which implies that an expansionary monetary policy lowers unemployment and raises inflation. The voting function can be rewritten as

$$V = f(w(M), p(M)).$$

The derivative of the vote ratio with respect to monetary policy is

$$\frac{dV}{dM} = \underset{\text{(negative)}}{f_U} \cdot \underset{\text{(negative)}}{\frac{dU}{dM}} + \underset{\text{(negative)}}{f_\pi} \cdot \underset{\text{(positive)}}{\frac{d\pi}{dM}},$$

where we have used notation for derivatives for the univariate unemployment and inflation functions and notation for partial derivatives for the multivariate voting function.

This result shows how the vote ratio changes as a result of small changes in monetary policy. The derivative dV/dM is the sum of two terms, each of which is the product of a partial derivative of the voting function and the derivative of either the unemployment function or the inflation function. The first term is positive because an expansionary monetary policy lowers unemployment and raises the proportion of votes going to the incumbent. The second term is negative because the higher inflation associated with an expansionary monetary policy turns the voters against the incumbent. While on the one hand, an expansionary monetary policy may help the incumbent, on the other hand, it may hurt his chances of reelection.

A natural extension of the chain rule concerns a situation where the arguments of a composite function are themselves multivariate functions rather than univariate functions.

Multivariate Chain Rule (II) If the arguments of the differentiable function

$$y = f(x_1, x_2, \ldots, x_n)$$

are themselves differentiable functions of the variables $t_1, \ldots, t_m$ such that

$$x_1 = g^1(t_1, \ldots, t_m), \quad x_2 = g^2(t_1, \ldots, t_m), \quad \ldots, \quad x_n = g^n(t_1, \ldots, t_m),$$

where $g^i(t_1, \ldots, t_m)$ is the ith multivariate function, then

$$\frac{\partial y}{\partial t_i} = f_1 \cdot \frac{\partial x_1}{\partial t_i} + f_2 \cdot \frac{\partial x_2}{\partial t_i} + \cdots + f_n \cdot \frac{\partial x_n}{\partial t_i},$$

where

$$f_i = \frac{\partial y}{\partial x_i}.$$

We can extend the voting example to illustrate this version of the chain rule by considering unemployment and inflation as a function of both tax policy and monetary policy such that

$$U = w(\underset{-}{M}, \underset{+}{T}) \quad \text{and} \quad \pi = p(\underset{+}{M}, \underset{-}{T}),$$

where T represents tax rates and positive or negative signs under variables indicate the sign of the respective partial derivatives. In this case the total partial derivative of the vote ratio with respect to monetary policy equals

$$\frac{\partial V}{\partial M} = \underset{\text{(negative)}}{f_U} \cdot \underset{\text{(negative)}}{\frac{\partial U}{\partial M}} + \underset{\text{(negative)}}{f_\pi} \cdot \underset{\text{(positive)}}{\frac{\partial \pi}{\partial M}}.$$

where partial derivatives replace the derivatives used in the previous case. The total partial derivative of the vote ratio with respect to tax rates equals

$$\frac{\partial V}{\partial T} = \underset{\text{(negative)}}{f_U} \cdot \underset{\text{(positive)}}{\frac{\partial U}{\partial T}} + \underset{\text{(negative)}}{f_\pi} \cdot \underset{\text{(negative)}}{\frac{\partial \pi}{\partial T}}.$$

As with monetary policy, the effect of a change in tax rates on the vote ratio is ambiguous since lowering taxes not only lowers unemployment but also increases inflation.

Growth Accounting

Long-term economic growth reflects both an increase in the factors used to produce goods and services and technological progress. **Growth accounting** provides a framework for attributing overall growth to the accumulation of factors of production and to technological progress. Consider the production of national output at any moment t, $Y(t)$, as a function of the amount of labor in the economy at that moment, $L(t)$; the amount of capital at that moment, $K(t)$; and available technology at that moment, $A(t)$. Assume that the production function takes the Cobb-Douglas form

$$Y(t) = A(t) \cdot L(t)^{\alpha} \cdot K(t)^{1-\alpha} \equiv \Phi(A(t), L(t), K(t)),$$

where $\Phi(t)$ is a composite function. The chain rule shows that the derivative of national output with respect to time is

$$\frac{dY(t)}{dt} = \Phi_A(t)\frac{dA(t)}{dt} + \Phi_L(t)\frac{dL(t)}{dt} + \Phi_K(t)\frac{dK(t)}{dt},$$

where

$$\begin{aligned}\Phi_A(t) &= L(t)^{\alpha} \cdot K(t)^{1-\alpha}, \\ \Phi_K(t) &= \alpha A(t) \cdot L(t)^{\alpha-1} \cdot K(t)^{1-\alpha}, \quad \text{and} \\ \Phi_K(t) &= (1-\alpha)A(t) \cdot L(t)^{\alpha} \cdot K(t)^{-\alpha}.\end{aligned}$$

Since $Y(t) = \Phi(t)$, we can divide the left side of this derivative by $Y(t)$ and the right side by the $\Phi(t)$ to obtain

$$\frac{dY(t)}{dt}\frac{1}{Y(t)} = \frac{\Phi_A(t)}{\Phi(t)}\frac{dA(t)}{dt} + \frac{\Phi_L(t)}{\Phi(t)}\frac{dL(t)}{dt} + \frac{\Phi_K(t)}{\Phi(t)}\frac{dK(t)}{dt}.$$

Note that

$$\begin{aligned}\frac{\Phi_A(t)}{\Phi(t)} &= \frac{1}{A(t)} \\ \frac{\Phi_L(t)}{\Phi(t)} &= \frac{\alpha}{L(t)}, \quad \text{and} \\ \frac{\Phi_K(t)}{\Phi(t)} &= \frac{(1-\alpha)}{K(t)}.\end{aligned}$$

Therefore

$$\frac{dY(t)}{dt}\frac{1}{Y(t)} = \frac{dA(t)}{dt}\frac{1}{A(t)} + \alpha\frac{dL(t)}{dt}\frac{1}{L(t)} + (1-\alpha)\frac{dK(t)}{dt}\frac{1}{K(t)}.$$

This equation attributes the rate of growth in output,

$$\frac{dY(t)}{dt}\frac{1}{Y(t)},$$

to the sum of the rate of growth in the labor force,

$$\frac{dL(t)}{dt}\frac{1}{L(t)},$$

the rate of growth in the capital stock,

$$\frac{dK(t)}{dt}\frac{1}{K(t)},$$

and the rate of growth of technological progress,

$$\frac{dA(t)}{dt}\frac{1}{A(t)}.$$

Technological progress cannot be directly observed. Instead, it is measured as what is left over after accounting for the growth due to factors of production. This is called the **Solow residual,** after Robert Solow who first developed this technique for determining the contribution of technological advances to economic growth. Subsequent work by Edward Denison attributes over a third of the economic growth in the United States between 1929 and 1982 to technological progress.[6]

Homogeneous Functions and Euler's Theorem

An application of the chain rule enables us to derive **Euler's Theorem,** which shows the relationship between the partial derivatives of a homogeneous function and the value of the function itself. We begin our discussion of this theorem with a definition of a **homogeneous function.**

Homogeneous Function A function

$$y = f(x_1, \dots, x_n)$$

is **homogeneous of degree *k*** if, for any number s where $s > 0$,

$$s^k y = f(sx_1, \dots, sx_n).$$

This definition shows that multiplying each argument of a function that is homogeneous of degree k by s will increase the value of the function by a factor of s^k. For example, the univariate function

$$y = ax^b$$

is homogeneous of degree b since

$$a(sx)^b = ax^b s^b = ys^b.$$

The multivariate Cobb-Douglas production function is homogeneous of degree 1 in capital and labor since

$$A(sK)^{1-\alpha}(sL)^{\alpha} = s^{1-\alpha+\alpha} AK^{1-\alpha}L^{\alpha} = sQ.$$

Homogeneity of degree 1 is often called **linear homogeneity.** An important property of homogeneous functions is given by Euler's Theorem.

Euler's Theorem For any multivariate function

$$y = f(x_1, \dots, x_n)$$

that is homogeneous of degree k,

$$ky = x_1 f_1(x_1, \dots, x_n) + \cdots + x_n f_n(x_1, \dots, x_n)$$

for any set of values $(x_1, x_2, \dots, x_n)$, where $f_i(x_1, \dots, x_n)$ is the partial derivative of the function with respect to its ith argument.

[6] Edward F. Denison, *Trends in American Economic Growth, 1929–1982* (Washington, DC: The Brookings Institution, 1985).

We can prove Euler's Theorem by first noting that, by the definition of homogeneity, multiplying each of the arguments of a homogeneous function by any number s gives us

$$f(sx_1, \ldots, sx_n) = s^k y.$$

We can consider this a composite function, where each argument is itself a function of s. Taking the derivative of $f(sx_1, \ldots, sx_n)$ with respect to s, we have

$$\frac{d}{ds} f(sx_1, \ldots, sx_n) = x_1 f_1(sx_1, \ldots, sx_n) + \cdots + x_n f_n(sx_1, \ldots, sx_n).$$

We can also take the derivative of the simple univariate function $s^k y$ with respect to s (where we treat y as a constant), which gives us

$$\frac{d(s^k y)}{ds} = ks^{k-1} y = ks^{k-1} f(x_1, \ldots, x_n).$$

Since

$$s^k y = f(sx_1, \ldots, sx_n)$$

for any set of values $(x_1, x_2, \ldots, x_n)$, it is also true that

$$\frac{d}{ds} f(sx_1, \ldots, sx_n) = \frac{d(s^k y)}{ds}.$$

Therefore

$$\begin{aligned} x_1 f_1(sx_1, \ldots, sx_n) + \cdots + x_n f_n(sx_1, \ldots, sx_n) &= ks^{k-1} f(x_1, \ldots, x_n) \\ &= ks^{k-1} y. \end{aligned}$$

Since s can take any value, we can consider the case where $s = 1$. This gives us Euler's Theorem. The converse of Euler's Theorem is also true; that is, any function that has the property

$$ky = x_1 f_1(x_1, \ldots, x_n) + \cdots + x_n f_n(x_1, \ldots, x_n)$$

is homogeneous of degree k. The proof of this theorem is more complicated than the proof of its converse, and we do not present it here.[7]

Euler's Theorem is used in the following application.

The Division of National Income

The Cobb-Douglas production function was developed by the mathematician Charles Cobb and the economist (and later U.S. senator) Paul Douglas in the late 1920s in order to help explain the near-constant division of national income across time in the

[7] This proof can be found in the appendix of Chapter 24 in Carl Simon and Lawrence Bloom, *Mathematics for Economists* (New York: W. W. Norton, 1994).

United States. We can use Euler's Theorem to show how the Cobb-Douglas production function reflects constant factor shares of national income.

As noted previously, the Cobb-Douglas production function is homogeneous of degree 1 in capital and labor. Therefore, by Euler's Theorem,

$$Q = \frac{\partial Q}{\partial K}K + \frac{\partial Q}{\partial L}L.$$

As discussed in the previous section, factors of production are paid their marginal products in neoclassical theory. Thus the real wage paid to labor, w, is its marginal product. The total factor payment to labor, which equals wL, is

$$wL = \frac{\partial Q}{\partial L}L = [\alpha AK^{1-\alpha}L^{\alpha-1}]L = \alpha Q.$$

Likewise, the rent to capital, r, equals the marginal product of capital, and the total factor payment to capital is

$$rK = \frac{\partial Q}{\partial K}K = [(1-\alpha)AK^{-\alpha}L^{\alpha}]K = (1-\alpha)Q.$$

National income equals the value of national production (Q) and is wholly divided between payments to capital and payments to labor.

$$Q = wL + rK = \alpha Q + (1-\alpha)Q$$

A striking result here is that the parameter α, which shows how much a unit of labor contributes to production, also represents the share of national income going to labor under the assumption that factors are paid their marginal products. Similarly, the parameter $1-\alpha$ represents both how much a unit of capital contributes to production as well as the share of national income going to capital. In the United States, the estimated value of α is about 0.67, which means that payments to labor are about twice (that is, 0.67/0.33) the size of payments to capital.

The two functions that are the marginal products of the Cobb-Douglas production function and appear in the previous application,

$$\frac{\partial Q}{\partial L} = \alpha AK^{1-\alpha}L^{\alpha-1} \quad \text{and}$$
$$\frac{\partial Q}{\partial K} = (1-\alpha)AK^{-\alpha}L^{\alpha},$$

are each homogeneous of degree 0 since

$$\frac{\partial Q}{\partial L} = \alpha A(sK)^{1-\alpha}(sL)^{\alpha-1} = s^0\alpha AK^{1-\alpha}L^{\alpha-1} = \alpha AK^{1-\alpha}L^{\alpha-1} \quad \text{and}$$
$$\frac{\partial Q}{\partial K} = (1-\alpha)A(sK)^{-\alpha}(sL)^{\alpha} = s^0(1-\alpha)AK^{-\alpha}L^{\alpha} = (1-\alpha)AK^{-\alpha}L^{\alpha}.$$

These functions can be written such that the arguments K and L are expressed as a ratio. That is,

$$\frac{\partial Q}{\partial L} = \alpha A\left(\frac{K}{L}\right)^{1-\alpha} \quad \text{and}$$
$$\frac{\partial Q}{\partial K} = (1-\alpha)A\left(\frac{L}{K}\right)^{\alpha}.$$

More generally, we have the following property of any function which is homogeneous of degree 0.

Arguments of Functions That Are Homogeneous of Degree 0 Any function

$$f(x_1, x_2, \ldots, x_i, \ldots, x_n)$$

that is homogeneous of degree 0 can be written as

$$f\left(\frac{x_1}{x_i}, \frac{x_2}{x_i}, \ldots, 1, \ldots, \frac{x_n}{x_i}\right)$$

for any $i = 1, 2, \ldots, n$.

The proof of this result is straightforward. If the function $f(x_1, x_2, \ldots, x_i, \ldots, x_n)$ is homogeneous of degree 0, then

$$s^0 \cdot f(x_1, x_2, \ldots, x_i, \ldots, x_n) = f(sx_1, sx_2, \ldots, sx_i, \ldots, sx_n),$$

and, since $s^0 = 1$, we have

$$f(x_1, x_2, \ldots, x_i, \ldots, x_n) = f(sx_1, sx_2, \ldots, sx_i, \ldots, sx_n).$$

Then simply choose

$$s = \frac{1}{x_i}$$

to get

$$f(x_1, x_2, \ldots, x_i, \ldots, x_n) = f\left(\frac{x_1}{x_i}, \frac{x_2}{x_i}, \ldots, 1, \ldots, \frac{x_n}{x_i}\right).$$

The property that the first partial derivatives of the Cobb-Douglas production function are homogeneous of degree 0 is a particular example of the following general property of homogeneous functions.

First Partial Derivatives of Homogeneous Functions If the function

$$f(x_1, x_2, \ldots, x_i, \ldots, x_n)$$

is homogeneous of degree k, then each of its first partial derivatives,

$$f_i = \frac{\partial f(x_1, x_2, \ldots, x_i, \ldots, x_n)}{\partial x_i}$$

for any $i = 1, 2, \ldots, n$, is homogeneous of degree $k - 1$.

To prove this result, note that for a function that is homogeneous of degree k,

$$f(sx_1, sx_2, \ldots, sx_n) = s^k f(x_1, x_2, \ldots, x_n)$$

for any $(x_1, x_2, \ldots, x_n)$. Using the chain rule for taking the derivative of the function $f(sx_1, sx_2, \ldots, sx_n)$ with respect to x_i, we have

$$\frac{\partial f(sx_1, sx_2, \ldots, sx_n)}{\partial x_i} = \frac{\partial f(sx_1, sx_2, \ldots, sx_n)}{\partial (sx_i)} \cdot \frac{d(sx_i)}{dx_i} = s \cdot f_i(sx_1, sx_2, \ldots, sx_n).$$

Taking the partial derivative of the function $s^k f(x_1, x_2, \ldots, x_n)$ with respect to x_i gives us

$$\frac{\partial s^k f(x_1, x_2, \ldots, x_n)}{\partial x_i} = s^k f_i(x_1, x_2, \ldots, x_n).$$

Equating these two partial derivatives, we have

$$s \cdot f_i(sx_1, sx_2, \ldots, sx_n) = s^k f_i(x_1, x_2, \ldots, x_n)$$

or

$$f_i(sx_1, sx_2, \ldots, sx_n) = s^{k-1} f_i(x_1, x_2, \ldots, x_n),$$

which proves the result since it shows that the function f_i is homogeneous of degree $k - 1$. This result will be useful for the analysis of level curves discussed in the following section.

In the discussion of level curves, we also consider homothetic functions. A **homothetic function** is a monotonic transformation of a homogeneous function. Thus if

$$y = f(x_1, \ldots, x_n)$$

is a homogeneous function, then

$$z = g(y)$$

is a homothetic function if the function $g(y)$ is strictly monotonic, that is, if $g'(y) > 0$ for all y or if $g'(y) < 0$ for all y. For example, consider the function

$$y = x_1^\alpha x_2^\beta,$$

which is homogeneous of degree $\alpha + \beta$ because

$$(sx_1)^\alpha (sx_2)^\beta = s^{\alpha+\beta} x_1^\alpha x_2^\beta = s^{\alpha+\beta} y.$$

The function

$$z = \ln(y) = \alpha \ln(x_1) + \beta \ln(x_2)$$

is homothetic since the logarithmic function is strictly monotonic. But this homothetic function is not homogeneous in the arguments x_1 and x_2 since

$$\begin{aligned} \alpha \ln(sx_1) + \beta \ln(sx_2) &= \alpha \ln(x_1) + \beta \ln(x_2) + (\alpha + \beta) \ln(s) \\ &= z + (\alpha + \beta) \ln(s). \end{aligned}$$

Thus, while every homogeneous function is a homothetic function since we can simply choose the function $g(y) = y$, this example shows that not every homothetic function is a homogeneous function.

Exercises 8.3

1. Find the derivative dy/dz
   (a) $y = f(x, w) = 3x^2 - 2xw + w^2$, where $x = 8z - 18$ and $w = 4z$
   (b) $y = f(x, z) = 4x^3 + \frac{1}{4}xz^2 - 2z$, where $x = z^{-2}$
   (c) $y = f(v, w, z)$, where $v = g(z)$ and $w = h(z)$
   (d) $y = f(x, t) = (xt + 5)(2xt)$, where $x = \ln(z)$ and $t = \sqrt{z}$
2. Find the partial derivatives $\partial Z/\partial u$ and $\partial Z/\partial v$ for each set of functions.
   (a) $Z = f(x, y) = 4x^2 + 2xy + y^2$, where $x = 3u^2$ and $y = u - 2v$
   (b) $Z = f(x, y) = ax^3 - bx^2y + cy$, where $x = \gamma u + \theta v$ and $y = \theta u - \gamma v^2$
   (c) $Z = f(x, y) = 2e^x + \frac{1}{2}x^2y - 4\ln y$, where $x = \frac{1}{4}u$ and $y = u^2 + 6v$
   (d) $Z = f(x, y, u) = 2x^3 - 3xy^2 + 0.75yu - 5u^2$, where $x = \sqrt{u + v}$ and $y = v^2$
3. The United States has a significant negative trade balance with Japan, where the trade balance between the two countries is defined as exports minus imports. U.S. exports are a function of the exchange rate (E) and Japanese income (Y_J), and U.S. imports from Japan are a function of the exchange rate and U.S. income (Y_{US}). An increase in the exchange rate represents a depreciation of the U.S. dollar. The following functional notation captures these relationships, with the sign of the partial derivative indicated below each argument:

$$X = f(\underset{+}{E}, \underset{+}{Y_J})$$
$$IMP = g(\underset{-}{E}, \underset{+}{Y_{US}}).$$

   Assume that the exchange rate and U.S. income are affected by U.S. monetary policy (M_{US}), where the sign of the partial derivative is indicated below each argument, as shown by the functions,

$$E = r(\underset{+}{M}) \quad \text{and} \quad Y_{US} = s(\underset{+}{M}),$$

   and also assume Japanese national income is exogenous. The trade balance function can be written as

$$TB = X - IMP = h(r(M), s(M), Y_J).$$

   (a) Determine the derivative of the trade balance with respect to monetary policy, dTB/dM
   (b) Determine the impact (positive or negative) on the trade balance of a change in each of the variables.

4. Determine whether each function is homogeneous and, if so, of what degree.
   (a) $f(x, y, w) = \dfrac{x}{w} + \dfrac{3y}{5x}$
   (b) $f(x, y, w) = \dfrac{x^2}{w} + \dfrac{2w^2}{y}$
   (c) $f(x, y, w) = \dfrac{x^2y}{w} + 2xyw$
   (d) $f(x, y) = \sqrt{x^2 + y^2}$
   (e) $f(x, y, w) = 3x^2y - \dfrac{3y}{w^2}$
   (f) $f(x, y) = x^{1/2}y^{1/4} + y^{5/8}$
5. Show that each of the first partial derivatives of the homogeneous functions you found in question 4 is homogeneous of degree $k - 1$.
6. A proportional increase in all inputs in a production function increases the scale of production. If there are constant returns to scale, then output will increase equiproportionally to the increase in all inputs. If there are increasing returns to scale, an increase in all inputs leads to a more than proportionate increase in output. If there are decreasing returns to scale, then output increases less than proportionately with an increase in all inputs. Consider the production function
$$q = AK^{\alpha}L^{\beta}.$$
   (a) Using Euler's Theorem, prove that this production function exhibits constant returns to scale when $\alpha + \beta = 1$.
   (b) What condition on $\alpha + \beta$ is necessary for increasing returns to scale? For decreasing returns to scale?
7. Consider the production function
$$y = f(x_1, x_2) = x_1^{1/4}x_2^{1/3}.$$
   (a) Determine whether this production function is homogeneous. If so, of what degree?
   (b) Take the partial derivatives of the production function, and show that they are homogeneous of degree $k - 1$.
   (c) Now, using Euler's Theorem, show that
$$x_1 f_1(sx_1, sx_2) + x_2 f_2(sx_1, sx_2) = ks^{k-1}f(x_1, x_2).$$
8. Consider the following Cobb-Douglas production function, which is homogeneous of degree 1 in capital and labor,
$$Q = 50K^{0.4}L^{0.6}.$$
Show that the sum of the total factor payments to labor $(wL = \partial Q/\partial L\ L)$ and capital $(rK = \partial Q/\partial K\ K)$ equals the value of national production (Q), which is the value of national income such that
$$Q = wL + rK = \alpha Q + (1 - \alpha)Q,$$
where $\alpha = 0.6$.

9. Consider the function

$$y = f(x_1, x_2) = x_1 x_2$$

defined over the domain $x_1 > 0$ and $x_2 > 0$. Also, consider the functions

$$g(y) = \ln(y), \quad h(y) = 10y, \quad j(y) = y^2, \quad \text{and} \quad k(y) = e^y.$$

(a) Is $f(x_1, x_2)$ a homogeneous function? If so, what is its degree?
(b) Is $g(y)$ a homothetic function? Is $g(y)$ a homogeneous function in the arguments x_1 and x_2? If so, what is its degree?
(c) Is $h(y)$ a homothetic function? Is $h(y)$ a homogeneous function in the arguments x_1 and x_2? If so, what is its degree?
(d) Is $j(y)$ a homothetic function? Is $j(y)$ a homogeneous function in the arguments x_1 and x_2? If so, what is its degree?
(e) Is $k(y)$ a homothetic function? Is $k(y)$ a homogeneous function in the arguments x_1 and x_2? If so, what is its degree?

10. Show that each function is homothetic by transforming it back to its original homogeneous form.
(a) $y = \ln(x) + \ln(z)$
(b) $y = 0.30 \ln(L) + 0.70 \ln(K)$
(c) $y = 2\ln(x) + \ln(y) - \ln(w)$
(d) $y = e^{xz}$

8.4 TOTAL DIFFERENTIALS AND IMPLICIT DIFFERENTIATION

In Chapter 6 we introduced the concept of the differential of a univariate function. It was shown there that we can use the differential to approximate how small changes in the argument of a function affect its value and thereby avoid the more tedious calculations involved in obtaining an exact answer through the use of difference quotients. The multivariate analogue to this is the **total differential,** which shows how small changes in all the arguments of a function affect the value of the function.

Total Differential The total differential of the multivariate function

$$y = f(x_1, x_2, \ldots, x_n)$$

evaluated at the point $(x_1^0, x_2^0, \ldots, x_n^0)$ is

$$dy = f_1(x_1^0, x_2^0, \ldots, x_n^0)\,dx_1 + f_2(x_1^0, x_2^0, \ldots, x_n^0)\,dx_2 + \cdots + f_n(x_1^0, x_2^0, \ldots, x_n^0)\,dx_n,$$

where $f_i(x_1^0, x_2^0, \ldots, x_n^0)$ represents the partial derivative of the function $f(x_1, x_2, \ldots, x_n)$ with respect to its ith argument, evaluated at the point $(x_1^0, x_2^0, \ldots, x_n^0)$.

A numerical example illustrates the use of the total differential. Consider the utility function

$$U(M, C) = \frac{1}{4}\ln(M) + \frac{3}{4}\ln(C),$$

which describes the utility you derive from consuming boxes of cookies, C, and pints of milk, M, where $C > 0$ and $M > 0$. Notice that this utility function reflects an assumption of **nonsatiation** since more cookies or more milk always increases your utility because the partial derivatives are positive. These partial derivatives are

$$U_M(M, C) = \frac{1}{4M} > 0 \quad \text{and} \quad U_C(M, C) = \frac{3}{4C} > 0.$$

This utility function also reflects **diminishing marginal utility** since

$$U_{MM}(M, C) = -\frac{1}{4M^2} < 0 \quad \text{and} \quad U_{CC}(M, C) = -\frac{3}{4C^2} < 0.$$

We assume, initially, that $M = 1$ and $C = 1$, a pair of values that gives us $U(M, C) = 0$ since $\ln(1) = 0$. To obtain the differential approximation of these changes, we first obtain the total differential

$$dU = \frac{1}{4M}\,dM + \frac{3}{4C}\,dC.$$

Evaluating this at the point where $M = 1$ and $C = 1$, we have the differential approximation

$$dU = \frac{1}{4}\,dM + \frac{3}{4}\,dC.$$

The actual change in the value of the function when M changes from 1.0 to 1.1 is approximately 0.0238. The differential approximation is

$$dU = \frac{1}{4} \cdot 0.10 + \frac{3}{4} \cdot 0 = 0.025,$$

a difference that is about 5% greater than the actual change.

The actual change in the value of the function when both M and C change from 1.0 to 1.1 is about 0.095. The differential approximation is

$$dU = \frac{1}{4} \cdot 0.10 + \frac{3}{4} \cdot 0.10 = 0.10,$$

a difference that is about 0.5% greater than the actual change.

The actual change in the value of the function when both M and C change from 1 to 2 is about 0.69 (recall from the doubling times application in Chapter 3 that $\ln(2) \approx 0.70$). The differential approximation is

$$dU = \frac{1}{4} \cdot 1.00 + \frac{3}{4} \cdot 1.00 = 1.00,$$

a difference that is about 44% greater than the actual change.

The geometric interpretation of the total differential is a multidimensional version of the differential of a univariate function. Figure 6.8 in Chapter 6 shows that, in a univariate setting, the differential

$$dy = f'(x)\,dx$$

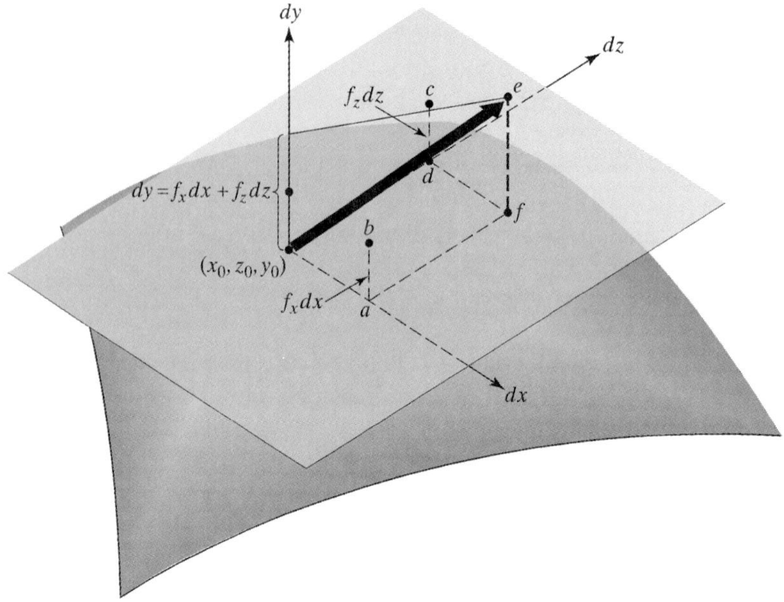

FIGURE 8.4 Differential of a Multivariate Equation at Point (x_0, z_0, y_0)

at point (x_0, y_0) can be interpreted as describing points on the line tangent to the function at that point. The slope of this line is $f'(x)$. In a multivariate function with two arguments x and z, the differential at point (x_0, z_0, y_0) can be interpreted as describing points on the two-dimensional plane that passes through (x_0, z_0, y_0) and is tangent to the surface of the original multivariate function. Points on the tangent plane satisfy the differential

$$dz = f_x(x, z)\, dx + f_z(x, z)\, dz.$$

This tangent plane is illustrated in Figure 8.4. The slope of a slice of this tangent plane along the dx axis is $f_x(x_0, z_0)$, and the slope of a slice along the dz axis is $f_z(x_0, z_0)$. In terms of Figure 8.4, the approximate change due to a small change in the arguments equal to dx and dz is represented by the difference in the height of the tangent plane dy. The overall change, dy, consists of that amount due to dx, which is $f_x(x_0, z_0)\, dx$, and that amount due to dz, which is $f_z(x_0, z_0)\, dz$. In Figure 8.4, $f_x(x_0, z_0)\, dx$ is represented by the distance *ab*, $f_z(x_0, z_0)\, dz$ is represented by the distance *cd*, and dy is represented by the distance *ef*.

Implicit Functions

The numerical example just presented shows how a change in the consumption of cookies and milk affects utility. This function could also be used to ask the question of how many more cookies one must receive in order to compensate for having one less pint of milk so that overall utility remains constant. You may recognize that this question is linked to the analysis of an indifference curve. In this section we discuss the analysis of implicit functions for addressing questions like this.

The functions we have discussed to this point are **explicit functions** since they represent a dependent variable (say y) as a function of a set of independent variables (say $x_1, x_2, \ldots, x_n$) in a form like

$$y = f(x_1, x_2, \ldots, x_n).$$

In contrast, an **implicit function** combines the dependent variable and the independent variables in a form like

$$F(y, x_1, x_2, \ldots, x_n) = k,$$

where k is a constant (and we may have $k = 0$). Sometimes it is easy to rewrite an implicit function in the form of an explicit function. For example, a trivial case is the implicit function

$$2y - 5x = 10,$$

which can be rewritten as the explicit function

$$y = \frac{5}{2}x + 5.$$

In other cases, however, it is quite difficult to rewrite an implicit function as an explicit function, as with the implicit function

$$\frac{1}{3}y^3 - 4y^2 + 16y + 3x^2 + 5x = 7.$$

In economic analysis, implicit functions are often used in the context of **level curves,** which show how the arguments of a function are related to a particular level of a variable. An **indifference curve** is a particular type of level curve that shows the combination of goods that provide a certain level of utility. For example, an implicit function that uses the utility function presented previously to describe an indifference curve is

$$\frac{1}{4}\ln(M) + \frac{3}{4}\ln(C) = 0.52.$$

An **isoquant** is another type of level curve that shows the combinations of factors of production that yield a given level of output. An implicit function that uses a Cobb-Douglas production function to describe an isoquant is

$$K^{1/3}L^{2/3} = 2.$$

We can derive the properties of level curves or other types of implicit functions through the use of the **Implicit Function Theorem.**

Implicit Function Theorem For an implicit function

$$F(y, x_1, x_2, \ldots, x_n) = k,$$

for which k is a constant, which is defined at the point $(y^0, x_1^0, x_2^0, \ldots, x_n^0)$ and which has continuous first partial derivatives at that point with $F_y(y^0, x_1^0, x_2^0, \ldots, x_n^0) \neq 0$, there is a function

$$y = f(x_1, x_2, \ldots, x_n)$$

defined in the neighborhood of $(x_1^0, x_2^0, \ldots, x_n^0)$ corresponding to $F(y, x_1, x_2, \ldots, x_n) = k$ such that

$$\text{i. } F(f(x_1^0, x_2^0, \ldots, x_n^0), x_1^0, x_2^0, \ldots, x_n^0) = k$$
$$\text{ii. } y^0 = f(x_1^0, x_2^0, \ldots, x_n^0)$$
$$\text{iii. } f_i(x_1^0, x_2^0, \ldots, x_n^0) = -\frac{F_{x_i}(y^0, x_1^0, x_2^0, \ldots, x_n^0)}{F_y(y^0, x_1^0, x_2^0, \ldots, x_n^0)},$$

where

$$F_{x_i}(y^0, x_1^0, x_2^0, \ldots, x_n^0) = \frac{\partial F(y, x_1, x_2, \ldots, x_n)}{\partial x_i} \quad \text{and}$$
$$F_y(y^0, x_1^0, x_2^0, \ldots, x_n^0) = \frac{\partial F(y, x_1, x_2, \ldots, x_n)}{\partial y},$$

with these derivatives evaluated at $(y^0, x_1^0, x_2^0, \ldots, x_n^0)$. ■

The results (i) and (ii) show that there is a correspondence between the explicit function $f(x_1, x_2, \ldots, x_n)$ and the implicit function $F(y, x_1, x_2, \ldots, x_n)$ in that the explicit function evaluated at $(x_1^0, x_2^0, \ldots, x_n^0)$ gives us y^0 and

$$F(f(x_1^0, x_2^0, \ldots, x_n^0), x_1^0, x_2^0, \ldots, x_n^0) = F(y^0, x_1^0, x_2^0, \ldots, x_n^0).$$

The third result shows that there is a correspondence between the ratio of the partial derivatives of the implicit function and the partial derivative of the explicit function.

We can illustrate the use of the third result with reference to the implicit functions given previously. This result shows that the implicit function

$$2y - 5x = 10$$

has the derivative

$$\frac{dy}{dx} = \frac{5}{2},$$

which is the same as the derivative of the explicit function corresponding to this implicit function. The derivative of the function

$$\frac{1}{3}y^3 - 4y^2 + 16y + 3x^2 + 5x = 7$$

is

$$\frac{dy}{dx} = -\frac{6x + 5}{y^2 - 8y + 16}.$$

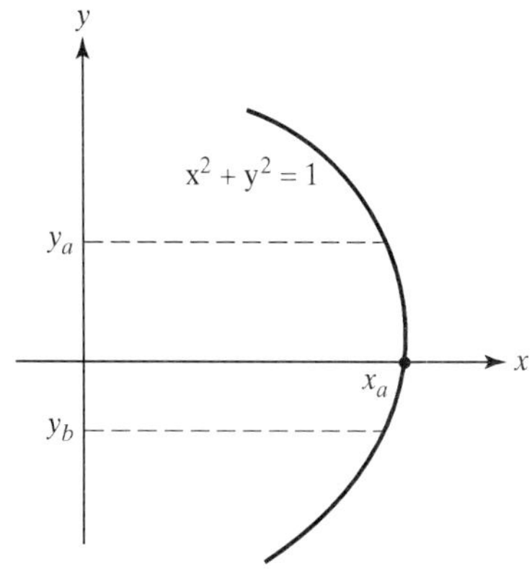

FIGURE 8.5 An Implicit Function

But note that this derivative does not exist in the neighborhood of $y = 4$ because

$$4^2 - 8(4) + 16 = 0.$$

In a similar manner, we can use the Implicit Function Theorem to find the derivative dy/dx for the implicit function

$$C(y, x) = y^2 + x^2 = 1.$$

The derivatives of the implicit function are

$$C_x(y, x) = 2x \quad \text{and} \quad C_y(y, x) = 2y,$$

and, therefore,

$$\frac{dy}{dx} = -\frac{x}{y}.$$

This derivative does not exist in the neighborhood of $y = 0$ because, as shown in Figure 8.5, $C_y(0, 1) = 0$. This is because y is not a single-valued function of x in the neighborhood of $y = 0$ and there are two values of y, y_a and y_b, that correspond to x_a in that neighborhood.

As an example of the use of the Implicit Function Theorem in an economic context, consider the implicit function

$$U(M, C) = \overline{U},$$

which gives the different combinations of cookies and milk that provide a level of utility equal to the constant $\overline{U}$. The Implicit Function Theorem shows that

$$\frac{dM}{dC} = -\frac{U_C(M, C)}{U_M(M, C)}.$$

This relationship indicates that the slope of the indifference curve in Figure 8.6(a) is -1 times the ratio of the marginal utility with respect to cookies to the marginal utility with

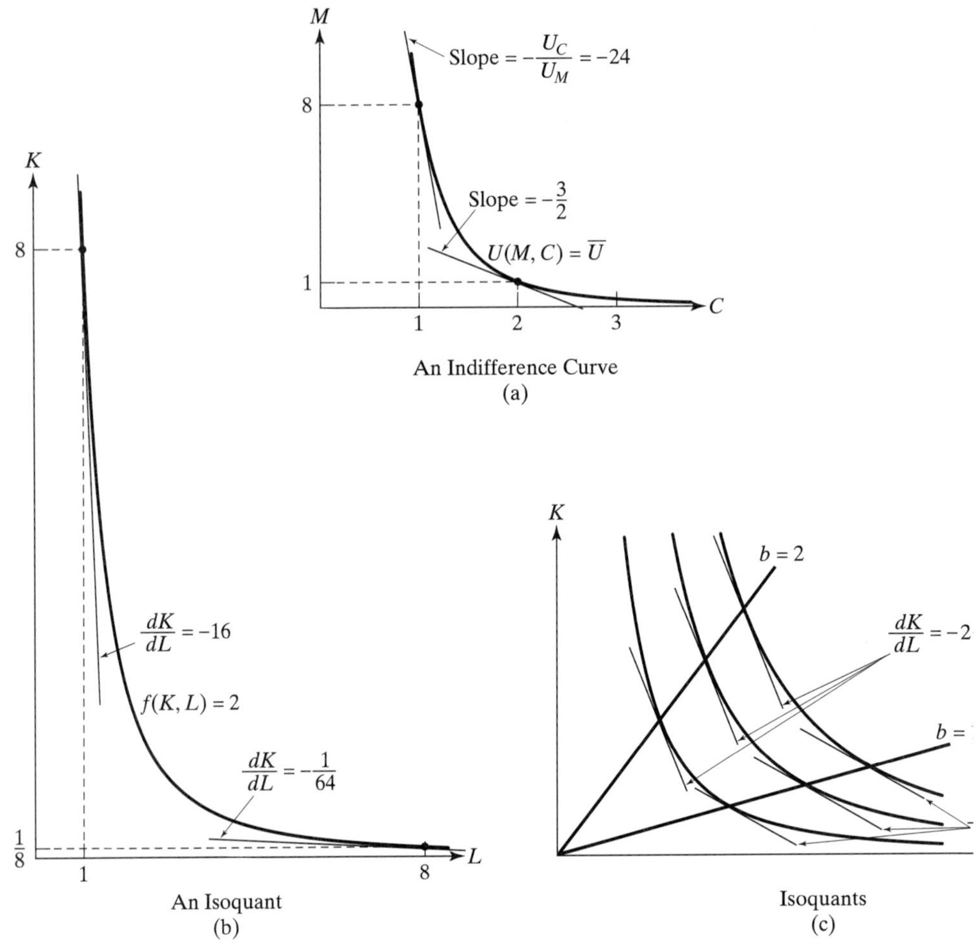

FIGURE 8.6 An Indifference Curve and Isoquants

respect to milk. In particular, with the logarithmic utility function presented previously,

$$U(M, C) = \frac{1}{4}\ln(M) + \frac{3}{4}\ln(C) = 0.52,$$

the slope of a line tangent to the indifference curve associated with this utility function is

$$\frac{dM}{dC} = -\frac{U_C(M, C)}{U_M(M, C)} = -\frac{3M}{C}.$$

A line tangent to this indifference curve is steeper at relatively low levels of cookie consumption and flatter at relatively low levels of milk consumption. In Figure 8.6(a) the slope of the line tangent to the indifference curve is -24 when $M = 8$ and $C = 1$, while the slope of the line tangent to the indifference curve is $-\frac{3}{2}$ when $M = 1$ and $C = 2$.

The Implicit Function Theorem shows that an isoquant associated with the Cobb-Douglas production function

$$K^{1/3}L^{2/3} = 2$$

has the property that

$$\frac{dK}{dL} = -2\frac{K}{L}.$$

As shown in Figure 8.6(b), a line tangent to this isoquant has the slope -16 when $K = 8$ and $L = 1$ and the slope $-\frac{1}{64}$ when $L = 8$ and $K = \frac{1}{8}$. More generally, for a Cobb-Douglas production function of the form

$$Q = AK^{1-\alpha}L^{\alpha},$$

a line tangent to its isoquant will have the slope

$$\frac{dK}{dL} = -\left(\frac{\alpha}{1-\alpha}\right)\frac{K}{L}.$$

An interesting property of the Cobb-Douglas production function is that the ratio of its marginal products depends upon the capital-labor ratio but not upon the overall level of production. This implies that, along a ray from the origin, the slopes of lines tangent to isoquants for a Cobb-Douglas production function are equal. This can be seen by noting that the equation for a ray from the origin is

$$K = bL$$

for any $b > 0$ and that any point on this ray takes the form of the ordered pair $(sK, sL) = (sbL, sL)$ for any $s \geq 0$. Therefore the slope of any line tangent to an isoquant along this ray is

$$\frac{dK}{dL} = -\left(\frac{\alpha}{1-\alpha}\right)\frac{sK}{sL} = -\left(\frac{\alpha}{1-\alpha}\right)\frac{sbL}{sL} = -\left(\frac{\alpha}{1-\alpha}\right)b.$$

The slope does not depend upon the scale, that is, the proportionate increase in K and L as represented by s. This is shown in Figure 8.6(c), which presents a number of isoquants and two rays from the origin, one corresponding to $b = 2$ and one corresponding to $b = 1$.

More generally, the slope of the level curves of any homogeneous function are constant along any ray from the origin. The slope of a level curve of a function $f(x_1, x_2)$ is

$$\frac{dx_2}{dx_1} = -\frac{f_1(x_1, x_2)}{f_2(x_1, x_2)}.$$

Recall from the previous section that, if the function $f(x_1, x_2)$ is homogeneous of degree k, then each of its partial derivatives are homogeneous of degree $k - 1$, and therefore,

$$f_i(sx_1, sx_2) = s^{k-1}f_i(x_1, x_2)$$

for $i = 1, 2$. Thus along a ray from the origin,

$$\begin{aligned}\frac{dx_2}{dx_1} &= -\frac{f_1(sx_1, sx_2)}{f_2(sx_1, sx_2)}\\ &= -\frac{s^{k-1}f_1(x_1, x_2)}{s^{k-1}f_2(x_1, x_2)}\\ &= -\frac{f_1(x_1, x_2)}{f_2(x_1, x_2)}.\end{aligned}$$

So for any proportionate scaling s of the two arguments x_1 and x_2, the slope of the level curve is unchanged.

Any homothetic function also exhibits the property of a constant slope of its level curves along a ray from the origin. This can be shown by considering the function

$$y = f(x_1, x_2),$$

which we assume is homogeneous of degree k in its arguments x_1 and x_2, and the homothetic function

$$z = g(y) = g(f(x_1, x_2)),$$

where $g'(y) > 0$ for all y or $g'(y) < 0$ for all y. Using the chain rule in conjunction with the Implicit Function Theorem, we find that

$$\begin{aligned}\frac{dx_2}{dx_1} &= -\frac{g'(y)f_1(sx_1, sx_2)}{g'(y)f_2(sx_1, sx_2)}\\ &= -\frac{f_1(sx_1, sx_2)}{f_2(sx_1, sx_2)}\\ &= -\frac{s^{k-1}f_1(x_1, x_2)}{s^{k-1}f_2(x_1, x_2)}\\ &= -\frac{f_1(x_1, x_2)}{f_2(x_1, x_2)}.\end{aligned}$$

Thus, as with homogeneous functions, the scaling factor s does not affect the slope of the level curve. This then shows that the slope of the level curves of any homothetic function, a class of functions that includes, but is not limited to, homogeneous functions, is not altered by a proportionate scaling of all of its arguments.

Exercises 8.4

1. Find the total differential for each function.

   (a) $w = 2x^2 + \frac{1}{2}xy - 3y^3$

   (b) $y = 4x_1^3 - \ln(x_1x_2) + 6x_2$

(c) $z = \dfrac{x^2}{y^3 + xy}$

(d) $y = 2x_1^2 e^{3x_2}$

2. For each function, use the total differential to approximate the change in y due to the given changes in x and z.
   (a) $y = x^2 + 4x - z^2 - 2xz$, where $x = 1, z = 4, \Delta x = 2, \Delta z = -2$
   (b) $y = e^{x^2+3z}$, where $x = 1, z = 2, \Delta x = 2, \Delta z = -2$
   (c) $y = \ln x^3 - 4z + 2xz$, where $x = 1, z = 2, \Delta x = 2, \Delta z = 4$
   (d) $y = x^2 + e^{z/2}$ for $x = 2, z = 2, \Delta x = 1$, and $\Delta z = -1$.
3. Assuming that $x = 2$ and $z = 1$, evaluate the function

$$y = 3x^2 - 2x + z^3 - 1.5z^2 - xz.$$

   (a) Use the total differential approximation to determine Δy for each set of changes in x and z:

$$\Delta x = 1.0, \quad \Delta z = 1.0$$
$$\Delta x = 0.5, \quad \Delta z = 0.5$$
$$\Delta x = 0.1, \quad \Delta z = 0.1.$$

   (b) Calculate the actual values of y for each pair of arguments x and z, and compare your results to the total differential approximations.
   (c) How well does the total differential approximate small changes in the value of the function?
4. Imagine that you have finished school and are working for a firm as an economist. Performance reviews are conducted annually, and salary increases are also awarded once a year. Your raise is dependent on your personal performance, as well as on other factors. Assume that your salary increase (I) is based on an index of the reliability of your forecasts (f), the current profitability of the firm (p), and your contribution to your department's projects (c) measured in revenue dollars. The salary increase function is:

$$I = f^{\alpha} + \ln\left(p^{\beta}\right) + \delta c.$$

   How would you determine the change in your salary due to changes in the arguments of this function? If the firm's profitability increases by 1%, by what factor will your salary increase?
5. Consider again the function for the demand for sugar presented in question 6 of Section 8.2,

$$Q_d = f(Y, P_C, P_S) = 0.05Y + 10P_C - 5P_S^2,$$

   where Q_d is the demand for sugar, Y is income, P_S is the price of sugar, and P_C is the price of saccharine.
   (a) Use the total differential to find the approximate change in the demand for sugar with an increase in income of \$1 if, initially, $Y = 10{,}000$, $P_S = 5$, and $P_C = 7$.

(b) Use the total differential to find the approximate change in the demand for sugar with a \$1 increase in the price of sugar if, initially, $Y = 10{,}000$, $P_S = 5$, and $P_C = 7$.

(c) Use the total differential to find the approximate change in the demand for sugar with a 1% increase in income if, initially, $Y = 10{,}000$, $P_S = 5$, and $P_C = 7$.

(d) Use the total differential to find the approximate change in the demand for sugar with a 1% increase in the price of sugar if, initially, $Y = 10{,}000$, $P_S = 5$, and $P_C = 7$.

6. Find the derivative of each implicit function, where $dY/dX = -F_X/F_Y$, provided that $F_Y \neq 0$.
   (a) $F(x, y) = x^2 + y^2 + (xy)^{1/3} = 0$
   (b) $F(x, y) = x^2y + y^2x + xy = 0$
   (c) $F(x, y) = \ln x^3 + (xy)^2 - 4y = 0$
   (d) $F(x, y, w) = w^3y^3 + x^3 + wxy + 7 = 0$ (Find $\partial y/\partial x$.)
   (e) $F(x, y) = xy^2e^y$

7. Consider the Cobb-Douglas production function

$$50K^{0.3}L^{0.7} = \overline{Q},$$

where $\overline{Q}$ is a given level of output, K is the amount of capital, and L is the amount of labor. The isoquant associated with this function reflects the levels of capital and labor that yield a constant level of output.

(a) Use the Implicit Function Theorem to derive an equation for the slope of an isoquant associated with this production function.

(b) When $K = 6$ and $L = 2$, what is the slope of a line tangent to this isoquant? What is the slope of the line when $K = 3$ and $L = 14$?

(c) The marginal rate of technical substitution (*MRTS*) is the rate at which the two production inputs can be substituted if output is held constant. It is the absolute value of the slope of the isoquant. Find the *MRTS* for both examples in part (b).

8. Consider the production function

$$Q = x_1^{0.25}x_2^{0.75}.$$

(a) Find the slope of the isoquant associated with this function, and determine the degree of homogeneity.

(b) Show that along any ray from the origin, the slopes of the isoquants are equal.

9. The implicit function

$$\overline{U} = U(A, B)$$

shows what combinations of apples (A) and bananas (B) provide the level of utility $\overline{U}$. The absolute value of the slope of the indifference curve is the marginal rate of substitution (*MRS*), which measures the rate at which one good can be substituted for another while maintaining the same level of utility. Find the derivative of the implicit function to determine the MRS of apples for bananas (MRS_{AB}) for each utility function.

(a) $\overline{U} = \sqrt{AB}$

(b) $\overline{U} = A^{0.25}B^{0.75}$

10. Consider the utility function for labor (L) and leisure (T)

$$\overline{U}(L, T) = LT,$$

where $\overline{U}$ is a given level of utility.

(a) Is this a homogenous function? If so, of what degree? Find the slope of an indifference curve associated with this utility function.

(b) Assume that there is a function $z = g(U)$ such that $z = \ln(U)$. Show that this function is homothetic.

(c) Using the chain rule in conjunction with the Implicit Function Theorem, show that the slope of the indifference curves associated with the homothetic function is not changed by a proportionate scaling of L and T.

11. Consider the following relationship among the infant mortality rate (M), national income per capita (Y), and the amount spent on health care per capita (H):

$$M = 8Y^{-0.25}H^{-0.1}.$$

What is the relationship between the national income per capita and health spending per capita such that the infant mortality rate is constant?

12. The Chapter 7 application about the money multiplier and the great depression presented the relationship between the money supply, M; the currency-deposit ratio, c; the reserve ratio, r; and the stock of high-powered money, H, as

$$M = \frac{1 + c}{c + r}H.$$

Determine the relationship between the change in the stock of high-powered money, dH, and the change in the currency-deposit ratio, dc, for a constant level of the money supply. Is dH/dc positive or negative? Also determine the relationship between dc and dr, the change in the reserve ratio, such that M is constant. Is dc/dr positive or negative?

Summary

Partial differentiation is the multivariate analogue of the differentiation of univariate functions. This chapter shows that the rules of partial differentiation are a straightforward extension of the rules of differentiation presented in Chapter 7. While there are some subtleties involved in moving from univariate derivatives to multivariate partial derivatives, much of the intuition carries over.

This chapter completes the part of the book that presents the rules of differentiation. The applications in the chapters in this part illustrate how important these rules are for economic analysis. In the next two chapters, we apply the techniques taught in Chapters 7 and 8 to a set of problems of central importance in economics: optimization.

Part Four

Optimization

Many models of economic behavior are based on the explicit assumption that people attempt to achieve the best result for themselves. Thus standard models of production, investment, or consumption identify the best or optimal outcome in terms of the lowest cost, the most rewarding return, or the highest level of well-being. Even models of seemingly noneconomic behavior, such as interactions within the family, crime, or political activity, are predicated on the assumption that there is an effort to achieve some type of optimal outcome.

Part Four contains three chapters that present mathematical techniques that are used by economists to identify optimal outcomes in economic models. Drawing on the methods of differentiation presented in Chapters 6 through 8, these techniques show how to find the ***extreme values*** *of a differentiable function. In many economic contexts, an extreme value represents the best outcome, and therefore, these mathematical techniques are often referred to as* ***optimization.*** *In other contexts, in which there is not an explicit assumption of optimizing behavior, it is still often important to be able to identify the extreme values of a function.*

This part opens with Chapter 9, which discusses ***unconstrained optimization*** *of univariate functions. The adjective "unconstrained" means that there are no limits on the argument of the function. This chapter draws on the techniques of univariate calculus presented in Chapters 6 and 7. Applications in this chapter demonstrate the use of* *univariate unconstrained optimization in various economic contexts, including micro economics, monetary theory, and economic growth.*

Chapter 10 extends the unconstrained optimization analysis to multivariate functions and employs the multivariate differentiation techniques presented in Chapter 8. This chapter begins with ***bivariate functions,*** *that is, functions with two arguments. A generalization of the results to functions with any number of arguments uses the tools of matrix algebra, which are presented in Chapters 4 and 5.*

Part Four closes with Chapter 11, which discusses **constrained optimization.** *Constrained optimization problems include conditions that limit the value of the arguments of a multivariate function. This mathematical method corresponds to the central economic problem of optimal choice in the face of scarcity. Applications in this chapter suggest the range of economic issues, such as the effects of college scholarship rules on household savings, intertemporal consumption, and the optimal allocation of time, that can be analyzed with constrained optimization.*

Chapter 9

Extreme Values of Univariate Functions

A solution to many types of economic models requires the identification of an optimal outcome. The basic model of the firm, for example, is predicated on the assumption that the goal of the firm is to achieve the highest level of profits. The solution to the problem facing the firm is to determine the point where the profit function achieves a maximum. More generally, the characterization of the best outcome requires the identification of an **extreme value** of a function, which may represent either a **maximum** or a **minimum.** The identification of the extreme value of economic functions is called **optimization** if that point represents the best or optimal economic outcome, such as maximum utility or minimum cost. Finding extreme values is also often important in other types of economic analysis that do not incorporate explicit optimizing behavior. For example, in this chapter we consider a cross-country statistical analysis of the link between pollution and per capita income to determine the level of income that corresponds to the highest level of pollution.

This chapter presents the techniques for identifying and characterizing the extreme values of univariate functions. The chapter begins with a presentation of the rules for finding extreme values in Section 9.1. Section 9.2 offers some applications of these techniques that illustrate their use in various economic contexts.

9.1 IDENTIFYING AND CHARACTERIZING EXTREME VALUES

The extreme value of a univariate function can occur either within the interval over which the function is defined or at its endpoints. Strictly monotonic functions, those which either increase or decrease continuously over their domain (such as linear functions, logarithmic functions, and exponential functions), do not have extreme values within the interior of their domain; extreme values occur only at their endpoints. Nonmonotonic functions, which we will study in this chapter, may have one or more extreme values within the interior of the domain over which they are defined. In this chapter we focus on the interior extreme values of functions that are differentiable.

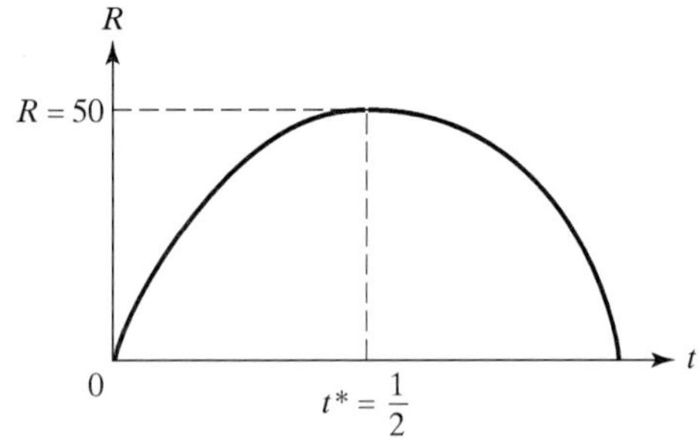

FIGURE 9.1 Tax Rate and Tax Revenue

The example of the relationship between the tax rate and tax revenue in Chapter 6 has already introduced the concept of extreme values. We return to this example to introduce the identification of an extreme value.

The First-Order Condition

In Chapter 6 we used the quadratic function

$$R = 200t - 200t^2$$

to illustrate the relationship between the tax revenue, R, and the tax rate, t. As shown in Figure 9.1, over the range $0 \leq t \leq 1$, this function first increases and then decreases, reaching a maximum at the tax rate t^*. The non-monotonic nature of this function reflects the reduction in the tax base that accompanies an increase in the tax rate, a reduction that eventually comes to dominate the effect of higher tax rates on tax revenues. In terms of calculus, the derivative $R'(t)$ is positive for values of t between 0 and t^*. At tax rates greater than t^*, however, the reduction in the tax base due to a small increase in the tax rate dominates the effect of the higher tax rate. Thus for tax rates above t^*, the derivative $R'(t)$ is negative, and tax revenue declines with a small increase in the tax rate.

As shown in Chapter 6, this function reaches its maximum value at the point where its derivative equals zero. To explicitly find the tax rate t^* that corresponds to maximum tax revenues, we note that the derivative of the revenue function is

$$R'(t) = 200 - 400t$$

This first derivative equals zero when $t = \frac{1}{2}$ since

$$R'\left(\frac{1}{2}\right) = 200 - 400\left(\frac{1}{2}\right) = 0.$$

Substituting the tax rate of $\frac{1}{2}$ into the revenue function, we find that the level of tax revenues at this tax rate is

$$R\left(\frac{1}{2}\right) = 200\left(\frac{1}{2}\right) - 200\left[\left(\frac{1}{2}\right)^2\right] = 50,$$

which represents the maximum obtainable tax revenues.

The identification of the tax rate that yields the maximum tax revenues uses the **stationary point** of the tax revenue function.

Stationary Point We say that x^* is a stationary point of a differentiable function $f(x)$ if

$$f'(x^*) = 0.$$

The single stationary point of the tax revenue function is $t^* = \frac{1}{2}$. The relationship between the stationary points of a function that is everywhere differentiable and the extreme values of that function is given by the following version of the **first-order condition,** so named for the use of the first derivative in identifying stationary points.

First-Order Condition (for Everywhere-Differentiable Functions) If the function $y = f(x)$ is everywhere differentiable on an interval and reaches a maximum or a minimum at the point x^* within that interval, then x^* is a stationary point; that is,

$$f'(x^*) = 0.$$

Some examples illustrate the use of the first-order condition. Consider the function

$$h(x) = -x^2 + 8x - 15,$$

which is graphed in Figure 9.2(a). The derivative of this function is

$$h'(x) = -2x + 8.$$

The first-order condition identifies the single stationary point of this function as $x^* = 4$. The function has the value $h(4) = 1$ at this stationary point. The figure shows this point as a maximum. Figure 9.2(b) depicts the function

$$j(x) = x^2 - 8x + 17,$$

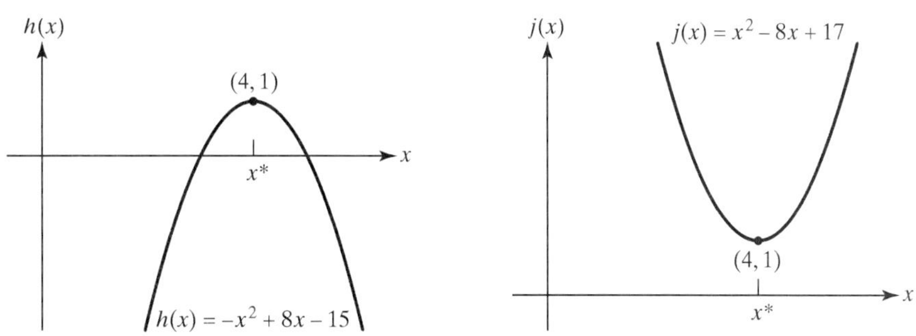

(a) A Stationary Point That Is a Maximum (b) A Stationary Point That Is a Minimum

FIGURE 9.2 Stationary Points

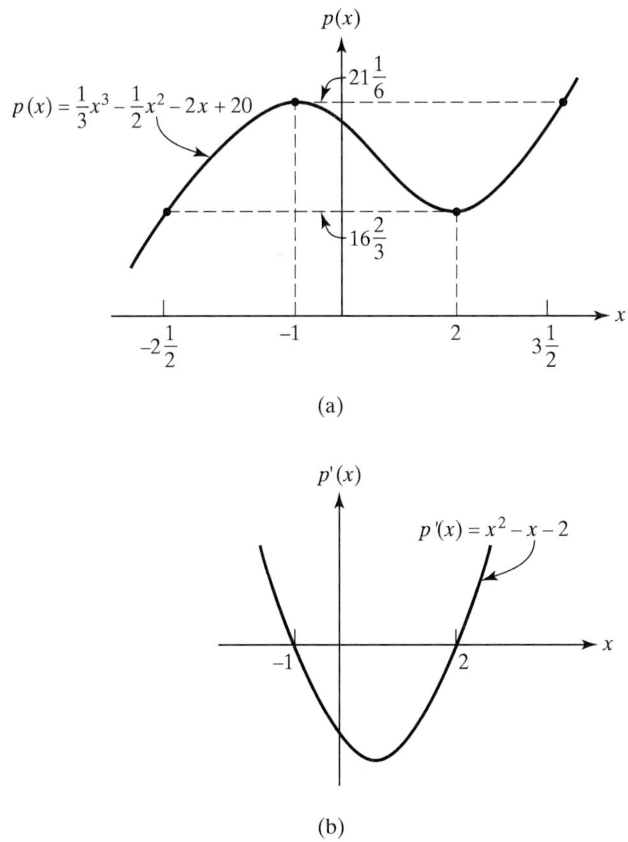

FIGURE 9.3 A Function with Two Extreme Points and Its Derivative

which has the derivative

$$j'(x) = 2x - 8.$$

The stationary point of this function is the same as that for the function graphed in Figure 9.2(a), $x^* = 4$. Also, the value of these functions at their single stationary points are the same; that is, $h(4) = j(4) = 1$. But, in the case of the function j, the graph indicates that it reaches a minimum at the point (4, 1). Thus the first-order condition only identifies stationary points; it cannot distinguish maxima or minima.

A function may have more than one stationary point. The function

$$p(x) = \frac{1}{3}x^3 - \frac{1}{2}x^2 - 2x + 20,$$

which is depicted in Figure 9.3(a), has the derivative

$$p'(x) = x^2 - x - 2.$$

This function has two stationary points, $x^* = 2$ and $x^* = -1$, since

$$p'(2) = 4 - 2 - 2 = 0 \quad \text{and}$$
$$p'(-1) = 1 - (-1) - 2 = 0.$$

Figure 9.3(b) depicts $p'(x)$.

Figure 9.3(a) illustrates that the extreme point $x^* = -1$ is a maximum because $p(x)$ achieves its largest value of $21\frac{1}{6}$ in the interval $(-\infty, 3\frac{1}{2})$ at that point. But this point is a **local maximum** since

$$p(x) > 21\frac{1}{6} \quad \text{if} \quad x > 3\frac{1}{2}.$$

Likewise, Figure 9.3b illustrates that $f(x)$ achieves its smallest value of $16\frac{2}{3}$ in the interval $(-2\frac{1}{2}, \infty)$ at the extreme point $x^* = 2$ but this is a **local minimum** since

$$p(x) < 16\frac{2}{3} \quad \text{if} \quad x < -2\frac{1}{2}.$$

In contrast, the extreme point of the quadratic function $h(x)$ in Figure 9.2(a) is a **global maximum,** and the extreme point of the quadratic function $j(x)$ in Figure 9.2(b) is a **global minimum.** All global maxima are also local maxima, and all global minima are also local minima. The converse is not true, however. Not all local maxima are global maxima, nor are all local minima also global minima.

These examples illustrate what may have been apparent to you from a careful reading of the first-order condition. The first-order condition provides a necessary but not a sufficient condition for identifying a local maximum or a local minimum. In other words, all extreme points are also stationary points, but not all stationary points are extreme points. Also, the first-order condition does not distinguish between stationary points that represent maxima and stationary points that represent minima. Finally, the first-order condition also cannot distinguish between local extreme points and global extreme points.

In fact, a stationary point may be neither a maximum nor a minimum. For example, the function

$$k(x) = 1 + (x - 4)^3,$$

which is graphed in Figure 9.4(a), has the derivative

$$k'(x) = 3(x - 4)^2,$$

which is graphed in Figure 9.4(b). This derivative is equal to zero at the stationary point $x^* = 4$, and, at that point, $k(4) = 1$. As shown in Figure 9.4(a), this stationary point represents neither a maximum nor a minimum. As will be discussed in more detail below, this point is called an **inflection point.**

The focus of the discussion in the chapters of Part IV, is on functions that are everywhere differentiable. For the sake of completeness, we briefly consider a wider class of functions that includes functions that may not be differentiable at some points. We define a **critical point** as follows.

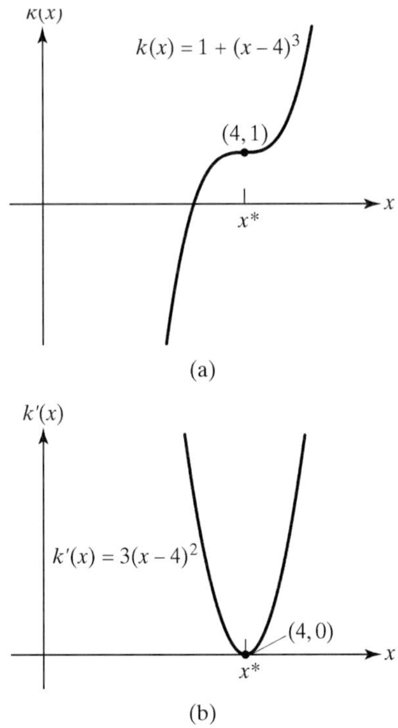

FIGURE 9.4 A Function with an Inflection Point and Its Derivative

Critical Point We say that x^* is a critical point of a function $f(x)$ if

$$f'(x^*) = 0$$

or if the derivative $f'(x)$ does not exist at x^*.

This definition shows that all stationary points are critical points, but not all critical points are stationary points. For example, the absolute value function

$$a(x) = |x|,$$

depicted in Figure 9.5(a), has no stationary points but has a critical point at $x^* = 0$ since $a'(0)$ does not exist. This function achieves a minimum at its critical point. A more general form of the first-order condition is expressed in terms of critical points rather than stationary points.

First-Order Condition If the function $f(x)$ achieves a maximum or a minimum at the point x^* within an interval on which it is defined, then x^* is a critical point of that function.

As with the previous first-order condition for differentiable functions, this condition provides a necessary but not a sufficient condition for identifying an extreme point. Figure 9.5(b) illustrates this. In that figure, the critical point x^* is not an extreme point of the function.

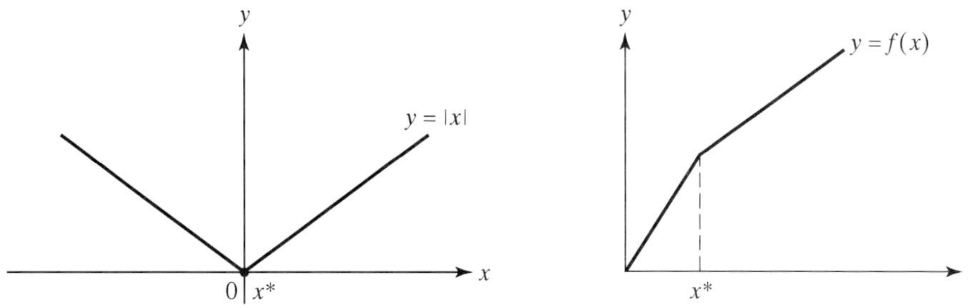

The Absolute Value Function

(a)

A Critical Point Which Is Not an Extreme Point

(b)

FIGURE 9.5 Critical Points

Characterizing Stationary Points

The preceding discussion shows that a stationary point of a function may be a maximum, a minimum, or an inflection point. Characterizing a particular stationary point as a maximum or a minimum can be accomplished by checking the sign of the first derivative at points around that critical point. A sufficient condition, though not a necessary condition, for a point to be a global maximum of a function $f(x)$ that has a continuous first derivative everywhere over some domain is as follows.

Global Maximum If a function $f(x)$ that is everywhere differentiable has the stationary point x^*, then this stationary point represents a global maximum if

$$f'(x) \geq 0 \quad \text{for all} \quad x \leq x^*, \quad \text{and} \quad f'(x) \leq 0 \quad \text{for all} \quad x \geq x^*.$$

This result requires that the function is increasing when the argument is less than the critical point x^* and decreasing when its argument is greater than the critical point x^*. Therefore for any nonnegative real number a, $f(x^* - a)$ will be no greater than $f(x^*)$ since$f'(x) \geq 0$ for any $x \leq x^*$. Likewise, $f(x^* + a)$ will be no greater than $f(x^*)$ since $f'(x) \leq 0$ for any $x \geq x^*$. This insures that $f(x^*)$ is a global maximum.

We can apply this rule to show that the tax rate identified as the stationary point in the example at the beginning of this section is a global maximum. The derivative of the tax revenue function,

$$R'(t) = 200 - 400t,$$

is positive for any $t < \frac{1}{2}$ and negative for any $t > \frac{1}{2}$. Thus the tax revenue at the tax rate $t = \frac{1}{2}$ is a global maximum. This result also shows that the stationary point $x = 4$ for the function $h(x)$ depicted in Figure 9.2(a) is a global maximum since the derivative

$$h'(x) = -2x + 8$$

is positive for any $x < 4$ and negative for any value of $x > 4$.

The identification of a global minimum can be obtained by simply switching the inequalities associated with the first derivatives in the global maximum rule. A sufficient condition, though not a necessary condition, for a point to be a global minimum of a function $f(x)$ that has a continuous first derivative everywhere over some domain is given by the following rule.

Global Minimum If a function $f(x)$ that is everywhere differentiable has the stationary point x^*, then this stationary point represents a global minimum if

$$f'(x) \leq 0 \quad \text{for all} \quad x \leq x^*, \quad \text{and} \quad f'(x) \geq 0 \quad \text{for all} \quad x \geq x^*.$$

The intuition behind this result follows exactly that of the global maximum rule. This result shows that the function depicted in Figure 9.2(b) achieves a global minimum at the critical point (4, 1) since the derivative of this function,

$$j'(x) = 2x - 8,$$

is negative for $x < 4$ and positive for $x > 4$.

Figure 9.3(a) depicts the function $p(x)$, which has an interior local maximum at the stationary point $x^* = -1$ and an interior local minimum at the stationary point $x^* = -2$. These local extreme points will not represent global extreme points if the function is defined on an interval with a lower endpoint less than $-2\frac{1}{2}$ and an upper endpoint greater than $3\frac{1}{2}$. We need conditions distinct from those presented previously for global extreme points to characterize a stationary point as a local maximum or a local minimum. These conditions are as follows.

Local Maximum If a function $f(x)$ that is everywhere differentiable has an interior local maximum at the stationary point x^*, then, throughout some interval to the left of the stationary point, (m, x^*),

$$f'(x) \geq 0$$

and, throughout some interval to the right of the stationary point, (x^*, n),

$$f'(x) \leq 0.$$

Local Minimum If a function $f(x)$ that is everywhere differentiable has an interior local minimum at the stationary point x^*, then, throughout some interval (m, x^*) to the left of the stationary point,

$$f'(x) \leq 0$$

and, throughout some interval (x^*, n) to the right of the stationary point,

$$f'(x) \geq 0.$$

Note that these rules are sufficient for functions with continuous first derivatives.

If the sign of the first derivative alternates around the stationary point in the manner discussed in one of these rules, then that stationary point is a local extreme point.

As an example of these rules, consider again the function

$$p(x) = \frac{1}{3}x^3 - \frac{1}{2}x^2 - 2x + 20,$$

which is depicted in Figure 9.3(a). Its first derivative is

$$p'(x) = x^2 - x - 2.$$

The stationary point $x^* = -1$ can be shown to be a local maximum since, for some positive number a,

$$\begin{aligned} p'(-1 - a) &= (-1 - a)^2 - (-1 - a) - 2 = a^2 + 3a > 0 \quad \text{for} \quad a > 0 \quad \text{and} \\ p'(-1 + a) &= (-1 + a)^2 - (-1 + a) - 2 = a^2 - 3a < 0 \quad \text{for} \quad 0 < a < 3. \end{aligned}$$

Thus, for example, if $a = 1$,

$$p'(-2) = 4 \quad \text{and} \quad p'(0) = -2$$

Therefore, around this critical point, the sign of the first derivative of the function switches from positive to negative. By a similar method, the stationary point $x^* = 2$ can be shown to be a local minimum since, for the points $x = 1$ and $x = 3$,

$$p'(1) = -2 \quad \text{and} \quad p'(3) = 4.$$

Therefore, around this critical point, the sign of the first derivative of the function switches from negative to positive.

The function graphed in Figure 9.3(a) also illustrates that the rules for global extreme points are sufficient but not necessary conditions. Suppose the function $p(x)$ given previously is defined only on the closed interval $[-2, 3]$. Over this interval, the global minimum value of the function is $p(2) = 16\frac{2}{3}$, and the global maximum is $p(-1) = 21\frac{1}{6}$, even though neither of the respective critical points meets the sufficient condition for a global maximum or a global minimum. These statements are true in this case because of the choice for the domain of the function. With the domain $[-3, 4]$, the two critical points are local but not global extreme points since the global minimum is the endpoint $p(-3) = 12\frac{1}{2}$ and the global maximum is the endpoint $p(4) = 25\frac{1}{3}$.

We can also apply the conditions for a local maximum and a local minimum to the function $k(x)$ depicted in Figure 9.4(a) to show that its stationary point, $x^* = 4$, is neither a local maximum nor a local minimum. As shown previously, the derivative of this function is

$$k'(x) = 3(x - 4)^2.$$

Evaluating this derivative at the two values $4 - a$ and $4 + a$ for any $a > 0$, we find

$$\begin{aligned} k'(4 - a) &= 3((4 - a) - 4)^2 = 3a^2 > 0 \quad \text{and} \\ k'(4 + a) &= 3((4 + a) - 4)^2 = 3a^2 > 0. \end{aligned}$$

Therefore this point is neither a local maximum nor a local minimum.

The Second-Order Condition

The signs of the first derivatives in an interval around a stationary point provide a sufficient condition for determining whether that point represents a local maximum or a local minimum. This method of characterizing a stationary point requires evaluating several first derivatives. A method that is often computationally more efficient is to check the sign of the second derivative of the function at the stationary point. This method, called the **second-order condition,** provides a sufficient condition but, as we will see, not a necessary condition, for characterizing a stationary point as a local maximum or a local minimum.

The intuition behind the second-order condition draws on the Chapter 7 discussion of the second derivative. The second derivative evaluated at a given point represents the instantaneous rate of change of the first derivative at that point. If the second derivative is negative, then the sign of the first derivative is changing from positive to the left of the stationary point to negative to the right of the stationary point. In this case the stationary point represents a local maximum. Conversely, if the second derivative is positive, then the sign of the first derivative is changing from negative to the left of the stationary point to positive to the right of the stationary point. In this case the stationary point represents a local minimum. Thus the second-order conditions for a local maximum and a local minimum are as follows.

Second-Order Condition for a Local Maximum If the second derivative of the differentiable function $y = f(x)$ is negative when evaluated at a stationary point x^* (that is, $f''(x^*) < 0$), then that stationary point represents a local maximum of that function.

Second-Order Condition for a Local Minimum If the second derivative of the differentiable function $y = f(x)$ is positive when evaluated at a stationary point x^* (that is, $f''(x^*) > 0$), then that stationary point represents a local minimum of that function.

We can use the second-order condition to characterize the two stationary points of the function $p(x)$ presented in Figure 9.3(a). The second derivative of this function is

$$p''(x) = 2x - 1.$$

This second derivative evaluated at the critical value $x^* = -1$ is negative since $p''(-1) = -3$. So this stationary point is a local maximum. The second derivative evaluated at the critical value $x^* = 2$ is positive since $p''(2) = 1$. So this point is a local minimum.

An example illustrates that the second-order condition is a sufficient but not a necessary condition for identifying a local extreme point. Consider the function

$$q(x) = x^4,$$

which is graphed in Figure 9.6. The first derivative of this function is

$$q'(x) = 4x^3,$$

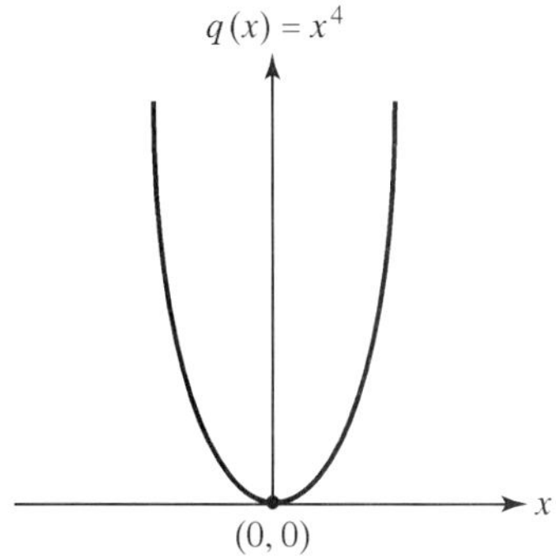

FIGURE 9.6 Failure of the Second-Order Condition

and, thus, the stationary point is $x^* = 0$. The second derivative of this function is

$$q''(x) = 12x^2.$$

Evaluating this second derivative at the stationary point, we find that $q''(0) = 0$, but, as shown in the figure, this point is a local (and global) minimum. In this case a problem arises because we are evaluating the second derivative at zero. The evaluation of this stationary point with the necessary and sufficient first-derivative condition shows that this function reaches a minimum at the stationary point $x^* = 0$ since the first derivative is negative for any negative value of x and positive for any positive value of x.

The rules for identifying and characterizing stationary points are used to analyze the empirical findings presented in the following application.

Income and the Environment

The bright promise of better living standards for the world's poor through economic growth is mitigated by the possible link between economic activity and ecological degradation. Will increasing economic activity in developing countries lead to a steady increase in environmental damage, or do higher living standards bring with them a demand for a cleaner environment? This question has been addressed in a cross-country study of the relationship between income per capita and pollution by Gene Grossman and Alan Krueger of Princeton University.[1]

Using data from the Global Environmental Monitoring System, Grossman and Krueger estimate a cubic relationship between a country's income per capita in thousands of dollars (Y) and the concentration level (in μg per cubic meter) of a variety of pollutants in its cities. They find that the relationship between the concentration of smoke (S), income, and other factors not related to income (X) is

$$S(Y) = 0.13Y^3 - 4.2Y^2 + 37.1Y + X.$$

[1] Gene M. Grossman and Alan B. Krueger, "Economic growth and the environment," *Quarterly Journal of Economics* 110, no. 2 (May 1995): 353–378.

The derivative of this equation with respect to income is the quadratic function[2]

$$S'(Y) = 0.39Y^2 - 8.4Y + 37.1.$$

The two values of income where this derivative equals zero, Y_1 and Y_2, can be found with the quadratic formula (see Chapter 2). The quadratic formula shows that the two stationary points of this function are

$$Y_1, Y_2 = \frac{8.4 \pm \sqrt{70.56 - 57.88}}{0.78} = 6.2, 15.3.$$

Substituting these values, we find that the estimated concentration of smoke is about $X + 99.6$ μg per cubic meter for $Y = 6.2$ and about $X + 50.1$ μg per cubic meter for $Y = 15.3$.

The second derivative of the concentration of smoke with respect to income is

$$S''(Y) = 0.78Y - 8.4.$$

At the stationary point of 6.2, the second derivative is

$$S''(6.2) = 0.78(6.2) - 8.4 = -3.6.$$

This point represents a local maximum of the function since the second derivative evaluated at this stationary point is negative. At the stationary point of 15.3, the second derivative is

$$S''(15.3) = 0.78(15.3) - 8.4 = -3.5,$$

which shows that this point is a local minimum.

These results suggest that, at relatively early stages of economic development (such as those currently found in Mexico or Malaysia), smoke concentration in cities is at a peak, while further economic growth (up to an annual income level of \$15,300 per capita) is associated with a reduction in this form of pollution. Similar results were found for other types of air and water pollution. The Grossman and Krueger study then provides the optimistic message that economic growth may not lead to further economic degradation since, as people become more wealthy, they will demand a higher level of environmental quality.

Concavity and Convexity

In Chapter 7 we introduced the link between concavity and the second derivative. Section 7.3 showed that if a differentiable function is strictly convex over some interval, then its second derivative is positive over that interval. That discussion also showed that if a differentiable function is strictly concave over some interval, then its second derivative is negative over that interval. Combining these definitions with maximum and minimum conditions, we get the following results for a function $f(x)$ that we assume is continuous and twice differentiable on the interval (m, n).

[2] Strictly speaking, this should be evaluated as a partial derivative since the pollution equation is a multivariate function. We assume here, however, that all variables other than income are constant to make this application consistent with the discussion in this section. As shown in the next chapter, the result would be the same in the multivariate case, as long as the other factors are themselves not linked to income.

Stationary Point of a Strictly Concave Function If the function $f(x)$ is strictly concave on the interval (m, n) and has the stationary point x^*, where $m < x^* < n$, then x^* is a local maximum in that interval. If a function is strictly concave everywhere, then it has, at most, one stationary point, and that stationary point is a global maximum. ■

Stationary Point of a Strictly Convex Function If the function $f(x)$ is strictly convex on the interval (m, n) and has the stationary point x^*, where $m < x^* < n$, then x^* is a local minimum in that interval. If a function is strictly convex everywhere, then it has, at most, one stationary point, and that stationary point is a global minimum. ■

A function switches from concave to convex or from convex to concave at an **inflection point.** A necessary and sufficient condition for an inflection point is as follows.

Inflection Point The twice-differentiable function $f(x)$ has an inflection point at $\tilde{x}$ if and only if the sign of the second derivative switches from negative in some interval $(m, \tilde{x})$ to positive in some interval $(\tilde{x}, n)$, in which case the function switches from concave to convex at $\tilde{x}$, or the sign of the second derivative switches from positive in some interval $(m, \tilde{x})$ to negative in some interval $(\tilde{x}, n)$, in which case the function switches from convex to concave at $\tilde{x}$. Note that, in either case, $m < \tilde{x} < n$. ■

As an example of these rules, consider again the function

$$p(x) = \frac{1}{3}x^3 - \frac{1}{2}x^2 - 2x + 20,$$

which is depicted in Figure 9.3(a). The second derivative of this function is

$$p''(x) = 6x - 2.$$

Thus $p''(x) < 0$ for any $x < \frac{1}{3}$, and the function is concave on the open interval $(-\infty, \frac{1}{3})$. The stationary point $x^* = -1$ in this interval is, therefore, a local maximum. We also note that $p''(x) > 0$ for any $x > \frac{1}{3}$ and the function is convex on the open interval $(\frac{1}{3}, \infty)$. The stationary point $x^* = 2$ in this interval is, therefore, a local minimum. The second derivative equals zero at the inflection point $x = \frac{1}{3}$, where the function switches from concave to convex.

As another example of an inflection point, consider the function

$$k(x) = 1 + (x - 4)^3,$$

which is depicted in Figure 9.4(a). The second derivative of this function, depicted in Figure 9.4(b), is

$$k''(x) = 6\,(x - 4).$$

The inflection point of this function is at $x = 4$ since

$$k''(4) = 0$$

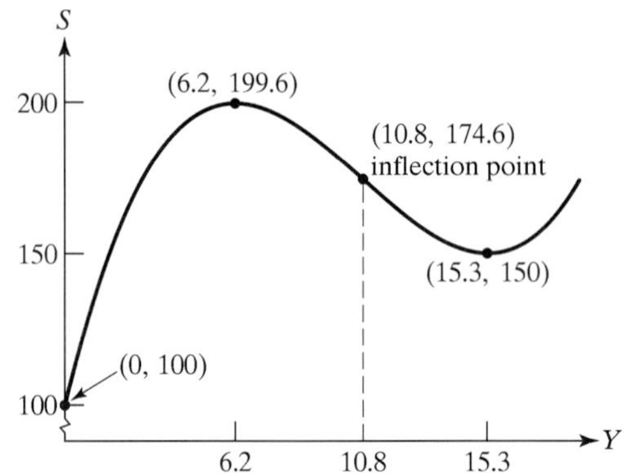

FIGURE 9.7 Identification of Inflection Point in Function Relating Income to Smoke Pollution Emissions ($X = 100$)

and the sign of $k''(x)$ switches from negative for $x < 4$ to positive for $x > 4$. Thus this function switches from concave to convex at this inflection point. As noted previously, this point is also the stationary point of the function, but it is not an extreme value. More generally, any stationary point that is an inflection point is neither a local minimum nor a local maximum.

A function may have a point where its second derivative equals zero but is not an inflection point. For example, the second derivative of the function

$$q(x) = x^4,$$

depicted in Figure 9.6, equals zero at $x = 0$ since

$$q''(0) = 12(0)^2 = 0.$$

But this is not an inflection point since the second derivative of this function does not switch signs in the neighborhood of the inflection point. For any real number $a \neq 0$, we have

$$q''(a) = 12a^2 > 0.$$

This function is convex on the open interval $(-\infty, \infty)$. Thus, as with the identification of an extreme point, the sign of the second derivative provides a sufficient but not a necessary condition for identifying an inflection point.

The identification of an inflection point is often useful for sketching the graph of a function. For example, we have already determined a good deal of information about the function relating income to smoke emissions $S(Y)$, which is discussed in the previous application. Assuming that $X = 100$, we graph this function in Figure 9.7. The single local maximum of this function, around which the function is concave, is the point (6.2, 199.6). The single local minimum of the function, around which the function is convex, is (15.3, 150.1). The function switches its concavity at $Y = 10.8$ since

$$S''(10.8) = 0.78(10.8) - 8.4 = 0.$$

Thus the inflection point is (10.8, 174.6). All of the information on local extreme points and the inflection point is used in the sketch in Figure 9.7.

Exercises 9.1

1. Identify the stationary points of each function, and determine whether they represent maxima, minima, or inflection points. Confirm your result by determining the sign of the first derivative in the neighborhood of the stationary points.
   (a) $y = x^2 - 10x + 10$
   (b) $y = \frac{1}{3}x^3 - 1.5x^2 + 2x - 4$
   (c) $y = -\frac{1}{2}x^6 - 5$
   (d) $y = \ln x^2 - 4x; x > 0$
   (e) $y = 2x^3 + 4x^2 - 5x + 3$
   (f) $y = \frac{\ln(x)}{x}; x > 0$
2. The second-order condition is a sufficient but not a necessary condition for identifying local extreme points. Using the second-order condition, confirm the results you obtained in question 1. Are there any functions in question 1 where the second-order condition does not work?
3. Consider the polynomial function of degree n
   $$y = a_n x^n + a_{n-1}x^{n-1} + \cdots + a_2x^2 + a_1x + a_0.$$
   What is the maximum number of "bends" (that is, extreme points) for this function? (*Hint:* Begin with $n = 1$, and then consider $n = 2, n = 3$, and so forth, to try to figure out the answer).
4. Continuing with the previous question, what is the maximum number of inflection points for a polynomial of degree n?
5. Find the formula for the stationary point(s) of the generic quadratic function
   $$y = \alpha + \beta X + \gamma X^2$$
   and for the generic cubic function
   $$y = \alpha + \beta X + \gamma X^2 + \theta X^3.$$
6. Show that a quadratic function does not have an inflection point. What is the geometric interpretation of this?
7. The student body president is facing reelection in what has proven to be a tight race between her and her opponent, a maverick outsider who has promised to change the way that students' resources will be used. An example of the voting function shows that the percentage of the vote going to the incumbent (V) is a function of the number of cups of free coffee made available (and drunk) in the student lounge (C) and the price of student sweatshirts imprinted with the school's logo (S) according to the function
   $$V = C^2 - 2S^2.$$
   Assuming that the incumbent has unlimited access to student resources (R), determine the amount she should spend if she wishes to obtain the largest possible vote. Assume that R affects the number of cups of free coffee and sweatshirts

as follows:

$$C = 3\sqrt{R} \quad \text{and} \quad S = \frac{1}{2}R.$$

What percentage of the vote will the incumbent president obtain? Confirm that this is a maximum.

8. Another result presented by Grossman and Krueger concerns sulfur dioxide emissions. They estimate the relationship between these emissions and income to be

$$SO_2 = 0.083Y^3 - 2.2Y^2 + 13.5Y + X,$$

where SO_2 represents μg per cubic meter of sulfur dioxide, Y is income, and X represents other factors not linked to income. Identify and characterize the extreme values of this function.

9. A firm's profits are maximized at that quantity where the difference between total revenues and total costs is at its greatest. Assume that total revenue is an upward-sloping linear function. Total cost is a cubic function with two stationary points, one which represents a minimum and one a maximum. Therefore the profit function, the difference between the first two functions, is also cubic with two stationary points. Plotting quantity on the horizontal axis and price on the vertical axis, sketch the three functions in one graph. Graph the three marginal functions. Identify the profit-maximizing level of output in both graphs.

10. William Baumol and James Tobin developed a model of money demand based on an individual's decisions on the trade-off between holding bonds, which pay interest, and holding money, which is used to purchase goods and services.[3] At the beginning of each month the individual gets income of Y and converts this costlessly to bonds. Over the course of the month, the individual makes n equal-sized withdrawals, each of which is in the amount Y/n. The cost of each withdrawal is c. This means that the average cash balance held during the month is $Y/2n$ and the total cost of managing the portfolio, TC, is

$$TC = (n \cdot c) + \left(i\frac{Y}{2n}\right),$$

where the first term in parentheses is the transaction cost and the second term is foregone interest. Find the value of n that minimizes total cost, and show the average cash holdings consistent with this value of n.

9.2 ECONOMIC APPLICATIONS

Identifying and characterizing extreme values is one of the most frequently used mathematical tools in economics. In this section we provide five examples of the use of this technique with univariate functions.

---

[3] William Baumol, "The transactions demand for cash: An inventory theoretic approach," *Quarterly Journal of Economics* (1952): 545–556; and James Tobin, "The interest rate elasticity of the transactions demand for cash," *Review of Economics and Statistics* (1956): 241–247.

A Monopolist's Optimal Pricing Scheme

Suppose the inverse demand function facing a monopolist is

$$p = q^{-1/\beta},$$

where p is the price of the good and q is its quantity. As shown in Chapter 7, this inverse demand function implies that the elasticity of demand for this good is constant and equal to β. The monopolist's total revenue equals

$$TR = p \cdot q = q^{1-1/\beta}.$$

Assume that total cost is linear in quantity so that

$$TC = c \cdot q,$$

which implies constant marginal cost since

$$\frac{dTC}{dq} = c.$$

Then the monopolist's profit, Π, is

$$\Pi = TR - TC = q^{1-1/\beta} - c \cdot q.$$

The optimization problem facing the monopolist is to choose quantity such that profits are maximized. The first-order condition for the monopolist's profit maximization problem is

$$\frac{d\Pi}{dq} = \left(1 - \frac{1}{\beta}\right)q^{-1/\beta} - c = 0$$

Solving this, we find the optimal quantity for the monopolist, which we denote as q^*, is

$$q^* = \left(\frac{c}{1 - 1/\beta}\right)^{-\beta}.$$

The price corresponding to this quantity can be found by substituting this quantity into the demand equation. This gives us the optimal price

$$p^* = (q^*)^{-1/\beta} = \frac{c}{1 - 1/\beta}.$$

The optimal price is lower with higher values of β since the denominator in the price equation, $(1 - 1/\beta)$, increases with β. A monopolist facing a relatively high elasticity of demand therefore charges a lower price than a monopolist with identical marginal cost who is facing a relatively lower elasticity of demand. Thus, for example, firms that enjoy some monopoly power and can practice price discrimination charge relatively higher prices to people who have relatively lower elasticity of demand. For example, plane tickets for times of peak business-related travel cost more than plane tickets during weekends.

The second-order condition insures that we have identified a profit-maximizing price and quantity. The second derivative of the profit function is

$$\frac{d^2\Pi}{dq^2} = \left(-\frac{1}{\beta}\right)\left(1 - \frac{1}{\beta}\right)q^{-1/\beta - 1},$$

which is unambiguously less than zero as long as $\beta > 1$.

These results are sensible only if demand is elastic, that is, if $\beta > 1$. If demand is inelastic and $1 > \beta > 0$, then the first-order condition suggests that the optimal price is negative! This strange result can be understood by checking the second-order condition, which shows that the negative price solution represents the point of minimum profits.

Strategic Behavior of Duopolists

We next consider an analysis of a market consisting of two competing firms. We solve for the equilibrium price and quantity of computer chips in a market with the two firms, A and B. The actions of one firm affect the outcome for the other firm since the price of computer chips is a function of the supply from both firms. Therefore the optimal strategy for either firm is a function of the actions undertaken by the other firm. We first derive the **reaction function** for each firm, which describes its optimal quantity supplied as a function of the other firm's supply.[4] We then solve for an equilibrium, which is a set of actions such that each player's strategy is the optimal response to the other player's strategy.[5]

We assume that the price of computer chips, P, depends upon the quantity offered by Firm A, Q_A, and the quantity offered by Firm B, Q_B, as shown by the linear function

$$P = 1400 - 2(Q_A + Q_B).$$

The profits of Firms A and B, Π_A and Π_B, respectively, are price times quantity minus costs. Assuming that both firms face the constant marginal cost $C = 200$ and using the price equation, we have the two profit equations

$$\begin{aligned}\Pi_A &= Q_A(1400 - 2(Q_A + Q_B)) - 200Q_A \\ &= 1200Q_A - 2Q_A^2 - 2(Q_AQ_B) \quad \text{and} \\ \Pi_B &= Q_B(1400 - 2(Q_A + Q_B)) - 200Q_B \\ &= 1200Q_B - 2Q_B^2 - 2(Q_AQ_B).\end{aligned}$$

The reaction function for Firm A is found by taking the derivative of its profit function with respect to its output and then solving for its output as a function of the output of Firm B. The first derivative of Firm A's profit function is

$$\frac{d\Pi_A}{dQ_A} = 1200 - 4Q_A - 2Q_B.$$

[4] This is a Cournot game since the duopolists choose an optimal quantity. A Bertrand game is one in which the duopolists choose an optimal price. Somewhat surprisingly, the outcomes of a Cournot game and a Bertrand game are usually different, even if the basic structure of the model is the same in each case.

[5] This is a version of a Nash Equilibrium, which is named after John Nash of Princeton University, who shared the 1995 Nobel Prize in economics for his work in the field of game theory.

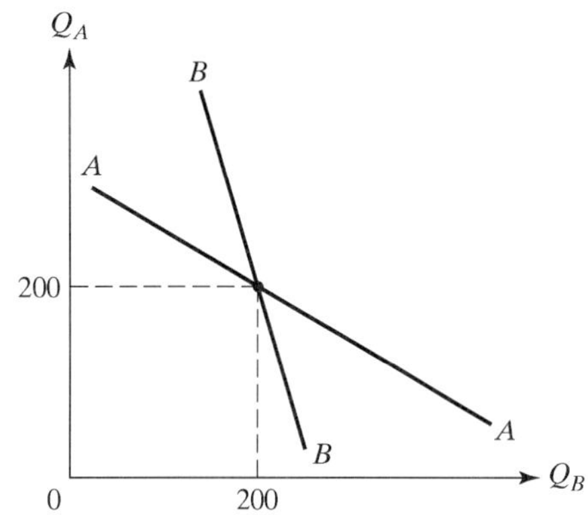

FIGURE 9.8 Reaction Functions of Firms *A* and *B*

The second derivative is

$$\frac{d^2\Pi_A}{dQ_A^2} = -4,$$

which is always negative. Therefore, by the second-order condition, the extreme value of Q_A will represent a global maximum.

Setting the first derivative equal to zero and solving for Q_A, we find Firm *A*'s reaction function to be

$$Q_A = 300 - \frac{Q_B}{2}.$$

This function is plotted as the line *AA* in Figure 9.8. Following the same procedure for Firm *B*, we find that its reaction function is

$$Q_B = 300 - \frac{Q_A}{2},$$

which is depicted as the line *BB* in Figure 9.8.

The point of intersection of the reaction functions *AA* and *BB* represents the unique equilibrium in this example since it is the only point where each firm's strategy is the optimal response to the other firm's strategy. An explicit solution is found by substituting the reaction function for Firm *B* into the reaction function for Firm *A* to obtain

$$Q_A = 300 - \frac{300 - Q_A/2}{2} = 150 + \frac{Q_A}{4},$$

and, therefore,

$$Q_A = 200 \quad \text{and} \quad Q_B = 200.$$

It is interesting to note that the level of total industry supply,

$$Q_A + Q_B = 400,$$

is greater than the amount firms would supply if they cooperated. In this case the monopoly formed by Firms A and B would have the profit function

$$\Pi = Q(1400 - 2Q) - 200Q,$$

where $Q \equiv Q_A + Q_B$ and $\Pi \equiv \Pi_A + \Pi_B$. In this case the first-order condition gives the optimal industry output of

$$Q = \frac{1}{2}\left(\frac{1200}{2}\right) = 300,$$

which is less than overall supply in the duopoly case.

An extension of this application demonstrates how a country might benefit from a strategic trade policy whereby it subsidizes its exports. Suppose Firm A is in America and Firm B is in Britain. The American government offers a subsidy of the amount S to Firm A for each chip it produces. This alters A's marginal cost to be $(200 - S)$ and its profit function to be

$$\Pi_A = Q_A(1400 - 2(Q_A + Q_B)) - (200 - S) \cdot Q_A.$$

With the subsidy, the reaction function for Firm A is

$$Q_A = \frac{1200 + S}{4} - \frac{Q_B}{2},$$

while the reaction function for Firm B is unchanged. Solving the two reaction functions for the output of each firm, we find

$$Q_A = 200 + \frac{S}{3} \quad \text{and} \quad Q_B = 200 - \frac{S}{6}.$$

The subsidy increases output by Firm A and reduces output by Firm B. The striking thing about this result is that it can be shown that, under certain conditions, the increase in profits by Firm A exceeds the cost of the subsidy. For example, without a subsidy, $\Pi_A = \$80{,}000$. With a subsidy of $S = \$30$ per chip, Q_A increases from 200 to 210, and Q_B decreases from 200 to 195. In this case $\Pi_A = \$88{,}200$. Thus the subsidy, which costs $\$30 \cdot 210 = \$6{,}300$, raises profits of America's chip-maker by \$8,200.[6]

Rules versus Discretion in Monetary Policy

Economists have long debated how best to conduct monetary policy. This debate is often framed as one of "rules versus discretion." Standard arguments for a monetary rule, whereby the central bank follows a preset and unvarying target for money growth or the inflation rate, focus on the difficulties of exactly calibrating policy to meet the economy's needs. In contrast, those who believe that the policy of a central bank should

[6] The potential role for subsidies is presented in James Brander and Barbara Spencer, "Export subsidies and international market share rivalry," *Journal of International Economics* 18 (1985): 83–100. For an overview of these types of strategic trade policies, see Paul Krugman, "Is free trade passé?" *Journal of Economic Perspectives* 1, no. 2 (Fall 1987): 131–144.

be subject to change at the discretion of its leaders argue that rules unnecessarily bind the actions of the monetary authority and do not allow it to respond to current conditions.

A more recent line of argument in this debate concerns the effects of discretionary policy on people's expectations that, in turn, have an impact on the underlying rate of inflation in an economy.[7] This argument emphasizes the possibility that the leaders of a central bank who undertake discretionary policy may face a **time inconsistency problem.** The time inconsistency problem occurs when an initial policy commitment may be reversed if it is no longer optimal and, since people know that the possibility of reversal exists, the initial policy is not credible, even at the outset.[8] In this context, a central bank would like the public to believe that it strongly opposes inflation. This belief would temper people's plans to raise wages and prices. But if the public believes that the central bank sometimes raises inflation to combat unemployment, then the underlying inflation rate in the economy would be higher than if the central bank credibly committed itself to a rule that precluded its ability to act with discretion. The higher inflation rate occurring in an environment of discretionary policy, however, may not be associated with unemployment lower than that found a low-inflation environment in which the central bank follows a rule.

A model that illustrates the time inconsistency problem includes two relationships. The **expectations-augmented Phillips curve** shows that there is a negative relationship between the level of unemployment, U, and the difference between actual inflation, π, and expected inflation, E

$$U = N - \alpha(\pi - E),$$

where N is the "natural rate" of unemployment and the parameter $\alpha > 0$. Note that inflation can only affect unemployment to the extent that it is unanticipated and $\pi \neq E$. The other relationship models the preferences of the central bank with a **loss function** that shows the central bank dislikes both unemployment and inflation. In particular, the central bank will attempt to minimize L where

$$L = U + \beta\pi^2.$$

Substituting the Phillips curve into the loss function, we can express L as a function of the inflation rate, the expected inflation rate, and the natural rate of unemployment as

$$L = N - \alpha(\pi - E) + \beta\pi^2.$$

A further assumption of this model is that the public first forms its expectation of inflation, E, and, after this, the central bank chooses the inflation rate, π. The unemployment

[7] Some early and influential contributions in this area are Finn E. Kydland and Edward C. Prescott, "Rules rather than discretion: The inconsistency of optimal plans," *Journal of Political Economy* 85, no. 3 (June 1977): 473–492; Guillermo Calvo, "On the time consistency of optimal policy in a monetary economy," *Econometrica* 46, no. 6 (November 1978): 1411–1428; and Robert Barro and David Gordon, "A positive theory of monetary policy in a natural rate model," *Journal of Political Economy* 91 (August 1983): 589–610.

[8] Another important example of a time inconsistency problem is that of patents. The optimal policy initially is to award strong patent protection, but once the innovation is developed, the optimal policy is one that allows its widest dissemination.

rate, U, follows from E and π according to the expectations-augmented Phillips curve relationship.

The key insights from this model derive from the determination of the public's expectations of inflation, E. Expectations are anchored at $E = 0$ when the central bank follows a credible rule that permanently sets the inflation rate to zero. In this situation, with $E = \pi = 0$ and $U = N$, the loss of the central bank will be

$$L = N - \alpha(0 - 0) + \beta 0^2 = N.$$

Under a policy of discretion, the public believes that the central bank will minimize its loss given the public's expectation of inflation, E. The optimal inflation rate is found by first differentiating the loss function with respect to the inflation rate and then setting this equal to zero. This gives us

$$\frac{dL}{d\pi} = -\alpha + 2\beta\pi = 0,$$

which yields an optimal inflation rate of $\pi = \alpha/2\beta$. This can be shown to minimize the loss function since the second derivative is $d^2L/d\pi^2 = 2\beta > 0$. The public, recognizing the motivations of the central bank as well as its constraints, sets the expected inflation rate equal to the optimal rate calculated here, so we have, under discretion,

$$E = \pi = \frac{\alpha}{2\beta}.$$

Substituting this into the loss function, we find that, under discretion, the loss is

$$L = N - \alpha\left(\frac{\alpha}{2\beta} - \frac{\alpha}{2\beta}\right) + \beta\left(\frac{\alpha}{2\beta}\right)^2 = N + \frac{\alpha^2}{4\beta},$$

which exceeds the loss under the rule of $\pi = 0$.

The source of the relatively poor outcome under a policy of discretion as compared to a rule is that the central bank cannot manage the public's expectations unless it commits itself to a rule. This result has a number of theoretical implications; for example, it may be useful to appoint a central banker who cares relatively little about inflation (that is, one who has a large value of β) in order to achieve a lower level of inflation while not suffering, at least in the context of this model, higher unemployment. Along these same lines, it may be useful to have an institutional framework in which the central bank enjoys independence from political pressures. Indeed, evidence suggests that economies with more independent central banks have, on average, lower inflation but not higher rates of unemployment.[9]

[9]On the desirability of appointing a "conservative" central banker, see Kenneth Rogoff "The Optimal degree of commitment to an intermediate monetary target," *Quarterly Journal of Economics* 100, no. 4 (November 1985): 1169–1190. Evidence that economies with more independent central banks lower average inflation but do not have higher average unemployment is presented in Alberto Alesina and Lawrence H. Summers "Central Bank independence and macroeconomic performance," *Journal of Money, Credit and Banking* 25, no. 2 (May 1993): 151–162.

The Inflation Tax

Very high inflation often goes hand in hand with severe fiscal problems. A government may be forced to resort to simply printing money to pay for its expenditures when it cannot raise sufficient revenues through conventional taxes. This rapid expansion of the money supply leads to a corresponding high rate of inflation.

In a classic study of the fiscal consequences of hyperinflation, Phillip Cagan of Columbia University presents a model of the **inflation tax** and the **seigniorage** raised by the government.[10] Seigniorage is the amount of real resources the government obtains by printing money. This is closely linked to the inflation tax, which is the decline in the value of real money balances caused by inflation. In many ways, the inflation tax resembles the income tax discussed at the beginning of this chapter. In both cases, tax revenues are the product of a tax rate and a tax base. The tax rate for the inflation tax is the rate of inflation, π, while the tax base is the level of real balances, which is the quotient of the nominal money supply over the price level, M/P.

As in the case of the income tax, the tax base of the inflation tax declines with an increase in the "tax rate," that is, the expected inflation rate. People attempt to hold fewer real balances and more of other assets when the expected inflation rate rises. This is reflected in the money demand equation

$$\frac{M}{P} = e^{-\lambda\,(\pi^e + r) + \alpha Y},$$

where π^e is expected inflation, r is the real interest rate, and Y is income. The sum of expected inflation and the real interest rate equals the nominal interest rate, which represents the opportunity cost of holding money. Money demand decreases with an increase in the nominal interest rate. Money demand also increases with an increase in income as people want more real balances to fund the increased purchases that accompany higher income.

We consider the situation where actual inflation equals expected inflation ($\pi = \pi^e$). In this case the seigniorage revenues raised by the government, S, equal the inflation tax.

$$S = \pi\frac{M}{P} = \pi\, e^{-\lambda\,(\pi + r) + \alpha Y}.$$

We can determine the maximum level of seigniorage revenues that a government can raise by finding the critical value of this function and checking whether it represents a maximum or a minimum. Treating the real interest rate and income as constant, the first-order condition sets the derivative of seigniorage with respect to inflation equal to zero,

$$\frac{dS}{d\pi} = e^{-\lambda(\pi + r) + \alpha Y} - \lambda\pi e^{-\lambda(\pi + r) + \alpha Y} = 0.$$

[10] Phillip Cagan, "The Monetary Dynamics of Hyperinflation," *Studies in the Quantity Theory of Money* (Chicago: University of Chicago Press, 1956).

This implies that the single stationary point is

$$\pi = \frac{e^{-\lambda(\pi+r)+\alpha Y}}{\lambda e^{-\lambda(\pi+r)+\alpha Y}} = \frac{1}{\lambda}.$$

The second derivative of the seigniorage function with respect to inflation is

$$\frac{d^2S}{d\pi^2} = (-2\lambda + \lambda^2\pi)e^{-\lambda(\pi+r)+\alpha Y}.$$

Evaluating this at the critical value $\pi = 1/\lambda$ gives us

$$\frac{d^2S}{d\pi^2} = (-2\lambda + \lambda)e^{-1-\lambda r+\alpha Y} < 0,$$

where the sign of this second derivative is unambiguously negative since $(-2\lambda + \lambda) = -\lambda < 0$ and $e^{-1-\lambda r + \alpha Y} > 0$. Thus the second-order condition shows that seigniorage reaches its maximum level at the critical value $\pi = 1/\lambda$. Substituting this critical value into the seigniorage relationship shows that maximum seigniorage is

$$S^* = \frac{1}{\lambda}e^{-1-\lambda r+\alpha Y}.$$

Cagan studied seven different hyperinflation episodes, five of which occurred in the first half of the 1920s (in Germany, Austria, Poland, Russia, and Hungary) and two of which occurred in the mid-1940s (in Greece and, again, in Hungary). He found that actual average rates of inflation in each of the hyperinflations were well above the constant rates that would have maximized revenues.

The Golden Rule

What is the optimal level of savings? The answer to this question has both an economic and a moral component. The economic component links current savings to future income. Saving more today reduces current consumption, but it may lead to higher consumption in the future. This intertemporal trade-off raises the ethical issue of valuing consumption of the current generation relative to that of future generations.

One answer to the question of the optimal level of savings draws from the work of Robert Solow and a precept from the Bible. Solow's model of economic growth offers a framework for analyzing the long-run level of savings and consumption in an economy. The biblical precept of the Golden Rule, which states, "Do unto others as you would have them do unto you," commands us to try to maximize consumption across time rather than increasing consumption in the present at the expense of consumption for yet-unborn generations.[11]

---

[11] Solow won the 1987 Nobel Prize in Economics for his work on economic growth. The growth model was introduced in "A contribution to the theory of economic growth," *Quarterly Journal of Economics* (February 1956): 65–94. For the Golden Rule, see Edmund Phelps' article "The Golden Rule of accumulation: A fable for growthmen," *American Economic Review* 51 (September 1961): 638–643.

A central component of the Solow growth model is the Cobb-Douglas production function. This production function,

$$Y = K^{\alpha}L^{1-\alpha},$$

where Y is output, K is the capital stock, L is labor, and $1 > \alpha > 0$, can be written in "intensive" form by dividing each side by L to obtain

$$y = k^{\alpha},$$

which relates income per capita, $y = Y/L$, to capital per capita, $k = K/L$. Other relationships used in the Solow growth model are also expressed in per capita terms. The national income accounting identity

$$y = c + s$$

shows that, in an economy without a government sector, national income per capita equals the sum of consumption per capita, c, and savings per capita, s. Another national income accounting identity,

$$y = c + i,$$

shows that national income per capita equals the sum of spending on consumption goods per capita and investment spending per capita, i, since we are also assuming that this economy does not trade with the rest of the world. These two relationships imply

$$s = i.$$

Investment adds to the capital stock. The capital stock is diminished by depreciation. We assume that a constant proportion of the capital stock, δ, depreciates each period, so overall depreciation is δk. The net change in the capital stock, Δk, is the difference between investment and depreciation as shown by the equation

$$\Delta k = i - \delta k.$$

The final relationship,

$$s = \sigma y,$$

is a function that specifies savings per capita as a constant proportion of income per capita.

The long-run level of capital per capita is constant in this model. This has several implications that allow us to solve for the long-run level of consumption as a function of the long-run level of capital. First note that $\Delta k = 0$ implies $i = \delta k$, and, since the national income accounting identities show that $i = s$, then, in the long run, $s = \delta k$. Using the intensive production function and this long-run relationship, we then have

$$c = y - s = y - i = k^{\alpha} - \delta k$$

in the long run.

We can use this function to solve for the maximum level of long-run consumption. The first-order condition for the consumption per capita function is

$$\frac{dc}{dk} = \alpha k^{\alpha-1} - \delta = 0,$$

which shows that the stationary point of this function occurs where the marginal product of capital, $\alpha k^{\alpha-1}$, equals the depreciation rate, δ. The second derivative of this function,

$$\frac{dc}{dk} = \alpha(\alpha - 1)k^{\alpha-2},$$

is negative since $\alpha(\alpha - 1) < 0$ and, therefore, following the Golden Rule of acquiring capital to the point where $\alpha k^{\alpha-1} = \delta$, provides for the highest level of sustained consumption. If the capital stock were below its Golden Rule level, then increasing the capital stock by a small amount would increase output by more than it would contribute to depreciation. A small addition to the capital stock beyond the level dictated by the Golden Rule would increase depreciation by more than it would increase output.

An application of the Golden Rule to the real world can be accomplished by the straightforward extension of the model presented here to incorporate growth in the labor force and technological change. Evidence suggests that the capital stock in the United States is below its Golden Rule level.[12]

Exercises 9.2

1. Find the inflection point(s) for the function used in the inflation tax application,

$$S = \frac{M}{P} = \pi e^{-\lambda(\pi+r)+\alpha Y}.$$

2. In the model of perfect competition, all firms are price-takers since they treat price as a market-determined constant. Firm Perfcomp's total revenue function is

$$TR(Q) = P \cdot Q,$$

in which P equals the output price. Assume that $P = 12$ and the total cost function is

$$TC(Q) = Q^3 - 4.5Q^2 + 18Q - 7.$$

(a) Determine the firm's profit function and the level of output at which Firm Perfcomp should produce in order to maximize profits. Confirm that this quantity represents maximum profits for the firm by using the second-order condition.

(b) According to microeconomic theory, perfectly competitive firms will maximize profits by producing at the quantity where price equals marginal cost and where the slope of the marginal revenue curve is less than that of the marginal cost curve. Show that the theory holds in this example.

3. Consider a monopolist's linear demand function

$$P = 12 - 2Q,$$

---

[12] For a discussion of the relationship between the actual capital stock in the United States and its Golden Rule level, see N. Gregory Mankiw, *Macroeconomics*, 3d ed. (New York: Worth Publishers, 1997): 108–109.

where P is the price of the good and Q is its quantity. The monopolist's total cost function is

$$TC = \frac{1}{3}Q^3 - 5Q^2 + 17Q + 25.$$

Determine the level of output at which the monopolist should produce in order to maximize her profits. What is the optimal price that corresponds with this quantity?

4. Babydrink is a profit-maximizing monopolist that produces infant formula. The demand curve facing the firm is given by

$$P = a - bQ,$$

where both a and b are positive parameters. This firm's total cost function is linear in quantity with constant marginal cost c per unit of output and fixed costs of F.

   (a) Remembering that profit $\pi = TR - TC$, determine this firm's profit function. Maximize the profit function, and calculate the optimal levels of price and output.

   (b) Now assume that the government imposes a tax t per unit of output sold by the firm. Using the same procedure as in part (a), obtain the new profit-maximizing levels of price and output.

   (c) The government decides to choose t so that it maximizes the revenues it can obtain from taxing Babydrink's output. Remembering that tax revenues equal the tax rate times the tax base, or Q, in this example, what level of t should the government choose?

5. The Bertrand model of duopoly assumes that firms determine prices and then respond to market demand by producing the quantity consumers wish to purchase. Consider two firms that make slightly different products. Demand for the two firms' output is a linear function of prices,

$$Q_A = a - p_A + bP_B$$
$$Q_B = a - p_B + bP_A.$$

There is a negative relationship between a firm's price and its quantity demanded. Assume that $0 < b < 1$ and that marginal costs are constant and the same for the two firms.

   (a) Determine each firm's profit function.

   (b) Using the first-order condition for profit maximization, determine each firm's reaction function.

   (c) Solve for the equilibrium price.

6. An extension of the Solow growth model includes the effect of an increase in the labor force on an economy. Consider the Cobb-Douglas intensive production function

$$y = k^a,$$

where

$$y = \frac{Y}{L} \quad \text{and} \quad k = \frac{K}{L}.$$

All other national income accounting identities are the same as in the text application except that

$$\Delta k = i - \delta k - nk,$$

where n represents population growth, which suggests that the change in an economy's capital stock is now affected by investment, depreciation, and population growth.

(a) Assuming that in the long run, $\Delta k = 0$, set up the function for long-run consumption per capita. Use the first-order condition to determine the level of k that maximizes consumption.

(b) What is the Golden Rule level of capital accumulation? If two economies have identical production functions and the same rate of depreciation but one's population is growing faster than the other's, which economy has the higher marginal product of capital? Graph this relationship, and explain its significance.

(c) What is the impact of higher population growth on the steady-state levels of capital per worker and output per worker?

7. Technological progress can be incorporated into the Solow growth model as an increase in the efficiency of labor (E), so that the economy's production function becomes $Y = f(K, L \times E)$. The efficiency of labor grows at some constant rate g so that each unit of labor becomes g percent more efficient each year. Output therefore increases as if the labor force had increased g percent. Allowing

$$y = \frac{Y}{L \times E} \quad \text{and} \quad k = \frac{K}{L \times E},$$

which are measures of output and capital per efficiency unit of labor, respectively, the intensive production function is again $y = k^a$, and

$$\Delta k = i - (\delta + n + g)k.$$

Consider an economy with the production function $Y = K^{1/2} L^{1/2}$ and that is experiencing labor-augmenting technological change, that is, E is increasing at the rate $g = 0.02$ (2% annual growth). The capital stock is diminishing at a rate of 10% a year, while the population grows at 2.5% per year. The efficiency of labor is improving at a rate of 2% annually. What is the Golden Rule level of capital accumulation that maximizes consumption per efficiency unit of labor? How does the effect of labor-augmenting technological progress on k^* compare with the effect of population growth?

8. A sugar refiner is located in an isolated geographic area. It is a price-taker in the output market. The price facing the firm equals 9, and its total revenue is $TR = 9Q$, where Q is the rate of output. The refiner's production function is $Q = 3L^{1/3}$, where L is the amount of labor employed. Because of its isolated location, the amount of labor the firm employs has an effect on the level of compensation paid. The firm's compensation function is

$$wL = 6L^{4/3},$$

where w equals wages. The refiner's profit function is

$$\pi = TR(Q(L)) - wL.$$

(a) Set up the first-order condition, and determine the optimal amount of labor the refiner should employ in order to maximize profits.

(b) Use the second-order condition to confirm that this value represents a maximum. What is the economic interpretation of the second-order condition in this example?

9. A domestic auto producer is facing intense competition in the U.S. market from Asian auto imports. The executive officer decides that one way to counter this competition is by producing at the quantity at which total costs are minimized. The firm's cost structure can be illustrated by the function

$$TC = \frac{1}{3}Q^3 - 10Q^2 + 80Q + 500.$$

Calculate, for the executive officer, the cost-minimizing quantity, and provide him with a sketch of the original function by determining its y-intercept and its stationary point(s). As a consultant, you suggest that, according to economic theory, the firm should be producing at the quantity that maximizes profit, not minimizes cost. Assuming that the total revenue function is

$$TR(Q) = 8Q - Q^2,$$

calculate the profit-maximizing output. How does this answer differ from the one that minimizes cost?

10. The compensation firms pay workers typically includes benefits as well as salary. The cost of one particular benefit, health insurance, has been rising rapidly. Consider a firm that uses only labor as its input and has the production function

$$f(L) = \alpha L^{\beta},$$

where L is the number of workers employed, $\alpha > 0$, and $1 > \beta > 0$. The profits of this firm, Π, equal

$$\Pi = p \cdot f(L) - (w + b)L,$$

where p is the price of the firm's product, w is the wage paid to a worker, and b is the cost of providing a worker with benefits.

(a) Find the number of workers the firm will demand in order to maximize its profits. Assume that the firm takes as given p, w, and b. How does the optimal number of workers demanded vary with the value of b?

(b) Show that your solution represents the maximization of profits as opposed to the minimization of profits.

Summary

This chapter shows how to identify and characterize extreme values of univariate functions with the tools of differentiation presented in Chapters 6 and 7. The key insight is that the extreme point of a differentiable function is found at a point where its first derivative equals zero. This first-order condition, while necessary, is not sufficient for showing that a point is a maximum or a minimum. Necessary and sufficient conditions are obtained by considering the value of the first derivative in the neighborhood of the stationary point. Alternatively, the second-order condition provides a sufficient condition, though not a necessary condition.

The techniques presented in this chapter have a wide range of uses in a variety of fields of economics, as demonstrated by the applications in this chapter. These techniques are important for models that assume optimizing behavior, as well as for other situations in which the identification of an extreme point is useful.

The next chapter extends the material presented here to multivariate functions. Much of the intuition for understanding the techniques of identifying and characterizing the extreme points of multivariate functions directly follows from the intuition and rules developed in this chapter.

Chapter 10

Extreme Values of Multivariate Functions

Many problems in economics reflect a need to choose among alternatives. For example, consumers choose among a wide set of goods, producers choose from a number of possible input sets or output mixes, and policy-makers may have several instruments at hand for achieving a particular end. Formal economic analyses of these types of problems require a technique for identifying and characterizing the extreme points of multivariate functions. We present these techniques in this chapter.

The multivariate techniques featured in this chapter are a generalization of the univariate techniques presented in Chapter 9. We will make this clear by reinterpreting the results from the previous chapter in the context of the differential. Placing the univariate results in this context demonstrates a natural and straightforward link between the univariate and multivariate first-order conditions. In Section 10.1 we present the first-order condition for a multivariate function and use the results in three applications. The use of the differential also provides a link between the second-order conditions in the univariate and multivariate cases. The second-order conditions are more complicated in the multivariate case than in the univariate case due to the presence of cross partial derivatives. Therefore we begin with the general results for the simplest multivariate case and, in Section 10.2, develop the second-order conditions for a bivariate function. Section 10.3 extends the second-order conditions to a more general multivariate setting.

10.1 THE MULTIVARIATE FIRST-ORDER CONDITION

The discussion in Chapter 9 demonstrates that extreme values of a univariate function are found at the points where the derivative of that function equals zero. In this section we show that this has a natural interpretation in the context of the differential. This interpretation permits a straightforward extension from the univariate case to the multivariate case. We use the differential to develop the first-order condition for a multivariate function.

Recall from Chapter 6 that the differential dy of the univariate function $y = f(x)$ evaluated at the point x_0 is

$$dy = f'(x_0)\, dx.$$

This differential defines a line tangent to the function $f(x)$ at the point x_0. At a stationary point x^*, where $f'(x^*) = 0$, the differential dy equals zero for any dx. Since all interior extreme points of functions that are everywhere differentiable are also stationary points, it follows that the differential equals zero at all interior extreme points of functions that are everywhere differentiable.

The multivariate analogue to the differential is the total differential. As discussed in Chapter 8, the total differential dy of the multivariate function $y = f(x_1, x_2, \ldots, x_n)$ is

$$dy = f_1(x_1, x_2, \ldots, x_n)\, dx_1 + f_2(x_1, x_2, \ldots, x_n)\, dx_2 + \cdots + f_n(x_1, x_2, \ldots, x_n)\, dx_n,$$

where $f_i(x_1, x_2, \ldots, x_n)$ represents the partial derivative of the function with respect to the ith argument. Extending the logic of the univariate case, we say that a stationary point of a multivariate function is a set of values of the arguments of that function $(x_1^*, x_2^*, \ldots, x_n^*)$ such that the total differential dy equals zero for any set of values $(dx_1, dx_2, \ldots, dx_n)$. This occurs at the point where all partial derivatives equal zero. The first-order condition for a multivariate function follows from this result.

First-Order Condition for a Multivariate Function If the function

$$y = f(x_1, x_2, \ldots, x_n)$$

is differentiable with respect to each of its arguments on a domain and reaches a maximum or a minimum at the stationary point $(x_1^*, x_2^*, \ldots, x_n^*)$ within that domain, then each of the partial derivatives evaluated at that point equals zero. That is,

$$\begin{aligned} f_1(x_1^*, x_2^*, \ldots, x_n^*) &= 0,\\ f_2(x_1^*, x_2^*, \ldots, x_n^*) &= 0,\\ &\vdots\\ f_n(x_1^*, x_2^*, \ldots, x_n^*) &= 0. \end{aligned}$$

Two examples illustrate the use of this multivariate first-order condition. Consider the bivariate function

$$g(x_1, x_2) = 6x_1 - x_1^2 + 16x_2 - 4x_2^2.$$

The first-order conditions for this function are

$$\begin{aligned} g_1(x_1, x_2) &= 6 - 2x_1 = 0 \quad \text{and}\\ g_2(x_1, x_2) &= 16 - 8x_2 = 0. \end{aligned}$$

The single stationary point of this function is therefore $x_1^* = 3, x_2^* = 2$, and the value of the function at this point is $g(x_1^*, x_2^*) = g(3, 2) = 25$. As we show in Section 10.3, this represents a maximum.

As another example, consider the function

$$h(x_1, x_2) = x_1^2 + 4x_2^2 - 2x_1 - 16x_2 + x_1x_2.$$

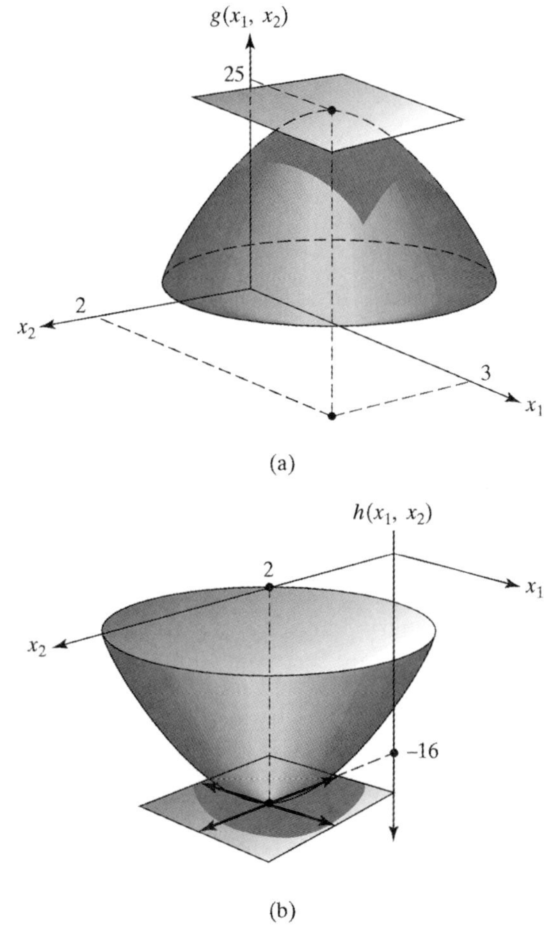

FIGURE 10.1 Stationary Points and the Tangent Planes of Bivariate Functions

The first-order conditions for this function are

$$h_1(x_1, x_2) = 2x_1 - 2 + x_2 = 0 \quad \text{and}$$
$$h_2(x_1, x_2) = 8x_2 - 16 + x_1 = 0.$$

Solving these two equations for the critical values of the two arguments, we find that the single stationary point of this function is $x_1^* = 0, x_2^* = 2$. At this point, the function has the value $h(0, 2) = -16$. As we demonstrate in Section 10.3, this point represents a minimum.

Figure 10.1(a) depicts the bivariate functions $g(x_1, x_2)$ and identifies its stationary point $x_1 = 3, x_2 = 2$, while Figure 10.1(b) depicts $h(x_1, x_2)$ and identifies its stationary point $x_1 = 0, x_2 = 2$. Each figure also includes the plane tangent to the function at the stationary point. The tangent planes in Figure 10.1(a) and Figure 10.1(b) are each parallel to the (x_1, x_2) surface. This is analogous to the condition that, for a univariate

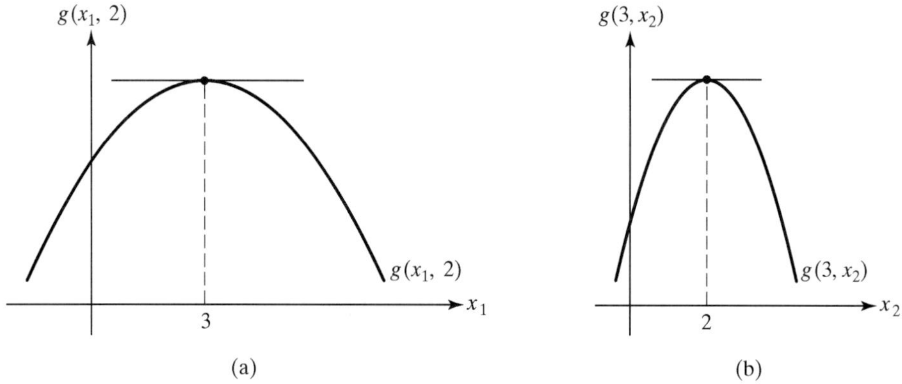

FIGURE 10.2 Slices of a Bivariate Function

function, the tangent line representing the differential has a slope of zero at a stationary point.

Figure 10.2(a) and Figure 10.2(b) further demonstrate this analogy between the tangent line at a stationary point of a univariate function and the tangent plane at a stationary point of a bivariate function. Figure 10.2(a) presents a slice of the function $g(x_1, x_2)$ for $x_2 = 2$, and Figure 10.2(b) presents a slice of this function for $x_1 = 3$.[1] Collapsing the three-dimensional function by considering a two-dimensional slice results in the tangent plane collapsing to a line. The tangent line at the point $x_1 = 3$ in Figure 10.2(a) and the tangent line at the point $x_2 = 2$ in Figure 10.2(b) each have a slope equal to zero.

As in the univariate case, the multivariate first-order condition provides a necessary but not a sufficient condition for identifying an extreme point. This first-order condition cannot distinguish between extreme points that represent local maxima, local minima, or saddle points that are neither local maxima nor local minima. We return to this point in Section 10.3. But first, using the multivariate first-order condition, we present three applications.

A Monopolist Selling to Segmented Markets

Many firms have the opportunity to sell their products at different prices to different sets of consumers. For example, movie theatres charge more for an adult's ticket than for a child's ticket, airlines charge different fares depending upon the time of travel, and museums charge a reduced admission fee to senior citizens. A firm may be able to enjoy higher profits if it sets different prices than if it has a uniform price for all consumers.

[1] Recall Figure 8.2 in which slices of a bivariate production function provided two-dimensional depictions of the relationship between labor and output for a given amount of capital and between capital and output for a given amount of labor.

To illustrate this, we study the optimal pricing schedule of an electric utility that is the sole supplier of electricity to industrial users as well as to households in a particular region. We assume that the utility can set separate prices in each market. Among industrial firms, the demand for millions of kilowatt-hours (million-kwh) per month of electric power, K_F, is a function of the price charged to those firms in dollars per kwh, P_F, as represented by the demand function

$$K_F = 0.729P_F^{-3}.$$

We also assume that, among households, the demand for million-kwh per month of electric power, K_H, is a function of the price charged to households in dollars per kwh, P_H, as shown by the demand function

$$K_H = 7.2P_H^{-2}.$$

Total cost facing the monopolist consists of a fixed cost of Φ million dollars plus a constant marginal cost of \$0.06 per kwh, as shown by the function

$$TC = \Phi + 0.06(K_F + K_H).$$

The electric utility maximizes its total profit, which equals its total revenue from both markets minus total cost,

$$\Pi = K_F P_F + K_H P_H - (\Phi + 0.06(K_F + K_H)).$$

Substituting the two demand functions, we find

$$\Pi = 0.729P_F^{-2} + 7.2P_H^{-1} - (\Phi + 0.06(0.729P_F^{-3} + 7.2P_H^{-2})).$$

There are two first-order conditions, one taking the partial derivative with respect to P_F and one taking the partial derivative with respect to P_H. These are

$$\frac{\partial \Pi}{\partial P_F} = -2 \cdot 0.729P_F^{-3} + 0.18 \cdot 0.729P_F^{-4} = 0 \quad \text{and}$$
$$\frac{\partial \Pi}{\partial P_H} = -7.2P_H^{-2} + 0.12 \cdot 7.2P_H^{-3} = 0.$$

We can solve for the prices that maximize the utility's profit. These are

$$P_F = \$0.09 \text{ per kwh} \quad \text{and}$$
$$P_H = \$0.12 \text{ per kwh}.$$

At these prices, the quantity of kilowatt-hours consumed by firms and households will be

$$K_F = 1000 \text{ million-kwh per month} \quad \text{and}$$
$$K_H = 500 \text{ million-kwh per month}.$$

In this example, the elasticity of demand for firms is 3, and the elasticity of demand for households is 2 (see Chapter 7 for a discussion of elasticity). The optimal pricing strategy involves charging a higher price to the group with the lower elasticity of demand. Thus the result here is very similar to the result in the application concerning the optimal price set by a monopolist, presented in Chapter 9, in which the price that maximizes profits decreases with the elasticity of demand.

Advertising

Advertising is ubiquitous. But what role does it play? Some people view advertising as an insidious attempt to foist desires for unneeded products upon a gullible public. Others see it as a useful way for people to obtain information about goods and services. And there are those who like to watch commercials and enjoy advertisements as a form of entertainment.

Economists have identified a number of possible motives for advertising.[2] Advertising may be one dimension along which firms compete. But even in the absence of competition, a firm may advertise to increase the demand for its product. We can derive the profit-maximizing amount of advertising undertaken by a monopolist in order to illustrate how the expenditure on advertising is a function of both its efficacy and the responsiveness of demand to price.

The model we use focuses on the role of advertising in informing people about a product. Assume that there are N potential customers for a monopolist's product. Each advertisement is viewed by $1/N$ people. Therefore, the probability that any particular consumer is not informed from a given advertisement is $(1 - 1/N)$. When the monopolist places two advertisements, the likelihood that a particular consumer does not view that ad is $(1 - 1/N)^2$. More generally, if S ads are placed, the probability that any one person does not see any of those ads is $(1 - 1/N)^S$. Consider the case where there are many potential consumers and N is a large number. From one of the central results in Chapter 3, we find

$$\lim_{N\to\infty}\left(1 - \frac{1}{N}\right)^S = \lim_{N\to\infty}\left[\left(1 + \frac{1}{-N}\right)^{-N}\right]^{S/(-N)} = e^{-S/N}.$$

We use this result and assume that, given a large value of N, we can approximate $(1 - 1/N)^S$ by $e^{-S/N}$. Then the probability that any particular consumer does see an ad is $(1 - e^{-S/N})$. With N consumers, the number who see ads is an increasing function of S and equal to

$$(1 - e^{-S/N})N.$$

In this model we assume that advertising serves to promote brand recognition and a consumer demands the monopolist's product only if she has learned about it from an advertisement. Once informed, a consumer will demand the quantity q, which is a linear function of price, as shown by the function

$$q = a - bP.$$

The total market demand for the product, Q, is the number of informed consumers times the demand function of each consumer,

$$Q = (1 - e^{-S/N})Nq = (1 - e^{-S/N})N(a - bP).$$

[2] For an excellent discussion of the theories of advertising and the evidence of its use by firms, see Chapter 10 of Lynne Pepall, Daniel J. Richards, and George Norman, *Industrial Organization: Contemporary Theory and Practice* (New York: South-Western College Publishing, 1999). The model in this application is drawn from that chapter.

With a constant marginal cost of production equal to C and the cost of each of the S advertisements equal to A, the profit of the monopolist, Π, is determined by the function

$$\begin{aligned}\Pi &= PQ - CQ - AS \\ &= (1 - e^{-S/N})N(aP - bP^2) - C(1 - e^{-S/N})N(a - bP) - AS.\end{aligned}$$

The monopolist must choose both the price at which to sell her good, P, and the number of advertisements to place, S. The first-order conditions for this multivariate optimization problem are

$$\frac{\partial \Pi}{\partial P} = (1 - e^{-S/N})N(a - 2bP) + bC(1 - e^{-S/N})N = 0 \quad \text{and}$$

$$\frac{\partial \Pi}{\partial S} = e^{-S/N}[(aP - bP^2) - C(a - bP)] - A = 0.$$

These conditions can be somewhat simplified by using the individual's and the market demand functions to obtain

$$\frac{\partial \Pi}{\partial P} = Q - (P - C)\frac{Qb}{q} = 0 \quad \text{and}$$

$$\frac{\partial \Pi}{\partial S} = e^{-S/N}q(P - C) - A = 0.$$

These two conditions imply that the profit-maximizing levels of P and Q meet the condition

$$\frac{q}{b} = \frac{A}{e^{-S/N}q}.$$

Further simplification is possible by noting that the elasticity of demand with respect to the market price, η_P, and the elasticity of demand with respect to the number of advertisements, η_S, are

$$\eta_P = -\frac{\partial Q}{\partial P}\cdot\frac{P}{Q} = \frac{bP}{Q} \quad \text{and}$$

$$\eta_S = \frac{\partial Q}{\partial S}\cdot\frac{S}{Q} = e^{-S/N}\cdot\frac{Sq}{Q}.$$

Finally, we multiply each side of the optimal condition by Q, multiply and divide the left side by P, and multiply and divide the right side by S to express this condition as

$$\frac{AS}{PQ} = \frac{\eta_S}{\eta_P}.$$

This result, from a paper by Robert Dorfman and Peter Steiner published in 1954, shows that the profit-maximizing combination of price and advertising is one where the amount spent on advertising as a proportion of total revenues, AS/PQ, equals the elasticity of demand with respect to advertising divided by the elasticity of demand with respect to price.[3] We can gain some intuition concerning the role of price elasticity by noting that the markup of price over marginal cost, $P - C$, increases with a decrease in the elasticity of demand.[4] There is more to be gained by increasing demand when the markup is high than when it is low, and therefore, the marginal contribution of advertising to profits is higher when the elasticity of demand with respect to price is low. The second of the two first-order conditions shows that the profit-maximizing level of S rises with $P - C$.

The Dorfman-Steiner result has an interesting implication concerning the observed correlation between advertising and market structure. It is often argued that advertising has the goal of decreasing price elasticity. Evidence links low elasticity of demand to higher advertising revenues. One could draw the conclusion that this proves that advertising alters people's demands. But the Dorfman-Steiner result shows that low price elasticity of demand may lead to higher advertising expenditures rather than the other way around. Thus, the issue of cause and effect with respect to advertising expenditures and elasticity of demand is not clear-cut.

Ordinary Least Squares Estimators

Econometrics is the branch of economics that applies statistical analysis to economic data. We have seen econometric results in a number of applications in earlier chapters, including the international pattern of women labor-force participation in Chapter 6, the relationship between income per capita and infant mortality in Chapter 7, and the determination of wages in Chapter 8. In each of these cases, the econometric method of Ordinary Least Squares (OLS) provides an estimate of the relationship between a dependent variable and one or more independent variables.

To illustrate OLS in a bivariate regression, consider the set of points (X_i, Y_i) in Figure 10.3, where Y_i represents the dependent variable and X_i represents the independent variable. OLS provides an estimate for $\hat{\alpha}$ and $\hat{\beta}$ in the regression equation

$$Y_i = \hat{\alpha} + \hat{\beta}X_i + e_i,$$

where e_i is the residual term. Figure 10.3 includes the regression line that contains the points $(X_i, \hat{Y}_i)$, where $\hat{Y}_i$ is the predicted value of the dependent variable corresponding to the ith value of the independent variable such that

$$\hat{Y}_i = \hat{\alpha} + \hat{\beta}X_i.$$

For example, in Figure 10.3, the value of one of the independent variables is labeled as X_3, the value of the corresponding dependent variable is labeled as Y_3, and the corresponding predicted value is labeled as $\hat{Y}_3$. The distance corresponding to the residual

[3] Robert Dorfman and Peter O. Steiner, "Optimal advertising and optimal quality," *American Economic Review* 44, no. 4 (December 1954): 826–836.

[4] The previous application shows that a monopolist maximizes profits by setting a higher price to that segment of the market that has a lower elasticity of demand. This implies, of course, that with a given marginal cost, the markup of price over marginal cost rises with a decrease in the elasticity of demand.

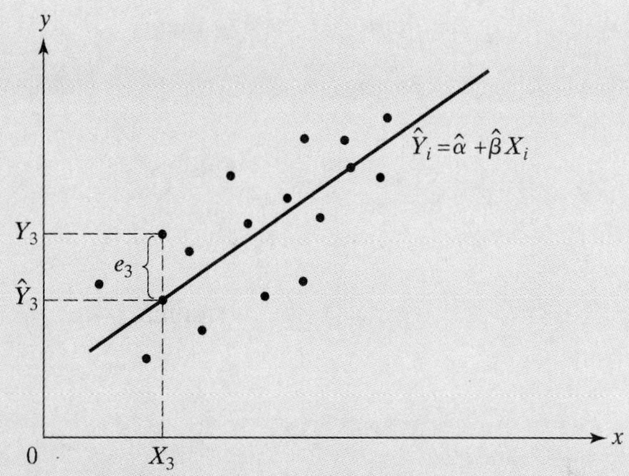

FIGURE 10.3 A Regression Line

for the third observation is labeled as e_3. This represents the difference between the actual and the predicted value of the dependent variable. In general,

$$e_i = Y_i - \hat{Y}_i.$$

As the name "least squares" suggests, OLS offers a formula for $\hat{\alpha}$ and $\hat{\beta}$ that minimizes the sum of squared residuals (SSR). With n observations,

$$\begin{aligned} SSR &= \sum_{i=1}^{n}(e_i^{\,2}) \\ &= \sum_{i=1}^{n}(Y_i - \hat{Y}_i)^2 \\ &= \sum_{i=1}^{n}(Y_i - (\hat{\alpha} + \hat{\beta}X_i))^2 \\ &= \sum_{i=1}^{n}Y_i^{\,2} + \sum_{i=1}^{n}(\hat{\alpha} + \hat{\beta}X_i)^2 - 2\sum_{i=1}^{n}Y_i \cdot (\hat{\alpha} + \hat{\beta}X_i). \end{aligned}$$

We can determine the formulas for $\hat{\alpha}$ and $\hat{\beta}$ by using the multivariate first-order condition. In this case the first-order condition requires

$$\frac{\partial SSR}{\partial \hat{\alpha}} = 2\sum_{i=1}^{n}(\hat{\alpha} + \hat{\beta}X_i) - 2\sum_{i=1}^{n}Y_i = 0 \quad \text{and}$$

$$\frac{\partial SSR}{\partial \hat{\beta}} = 2\sum_{i=1}^{n}X_i(\hat{\alpha} + \hat{\beta}X_i) - 2\sum_{i=1}^{n}Y_i \cdot X_i = 0,$$

where we have used the sum-difference rule, which shows

$$\frac{\partial}{\partial u}\sum_{i=1}^{n} f(u, v_i) = \sum_{i=1}^{n} f_u(u, v_i).$$

We can simplify the first equation by noting that

$$2\sum_{i=1}^{n}(\hat{\alpha} + \hat{\beta}X_i) = 2n\hat{\alpha} - 2\hat{\beta}\sum_{i=1}^{n}X_i.$$

Solving the first equation, we find that

$$n\hat{\alpha} = \sum_{i=1}^{n}Y_i - \hat{\beta}\sum_{i=1}^{n}X_i.$$

Dividing through by n and recognizing that the averages of X_i and Y_i, denoted $\overline{X}$ and $\overline{Y}$, respectively, are

$$\overline{X} = \frac{1}{n}\sum_{i=1}^{n}X_i \quad \text{and} \quad \overline{Y} = \frac{1}{n}\sum_{i=1}^{n}Y_i,$$

we find

$$\hat{\alpha} = \overline{Y} - \hat{\beta}\overline{X}.$$

Therefore, once we find $\hat{\beta}$, given the average values for X and Y, we can determine $\hat{\alpha}$.

To find $\hat{\beta}$, we substitute the solution for $\hat{\alpha}$ in the first-order condition $\partial SSR/\partial\hat{\beta} = 0$ to obtain

$$\overline{Y}\sum_{i=1}^{n}X_i - \hat{\beta}\overline{X}\sum_{i=1}^{n}X_i + \hat{\beta}\sum_{i=1}^{n}X_i^2 = \sum_{i=1}^{n}Y_i \cdot X_i.$$

Dividing each term of this equation by n, we get

$$\overline{X}\cdot\overline{Y} - \hat{\beta}(\overline{X})^2 + \hat{\beta}\frac{1}{n}\sum_{i=1}^{n}X_i^2 = \frac{1}{n}\sum_{i=1}^{n}Y_i \cdot X_i,$$

which can be rearranged to show that[5]

$$\hat{\beta} = \frac{(1/n)\sum_{i=1}^{n}Y_i \cdot X_i - (\overline{X}\cdot\overline{Y})}{(1/n)\sum_{i=1}^{n}X_i^2 - (\overline{X})^2}.$$

This numerator can be rewritten as

$$\frac{1}{n}\sum_{i=1}^{n}(Y_i - \overline{Y})(X_i - \overline{X}),$$

[5] Recall from the discussion in Chapter 4 that, in general,

$$\sum_{i=1}^{n}X_iY_i \neq \sum_{i=1}^{n}X_i \cdot \sum_{i=1}^{n}Y_i$$

and, therefore,

$$\frac{1}{n^2}\sum_{i=1}^{n}X_i \cdot Y_i \neq \overline{X}\cdot\overline{Y}.$$

and the denominator can be written as[6]

$$\frac{1}{n}\sum_{i=1}^{n}(X_i - \overline{X})^2.$$

Canceling out the term $1/n$ in the numerator and denominator and then dividing both the numerator and denominator by $n - 1$, we can write the quotient as

$$\hat{\beta} = \frac{[1/(n-1)]\,\Sigma_{i=1}^{n}\Sigma_{i=1}^{n}(Y_i - \overline{Y})(X_i - \overline{X})}{[1/(n-1)]\,\Sigma_{i=1}^{n}(X_i - \overline{X}\,)^2} = \frac{s_{XY}}{s_X^2},$$

where s_{XY} is the estimated **covariance** of X and Y and s_X^2 is the estimated **variance** of the variable X.

We present regression results in Chapter 7, in the application concerning the relationship between the dependent variable of the logarithm of infant mortality, $\ln(INF)$, and the independent variable of the logarithm of per capita national income, $\ln(INC)$, for a sample including over three hundred countries. The estimated slope and intercept of this regression equation can be determined from the estimated variance of the natural logarithm of income, the estimated covariance of the two variables, and the averages of the two variables. The variance of the logarithm of per capita national income is 2.36, and the covariance of the logarithm of infant mortality and the logarithm of per capita national income is -1.30. Therefore

$$\hat{\beta} = \frac{-1.30}{2.36} = -0.55.$$

The average of the logarithm of infant mortality is 3.42, and the average of the logarithm of per capita national income is 7.45. Therefore the intercept of the regression line is

$$\hat{\alpha} = \overline{Y} - \hat{\beta}\overline{X} = 3.42 - (-0.55)\cdot 7.45 = 7.52.$$

Thus, as reported in that application, the regression equation depicted in Figure 7.2(b) is

$$\ln(INF) = 7.52 - 0.55 \cdot \ln(INC).$$

Exercises 10.1

1. Find the stationary point(s) of each function.
   (a) $f(x, z) = 4x - 2z^2 + x^2 + z$
   (b) $f(x, z) = 8x - x^2 + 14z - 7z^2$

[6]Note that

$$\frac{1}{n}\sum_{i=1}^{n}(Y_i - \overline{Y})(X_i - \overline{X}) = \frac{1}{n}\left(\sum_{i=1}^{n} Y_iX_i - \sum_{i=1}^{n} Y_i\overline{X} - \sum_{i=1}^{n}\overline{Y}X_i + \sum_{i=1}^{n}\overline{YX}\right).$$

(c) $f(x, z) = 4x - x^{1/2} + \frac{1}{3}z - 2z^{1/2}$

(d) $f(x, z) = x + 3e^{z} - e^{x} - e^{3z}$

2. Find the stationary point(s) of each function.

(a) $g(u, v) = 10 + 20u - 2u^2 + 16v - v^2 - 2uv$

(b) $g(u, v) = 100 - 5u + 4u^2 - 9v + 5v^2 + 8uv$

(c) $g(u, v) = \frac{1}{3}u^3 + 3uv + 2u - \frac{3}{2}v^2$

(d) $g(u, v) = 72u^{1/3}v^{1/3} - 6u - 3v$

3. Find the stationary points for each function.

(a) $h(a, b) = (a + 5)^2 - (b + 3)^2$

(b) $h(a, b) = \frac{1}{2}a^4 - b^6$

(c) $h(a, b) = 3a^2 + 6a - b^2 + 4b - 2ab$

(d) $h(a, b) = a^{-1} + b^{-1} + ab$

4. Use the first-order condition to identify the stationary points of each function below. Evaluate each function in the neighborhoods of its stationary points

$$x^* + a, \quad z^* + a, \quad x^* - a, \quad \text{and} \quad z^* - a,$$

where x^* and z^* are the critical points of the function $f(x, z)$ and $a = 1$. Determine whether the stationary points identified represent a maximum, minimum, or saddle point.

(a) $f(x, z) = 6x - x^2 + 16z - 4z^2$

(b) $f(x, z) = 50 + 10x - \frac{1}{2}x^2 + 14z - 2z^2 + xz$

(c) $f(x, z) = 4x^2z^2 - 16x - 4z$

(d) $f(x, z) = 6x + 2z^2 - x^2 + 4z$

5. Governments have a variety of means of raising revenue. As discussed in Chapter 9, the Central Bank can raise seigniorage revenues, S, through inflation (π). The Treasury can raise income tax revenue, T, by imposing an income tax rate, t. Total government revenue, R, therefore, is $R = S + T$. Both inflation and income taxes affect income. Assume that the equation for actual income is

$$Y = X - ct + g\pi,$$

where X is potential income.

(a) Seigniorage is the product of the inflation rate and the level of real balances (M/P). Assume that

$$\frac{M}{P} = -a\pi + bY,$$

so that

$$S = \pi(-a\pi + bY).$$

Taking into account the effect of inflation on income, find the level of inflation that maximizes seigniorage revenue.

(b) Income tax revenue equals the tax rate times the level of income as follows:

$$T = tY = t(X - ct + g\pi).$$

Given the inflation rate, find the tax rate that maximizes income tax revenues.

(c) If the Central Bank and the Treasury act as a single decision-maker and jointly set the inflation rate and the tax rate in order to maximize R, would they choose the same rates as they would when acting independently? Are π and t higher or lower when there is cooperation between the two? Is R higher or lower when there is cooperation? Give an intuitive interpretation of your answers concerning π, t, and R.

6. Assume that an individual's total labor compensation is a function of that person's education level, E, and years of experience, X, in a given profession. This compensation function (C) is

$$C = -2E^2 + 78E - 2X^2 + 66X - 2EX.$$

Find the stationary point that maximizes the compensation function to determine what combination of education and experience gives the highest level of this individual's labor compensation.

7. As financial advisor to the *The Journal of Important Stuff*, you need to determine the effect on sales of the number of pages devoted to important stuff about economics (E) and (un)important stuff about everything else (U). After careful consideration, you decide that the function describing the relationship between sales (S) and number of pages on economics and other stuff is

$$S = 100U + 310E - \frac{1}{2}U^2 - 2E^2 - UE.$$

What is your recommendation for the number of pages devoted to economics articles and the number of pages devoted to articles on other topics in order to maximize sales?

8. A firm uses inputs of labor, L, and capital, K, to produce its output, Q, according to the production function

$$Q = f(K, L) = 9L^{1/3}K^{1/3}.$$

The firm is a price-taker in the input markets. Labor is paid an hourly wage of $w = 12$, and the price of capital is $r = 6$. The firm sells its output at a price of $P = 4$ per unit. Maximize the profit function

$$\Pi(K, L) = Pf(K, L) - wL - rK$$

to determine the optimum level of each input the firm should use.

9. The profits of two cigarette manufacturing firms, Cambells (C) and Marlbury (M), depend upon the firms' own advertising budgets and the advertising budgets of

their respective rivals as follows:

$$\Pi_C = 1000A_C - A_C^2 - A_M^2$$
$$\Pi_M = 1000A_M - A_M A_C - A_M^2$$

In these equations, Π_C and A_C represent the profits and advertising budget of Cambells, and Π_M and A_M represent the profits and advertising budget of Marlbury.

(a) Suppose, initially, that each firm considers the other firm's advertising budget as an exogenous parameter. Find the optimal advertising budget for each firm. Also find each firm's profits. Show that this level represents maximum profits.

(b) Now the two firms merge, and, while keeping separate brands, the directors of the unified firm choose A_C and A_M in order to maximize the sum $\Pi = (\Pi_C + \Pi_M)$. Determine A_C and A_M. Are the joint profits higher after the merger or when the firms compete? (Rather than solving for Π, consider whether A_C and A_M here differ from those in part (a) and, if so, what this implies.)

(c) The directors of the unified firm must decide whether to keep separate brands and differentiated products (and thus have two separate advertising campaigns) or to have only one brand. If the firm has only one brand, then there is no differentiation in advertising. With one brand, the joint profit function, Π, is the sum of the profit functions given above with the difference that $A = A_M = A_C$. What is P when the products are not differentiated and $A = A_M = A_C$? Which strategy leads to higher Π, differentiated or undifferentiated products? (*Hint:* Refer to your answers from parts (a) and (b)).

10. The publishing firm America's Western Lore (AWL) sells its cowboy novels in two regions of the country, Texas and Massachusetts. The demand for these books in Texas is given by the inverse demand function

$$P_T = \alpha - \beta Q_T,$$

while the inverse demand function in Massachusetts is

$$P_M = \gamma - \theta Q_M,$$

where Q refers to quantity, P refers to price, and the subscripts refer to Texas or Massachusetts. We initially assume that books cannot be shipped between Texas and Massachusetts. We also assume that $\beta > \theta$ and $\alpha > \gamma$.

(a) Find the optimal quantities to sell in Massachusetts and in Texas under the assumption that the total cost function for AWL is linear and

$$TC = \Psi + c(Q_M + Q_T),$$

where c is a parameter and Ψ represents fixed costs. Determine the profits earned by AWL.

(b) Find the optimal quantities to sell in Massachusetts and in Texas under the assumption that the total cost function for AWL is quadratic and

$$TC = \Psi + c(Q_M + Q_T)^2,$$

where c is a parameter and Ψ represents fixed costs.

(c) Now suppose some residents of Texas and Massachusetts begin transporting books such that $P_T = P_M$, and then AWL faces the overall inverse demand function

$$P = \left(\frac{\alpha\theta + \gamma\beta}{\beta + \theta}\right) - \left(\frac{\beta\theta}{\beta + \theta}\right)Q,$$

where P is the common price in Texas and Massachusetts and $Q = Q_M + Q_T$. Determine the profits AWL would have earned in this case.

11. A monopolist produces an identical product in two plants, one in Busytown and one in Slackerville. The total cost of output Q_B produced in Busytown is

$$C_B = Q_B + Q_B^2.$$

The total cost of output Q_S produced in Slackerville is

$$C_S = 6Q_S + 1.5Q_S^2.$$

The total demand for the firm's product is

$$P = 56 - 2Q_T,$$

where total quantity is $Q_T = Q_S + Q_B$. What levels of output should the firm produce in each plant in order to maximize profits?

12. Suppose that a monopolist produces an identical product in three plants and faces an inverse demand function

$$P = 40 - Q_T,$$

where the total quantity in all three plants is $Q_T = Q_1 + Q_2 + Q_3$. The output from the three plants is produced at the costs

$$C_1 = Q_1 + Q_1^2, \quad C_2 = 3Q_2, \quad \text{and} \quad C_3 = 2Q_3^2 - Q_3,$$

where C_i refers to the total cost required to produce Q_i units from each facility.

(a) Assuming that total revenue $TR = P \cdot Q$ and total cost $TC = C_1 + C_2 + C_3$, determine the profit function.

(b) Determine the levels of output, Q_1, Q_2, and Q_3 that maximize this firm's profits.

10.2 THE SECOND-ORDER CONDITION IN THE BIVARIATE CASE

In Section 10.1 we used the differential to draw a direct correspondence between the first-order conditions for the univariate and multivariate cases. In this section we again turn to the differential to develop intuition for the multivariate second-order condition by focusing on bivariate functions. These conditions are sufficient, though not necessary, for characterizing an extreme point as a local maximum or a local minimum. The results for bivariate functions developed in this section are extended in Section 10.3 to the more general multivariate case.

In Chapter 9 we present the second-order condition for a univariate function with respect to that function's second derivative. To extend this result to a bivariate function, we recast these conditions in terms of the **second differential.** The second differential of a function can be considered as the differential of the first differential, and, therefore, it is denoted as $d(dy) = d^2y$. The second differential of the univariate function $y = f(x)$ equals

$$d^2y = \frac{d(f'(x)\,dx)}{dx}\,dx = (f''(x)\,dx)\,dx = f''(x)\,(dx)^2,$$

which is the product of the second derivative and the term $(dx)^2$, which is positive for any dx.

A sufficient condition for a stationary point of a univariate function to be a local maximum is that the second derivative evaluated at that point is negative. In the context of the second differential, a sufficient condition for a stationary point to be a local maximum is that, for any dx, the second differential evaluated at the stationary point is negative. A sufficient condition for a local minimum of a univariate function is that the second derivative evaluated at that point is positive for any dx.

We find the **second total differential** of the general bivariate function $y = f(x_1, x_2)$ by first obtaining the total differential

$$dy = f_1(x_1, x_2)\,dx_1 + f_2(x_1, x_2)\,dx_2.$$

Taking the total derivative of the total differential by treating the dx_i terms as constants and f_i terms as functions, we get the second total differential

$$d^2y = \frac{\partial(f_1\,dx_1 + f_2\,dx_2)}{\partial x_1}\,dx_1 + \frac{\partial(f_1\,dx_1 + f_2\,dx_2)}{\partial x_2}\,dx_2$$

or

$$d^2y = f_{11}\cdot(dx_1)^2 + f_{22}\cdot(dx_2)^2 + 2f_{12}\cdot(dx_1\cdot dx_2),$$

where f_i represents $f_i(x_1, x_2)$, f_{ij} represents $f_{ij}(x_1, x_2)$, and we use Young's Theorem, which states that $f_{12}(x_1, x_2) = f_{21}(x_1, x_2)$ (see Chapter 8).

Analogous to the univariate case, sufficient conditions for identifying a stationary point of a bivariate function $f(x_1, x_2)$ as a local maximum or a local minimum depend upon the value of the second total differential for any dx_1 and dx_2, as shown in the following rules.

Sufficient Condition for a Local Maximum If the second total differential evaluated at a stationary point of a function $f(x_1, x_2)$ is negative for any dx_1 and dx_2, then that stationary point represents a local maximum of the function.

Sufficient Condition for a Local Minimum If the second total differential evaluated at a stationary point of a function $f(x_1, x_2)$ is positive for any dx_1 and dx_2, then that stationary point represents a local minimum of the function.

To use these sufficient conditions in the bivariate case, we need to identify a specific set of rules that ensure that the sign of the second total differential is either positive or negative for any values of dx_1 and dx_2. Two conditions for assigning a sign to d^2y are immediately apparent. If dx_1 equals zero, then $d^2y = f_{22}(x_1, x_2) \cdot (dx_2)^2$. In this case the sign of d^2y is the same as the sign of $f_{22}(x_1, x_2)$ since $(dx_2)^2$ is necessarily nonnegative. By extension, if dx_2 equals zero, then the sign of d^2y is the same as the sign of $f_{11}(x_1, x_2)$. Thus a necessary condition for d^2y to be positive for any set of values for dx_1 and dx_2 is that $f_{11}(x_1, x_2)$ and $f_{22}(x_1, x_2)$ are each positive, and a necessary condition for d^2y to be negative for any set of values for dx_1 and dx_2 is that $f_{11}(x_1, x_2)$ and $f_{22}(x_1, x_2)$ are each negative.

A complete set of conditions that ensures that d^2y is either positive or negative must also take into account the value of the cross partial derivative $f_{12}(x_1, x_2)$. We can develop these conditions by completing the square of the second total differential. Adding and subtracting $(f_{12})^2(dx_2)^2/f_{11}$ to the second total differential and rearranging terms, we find

$$d^2y = f_{11}\left[(dx_1)^2 + 2 \cdot \frac{f_{12}}{f_{11}} \cdot (dx_1)(dx_2) + \left(\frac{(f_{12})}{(f_{11})}\right)^2 (dx_2)^2\right] + \left[f_{22} - \frac{(f_{12})^2}{f_{11}}\right] \cdot (dx_2)^2.$$

The first term in parentheses can be rewritten as $(dx_1 + f_{12}/f_{11}\, dx_2)^2$, which is unambiguously positive since it is squared. Thus the second differential can be written as

$$d^2y = f_{11}\left(dx_1 + \frac{(f_{12})}{(f_{11})}\, dx_2\right)^2 + \left(f_{22} - \frac{(f_{12})^2}{f_{11}}\right)(dx_2)^2.$$

The second total differential is positive for any values of dx_1 and dx_2 if f_{11} is positive and if

$$f_{22} - \frac{(f_{12})^2}{f_{11}} > 0$$

or, equivalently, if f_{11} is positive and if

$$f_{11}f_{22} > (f_{12})^2.$$

The second total differential is negative for any values of dx_1 and dx_2 if f_{11} is negative and if

$$f_{22} - \frac{(f_{12})^2}{f_{11}} < 0$$

or, equivalently, if f_{11} is negative and if

$$f_{11}f_{22} > (f_{12})^2.$$

While these conditions do not explicitly include the sign of f_{22}, the condition $f_{11}f_{22} > (f_{12})^2$ requires that f_{22} is nonzero and has the same sign as f_{11} since $(f_{12})^2$ is necessarily greater than or equal to zero.[7]

[7]This strict inequality $f_{11}f_{22} > (f_{12})^2$, rather than the weak inequality $f_{11}f_{22} \geq (f_{12})^2$, is required to cover the special case of $dx_1 = -f_{12}/f_{11}\, dx_2$, which causes $f_{11}(dx_1 + (f_{12})/(f_{11})\, dx_2)^2$ to equal zero and the second total differential to be

$$d^2y = \left(f_{22} - \frac{f_{12}}{f_{11}}\right)(dx_2)^2.$$

These results provide the following sufficient conditions for characterizing stationary points of bivariate functions as local minima or local maxima.

Second-Order Condition for a Local Maximum of a Bivariate Function If the function $y = f(x_1, x_2)$ has the stationary point (x_1^*, x_2^*) and if $f_{11}(x_1^*, x_2^*) < 0$ and

$$f_{11}(x_1^*, x_2^*)f_{22}(x_1^*, x_2^*) > (f_{12}(x_1^*, x_2^*))^2,$$

then the function reaches a local maximum at this stationary point. These two conditions also imply that $f_{22}(x_1^*, x_2^*) < 0$ at this stationary point. ■

Second-Order Condition for a Local Minimum of a Bivariate Function If the function $y = f(x_1, x_2)$ has the stationary point (x_1^*, x_2^*) and if $f_{11}(x_1^*, x_2^*) > 0$ and

$$f_{11}(x_1^*, x_2^*)f_{22}(x_1^*, x_2^*) > (f_{12}(x_1^*, x_2^*))^2,$$

then the function reaches a local minimum at this stationary point. These two conditions also imply that $f_{22}(x_1^*, x_2^*) > 0$ at this stationary point. ■

We can use these conditions to characterize the stationary points of the two functions used as examples in Section 10.1. The second partial derivatives of the bivariate function

$$g(x_1, x_2) = 6x_1 - x_1^2 + 16x_2 - 4x_2^2$$

are

$$g_{11}(x_1, x_2) = -2 \quad \text{and} \quad g_{22}(x_1, x_2) = -8,$$

and the cross partial derivative $g_{12}(x_1, x_2)$ is zero. Therefore this stationary point is a maximum since the second partial derivatives are each negative and their product, which is 16, is greater than the square of the cross partial derivative, which is 0. The second partial derivatives of the function

$$h(x_1, x_2) = x_1^2 + 4x_2^2 - 2x_1 - 16x_2 + x_1x_2$$

are

$$h_{11}(x_1, x_2) = 2 \quad \text{and} \quad h_{22}(x_1, x_2) = 8,$$

which are both positive. The cross partial derivative is

$$h_{12}(x_1, x_2) = 1,$$

and

$$h_{11}h_{22} > (h_{12})^2 \quad \text{since} \quad 16 > 1.$$

Therefore the stationary point of this function, (0, 2), is a minimum.

We can also use the second-order condition to check that the optimal prices in the electric utility application in Section 10.1 maximize profits. Recall that the partial derivatives of the profit function in that application are

$$\frac{\partial \Pi}{\partial P_F} = -2 \cdot 0.729P_F^{-3} + 0.18 \cdot 0.729P_F^{-4} \quad \text{and}$$
$$\frac{\partial \Pi}{\partial P_H} = -7.2P_H^{-2} + 0.12 \cdot 7.2P_H^{-3}.$$

The second partial derivatives of this function evaluated at the stationary point $P_F = 0.09$ and $P_H = 0.12$ are

$$\frac{\partial^2 \Pi}{\partial P_F^2} = 0.729(6P_F^{-4} - 0.72P_F^{-5}) = (0.729)\left(\frac{-0.18}{0.09^4}\right) < 0 \quad \text{and}$$
$$\frac{\partial^2 \Pi}{\partial P_H^2} = 7.2(2P_H^{-3} - 0.36P_H^{-4}) = (7.2)\left(\frac{-0.12}{0.12^3}\right) < 0,$$

and the cross partial derivative is

$$\frac{\partial^2 \Pi}{\partial P_H \, \partial P_F} = 0.$$

Therefore these prices maximize profits since

$$\left(\frac{\partial^2 \Pi}{\partial P_F^2}\right)\left(\frac{\partial^2 \Pi}{\partial P_H^2}\right) > \left(\frac{\partial^2 \Pi}{\partial P_H \, \partial P_F}\right)^2$$

and the second order condition for a maximum is met.[8]

One possibility not covered by these sufficient conditions is that one partial derivative is positive and the other is negative, for example, $f_{11} > 0$ and $f_{22} < 0$. In this case the stationary point is called a **saddle point,** so named because the function looks like a saddle. The "stationary point" of a real saddle appears as a minimum when viewed from the side of a horse since, from this point, the saddle rises toward the front of the horse and toward the rear of the horse. This point looks like a maximum when viewed from the front or the rear of the horse since the saddle slopes downward over the horse's flanks. Likewise, as shown in Figure 10.4, the saddle point of a function with two arguments is a minimum from the perspective of one direction and a maximum from the perspective of another.

The stationary point of the function

$$y = (x_1 - 2)^2 - (x_2 + 1)^2$$

can be shown to be a saddle point. Solving for the values of x_1 and x_2 when the two first partial derivatives are zero, we find that the stationary point is $x_1 = 2$ and $x_2 = -1$. The second partial derivatives are

$$\frac{\partial^2 y}{\partial x_1^2} = 2 \quad \text{and} \quad \frac{\partial^2 y}{\partial x_2^2} = -2.$$

Thus the stationary point $(2, -1)$ is a saddle point of this function.

[8] See question 11 at the end of this section for an example that highlights the condition $f_{11}f_{22} > (f_{12})^2$.

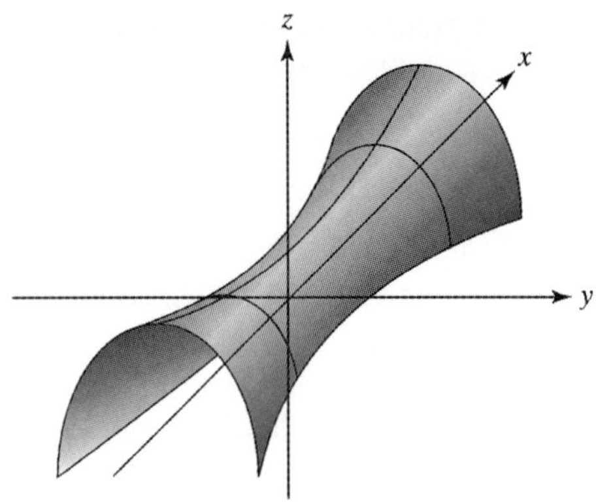

FIGURE 10.4 A Saddle Point

It is important to remember that these second-order conditions are sufficient but not necessary. In particular, these conditions do not allow us to characterize a stationary point (x_1^*, x_2^*) if

$$f_{11}(x_1^*, x_2^*) = 0,$$
$$f_{22}(x_1^*, x_2^*) = 0, \quad \text{or}$$
$$f_{11}(x_1^*, x_2^*)f_{22}(x_1^*, x_2^*) = (f_{12}(x_1^*, x_2^*))^2.$$

For example, the function

$$z = w_1^4 + w_2^4 + 5$$

has the stationary point (0, 0) where the value of the function is $z = 5$. The second partial derivatives of this function are

$$\frac{\partial^2 z}{\partial w_1^2} = 12w_1^2 \quad \text{and} \quad \frac{\partial^2 z}{\partial w_2^2} = 12w_2^2.$$

These partial derivatives are each zero when evaluated at the stationary point, but this stationary point represents a minimum of this function. The value of the function is clearly greater than zero for any point (w_1, w_2) other than (0, 0).

Exercises 10.2

1. Determine whether the stationary points (x^*, z^*) for each function $f(x, z)$ in parts (a) through (d) of question 1 in Section 10.1 represent maxima, minima, or saddle points.
2. Determine whether the stationary points (u^*, v^*) for each function $g(u, v)$ in parts (a) through (d) of question 2 in Section 10.1 represent maxima, minima, or saddle points.

3. Determine whether the stationary points (a^*, b^*) for each function $h(a, b)$ in parts (a) through (d) of question 3 in Section 10.1 represent maxima, minima, or saddle points.
4. Show that the choice of inflation, π, and the tax rate, t, in question 5(c) of Section 10.1 leads to maximum government revenues.
5. Show that the education level, E, and years of experience, X, identified as the stationary point in question 6 of Section 10.1 provides for maximum compensation.
6. Show that the number of pages devoted to economic and noneconomic articles in question 7 of Section 10.1 yields maximum sales.
7. Show that the optimal quantities of books sold in Texas and Massachusetts by AWL in question 10(a) of Section 10.1 yield maximum profits. Also, show that the solution for the optimal quantities of books sold in Texas and Massachusetts in question 10(b), when total cost differs from the specification in 10(a), yields maximum profits.
8. Show that the solution to the two-plant production problem in question 11 of Section 10.1 provides maximum profits.
9. Given the function $z = \theta r^2 + \gamma s^2$, find the stationary points r^* and s^*, and determine whether the stationary point represents a maximum, a minimum, or a saddle point under each of the following conditions.
   (a) $\theta > 0; \gamma > 0$
   (b) $\theta < 0; \gamma < 0$
   (c) θ and γ are different signs
10. Show that the optimal levels of P and S in the application about advertising represent a point where profits are maximized using the second-order conditions.
11. Consider the function

$$y = -2x^2 - 4x - \frac{1}{2}z^2 + 4z + 4xz.$$

   (a) Find the values of x and z that correspond to the stationary point of this function.
   (b) Is the point you identified in part (a) a maximum, a minimum, or neither?

10.3 THE SECOND-ORDER CONDITION IN THE GENERAL MULTIVARIATE CASE

In Section 10.2 we developed a set of second-order conditions for bivariate functions based on the second total differential of a general bivariate function. In this section we use the tools of matrix algebra to develop a set of conditions that enables us to find the sign of the second total differential of a multivariate function. These conditions provide sufficient conditions for characterizing a stationary point as a local maximum or a local minimum in the general multivariate case.

To illustrate the use of matrix algebra, we first consider the bivariate case for which

$$d^2y = f_{11} \cdot (dx_1)^2 + f_{22} \cdot (dx_2)^2 + 2f_{12} \cdot (dx_1 \cdot dx_2),$$

where, again, f_{ij} represents $f_{ij}(x_1, x_2)$. This can be rewritten in matrix format as the **quadratic form** of the two variables dx_1 and dx_2.

$$d^2y = [dx_1 \quad dx_2] \cdot \begin{bmatrix} f_{11} & f_{12} \\ f_{21} & f_{22} \end{bmatrix} \cdot \begin{bmatrix} dx_1 \\ dx_2 \end{bmatrix}.$$

More generally, to extend this to any multivariate function, we first define the quadratic form of the n variables as

$$Q = a_{11} \cdot z_1^2 + 2a_{12} \cdot z_1 \cdot z_2 + \cdots + 2a_{ij} \cdot z_i \cdot z_j + \cdots + a_{nn} \cdot z_n^2.$$

This quadratic form can be written in matrix notation as

$$Q = z'Az = [z_1 \quad z_2 \quad \ldots \quad z_n] \cdot \begin{bmatrix} a_{11} & a_{12} & \ldots & a_{1n} \\ a_{21} & a_{22} & \ldots & a_{2n} \\ \ldots & \ldots & \ldots & \ldots \\ a_{n1} & a_{n2} & \ldots & a_{nn} \end{bmatrix} \cdot \begin{bmatrix} z_1 \\ z_2 \\ \ldots \\ z_n \end{bmatrix},$$

where the matrix A is symmetric.

We are interested, here, in quadratic forms in which the vector represents the differentials $[dx_1 \quad dx_2 \quad \ldots \quad dx_n]$ and the matrix consists of the second partial derivatives, where the (i, j)th element of the matrix is the second partial derivative $f_{ij}(x_1, \ldots, x_i, \ldots, x_j, \ldots, x_n)$. This $n \times n$ matrix is called the **Hessian matrix** of the function $f(x_1, \ldots, x_n)$. Young's Theorem, which states that $f_{ij}(x_1, \ldots, x_n) = f_{ji}(x_1, \ldots, x_n)$ for any i and j if the function is differentiable, ensures that Hessian matrices are symmetric. Thus the second total differential for a multivariate function with four arguments is

$$d^2y = dx' \cdot H \cdot dx = [dx_1 \quad dx_2 \quad dx_3 \quad dx_4] \cdot \begin{bmatrix} f_{11} & f_{12} & f_{13} & f_{14} \\ f_{21} & f_{22} & f_{23} & f_{24} \\ f_{31} & f_{32} & f_{33} & f_{34} \\ f_{41} & f_{42} & f_{43} & f_{44} \end{bmatrix} \cdot \begin{bmatrix} dx_1 \\ dx_2 \\ dx_3 \\ dx_4 \end{bmatrix},$$

where H is the Hessian matrix and dx is the column vector of differentials.

A quadratic form $z'Az$ is **positive definite** if, for any column vector z consisting of the n elements z_i, $i = 1, \ldots, n$, other than the zero vector (where $z_i = 0$ for all $i = 1, \ldots, n$), the quadratic form is positive. A quadratic form $z'Az$ is **negative definite** if, for any column vector z consisting of the n elements z_i, $i = 1, \ldots, n$, other than the zero vector (where $z_i = 0$ for all $i = 1, \ldots, n$), the quadratic form is negative.

A matrix A is positive definite if its quadratic form $z'Az$ is positive definite, and it is negative definite if its quadratic form is negative definite. Necessary and sufficient conditions for determining whether a matrix is positive definite or negative definite concern the sign of its **leading principal minors.** The leading principal minors of a matrix are the determinants of its **leading principal submatrices.** The kth leading principal submatrix of any $n \times n$ matrix is the $k \times k$ matrix obtained by deleting the last $n - k$ rows and the last $n - k$ columns of the matrix. Since we have $k = 1, 2, \ldots, n$, an $n \times n$ matrix has n leading principal submatrices and n leading principal minors.

To illustrate this, consider the matrix

$$\begin{bmatrix} a & b & c & d \\ e & f & g & h \\ i & j & k & l \\ m & n & o & p \end{bmatrix}.$$

The first leading principal submatrix is obtained by eliminating the last $n - k = 4 - 1 = 3$ rows and columns, which gives us the 1×1 matrix

$$[a].$$

The first leading principal minor is a. The second leading principal submatrix is obtained by eliminating the last $4 - 2 = 2$ rows and columns, which gives us the 2×2 matrix

$$\begin{bmatrix} a & b \\ e & f \end{bmatrix}.$$

The determinant of this matrix, $af - be$, is the second leading principal minor. The determinant of the third leading principal submatrix

$$\begin{bmatrix} a & b & c \\ e & f & g \\ i & j & k \end{bmatrix}$$

is the third leading principal minor. The determinant of the original matrix, which is the fourth leading principal submatrix, is the fourth leading principal minor.

The following rules link the value of the leading principal minors to whether a matrix is positive definite or negative definite.

Negative Definite Matrix An $n \times n$ matrix is negative definite if and only if all of its n leading principal minors alternate in sign with the first principal minor negative, the second principal minor positive, the third principal minor negative, and so on.

Positive Definite Matrix An $n \times n$ matrix is positive definite if and only if all of its n leading principal minors are strictly positive.

We can identify a stationary point of a multivariate function as a local maximum or a local minimum by determining whether the Hessian matrix of that function evaluated at that stationary point is negative definite or positive definite. If the Hessian matrix of the multivariate function $y = f(x_1, \ldots, x_n)$ evaluated at a stationary point is negative definite, then d^2y is negative for any set of differentials $(dx_1, \ldots, dx_n)$ as long as $dx_i \neq 0$ for all i. In this case that stationary point represents a local maximum. If the Hessian matrix evaluated at a stationary point is positive definite, then d^2y is positive for any set of differentials $(dx_1, \ldots, dx_n)$ as long as

$dx_i \neq 0$ for all i. In this case that stationary point represents a local minimum. Therefore we have the following sufficient conditions for characterizing the stationary points of a multivariate function.

Sufficient Condition for a Local Maximum of a Multivariate Function If the function $y = f(x_1, \ldots, x_n)$ has the stationary point $(x_1^*, \ldots, x_n^*)$ and the Hessian of this function evaluated at that stationary point is negative definite, then this stationary point represents a local maximum of this function.

Sufficient Condition for a Local Minimum of a Multivariate Function If the function $y = f(x_1, \ldots, x_n)$ has the stationary point $(x_1^*, \ldots, x_n^*)$ and the Hessian of this function evaluated at that stationary point is positive definite, then this stationary point represents a local minimum of this function.

Saddle Point of a Multivariate Function If the function $y = f(x_1, \ldots, x_n)$ has the stationary point $(x_1^*, \ldots, x_n^*)$ and the nonzero leading principal minors of the Hessian of this function evaluated at that stationary point do not follow the sign pattern of either a positive definite or a negative definite matrix, then this stationary point represents a saddle point of this function.

It is easy to show that the sufficient conditions for a bivariate function, presented in Section 10.2, conform to these conditions. The Hessian matrix for the bivariate function $f(x_1, x_2)$ evaluated at the stationary point (x_1^*, x_2^*) is

$$\begin{bmatrix} f_{11}(x_1^*, x_2^*) & f_{12}(x_1^*, x_2^*) \\ f_{12}(x_1^*, x_2^*) & f_{22}(x_1^*, x_2^*) \end{bmatrix}.$$

The first leading principal submatrix is the 1×1 matrix $[f_{11}(x_1^*, x_2^*)]$, and the first principal minor is simply $f_{11}(x_1^*, x_2^*)$. The second principal minor is the determinant of the matrix itself, which is

$$f_{11}(x_1^*, x_2^*) \cdot f_{22}(x_1^*, x_2^*) - (f_{12}(x_1^*, x_2^*))^2.$$

Therefore the 2×2 Hessian matrix is positive definite if $f_{11}(x_1^*, x_2^*) > 0$ and if

$$f_{11}(x_1^*, x_2^*)f_{22}(x_1^*, x_2^*) > (f_{12}(x_1^*, x_2^*))^2.$$

These conditions are identical to the sufficient condition for a local minimum presented earlier. The Hessian matrix is negative definite if $f_{11}(x_1^*, x_2^*) < 0$ and if

$$f_{11}(x_1^*, x_2^*)f_{22}(x_1^*, x_2^*) > (f_{12}(x_1^*, x_2^*))^2.$$

These conditions are identical to the sufficient condition for a local maximum presented earlier.

As a concrete example of a function with three arguments, we consider

$$r(x_1, x_2, x_3) = 15x_1 + x_1x_2 - 4x_1^2 - 2x_2^2 - x_3^2 + 2x_2x_3 + 7.$$

The three first derivatives of this function are

$$\frac{\partial y}{\partial x_1} = 15 + x_2 - 8x_1,$$
$$\frac{\partial y}{\partial x_2} = x_1 - 4x_2 + 2x_3, \quad \text{and}$$
$$\frac{\partial y}{\partial x_3} = -2x_3 + 2x_2.$$

The first-order conditions set each of these partial derivatives equal to zero. Solving the three first-order conditions, we find that the stationary point of this function is $x_1 = 2$, $x_2 = 1$, and $x_3 = 1$. At this stationary point, $r(2, 1, 1) = 22$. The Hessian matrix of this function is

$$\begin{bmatrix} -8 & 1 & 0 \\ 1 & -4 & 2 \\ 0 & 2 & -2 \end{bmatrix}.$$

The first leading principle submatrix is $[-8]$, and the first leading principal minor is simply -8. The second leading principal submatrix is

$$\begin{bmatrix} -8 & 1 \\ 1 & -4 \end{bmatrix},$$

and, therefore, the second leading principal minor is

$$(-8)(-4) - 1^2 = 31.$$

The third leading principal submatrix is the Hessian matrix itself. The determinant of this matrix can be found with a Laplace expansion along the third row (see Chapter 5), and this determinant is equal to

$$-2(-16) + (-2)(32 - 1) = -30.$$

The signs of the leading principal minors alternate from negative to positive to negative. Therefore the Hessian matrix is negative definite, and the stationary point of this function is a maximum.

More generally, the Hessian matrix of a multivariate function with three arguments $f(x_1, x_2, x_3)$ evaluated at the stationary point (x_1^*, x_2^*, x_3^*) is

$$\begin{bmatrix} f_{11}(x_1^*, x_2^*, x_3^*) & f_{12}(x_1^*, x_2^*, x_3^*) & f_{13}(x_1^*, x_2^*, x_3^*) \\ f_{12}(x_1^*, x_2^*, x_3^*) & f_{22}(x_1^*, x_2^*, x_3^*) & f_{23}(x_1^*, x_2^*, x_3^*) \\ f_{13}(x_1^*, x_2^*, x_3^*) & f_{23}(x_1^*, x_2^*, x_3^*) & f_{33}(x_1^*, x_2^*, x_3^*) \end{bmatrix}.$$

This matrix is positive definite if

$$f_{11} > 0,$$
$$f_{11}f_{22} > (f_{12})^2, \quad \text{and}$$
$$f_{11}f_{22}f_{33} + 2f_{12}f_{23}f_{13} > f_{11}(f_{23})^2 + f_{22}(f_{13})^2 + f_{33}(f_{12})^2,$$

where $f_{ij} = f_{ij}(x_1^*, x_2^*, x_3^*)$, that is, f_{ij} is the second partial or cross partial derivative evaluated at the stationary point (x_1^*, x_2^*, x_3^*). The Hessian matrix is negative definite if

$$f_{11} < 0,$$
$$f_{11}f_{22} > (f_{12})^2, \quad \text{and}$$
$$f_{11}f_{22}f_{33} + 2f_{12}f_{23}f_{13} < f_{11}(f_{23})^2 + f_{22}(f_{13})^2 + f_{33}(f_{12})^2.$$

Concavity and Convexity Once Again

In Chapter 7 we present conditions for the concavity and convexity of univariate functions based upon their second derivative. As discussed there, a univariate function $f(x)$ is strictly convex over an interval if $f''(x) > 0$ for all x within that interval, and it is strictly concave over an interval if $f''(x) < 0$ for all x within that interval.

Multivariate functions can also be classified as strictly concave or strictly convex. This classification depends upon the sign definiteness of the Hessian matrix of the function. If a Hessian matrix of a function is positive definite within a domain inside of which its partial derivatives are continuous, then that function is strictly convex within that domain. If a Hessian matrix of a function is negative definite within a domain inside of which its partial derivatives are continuous, then that function is strictly concave within that domain.

There is also a multivariate version of the distinction between strictly convex and convex functions or strictly concave and concave functions. Recall that a univariate function $f(x)$ is convex over an interval if $f''(x) \geq 0$ for all x within that interval. Thus all strictly convex functions are also convex, but not all convex functions are also strictly convex. The same type of distinction holds for concave and strictly concave functions. In the multivariate case, a quadratic form is **positive semidefinite** if, for any column vector z, the quadratic form $z'Az$ is nonnegative. A quadratic form is **negative semidefinite** if, for any column vector z, the quadratic form $z'Az$ is nonpositive.

The conditons for a quadratic form $z'Az$ to be positive semidefinite or negative semidefinite require checking the sign of all of the principal minors of the matrix A, not just the leading principal minors. This, in turn, requires us to define some new terms. A ***k*th order principal submatrix** of matrix A is obtained by eliminating any $n - k$ rows along with the corresponding $n - k$ columns from A. For example, we consider the 3×3 matrix H where

$$H = \begin{bmatrix} 1 & 0 & 1 \\ 0 & 1 & 1 \\ 1 & 1 & 2 \end{bmatrix}.$$

This matrix has one third-order principal submatrix, which is H itself, since this is obtained by eliminating $3 - 3 = 0$ rows and columns. This matrix has three second-order principal submatrices, each of which involves eliminating $3 - 2 = 1$ row and its associated column. These three second-order principal submatrices, obtained by eliminating the first column and row, the second column and row, and the third column and row, respectively, are

$$\begin{bmatrix} 1 & 1 \\ 1 & 2 \end{bmatrix}, \quad \begin{bmatrix} 1 & 1 \\ 1 & 2 \end{bmatrix}, \quad \text{and} \quad \begin{bmatrix} 1 & 0 \\ 0 & 1 \end{bmatrix}.$$

There are three first-order principal submatrices, each obtained by eliminating $3 - 1 = 2$ rows and associated columns. Eliminating the last two rows and columns gives us the principal submatrix [1] (that is, the element a_{11}), eleminating the first two rows and columns gives us the principal submatrix [2] (that is, the element a_{33}), and eliminating the first and third row and column gives us the principal submatrix [1] (that is, the element a_{22}).

A ***k*th-order principal minor** of a matrix is the determinant of one of its kth-order principal submatrices. The single third-order principal minor of a 3×3 matrix is its determinant. The determinant of the matrix H defined here, which we evaluate with a Laplace expansion along its first row, equals

$$|H| = (-1)^2 1 (2 - 1) + (-1)^3 0 (0 - 1) + (-1)^4 1 (0 - 1) = 0.$$

Each of the principal minors associated with the three second-order principal submatrices equals 1 since the determinant of each of these 2×2 principal submatrices is 1. The principal minor of each of three first-order principal submatrices is simply the value of the single element of those submatrices.

With these terms defined, we can now present the necessary and sufficent conditions for a matrix to be positive semidefinite or negative semidefinite.

Positive Semidefinite Matrix An $n \times n$ matrix A is positive semidefinite if and only if all of its principal minors are greater than or equal to zero. If A is positive semidefinite, then the quadratic form $z'Az$, where z is an $n \times 1$ vector with at least one element not equal to zero, is positive semidefinite.

Negative Semidefinite Matrix An $n \times n$ matrix A is negative semidefinite if and only if all of its principal minors of order k either have the same sign as $(-1)^k$ or equal 0. If A is negative semidefinite, then the quadratic form $z'Az$, where z is an $n \times 1$ vector with at least one element not equal to zero, is negative semidefinite.

The 3×3 matrix H given above is positive semidefinite since each of its seven principal minors, 0, 1, 1, 1, 1, 2, 1, are nonnegative. Note that this matrix is not positive definite, however, since its third leading principal minor, which is just the determinant of H itself, is 0.

As another example, we consider the matrix

$$\begin{bmatrix} 0 & 0 \\ 0 & a \end{bmatrix}.$$

This matrix has the two first-order principal minors, 0 and a (corresponding to its two diagonal elements) and the second-order principal minor 0 (the determinant of the matrix). This matrix is neither positive definite nor negative definite since both of its leading principal minors are 0. The matrix is positive semidefinite if $a \geq 0$, and it is negative semidefinite if $a \leq 0$.

The concavity and convexity of multivariate functions can be related to the characterization of the stationary points of these functions. A stationary point in a concave interval, that is, an interval in which the function is negative semidefinite, is a local maximum. A stationary point in a convex interval, that is, an interval in which the function is positive semidefinite, is a local minimum. Furthermore, these conditions can be used to identify sufficient conditions for a global maximum or a global minimum.

Global Maximum If a function is everywhere concave within a domain, that is, if the Hessian matrix of the function is negative semidefinite within a domain, then a stationary point in that domain is a global maximum. ■

Global Minimum If a function is everywhere convex within a domain, that is, if the Hessian matrix of the function is positive semidefinite within a domain, then a stationary point in that domain is a global minimum. ■

These conditions show that the stationary point of the function $r(x_1, x_2, x_3)$ presented earlier is a global maximum since the Hessian matrix of this function is negative semidefinite for a domain consisting of real numbers for x_1, x_2, and x_3. These conditions for a global maximum or a global minimum can be viewed as a multivariate generalization of the conditions for global extreme points of univariate functions presented in the previous chapter.

Exercises 10.3

1. What is the sufficient condition for identifying the stationary point of the multivariate function

$$y = x_1^2 + x_2^2 + x_3^2?$$

2. Generalizing your results to question 1, give the sufficient condition for identifying a stationary point of a multivariate function $y = f(x_1, x_2, x_3)$ as a local minimum if all cross partial derivatives are zero, that is, if $f_{ij} = 0$ for all $i \neq j$. What is the sufficient condition for a local maximum in this case?
3. Generalize your answer to question 2 by discussing the sufficient condition for identifying the stationary point of a multivariate function with n arguments as a local maximum or a local minimum if all cross partial derivatives equal zero.
4. Identify the stationary points of the function

$$f(x_1, x_2, x_3) = 2x_1^2 - 21x_1 - 3x_1x_2 + 3x_2^2 - 2x_2x_3 + x_3^2,$$

and use the sufficient condition to determine if they represent local maxima or local minima.

5. Identify the stationary points of the function

$$f(x_1, x_2, x_3) = 2x_1x_2 - \frac{1}{2}x_1^2 - 3x_2^2 + x_2x_3 - 1.5x_3^2 + 10x_3,$$

and use the sufficient condition to determine if they represent local maxima or local minima.

6. Show that the output levels Q_1, Q_2, and Q_3, identified as the stationary points in question 12 of Section 10.1 represent a point of maximum profits.
7. Find all the principal minors of the following matrices, and determine whether the matrices are negative definite, negative semidefinite, positive definite, or positive semidefinite.

(a) $\begin{bmatrix} -1 & 2 \\ -1 & 0 \end{bmatrix}$

(b) $\begin{bmatrix} 0 & 1 \\ -1 & 2 \end{bmatrix}$

(c) $\begin{bmatrix} 0 & -1 \\ 2 & -1 \end{bmatrix}$

(d) $\begin{bmatrix} 1 & 0 \\ 1 & 1 \end{bmatrix}$

8. How many leading principal minors are there in a 4×4 matrix? How many principal minors are there in a 4×4 matrix?

Summary

This chapter uses the tools of differentiation presented in Chapter 8 to develop a set of conditions for identifying and characterizing the extreme points of multivariate functions. The intuition developed in Chapter 9 is extended through the use of the differential. The identification of a stationary point is a relatively straightforward extrapolation of the conditions in the previous chapter. The second-order conditions, however, are complicated by the presence of cross partial derivatives. Results are first derived for the bivariate case and then extended to the multivariate case. In the multivariate situation, tools from matrix algebra are used.

The examples and end-of-section problems in this chapter demonstrate some of the uses of the techniques of multivariate optimization in economic applications. An important extension of these techniques involves problems in which the arguments of a multivariate function are limited by a constraint. These types of constrained optimization problems are the subject of the next chapter. The material presented there builds on the concepts and techniques developed in this chapter.

Chapter 11

Constrained Optimization

A basic concept in economics is opportunity costs. Choosing more of one desirable thing usually means choosing less of some other desirable thing. This trade-off arises because of scarce resources; a consumer has a limited budget, a producer has limited funds to purchase inputs, a government has limited revenues, and each of us has only 24 hours in a day.

Much of economic analysis models optimal choice in the face of trade-offs in one form or another. Constrained optimization problems appear in virtually every area of economics. This chapter presents the technique that identifies an optimal outcome under constraints, which is one of the core mathematical tools in economics.

The basic constrained optimization problem reflects a tension between what is desired and what is obtainable. The framework of any constrained optimization problem includes an **objective function** and one or more **constraints.** An objective function links the level of several choice variables to the ultimate goal of the problem; for example objective functions link the level of inputs to the production of output or the consumption of goods to the utility derived from that consumption. Objective functions, typically, are monotonic. For example, multivariate utility functions are increasing in each of their arguments and thus reflect the assumption of nonsatiation, that is, "more is better."

The constraint is the source of the trade-off among different options and presents the attainable limits on the value of the arguments of the objective function. These limits may be financial, as with a budget constraint, or physical, such as the amount of time or resources available for undertaking different activities. The **feasible set** of a constrained optimization problem is the set of arguments of the objective function that satisfies all the constraints of the problem simultaneously. **Equality constraints** are constraints that hold exactly, such as the constraint that total expenditure must equal total income. **Inequality constraints** allow a function of one or more of the choice variables to be less than or greater than some level, as with the constraint that total production must use no more than available capacity.

The techniques of constrained optimization presented in this chapter build on the method for identifying the stationary point of a function discussed in Chapters 9 and 10. The first technique, presented in Section 11.1, substitutes equality constraints directly into an objective function. We identify the optimal set of choice variables by finding the extreme value of an objective function that has "internalized" the constraints and by using the techniques presented in the previous chapters for an unconstrained optimization problem. Section 11.2 offers another approach, the **Lagrange multiplier method.** This method is often computationally simpler than the substitution method. It also provides direct information on the effect of relaxing the constraint. Section 11.3 illustrates the use of these techniques in a number of economic settings. Section 11.4 concludes this chapter with an introduction to techniques for solving constrained optimization problems with inequality constraints.

11.1 SOLVING CONSTRAINED OPTIMIZATION PROBLEMS THROUGH SUBSTITUTION

Constraints arise naturally in economic problems. A consumer purchasing goods can spend no more than his budget permits. A worker deciding on how to divide up her activities between labor and leisure is bound by the number of waking hours in a day. A producer selecting the cost-minimizing set of inputs may be obliged to produce a certain level of output. Economic models of decision making in each of these types of situations identify an optimum outcome subject to the constraints facing the consumer, producer, or worker.

Constraints limit the feasible set of choices in an optimization problem. One method for solving a constrained optimization problem is to convert it to an unconstrained optimization problem by "internalizing" the constraint (or constraints) directly into the objective function. The constraint is internalized when we express it as a function of one of the arguments of the objective function and then substitute out that argument using the constraint. We can then solve the internalized objective function by using the unconstrained optimization techniques presented in Chapters 9 and 10.

To illustrate this technique, we identify the maximum value of the bivariate objective function

$$f(x_1, x_2) = 2\sqrt{x_1} + \frac{1}{2}\sqrt{x_2}$$

subject to the linear constraint

$$4x_1 + x_2 = 20.$$

Note that the objective function is monotonic in its two arguments. Thus, if this were an unconstrained optimization problem, there would not be an interior solution. The constraint, however, limits the feasible set of values for x_1 and x_2 such that an interior solution exists.

The constraint can be rewritten as $x_2 = 20 - 4x_1$. The objective function that internalizes this constraint, $\bar{f}(x_1)$, is the univariate function

$$\bar{f}(x_1) = 2\sqrt{x_1} + \frac{1}{2}\sqrt{20 - 4x_1}.$$

The first-order condition of this function is

$$\bar{f}'(x_1) = \frac{1}{\sqrt{x_1}} - \frac{1}{\sqrt{20 - 4x_1}} = 0.$$

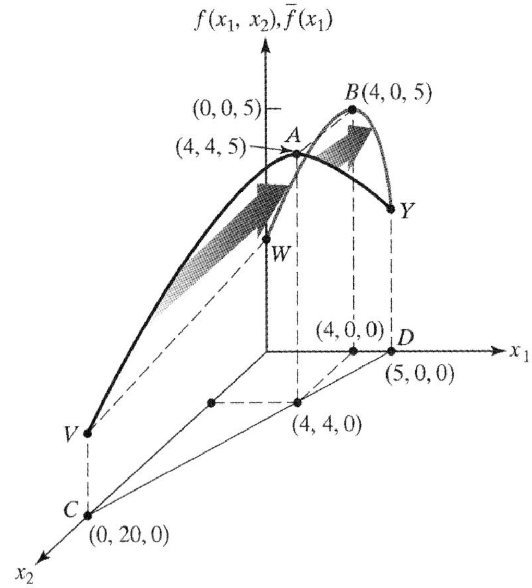

FIGURE 11.1 Constrained Optimization and an Internalized Function

Solving this equation, we find an extreme point of this function occurs when $x_1 = 4$. Using the constraint, we then see that $x_2 = 20 - 4(4) = 4$. The maximum value for the internalized function $\bar{f}(x_1)$ or, equivalently, the maximum value for the function $f(x_1, x_2)$ subject to the constraint $4x_1 + x_2 = 20$ is therefore $2\sqrt{4} + \frac{1}{2}\sqrt{4} = 5$.

We can check the second-order condition of the internalized function to ensure that this extreme value is a maximum. The second derivative of the internalized function is

$$\bar{f}''(x_1) = -\frac{1}{2}(x_1)^{-3/2} - 2\cdot(20 - 4x_1)^{-3/2}.$$

This second derivative evaluated at the stationary point $x_1 = 4$ equals $-\frac{5}{16}$, indicating that the extreme point is a maximum.

A geometric interpretation of this problem is presented in the three-dimensional depiction in Figure 11.1. The height of the plane represents the value of the bivariate objective function $y = f(x_1, x_2)$, and any point in this diagram can be identified by the triplet (x_1, x_2, y). The feasible set of the arguments of the function, that is, the pairs of values of x_1 and x_2 that are consistent with the constraint, are represented by the straight line CD plotted in the plane where $y = 0$. The value of the function for the combinations of x_1 and x_2 that are in the feasible set are represented by the curve VY. The figure indicates that the plane reaches its maximum height along this curve at point A, representing the point (4, 4, 5).

This figure can also be used to illustrate the solution technique incorporating the function that internalizes the constraint. The substitution method reduces the objective function from the bivariate function $y = f(x_1, x_2)$ to the univariate function $y = \bar{f}(x_1)$. This univariate function is the projection of the feasible values of $f(x_1, x_2)$ onto a plane in which the horizontal axis represents x_1 and the vertical axis represents values of $\bar{f}(x_1)$. In Figure 11.1, the graph of $\bar{f}(x_1)$ is represented by the curve *WY*. The maximum value of this function is represented by the point *B* on this curve.

The following problem illustrates the use of this method for solving a constrained optimization problem in an economic context.

A Consumption Problem

Suppose you have \$6.00 to spend on a lunch of soup and salad. The restaurant at which you dine sells both soup and salad by weight. An ounce of soup costs \$0.25, and an ounce of salad costs \$0.50. How many ounces of each will you purchase?

We first set up the budget constraint of this problem. If you wanted only soup, you would be able to buy 24 ounces (\$6.00/(\$0.25/oz)). If you wanted only salad, you would be able to buy 12 ounces (\$6.00/(\$0.50/oz)). More generally, any combination of soup (S) and salad (V) you purchase must satisfy the constraint

$$6 = \frac{S}{4} + \frac{V}{2}. \tag{11.1}$$

The objective function is a bivariate function that describes the amount of satisfaction (or utility) you derive from the consumption of soup and salad. We employ, here, the utility function

$$U(S, V) = \frac{1}{2}\ln(S) + \frac{1}{2}\ln(V). \tag{11.2}$$

This utility function reflects nonsatiation in both soup and salad since the natural logarithm function is monotonic and increasing. It also reflects a preference for diversity and a more balanced lunch selection.[1] For example, two ounces of soup and two ounces of salad provides the utility

$$\frac{1}{2}\ln(2) + \frac{1}{2}\ln(2) = 0.69,$$

while the less balanced choice of three ounces of soup and one ounce of salad provides the utility

$$\frac{1}{2}\ln(3) + \frac{1}{2}\ln(1) = 0.55.$$

The substitution method presented above reduces the problem of identifying an optimal set of two variables subject to an equality constraint to the problem of identifying the extreme value of a univariate function. In this example, the budget constraint

[1]Note that utility as described by this function approaches negative infinity as the amount of salad consumed goes to zero or as the amount of soup consumed goes to zero.

requires that the optimal amount of soup is $S = 24 - 2V$. Substituting this into the bivariate utility function, we get

$$\overline{U}(V) = \frac{1}{2}\ln(24 - 2V) + \frac{1}{2}\ln(V),$$

where $\overline{U}(V)$ represents the univariate utility function obtained by internalizing the constraint into the bivariate utility function $U(S, V)$. The first-order condition for the function $\overline{U}(V)$ is

$$\frac{d\overline{U}(V)}{dV} = \frac{-1}{24 - 2V} + \frac{1}{2V} = 0.$$

Solving for V, we find that the optimal amount of salad to purchase is 6 ounces. Substituting this solution into the budget constraint, we find that the optimal amount of soup is 12 ounces.

The second-order condition shows that this amount of soup and salad represents the maximum amount of utility. The second derivative of the function $\overline{U}(V)$ is

$$\frac{d^2\overline{U}(V)}{dV^2} = \frac{-2}{(24 - 2V)^2} - \frac{2}{(2V)^2},$$

which is unambiguously negative.

This solution is depicted in Figure 11.2 in which the amount of soup is measured along the y-axis and the amount of salad is measured along the x-axis. The feasible set in this figure is represented by the line FF, which includes any points that satisfy the budget constraint (11.1). The slope of this budget line is constant and equal to

$$\frac{dS}{dV} = -2.$$

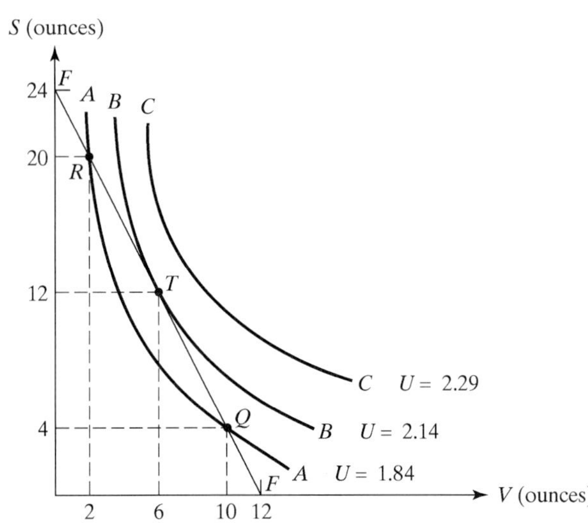

FIGURE 11.2 Constrained Optimization with a Budget Line and Indifference Curves

The figure includes three level curves, which, in this case, are indifference curves, consistent with the utility function (11.2). The indifference curve AA represents combinations of soup and salad that provide a level of utility equal to 1.84, the indifference curve BB represents combinations that provide a level of utility equal to 2.14, and the indifference curve CC represents combinations that provide a level of utility equal to 2.29. The optimal combination of 6 ounces of salad and 12 ounces of soup, labeled as T in the graph, is the point of tangency between the indifference curve BB and the budget line. Any point on the indifference curve CC is not attainable. The two feasible points R and Q, corresponding to the indifference curve AA, are suboptimal since they represent a lower level of utility than that obtained at T.

The optimality of the tangency solution T can be understood in the context of equating the ratio of marginal utilities to the price ratio of the goods. As discussed in Chapter 8, the slope of a line tangent to any of these indifference curves at the point (V_0, S_0) is the ratio of marginal utilities, and, for the utility function (11.2),

$$\frac{dS}{dV} = -\frac{U_V(S_0, V_0)}{U_S(S_0, V_0)} = -\frac{S_0}{V_0}.$$

At the optimal point T, any decrease in utility due to a small reduction in the consumption of one good is just matched by the increase in utility due to the increase in consumption of the other good since the ratio of marginal utilities equals the price ratio of the goods. If salad consumption drops by dV, then utility decreases by

$$U_V\, dV = \frac{1}{2V}\, dV = \frac{1}{12}\, dV$$

when evaluated at the optimal point where $V = 6$. This reduction in salad consumption allows an increase in soup consumption equal to $dS = 2\, dV$. This raises utility by

$$U_S\, dS = U_S 2\, dV = \frac{1}{2S} 2\, dV = \frac{1}{12}\, dV$$

when evaluated at the optimal point where $S = 12$. Thus the reduction in utility from a decrease in salad consumption is matched by an increase in utility due to an increase in soup consumption for small shifts in the consumption bundle.

This result can also be demonstrated through a numerical example. The difference in utility between the optimum amount, $U(12, 6)$, and the amount derived from consuming 5.5 ounces of salad and 13 ounces of soup is

$$\begin{aligned} U(12, 6) - U(13, 5.5) &= \left[\frac{1}{2}\ln(12) + \frac{1}{2}\ln(6)\right] - \left[\frac{1}{2}\ln(13) + \frac{1}{2}\ln(5.5)\right] \\ &= 2.13833 - 2.13485 = 0.0035, \end{aligned}$$

which represents a change of 0.16%. At any other feasible point, however, utility changes by a much greater percentage with a similar readjustment of consumption since the ratio of marginal utilities does not equal the price ratio of the goods. For example, the utility at point Q in the figure is $U(4, 10) = 1.84$. If consumption occurs instead at the feasible point $S = 5$ and $V = 9.5$, then $U(5, 9.5) = 1.93$, and utility increases by more than 4.7%.

Exercises 11.1

1. Using the substitution method, solve each bivariate constrained optimization problem. Determine the optimum values of the choice variables, and use the second-order condition to verify that they are minima or maxima.
   (a) $y = x^2 + 2xz + 4z^2$ subject to $x + z = 8$
   (b) $y = 3x^2 + z^2 - 2xz$ subject to $x + z = 1$
   (c) $y = 10x + 40z$ subject to $x^{1/2}z^{1/2} = 2$
   (d) $y = \ln 2x + 2 \ln z$ subject to $z = 16 - 4x$
   (e) $y = 2x^{1/2}z^{1/2}$ subject to $x + z = 1$
2. You own a farm that produces two types of wheat, type x and type z. You are under contract to deliver 12 tons of wheat, in any combination of your choosing, to the bread manufacturer operating in your farm district. Find the combination of crops that minimize the cost of fulfilling this contract given your cost function $C = 3x^2 - 4xz + 9z^2 - 8z + 36$.
3. In the theory of individual labor supply, it is assumed that an individual derives utility from both income, which is earned through work, and leisure. Income (I) is determined by the number of hours worked (L) multiplied by the hourly wage rate (w), so that $I = wL$. Assume that in each day, a total number of 24 hours is available for either work (L) or leisure (R) such that $L + R = 24$ and that the hourly wage is \$4. The individual's labor-leisure utility function is $U(I, R) = 4IR^2$. Using the substitution method, determine how the individual will balance labor and leisure in order to maximize utility.
4. Use the lunch example where the choice is between soup and salad to show that the solution obtained from the internalized function $\overline{U}(S)$ is the same as the solution obtained (in this section) from the internalized function $\overline{U}(V)$.
5. Consider an extension of the consumption problem presented in this section in which a third item, juice, may be consumed at lunch. Assume the utility function is now

$$U(S, V, J) = \frac{1}{3}\ln(S) + \frac{1}{3}\ln(V) + \frac{1}{3}\ln(J),$$

   where J represents the number of ounces of juice consumed at lunch. Also, assume that 12 ounces of juice costs \$1.00 and that you can purchase any number of ounces of juice at this price. As in the example in this section, you have \$6.00 to spend on lunch.
   (a) Write the equation representing the budget constraint in this three-good case.
   (b) Determine the utility function $\overline{U}(V, J)$ that internalizes this constraint by solving to remove the soup variable. Use the first-order conditions to obtain the optimal relationship between salad and juice.
   (c) Determine the utility function $\overline{U}(S, J)$ that internalizes this constraint by solving to remove the salad variable. Use the first-order conditions to obtain the optimal relationship between soup and juice.
   (d) Use the optimal ratios from parts (b) and (c), along with the budget constraint, to find the optimal amounts of soup, salad, and juice.

(e) Show that this solution provides a maximum level of utility by employing the second-order conditions presented in Chapter 10.

6. Suppose you have completed your soup and salad and have moved on to dessert. You decide to have some combination of cappuccino and pudding that minimizes the amount of calories you consume, while still providing you with a certain level of gustatory pleasure. Each ounce of cappuccino has 50 calories, and each ounce of pudding has 100 calories. The utility from consuming cappuccino (C) and pudding (P) is measured in "utils," and the "production of utils" from consuming cappuccino and pudding is represented by the function

$$U(C, P) = C^{1/3}P^{2/3}.$$

You decide to consume 5 utils of dessert in a way that minimizes the number of calories. Set this up as a constrained minimization problem. Find the optimal number of ounces of cappuccino and pudding. Use the second-order condition to show that this solution represents a minimum rather than a maximum number of calories.

7. Use the substitution method to find the optimum values for the multivariate constrained optimization function

$$U = 2x^2 + 5xy - y^2 - 3xz$$

subject to $x + y + z = 14$. Use the second-order condition presented in Chapter 10 to confirm whether the extreme value represents a maximum or a minimum.

8. What is the optimal amount of soup, salad, and juice when your utility function is the same as the one presented in question 5 but you have \$9.00 to spend on lunch rather than \$6.00? Comment on the optimal relative proportions of each item.

9. To help your college, you decide to spend 12 hours each week in two activities: accompanying prospective students on tours of the college and phoning alumni to ask for donations. In consultation with members of the psychology and economics departments, the head of student volunteers has determined that the increase in the college's revenues, R, arising from the number of hours you spend guiding tours, T, and the number of hours you spend phoning alumni, P, can be expressed as the function

$$R(T, P) = \sqrt{T} + \sqrt{\frac{P}{2}}.$$

Solve the problem facing the head of student volunteers, and determine the optimal number of hours you should devote to guiding tours and the optimal number of hours you should devote to phoning alumni. Show that this represents a maximum amount of increase in revenues rather than a minimum amount of increase in revenues.

11.2 OPTIMIZATION WITH LAGRANGIAN FUNCTIONS

An alternative to substituting an equality constraint into an objective function as a method for solving optimization problems is the **Lagrange multiplier method.** This method involves forming a **Lagrangian function** that includes the objective function, the constraint, and a variable called a **Lagrange multiplier.** Constrained optimization problems are often easier to solve with the Lagrange multiplier method than with the substitution method discussed in the previous section. Also, as we demonstrate here, the Lagrange multiplier itself often has an important economic interpretation.

In this section we first show how to set up and solve optimization problems with equality constraints with the Lagrange multiplier method. We next discuss the interpretation of the Lagrange multiplier. We then extend this to problems with several constraints. This section concludes with sufficient conditions, in the context of the Lagrange multiplier method, for determining if a solution represents a maximum or a minimum.

Setting Up and Solving Lagrangian Functions

The Lagrangian function for a constrained maximization or a constrained minimization problem with the objective function $f(x_1, x_2)$ subject to the equality constraint that $g(x_1, x_2) = c$ is

$$L(x_1, x_2, \lambda) = f(x_1, x_2) - \lambda(g(x_1, x_2) - c), \tag{11.3}$$

where x_1 and x_2 are the two variables to be chosen. Notice that the arguments of the Lagrangian function include both the arguments of the objective function and the Lagrange multiplier, λ. Also, note that the value of the Lagrangian function is the same as the value of the objective function when the constraint holds. This shows that the values of x_1 and x_2 that maximize or minimize the Lagrangian function also maximize or minimize the objective function when the constraint holds.

We begin to solve the constrained optimization problem corresponding to the Lagrangian function (11.3) by solving a system of equations. These equations include the first-order conditions for the Lagrangian function with respect to each of the arguments of the objective function and the equality constraint, and they are the set of values of x_1, x_2, and λ that satisfy[2]

$$\begin{aligned} \frac{\partial L(x_1, x_2, \lambda)}{\partial x_1} &= 0, \\ \frac{\partial L(x_1, x_2, \lambda)}{\partial x_2} &= 0, \quad \text{and} \\ g(x_1, x_2) &= c. \end{aligned} \tag{11.4}$$

We illustrate the Lagrange multiplier method by setting up and solving the consumption problem presented in Section 11.1. The Lagrangian function for this problem is

$$L(S, V, \lambda) = \frac{1}{2}\ln(S) + \frac{1}{2}\ln(V) - \lambda\left(\frac{1}{4}S + \frac{1}{2}V - 6\right).$$

---

[2]Sometimes the method for solving a Lagrangian function is presented as finding the solution to the equations representing the first-order conditions for the Lagrangian function with respect to each of its arguments. Therefore one equation is found by setting the partial derivative

$$\frac{\partial L(x_1, x_2, \lambda)}{\partial \lambda}$$

equal to zero. This, of course, just gives us the third equation in (11.4), which is that the constraint must hold with equality.

The first-order conditions for this function with respect to S and V are

$$\frac{\partial L(S, V, \lambda)}{\partial V} = \frac{1}{2S} - \frac{1}{4}\lambda = 0 \quad \text{and}$$

$$\frac{\partial L(S, V, \lambda)}{\partial V} = \frac{1}{2V} - \frac{1}{2}\lambda = 0.$$

The third equation required to solve this constrained optimization problem is the constraint itself, that is,

$$\frac{1}{4}S + \frac{1}{2}V = 6.$$

These three equations contain three unknowns, S, V, and λ. Solving for λ in the first two equations, we find

$$\frac{2}{S} = \lambda = \frac{1}{V}$$

or $S = 2V$. We can then use this relationship along with the third equation, the budget constraint, to obtain the solutions of $V = 6$ ounces and $S = 12$ ounces presented earlier.

The extension of this method to the case of more than two arguments in the objective function is straightforward. In this case the Lagrangian function takes the form

$$L(x_1, x_2, \ldots, x_n, \lambda) = f(x_1, x_2, \ldots, x_n) - \lambda(g(x_1, x_2, \ldots, x_n) - c). \tag{11.5}$$

The solution to this problem is the set of values of $x_1, x_2, \ldots, x_n$, and λ that satisfy the equations

$$\frac{\partial L(x_1, x_2, \ldots, x_n, \lambda)}{\partial x_i} = 0 \quad \text{for} \quad i = 1, 2, \ldots, n \quad \text{and}$$

$$g(x_1, x_2, \ldots, x_n) = c. \tag{11.6}$$

To illustrate this, we extend the consumption example presented earlier by considering a third item consumed at lunch. Assume the utility function is now

$$U(S, V, J) = \frac{1}{3}\ln(S) + \frac{1}{3}\ln(V) + \frac{1}{3}\ln(J),$$

where J represents the number of ounces of juice consumed at lunch. Also, assume that 12 ounces of juice costs \$1.00 and that you can purchase any number of ounces of juice at this price. The budget constraint is now

$$6 = \frac{S}{4} + \frac{V}{2} + \frac{J}{12}.$$

The Lagrangian function for this three-item example is

$$L(S, V, J, \lambda) = \frac{1}{3}\ln(S) + \frac{1}{3}\ln(V) + \frac{1}{3}\ln(J) - \lambda\left(\frac{S}{4} + \frac{V}{2} + \frac{J}{12} - 6\right).$$

The first-order conditions for this function are

$$\frac{\partial L(S,V,J,\lambda)}{\partial S} = \frac{1}{3S} - \frac{\lambda}{4} = 0,$$
$$\frac{\partial L(S,V,J,\lambda)}{\partial V} = \frac{1}{3V} - \frac{\lambda}{2} = 0, \quad \text{and}$$
$$\frac{\partial L(S,V,J,\lambda)}{\partial J} = \frac{1}{3J} - \frac{\lambda}{12} = 0.$$

Solving for λ, we obtain the optimal ratios of $S = 2V$, $J = 6V$, and $S = \frac{1}{3}J$. Combining these ratios with the budget constraint

$$6.00 = \frac{S}{4} + \frac{V}{2} + \frac{J}{12},$$

we get the solution $J = 24$ ounces, $V = 4$ ounces, and $S = 8$ ounces.

Interpreting the Lagrange Multiplier

The Lagrange multiplier method generates a variable not obtained with the substitution method, the Lagrange multiplier. It is useful to calculate the value of the Lagrange multiplier because it represents the effect of a small change in the constraint on the optimal value of the objective function.

We can demonstrate this analytically by using the chain rule. Consider the optimal value of a constrained maximization problem in which the objective function is $f(x, y)$ and there is one constraint $g(x, y) = c$. Call the optimal value of the two arguments $x^*(c)$ and $y^*(c)$, where the asterisks reflect the fact that these are the optimal values and the c in parentheses reflects the fact that the optimal values are themselves functions of the constraint. At the optimum,

$$g(x^*(c), y^*(c)) = c.$$

Using the chain rule to take the derivative of each side of this expression with respect to c, we have

$$\frac{\partial g(x^*(c), y^*(c))}{\partial x}\frac{dx^*(c)}{dc} + \frac{\partial g(x^*(c), y^*(c))}{\partial y}\frac{dy^*(c)}{dc} = 1. \tag{11.7}$$

Also, using the chain rule to differentiate the optimum value of the objective function with respect to the constraint, we have

$$\frac{df(x^*(c), y^*(c))}{dc} = \frac{\partial f(x^*(c), y^*(c))}{\partial x}\frac{dx^*(c)}{dc} + \frac{\partial f(x^*(c), y^*(c))}{\partial y}\frac{dy^*(c)}{dc}. \tag{11.8}$$

The first-order conditions require that

$$\frac{\partial f(x^*(c), y^*(c))}{\partial x} = \lambda\frac{\partial g(x^*(c), y^*(c))}{\partial x}$$

and

$$\frac{\partial f(x^*(c), y^*(c))}{\partial y} = \lambda \frac{\partial g(x^*(c), y^*(c))}{\partial y}.$$

Substituting these first-order conditions into (11.8) gives us

$$\frac{df(x^*(c), y^*(c))}{dc} = \lambda\left[\frac{\partial g(x^*(c), y^*(c))}{\partial x}\frac{dx^*(c)}{dc} + \frac{\partial g(x^*(c), y^*(c))}{\partial y}\frac{dy^*(c)}{dc}\right]. \quad (11.9)$$

The result in (11.7) shows that the term in square brackets in (11.9) equals 1. Therefore we find that

$$\frac{df(x^*(c), y^*(c))}{dc} = \lambda.$$

That is, the Lagrange multiplier represents the change in the optimum value of the objective function with a small change in the constraint.

A numerical example illustrates this property of the Lagrange multiplier. In the two-item lunch problem presented earlier, the optimal ratio of soup to salad is $S = 2V$, and the Lagrange multiplier is $\lambda = 1/V$ (or, equivalently, $2/S$). The utility derived when \$6.00 is spent optimally by consuming 12 ounces of soup and 6 ounces of salad is $U(S, V) = U(12, 6) = 2.14$, and, in this case, the Lagrange multiplier is $1/6$. If, instead, \$7.00 is available for lunch, the optimal quantities of salad and soup are $V = 7$ ounces and $S = 14$ ounces. The utility obtained from consuming this combination of soup and salad is $U(14, 7) = 2.29$. The Lagrange multiplier in this case is $1/7$. The difference in utility as the budget for lunch increases from \$6.00 to \$7.00, which is equal to $2.29 - 2.14 = 0.15$, is approximately equal to the average of the two respective Lagrange multipliers (that is, $(1/6 + 1/7)/2 \approx 0.15$). Thus the Lagrange multiplier can be interpreted as the marginal utility of money available for lunch. The decrease in the Lagrange multiplier with an increase in the money available for lunch reflects diminishing marginal utility.

In other contexts, the Lagrange multiplier may be interpreted differently. For example, if the objective function represents the profit function from undertaking an activity and the constraint reflects a limit on using an input to that activity, the Lagrange multiplier reflects the marginal benefit from having additional input. In this case the Lagrange multiplier represents the price a firm would be willing to pay per unit of additional input, which is known as the **shadow price** of the input.

The Envelope Theorem

In the 1930s, the economist Jacob Viner was studying the theory of short-run and long-run cost functions of a firm. Viner defined the short-run as a period when capital is fixed and labor is variable and the long-run as a period when both capital and labor are variable. This definition seemed to have two implications for the relationship between short-run average cost and long-run average cost. First, long-run average cost should always be less than or equal to short-run average cost because the ability to vary capital inputs allows for lower cost production. This implies that the long-run cost curve is

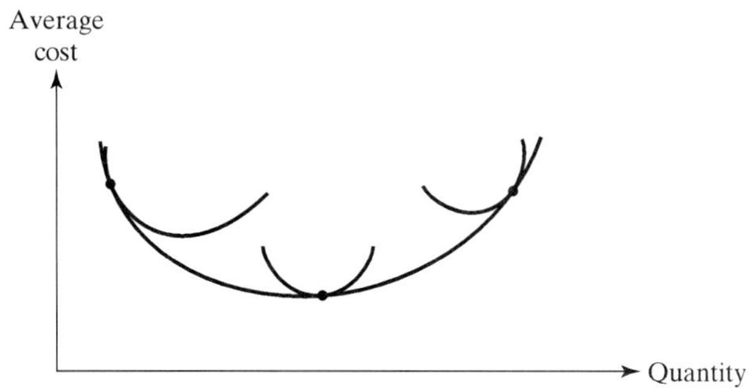

(a)

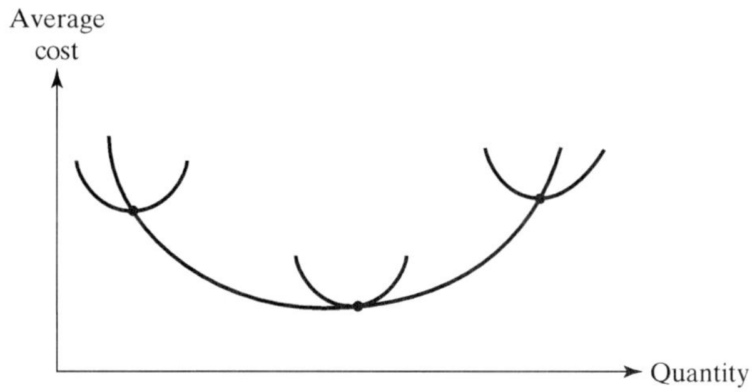

(b)

FIGURE 11.3 Short-Run Cost and Long-Run Cost Functions

the "envelope" of the set of short-run cost curves as shown in Figure 11.3(a). Viner also reasoned that the long-run average cost curve should be the collection of minimum points of the various short-run average cost curves as in Figure 11.3(b). Viner's draftsman reported back to him, however, that he could not draw a long-run average cost curve that was an envelope to all the short-run curves and that also passed through the minimum point of each of the short-run curves. This is apparent from the graphs presented here. Figure 11.3(a) shows that a long-run average cost curve that is an envelope to the various short-run average cost curves does not pass through their minimum points, and Figure 11.3(b) shows that a long-run average cost curve that passes through the minimum of various short-run average cost curves is not an envelope.

As you may know from microeconomic theory, the correct long-run average cost curve is the one in Figure 11.3(a), which is an envelope.[3] But the economic puzzle posed by this particular geometric problem has broader implications. The general issue concerns whether or not altering one argument of a multivariate function affects the derivative of that function with respect to another argument when the derivative is

[3] Viner chose to include in his article a long-run cost curve that passes through the minimum points of all the short-run cost curves, like the one in Fig. 11.3(b).

evaluated at an optimum. This problem was analyzed by Paul Samuelson, and its resolution is known as the **Envelope Theorem.**[4]

Consider a generic problem involving the determination of the maximum value of an objective function

$$f(x_1, \ldots, x_n; \beta_1, \ldots, \beta_m),$$

subject to a constraint

$$g(x_1, \ldots, x_n; \beta_1, \ldots, \beta_m) = 0,$$

where the set of x_i's are choice variables and the set of β_i's are parameters. (It need not be the case that every choice variable and every parameter appear in both the objective function and the constraint.) The Lagrangian, in this case, is

$$L(x_1, \ldots, x_n; \beta_1, \ldots, \beta_m) = f(x_1, \ldots, x_n; \beta_1, \ldots, \beta_m) - \lambda g(x_1, \ldots, x_n; \beta_1, \ldots, \beta_m).$$

We assume that all partial derivatives are continuous. The first-order conditions for this problem are

$$f_{x_i} - \lambda g_{x_i} = 0 \quad \text{for} \quad i = 1, \ldots, n \quad \text{and}$$

$$g(x_1, \ldots, x_n; \beta_1, \ldots, \beta_m) = 0.$$

Given a solution to this problem, we define the **maximum value function** as

$$F(\beta_1, \ldots, \beta_m) = f(x_1^*(\beta_1, \ldots, \beta_m), \ldots, x_n^*(\beta_1, \ldots, \beta_m);\ \beta_1, \ldots, \beta_m),$$

where $x_i^*(\beta_1, \ldots, \beta_m)$ is the optimal choice for the ith variable, given the parameters $\beta_1, \ldots, \beta_m$. The chain rule shows that the derivative of the maximum value function with respect to the parameter β_i is

$$F_{\beta_i} = f_{x_1} \frac{\partial x_1^*}{\partial \beta_i} + \cdots + f_{x_n} \frac{\partial x_n^*}{\partial \beta_i} + f_{\beta_i}.$$

The first-order conditions $f_{x_i} = \lambda g_{x_i}$ for $i = 1, \ldots, n$, can be used to show that, at the optimum, the derivative of the maximum value function is

$$F_{\beta_i} = \lambda g_{x_1} \frac{\partial x_1^*}{\partial \beta_i} + \cdots + \lambda g_{x_n} \frac{\partial x_n^*}{\partial \beta_i} + f_{\beta_i}.$$

$$= \lambda\left(g_{x_1} \frac{\partial x_1^*}{\partial \beta_i} + \cdots + g_{x_n} \frac{\partial x_n^*}{\partial \beta_i}\right) + f_{\beta_i}.$$

Differentiating the constraint evaluated at the optimal level of the variables, in a manner analogous to (11.7), we have

$$g_{x_1} \frac{\partial x_1^*}{\partial \beta_i} + \cdots + g_{x_n} \frac{\partial x_n^*}{\partial \beta_i} + g_{\beta_i} = 0,$$

[4]The original Viner article, "Cost Curves and Supply Curves," is reprinted in *AEA Readings in Price Theory* (Homewood, IL: Irwin, 1952). Samuelson's analysis is found in his *Foundations of Economic Analysis* (Cambridge, MA: Harvard University Press, 1947).

or, equivalently, we find that the term in parentheses in the second line of the derivative of the maximum value function is

$$\left(g_{x_1} \frac{\partial x_1^*}{\partial \beta_i} + \cdots + g_{x_n} \frac{\partial x_n^*}{\partial \beta_i} \right) = -g_{\beta_i}.$$

Substituting this expression into the derivative of the maximum value function, we have the general statement of the Envelope Theorem,

$$F_{\beta_i} = f_{\beta_i} - \lambda g_{\beta_i}.$$

We can also express this result in terms of the Lagrangian function for the constrained optimization problem as

$$F_{\beta_i} = L_{\beta_i} \big|_{x_1, \ldots, x_n},$$

where $L_{\beta_i} \big|_{x_1, \ldots, x_n}$ represents the derivative of the Lagrangian function with respect to the parameter β_i when the set of choice variables $x_1, \ldots, x_n$ is held constant. This result shows that the effect of a small change in a parameter of a constrained optimization problem on its maximum value can be determined by considering only the partial derivative of the objective function and the partial derivative of the constraint with respect to that parameter. Thus, to a first approximation, it is not necessary to consider how a small change in a parameter affects the optimal value of the variables of the problem in order to evaluate the change in its maximum value.

The Envelope Theorem can be used to show that the correct depiction of short-run cost curves and a long-run cost curve is as shown in Figure 11.3(a) and not as shown in Figure 11.3(b). The distinction between the short run and the long run is the assumption that in the short run, the capital input is fixed and the labor input is variable, while in the long run, both capital and labor are variable inputs. The Lagrangian function corresponding to the short-run problem of minimizing costs while producing a level of output Y, given a fixed capital input, can be written as

$$L(N, \overline{K}, \lambda, r, w, Y) = -[wN + r\overline{K} - \lambda(f(N, \overline{K}) - Y)],$$

where N is the labor input, r is the rental rate on capital, w is the wage, and $\overline{K}$ is the fixed input of capital. The maximum value function is

$$C(\overline{K}, r, w, Y),$$

and its partial derivative with respect to output is

$$C_Y = \frac{\partial L(N^*, \overline{K}, \lambda, r, w, Y)}{\partial Y} \bigg|_N = -\lambda.$$

The Lagrangian function corresponding to the long-run problem of minimizing costs while producing a level of output Y is

$$L(N, K, \lambda, w, r, Y) = -[wN + rK - \lambda(f(N, K) - Y)],$$

where the capital input, K, is variable. The maximum value function for the long-run problem is

$$C(w, r, Y),$$

and its partial derivative with respect to output is

$$C_Y = \left.\frac{\partial L(N^*, K^*, \lambda, r, w, Y)}{\partial Y}\right|_{N,K} = -\lambda.$$

Thus, at given levels of output, the slope of the short-run total cost curve reflecting fixed capital input equals the slope of the long-run total cost curve reflecting variable capital input. It follows that this same tangency relationship holds for average costs, as in Figure 11.3(a).

The Envelope Theorem has a wide range of other applications in economics. You may have noticed that we essentially used the Envelope Theorem already in our discussion of the interpretation of the Lagrange multiplier. In that example, the Lagrangian function is

$$L(x, y, c, \lambda) = f(x, y) - \lambda(g(x, y) - c).$$

In this case the parameter c, which represents the value of the constraint, does not appear in the objective function. At the optimal values x^* and y^*, the derivative of the maximum value function $F(c)$ with respect to the parameter representing the constraint, c, is

$$F_c = \left.\frac{\partial L(x^*, y^*, c, \lambda)}{\partial c}\right|_{x,y} = \lambda,$$

which is the result we obtained previously.

We can also use the Envelope Theorem to study properties of a profit maximization problem. Consider a firm that uses the two inputs x_1 and x_2, which cost w_1 and w_2, respectively, to produce the good y, which it sells for the price p. The production function is $f(x_1, x_2)$. The constrained maximization problem facing this firm can be represented by the Lagrangian function

$$L(x_1, x_2, y, p, w_1, w_2, \lambda) = py - w_1x_1 - w_2x_2 - \lambda(f(x_1, x_2) - y).$$

The Envelope Theorem shows that the derivatives of the maximum value profit function, $\Pi(p, w_1, w_2)$, evaluated at the optimal values of the choice variables y^*, x_1^*, and x_2^*, are

$$\frac{\partial \Pi(p, w_1, w_2)}{\partial p} = \left.\frac{\partial L(x_1^*, x_2^*, y^*, p, w_1, w_2, \lambda)}{\partial p}\right|_{x_1,x_2} = y^* > 0,$$

$$\frac{\partial \Pi(p, w_1, w_2)}{\partial w_1} = \left.\frac{\partial L(x_1^*, x_2^*, y^*, p, w_1, w_2, \lambda)}{\partial w_1}\right|_{x_1,x_2} = -x_1^* < 0, \quad \text{and}$$

$$\frac{\partial \Pi(p, w_1, w_2)}{\partial w_2} = \left.\frac{\partial L(x_1^*, x_2^*, y^*, p, w_1, w_2, \lambda)}{\partial w_1}\right|_{x_1,x_2} = -x_2^* < 0,$$

which shows that profits increase with an increase in the price of the good and decrease with an increase in the price of the input. These results are known as **Hotelling's Lemma.**

Lagrangian Functions with Multiple Constraints

We can solve the solution to a constrained optimization problem with more than one constraint by using a Lagrangian function with a Lagrange multiplier corresponding to each constraint. In general, the Lagrangian function for a constrained optimization problem with an objective function with n variables subject to m equality constraints is written as

$$L(x_1, \ldots, x_n, \lambda_1, \ldots, \lambda_m) = f(x_1, \ldots, x_n) - \sum_{i=1}^{m} \lambda_i (g^i(x_1, \ldots, x_n) - c_i), \quad (11.10)$$

where $g^i(x_1, \ldots, x_n) = c_i$ represents the ith constraint.

To illustrate a problem with more than one constraint, suppose that you wish to limit your consumption of juice and soup at lunch such that you drink exactly 24 ounces of liquid. We might think of this as a "liquidity constraint." Recall from the solution earlier that, in the absence of this constraint, you would drink 32 ounces of liquid since the optimal solution consists of 24 ounces of juice and 8 ounces of soup. A Lagrangian function with the liquidity constraint as well as the financial constraint is

$$\begin{aligned} L(S, V, J, \lambda, \mu,) = {} & \frac{1}{3}\ln(S) + \frac{1}{3}\ln(V) + \frac{1}{3}\ln(J) \\ & -\lambda\left(\frac{S}{4} + \frac{V}{2} + \frac{J}{12} - 6\right) - \mu(S + J - 24), \end{aligned}$$

where μ is the Lagrange multiplier for the liquidity constraint. The first-order conditions for the function $L(S, V, J, \lambda, \mu)$ are

$$\begin{aligned} \frac{\partial L(S, V, J, \lambda, \mu)}{\partial S} &= \frac{1}{3S} - \frac{\lambda}{4} - \mu = 0, \\ \frac{\partial L(S, V, J, \lambda, \mu)}{\partial V} &= \frac{1}{3V} - \frac{\lambda}{2} = 0, \quad \text{and} \\ \frac{\partial L(S, V, J, \lambda, \mu)}{\partial J} &= \frac{1}{3J} - \frac{\lambda}{12} - \mu = 0. \end{aligned}$$

A solution also requires that the two constraints are met. That is,

$$\begin{aligned} \frac{S}{4} + \frac{V}{2} + \frac{J}{12} &= 6 \quad \text{and} \\ S + J &= 24. \end{aligned}$$

These five equations have five unknown variables, S, V, J, λ, and μ. Using the first-order conditions to solve for these variables, we find that

$$V = \frac{SJ}{3(J - S)}.$$

Then, using the two constraints, we find that the optimal consumption levels are 8 ounces of soup, 16 ounces of juice, and $5\frac{1}{3}$ ounces of salad. It is not surprising that this additional constraint has altered the optimal consumption set. Also, it should not be surprising that the utility derived from this consumption set is lower than that obtained when there is no liquidity constraint. The utility, in this case, is

$$\frac{1}{3}\ln(8) + \frac{1}{3}\ln\left(5\frac{1}{3}\right) + \frac{1}{3}\ln(16) = 2.17,$$

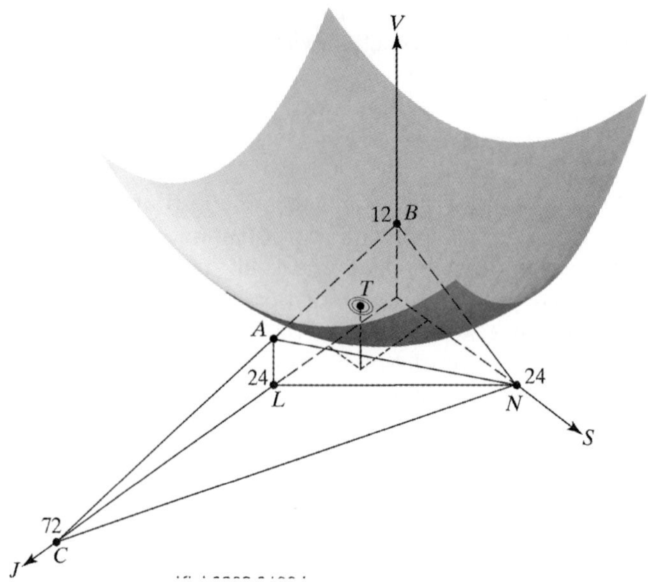

FIGURE 11.4 Optimal Consumption with Two Constraints

while the utility obtained when any amount of liquid can be consumed is

$$\frac{1}{3}\ln(8) + \frac{1}{3}\ln(4) + \frac{1}{3}\ln(24) = 2.21.$$

This solution is depicted in the three-dimensional graph in Figure 11.4. This figure is similar to the graph in Figure 11.2, which depicts the solution to the two-item consumption problem. Figure 11.4 includes two constraints: the liquidity constraint, represented by the line LN, and the budget constraint, represented by the plane BCN. The feasible set for this problem is the surface $BNLAB$ since this surface represents the set of points that simultaneously solves both constraints. The optimal combination of items is labeled as point T on the graph. At this point, a surface representing an indifference plane is tangent to the plane representing the feasible set of items.

Of course, it is necessary that the set of constraints in an optimization problem provide a feasible set of values of the arguments of the function. Otherwise, the problem cannot be solved. For example, in the three-item lunch example, suppose you wanted to consume 100 ounces of liquid. This constraint and the budget constraint cannot be simultaneously satisfied since there is no way to purchase enough soup and juice with the \$6.00 available.

Sufficient Conditions for the Lagrangian Function

The discussion of the Lagrange multiplier method has focused, to this point, on necessary conditions for identifying an extreme point. These necessary conditions do not distinguish between a maximum and a minimum. In this section we present sufficient conditions for determining whether an optimum set of values represents a minimum or a maximum of the objective function in the context of the Lagrange multiplier method.

The sufficient conditions for characterizing the stationary point of a multivariate function presented in Chapter 10 are based on whether the Hessian matrix of the function is positive definite or negative definite when evaluated at the stationary point. The sufficient conditions for a constrained maximization problem, likewise, depend upon whether the Lagrangian function is positive definite or negative definite when evaluated at a stationary point.

The conditions for establishing whether a function is negative definite or positive definite when some of its arguments are constrained differ from the conditions when all arguments of a function are free to vary. To demonstrate this, we begin by developing conditions that ensure that a bivariate quadratic form subject to a linear constraint is negative definite. Recall from Chapter 10 that the bivariate quadratic equation

$$Q(x, y) = ax^2 + 2bxy + cy^2$$

can be represented by the matrix system

$$Q(x, y) = [x \quad y]\begin{bmatrix} a & b \\ b & c \end{bmatrix}\begin{bmatrix} x \\ y \end{bmatrix}.$$

The quadratic form $Q(x, y)$ is negative definite if

$$a < 0 \quad \text{and} \quad ac - b^2 > 0,$$

where $ac-b^2$ is the determinant of the 2×2 matrix. This quadratic form is positive definite if

$$a > 0 \quad \text{and} \quad ac - b^2 > 0.$$

Now suppose that x and y are constrained by the linear relationship $Ax + By = 0$. In this case the quadratic equation can be written as

$$\begin{aligned} Q\left(x, -\frac{A}{B}x\right) &= ax^2 + 2bx\left(-\frac{A}{B}x\right) + c\left(-\frac{A}{B}x\right)^2 \\ &= ax^2 - 2b\frac{A}{B}x^2 + c\frac{A^2}{B^2}x^2 \\ &= -\frac{x^2}{B^2}[2bAB - aB^2 - cA^2]. \end{aligned}$$

The term in square brackets is the determinant of the matrix

$$H = \begin{bmatrix} 0 & A & B \\ A & a & b \\ B & b & c \end{bmatrix}$$

since we can expand along the first row of this matrix to obtain the determinant

$$\det H = 0(ac - b^2) - A(Ac - bB) + B(Ab - aB).$$

Sufficient Condition for a Maximum with One Constraint Consider a Lagrangian function consisting of an objective function with n arguments and one constraint. If the determinant of the bordered Hessian of that Lagrangian function evaluated at a stationary point has the same sign as $(-1)^n$ and the largest $n - 1$ leading principal minors alternate in sign, then the quadratic form is negative definite on the constraint, and the stationary point represents a maximum. ■

Sufficient Condition for a Minimum with One Constraint Consider a Lagrangian function consisting of an objective function with n arguments and one constraint. If all of the largest $n - 1$ leading principal minors of its bordered Hessian evaluated at the stationary point are negative, including the determinant of bordered Hessian itself, then the quadratic form is positive definite on the constraint, and the stationary point represents a minimum. ■

If these conditions are violated by the $n - 1$ nonzero leading principal minors, then the stationary point is neither a maximum nor a minimum.

Applying this more general result to our two-item lunch choice example, we find that $n - 1 = 1$, and, therefore, we only need to check the sign of the largest leading principal minor, which is the determinant of H. The determinant of H is positive, and, therefore, the quadratic form representing the second total differential is negative because $(-1)^2 = 1$.

In the three-item lunch choice example, in which we find the optimal combination of soup, salad, and juice with the Lagrangian function $L(S, V, J, \lambda)$, the Hessian matrix is

$$H = \begin{bmatrix} 0 & \frac{1}{4} & \frac{1}{2} & \frac{1}{12} \\ \frac{1}{4} & -\frac{1}{3S^2} & 0 & 0 \\ \frac{1}{2} & 0 & -\frac{1}{3V^2} & 0 \\ \frac{1}{12} & 0 & 0 & -\frac{1}{3J^2} \end{bmatrix}.$$

The $n - 1 = 3 - 1 = 2$ largest principal minors of this Hessian are the determinant of the third leading principal submatrix, which is

$$\begin{vmatrix} 0 & \frac{1}{4} & \frac{1}{2} \\ \frac{1}{4} & -\frac{1}{3S^2} & 0 \\ \frac{1}{2} & 0 & -\frac{1}{3V^2} \end{vmatrix} = \frac{1}{12S^2} + \frac{1}{48V^2} > 0 \quad \text{for any } S, V,$$

and the determinant of the matrix itself, which is

$$|H| = -\left(\frac{1}{1296S^2V^2} + \frac{1}{144J^2V^2} + \frac{1}{36S^2J^2}\right) < 0 \quad \text{for any } S, V, J.$$

Since the forth leading principal minor, which is the determinant of the Hessian matrix itself, has the same sign as $(-1)^3$ and the third leading principal minor is positive, the quadratic form is negative definite on the constraint, and the stationary point $S = 8$, $V = 4$, and $J = 24$ identified earlier represents a maximum.

We close by generalizing this result further to the case of a Lagrangian function with n variables and m constraints. Denote this function as $L(x_1, x_2, \ldots, x_n)$, the ith constraint as $g_i(x_1, x_2, \ldots, x_n) = c_i$, and the associated Lagrange multiplier as λ_i. The bordered Hessian, in this case, is

$$H = \begin{bmatrix} 0 & \hat{0} & 0 & \frac{\partial g_1}{\partial x_1} & \cdots & \frac{\partial g_1}{\partial x_n} \\ \tilde{0} & \hat{\hat{0}} & \tilde{0} & \cdots & \cdots & \cdots \\ 0 & \hat{0} & 0 & \frac{\partial g_m}{\partial x_1} & \cdots & \frac{\partial g_m}{\partial x_n} \\ \frac{\partial g_1}{\partial x_1} & \cdots & \frac{\partial g_m}{\partial x_1} & \frac{\partial^2 L}{\partial x_1^2} & \cdots & \frac{\partial^2 L}{\partial x_1 \partial x_n} \\ \vdots & \vdots & \vdots & \vdots & \vdots & \vdots \\ \frac{\partial g_1}{\partial x_n} & \cdots & \frac{\partial g_m}{\partial x_n} & \frac{\partial^2 L}{\partial x_1 \partial x_n} & \cdots & \frac{\partial^2 L}{\partial x_1^2} \end{bmatrix}$$

where $\tilde{0}$ represents an $(m - 2) \times 1$ column vector with each element equal to 0; $\hat{0}$ represents a $1 \times (m - 2)$ row vector with each element equal to 0; and $\hat{\hat{0}}$ represents an $(m - 2) \times (m - 2)$ matrix with each element equal to 0. For example, in the three-item lunch example with both a budget constraint and a liquidity constraint, the bordered Hessian matrix is

$$H = \begin{bmatrix} 0 & 0 & \frac{1}{4} & \frac{1}{2} & \frac{1}{12} \\ 0 & 0 & 1 & 0 & 1 \\ \frac{1}{4} & 1 & -\frac{1}{3S^2} & 0 & 0 \\ \frac{1}{2} & 0 & 0 & -\frac{1}{3V^2} & 0 \\ \frac{1}{12} & 1 & 0 & 0 & -\frac{1}{3J^2} \end{bmatrix}.$$

The sufficient conditions, in this case, require checking the sign of the largest $n - m$ principal minors of H. The sufficient conditions for a maximum and a minimum are as follows.

Sufficient Condition for a Constrained Maximum Consider a Lagrangian function consisting of an objective function with n arguments and m constraints. If the determinant of the bordered Hessian of that Lagrangian function evaluated at a stationary point has the same sign as $(-1)^n$ and the largest $n - m$ leading principal minors alternate in sign, then the quadratic form is negative definite on the set of constraints, and the stationary point represents a maximum.

Sufficient Condition for a Constrained Minimum Consider a Lagrangian function consisting of an objective function with n arguments and m constraints. If all of the largest $n-m$ leading principal minors of its bordered Hessian evaluated at the stationary point have the sign $(-1)^m$, including the determinant of the bordered Hessian itself, then the quadratic form is positive definite on the set of constraints, and the stationary point represents a minimum.

If these two conditions are violated by nonzero principal minors, then the point represents neither a maximum nor a minimum.

In the three-item, two-constraint example, we need to check the last $n - m = 3 - 2 = 1$ principal minor, that is, the sign of the determinant of the bordered Hessian matrix itself. In this case

$$|H| = -\left(\frac{1}{12S^2} + \frac{1}{12J^2} + \frac{1}{108V^2}\right) < 0,$$

which has the same sign as $(-1)^3$. Therefore this shows that the quadratic form is negative definite on the set of constraints and the stationary point $S = 8, V = 5\frac{1}{3}$, and $J = 16$ identified earlier represents a maximum.

Notice that these three sets of conditions—for the bivariate case with one constraint, for the n variable case with one constraint, and for the case with n variables and m constraints—are progressively more general. The first case is a special case of the second, which is itself a special case of the third.

Exercises 11.2

1. Use the Lagrangian multiplier method to determine the optimal values for each constrained optimization problem's choice variables, and solve for the Lagrange multiplier, λ.
   (a) $U = x^2 + 2x + 3z^2 - 6z + xz$ subject to $2x + 2z = 32$
   (b) $U = \frac{1}{2}a^2 + 4b^2 - 4a + 8c^2$ subject to $\frac{1}{2}a + 3b + c = 25$
   (c) $U = x^3z^4$ subject to $\frac{x}{50} + z = 34$
   (d) $Z = \ln(x + y)$ subject to $xy = 16$
2. You allocate \$24 per week for the purchase of cookies and apples at your school's cafeteria. Your utility from eating cookies and apples is given by
$$U(C, A) = 2C^{1/2} + A^{1/2}.$$

Assume that cookies cost \$1 each and apples cost \$0.50.

(a) Set up the Lagrangian function associated with this problem. Solve for the optimal proportion of cookies to apples. Given your budget constraint, how many cookies and apples will you buy each week?

(b) Solve for the Lagrangian multiplier. What is your interpretation of this parameter? What happens to this parameter if you allocate twice as much per week to the purchase of cookies and apples? How do you interpret this change?

3. The utility you derive from exercise (X) and watching movies (M) is described by the function

$$U(X, M) = 100 - e^{-2X} - e^{-M}.$$

Currently you have four hours each day that you can devote either to watching movies or exercising. Set up the Lagrangian function for finding the optimal amount of time spent at each activity. Solve for the optimal amounts of time exercising and watching movies. Also, provide an interpretation of the Lagrange multiplier in this problem.

4. Your favorite pastries are Twinkies and RingDings. The utility you derive from these is given by the function

$$U(T, R) = \frac{1}{2}\ln(T) + \frac{1}{2}\ln(R),$$

where T is the number of cases of Twinkies and R is the number of cases of RingDings consumed each month. A case of RingDings costs \$8, and a case of Twinkies costs \$4.

(a) Using the Lagrangian multiplier method, determine the optimal choices of cases of RingDings and Twinkies if you have \$32 to spend on pastries each month.

(b) One day, after eating pastries, you write a letter to the manufacturer who responds with an offer that allows you to purchase cases of Twinkies and cases of RingDings at a discount such that the total cost, C, for any purchase is

$$C = 8\sqrt{T} + 4\sqrt{R}.$$

How many cases of Twinkies and RingDings will you purchase with this special arrangement?

(c) Which of the following, (i), (ii), or (iii), correctly completes this sentence? The utility obtained with the budget constraint in part (b) is

(i) less than twice as much as the utility with the budget constraint in part (a).

(ii) exactly twice as much as the utility with the budget constraint in part (a).

(iii) more than twice as much as the utility with the budget constraint in part (a).

5. Suppose it is late in the semester and you have two exams left. You must decide how to allocate your working time during the study period. After eating, sleeping, exercising, and maintaining some human contact, you have 12 hours each day in which to study for your exams. You have figured out that your grade point average,

GPA, from your two courses, Mathematical Methods and Literary Methods, takes the form

$$GPA = \frac{2}{3}\left(\sqrt{M} + \sqrt{2L}\right),$$

where M is the number of hours per day spent studying for Mathematical Methods and L is the number of hours per day spent studying for Literary Methods. What is the optimal number of hours per day spent studying for each course? If you follow this strategy, what will your *GPA* be?

6. The Cobb-Douglas production function takes the form

$$Q = AK^{\alpha}L^{1-\alpha},$$

where Q is the amount of output, K is the amount of capital input, and L is the amount of labor input. Suppose that a firm faces a linear cost-of-inputs function

$$C = wL + rK,$$

where C is the cost of inputs, w is the wage rate, and r is the rental rate on capital.

(a) Set up a Lagrangian function reflecting the constrained optimization problem of obtaining the most output given a budget $\overline{C}$ to spend on inputs. Solve this for the optimal levels of capital and labor.

(b) Set up a Lagrangian function reflecting the constrained optimization problem of spending the least amount on inputs given that the level of output must equal the amount $\overline{Q}$. Solve this for the optimal levels of capital and labor.

7. Use the Lagrange multiplier method to determine the extreme values of the function

$$Z = x^2 + 2xy + w^2$$

subject to the two constraints

$$2x + y + 3w = 24 \quad \text{and} \quad x + w = 8.$$

8. Use the sufficient condition to determine whether the stationary points identified in parts (a), (b) and (d) of question 1 represent maxima, minima, or saddle points.

9. After graduation, you decide to serve those who can no longer abide cafeteria food by opening a restaurant near your university. One of your first tasks is to determine how many graduate students to hire and how many undergraduate students to hire. The number of meals you can serve, M, is a function of the number of graduate students you employ, G, and the number of undergraduate students you employ, U, as shown by the production function

$$M = G^{1/3}U^{2/3}.$$

(a) You want to maximize the number of meals you serve, given your wage bill. Determine the optimal ratio of graduate students to undergraduate students if the wage paid to graduate students is W_G and the wage paid to undergraduate students is W_U.

(b) Does the optimal ratio of graduate students to undergraduate students change if undergraduate students unionize and their wages rise?

(c) How many graduate students will you hire, and how many undergraduate students will you hire if you want to maximize the number of meals you serve and your daily wage bill can be no greater than $1,500? Assume that graduate students work for \$50 per day and undergraduate students can be hired for \$25 per day.

11.3 ECONOMIC APPLICATIONS

The Lagrange multiplier method has many applications in economics. The following five applications illustrate its use.

Constant Expenditure-Share Utility Functions

You may have noticed that, in the two-item case presented earlier, the optimal solution calls for equal expenditures on soup and salad and, in the three-item case, the optimal solution calls for equal expenditures on soup, salad, and juice. This is a consequence of the type of utility function used in those examples and the fact that the coefficients in those particular functions were identical across commodities. The log-linear utility function used in these examples represents the logarithm of a Cobb-Douglas function in which the exponents on each good are equal. More generally, the optimal budget share on the ith item is α_i when the utility function takes the form

$$U(x_1, x_2, \ldots, x_n) = \sum_{i=1}^{n} \alpha_i \ln(x_i),$$

where $\sum_{i=1}^{n} \alpha_i = 1$, and when the constraint takes the linear form

$$\sum_{i=1}^{n} p_i x_i = c.$$

We prove the proposition that the optimal budget share on the ith item is α_i, in this case, by solving the optimization problem with the Lagrange multiplier method. The Lagrangian function takes the form

$$L(x_1, x_2, \ldots, x_n, \lambda) = \sum_{i=1}^{n} \alpha_i \ln(x_i) - \lambda\left(\sum_{i=1}^{n} p_i x_i - c\right).$$

The n first-order conditions are

$$\frac{\partial L(x_1, x_2, \ldots, x_n, \lambda)}{\partial x_i} = \frac{\alpha_i}{x_i} - \lambda p_i = 0 \quad \text{for} \quad i = 1, \ldots, n,$$

which implies that $\lambda p_i x_i = \alpha_i$ for $i = 1, 2, \ldots, n$. The sum of each of these n conditions gives us

$$\lambda \sum_{i=1}^{n} p_i x_i = \sum_{i=1}^{n} \alpha_i.$$

The budget constraint shows that $\sum_{i=1}^{n} p_i x_i = c$, and we have assumed that $\sum_{i=1}^{n} \alpha_i = 1$. Therefore we have

$$\lambda \sum_{i=1}^{n} p_i x_i = \lambda c = \sum_{i=1}^{n} \alpha_i = 1$$

or

$$\lambda = \frac{1}{c}.$$

This result for λ, along with the previous result that the optimal solution for consumption of the ith good is $\lambda p_i x_i = \alpha_i$, shows that the optimal expenditure on the ith good as a proportion of total expenditures is

$$\frac{p_i x_i}{c} = \alpha_i.$$

The Constant Elasticity of Substitution Production Function

The elasticity of substitution between two factors of production represents the percentage change in the optimal ratio of those two factors in response to a 1% change in the ratio of their cost. For example, the elasticity of substitution between capital and labor, σ, equals

$$\sigma = \frac{d \ln(K^*/N^*)}{d \ln(w/r)},$$

where K^* is the optimal amount of capital, N^* is the optimal amount of labor, r is the rental cost of capital, and w is the wage rate (see Chapter 7 for a discussion of elasticities).

A commonly studied production function is

$$Q = (\alpha K^\rho + (1-\alpha)N^\rho)^{1/\rho},$$

where $\rho \le 1$. This is the **constant elasticity of substitution (CES) production function.** We can use the Lagrange multiplier method to solve for the elasticity of substitution for this production function.

The Lagrangian function that is used to solve for the minimum cost of producing a given level of output $\overline{Q}$ is

$$L(K, N, \lambda) = rK + wN - \lambda[(\alpha K^\rho + (1-\alpha)N^\rho)^{1/\rho} - \overline{Q}],$$

where rK is the amount spent on capital and wN is the wage bill. The first-order conditions are

$$\frac{\partial L(K, N, \lambda)}{\partial K} = r - \lambda\alpha K^{\rho-1}(\alpha K^\rho + (1-\alpha)N^\rho)^{(1/\rho)-1} = 0$$

$$\frac{\partial L(K, N, \lambda)}{\partial N} = w - \lambda(1-\alpha)N^{\rho-1}(\alpha K^\rho + (1-\alpha)N^\rho)^{(1/\rho)-1} = 0.$$

Solving to remove λ in these two first-order conditions, we have

$$\frac{r}{\alpha K^{\rho-1}(\alpha K^\rho + (1-\alpha)N^\rho)^{(1-\rho)/\rho}} = \frac{w}{(1-\alpha)N^{\rho-1}(\alpha K^\rho + (1-\alpha)N^\rho)^{(1-\rho)/\rho}},$$

where we have written $(1/\rho) - 1$ as $(1 - \rho)/\rho$. This relationship can be rearranged to obtain the optimal capital-labor ratio, which is

$$\frac{K^*}{N^*} = \left(\frac{w}{r} \cdot \frac{\alpha}{(1 - \alpha)}\right)^{1/(1-\rho)}.$$

The elasticity of substitution is simply the derivative of the logarithm of the optimal ratio of capital to labor with respect to the ratio of the wage rate to the rental rate, w/r. Taking logarithms of both sides of the above equation, we have

$$\ln\left(\frac{K^*}{N^*}\right) = \frac{1}{1 - \rho} \ln\left(\frac{w}{r}\right) + \frac{1}{1 - \rho} \ln\left(\frac{\alpha}{(1 - \alpha)}\right),$$

and, therefore, the elasticity of substitution is

$$\sigma = \frac{d\ln\left(K^*/N^*\right)}{d\ln(w/r)} = \frac{1}{1 - \rho}.$$

This production function allows for any positive elasticity of substitution. As ρ approaches 1, the elasticity of substitution approaches infinity, and any small increase in the relative factor prices causes a very large increase in the demand for capital relative to labor. There is unitary elasticity when $\rho = 0$, in which case a 1% change in the wage-rental ratio leads to a 1% change in the capital-labor ratio. The elasticity falls below 1 for negative values of ρ. For example, if $\rho = -1$, then a 1% increase in the wage-rental ratio leads to a 1/2% increase in the optimal ratio of capital to labor. As ρ approaches negative infinity, the elasticity of substitution approaches zero, a situation where there is no scope for substituting capital for labor in production.

Intertemporal Consumption

The lunch example presented earlier solves for the optimal amount of consumption of different goods. Other types of constrained optimization problems focus on consumption across time. In these problems, goods are distinguished by their date of consumption ("consumption today" or "consumption tomorrow") rather than by the type of good ("soup" or "salad"). These types of intertemporal consumption problems are used extensively in macroeconomics and finance.

We present, here, a basic two-period intertemporal consumption problem. The first period represents "the present," and the second period represents "the future." At the beginning of each period, a certain amount of income is received, I_j, where $j = 1, 2$. During the first period, a person must decide how much of that income to use for consumption, C_1, and how much of that income to save, S. At the beginning of the second period, the person has the income from that period, I_2, as well as the principal and interest from the amount saved from the first period, $(1 + R)S$, where R is the real interest rate. There is no saving in the second period because there is no third period.

The following budget constraints capture this situation. The first-period budget constraint is

$$I_1 = C_1 + S,$$

and the second-period budget constraint is

$$(1 + R)S + I_2 = C_2.$$

An intertemporal budget constraint can be derived by substituting to remove savings. This gives us

$$I_1 + \frac{I_2}{(1 + R)} = C_1 + \frac{C_2}{(1 + R)}.$$

You might recognize, from the discussion in Chapter 3, that the left-hand side of the previous expression is the present value of income and the right-hand side is the present value of consumption.

We consider a general utility function that takes the form

$$U(C_1, C_2) = u(C_1) + \beta u(C_2),$$

where β is the subjective discount rate and $1 > \beta > 0$. The subjective discount rate reflects a preference for current consumption relative to future consumption. We assume that $u'(C_i) > 0$ and $u''(C_i) < 0$. Define the discounted value of the stream of income as

$$\tilde{I} = I_1 + \frac{I_2}{(1 + R)}.$$

The Lagrangian function for this optimization problem is

$$L(C_1, C_2, \lambda) = u(C_1) + \beta u(C_2) - \lambda\left(C_1 + \frac{C_2}{(1 + R)} - \tilde{I}\right).$$

The first-order conditions are

$$\frac{\partial L(C_1, C_2, \lambda)}{\partial C_1} = u'(C_1) - \lambda,$$

$$\frac{\partial L(C_1, C_2, \lambda)}{\partial C_2} = \beta u'(C_2) - \frac{\lambda}{1 + R}, \quad \text{and}$$

$$\tilde{I} = C_1 + \frac{C_2}{(1 + R)}.$$

Substituting to remove λ in the first two of these equations gives us the **Euler equation** for consumption

$$u'(C_1) = (1 + R)\beta u'(C_2).$$

The Euler equation requires that consumption across time cannot be readjusted in a way that raises total utility. The intuition here follows directly the intuition for the two-item consumption problem discussed at the end of Section 11.1. If a consumer lowers first-period consumption by the small amount dC_1, then this decreases utility by the amount $u'(C_1)\,dC_1$. This reduction in first-period consumption allows consumption in the second period to increase by

$$dC_2 = (1 + R)\,dC_1.$$

The increase in utility from this extra second-period consumption is

$$\beta u'(C_2)\,dC_2 = \beta u'(C_2)(1 + R)\,dC_1.$$

The Euler equation requires that, at an optimum, the decrease in utility from a reduction in first-period consumption just matches the increase in consumption from an increase in second-period consumption for small changes in consumption across periods that do not violate the budget constraint.

The Euler equation can be rewritten as

$$\frac{\beta u'(C_2)}{u'(C_1)} = \frac{1}{(1 + R)}.$$

Note that the ratio of the marginal utilities of consumption does not depend upon income in either period. Therefore the ratio of future consumption to present consumption does not depend upon income in either period. This is because consumption in each period depends upon "permanent income," $\tilde{I}$, rather than period-specific income. The interest rate does affect relative levels of income in each period. An increase in the interest rate must be accompanied by some combination of an increase in the second-period consumption (which decreases $u'(C_2)$) and a decrease in the first-period consumption (which increases $u'(C_1)$). Also, greater "impatience," reflected by a decrease in β, will result in a decrease in the second-period consumption (which increases $u'(C_2)$) and an increase in the first-period consumption (which decreases $u'(C_1)$).

College Scholarships and National Savings

The model in the previous application can be extended to show how a variety of factors affect savings. People save for a variety of reasons including financing retirement or large expenditures like college tuitions. Factors that affect the relative cost of future expenditures may have an impact on savings. Martin Feldstein of Harvard University has studied the effect of one such factor, college scholarship rules.[5]

The central point of Feldstein's analysis is that scholarship rules act as a capital levy on the wealth that a family accumulates before and during the time its children are in college and thus serve to discourage household savings. Feldstein considers a scholarship rule of the form

$$S = \alpha(E - \theta A) + \beta,$$

where S is the amount of scholarship money, E is the cost of tuition, θA is the expected parental contribution to the cost of education, α is the extent to which scholarship aid covers the shortfall between tuition and expected parental contribution $(1 \geq \alpha \geq 0)$, and β is the amount of scholarship aid (if β is positive) or the financing gap (if β is negative) not tied to a family's wealth. The variable A is the wealth of the family, and θ is a parameter that represents the extent to which an additional dollar of wealth reduces scholarship awards $(1 \geq \theta \geq 0)$. It is assumed that $E \geq S \geq 0$.

[5] Martin Feldstein, "College scholarship rules and private savings," *American Economic Review* 85, no. 3 (June 1995): 552–566.

This model has two periods, and its structure is simplified to highlight the issue at hand. In the first period, families earn income Y. This income is used either to consume an amount C or save an amount A according to the first-period budget constraint

$$A = Y - C.$$

In the second period, families use their savings from the first period, A (for simplicity, we assume the interest rate is zero) either to finance their retirement, R, or finance education. The amount spent on education equals the cost of tuition minus the scholarship award, $E - S$. Thus the second-period budget constraint is

$$A = R + (E - S).$$

We can combine the budget constraints for the two periods into a single budget constraint by solving for A. This gives us

$$Y - C = R + (E - S).$$

Using the scholarship rule $S = \alpha(E - \theta A) + \beta$, we solve for S. After some rearranging, we then have a consolidated budget constraint

$$(1 - \alpha\theta)Y = (1 - \alpha\theta)C + R + (1 - \alpha)E - \beta.$$

Families are assumed to have a utility function defined over the amount of first-period consumption, education, and retirement consumption. We assume that this utility function takes the form

$$U(C, E, R) = 2\sqrt{C} + 2\sqrt{E} + 2\sqrt{R}.$$

The Lagrangian function for the constrained optimization problem facing families is

$$L(C, E, R, \lambda) = 2\sqrt{C} + 2\sqrt{E} + 2\sqrt{R}$$
$$- \lambda([(1 - \alpha\theta)C + R + (1 - \alpha)E - \beta] - (1 - \alpha\theta)Y).$$

The first-order conditions are

$$\frac{\partial L(C, E, R, \lambda)}{\partial C} = \frac{1}{\sqrt{C}} - \lambda(1 - \alpha\theta) = 0,$$
$$\frac{\partial L(C, E, R, \lambda)}{\partial E} = \frac{1}{\sqrt{E}} - \lambda(1 - \alpha) = 0, \quad \text{and}$$
$$\frac{\partial L(C, E, R, \lambda)}{\partial R} = \frac{1}{\sqrt{R}} - \lambda = 0.$$

These first-order conditions can be solved for the optimal ratios of first-period consumption, expenditures on education, and savings for retirement. These ratios are

$$\frac{R}{E} = (1 - \alpha)^2,$$
$$\frac{R}{C} = (1 - \alpha\theta)^2, \quad \text{and}$$
$$\frac{E}{C} = \left(\frac{1 - \alpha\theta}{1 - \alpha}\right)^2.$$

These results demonstrate that an increase in the expected parental contribution for any level of wealth (that is, an increase in θ) will increase the amount of current consumption relative to the amount saved since the ratios R/C and E/C both decrease with an increase in θ.

The budget constraint can be used in conjunction with the first-order conditions to solve for the optimal level of R, E, and C. These are

$$R = (1 - \alpha\theta)(1 - \alpha)\Omega((1 - \alpha\theta)Y + \beta),$$

$$E = \left(\frac{1 - \alpha\theta}{1 - \alpha}\right)\Omega((1 - \alpha\theta)Y + \beta), \quad \text{and}$$

$$C = \left(\frac{1 - \alpha}{1 - \alpha\theta}\right)\Omega((1 - \alpha\theta)Y + \beta),$$

where $\Omega = [(1 - \alpha) + (1 - \alpha\theta)(2 - \alpha)]^{-1}$. An increase in θ, the expected parental contribution for any level of wealth, decreases R and E (and, therefore, current savings) and increases current consumption. Feldstein empirically estimates that wealth-based college scholarship rules have reduced the accumulation of wealth by U.S. households by about one-third.

The Optimal Allocation of Time

Time is the most common scarce resource. In the text of his 1992 Nobel Prize acceptance lecture, Gary Becker of the University of Chicago writes

> Economic and medical progress have greatly increased length of life, but not the physical flow of time itself, which always restricts everyone to 24 hours per day. So while goods and services have expanded enormously in rich countries, the total time available to consume has not. Thus wants remain unsatisfied in rich countries as well as in poor ones. For while the growing abundance of goods may reduce the value of additional goods, time becomes more valuable as goods become more abundant. The welfare of people cannot be improved in a utopia in which everyone's needs are fully satisfied, but the constant flow of time makes such a utopia impossible.

Becker modeled the optimal allocation of time in a paper published in the mid-1960s.[6] This research has important implications for a wide range of economic issues, such as labor supply and the effects of technological change, as well as for such seemingly noneconomic issues as the determination of family size.

A key aspect of Becker's model is that utility is derived from the process of consuming a good rather than from the good itself. Accordingly, the arguments of the utility function that serves as the objective function in this problem,

$$U(A_1, A_2, \ldots, A_n),$$

[6] The Nobel lecture is published in *Journal of Political Economy* 101, no. 3 (June 1993); 385–409. The above quote is on page 386. The optimal allocation of time is presented in Gary S. Becker, "A theory of the allocation of time," *Economic Journal* 75 (September 1965): 493–517.

are the set of activities A_i rather than the goods used to undertake those activities, G_i. The ith activity requires G_i/n_i units of a good and t_i/h_i hours of time, where n_i and h_i are units of goods and units of time, respectively, per one unit of activity i. Productivity advances may reduce the amount of a good, G_i, needed to undertake the ith activity, which is reflected by a decrease in n_i. Time-saving advances lower the time-cost of the ith activity, which is reflected by a decrease in h_i.

We consider a situation with two activities. People face both time and financial constraints. The total time available to a person, T, is spent in work, W; in activity 1, t_1; or in activity 2, t_2. This constraint is written as

$$T = W + t_1 + t_2.$$

The financial constraint reflects the assumption that total income, which is the product of the average wage, w, and the number of hours worked, W, is spent on either good 1 or good 2. With the prices of these goods given by the exogenous parameters P_1 and P_2, respectively, this constraint is

$$wW = P_1 G_1 + P_2 G_2.$$

Defining the money value of total time as wT and using these two constraints, we can write a consolidated money and time constraint as

$$wT = P_1 G_1 + P_2 G_2 + wt_1 + wt_2.$$

We can write this constraint in terms of activities rather than goods by using the requirements that undertaking the ith activity at a level A_i requires G_i/n_i of the ith good and t_i/h_i hours. The consolidated money and time constraint in terms of activities is

$$wT = P_1 n_1 A_1 + P_2 n_2 A_2 + wh_1 A_1 + wh_2 A_2.$$

The utility function $U(A_1, A_2)$ is assumed to be monotonically increasing in each of its arguments and to have strictly negative second partial derivatives. The corresponding Lagrangian function is

$$L(A_1, A_2, \lambda) = U(A_1, A_2) - \lambda(P_1 n_1 A_1 + P_2 n_2 A_2 + wh_1 A_1 + wh_2 A_2 - wT).$$

The first-order conditions are

$$\frac{\partial L(A_1, A_2, \lambda)}{\partial A_1} = U_1(A_1, A_2) - \lambda(P_1 n_1 + wh_1),$$

$$\frac{\partial L(A_1, A_2, \lambda)}{\partial A_2} = U_2(A_1, A_2) - \lambda(P_2 n_2 + wh_2), \quad \text{and}$$

$$wT = P_1 n_1 A_1 + P_2 n_2 A_2 + wh_1 A_1 + wh_2 A_2,$$

where $U_i(A_1, A_2)$ is the derivative of the utility function with respect to its ith argument. The first two equations can be solved to show

$$\frac{U_1(A_1, A_2)}{U_2(A_1, A_2)} = \frac{wh_1 + P_1 n_1}{wh_2 + P_2 n_2}.$$

The left-hand side of this solution represents the ratio of marginal utilities of the activities, and the right-hand side is the ratio of the "costs" of the activities. These costs include both the financial costs of the goods and the time costs.

The solution to this model presents a variety of interesting implications. The solution implies that any exogenous change that affects the ratio of costs of the activities requires a change in the same direction in the ratio of marginal utilities of the activities. Technological change that makes undertaking an activity less costly in terms of time (that is, a decrease in h_i) or the goods (a decrease in n_i) will lead to an increase in the relative amount of that activity since $U_i(A_1, A_2)$ decreases with an increase in A_i. For example, people probably view more movies now than in years past since VCRs make it both cheaper and less time-consuming to watch a movie. This model also predicts that an increase in wages decreases the consumption of those activities that are more time-intensive since the right-hand side of the previous expression increases with w if $h_1 > h_2$. Thus people may watch more movies and read fewer books as their wages rise. This result also implies that people may choose to have fewer children, itself a very time-intensive activity, with an increase in wages. This is especially true if wages to both members of a household increase. Empirical evidence suggests, in fact, that married women with higher earning potential have fewer children than married women with lower earning potential and that average family size is smaller in countries where the earning potential of women is higher.[7]

Exercises 11.3

1. Consider the student with an insatiable appetite for fast-food hamburgers. Assume that his utility can be expressed as the Cobb-Douglas function
$$U(x_1, x_2) = x_1^{1/2}x_2^{1/2},$$
where x_1 is the number of McBurger hamburgers and x_2 represents the number of King of Burger hamburgers. Assume that McBurger hamburgers cost \$4, King of Burger hamburgers cost \$2 each, and the student has \$120 to spend on hamburgers each semester.
   (a) Find the values of x_1 and x_2 that maximize this student's utility, and use the sufficient condition to confirm that your answer represents a maximum.
   (b) Find the values of x_1 and x_2 that maximize this student's utility when the utility function is the natural logarithm of $U(x_1, x_2)$ such that
$$V(x_1, x_2) = \ln U(x_1, x_2).$$
   (c) Find the value of the Lagrangian, λ, in each case. Do they differ and why?
2. In what is called the dual of constrained utility maximization, a consumer might seek to minimize expenditures in order to achieve some specified level of utility, instead of maximizing utility given a budget constraint. In this setting, the roles of the objective function and the constraint are reversed in order to solve

[7] Recall the application about the international pattern of women's work in Chapter 6.

the problem

$$\min \quad e = p_1x_1 + p_2x_2 \quad \text{subject to} \quad u(x_1, x_2) = \bar{u}.$$

(a) Continuing with question 1, find the values of x_1 and x_2 that minimize the following expenditure function given the utility constraint

$$e = p_1x_1 + p_2x_2$$
$$\bar{u}(x_1, x_2) = x_1^{1/2}x_2^{1/2} = 17.67,$$

where $p_1 = 4$ and $p_2 = 2$.

(b) How do the answers for x_1, x_2, total expenditure, and total utility compare with your results for question 1? What is the intuition behind this result?

(c) If the given utility rises to $\bar{u} = 20$, how does this affect your answers?

3. What is the elasticity of substitution for the Cobb-Douglas production function, $Q = K^{\alpha}L^{1-\alpha}$?

4. In a model of monopolistic competition, Avinash Dixit and Joseph Stiglitz propose a utility function that reflects a preference for a range of differentiated products in consumption.[8] In the three-good case, their utility function takes the form

$$U(X_1, X_2, X_3) = (X_1^{\alpha} + X_2^{\alpha} + X_3^{\alpha})^{1/\alpha},$$

where the three goods are X_1, X_2, and X_3 and $1 > \alpha > 0$. Solve for the elasticity of substitution between any two goods in this model.

5. Determine the Euler equations for a two-period intertemporal optimization problem when the utility function takes the following form.

(a) $U(C_1, C_2) = \ln(C_1) + \beta \ln(C_2)$

(b) $U(C_1, C_2) = \dfrac{C_1}{1-\gamma} + \beta\dfrac{C_2}{1-\gamma}$

(c) $U(C_1, C_2) = \Psi - \left(\dfrac{1}{\alpha}\right)e^{(-\alpha C_1)} - \left(\dfrac{\beta}{\alpha}\right)e^{(-\alpha C_2)}$

6. Develop and solve a Lagrangian function for a three-period intertemporal consumption model. In this model there will be savings in the first and second periods but not in the third period. The utility function is

$$U(C_1, C_2, C_3) = U(C_1) + \alpha U(C_2) + \beta U(C_3),$$

where $0 < \beta < \alpha < 1$.

7. Consider an extension of the model of the effect of college scholarship rules on savings by considering a problem in which there is an exogenous level of second-period income, Y_2; families enjoy second-period consumption, C_2; and retirement spending occurs after the second period. (You can still use a two-period model in this case.) Also assume that there is a positive interest rate *r*.

(a) Develop the first-period and second-period budget constraints in this case, and use these to develop a consolidated intertemporal budget constraint.

---

[8]"Monopolistic competition and optimum product diversity," *American Economic Review* 67, no. 2 (June 1977): 297–308.

(b) Assume the utility function is

$$U(C_1, C_2, E, R) = 2\sqrt{C_1} + 2\beta\sqrt{C_2} + 2\beta\sqrt{E} + 2\beta^2\sqrt{R},$$

where β is the subjective discount rate and $1 > \beta > 0$. Set up and solve the Lagrangian function

8. Extend the two-period intertemporal consumption model by assuming that the consumer has an initial stock of wealth, W_0. How does a nonzero initial stock of wealth alter the ratio of optimal consumption in the two periods?

9. Consider the application on Gary Becker's model of optimal allocation of time. As with Becker's model, assume your utility is derived from the consumption process rather than from the good itself so that your utility function is

$$U(A_1, A_2) = \frac{1}{2}\ln(A_1) + \frac{1}{2}\ln(A_2),$$

where A_i are the set of activities in which you consume the set of goods G_i. The ith activity requires G_i/n_i units of a good and t_i/h_i hours of time, where n_i and h_i are units of goods and units of time, respectively, per one unit of activity i. Assume that there are only two activities and

$$n_1 = 2, \quad n_2 = 6, \quad h_1 = 2, \quad \text{and} \quad h_2 = 2.4.$$

Assume that you are a working parent facing both time and financial constraints. The total time available to you is

$$T = W + t_1 + t_2 = 24,$$

where W represents work, t_1 is the time you spend caring for your children and household, and t_2 is the time you have exclusively for yourself. Your financial constraint reflects the assumption that your total income, wW, is spent on either good 1 or good 2 as given by

$$wW = P_1G_1 + P_2G_2,$$

where $P_1 = 3$, $P_2 = 2$, and $w = 5$. Combining the time and financial constraints into a consolidated constraint that defines the money value of total time and rewriting the constraint in terms of activities rather than goods, we have

$$wT = P_1n_1A_1 + P_2n_2A_2 + wh_1A_1 + wh_2A_2.$$

(a) Set up a Lagrangian function, and determine the values of A_1 and A_2. Use your results to calculate how much time you would spend at work, caring for your household, and pursuing your own leisure activities given your time constraint.

(b) Solve for G_1 and G_2 to determine how your total income is spent.

(c) Suppose that a new, high-powered vacuum cleaner that dramatically reduces the amount of time you spend cleaning your house is invented. Predict the impact of this technological change on the relative amount of activity A_1.

(d) Suppose that, in your limited free time, you decide to get in shape. After months of going to the gym, you can now run five miles in the same amount of time that it used to take you to run three (a decrease in n_2). Predict the impact of this change on the relative amount of activity A_2.

(e) Suppose your manager gives you a significant raise. What is the impact on consumption of A_1 and A_2 given that, initially, $h_1 < h_2$?

11.4 OPTIMIZATION WITH INEQUALITY CONSTRAINTS

The optimization problems presented in Sections 11.1, 11.2, and 11.3 have constraints that hold with equality. Optimization problems may have constraints that take the form of inequalities rather than equalities. Sometimes these inequality constraints require that the consumption of a good is nonnegative, that is, $C \geq 0$. In other problems, constraints may be more naturally expressed as inequalities rather than equalities. For example, the liquidity constraint presented previously may be thought of as $S + J \leq 24$ rather than $S + J = 24$. A modification of the Lagrange multiplier method offers a technique for solving optimization problems in which the constraints take the form of inequalities. This technique is outlined in this section.

The basic framework for maximizing a multivariate function $f(x_1, x_2, \ldots, x_n)$ subject to the m inequality constraints $g^i(x_1, x_2, \ldots, x_n) \leq c_i$ uses the Lagrangian function

$$L(x_1, \ldots, x_n, \lambda_1, \ldots, \lambda_m) = f(x_1, \ldots, x_n) - \sum_{i=1}^{m} \lambda_i(g^i(x_1, \ldots, x_n) - c_i), \quad (11.11)$$

which is identical to the one presented in (11.10). The solution to this problem satisfies the conditions

$$\begin{aligned} \frac{\partial L(x_1, \ldots, x_n, \lambda)}{\partial x_j} &= 0 \quad \text{for} \quad j = 1, 2, \ldots, n, \\ g^i(x_1, \ldots, x_n) &\leq c_i \quad \text{for} \quad i = 1, 2, \ldots, m, \\ \lambda_i &\geq 0 \quad \text{for} \quad i = 1, 2, \ldots, m, \quad \text{and} \\ \lambda_i(c_i - g^i(x_1, \ldots, x_n)) &= 0 \quad \text{for} \quad i = 1, 2, \ldots, m. \end{aligned} \quad (11.12)$$

These are the **Kuhn-Tucker conditions** for the solution of optimization problems with inequality constraints.

Just as the Lagrangian function (11.11) looks much like the Lagrangian function (11.10), some of the Kuhn-Tucker conditions (11.12) are much like those for problems with equality constraints which are given in (11.4). The condition setting the derivatives of the Lagrangian function with respect to the arguments of the objective function equal to zero is identical to the condition for optimization problems with equality constraints. The condition that

$$g^i(x_1, x_2, \ldots, x_n) \leq c_i$$

for all constraints is comparable to the condition requiring all constraints to hold with equality, which is used in problems with equality constraints.

The other two Kuhn-Tucker conditions are called the **complementary slackness conditions.** These can be understood with reference to the discussion in Section 11.2, which shows that the value of the Lagrange multiplier represents the marginal benefit from relaxing the constraint. The first of these, the condition requiring all Lagrange multipliers to be nonnegative, means that relaxing any constraint does not decrease the optimal value of the objective function. The final Kuhn-Tucker condition,

$$\lambda_i(c_i - g^i(x_1, x_2, \ldots, x_n)) = 0,$$

requires that either $\lambda_i = 0$ or $c_i = g^i(x_1, x_2, \ldots, x_n)$ or that both of these hold. In the case where $c_i = g^i(x_1, x_2, \ldots, x_n)$, the constraint is **binding** or **active.** In this case the ith Lagrange multiplier need not equal zero, which reflects the fact that an increase in the constraint increases the value of the objective function. In contrast, the fourth condition requires that the ith Lagrange multiplier equals zero when the constraint is **nonbinding** or **inactive,** that is, when $c_i > g^i(x_1, x_2, \ldots, x_n)$. The intuition here is that there must be no benefit from relaxing the constraint at the optimum if the constraint is not binding there.

As an example of the use of the Kuhn-Tucker conditions, consider the problem of maximizing the objective function

$$f(x, y) = x - \frac{x^2}{2} + y^2$$

subject to the constraints

$$\frac{x^2}{2} + y^2 \leq \frac{9}{8}$$
$$-y \leq 0.$$

Notice that the constraint that y is nonnegative is written in a way to make it conformable with the setup of the problem given above. The Lagrangian, in this case, is

$$L = x - \frac{x^2}{2} + y^2 - \lambda\left(\frac{x^2}{2} + y^2 - \frac{9}{8}\right) - \mu(-y).$$

The optimal choice of x and y satisfies the conditions

$$\begin{aligned}
\frac{\partial L}{\partial x} &= 1 - x - \lambda x = 0, \\
\frac{\partial L}{\partial y} &= 2y - 2\lambda y + \mu = 0, \\
\frac{x^2}{2} + y^2 &\leq \frac{9}{8}, \\
-y &\leq 0, \\
\lambda &\geq 0, \\
\mu &\geq 0, \\
\lambda\left(\frac{9}{8} - \frac{x^2}{2} - y^2\right) &= 0, \quad \text{and} \\
\mu y &= 0.
\end{aligned}$$

We proceed by considering solutions that arise in four cases corresponding to the four possible ways in which the complementary slackness conditions may be met. These cases are

$$\begin{aligned}
\lambda = 0 &\quad \text{and} \quad \mu = 0, \\
\lambda \neq 0 &\quad \text{and} \quad \mu = 0, \\
\lambda = 0 &\quad \text{and} \quad \mu \neq 0, \\
\lambda \neq 0 &\quad \text{and} \quad \mu \neq 0.
\end{aligned}$$

We then compare the value of the objective function for each solution to find the optimal choice of x and y.

We first find a solution where $\lambda = 0$ and $\mu = 0$. In this case the condition $\partial L/\partial x = 0$ shows that $x = 1$, and the condition $\partial L/\partial y = 0$ shows that $y = 0$. The pair of values $x = 1$, $y = 0$ satisfies the constraint

$$\frac{x^2}{2} + y^2 \leq \frac{9}{8}$$

as well as the constraint that y is nonnegative. The value of the objective function for these values of x and y is $f(1, 0) = \frac{1}{2}$.

We next find a solution where $\lambda \neq 0$ and $\mu = 0$. In this case the first-order condition $\partial L/\partial y = 0$ requires that $\lambda = 1$, which satisfies the condition that $\lambda \geq 0$. This, in turn, requires that $x = \frac{1}{2}$ satisfy the condition $\partial L/\partial x = 0$. The complementary slackness condition requires that

$$\frac{9}{8} - \frac{(1/2)^2}{2} - y^2 = 0,$$

which is satisfied for $y = 1$ or $y = -1$. But the constraint that y is nonnegative allows us to consider only the solution $y = 1$. The value of the objective function for $x = \frac{1}{2}$ and $y = 1$ is $f\left(\frac{1}{2}, 1\right) = \frac{11}{8}$.

We next consider a solution where $\lambda = 0$ and $\mu \neq 0$. In this case the condition $\partial L/\partial x = 0$ shows that $x = 1$. The condition $\mu y = 0$ requires that $y = 0$. Therefore this solution is identical to the one found for $\lambda = 0$ and $\mu = 0$, and, as in that case, the value of the objective function is $f(1, 0) = \frac{1}{2}$.

Finally, we consider whether we can find a solution where $\lambda \neq 0$ and $\mu \neq 0$. The condition $\mu y = 0$ requires that $y = 0$. But if $y = 0$, then the condition $\partial L/\partial y = 0$ requires $\mu = 0$. Therefore there is no solution in which $\lambda \neq 0$ and $\mu \neq 0$.

Ranking these solutions by the value of the objective function, we find that the optimum is $x = \frac{1}{2}$ and $y = 1$ since

$$f\left(\frac{1}{2}, 1\right) > f(1, 0).$$

This optimal solution is one where $\lambda \neq 0$ and $\mu = 0$. Therefore, at the optimal solution,

$$\frac{x^2}{2} + y^2 = \frac{9}{8},$$

and this constraint is binding, while

$$-y < 0,$$

and this constraint is not binding.

The general formulation outlined here can be modified as needed to fit the problem. For example, if the problem is one of finding the constrained minimum value of the function $h(x_1, x_2)$, just define $f(x_1 x_2) = -h(x_1, x_2)$, and then proceed with the method for maximizing the function presented above. In a similar manner, the inequality constraint $j(x_1, x_2) \geq z$ can be made conformable to the conditions required above by rewriting it as $-j(x_1x_2) \leq z$. In mixed problems with equality and inequality constraints, the equality constraints must hold exactly (as with the examples in Section 11.2), while the inequality constraints may be binding or nonbinding.

Exercises 11.4

1. Find the maximum value of the function
$$h(x, y) = 2x^2 - y^2$$
subject to the constraint that
$$x^2 + y^2 = 1$$
and the constraint that x and y are nonnegative.

2. Find the maximum value of the function
$$r(a, b) = 2a^2 + b^2$$
subject to the constraints
$$2a + b \leq 9 \quad \text{and}$$
$$a^2 + b^2 \geq 16.$$

3. Consider the three-item lunch problem presented earlier where the utility function is
$$U(S, V, J) = \frac{1}{3}\ln(S) + \frac{1}{3}\ln(V) + \frac{1}{3}\ln(J)$$
but the constraints are
$$\frac{S}{4} + \frac{V}{2} + \frac{J}{12} \leq 6 \quad \text{and}$$
$$S + J \leq 40,$$
where S represents ounces of soup, V represents ounces of salad, and J represents ounces of juice.
   (a) Set up the Lagrangian function for this problem.
   (b) Find the optimal solution for this problem. Be sure to check that this solution satisfies all the complementary slackness conditions.

4. In question 6 of Section 11.2, we present a firm with the Cobb-Douglas production function
$$Q = AK^{\alpha}L^{1-\alpha},$$
where $L \geq 0$ and $K \geq 0$. This firm faces the linear cost function
$$C = wL + rK,$$
where w is the wage rate and r is the rental rate paid on capital.
   (a) Set up a Lagrangian function reflecting the constrained optimization problem of obtaining the most output given that the cost of inputs must be less than or equal to a given budget $\overline{C}$. Solve for the optimal levels of capital and labor.

(b) Set up a Lagrangian function reflecting the constrained optimization problem of minimizing input costs given that the level of output must be less than or equal to an amount $\bar{Q}$. Solve this for the optimal levels of capital and labor. Remember to define the objective function in a constrained minimization problem as $f(x_1, x_2) = -h(x_1, x_2)$.

(c) How do your results compare to those obtained in question 6 of Section 11.2? What is the intuition behind these results?

5. Consider again the issue of optimal time allocation. Assume that you have a utility function defined over two goods, x_1 and x_2, such that your utility function is $u(x_1, x_2)$. Suppose it takes t_1 units of time to consume x_1 units of pizza and t_2 units of time to consume x_2 units of beer. The total time available for consumption is T. Your challenge is to maximize your utility subject to your income constraint

$$p_1x_1 + p_2x_2 \leq m$$

and time constraint

$$t_1x_1 + t_2x_2 \leq T.$$

Assume that both $x_1$and x_2 are strictly positive at the optimum and $u_i(x_1, x_2)$ is positive, reflecting nonsatiation.

(a) Set up a Lagrangian function in which utility is maximized subject to both the income and time constraint.

(b) Consider the four solution possibilities to this problem based on the four possible ways in which the complementary slackness conditions might be met:

$$\lambda = 0 \quad \text{and} \quad \mu = 0,$$
$$\lambda = 0 \quad \text{and} \quad \mu \neq 0,$$
$$\lambda \neq 0 \quad \text{and} \quad \mu = 0,$$
$$\lambda \neq 0 \quad \text{and} \quad \mu = 0.$$

Which is most likely to yield the optimal solution?

Summary

The constrained optimization framework reflects the basic economic problem of obtaining the best outcome when faced with constraints. This chapter presents several techniques for explicitly solving constrained optimization problems. One method for solving constrained optimization problems involves using the constraint to substitute for one variable and then using the techniques presented in Chapters 9 and 10 to find the optimum value of the function that internalizes the constraint.

A second technique for solving problems with equality constraints is the Lagrange multiplier method. This technique requires the construction of a Lagrangian function that incorporates the objective function, any constraints, and Lagrange multipliers. The computation of the solution is often simpler with the Lagrange multiplier method than with the substitution method. Another advantage of this technique is that the Lagrange multiplier provides information on the effect on the objective function of small changes in the constraint.

The solution technique for optimization problems with inequality constraints is outlined in Section 11.4. Some of the Kuhn-Tucker conditions presented there are comparable to the conditions required by the Lagrange multiplier method presented in Section 11.2. In addition, the Kuhn-Tucker conditions require complementary slackness such that the Lagrange multiplier is zero if the constraint is nonbinding or nonzero if the constraint is binding.

The discussions in Section 11.3, as well as the end-of-section problems, reflect the range of economic applications of constrained optimization. A mastery of the material presented in this chapter is very important in virtually all fields of economics.

Part Five

Integration and Dynamic Analysis

Time plays a central role in many areas of economics, including finance, macroeconomics, and environmental economics. The four chapters that constitute this part of the book present techniques and tools that will enable you to understand ***dynamic analysis.*** *Dynamic analysis focuses on the evolution of variables over time. The applications in this part of the book draw from finance, macroeconomics, microeconomics, international economics, and resource economics.*

Part Five begins with Chapter 12, which presents ***integral calculus.*** *An important use of integral calculus in economics is valuing a stream of payments. We develop the basic concepts of integration by determining the present value of the stream of payments from a bond. An application in this chapter uses integration to explain why the price of a long-maturity bond is more volatile than the price of a bond that has a shorter maturity but is otherwise similar. There are other uses of integration in economics. One application* *demonstrates how integration is used to determine consumer's surplus. Another application uses integration to estimate the social cost of inflation. We show the use of integration in developing measures of income inequality. Integration is also important for the study of probability and statistics, as is illustrated by another application in Chapter 12.*

Chapters 13 and 14 present methods for studying dynamic equations. The equations studied in Chapter 13 are called ***difference equations.*** *A difference equation links the value of a variable in one period to its value in one or more other periods and treats time as a sequence of distinct periods. In contrast,* ***differential equations,*** *the subject of Chapter 14, treat time as a continuous stream of moments. Differential equations link the instantaneous rate of change of a variable to its level. Despite the distinctions between difference equations and differential equations, these chapters show the many common links between them. The applications in these chapters include a model of equity prices, three different models of the exchange rate, a model of income determination, and a mathematical presentation of an economic framework first presented by David Hume in the eighteenth century.*

This book concludes with a chapter on ***dynamic optimization.*** *Dynamic optimization offers a technique for determining the optimal time path of a variable given some objective function and some dynamic relationship that serves as a constraint. The first part of this chapter uses the Lagrange multiplier method to solve dynamic optimization problems in discrete time. The particular example used to illustrate this technique is a firm's optimal investment activity. The chapter then presents the method for solving a similar problem in continuous time. The continuous time result, known as the* ***Maximum Principle,*** *is shown to be analogous to the discrete time result presented in the first section of the chapter. Applications in this chapter include optimal consumption for a family and the optimal rate of depletion of a natural resource.*

Chapter 12

Integral Calculus

Many concepts in economics reflect the summation of values over a number of goods, individuals, firms, or time periods. For example, the aggregation of net value over goods purchased is used in constructing the welfare measure of consumer's surplus. Summing consumer's surplus over all individuals yields the market-wide measures of surplus for all consumers. Aggregation over time is important in macroeconomic analysis and finance theory. The macroeconomic concept of permanent income represents the discounted sum of the stream of future income. The price of an asset reflects the discounted sum of the value of the stream of payments it offers.

These aggregate values can often be expressed as sums, but sums may be cumbersome to calculate when there are a large number of individuals, items, or time periods. Moreover, functions used in economics are often continuous rather than discrete since they identify a continuum of goods, individuals, firms, or time periods. Aggregation over a continuum can only be approximated by a summation. The actual value can be calculated through the mathematical technique of **integration,** a technique that is the focus of **integral calculus.**

This chapter presents integral calculus. Section 12.1 develops the intuition for integration through a geometric representation of the area under the graph of a continuous function. This is followed by a presentation of the basic result of integral calculus, which is then supported by a discussion of the Fundamental Theorem of Calculus. Section 12.2 applies this concept to developing rules of integration. Section 12.3 offers some applications that demonstrate the use of integral calculus in economics.

12.1 INTEGRALS AS THE AREA UNDER A CURVE

The area between the graph of a function and the x-axis is a geometric representation of the aggregate value of that function over an interval. There are many examples in economics in which the aggregate value of a function is important. For example, in elementary microeconomics, you are taught that the area under a marginal revenue function represents total revenue. Figure 12.1 provides an example of this. This figure presents the demand curve facing a monopolist who sells access to the Web site "Portraits of Famous Economists" on the Internet. The inverse demand function represented in this diagram is

$$P = 100 - 2Q,$$

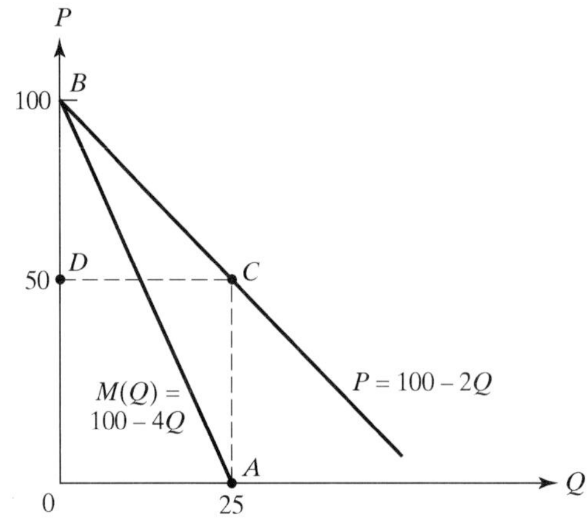

FIGURE 12.1 Demand and Marginal Revenue for a Web Site

where P is the price of an annual subscription to the Web site and Q is the number of subscribers per year. We find the marginal revenue function by taking the derivative of total revenue with respect to quantity. In this case the marginal revenue function $M(Q)$ is

$$M(Q) = 100 - 4Q.$$

We assume that the marginal cost of providing access to the Web site is zero. Therefore the profit-maximizing quantity, where marginal revenue equals marginal cost, is $Q = 25$. At this quantity, $P = 50$. The area under the marginal revenue function, represented by the triangle $0AB$ in the figure, equals one-half of the product of its base times its height. This triangle has a base equal to 25 and a height equal to 100, so its area is $1/2 \times 25 \times 100 = 1250$. This is also equal to the area of the rectangle $0ACD$. The area of a rectangle is the product of its base and its height, which, in this case, is quantity (25) times price $(P = 100 - 2 \cdot 25 = 50)$.

While it is a simple matter to calculate the area of a rectangle or a triangle traced out by a linear function, it is not clear what we mean by the area under the graph of a continuous nonlinear function. Integral calculus offers a way to both precisely define and evaluate such areas. We begin our study of integral calculus with an economic problem that involves finding the area under a nonlinear function: the calculation of the present value of a stream of continuous payments.

Valuing a Stream of Payments

Present value represents the equivalent value today of some amount received in the future. As discussed in Chapter 3, the present value of a one-time payment of $\$X$ received at a time T periods from the current period, when compounded continuously at the interest rate r, is

$$\$X \cdot e^{-rT}.$$

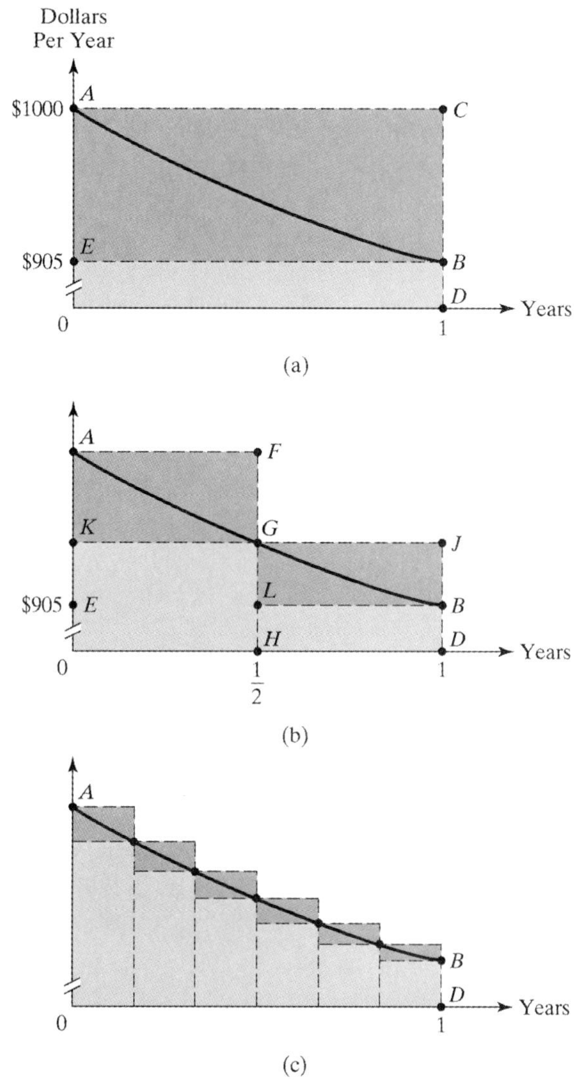

FIGURE 12.2 Discrete Approximation to a Continuous Payment

This formula shows that the present value of a given payment decreases as the time of payment moves further into the future.

A series of discrete payments can be valued by summing the present value of each payment. The value of a stream of continuous payments, however, can only be approximated by the sum of a series of discrete payments. As an example of this, consider an asset that provides a continuous stream of payments such that it pays $1,000 over the course of one year and the relevant interest rate on an alternative asset is 10% (that is, $r = 0.10$). How much is that asset worth at the beginning of the year, or equivalently, what is the asset's price? Figure 12.2(a) presents a geometric representation of this problem. The y-axis in this figure represents the value of the payment in dollars per year, and the x-axis represents time in years. We see that the exact value of this asset is represented by the area under the graph of the function

$$\$1{,}000 \cdot e^{-0.10t}$$

for $t = 0$ to 1, which is represented by the irregularly shaped figure $0ABD$ in Figure 12.2(a).

We can find an upper bound to the value of the asset by calculating the present value as if the bond were paid immediately. This represents an overestimate of the value of the stream of continuous payments. An asset that pays \$1,000 immediately is obviously worth \$1,000, and this value is represented by the area of the rectangle $0ACD$ in Figure 12.2(a). Using the present value formula, we find that the height $0A$ is equal to

$$\$1{,}000/\text{year} \cdot e^{-0.10/\text{year}\cdot 0\text{ years}} = \$1{,}000/\text{year}.$$

The base of $0ACD$ is 1 year. Therefore the value corresponding to the area $0ACD$ is \$1,000.

We can also find a lower bound to the value of the asset by calculating the present value as if no payments were made until the end of the year. This represents an underestimate of the value of the stream of continuous payments. The value of an asset that pays \$1,000 only at the end of the year is represented by the rectangle $0EBD$. The height of this rectangle, represented by the distance $0E$, equals

$$\$1{,}000/\text{year} \cdot e^{-0.10/\text{year}\cdot 1\text{ year}} = \$905/\text{year}.$$

The base of this rectangle is 1 year, and, therefore, the value represented by $0EBD$ is \$905.

More accurate approximations of the area $0ABD$ can be obtained by splitting the period into two subperiods and then either summing the two rectangles representing the overestimate of each period or the two rectangles representing the underestimate of each period. A smaller overestimate of the area $0ABD$ is presented in Figure 12.2(b). Here the area of the rectangle $0AFH$ represents an approximation of the value of the asset over the first 6 months, and the area of the rectangle $HGJD$ represents the value of the asset over the second 6 months. The area of $0AFH$ equals

$$\$1{,}000/\text{year} \cdot e^{0.10/\text{year}\cdot 0\text{ years}} \cdot \frac{1}{2}\text{ year} = \$500,$$

and the area of $HGJD$ equals

$$\$1{,}000/\text{year} \cdot e^{-0.10/\text{year}\cdot 1/2\text{ year}} \cdot \frac{1}{2}\text{ year} = \$476.$$

This overestimate of \$976, which is the sum of the areas of $0AFH$ and $HGJD$, is less than the overestimate of \$1,000 from the single rectangle $0ACD$. Likewise, an underestimate of $0ABD$ based on the sum of the areas of two rectangles, one evaluating the value of the stream of payments over the first 6 months ($0KGH$) and one evaluating the value of the stream of payments over the second 6 months ($HLBD$), is

$$\$1{,}000/\text{year} \cdot e^{-0.10/\text{year} \cdot 1/2\ \text{year}} \cdot \frac{1}{2}\ \text{year} = \$476$$

plus

$$\$1{,}000/\text{year} \cdot e^{-0.10/\text{year} \cdot 1\ \text{year}} \cdot \frac{1}{2}\ \text{year} = \$452.$$

This sum, \$928, is greater than the approximation based on the area of the single rectangle $0EBD$.

We could further refine our estimates of the area $0ABD$ by splitting the year into more subperiods. The number of subperiods used in an approximation equals the number of rectangles employed in either an overestimate or an underestimate. For example, in Figure 12.2(c), there are six subperiods. The area of the six rectangles that overestimate the area $0ABD$ is

$$\sum_{i=0}^{5} \$1{,}000/\text{year} \cdot e^{-0.10/\text{year} \cdot (i \cdot 1/6\ \text{year})} \cdot \frac{1}{6}\ \text{year} = \$960.$$

The area of the six rectangles that underestimate the area $0ABD$ is

$$\sum_{i=1}^{6} \$1{,}000/\text{year} \cdot e^{-0.10/\text{year} \cdot (i \cdot 1/6\ \text{year})} \cdot \frac{1}{6}\ \text{year} = \$944.$$

More generally, the formula for an overestimate of the area $0ABD$ based upon a division of the year into n equal-sized subperiods is

$$\sum_{i=0}^{n-1} \$1{,}000/\text{year} \cdot e^{-0.10/\text{year} \cdot (i \cdot 1/n\ \text{year})} \cdot \frac{1}{n}\ \text{year}, \tag{12.1}$$

while a general formula for an underestimate of the area with n subperiods is

$$\sum_{i=1}^{n} \$1{,}000/\text{year} \cdot e^{-0.10/\text{year} \cdot (i \cdot 1/n\ \text{year})} \cdot \frac{1}{n}\ \text{year}. \tag{12.2}$$

The two formulas (12.1) and (12.2) differ only in the limits of the sums. In particular, denoting the area of the overestimate as A_1 and the area of the underestimate as A_2, we have

$$A_1 = \frac{\$1000/\text{year}}{n} \cdot e^0 + A_C$$

and

$$A_2 = A_C + \frac{\$1000/\text{year}}{n} \cdot e^{-0.10},$$

where the amount common to each sum, A_C, is

$$A_C = \sum_{i=1}^{n-1} \$1{,}000/\text{year} \cdot e^{-0.10/\text{year} \cdot (i \cdot 1/n\text{year})} \cdot \frac{1}{n}\ \text{year}.$$

The difference between the overestimate and the underestimate equals

$$A_1 - A_2 = \frac{\$1{,}000}{n}(e^0 - e^{-0.10})$$
$$= \frac{\$1000}{n}(0.095).$$

This result shows that the difference between the overestimate and the underestimate is \$47.50 when the estimates are based on two 6-month periods and \$15.83 when the estimates are based on six 2-month periods. It is easy to see from this formula that the difference between the overestimate and the underestimate approaches zero as the number of subperiods approaches infinity since

$$\lim_{n\to\infty}[A_1 - A_2] = \lim_{n\to\infty}\left[\frac{\$1{,}000/\text{year}}{n}(e^0 - e^{-0.10})\right] = 0.$$

Therefore the exact value of A_C is the limit of the previous sum as $n \to \infty$.

Generalizing these results, we find that the formulas for an overestimate of the area under a graph of a decreasing monotonic function $f(x)$ over the range of the value of x from a to b is

$$A_1 = \sum_{i=0}^{n-1} f(x_i)\cdot\frac{b-a}{n}$$

and the formula for an underestimate of the area is

$$A_2 = \sum_{i=1}^{n} f(x_i)\cdot\frac{b-a}{n},$$

where $x_i = a + i\cdot(b-a)/n$. If, instead, the function is increasing over the range from a to b, these formulas still provide the appropriate approximations, but $A_2 > A_1$ since, in this case, A_2 represents the overestimate and A_1 represents the underestimate.

We define

$$\Delta x = x_{i+1} - x_i = \frac{b-a}{n}.$$

This allows us to write the formulas for the areas as

$$A_1 = \sum_{i=0}^{n-1} f(x_i)\cdot\Delta x \tag{12.3}$$

and

$$A_2 = \sum_{i=1}^{n} f(x_i)\cdot\Delta x. \tag{12.4}$$

More accurate measures of the true area under the graph of the function $f(x)$ over the interval (a, b), which we call A_a^b, are obtained as we divide the range (a, b) into a larger number of equal-sized increments. As the number of increments increases and n

approaches infinity, we have

$$\lim_{n\to\infty} A_1 = \lim_{n\to\infty} A_2 = A_a^b.$$

We next turn to the evaluation of A_a^b.

The Definite Integral

The previous discussion leads us to define the **definite integral,** also called the **Riemann integral,** as

$$\int_a^b f(x)\,dx = \lim_{n\to\infty} \sum_{i=0}^{n-1} f(x_i)\cdot\Delta x,$$

where $\int_a^b f(x)\,dx$ is read as "the integral of $f(x)$ from a to b" and x_i and Δx are as we defined them earlier. We define the area under a curve over the range a to b, which we denote as A_a^b, as

$$A_a^b = \int_a^b f(x)\,dx. \tag{12.5}$$

This definite integral has the **lower limit** a and the **upper limit** b. The integral sign, $\int$, was chosen by the mathematician Gottfried von Leibnitz (who, with Issac Newton, developed calculus) because it is similar to the printed letter *S*, which begins the German word for summation. As with Σ, which is the Greek letter closest to *S*, you can think of $\int$ as representing a type of sum. The integral sign and the term dx form a kind of package. The x in dx is the **variable of integration,** and it indicates the variable in the function $f(x)$, which is called the **integrand,** over which the integration occurs. For example, the integral

$$\int_a^b f(x, y)\,dx$$

requires integrating the bivariate function $f(x, y)$ over the value of x, while the integral

$$\int_a^b f(x, y)\,dy$$

requires integrating the bivariate function $f(x, y)$ over the variable y.

The discussion in the previous section shows that we can think of the definite integral as

$$\int_a^b f(x)\,dx = \lim_{n\to\infty} A_1 = \lim_{n\to\infty} A_2.$$

The upper and lower limits of the integral can be understood in terms of the limits of the sums. Consider the formulas (12.3) and (12.4) where $x_0 = a$, $x_n = b$, and $\Delta x = (b - a)/n$. The lower limit of the sum

$$A_1 = \sum_{i=0}^{n-1} f(x_i)\cdot\Delta x$$

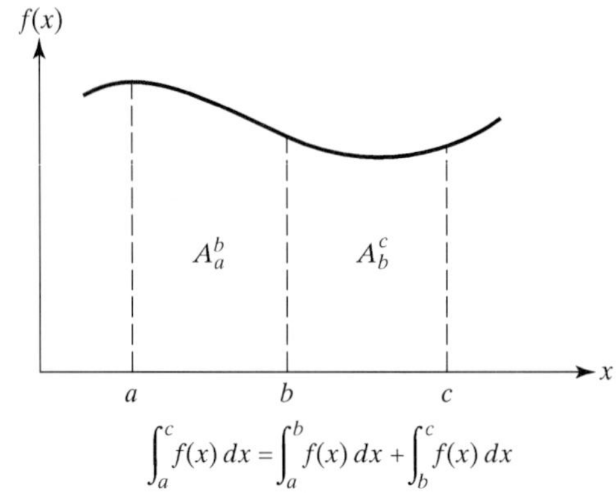

FIGURE 12.3 The Additive Rule for Integrals

is $x_0 = a$, and its upper limit is $x_{n-1} = (a + (n - 1)\,\Delta x) = (a + (n - 1)((b - a)/n))$. As n approaches infinity, this upper limit of the sum approaches b since

$$\lim_{n\to\infty} x_{n-1} = \lim_{n\to\infty}\left(a + (n - 1)\frac{b - a}{n}\right) = \lim_{n\to\infty}\left(a + \frac{n - 1}{n}(b - a)\right) = b.$$

The upper limit of the sum

$$A_2 = \sum_{i=1}^{n} f(x_i)\cdot\Delta x$$

is $x_n = b$, and its lower limit is $x_1 = (a + \Delta x) = (a + (b-a)/n)$. As n approaches infinity, the lower limit of this sum approaches a.

Some properties of the definite integral with respect to its limits can be understood in the context of its definition as the area under a curve. If the limits of an integral are the same, then the base of the shape under the curve is zero, and the area must equal zero. This gives us the rule that

$$\int_a^a f(x)\,dx = 0. \tag{12.6}$$

The area over a given range of the argument of a function, say a to c, can be expressed as the sum of the area over two parts of that range, say a to b and b to c, as shown in Figure 12.3. The **additive rule for integrals** states that

$$A_a^c = A_a^b + A_b^c$$

or, in terms of the definite integrals,

$$\int_a^c f(x)\,dx = \int_a^b f(x)\,dx + \int_b^c f(x)\,dx. \tag{12.7}$$

This discussion of the definite integral as the representation of the area under a function from a to b supposes that b is greater than a. If a is greater than b, then the integral is defined to be negative since we are moving from a greater to a lesser value of the variable of integration. Therefore

$$\int_b^a f(x)\,dx = -\int_a^b f(x)\,dx. \tag{12.8}$$

Although we have presented the definite integral, we have not yet shown how to evaluate it. Next we turn to the basic result required for evaluating integrals. This result, called the Fundamental Theorem of Calculus, links integration and differentiation.

Evaluating Definite Integrals

Evaluating the definite integral

$$\int_a^b f(t)\,dt$$

to calculate the area under the graph of the continuous function $f(t)$ from $t = a$ to $t = b$ involves two steps. First we need to find the **antiderivative** of the function $f(t)$, which we call $F(t)$. The derivative of $F(t)$ is the function $f(t)$. For example, the function

$$f(t) = 5t$$

has an antiderivative

$$F(t) = \frac{5t^2}{2}$$

since

$$\frac{dF(t)}{dt} = 5t = f(t).$$

But note that the function $H(t) = F(t) + C$, where C is a constant, is also an antiderivative of $f(t)$ since

$$\frac{dH(t)}{dt} = \frac{dF(t)}{dt} + \frac{dC}{dt} = f(t).$$

Therefore, given one antiderivative of a function, we can find another antiderivative of that function by simply adding a constant to the first antiderivative.

The second part of the Fundamental Theorem of Calculus (which corresponds to the second step) shows that

$$\int_a^b f(t)\,dt = H(b) - H(a), \tag{12.9}$$

where $H(b)$ is any antiderivative evaluated at the upper limit, b, and $H(a)$ is the same antiderivative evaluated at the lower limit, a. For example, we could evaluate the integral $\int_4^6 5t\,dt$ as follows.

$$\begin{aligned}\int_4^6 5t\,dt &= \left.\frac{5t^2}{2}\right|_4^6 \\ &= \frac{5(6^2)}{2} - \frac{5(4^2)}{2} = 50,\end{aligned}$$

where t is the variable of integration, $5t$ is the integrand, and

$$\left.\frac{5t^2}{2}\right|_4^6$$

is a shorthand way to denote

$$\frac{5(6^2)}{2} - \frac{5(4^2)}{2}.$$

Some examples illustrate the two steps of evaluating a definite integral, finding the antiderivative and subtracting the antiderivative evaluated at the lower limit from the antiderivative evaluated at the upper limit. The triangle $0AB$ in Figure 12.1 is defined by the function

$$M(Q) = 100 - 4Q$$

over the range $Q = 0$ to $Q = 25$. The area of this triangle can be found by evaluating the integral

$$\int_0^{25} (100 - 4Q)\, dQ,$$

where Q is the variable of integration and $M(Q) = 100 - 4Q$ is the integrand. The antiderivative of the integrand is easily confirmed to be

$$R(Q) = 100Q - 2Q^2 + C$$

since $dR(Q)/dQ = M(Q)$. Evaluating the function $R(Q)$ over the limits of the integral, we find

$$\begin{aligned} R(25) - R(0) &= (100 \cdot 25 - 2 \cdot 25^2 + C) - (100 \cdot 0 - 2 \cdot 0^2 + C) \\ &= 1250. \end{aligned}$$

We can determine the area of the rectangle $0DCA$ in Figure 12.1, which represents the constant-value function $w(Q) = 50$ over the range $Q = 0$ to $Q = 25$, by evaluating the integral

$$\int_0^{25} 50\, dQ,$$

where Q is the variable of integration. The antiderivative of the constant-value integrand is

$$W(Q) = 50Q + C.$$

Evaluating this over the appropriate range, we have

$$W(25) - W(0) = (50(25) + C) - (50(0) + C) = 1250.$$

We can also use this method to solve the problem of valuing a continuous stream of payments. The definite integral representing the present value of a constant stream of payments of $\$X$ per year at an annual interest rate of r percent over n years is the area under a curve like that in Figure 12.2 and is equal to the definite integral

$$\int_0^n Xe^{-rt}\,dt,$$

where t is the variable of integration. For example, the present value of a continuous stream of payments of \$1,000 per year over three years when the interest rate is 5% is

$$\int_0^3 1000e^{-0.05\cdot t}\,dt.$$

You can confirm that the antiderivative of the integrand

$$v(t) = 1000\cdot e^{-0.05\cdot t}$$

is

$$V(t) = -1000\frac{1}{0.05}e^{-0.05t} + C$$

since

$$\frac{dV(t)}{dt} = -1000\frac{1}{0.05}(-0.05)e^{-0.05\cdot t} = 1000e^{-0.05\cdot t} = v(t).$$

Evaluating this for the lower limit 0 and the upper limit 3, we find

$$\begin{aligned} V(3) - V(0) &= \left(-\frac{1000}{0.05}e^{-0.15} + C\right) - \left(-\frac{1000}{0.05}e^{0} + C\right) \\ &= 20{,}000(1 - e^{-0.15}) \\ &\approx 2786. \end{aligned}$$

The Fundamental Theorem of Calculus

The technique we have presented for evaluating definite integrals draws on a link between integration and differentiation of continuous functions. The logic behind this link is most likely not readily apparent to you. This is to be expected since the theorem that demonstrates this link, the **Fundamental Theorem of Calculus,** is, according to the authors of a leading calculus textbook, "beautiful, powerful, deep, and unexpected. . . ."[1] In this section we present the Fundamental Theorem of Calculus and show how it supports the result (12.9).

Our development of the Fundamental Theorem of Calculus uses the **Mean Value Theorem for Definite Integrals,** which, in turn, draws on the **Max-Min Rule for Definite Integrals.** The Max-Min Rule states that if $\max(f)$ is the maximum value of the function $f(x)$ over an interval $[a, b]$ and $\min(f)$ is its minimum value over that

[1] George B. Thomas, Jr., and Ross L. Finney, *Calculus and Analytic Geometry,* 8th ed. (Reading, MA: Addison-Wesley, 1994.)

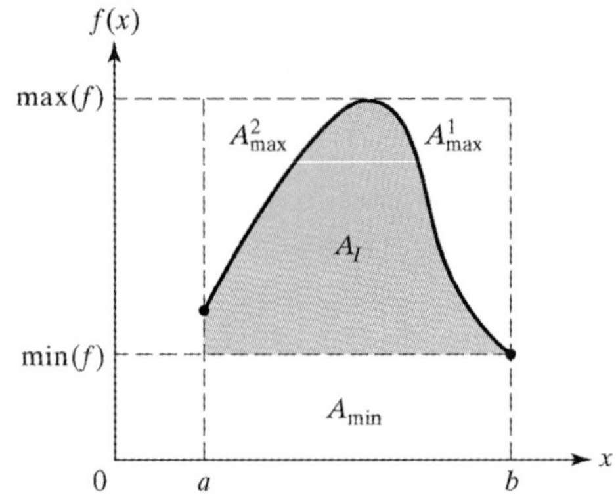

FIGURE 12.4 The Max-Min Rule

interval, then

$$\min(f)\cdot(b-a) \le \int_a^b f(x)\,dx \le \max(f)\cdot(b-a).$$

This rule is apparent from Figure 12.4. This figure includes the rectangle $A_{\min}$ which has base *ab* and height $\min(f)$, the shaded area A_I, and the two areas $A^1_{\max}$ and $A^2_{\max}$. In this figure

$$\min(f)\cdot(b-a) = A_{\min},$$
$$\int_a^b f(x)\,dx = A_{\min} + A_I,$$
$$\max(f)\cdot(b-a) = A_{\min} + A_I + A^1_{\max} + A^2_{\max},$$

and

$$A_{\min} \le A_{\min} + A_I \le A_{\min} + A_I + A^1_{\max} + A^2_{\max}.$$

The Mean Value Theorem for Definite Integrals states that there exists some number n in the interval $[a, b]$ such that

$$f(n) = \frac{1}{b-a}\int_a^b f(x)\,dx.$$

We obtain this theorem from the Max-Min Rule by dividing through the terms in that rule by $(b-a)$ and noting that

$$\min(f) \le \frac{1}{b-a}\int_a^b f(x)\,dx \le \max(f).$$

The Mean Value Theorem holds because $f(x)$ is a continuous function and because the integral in the above expression lies between $\min(f)$ and $\max(f)$. Therefore there is some n where $a \le n \le b$ such that $f(n)$ equals the integral.

We use the Mean Value Theorem in the first part of the Fundamental Theorem of Calculus to show that the function defined by

$$F(x) = \int_a^x f(t)\,dt$$

satisfies the relationship

$$\frac{dF(x)}{dx} = f(x).$$

We can analyze the derivative of the function $F(x)$ by first using the definition of the derivative from Chapter 6. This gives us

$$\frac{dF(x)}{dx} = \lim_{\Delta x \to 0} \frac{F(x + \Delta x) - F(x)}{\Delta x},$$

where, by the definition of the definite integral,

$$F(x + \Delta x) = \int_a^{x+\Delta x} f(t)\,dt.$$

Therefore the derivative of $F(x)$ can be written as

$$\begin{aligned}\frac{dF(x)}{dx} &= \lim_{\Delta x \to 0} \frac{1}{\Delta x}\left[\int_a^{x+\Delta x} f(t)dt - \int_a^x f(t)\,dt\right]\\ &= \lim_{\Delta x \to 0} \frac{1}{\Delta x}\left[\int_x^{x+\Delta x} f(t)\,dt\right].\end{aligned}$$

The Mean Value Theorem shows that, for some number n in the interval $[x, x + \Delta x]$,

$$f(n) = \frac{1}{(x + \Delta x) - x}\int_x^{x+\Delta x} f(t)\,dt = \frac{1}{\Delta x}\int_x^{x+\Delta x} f(t)\,dt.$$

As Δx approaches zero, the interval $[x, x + \Delta x]$ shrinks, and the number n must therefore approach x. Thus, since $f(x)$ is continuous,

$$\lim_{\Delta x \to 0} f(n) = \lim_{n \to x} f(n) = f(x)$$

and, therefore,

$$\lim_{\Delta x \to 0} \frac{1}{\Delta x}\left[\int_x^{x+\Delta x} f(t)\,dt\right] = f(x),$$

which gives us the result

$$\frac{dF(x)}{dx} = f(x).$$

This proves the first part of the Fundamental Theorem of Calculus; that is, $F(x)$ is an antiderivative of $f(x)$. The family of all antiderivatives of a function is also (and more commonly) called its **indefinite integral.** We write the indefinite integral of the function $f(x)$ as

$$\int f(x)\,dx.$$

The first part of the Fundamental Theorem of Calculus therefore shows that

$$\int f(x)\,dx = F(x) + C,$$

where C is an arbitrary constant called the **constant of integration,** which is included because the antiderivative is defined only up to an additive constant. Defining $H(x) = F(x) + C$, we have

$$\frac{dH(x)}{dx} = \frac{d(F(x) + C)}{dx} = \frac{dF(x)}{dx}.$$

The second part of the Fundamental Theorem of Calculus illustrates how to evaluate a definite integral. We have shown that, with the lower limit a and the upper limit x,

$$F(x) = \int_a^x f(t)\,dt = H(x) - C$$

for any arbitrary x. For a particular value of x, say $x = b$, we have

$$F(b) = \int_a^b f(t)\,dt = H(b) - C,$$

while $F(a)$ is

$$F(a) = \int_a^a f(t)\,dt = H(a) - C.$$

But also note that by (12.6)

$$F(a) = \int_a^a f(t)\,dt = 0.$$

Therefore $H(a) = C$, and, thus,

$$F(b) - F(a) = \int_a^b f(t)\,dt = H(b) - H(a) \tag{12.10}$$

for any antiderivative $H(x)$.

The Fundamental Theorem of Calculus shows that the definite integral evaluated at an upper and lower limit equals the difference between the antiderivatives evaluated at those limits. To use this result, we need to be able to evaluate the antiderivative of various integrands. Rules of integration that show how to evaluate antiderivatives of various functions are presented in the next section.

Exercises 12.1

1. Assume that you own an asset that provides you with a continuous stream of interest payments of \$1,000 over the course of one year, where the relevant interest rate

on an alternative asset is 6%. The exact representation of this asset is represented by the area under the function

$$1000e^{-0.06t}.$$

Answer the following to understand how the value of a continuous stream of payments is a approximated by a series of discrete payments.

(a) Find an upper bound to the value of this asset by calculating its present value as if it were paid today.

(b) Find the lower bound to the value of this asset as if it were paid only at the end of the year.

(c) Assume that the one-year period is split into 2 subperiods. Calculate the overestimate and underestimate of the area under the function.

(d) Assume that the one-year period is now split into 4 subperiods. Calculate the overestimate and underestimate of the area under the function.

(e) Finally, assume that the one-year period is now split into 12 subperiods. Calculate the overestimate and underestimate of the area under the function.

(f) Determine the exact value of the continous stream of payments with the definite integral

$$\int_0^1 1000e^{-0.06t}\,dt.$$

2. Find the exact representation of the price of a bond that offers a continuous stream of payments when

(a) the stream of payments of \$1,000 per year lasts one year and the interest rate is 5%.

(b) the stream of payments of \$1,000 per year lasts for two years and the interest rate is 10%.

(c) the stream of payments of \$2,000 per year lasts for two years and the interest rate is 10%.

(d) the stream of payments is \$1,000 over the first year and \$2,000 over the second year and the interest rate is 10%.

3. Confirm that each function $f(x)$ has the listed antiderivative $F(x)$.

(a) $f(x) = 6x, F(x) = 3x^2 + C$

(b) $f(x) = x^2 + 2x + 7, F(x) = \frac{x^3}{3} + x^2 + 7x + C$

(c) $f(x) = e^{4x}, F(x) = \frac{1}{4}e^{4x} + C$

(d) $f(x) = \frac{1}{2x}, F(x) = \frac{1}{2}\ln(x) + C$

4. Find the antiderivatives of each function.

(a) $f(x) = -5x$

(b) $g(x) = x^2$

(c) $h(x) = -5x + x^2$
(d) $j(x) = e^{x/2}$
(e) $k(x) = 2x \cdot e^{x^2}$

5. Evaluate the antiderivatives (indefinite integrals) you found in parts (a) through (e) of question 3 over the interval $x = 1$ to $x = 5$.
6. You are offered a job with a company that will pay you an initial annual wage of \$40,000 per year and will provide a guarantee that your income will rise at the continuously compounded rate of 5% per year over the next ten years.
   (a) How many dollars will this company pay you over these ten years?
   (b) If your discount rate is 3% per year, what is the present discounted value of the income stream offered by this company over the next decade?
   (c) Suppose that the company now offers you the option of a higher starting salary of \$50,000 but with the slower growth rate of 4% per year. Which offer is more attractive in terms of present value?
7. Durable goods provide a stream of services to their occupants. We can think of the price of a durable good as the net present value of this stream of services. If we denote the annual value of services provided by a durable good as D and the length of time the good is useful as T, how does the price of the durable good vary with the interest rate?
8. Continuing with question 7, suppose that the usefulness of a durable good depreciates at a rate v such that its usefulness n years from the time it is purchased is

$$D \cdot e^{(-v \cdot n)}.$$

   Determine the relationship between the rate of depreciation of the durable good and its price for a given length of time over which the good can be used.
9. Assume you have a revenue function $z = f(x)$ such that the second derivative of the function is $d^2z/dx = 2e^{0.5x} + x$. The second derivative can be used to determine the area under the graph of the marginal revenue function. Derive the marginal revenue function, dz/dx, by integrating d^2z/dx over the value of x.
10. Given a total function, such as total cost, a marginal function can be derived through the process of differentiation. Conversely, the process of integration will generate a total function on the basis of a given marginal function. Assume that a firm has the marginal cost function

$$C'(Q) = 4e^{(0.2Q)}.$$

   (a) Derive this firm's total cost function by integrating $C'(Q)$ with respect to Q.
   (b) Now assume that the firm's fixed costs are $C_F = 120$. Determine the firm's total cost function by setting $Q = 0$. Is there a difference between the value of the constant in the total cost function, c, and the initial value of the total function?

12.2 RULES OF INTEGRATION

Evaluating definite integrals requires identifying the antiderivative of a continuous function. The previous section shows that the antiderivative of a function $F(t)$ has the property that

$$\frac{d(F(t) + C)}{dt} = \frac{dF(t)}{dt} = f(t).$$

We can use this result to derive rules of integration by "working backwards" through the rules of differentiation to find what functions $F(t)$ match the integrands $f(t)$. In this section we present a number of rules of integration that are used frequently in economics.

Before beginning, it should be noted that extending the rules presented here to other functions often involves trial and error. It should also be noted that not every integral of a continuous function has a simple representation. For example, there is no simple representation of the solution for the integral

$$\int e^{-x^2}\,dx$$

because there is no simple function $F(x)$ such that $dF(x)/dx = e^{-x^2}$.

The following rules of integration can be verified with the rules for differentiation presented in Chapters 6 and 7.

Constants in the Integral

As noted earlier, the variable x in dx is the variable of integration, and it indicates the variable in the integrand over which integration occurs. Any other variable or parameter in the integrand can be taken "outside the integral sign" and treated as a constant for purposes of integration. If the variable k does not depend upon the variable x, then

$$\int kf(x)\,dx = k\int f(x)\,dx. \tag{12.11}$$

For example,

$$\begin{aligned}\int 2y(100 - 2x)\,dx &= 2y\int (100 - 2x)\,dx \\ &= 2y(100x - x^2 + C)\end{aligned}$$

since

$$\frac{d}{dx}2y(100x - x^2 + C) = 2y(100 - 2x).$$

The rule concerning constants in the integral is useful for altering the integrand in a way that makes it explicitly conform to a rule for integration. This strategy was used in evaluating the integral

$$\int Xe^{-rt}\,dt,$$

which represents the present value of a stream of payments. The variable of integration here is t. Multiplying and dividing by $-r$ and taking X outside the integral, we have

$$-\frac{X}{r}\int -re^{-rt}\,dt.$$

Defining $f(t) = -re^{-rt}$, we can easily confirm that $F(t) = e^{-rt} + C$ since

$$\frac{dF(t)}{dt} = \frac{de^{-rt}}{dt} + \frac{dC}{dt} = -re^{-rt}.$$

It is very important to note that it is not possible to multiply and divide through by the variable of integration. Thus, as noted earlier, there is no straightforward solution for the integral

$$\int e^{-x^2}\,dx$$

since it *cannot* be rewritten as

$$-\frac{1}{2x}\int -2xe^{-x^2}\,dx$$

because x is the variable of integration in this case.

Power Rule of Integration

By basic differentiation, we can show

$$\int x\,dx = \frac{x^2}{2} + C$$

because

$$\frac{d}{dx}\left(\frac{x^2}{2} + C\right) = x.$$

More generally, it is easy to verify that

$$\int x^n\,dx = \frac{x^{n+1}}{n+1} + C \qquad (12.12)$$

for $n \neq -1$ by simply taking the derivative of the right-hand side and noting that the resulting expression equals the integrand on the left-hand side. In the case of $n = -1$,

$$\int \frac{1}{x}\,dx = \ln(x) + C \quad \text{for} \quad x > 0 \qquad (12.13)$$

since, as shown in Chapter 7,

$$\frac{d(\ln(x) + C)}{dx} = \frac{d(\ln(x))}{dx} = \frac{1}{x}.$$

Integrals of Exponential Functions

The example of valuing a stream of payments requires identifying an antiderivative for a simple exponential function. In that example, it is necessary to multiply and divide by a constant to evaluate the integral. A general restatement of that result is

$$\int Ae^{kx}\,dx = \frac{A}{k}e^{kx} + C, \tag{12.14}$$

where A and k are not functions of x. We can confirm this general result by simply taking the derivative of the right-hand side of this equation.

Sum-Difference Rule

In Chapter 7 it is shown that

$$\frac{d}{dx}(F(x) \pm G(x)) = \frac{dF(x)}{dx} \pm \frac{dG(x)}{dx}.$$

A similar result holds for integration. That is,

$$\int (f(x) \pm g(x))\,dx = \int f(x)\,dx \pm \int g(x)\,dx. \tag{12.15}$$

For example, the integral of a quadratic function can be separated into three separate integrals.

$$\begin{aligned}\int (ax^2 + bx + c)\,dx &= \int ax^2\,dx + \int bx\,dx + \int c\,dx\\ &= \frac{ax^3}{3} + \frac{bx^2}{2} + cx + C,\end{aligned}$$

where C is a composite of the constants of integration of the three separate integrals.

Substitution

The chain rule provides a way to differentiate a composite function. For example, given the composite function consisting of the outside function $g(\bullet)$ and the inside function $h(\bullet)$, the discussion in Chapter 7 shows that

$$\frac{d(g(h(x)) + C)}{dx} = g'(h(x)) \cdot h'(x),$$

where C is a constant. By the Fundamental Theorem of Calculus, we integrate each side of this expression with respect to x to obtain

$$g(h(x)) + C = \int g'(h(x)) \cdot h'(x)\,dx. \tag{12.16}$$

Another way to remember this result is to define $u = h(x)$ so that $du = h'(x)\,dx$. In this case we use the ***u*-substitution method** to obtain.

$$\int g'(h(x)) \cdot h'(x)\,dx = \int g'(u) \cdot du = g(u) + C.$$

As an example of the use of the u-substitution rule, consider the integral

$$\int (x^2 + 4)^3 2x\,dx.$$

Let $u = x^2 + 4$ and $g(u) = u^3$. Then $du = 2x\,dx$, and

$$\begin{aligned}\int (x^2 + 4)^3 2x\,dx &= \int u^3\,du \\ &= \frac{u^4}{4} + C \\ &= \frac{(x^2 + 4)^4}{4} + C.\end{aligned}$$

If this were a definite integral with the lower limit 0 and the upper limit 2, we would then have

$$\int_0^2 (x^2 + 4)^3\, 2x\,dx = \frac{(2^2 + 4)^4}{4} - \frac{(0^2 + 4)^4}{4} = 960.$$

If, instead, we used the u-substitution method with $u = h(x)$, we would need to change the limits of integration as follows:

$$\int_a^b g'(h(x)) \cdot h'(x)\,dx = \int_{h(a)}^{h(b)} g'(u) \cdot du = g(u)\Big|_{h(a)}^{h(b)}.$$

For example, with the original integrand $(x^2 + 4)^3 2x$, we define $u = h(x) = x^2 + 4$, and, therefore, $du = h'(x) = 2x\;dx$. The limits are adjusted such that the upper limit equals $h(2) = 2^2 + 4 = 8$ and the lower limit equals $h(0) = 0^2 + 4 = 4$. We then have

$$\int_0^2 (x^2 + 4)^3 2x\,dx = \int_4^8 u^3\,du = \frac{u^4}{4}\Big|_4^8 = 960.$$

The chain rule is used in Chapter 7 to generate general forms of specific rules of differentiation. The result (12.16) can likewise be used to find more general forms of the rules (12.12), (12.13), and (12.14). The general form of the power rule of integration (for $n \neq -1$) is

$$\int f(x)^n f'(x)\,dx = \frac{f(x)^{n+1}}{n + 1} + C. \tag{12.17}$$

We can prove this rule by using the chain rule to show

$$\frac{d}{dx}\left(\frac{f(x)^{n+1}}{n + 1}\right) = f(x)^n f'(x).$$

This rule can be used in a variety of settings. For example, consider the indefinite integral

$$\int (x + 1)^2\,dx.$$

To see whether this integral conforms to the power rule of integration, we define $f(x) = x + 1$ and note that $f'(x) = 1$. Thus this integral, as written, conforms to the power rule, and, therefore,

$$\int (x+1)^2\,dx = \frac{(x+1)^3}{3} + C.$$

The indefinite integral

$$\int (2x+1)^2\,dx$$

does not, as written, conform to the power rule because $f'(x) = 2$. But we can multiply and divide this integral by 2 to obtain the solution

$$\frac{1}{2}\int (2x+1)^2 2\,dx = \frac{(2x+1)^3}{6} + C.$$

A general form of the result for the case where the integrand $f(x) = 1/x$ is the rule

$$\int \frac{f'(x)}{f(x)}\,dx = \ln(f(x)) + C \quad \text{for} \quad f(x) > 0. \tag{12.18}$$

We can confirm this by recalling from the results presented in Chapter 7 that

$$\frac{d[\ln(f(x)) + C]}{dx} = \frac{f'(x)}{f(x)}.$$

Some uses of this rule are

$$\int \frac{2}{x}\,dx = 2\ln(x) + C \quad \text{for} \quad x > 0$$

and

$$\int \frac{x}{(4x^2+1)}\,dx = \frac{1}{8}\int \frac{8x}{(4x^2+1)}\,dx = \frac{1}{8}\ln(4x^2+1) + C.$$

A general form for the integral of an exponential function is

$$\int Ae^{f(x)}f'(x)\,dx = Ae^{f(x)} + C, \tag{12.19}$$

which we can confirm by using the chain rule to show

$$\frac{d[Ae^{f(x)} + C]}{dx} = Ae^{f(x)}f'(x).$$

An example of an application of this rule is

$$\int xe^{x^2}\,dx = \frac{1}{2}e^{x^2} + C.$$

Integration by Parts

The product rule presented in Chapter 7, written in terms of the differential, states that

$$\frac{d[f(x)g(x)]}{dx} = f'(x)g(x) + g'(x)f(x).$$

Multiplying each side by dx and taking the integral, we have

$$\int \frac{d[f(x)g(x)]}{dx}\,dx = \int f'(x)g(x)\,dx + \int g'(x)f(x)\,dx. \tag{12.20}$$

We know

$$\int \frac{d[f(x)g(x)]}{dx}\,dx = f(x)g(x) + C,$$

and, therefore, (12.20) can be rewritten as

$$f(x)\cdot g(x) + C = \int f'(x)g(x)\,dx + \int g'(x)f(x)\,dx.$$

The use of this result for evaluating integrals can be made apparent if we rearrange terms and, for the sake of simplicity, define $u = f(x)$, $du = f'(x)\,dx$, $v = g(x)$, and $dv = g'(x)\,dx$. We then have

$$\int u\,dv = uv - \int v\,du + C, \tag{12.21}$$

which is the formula for **integration by parts.**

Evaluating an integral with integration by parts involves deciding what to define as u and what to define as dv. For example, consider the integral

$$\int x\ln(x)\,dx.$$

This integral does not fit into any of the categories discussed so far. Its evaluation with integration by parts, however, may provide a solution. Begin by defining $u = \ln(x)$ and $dv = x\,dx$. Then $du = (1/x)\,dx$, and $v = \int x\,dx = x^2/2$. Using the formula for integration by parts, we have

$$\begin{aligned}\int x\ln(x)\,dx &= \frac{x^2}{2}\ln(x) - \int \frac{x^2}{2}\cdot\frac{1}{x}\,dx\\ &= \frac{x^2}{2}\ln(x) - \int \frac{x}{2}\,dx\\ &= \frac{x^2}{2}\ln(x) - \frac{x^2}{4} + C.\end{aligned}$$

It is straightforward to confirm that this is the antiderivative of the integrand. Thus integration by parts enables us to evaluate this integral, which does not conform to any of the categories previously presented, by rewriting it in a way that involves an integral that does conform to one of the categories.

What if we had attempted a solution by defining $u = x$ and $dv = \ln(x)dx$? In that case $du = dx$, but there is no rule given previously for evaluating $\int \ln(x)\,dx$. This illustrates the trial and error nature of the evaluation of integrals, especially with the method of integration by parts.

Improper Integrals

The rules of integration previously presented show how to find the indefinite integrals of a range of functions. We then calculate the definite integral by subtracting the indefinite integral evaluated at the upper limit from the indefinite integral evaluated at the lower limit. That is,

$$\int_a^b f(x)\,dx = F(b) - F(a).$$

A special category of the definite integral is called the **improper integral.** An improper integral is an integral in which the upper limit approaches positive infinity,

$$\int_a^\infty f(x)\,dx = \lim_{b\to\infty}\int_a^b f(x)\,dx,$$

the lower limit approaches negative infinity,

$$\int_{-\infty}^b f(x)\,dx = \lim_{a\to-\infty}\int_a^b f(x)\,dx,$$

or the lower limit approaches negative infinity and the upper limit approaches positive infinity,

$$\int_{-\infty}^\infty f(x)\,dx = \lim_{m\to-\infty}\int_m^c f(x)\,dx + \lim_{m\to\infty}\int_c^m f(x)\,dx,$$

where c is an arbitary fixed real number. An improper integral also occurs when the integrand $f(x)$ is not defined at the point a, but is defined and continuous in the half-closed interval $(a, b]$, or is not defined at the point b, but is defined and continuous in the half-closed interval $[a, b)$. In the first case,

$$\int_a^b f(x)\,dx = \lim_{\delta\to a^+}\int_\delta^b f(x)\,dx,$$

where $\lim\limits_{\delta\to a^+}$ is a right-hand limit, and, in the second case,

$$\int_a^b f(x)\,dx = \lim_{\delta\to b^-}\int_a^\delta f(x)\,dx,$$

where $\lim\limits_{\delta\to b^-}$ is a left-hand limit. If an improper integral has a finite limit, then it **converges;** while if it does not have a finite limit, it **diverges.**

A common use of improper integrals in economics is the valuation of a stream of payments that continues forever. For example, a consul is a bond that offers a level stream of payments forever. The price of a consul will be finite if the present value of the income stream converges. It is easy to check for convergence in this case. Consider a consul that pays \$10,000 per year forever. Following the present value formula (12.7), we find that the value of the bond at time 0 (that is, at present) when the interest rate is 4% is

$$\begin{aligned}\int_0^{\infty} \$10{,}000 \cdot e^{-0.04 \cdot t}\,dt &= \lim_{b \to \infty} -\frac{\$10{,}000}{0.04}e^{-0.04 \cdot b} - \left(-\frac{\$10{,}000}{0.04}e^{0}\right)\\ &= -\frac{\$10{,}000}{0.04} \cdot 0 - \left(-\frac{\$10{,}000}{0.04}\right)\\ &= \frac{\$10{,}000}{0.04}\\ &= \$250{,}000.\end{aligned}$$

More generally,

$$\int_0^{\infty} X \cdot e^{-r \cdot t}\,dt = \frac{X}{r}.$$

This simple formula allows for easy calculation of the present discounted value of an infinite stream of payments.

Exercises 12.2

1. Using the basic rules presented in this section, integrate each function.

   (a) $\int x^3\,dx$

   (b) $\int dx$

   (c) $\int \sqrt{x^5}\,dx$

   (d) $\int \frac{3}{x^2}\,dx$

   (e) $\int 4e^{2x}\,dx$

   (f) $\int \frac{x}{2}e^{(x^2/4)}\,dx$

   (g) $\int \frac{18x^2}{6x^3 + 2}\,dx$

2. Evaluate the integrals you derived in parts (a) through (g) in question 1 over the interval $x = 2$ to $x = 5$.

3. Use the sum-difference rule to evaluate each function.

   (a) $\int (x^3 + 2x^2 + 4)\,dx$

(b) $\int \left(2e^{-2x} - \frac{6x}{3x^2 - 1} + 5\sqrt{x^3}\right) dx$

(c) $\int \left(2x - 2 - \frac{2}{x}\right) dx$

(d) $\int (x^{3/2} + x^{1/2} + x^{-5/2})\, dx$

4. Use the u-substitution rule to evaluate each function.

(a) $\int \frac{2x}{x^2 + 4} dx$

(b) $\int \frac{1}{\sqrt{x}} e^{\sqrt{x}}\, dx$

(c) $\int x(x^2 - 1)^5\, dx$

(d) $\int 4xe^{x^2}\, dx$

5. Use integration by parts to evaluate each function.

(a) $\int \ln(x)\, dx$

(b) $\int x^2 \ln(x)\, dx$

(c) $\int x^3 e^{4x}\, dx$

(d) $\int x^3 \sqrt{1 + x^2}\, dx$

6. Evaluate the integrals you derived in parts (a) through (d) in question 4 over the interval $x = 1$ to $x = 3$.

7. Capital formation is the process of adding to a given stock of capital. In a continuous-time model, capital stock can be expressed as a function of time, $K(t)$. Investment, $I(t)$, represents the rate of capital formation and can be expressed as the derivative of capital stock with respect to time,

$$I(t) = \frac{dK(t)}{dt}.$$

Suppose that the investment varies with time in the following fashion: $I(t) = t^{-1/2}$. At time $t = 9$, the capital stock is 100. What is the capital stock at the end of period 25?

8. The capital stock in Eastern Europe depends upon capital generated internally by the countries themselves and foreign direct investment from the West. Suppose the rate of internal investment is a function of domestic income such that $I = Y^{1/2}$. Income at any moment in Eastern Europe, $Y(t)$, is

$$Y(t) = (\$100 \cdot 1.21t) + \$100,$$

where $t = 0$ in 1989. Capital is also available from the West, which invests 1% of its total output in the Eastern European countries. Output in the West grows at 4% per year, and its initial level is \$1,000 million (that is $Y_w(t) = \$1{,}000e^{0.04t}$).

(a) How much capital will Eastern Europe accumulate between 1989 (year 0) and 2014 (year 25)?

(b) Western capital flows depend upon the prospects for reform. If these prospects are dim and the West stops its flow of direct investment to Eastern Europe in 1998 (years 1 through 10 only), how much capital will the Eastern Europeans have accumulated between 1989 and 2014?

(c) Western capital flows also depend upon growth in the West. How much capital will Eastern Europe have accumulated by 2014 (that is, from years 10 through 25) if growth in the West slows to 2% per year after 1999?

9. The generation of greenhouse gases, $P(t)$, in any year t is related to the production of industrial output by the formula

$$P(t) = 0.5Q(t)e^{-0.02t},$$

where $Q(t)$ is the units of output in year t. The exponent term reflects the absorptive capacity of the earth's atmosphere. The number of units of output produced each year increases at a steady rate such that

$$Q(t) = 800 \cdot e^{0.06t}$$

in year t, where $t = 0$ for 1970. Also, at the beginning of 1970, there are 500 million tons of greenhouse gases in the atmosphere.

(a) If this is a complete characterization of the change in the level of greenhouse gases each year, what are the number of tons of greenhouse gases at the end of 1994 (that is, after 25 years)? Recall that $e \approx 2.72$.

(b) Deforestation has reduced the absorptive capacity of the atmosphere. Suppose that there is a sudden shift in this capacity after 10 years such that for the first 10 years, the equation above held, but afterward (from years 10 through 25), the equation for pollution is

$$P(t) = 0.5Q(t)e^{-0.01t},$$

while the production equation remains unchanged. Solve for the level of pollution at the end of 1994.

10. Land is an indestructible capital asset that offers a perpetual revenue flow. You own a piece of land that returns \$20,000 per year forever. The relevant real interest rate to consider is 4%. What is the present value of this land at time 0?

12.3 ECONOMIC APPLICATIONS

In this section we present economic applications of integral calculus. Beyond demonstrating some of the uses of integration in economics, the applications in this section also provide a context for understanding integral calculus and offer some examples that will help you master the rules of integration.

Bond Price Volatility and Bond Maturity

The price of a bond is the present value of its stream of payments. The result in (12.9) shows that the price of an n-year bond that offers a continuous stream of payments of $\$X$ per year over n years, P_n, is

$$P_n = \int_0^n \$X \cdot e^{-rt}\, dt,$$

where r is the interest rate offered on comparable assets. Following the results given previously, we find that this definite integral equals

$$P_n = \frac{\$X}{r}(1 - e^{-rn}).$$

For example, when the interest rate is 10%, the price of a five-year bond that offers a stream of payments of \$1,000 per year will be (rounded to the nearest dollar)

$$\frac{\$1{,}000}{0.10}(1 - e^{-0.10 \times 5}) = \$3{,}935.$$

The price of a ten-year bond that offers a stream of payments of \$1,000 per year is

$$\frac{\$1{,}000}{0.10}(1 - e^{-0.10 \times 10}) = \$6{,}321.$$

If the interest rate falls to 6%, then the price of the five-year bond rises by about 10% to \$4,320, and the price of the ten-year bond rises by about 19% percent to \$7,520.

In this example the price of the bond with the longer duration is more volatile than the price of the bond with the shorter duration. This is a general result that we can show by considering the ratio of the prices of two bonds that differ in their duration. Suppose that both bonds offer a stream of payments of $\$X$ per year and the appropriate interest rate to use when valuing each bond is r. The ratio of the price of the bond of duration n to the price of the bond of duration m is

$$\frac{P_n}{P_m} = \frac{\int_0^n \$Xe^{-rt}\, dt}{\int_0^m \$Xe^{-rt}\, dt} = \frac{1 - e^{-rn}}{1 - e^{-rm}}$$

since the term $\$X/r$ is common to both prices and, therefore, cancels out. The elasticity of the ratio of these prices with respect to r is

$$\frac{\frac{d}{dr}\left(\frac{P_n}{P_m}\right)}{P_n/P_m} = \frac{ne^{-rn} - me^{-rm} + (m - n)e^{-rm-rn}}{(1 - e^{-rm})(1 - e^{-rn})}.$$

It can be shown that this ratio (in absolute value) is greater than 1 if $n > m$, implying that long bond prices are more volatile with respect to changes in interest rates than are the prices of bonds of shorter duration.

Consumer's Surplus

Consumer's surplus is a measure of the net benefit to a consumer from purchasing a commodity at a certain price. One measure of consumer's surplus is the area under a

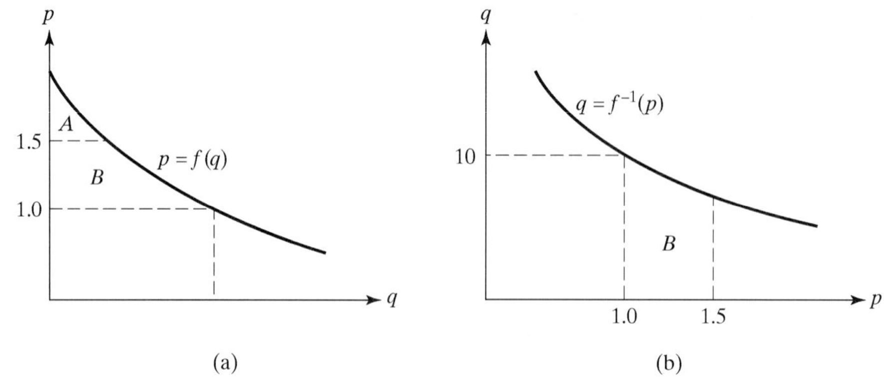

FIGURE 12.5 Consumer's Surplus

demand curve and above the price paid by the consumer. For example, in Figure 12.5(a), the consumer's surplus at price 1.0 equals the area $A + B$, while consumer's surplus at price 1.5 equals only the area A. The change in consumer's surplus with an increase in price, therefore, is approximated by the area B.[2]

We can use integration to calculate the change in consumer's surplus by writing the demand function in the form of quantity as a function of price and then finding the area corresponding to B in Figure 12.5(b) (which equals the area B in Figure 12.5(a)). In this application, we find the change in consumer's surplus for three different demand curves. In each of these cases, we assume that, initially, price equals 1.0 and quantity equals 10. The calculation is then the change in consumer's surplus when price rises to 1.5.

We begin with the linear demand curve

$$q = 15 - 5p.$$

The decrease in consumer's surplus, in this case, is

$$\int_{1}^{1.5} (15 - 5p)\, dp = 15p - \frac{5p^2}{2}\bigg|_{1}^{1.5}$$
$$= (16.875) - (12.5) = 4.375.$$

Next we consider the constant elasticity of substitution demand curve

$$q = 10 \cdot p^{-1/2}.$$

[2]This is only an approximation because the appropriate demand curve to use when evaluating consumer's surplus is the compensated demand curve (also known as the Hicksian demand curve), which does not reflect income effects. In practice, the difference between the measure of consumer's surplus derived from the demand curve that does reflect income effects, the so-called Marshallian demand curve, and the types of consumer's surplus derived from the compensated demand curve are small. See Robert Willig, "Consumer's surplus without apology," *American Economic Review* 66 (1976): 589–597. The examples presented here are drawn from Hal Varian's *Intermediate Microeconomics: Theory and Practice,* 3d ed. (New York: W. W. Norton, 1993).

The decrease in consumer's surplus, in this case, is

$$\int_{1}^{1.5} 10 \cdot p^{-1/2} dp = 20p^{1/2} \Big|_{1}^{1.5}$$
$$= (24.49) - (20) = 4.49.$$

Finally, consider the demand curve

$$q = \frac{10}{p}.$$

The decrease in consumer's surplus, in this case, is

$$\int_{1}^{1.5} \frac{10}{p} dp = 10 \ln (p) \Big|_{1}^{1.5}$$
$$= (4.055) - (0) = 4.055.$$

Consumer's surplus is an important concept for gauging the welfare effects of policies. This is evident from the following application, which uses this concept in a macroeconomic context.

The Cost of Inflation

Inflation is widely disliked by the public. During the late 1970s, when inflation in the United States exceeded 13% per year, public opinion polls indicated that inflation was viewed as the most pressing problem facing the country. The economic costs of inflation, however, do not seem to warrant this level of concern. In particular, fully anticipated, long-run inflation may impose little cost on an economy.

A quantitative measure of the economic cost of inflation is suggested by Bennett McCallum.[3] McCallum starts with a money demand equation

$$m = \theta Y^{\beta} R^{-\gamma},$$

where m represents real money balances, Y is real income, R is the nominal interest rate, and $\theta, \beta,$ and γ are parameters. Empirical studies of money demand in the United States suggest that $\beta = 1$ and $-\gamma = -0.2$. McCallum studies the benefit of reducing inflation measured as a percentage of real income. Defining the ratio of money to income as $M = m/Y$ and using the parameter estimates for β and γ, we can write the relevant money demand function as

$$R = \left(\frac{1}{\theta} \cdot M\right)^{-5}.$$

This function is graphed in Figure 12.6, which has the nominal interest rate along the y-axis and the ratio of money to income along the x-axis.

---

[3] See pages 124–131 of his book *Menetary Economics: Theory and Policy* (New York: Macmillan, 1989).

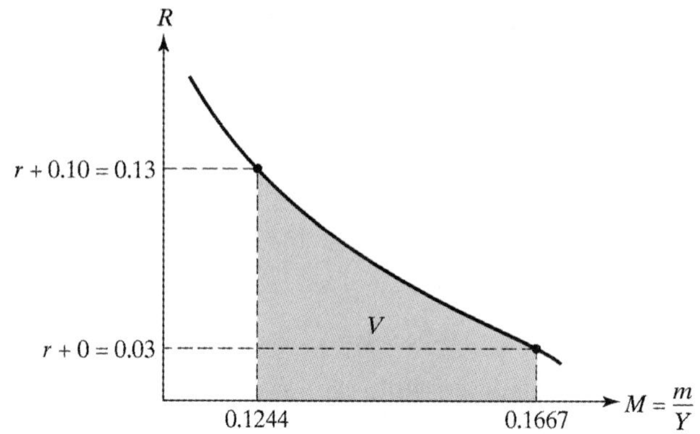

FIGURE 12.6 The Cost of Inflation

We can find a value of θ by first noting that M is about $\frac{1}{6}$ for the United States. Also, by the Fisher equation,

$$R = r + \pi,$$

where r is the real interest rate and π is expected inflation. We assume that actual inflation and expected inflation are the same in the long run. An approximate value of the long-run real interest rate is $r = 0.03$. Therefore, in the absence of inflation, $R = 0.03$, and the money demand function implies

$$\theta = \frac{(0.03)^{0.2}}{6} = 0.0827.$$

Just as the change in consumer's surplus is represented by the area B in Figure 12.5, the benefit from lowering inflation is represented by the area labeled as V under the money demand curve in Figure 12.6 when we assume that the cost of supplying money is zero. To integrate the area under the money demand curve, we first need to decide on the change in inflation we wish to study and then determine the implied changes in real balances in order to have the limits of integration. McCallum considers the benefit of a long-run permanent reduction in inflation from 10% per year to 0% per year. At a 10% inflation rate, real balances as a percentage of national income are

$$M = (0.0827)\,(0.13)^{-0.2} = 0.1244,$$

and, at 0% inflation, real balances as a percentage of national income are

$$M = (0.0827)\,(0.03)^{-0.2} = 0.1667.$$

Thus the integral that represents the benefit from reducing inflation is

$$\int_{0.1244}^{0.1667} R \cdot dM = \int_{0.1244}^{0.1667} (0.0827)^5 M^{-5} \cdot dM = 0.0028.$$

Thus the cost of 10% inflation as compared to 0% inflation is less than three-tenths of a percent of one year's national income.

While this seems quite low, Martin Feldstein has made the point that the permanent benefit of this could be substantial when the inflation rate is reduced once and for all.[4] The loss from inflation is typically expressed as a percentage of national income. As national income grows, so does the benefit from permanently eradicating inflation. The instantaneous, nondiscounted benefit t years after the reduction of inflation is Ve^{rt} if the economy's growth rate is r per year. If we discount this benefit by some factor ρ, then the instantaneous discounted benefit at time t is

$$Ve^{rt}e^{-\rho t} = Ve^{(r-\rho)t},$$

and the value of the stream of benefits is represented by the integral of this expression evaluated from 0 to t. For example, if the economy grows at 2% per year ($r = 0.02$) and the real discount rate is 1% per year ($\rho = 0.01$), then the present value of the benefit over 50 years is

$$\begin{aligned}\int_0^{50} Ve^{(0.02-0.01)t}\,dt &= \int_0^{50} Ve^{0.01t}\,dt \\ &= 100(e^{0.5} - 1)\,V \\ &= 64.9V.\end{aligned}$$

Looking at it this way, we see that the present value of reducing inflation from 10% to a permanent level of 0% when V is 0.0028% of national income is $64.9 \cdot (0.0028) =$ 18% of a year's national income.

Measuring Inequality

The distribution of income has profound economic, social, and political implications. Any empirical study of the extent of income inequality, or of its causes or effects, must employ some measure of the degree of inequality in an economy. One widely used measure of inequality is the **Gini coefficient.** In this application we use integration to show how this coefficient reflects the distribution of income.

The Gini coefficient is derived from the **Lorenz curve.** The Lorenz curve is plotted in a graph where the horizontal axis represents the population, ordered from poorest to richest, and the vertical axis represents the cumulative percentage of income. The horizontal axis can be scaled from 0 to 1. In this application, the x-value 0.2 represents the poorest fifth of the population, 0.5 represents the poorer half of the population, 0.9 represent all but the richest tenth of the population, and so on. If the poorest fifth of the population collectively earns one-twenty-fifth of all income, then the Lorenz curve includes the point (0.2, 0.04), and if the poorer half of the population earns one-quarter of all income, then the Lorenz curve also includes the point (0.5, 0.25). A Lorenz curve that includes these two points, (0.2, 0.04) and (0.5, 0.25), is plotted in Figure 12.7. This figure also includes a 45° line. The 45° line is a benchmark since it represents a Lorenz

[4]Martin Feldstein, "The welfare cost of permanent inflation and optimal short-run economic policy," *Journal of Political Economy* 87, no. 4 (1979): 749–768.

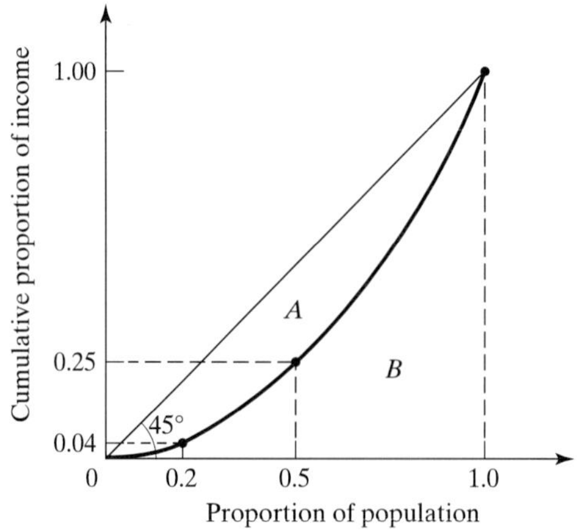

FIGURE 12.7 A Lorenz Curve

curve for a perfectly egalitarian country in which any proportion of the population earns that proportion of total income in the economy.

The Gini coefficient represents the area between the 45° line and the actual Lorenz curve of an economy relative to the entire area under the 45° line. For example, in Figure 12.7, where the area between the Lorenz curve and the 45° line is labelled A and the area between the Lorenz curve and the horizontal axis is labelled B, the Gini coefficient is the ratio $A/A + B$. Smaller values of the Gini coefficient represent more egalitarian societies. A perfectly egalitarian society, in which the Lorenz curve is the 45° line, has a Gini coefficient of 0. A completely inegalitarian society, in which one person earns all income (and, therefore, the Lorenz curve is shaped like a backwards L), has a Gini coefficient of 1.

In practice, Gini coefficients tend to range from about 0.25 to about 0.6. For example, in her study of the relationship between inequality and growth, Kristin Forbes reports Gini coefficients in 1990 that range from the most egalitarian values of 0.233 for Hungary and 0.245 for Bulgaria to the most inegalitarian values of 0.550 and 0.596 for Mexico and Brazil, respectively.[5] In 1970, the Gini coefficient for the United States was 0.341, and it has increased since then, reaching a value of 0.378 in 1990.

Typically, the Gini coefficient is estimated from discrete data on the income going to each quintile, decile, or some other proportion of the population. But Lorenz curves are also fitted to large numbers of observations, and these parametrized continuous Lorenz curves are used to generate Gini coefficients. The Gini coefficient associated with a continuous Lorenz curve is

$$G = \frac{1/2 - \int_0^1 L(p)\,dp}{1/2} = 1 - 2\int_0^1 L(p)\,dp$$

[5]See Table 2 in Kristin Forbes, "The relationship between inequality and growth," *American Economic Review* 90, no. 4 (September 2000).

since the area of the triangle $A + B$ equals $\frac{1}{2}$ and the area A is the area of the triangle $A + B$ minus the area under the Lorenz curve function $L(p)$.

One particular Lorenz curve takes the form

$$L(p) = p - \theta p(1 - p)^{\beta},$$

where p ranges from 0 to 1 and represents the cumulative proportion of the population; $L(p)$ is the Lorenz curve and shows the amount of national income, as a percentage earned by the pth poorest proportion of the population; $0 < \beta \leq 1$; and $\theta > 0$.[6] Note that $L(0) = 0$ and $L(1) = 1$. The Gini coefficient associated with this Lorenz curve function is

$$G = 1 - 2\int_0^1 [p - \theta p(1 - p)^{\beta}]\,dp.$$

To evaluate this integral, we first note that

$$\begin{aligned}\int_0^1 [p - \theta p(1 - p)^{\beta}]\,dp &= \int_0^1 p\,dp - \int_0^1 \theta p(1 - p)^{\beta}\,dp \\ &= \frac{p^2}{2}\bigg|_0^1 - \int_0^1 \theta p(1 - p)^{\beta}\,dp \\ &= \frac{1}{2} - \int_0^1 \theta p(1 - p)^{\beta}\,dp.\end{aligned}$$

We can then solve the remaining integral by using integration by parts. Let $u = \theta p$ and $dv = (1 - p)^{\beta}dp$. Then $du = \theta\,dp$ and $v = -(1/(\beta + 1))(1 - p)^{\beta+1}$. Using the integration-by-parts formula, we have

$$\begin{aligned}\int_0^1 \theta p(1 - p)^{\beta}\,dp &= -\frac{\theta}{\beta + 1}p(1 - p)^{\beta+1}\Big|_0^1 - \int_0^1 -\frac{\theta}{\beta + 1}(1 - p)^{\beta+1}\,dp \\ &= -\frac{\theta}{\beta + 1}p(1 - p)^{\beta+1}\Big|_0^1 - \frac{\theta(1 - p)^{\beta+2}}{(\beta + 1)(\beta + 2)}\bigg|_0^1 \\ &= \frac{\theta}{(\beta + 1)(\beta + 2)}.\end{aligned}$$

[6]The particular Lorenz curve presented in this application is a specific case of a Beta Lorenz curve. The Beta Lorenz curve takes the form

$$L(p) = p - \theta p^{\alpha}(1 - p)^{\beta},$$

where $\theta > 0$, $0 < \alpha \leq 1$, and $0 < \beta \leq 1$. Thus the Beta Lorenz curve we consider sets $\alpha = 1$. See Nanak Kakwani, "On a class of povery measures," *Econometrica* 48, no. 2 (March 1980): 437–446.

Thus the Gini coefficient associated with this Lorenz curve is

$$G = 1 - 2\int_0^1 L(p)\,dp$$
$$= 1 - 2\left[\frac{1}{2} - \int_0^1 \theta p(1-p)^\beta\,dp\right]$$
$$= \frac{2\theta}{(\beta+1)(\beta+2)}.$$

This result shows that, with $\beta = 1$, $G = \theta/3$. In the limit, as β approaches 0, $G = \theta$.

A Lorenz curve like this one can be estimated from large samples. The associated Gini coefficients then provide a measure of income inequality. Using a slightly more general function for the Lorenz curve than the one presented here, Gaurav Datt and Martin Ravallion estimate the 1988 values of Gini coefficients of 0.283 for rural India, 0.328 for urban India, and 0.615 for Brazil.[7]

Some Elements of Probability and Statistics

Economists use statistical tools in both theoretical modeling and empirical testing of models. A basic concept in statistics is that of a **random variable,** which is the outcome of a random event like the flip of a coin or the roll of a die. The possible set of outcomes of flipping a coin or rolling a die can be described by a set with a discrete number of elements: heads or tails, in the case of the coin, and the integers 1 through 6, in the case of the die. In these cases, the random variables are discrete. Alternatively, the random variable is continuous in cases in which the set of outcomes is drawn from a continuous domain. We can use integration to describe some properties of continuous random variables.

A listing of the values x of a random variable X with the associated probability of each outcome is a **probability distribution.** For example, a coin toss has two possible outcomes, x = heads or x = tails. The **probability distribution function,** $f(x)$ in this case, is

$$f(\text{heads}) = \Pr(X = \text{heads}) = \frac{1}{2} \quad \text{and}$$
$$f(\text{tails}) = \Pr(X = \text{tails}) = \frac{1}{2},$$

where $\Pr(X = i)$ represents the probability that event i occurs. In general, for discrete random variables with the probability distribution function $f(x)$, we have

$$0 \leq f(x) \leq 1 \quad \text{and} \quad \sum_x f(x_i) = 1,$$

where Σ_x represents the sum over all possible outcomes of x.

[7] See Guarav Datt and Martin Ravallion, "Growth and redistribution components of changes in poverty measures: A decomposition with applications to Brazil and India in the 1980s." *Journal of Development Economics* 38, no. 2, (April 1992): 275–295. Datt and Ravaillon estimate a Beta Lorenz cure in which they do not constrain $\alpha = 1$.

A continuous random variable can take any value between its upper limit and its lower limit. For example, consider a random-number generator that selects a real number between 0 and 100. In this case x is a real number, but the probability associated with any particular point is zero since there is essentially a zero probability that the random number chosen is, say, 5.324. For continuous random variables, we have a nonnegative probability distribution function $f(x)$ such that[8]

$$\Pr(a \le x \le b) = \int_a^b f(x)\, dx \ge 0.$$

We also have

$$\int_{-\infty}^{\infty} f(x)\, dx = 1,$$

where it is understood that $f(x) = 0$ for x less than the lower limit of a distribution or greater than the upper limit of a distribution. The condition involving this improper integral is analogous to the condition for the sum of the probability distribution functions over all x in the discrete case.

As an example of a continuous distribution, consider the **uniform distribution.** A uniform distribution is completely described by its lower limit and its upper limit since the probability distribution function for a random variable with a uniform distribution with lower limit a and upper limit b is

$$\begin{aligned} u(x) &= \frac{1}{b-a} \quad \text{for} \quad x \text{ in } [a, b] \\ u(x) &= 0 \quad \text{otherwise.} \end{aligned}$$

Figure 12.8(a) presents a uniform distribution with lower limit 0 and upper limit 100. With this distribution, there is an equal probability that the realization of the continuous random variable X is in the closed interval $[0, 1]$ as in the closed interval $[98, 99]$ or in the closed interval $[22, 23]$. Specifically, we have the probability distribution function $u(x) = \frac{1}{100}$ and

$$\begin{aligned} \Pr(a \le x \le b) &= \int_a^b \frac{1}{100}\, dx \\ &= \frac{x}{100}\bigg|_a^b \\ &= \frac{b-a}{100}. \end{aligned}$$

[8] Since the probability associated with any particular point in a continuous distribution is zero, we also have

$$\Pr(a \le x \le a) = \int_a^a f(x)\, dx = 0$$

and

$$\Pr(a \le x \le b) = \Pr(a < x < b).$$

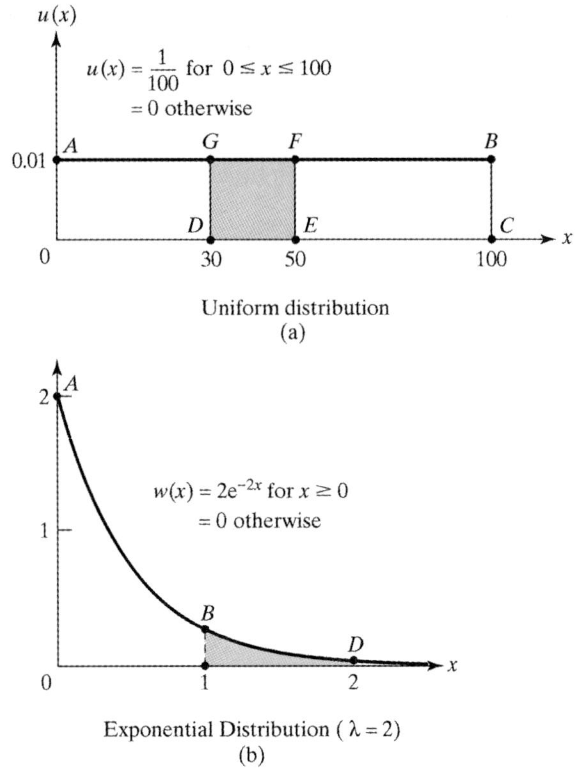

FIGURE 12.8 A Uniform Distribution and an Exponential Distribution

The probability that the random variable is between any two consecutive integers is therefore $\frac{1}{100}$. The probability that the random variable is greater than or equal to 30 and less than or equal to 50 is

$$\Pr(30 \leq x \leq 50) = \int_{30}^{50} \frac{1}{100}\,dx = 0.20.$$

In Figure 12.8(a) this probability is represented by the ratio of the area of the rectangle *DEFG* to the area of the rectangle $0ABC$.

As another example, we consider the **exponential distribution.** This distribution is useful for modeling the time when a certain event occurs, such as the time when a recession ends. The probability distribution function of an exponential distribution is

$$w(x) = \lambda e^{-\lambda x} \quad \text{for} \quad 0 < x < \infty.$$

The parameter λ is positive, and, as we will see, $1/\lambda$ represents the average time until an event occurs. Figure 12.8(b) depicts this distribution function for the case of $\lambda = 2$. As shown in this figure, the probability of the occurrence of an event during any given unit of time (which we call a "period") is highest at the outset. In the case of $\lambda = 2$, the probability of a certain event occurring at some moment between time a and time b is

$$\begin{aligned} \Pr(a < x < b) &= \int_a^b 2e^{-2x}\,dx \\ &= -e^{-2x}\Big|_a^b \\ &= -e^{-2b} - (-e^{-2a}). \end{aligned}$$

Thus the probability of an event occurring between time 0 and time 1 when $\lambda = 2$ is

$$-e^{-2} - (-e^{0}) = -0.135 + 1 = 0.865,$$

and, therefore, the area $0AB1$ in Figure 12.8(b) is about 86.5% of the total area under the curve since the total area under the curve for any value of λ is

$$\begin{aligned} \Pr(0 < x < \infty) &= \int_a^b \lambda e^{-\lambda x}\,dx \\ &= -e^{-\lambda x}\Big|_0^\infty \\ &= 1. \end{aligned}$$

The probability of an event occurring between time 1 and time 2 is

$$-e^{-4} - (-e^{-2}) = -0.018 + 0.135 = 0.117,$$

and, therefore, the area $1BD2$ is about 11.7% of the total area under the curve in Figure 12.8(b).

A **cumulative distribution function,** $F(x)$, associated with the probability function $f(x)$, is the probability that the random variable is less than or equal to the value x. The cumulative distribution function is defined as

$$F(x) = \Pr(X \le x) = \int_{-\infty}^{x} f(x)\,dx,$$

where it is understood that $f(x) = 0$ for x less than the lower limit of a distribution. The uniform distribution $u(x)$ described previously has the cumulative distribution function $U(x)$ where

$$U(x) = \Pr(X \le x) = \int_0^x \frac{1}{100}\,dx = \frac{x}{100}.$$

Thus, for example, $U(20) = 0.20$ and $U(75) = 0.75$. The exponential distribution with the probability distribution function $w(x)$ has the cumulative probability distribution function $W(x)$ where

$$W(x) = \Pr(X \le x) = \int_0^x \lambda e^{-\lambda x}\,dx = 1 - e^{-\lambda x}.$$

In the case where $\lambda = 2$, we have $W(1) = 1 - e^{-2} = 0.865$ and $W(2) = 1 - e^{-4} = 0.982$.

Statistics are parameters associated with probability distributions that describe that distribution. You are probably familiar with a frequently used statistic, the **average,** which is also called the **mean.** The mean of a random variable is a measure of its "central tendency." The mean of a continuous random variable with probability distribution $f(x)$, often denoted as μ, is

$$\mu = \int_{-\infty}^{\infty} x f(x)\, dx.$$

Thus the mean of the uniform distribution with lower bound a and upper bound b, μ_u, is

$$\begin{aligned}
\mu_u &= \int_a^b \frac{x}{b-a}\, dx \\
&= \left.\frac{x^2}{2(b-a)}\right|_a^b \\
&= \frac{b^2 - a^2}{2(b-a)} \\
&= \frac{(b-a)(b+a)}{2(b-a)} \\
&= \frac{1}{2}(b+a).
\end{aligned}$$

Therefore the mean of the uniform distribution with lower limit 0 and upper limit 100, depicted in Figure 12.8(a) is 50.

The mean of the exponential distribution $w(x) = \lambda e^{-\lambda x}$, which we denote as μ_e, is

$$\mu_e = \int_0^{\infty} x\lambda e^{-\lambda x}\, dx.$$

We can solve this integral with integration by parts. Let $u = x$ and $dv = \lambda e^{-\lambda x}\, dx$. Then $du = dx$ and $v = -e^{-\lambda x}$. Then we have

$$\begin{aligned}
\mu_e &= -xe^{-\lambda x}\big|_0^{\infty} - \int_0^{\infty} -e^{-\lambda x}\, dx \\
&= -xe^{-\lambda x}\big|_0^{\infty} + \frac{1}{-\lambda}\int_0^{\infty} (-\lambda)e^{-\lambda x}\, dx \\
&= -xe^{-\lambda x}\big|_0^{\infty} - \left.\frac{e^{-\lambda x}}{\lambda}\right|_0^{\infty} \\
&= -\left(x + \frac{1}{\lambda}\right) e^{-\lambda x}\big|_0^{\infty} \\
&= \frac{1}{\lambda}
\end{aligned}$$

since

$$\lim_{x\to\infty}\left(x + \frac{1}{\lambda}\right)e^{-\lambda x} = 0.$$

As discussed above, this result then gives us an interpretation of the single parameter of the exponential distribution. Thus for the case where $\lambda = 2$, which is depicted in Figure 12.8(b), the average time until an event occurs is $1/2$ period. With smaller values of λ, the average time until an event occurs is larger. For example, the mean time until an event occurs for an exponential distribution with $\lambda = 1/10$ is 10 periods.

Another statistic associated with a probability distribution is **variance,** which is a measure of the dispersion of the distribution. The variance of a random variable with probability distribution x, denoted as σ^2, is

$$\sigma^2 = \int_{-\infty}^{\infty} (x - \mu)^2 f(x)\, dx,$$

where μ is the mean of the distribution. For example, consider a uniform distribution with lower limit 0 and upper limit 100. We have seen that the mean of this distribution is $(0 + 100)/2 = 50$. The variance of this distribution is

$$\begin{aligned}\sigma^2 &= \int_0^{100} (x - 50)^2 \frac{1}{100}\, dx \\ &= \frac{(x-50)^3}{300}\bigg|_0^{100} \\ &= 833\frac{1}{3}.\end{aligned}$$

The continuous probability distribution functions presented here and in the exercises can be integrated. Other important continuous probability distribution functions, most notably the normal distribution (the graph of which is the familiar "bell-shaped curve"), do not have simple representations for their integrals. Therefore we obtain the cumulative probability of a normal distribution by referring to a table (found in most statistics textbooks) rather than by directly using a formula obtained from integrating the function.

Exercises 12.3

1. In a Chapter 3 problem on determining present value, we looked at the impact of fluctuating interest rates on the value of the bond investment your parents made in order to help finance your college tuition. Use the definite integral to obtain the present value of each of the following scenarios.
   (a) Your parents purchase a bond that will pay \$15,000 in one year plus a stream of interest payments equal to 7% of the bond's value when the interest rate on comparable assets is also 7%. How does your answer to this question differ from the answer obtained when the interest payment is made once at the end of the year?
   (b) Interest rates fall to 5% after the bond purchase, but the stream of interest payments is still equivalent to 7% of the bond's face value.
   (c) Interest rates rise to 9.5% after the bond purchase.

(d) Assume now that you have inside information that the Federal Reserve will lower interest rates three months after your parents must make their investment decision. Today your parents are considering two different bond maturity alternatives: 5 years and 10 years. Using your secret information that rates are expected to drop, which investment alternative will you recommend your parents take in order to obtain the biggest increase in their investment's value after three months?

2. In Chapter 3, we present a problem in which an antique stamp collection is discovered. In that problem, it is assumed that the value of the collection is expected to appreciate, but the stamps had to be stored in a special facility.

   (a) Assume that this storage cost is a constant stream at the rate of $s = \$100$ per year and the relevant discount rate, r, is 5%. Determine the total present value of the storage cost over m years with the integral

$$\int_{t=0}^{m} se^{-rt}\,dt.$$

   (b) As the owner of this stamp collection, your objective is to maximize the net present value of your investment, which is represented by the difference between the present value of the stamp collection and the present value of the stream of storage payments. Set up the function for net present value, $NPV(t)$, by using your answer to part (a) above and recalling that the formula for present value is $V(t)e^{-rt}$. Assume for this problem that $V = 1000$.

   (c) Maximize the NPV function with respect to t to determine the optimal number of years to hold the antique stamp collection.

3. Producer's surplus is related to the concept of consumer's surplus, but it represents the net benefit to a supplier of producing a commodity at a certain price. Producer's surplus can be measured as the area above the supply curve but below the market price.

   (a) Given the linear supply curve $q = 10p + 50$, assume that the initial price equals 1 and the quantity supplied equals 60. Use integration to determine the change in producer's surplus when the price rises to 2. Does this represent an increase or decrease in producer's surplus?

   (b) Producer's surplus might also be considered as the benefit accruing to a supplier of a factor of production in excess of what is required. In the case of labor, producer's surplus can be measured as the area above the supply curve and below the wage rate. Consider Sally, who is willing to supply her labor according to the function $q = 15\sqrt{p^3}$. Use integration to evaluate the change in producer's surplus when the wage rate rises from \$2 per hour to \$4 per hour.

4. International trade policy makers often consider the welfare effects on producers and consumers of imposing tariffs on imported goods. One way to measure these welfare effects is to evaluate changes in consumer's and producer's surplus due to changes in the tariff structure. Assume you are a policy maker in a small country. The demand for bananas is very high, and although there is some domestic

production, bananas are also imported. The demand for bananas is

$$q_d = 20 - 4p,$$

and the domestic supply of bananas is given by the function

$$q_s = 0.5p + 4.$$

As a small producer, you take the world price of bananas as given, where $p_w = 3$.

(a) If imports are defined as the difference between the quantity demanded and the quantity supplied at a given price, or excess demand, determine the level of imports when $p_w = 3$.

(b) Now assume that you, as policy maker, determine that it is in your country's best interest to stimulate domestic production of bananas. You decide to impose a tariff on banana imports so as to raise the domestic price sufficiently such that there will be no imports. What is this new domestic price, p_d?

(c) Use integration to evaluate the changes in consumer's surplus and producer's surplus due to the imposition of this tariff. Assume that the demand curve is not a compensated demand curve because it does not reflect income effects. Who benefits and who loses?

5. The discussion of the benefits of the reduction in inflation assumes a time horizon of 50 years.

(a) What is the present value of the benefit of the reduction in inflation if the appropriate time horizon is the entire future?

(b) What is the present value of the benefit of the reduction in inflation if the discount rate equals the rate of growth of the economy?

(c) Discuss the present value of the benefit of the reduction in inflation if the real discount rate exceeds the economy's growth rate.

6. Consider a probability distribution function $f(x)$ where

$$f(x) = 3x^2 \quad \text{for } 0 \le x \le 1$$
$$f(x) = 0 \quad \text{otherwise.}$$

(a) What is the probability that $\frac{1}{4} \le x \le \frac{3}{4}$?

(b) What is the probability that $\frac{1}{2} \le x \le 1$?

(c) What is the mean of this distribution?

(d) Show that the probability distribution function integrated from 0 to 1 equals 1.

(e) What is the variance of this distribution?

7. Consider a probability distribution function $f(x)$ where

$$f(x) = \frac{1}{x} \quad \text{for } 1 \le x \le U$$
$$f(x) = 0 \quad \text{otherwise.}$$

(a) As discussed in this section, a necessary condition for a probability distribution function is that its cumulative distribution equals 1 when evaluated at its upper limit. Find U, the upper limit of this distribution, such that $F(U) = 1$.

(b) Determine $\Pr\left(1 \le x \le \frac{U}{2}\right)$.

(c) Determine $\Pr\left(\frac{U}{2} \le x \le \mathrm{U}\right)$.

(d) What is the mean of this distribution?

8. The probability distribution function of the **Weibull distribution** is

$$g(x) = \alpha\beta x^{\alpha-1}e^{-\beta x^{\alpha}} \quad \text{for} \quad x \ge 0$$
$$g(x) = 0 \quad \text{otherwise,}$$

where $\alpha \ge 1$ and $\beta > 0$. This distribution function, like the exponential, is useful for modeling time until an event occurs.

(a) Consider the case where $\alpha = 2$ and $\beta = \frac{1}{2}$. What is the probability of $0 \le x \le 1$?

(b) Again, considering the case where $\alpha = 2$ and $\beta = \frac{1}{2}$, find the probability of $1 \le x \le 2$.

(c) Show that the probability distribution function integrated from 0 to ∞ equals 1.

9. Determine a general formula for the variance of a uniform distribution with a lower limit *a* and an upper limit *b*.

10. We have seen that an exponential distribution with probability distribution function,

$$w(x) = \frac{1}{2}e^{-x/2},$$

where the lower limit is 0 and the upper limit is ∞, has the mean

$$\mu = \frac{1}{\lambda} = \frac{1}{1/2} = 2.$$

Show that the variance of this distribution is $(1/\lambda)^2 = 4$ by evaluating the integral

$$\sigma^2 = \int_0^{\infty} \frac{(x-4)^2}{2} e^{-x/2} dx.$$

(*Hint*: One way to evaluate this integral is to multiply out the term $(x - 4)^2$ and then use integration by parts. Note the way integration by parts is used previously to find the mean of an exponential distribution.)

11. Determine the Gini coefficient associated with the Lorenz curve

$$L(p) = p - 0.375\sqrt{p}(1 - p).$$

Summary

Integration provides a method for finding the aggregate value for a variable described by a continuous function. A definite integral corresponds to the area under a curve. Definite integrals are used when economists calculate an aggregate value in models that treat time as a continuous variable; that assume a very large number of goods, firms, or individuals; or that make the simplifying assumption of continuous functions. The applications in this chapter illustrate some of these uses of integration in economic contexts.

The Fundamental Theorem of Calculus shows that integration is the inverse of differentiation. This result then paves the way for our deriving rules of integration. A number of these rules are presented in this chapter. The Fundamental Theorem also shows how to evaluate definite integrals when the limits of integration are provided. Integrals in which one of the limits is either positive or negative infinity, so-called improper integrals, can also be evaluated and may provide finite solutions if the integral converges.

Integrals appear again in Chapters 14 and 15. In Chapter 14 we discuss the integral solution to a differential equation, that is, an equation in which the rate of change of a variable is a function of its level. The objective functions of the maximization problems discussed in Chapter 15 are integrals representing the present value of a stream of payments. The techniques taught in this chapter are important for a full understanding of these topics, as well as for addressing the kind of economic questions presented in this chapter.

Chapter 13

Difference Equations

Many of the topics studied by economists can be characterized as decisions taken in one period that have consequences in some other period. Current savings finance future consumption. Investment this year increases the potential for production next year. Assets purchased today reward investors with a payoff tomorrow. A monopolist setting her price today must consider the potential for subsequent entry by other firms.

Each of these activities can only be properly addressed in the context of a dynamic analysis that includes an explicit role for events occurring at different moments in time. In this chapter we study one type of dynamic analysis called **discrete time analysis.** Discrete time analysis treats time as a series of distinct **periods** that are identified by integer values. Periods can be represented by any arbitrary length of time, such as a day, a month, or a year. The important characteristic of a period is that any variable takes only one value during any single period.

A central tool of discrete time analysis is a **difference equation.** A difference equation links the value of an endogenous variable in one period to its value in one or more other periods, as well as to the value of other variables. In this chapter we show how to solve linear difference equations. We begin by analyzing the most basic type of difference equation by using repeated substitution and with a graphical technique. Section 13.1 presents explicit solutions for these simple types of difference equations. These solutions are used in Section 13.2 in a number of economic applications. Section 13.3 shows how to solve a more complicated difference equation and systems of difference equations.

13.1 AN INTRODUCTION TO FIRST-ORDER DIFFERENCE EQUATIONS

Dynamic analysis provides an explicit solution for the values of a dependent variable over time. These values are represented in discrete time analysis as a **sequence.** A sequence is a set of values of some variable, such as

$$x_1, x_2, x_3, x_4, \ldots,$$

where each term of the sequence, x_n, is indexed by an integer that, in this context, represents a particular time period. The sequence of the variable x_t from period i to period

j can be expressed compactly as

$$\{x_t\}_{t=i}^{j} = x_i, x_{i+1}, \ldots, x_{j-1}, x_j.$$

The basic building block of discrete time analysis is the **difference equation.** A difference equation relates the value of a dependent variable in one period to its value in one or more adjacent periods, as well as to the value of one or more independent variables. An example of a difference equation is

$$x_t = ax_{t-1} + y_t, \tag{13.1}$$

where the sequence of dependent variables is represented by $\{x_t\}$, the sequence of independent variables is represented by $\{y_t\}$, and a is an exogenous parameter. This is a **first-order difference equation** since it includes x_t and its lagged value, x_{t-1}. The difference between the largest and smallest time period indexing the sequence of dependent variables in a second-order difference equation, such as

$$x_t = ax_{t-1} + bx_{t-2} + y_t,$$

equals 2 (that is, t minus $t - 2$). Both of these equations are **linear difference equations** since x_t is a linear function of the other variables.

A **solution** to the difference equation (13.1) is a representation of the entire sequence of $\{x_t\}$ as a function of time itself and of the sequence of the independent variable. The solution also depends upon one given value of the dependent variable. Typically there is a specification of an **initial value** of the dependent variable, that is, its value in the beginning of the sequence. Sometimes a model provides, instead, the endogenous variable's **terminal value,** which represents the last term in its sequence. As we will see in Section 13.3, the solution to a second-order difference equation requires specifying two values of the dependent variable, such as the initial values in the first two periods.

Numerical Examples of Dynamics

We introduce the analysis of difference equations by solving for consecutive values of a sequence generated by a linear first-order difference equation of the form

$$x_t = ax_{t-1} + y$$

through repeated substitution. The main difference across the four equations studied in this section concerns the value of the coefficient a. The particular difference found for these equations points to more general results, which we also present here. We first consider the difference equation

$$x_t = \frac{1}{2}x_{t-1} + 300. \tag{13.2}$$

We assume that $x_0 = 400$. The sequence of x can be determined by repeated use of the difference equation (13.2). For example,

$$\begin{aligned} x_0 &= 400 \quad \text{(given)}, \\ x_1 &= \frac{1}{2}x_0 + y = \frac{1}{2} \cdot 400 + 300 = 500, \end{aligned}$$

$$x_2 = \frac{1}{2}x_1 + y = \frac{1}{2}\cdot 500 + 300 = 550,$$

$$x_3 = \frac{1}{2}x_2 + y = \frac{1}{2}\cdot 550 + 300 = 575,$$

$$x_4 = \frac{1}{2}x_3 + y = \frac{1}{2}\cdot 575 + 300 = 587\frac{1}{2},$$

and so on. The dynamics generated by this difference equation are **monotonic** since the sign of $(x_t - x_{t-1})$ is the same for any t. The sequence of values $\{x_t\}$ for this equation is depicted in Figure 13.1.

We next use repeated substitution to generate the sequence consistent with the difference equation

$$x_t = -\frac{1}{2}x_{t-1} + 300, \tag{13.3}$$

and, again, we assume $x_0 = 400$. The sequence of values of x_t is

$$x_0 = 400 \text{ (given)},$$

$$x_1 = -\frac{1}{2}x_0 + y = -\frac{1}{2}\cdot 400 + 300 = 100,$$

$$x_2 = -\frac{1}{2}x_1 + y = -\frac{1}{2}\cdot 100 + 300 = 250,$$

$$x_3 = -\frac{1}{2}x_2 + y = -\frac{1}{2}\cdot 250 + 300 = 175,$$

$$x_4 = -\frac{1}{2}x_3 + y = -\frac{1}{2}\cdot 175 + 300 = 212\frac{1}{2}.$$

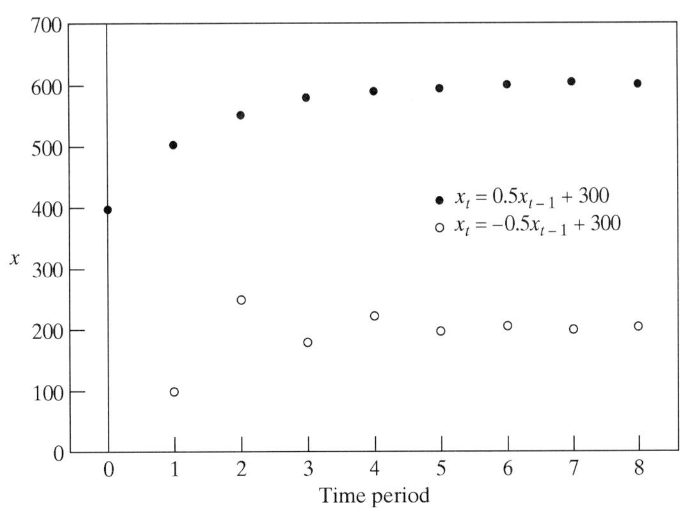

FIGURE 13.1 Stable Difference Equations (13.2) and (13.3)

The dynamics generated by this difference equation are **oscillatory** rather than monotonic since the sign of $(x_t - x_{t-1})$ alternates from one period to the next. For example, $(x_1 - x_0) = -300$, $(x_2 - x_1) = 150$, $(x_3 - x_2) = -75$, and so on. The sequence of values $\{x_t\}$ for this equation is also depicted in Figure 13.1.

These two specific examples point to a more general result for a linear first-order difference equation like (13.1).

Monotonic The differences between adjacent terms in the sequence generated by the difference equation

$$x_t = ax_{t-1} + y,$$

that is, $(x_t - x_{t-1})$, will be of the same sign if $a > 0$. In this case the dynamics generated by this equation are monotonic.

Oscillatory The differences between adjacent terms in the sequence generated by the difference equation

$$x_t = ax_{t-1} + y,$$

that is, $(x_t - x_{t-1})$, will alternate in sign if $a < 0$. In this case the dynamics generated by this equation are oscillatory.

The Steady State

One part of the solution of a difference equation is the **steady state value** of the endogenous variable for a given value of the exogenous variable. This steady state value is also called the **equilibrium value,** the **stationary value,** or the **long-run value.** We introduce an analysis of the steady state here by first focusing on the case where the independent variable is constant over all time periods. Subsequently, we will consider the steady state with a time-varying sequence of the independent variable.

Consider a version of the linear first-order difference equation (13.1), where $y_t = y$ for all t.

$$x_t = ax_{t-1} + y \tag{13.4}$$

The steady state value, which we denote as x_∞, exists if the sequence $\{x_t\}$ **converges.** A sequence converges to x_∞ if

$$\lim_{t\to\infty} x_t = x_\infty.$$

We can think of the steady state value as the long-run level of the variable after all dynamic adjustment has taken place. If there is no unique real number x_∞, then the sequence **diverges.** For example, if

$$\lim_{t\to\infty} x_t = \infty,$$

then the sequence $\{x_t\}$ diverges.

Thus

$$\lim_{t\to\infty} x_t = \lim_{t\to\infty} x_{t-1} = x_\infty$$

if the sequence generated by the difference equation (13.4) converges. If this is the case, then

$$\lim_{t\to\infty} x_t = \lim_{t\to\infty} (ax_{t-1} + y).$$

The steady state value of (13.4) therefore satisfies the condition

$$x_\infty = ax_\infty + y$$

or

$$x_\infty = \frac{1}{1-a}y.$$

The steady state is not well defined for the special case of $a = 1$. We discuss this special case later.

The steady state value of the difference equation (13.2) is

$$x_\infty = \frac{1}{1-1/2}300 = 600.$$

The first five numbers of the sequence for (13.2) presented earlier, along with its steady state value, suggest that there is convergence to the steady state value of $x_\infty = 600$ since $|x_t - x_{t-1}|$ decreases with an increase in t. This is an example of a **stable** difference equation since the sequence generated by it converges to the value 600. The steady state value of the difference equation (13.3) is

$$x_\infty = \frac{1}{1-(-1/2)}300 = 200.$$

This difference equation is also stable since $|x_t - x_{t-1}|$ decreases with an increase in t, and, in this case, there is convergence to the steady state value of $x_\infty = 200$.

The difference equation in each of these two examples is stable. A difference equation that generates a sequence $\{x_t\}$ for which

$$\lim_{x\to\infty} x_t = \infty \quad \text{or} \quad \lim_{x\to\infty} x_t = -\infty$$

is **unstable.** As an example of an unstable difference equation, consider

$$x_t = 2x_{t-1} - 300, \tag{13.5}$$

where, again, we assume $x_0 = 400$. The steady state value for this equation is

$$x_\infty = \frac{1}{1-(2)}(-300) = 300.$$

The sequence of the endogenous variable, beginning with x_0, is

$$\begin{aligned} x_0 &= 400 \text{ (given)}, \\ x_1 &= 2x_0 + y = 2\cdot 400 - 300 = 500, \end{aligned}$$

$$x_2 = 2x_1 + y = 2 \cdot 500 - 300 = 700,$$
$$x_3 = 2x_2 + y = 2 \cdot 700 - 300 = 1100,$$
$$x_4 = 2x_3 + y = 2 \cdot 1100 - 300 = 1800.$$

This sequence diverges as time progresses since $|x_t - x_{t-1}|$ increases with an increase in t. This monotonic divergence would hold for any x_0 other than $x_0 = x_\infty = 300$. If the initial value $x_0 = 300$, then

$$x_1 = 2(300) - 300 = 300,$$
$$x_2 = 2(300) - 300 = 300,$$

and $x_t = 300$ for any t.

The difference equation

$$x_t = -2x_{t-1} + 900 \tag{13.6}$$

is also unstable since, beginning at any x_0 other than $(1/(1 - (-2))(600) = 300$, the resulting sequence diverges. But in contrast to the previous example, the divergence will be oscillatory rather than monotonic since the coefficient is negative. This is shown by the following sequence, which begins with an initial value $x_0 = 400$.

$$x_0 = 400 \quad \text{(given)},$$
$$x_1 = -2x_0 + y = -2 \cdot 400 + 900 = 100,$$
$$x_2 = -2x_1 + y = -2 \cdot 100 + 900 = 700,$$
$$x_3 = -2x_2 + y = -2 \cdot 700 + 900 = -500,$$
$$x_4 = -2x_3 + y = -2 \cdot -500 + 900 = 1900.$$

The sequences corresponding to the difference equations (13.5) and (13.6) are presented in Figure 13.2.

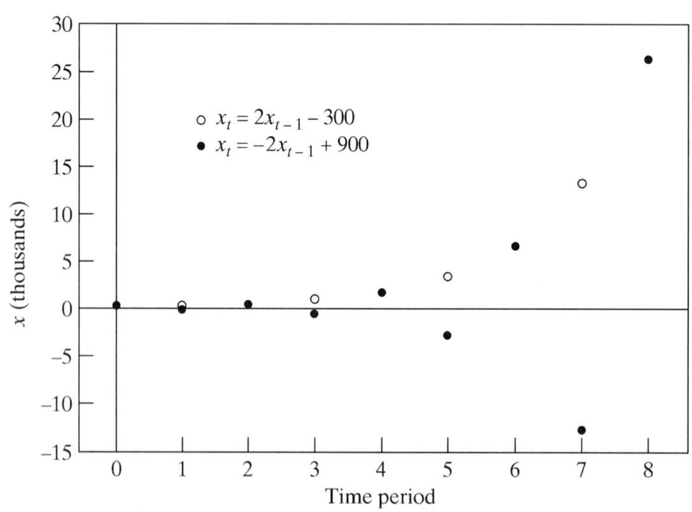

FIGURE 13.2 Unstable Difference Equations (13.5) and (13.6)

These specific examples suggest a more general result concerning the stability of a first-order linear difference equation.

Stable The sequence generated by the difference equation

$$x_t = ax_{t-1} + y$$

converges to the steady state value

$$x_\infty = \frac{1}{1-a}y,$$

regardless of the initial value x_0 if $-1 < a < 1$. In this case the equilibrium solution is stable.

Unstable The sequence generated by the difference equation

$$x_t = ax_{t-1} + y$$

diverges if $a > 1$ or $a < -1$ and if the initial value, x_0, does not equal $(1/(1-a))y$. In this case the equilibrium solution is unstable.

The Special Cases of a = 1 and a = −1

The strict inequalities in the results given previously do not cover the cases of $a = 1$ or $a = -1$. Let $a = 1$. We can examine the properties of the difference equation

$$x_t = x_{t-1} + y,$$

with the initial condition $x_0 = k$, by explicitly solving for its sequence over a number of periods and then drawing some conclusions. For example, the sequence $\{x_t\}_{t=0}^4$ is

$$\begin{aligned} x_0 &= k, \\ x_1 &= k + y, \\ x_2 &= (k + y) + y = k + 2y, \\ x_3 &= (k + 2y) + y = k + 3y, \quad \text{and} \\ x_4 &= (k + 3y) + y = k + 4y. \end{aligned}$$

By induction, we see that the solution to this difference equation is

$$x_t = x_0 + ty.$$

Thus this difference equation generates a sequence that approaches positive infinity if $y > 0$ or negative infinity if $y < 0$. If $y = 0$, then $x_t = x_0$ in each period. Thus, except for the special case of $y = 0$, the sequence generated by this difference equation diverges monotonically from its initial value.

There are also some special properties of the difference equation

$$x_t = -x_{t-1} + y,$$

where $a = -1$. Again, defining the initial value $x_0 = k$ and then calculating the sequence $\{x_t\}_{t=0}^{4}$, we find

$$\begin{aligned} x_0 &= k, \\ x_1 &= -k + y, \\ x_2 &= -(-k + y) + y = k, \\ x_3 &= -k + y, \text{ and} \\ x_4 &= -(-k + y) + y = k. \end{aligned}$$

Thus this shows that $x_n = k$ for even values of n (including $n = 0$) and $x_n = -k + y$ for odd values of n. Note that if

$$x_0 = \frac{y}{2}\left(= \frac{1}{1-(-1)}y\right),$$

then $x_t = y/2$ for all $t \geq 0$. Thus, unless $x_0 = x_\infty = y/2$, this difference equation generates a sequence that oscillates between two values.

Solutions to First-Order Difference Equations

The previous discussion gives a sense of the sequences that correspond to some particular first-order linear difference equations through the use of numerical examples and graphical analysis. In this section we show how to find explicit solutions to a general form of first-order difference equations through **repeated iteration.**

We begin the technique of repeated iteration by recognizing that the difference equation

$$x_t = ax_{t-1} + y$$

holds for any t. In particular, this equation shows that

$$x_{t-1} = ax_{t-2} + y.$$

We can use this to substitute for x_{t-1} in the original equation to get

$$x_t = a(ax_{t-2} + y) + y = a^2x_{t-2} + ay + y.$$

Repeating this for $x_{t-2} = ax_{t-3} + y$ and substituting for x_{t-2} in the previous expression, we get

$$x_t = a^3x_{t-3} + a^2y + ay + y.$$

A pattern starts to emerge from this substitution. Defining the initial period as $t = 0$ and given an initial term in the sequence x_0, we find that after substituting t times, the expression for x_t is

$$x_t = a^t x_0 + \sum_{i=0}^{t-1} a^i y. \tag{13.7}$$

An alternative way to express this result uses the fact that

$$\sum_{i=0}^{t-1} a^i = \frac{1-a^t}{1-a}.$$

We prove this relationship by first defining

$$S = \sum_{i=0}^{t-1} a^i = 1 + a + a^2 + \cdots + a^{t-1}.$$

Then

$$Sa = a + a^2 + a^3 + \cdots + a^t,$$

and $S - Sa = S(1 - a) = 1 - a^t$. Therefore

$$S = \sum_{i=0}^{t-1} a^i = \frac{1 - a^t}{1 - a}.$$

Since $\sum_{i=0}^{t-1} a^i y = y\sum_{i=0}^{t-1} a^i$, we can write the solution for the difference equation (13.4) as

$$x_t = a^t x_0 + \frac{1 - a^t}{1 - a} y. \tag{13.8}$$

This solution can be used to derive the steady state results presented previously. The sequence $\{x_i\}$ converges to the steady state value $x_\infty = \lim_{t\to\infty} x_t$ if $|a| < 1$ since, in that case,

$$\begin{aligned}\lim_{t\to\infty} x_t &= \lim_{t\to\infty}\left(a^t x_0 + \frac{1 - a^t}{1 - a} y\right)\\ &= 0 \cdot x_0 + \frac{1}{1 - a} y\\ &= \frac{1}{1 - a} y.\end{aligned}$$

The sequence $\{x_t\}$ diverges if $|a| > 1$ since, in that case,

$$\begin{aligned}\lim_{t\to\infty} x_t &= \lim_{t\to\infty}\left(a^t x_0 + \frac{1 - a^t}{1 - a} y\right)\\ &= \frac{1}{1 - a} y + \left(x_0 - \frac{1}{1 - a} y\right)\lim_{t\to\infty}(a^t)\end{aligned}$$

and $\lim_{t\to\infty}(a^t)$ is either ∞ or $-\infty$.

The linear first-order difference equation introduced at the beginning of this chapter as (13.1),

$$x_t = ax_{t-1} + y_t,$$

differs from (13.4) since it allows for time-varying values of y_t. We can solve (13.1) through repeated iteration in a manner similar to that followed earlier. Substituting for x_{t-1} in (13.1) by using the relationship

$$x_{t-1} = ax_{t-2} + y_{t-1},$$

we get

$$x_t = a(ax_{t-2} + y_{t-1}) + y_t = a^2 x_{t-2} + ay_{t-1} + y_t.$$

Repeating this to substitute for x_{t-2}, we get

$$x_t = a^3 x_{t-3} + a^2 y_{t-2} + a y_{t-1} + y_t.$$

Continuing with this process t times, we obtain a solution much like that in the case of a constant y,

$$x_t = a^t x_0 + \sum_{i=0}^{t-1} a^i y_{t-i} \tag{13.9}$$

We cannot simplify this solution further by using the fact that $\Sigma_{t=0}^{t-1} a^i = (1 - a^t)/(1 - a)$ since the terms in the sequence $\{y_t\}$ are not necessarily constant.

In the context of a time-varying value of the terms of the sequence $\{y_t\}$, we define a stable solution with the concept of a bounded sequence.

Bounded Sequence A sequence $\{x_t\}$ is bounded if there is a real number δ such that, for any t,

$$|x_t| < \delta.$$

The difference equation (13.1) is stable if the sequence $\{x_t\}$ is bounded when the sequence $\{y_t\}$, is bounded. Thus, as with the difference equation (13.4), a linear first-order difference equation with a time-varying term y_t is stable if $-1 < a < 1$. Otherwise, in general, the term a^t approaches positive or negative infinity as t gets very large, and, therefore, $\{x_t\}$ can be unbounded even if $\{y_t\}$ is bounded.

Forward Solutions

In some economic contexts, it is natural to think of a difference equation that expresses the value of some variable today as a function of its value in the next period. For example, in the next section we discuss an application of difference equations to the determination of the price of a stock. One factor in determining the current price of a stock is its expected future price. In cases like this, we can analyze a difference equation that takes the form

$$u_t = b u_{t+1} + v_t \tag{13.10}$$

This equation can be solved through the same method of repeated iteration used earlier. Substituting for u_{t+1} by using the equation

$$u_{t+1} = b u_{t+2} + v_{t+1},$$

we have

$$u_t = b(b u_{t+2} + v_{t+1}) + v_t = b^2 u_{t+2} + b v_{t+1} + v_t.$$

Repeating this n times, we have the expression

$$u_t = b^n u_{t+n} + \sum_{i=0}^{n-1} b^i v_{t+i}.$$

In the limit as n approaches infinity,

$$u_t = \lim_{n\to\infty}\left[b^n u_{t+n} + \sum_{i=0}^{n} b^i v_{t+i} \right].$$

Assume that $|b| < 1$. If $\{v_t\}$ is a bounded sequence, then the only possible bounded solution to the difference equation (13.10) is

$$u_t = \sum_{i=0}^{\infty} b^i v_{t+i} \tag{13.11}$$

since

$$\lim_{n\to\infty} b^n u_{t+n} = 0$$

if $\{u_t\}$ is bounded. To check this solution, note that

$$bu_{t+1} = b\sum_{i=0}^{\infty} b^i v_{t+i+1}$$

and, therefore,

$$\begin{aligned} u_t - bu_{t+1} &= \sum_{i=0}^{\infty} b^i v_{t+i} - b\sum_{i=0}^{\infty} b^i v_{t+i+1} \\ &= (v_t + bv_{t+1} + b^2 v_{t+2} + \cdots) - (bv_{t+1} + b^2 v_{t+2} + \cdots) \\ &= v_t, \end{aligned}$$

which is just the original equation (13.10). This is a **forward solution** for the difference equation (13.10) since it expresses u_t as a function of the future sequence $\{v_i\}_{i=t}^{\infty}$.

It is interesting to consider the forward solution in the context of the difference equation (13.1) when $|a| > 1$. Rewrite (13.1) in the form

$$x_t = \frac{1}{a} x_{t+1} - \frac{1}{a} y_{t+1}.$$

Referring to the forward solution (13.11) and defining $x_t = u_t$, $v_t = -(1/a)y_{t+1}$, and $(1/a) = b$, we find that the solution to this difference equation is

$$x_t = -\sum_{i=0}^{\infty}\left(\frac{1}{a}\right)^i \frac{y_{t+1+i}}{a}.$$

This solution maps the bounded sequence $\{y_t\}$ to the bounded sequence $\{x_t\}$. Notice that the **backward solution** (13.9), in this case, would not provide a bounded sequence $\{x_t\}$. Thus if a difference equation like (13.1) or (13.10) has a coefficient other than 1 or -1, then there is either a backward solution or a forward solution that maps a bounded sequence $\{y_t\}$ to a bounded sequence $\{x_t\}$. The choice of either the backward or the forward solution in an economics problem is dictated by economic logic. Applications in the next section illustrate this point.

General Solution

We end this section with another method for obtaining a general solution. This method is useful for solving higher-order difference equations and is also used in the next chapter to solve dynamic equations in continuous time. Introducing this method here allows us to show that the solution obtained with this technique is the same as that obtained through the technique of repeated iteration.

A general solution to the difference equation (13.4),

$$x_t = ax_{t-1} + y,$$

can be obtained by first solving the **homogeneous equation**

$$x_t - ax_{t-1} = 0,$$

which is (13.4) with $y = 0$. Based on previous results in this section, we conjecture that a solution to this homogeneous equation takes the form

$$x_t = Ak^t,$$

where A and k are to be determined. We can immediately determine the value of k by noting that, at time $t - 1$, this conjectured solution is

$$x_{t-1} = Ak^{t-1}.$$

Substituting these solutions into the homogeneous equation, we have

$$Ak^t - aAk^{t-1} = 0,$$

which implies that $k = a$. Thus the solution to the homogeneous equation is

$$x_t = Aa^t,$$

where A is a constant to be determined.

The homogeneous equation differs from the overall solution to (13.4) by some constant that reflects its steady state value. A **particular solution** to (13.4) is any solution for that equation. It will prove convenient to consider a particular solution for the case where $x_t = x_\infty$ for all t. This solution can be found by considering the limit of (13.4) as $t \to \infty$, which gives us x_∞. As shown previously, for any value of a other than 1,

$$x_\infty = \frac{1}{1-a}y.$$

The **general solution** to the difference equation is the sum of the solution to the homogeneous equation and the particular solution, that is,

$$x_t = Aa^t + \frac{1}{1-a}y,$$

where A is still to be determined. We can determine A if we are given the initial value in the sequence of the endogenous variable, x_0. At time $t = 0$, the value of this general solution is

$$x_0 = Aa^0 + \frac{1}{1-a}y,$$

which implies

$$A = \left(x_0 - \frac{1}{1-a}y\right).$$

Thus the general solution to the first-order linear difference equation for $a \neq 1$ is

$$\begin{aligned} x_t &= \left(x_0 - \frac{1}{1-a}y\right)a^t + \frac{1}{1-a}y \\ &= a^t x_0 + \frac{1-a^t}{1-a}y, \end{aligned}$$

which is the same as the solution given in (13.8).

The Phase Diagram

A way to illustrate the dynamic path of a variable generated by a difference equation like (13.4) is through the use of a **phase diagram.** A phase diagram for the difference equation (13.2) is presented in Figure 13.3. The horizontal axis in this figure represents x_{t-1}, and the vertical axis represents x_t. There are two equations graphed in this figure, the difference equation and the equation $x_t = x_{t-1}$, which is represented by a 45° line. The point where these two lines intersect represents the steady state value x_∞.

The manner in which a phase diagram is used to trace out the sequence $x_0, x_1, x_2, \ldots$ is illustrated in Figure 13.3. The initial value $x_0 = 400$ is identified on the vertical axis. To find x_1, move horizontally from this point to the 45° line (point A in the figure) and then vertically to the line representing the difference equation (point B in the figure). Point B represents x_1. To find x_2, simply repeat these steps, which will take you to point C in the figure. This figure illustrates the monotonic convergence of the sequence $\{x_t\}$ to its steady state value of $x_\infty = 600$.

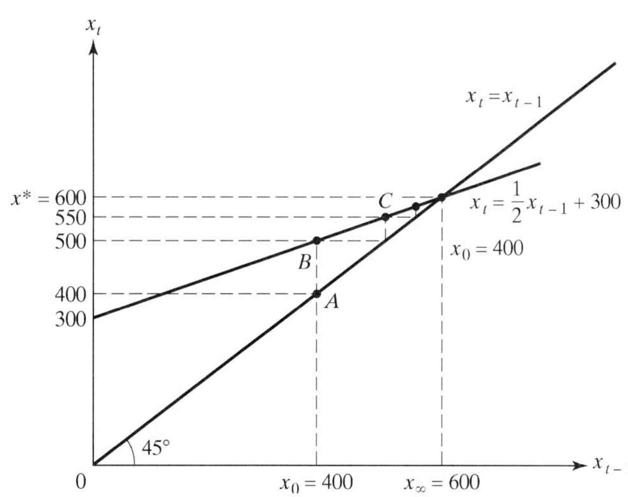

FIGURE 13.3 Phase Diagram for Equation (13.2)

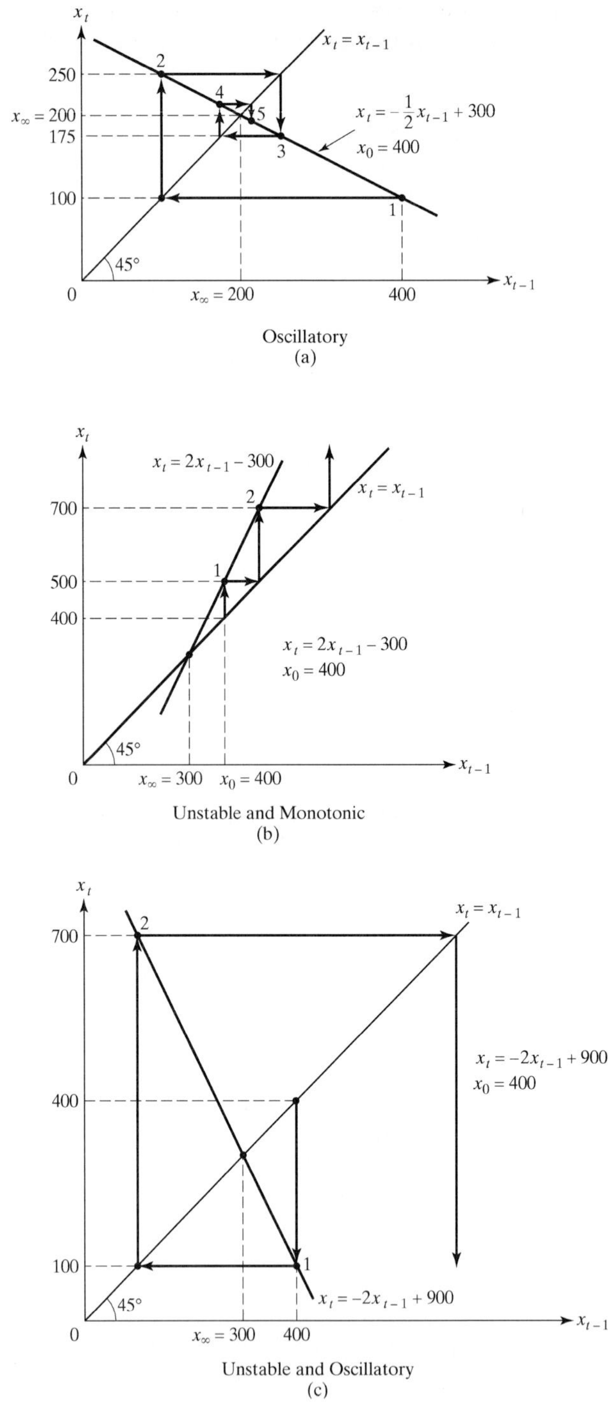

FIGURE 13.4 Phase Diagrams for Difference Equations (13.3), (13.5), and (13.6)

As discussed earlier and as shown in the phase diagram, the difference equation (13.2) exhibits monotonic convergence to the steady state. The three phase diagrams Figure 13.4(a), Figure 13.4(b), and Figure 13.4(c), which correspond to the difference equations (13.3), (13.5), and (13.6), respectively, exhibit different dynamics. Each of these phase diagrams includes a 45° line. The other lines in the diagrams are the graphs of the respective difference equations. In each case, the steady state value of the difference equation, x_∞, is represented by the intersection of the 45° line and the difference equation. The phase diagram in Figure 13.4(a) exhibits oscillatory convergence since the values of x alternate between being greater and less than x_∞ and the difference between x_t and x_∞ asymptotically approaches zero. The phase diagrams in Figures 13.4(b) and (c) represent unstable difference equations. The dynamics traced out by these phase diagrams show that x_t moves further and further from x_∞ as time progresses, as long as x_0 does not equal x_∞. The unstable sequence is monotonic in Figure 13.4(b) and oscillatory in Figure 13.4(c).

Phase diagrams are especially useful for getting a qualitative sense of the solution of a nonlinear difference equation. The method of determining the sequence of the endogenous variable in this case is the same as in the case of a linear solution. Beginning with an initial value, use the 45° line and the schedule representing the difference equation to find the next-period value of the endogenous variable. Each of the points where the difference equation crosses the 45° line represents a steady state. An important generalization of the linear examples previously presented can be used to characterize the one or more steady state points in a phase diagram of a difference equation with monotonic dynamics where the coefficient $a > 0$.

Stability in a Phase Diagram of a Strictly Increasing Difference Equation A difference equation is stable if, in a phase diagram, the graph of the difference equation is strictly increasing and it crosses the 45° line from above when moving from left to right.

A difference equation is unstable if, in a phase diagram, the graph of the difference equation is strictly increasing and it crosses the 45° line from below when moving from left to right.

The following application illustrates these properties.

Two Models of Economic Growth

Models of economic growth can be used to determine both the long-run level of income in an economy and the dynamic path of income. We can conduct a qualitative analysis of the dynamic path of income generated by a growth model by using a phase diagram. In this application we study the phase diagrams associated with two different growth models, the Solow model and a model in which there are increasing returns to scale over some interval of the production function.

Both of these growth models share the same set of variables and, also, some common equations. In both models, we define the capital stock per worker as k_t and the investment per worker as i_t, where subscripts refer to time periods. Investment is the gross addition to the capital stock. The net addition to the capital stock is the difference between investment and depreciation. We assume that, in each period, some proportion δ of capital depreciates and is not available for use in the following period $(0 < \delta < 1)$. This gives us the relationship

$$k_t - k_{t-1} = i_t - \delta k_{t-1}.$$

By national income accounting, $i_t = s_t$, where s_t represents savings per worker. We assume that savings per worker is a constant proportion σ of income per worker $(0 < \sigma < 1)$. Income per worker is determined by the production function $f(k_t)$. Substituting these values into the previous equation and rearranging, we have

$$k_t - \sigma f(k_t) = (1 - \delta)k_{t-1}.$$

Robert Solow combined these equations with an intensive Cobb-Douglas production function in his seminal 1956 article "A contribution to the theory of economic growth."[1] As discussed in the Golden Rule application in Chapter 9, the intensive Cobb-Douglas production function takes the form

$$f(k_t) = Ak_t^{\alpha},$$

where $0 < \alpha < 1$ and A is a constant. This production function exhibits decreasing returns to scale in $k = K/L$ along its entire range. Figure 13.5(a) plots the previous nonlinear difference equation when $f(k_t)$ is a Cobb-Douglas production function. There are two steady state values, 0 and k^*. The steady state value k^* is stable since it crosses the 45° line from above. This implies that, for any positive level of capital, the economy converges to k^* and income in the economy converges to $f(k^*)$. For example, one possible sequence with an initial value $k_0 < k^*$ is traced out in this figure by the points A, B, C, and D, where D is arbitrarily close to the steady state.

This convergence to a single steady state does not occur in an alternative formulation of the growth model, which is based upon a different type of production function. In a growth model in which there are increasing returns to scale over some range of the production function, there may be "poverty traps" that lead to permanent differences in income between rich and poor countries.[2] Increasing returns to scale may arise because a developing economy may experience a sectorial switch from agriculture to manufacturing and services, sectors that may have some increasing returns. This possibility would be reflected in a production function that has an interval in which the function is convex. The associated difference equation is sketched in the phase diagram in Figure 13.5(b). There are three steady states in this diagram (other than $k = 0$), k^*, k^{**}, and k^{***}. The steady states k^* and k^{***} are stable, and the steady state k^{**} is unstable. For any initial condition $k_0 > k^{**}$, the economy converges to the steady state k^{***}, as shown by the sequence labeled R in the figure. For any steady state $0 < k_0 < k^{**}$, the economy converges to k^*, as shown by the sequence labeled

[1] This article was cited when Solow was awarded the Nobel Prize in 1987. The article appears in the *Quarterly Journal of Economics* 70, no. 1 (February 1956): 65–94.

[2] Adapted from Robert J. Barro and Xavier Sala-i-Martin, *Economic Growth* (New York: McGraw-Hill, 1995): 49–52.

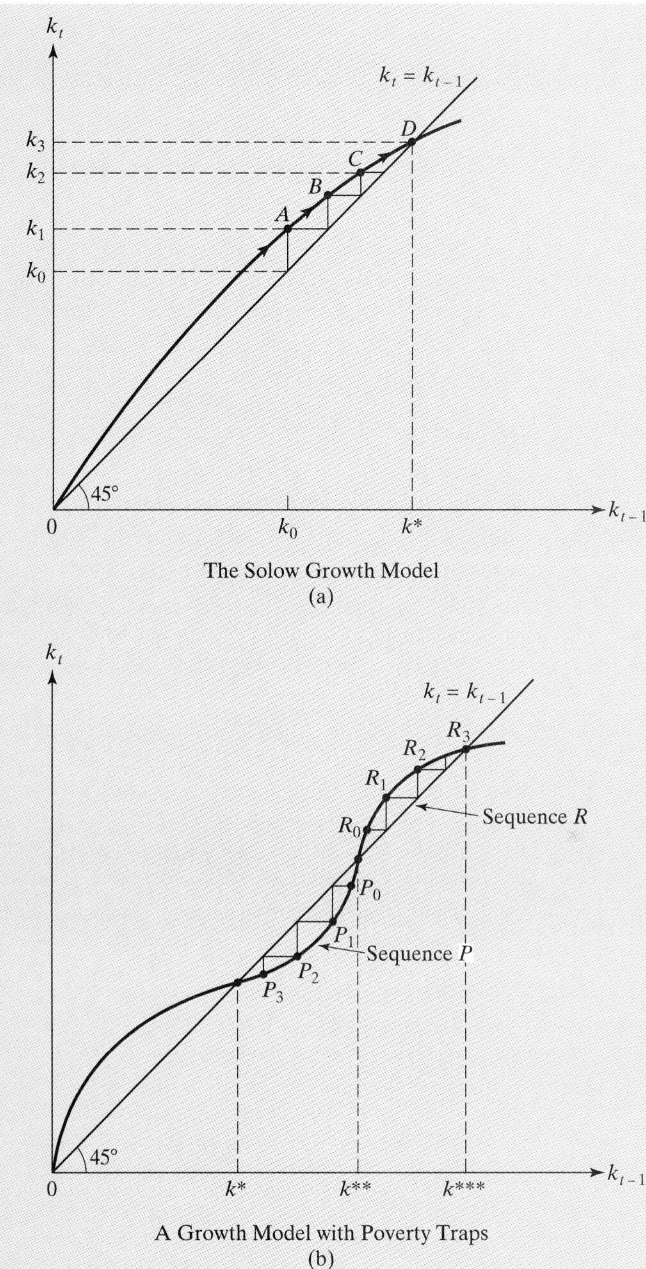

FIGURE 13.5 Two Growth Models

P in the figure. If the economy begins at k^{**}, then it stays at that steady state. The difference in ultimate outcomes due to the initial condition suggests a possible reason for poverty traps in which there are permanent differences in income between rich and poor countries.

Exercises 13.1

1. Given the initial value, calculate the first six values in the sequence for each first-order difference equation.

   (a) $v_t = \frac{7}{8}v_{t-1} + 30$ with $v_0 = 200$

   (b) $w_t = -\frac{1}{5}w_{t-1} + 6$ with $w_0 = 50$

   (c) $x_{t+1} = 0.25x_t + 60$ with $x_0 = 120$

   (d) $y_{t-1} = -y_{t-2} + 40$ with $y_0 = 30$

   (e) $4y_{t+1} - 2y_t = 10$ with $y_0 = 0$

2. For each equation in parts (a) through (e) of question 1,

   (a) discuss whether the sequence you calculated is monotonic or oscillatory and link the coefficient in the equation and this property.

   (b) discuss whether the sequence you calculated is stable or unstable and link the coefficient in the equation and this property.

3. Find the steady state for each equation in parts (a) through (e) of question 1.

4. Determine the steady state for each second-order difference equation.

   (a) $x_t = \frac{1}{4}x_{t-1} + \frac{1}{2}x_{t-2} + 15$

   (b) $y_t = y_{t-1} - \frac{1}{3}y_{t-2} + 20$

   (c) $z_t = 2z_{t-1} + 2z_{t-2} - 90$

5. Calculate the values of the second-order difference equations in question 4 for periods 2 through 5 given the following initial values.

   (a) $x_0 = 100, x_1 = 80$

   (b) $y_0 = 100, y_1 = 90$

   (c) $z_0 = 40, z_1 = 30$

   In each case assess whether the equation is stable or unstable based upon your calculations.

6. Graph a phase diagram for each difference equation below. Identify the steady state point in each phase diagram. Then use the phase diagram to plot the sequence of x_t and assume, in each case, that $x_0 = 24$.

   (a) $x_t = -\frac{1}{4}x_{t-1} + 20$

   (b) $x_t = \frac{1}{2}x_{t-1} + 5$

   (c) $x_t = -\frac{3}{2}x_{t-1} + 55$

   (d) $x_t = 3x_{t-1} - 50$

7. Your first job after graduation pays a salary and, after the first year, a bonus. Your initial salary is \$40,000, and you will not receive a bonus in your first year. In subsequent years, you will be paid 95% of the salary you received in the previous year plus a bonus. Your first bonus will be \$2,500. Your bonus will increase by 10% each year. Determine the sequence of your income (salary plus bonus) in your first six years on the job. Also calculate the percentage increase in salary each year.

8. Suppose that the market for hogs is characterized by the demand and supply equations

$$P_t = a - bQ_t^D + B \quad \text{and} \quad Q_t^S = c + gP_{t-1} - F,$$

where P_t is price, Q_t^D is quantity demanded, Q_t^S is quantity supplied, F is the price of feed $Q_t^S = Q_t^D$. The supply equation shows that farmers must decide in year $t - 1$ how many hogs to raise and bring to market in year t.

   (a) What is the steady state price and quantity, expressed as a function of the parameters a, b, c, and g as well as the exogenous variables B and F?

   (b) What values of the parameters a, b, c, and g give rise to a "hog cycle" in which a change in B or F leads to an oscillatory movement towards a new equilibrium?

9. The average number of cars stopped at a traffic light at a particular intersection from one moment when the light is red to another moment when the light is red follows the relationship

$$c_{t+1} = \frac{1}{11}c_t^2 + \frac{10}{11},$$

where c_t is the average number of cars in the intersection during the tth moment that the light is red. A value of $c_t = 0$ means that there are no cars waiting at the red light ($c_t \geq 0$).

   (a) Determine the steady state values of this relationship.

   (b) Construct a phase diagram for this difference equation. Discuss the stability of the steady state values.

   (c) Use the phase diagram to show the sequence of the average number of cars waiting at successive red lights if $c_0 = 0$, $c_0 = 4$, and $c_0 = 12$.

13.2 APPLICATIONS OF LINEAR FIRST-ORDER DIFFERENCE EQUATIONS

In this section we present dynamic economic models that employ a first-order difference equation.

Keynesian Income Determination

The simplest Keynesian model of income determination shows how a given change in an exogenous component of aggregate demand, like government spending, leads to a larger change in aggregate demand. This "multiplier" result is often presented as the consequence of an initial injection of government spending, setting off subsequent rounds of consumer spending. In this application, we explicitly model the sequence of a change of income in response to a change in government spending.

We use the simplest dynamic Keynesian model. Aggregate demand in period *t* is the sum of consumption and government spending in that period, as shown by

$$Y_t = C_t + G.$$

Permanent income, Y_t^P, is assumed to be a weighted average of income in the current period and income in the previous period, that is,

$$Y_t^P = \lambda Y_t + (1 - \lambda)Y_{t-1},$$

where $1 > \lambda > 0$. We assume that period-*t* consumption is a function of permanent income in that period, as shown by the simple function

$$C_t = \alpha + \beta Y_t^P,$$

where $\alpha > 0$ and $1 > \beta > 0$. Solving these equations, we get the difference equation in income and lagged income

$$Y_t = \frac{\beta(1 - \lambda)}{1 - \beta\lambda} Y_{t-1} + \frac{1}{1 - \beta\lambda}(a + G).$$

The coefficient

$$\frac{\beta(1 - \lambda)}{1 - \beta\lambda} = \frac{\beta - \beta\lambda}{1 - \beta\lambda}$$

is positive and less than one, which implies that this is a stable system that monotonically converges to its steady state value. The steady state value is

$$\begin{aligned} Y_\infty &= \frac{1}{1 - (\beta - \beta\lambda)/(1 - \beta\lambda)} \cdot \left[\frac{1}{1 - \beta\lambda}(\alpha + G)\right] \\ &= \frac{1}{1 - \beta}(a + G). \end{aligned}$$

The coefficient $1/(1 - \beta)$ is the familiar "Keynesian multiplier," which shows that the steady state of this model is identical to the simpler Keynesian model where consumption is a function of current income rather than permanent income. This correspondence occurs because, after all dynamic adjustment has taken place, $Y_{t-1} = Y_t = Y_\infty$ and, therefore, there is no difference between the values of permanent and current income.

We can examine the dynamics that move income to its steady state by considering what happens when government spending changes. Assume that $\alpha = 200$, $\beta = \frac{4}{5}$, and $\lambda = \frac{1}{2}$ and that we start out with an initial level of income of 2500, corresponding to the assumption that the initial level of government spending is 300. Figure 13.6 presents a phase diagram that shows what happens when government spending rises to 400. The difference equation line in this diagram, which reflects $G = 400$, is

$$Y_t = \frac{2}{3}Y_{t-1} + 1000.$$

The economy monotonically converges from $Y_0 = 2500$ to the new steady state of $Y^* = 3000$ with $Y_1 = 2667$, $Y_2 = 2778$, $Y_3 = 2852$, and so on. (Each of the previous numbers is rounded to the nearest integer.)

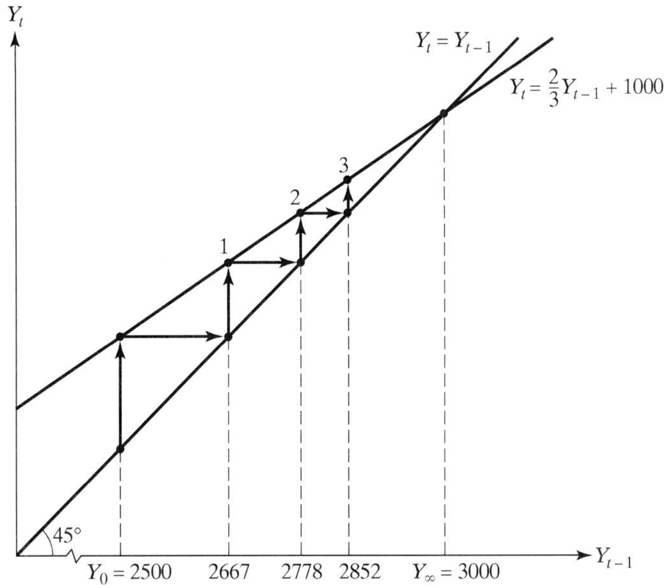

FIGURE 13.6 Keynesian Macroeconomic Model Phase Diagram ($G = 400$)

The Half-Life of Misalignments

One way to characterize the dynamic properties of a stable difference equation with monotonic dynamics is to calculate the **half-life,** which represents the number of periods it takes for a given deviation from the steady state value to be reduced by half. In this application we derive the formula for the half-life of a first-order stable difference equation with monotonic dynamics. We then use this to discuss the estimated half-life of deviations from the equilibrium value of the **real exchange rate,** which is a measure of the relative price competitiveness of goods sold in different countries.

We consider the first-order difference equation

$$x_t = ax_{t-1} + y,$$

where $1 > a > 0$ and where the starting value is denoted as x_0. As shown in Section 13.1, the steady state value, x_∞, is

$$x_\infty = \frac{y}{1 - a}.$$

The initial deviation between the starting value, x_0, and the steady state value, x_∞, is cut in half at time H if the value of x in that period, which we denote as x_H, is

$$x_H = \frac{x_\infty + x_0}{2}.$$

We use this result for the value of x at the time the initial deviation has been reduced by half to determine the value of H.

Equation (13.8) shows that

$$x_t = a^t x_0 + \frac{1 - a^t}{1 - a} y.$$

At time H, we have

$$x_H = a^H x_0 + \frac{1 - a^H}{1 - a} y = a^H x_0 + (1 - a^H) x_\infty,$$

where we use the definition for the steady state in replacing $((1 - a^H)/(1 - a))y$ with $(1 - a^H)x_\infty$. Combining this result with the definition of x_H, we have

$$\frac{x_\infty + x_0}{2} = a^H x_0 + (1 - a^H) x_\infty.$$

We need to determine H, given x_0, x_∞ and a. First we rewrite the equation above as

$$(1 - 2a^H) x_0 = (1 - 2a^H) x_\infty.$$

This can only be true, when $x_0 \neq x_\infty$, if

$$2a^H = 1.$$

We can solve for H by taking the natural logrithm of each side (recall from Chapter 3 that $\ln(1) = 0$ and $\ln(2) \approx 0.6931$), and after some simple algebra, we obtain

$$H = -\frac{\ln(2)}{\ln(a)} \approx -\frac{0.6931}{\ln(a)}.$$

Note that the half-life, H, representing the number of time periods for the initial deviation to be reduced in half, only depends upon the coefficient a and does not depend upon the initial value x_0 nor upon the constant term in the difference equation, y.

An example of the use of this formula involves the difference equation

$$x_t = \frac{1}{2} x_{t-1} + 8.$$

The half-life of the deviation between any initial value x_0, $x_0 \neq 16$, and the steady state value $x_\infty = 16$ is

$$-\frac{\ln(2)}{\ln(1/2)} = -\frac{\ln(2)}{\ln(1) - \ln(2)} = \frac{\ln(2)}{\ln(2)} = 1 \text{ period.}$$

The half-life of an equation with the coefficient $a = 0.9$, in contrast, is 6.58 periods[3] since

[3] Of course, with discrete-time analysis, the value of x in period 6 is maintained throughout that period; there is not a value $x_{6.58}$ distinct from x_6. Rounding H to the nearest integer tells you when the actual value of x is closest to the value $(x_0 + x_\infty)/2$. See question 3 at the end of this section.

$$-\frac{\ln(2)}{\ln(0.9)} \approx -\frac{0.6931}{-0.1054} = 6.58.$$

An economic application of the speed of convergence, as measured by the half-life of a deviation, involves the estimation of the dynamic properties of the real exchange rate. The real exchange rate represents the price of foreign goods relative to the price of domestic goods. Roughly speaking, we can consider the equilibrium value of the real exchange rate as one where the price of a basket of foreign goods equals the price of a similar basket of domestic goods. Deviations from this equilibrium may mark misalignments that, in turn, can contribute to trade imbalances across countries. Excess demand for a country's goods, or excess supply of a country's goods, however, exerts pressure on the real exchange rate to move towards its equilibrium value. It is important to know how quickly market pressures force the real exchange rate back to its equilibrium value.

Jeffrey Frankel studied the real exchange rate between the U.S. dollar and the British pound over the period 1869 to 1984. Using these annual data, he presents the estimated relationship.

$$q_t = 0.86q_{t-1} + \varepsilon_t$$

where q_t is the real exchange rate at time t and ε_t is a regression error term. This result implies a half-life of 4.6 years for the deviation of the real exchange rate from its long-run equilibrium level since

$$-\frac{\ln(2)}{\ln(0.86)} \approx -\frac{0.6931}{-0.1508} = 4.6 \text{ years.}$$

Other researchers, using somewhat different methodologies and other data, find a range of values for the half-life or deviations of the real exchange rate from its equilibrium value from about 3 years up to slightly more than 7 years.[4]

Money and Prices

Hyperinflations are dramatic episodes in which prices rise at a staggering rate. In a well-known study, Philip Cagan modeled the price process during a hyperinflation and empirically tested his model against 7 twentieth-century hyperinflations.[5] Cagan's model employed a money demand equation and a model of expectations. Each of these components of his model takes the form of first-order linear difference equations.

---

[4] See Jeffrey Frankel, "International Capital Mobility and Crowding Out in the U.S. Economy: Imperfect Integration of Financial Markets or Goods Markets?" in R. Hafer, ed., *How Open is the US Economy,* (Lexington, MA: Lexington Books, 1986). For an overview on this topic, see Kenneth A. Froot and Kenneth Rogoff, "Perspectives on PPP and Long-Run Real Exchange Rates," in Gene Grossman and Kenneth Rogoff, eds., *Handbook of International Economics, Volume 3* (Amsterdam, The Netherlands: Elsevier Science B.V., 1995), Chapter 32.

[5] Philip Cagan, "The Monetary Dynamics of Hyperinflation," *Studies in the Quantity Theory of Money,* Milton Friedman, ed. (Chicago: University of Chicago Press, 1956). See Chapter 9 for another reference to Cagan's study.

The money demand function studied by Cagan takes the form

$$\frac{M_t}{P_t} = \beta Y_t^{\alpha} \cdot e^{-\lambda Rt},$$

where M_t represents money supply, P_t represents the price level, Y_t represents income, R_t represents the nominal interest rate, and the parameters α, β, and λ are positive. The Fisher relationship shows that

$$R_t = r_t + \pi_t,$$

where r_t is the real interest rate and π_t is the expectation in period t of the inflation rate that will prevail from period t to period $t + 1$. Using the Fisher relationship and taking the natural logarithm of each side of this money demand equation, we get

$$m_t - p_t = \gamma - \lambda \pi_t, \tag{13.12}$$

where m_t is the natural logarithm of the money supply, p_t is the natural logarithm of the price level, and $\gamma = \ln \beta + \alpha \ln(y_t) - \lambda r_t$. To simplify the analysis, we assume that income and the real interest rate are constant in hyperinflation episodes (and, therefore, there is no time subscript on γ). This assumption is justified since the dominant factor affecting prices in these episodes is the behavior of the money supply and of expected inflation.

Equation (13.12) does not quite correspond to a first-order linear difference equation since π_t represents the difference between *expected* prices, not actual prices, in period $t + 1$ and actual prices in period t. A full solution to this model requires some specification of the manner in which price expectations are formed. Cagan presents an "adaptive expectations" model of inflation expectations. In this model the change in expected inflation rate, $\pi_t - \pi_{t-1}$, is a function of the difference between the actual change in prices, $\Delta p_t = p_t - p_{t-1}$, and the change that was expected over that interval, π_{t-1}, as shown by the relationship

$$\pi_t - \pi_{t-1} = \theta(\Delta p_t - \pi_{t-1}),$$

where θ represents how quickly expectations change and $0 \leq \theta \leq 1$. This adaptive expectations specification can be rewritten as

$$\pi_t = \theta \cdot \Delta p_t + (1 - \theta)\pi_{t-1},$$

which shows that expected inflation in period t is a weighted average of actual inflation, Δp_t, and the previous period's expected inflation.

To determine the actual sequence of prices, we first subtract $(1 - \theta)$ times the one-period lagged version of (13.12) from (13.12) itself to get

$$\begin{aligned}(m_t - p_t) - (1 - \theta)(m_{t-1} - p_{t-1}) &= -\lambda(\pi_t - (1 - \theta)\pi_{t-1}) \\ &= -\lambda\theta \cdot \Delta p_t,\end{aligned}$$

where the expression in the second line is obtained by using the adaptive expectations assumption. Rewriting this in the form of a difference equation by substituting $\Delta p_t = p_t - p_{t-1}$ and rearranging terms, we get the difference equation

$$p_t = \frac{1 - \lambda\theta - \theta}{1 - \lambda\theta} p_{t-1} + \frac{1}{1 - \lambda\theta}(m_t - (1 - \theta)m_{t-1}),$$

which is stable since $(1 - \lambda_\theta - \theta)/(1 - \lambda_\theta) < 1$. In fact, Cagan's empirical estimates indicated that $(1 - \lambda_\theta - \theta)/(1 - \lambda_\theta)$ was less than 1 for five of the seven hyperinflations he studied. The result (13.9) shows that the solution to this difference equation is

$$p_t = \left(\frac{1 - \lambda\theta - \theta}{1 - \lambda\theta}\right)^t p_0 + \sum_{i=0}^{t-1}\left(\frac{1 - \lambda\theta - \theta}{1 - \lambda\theta}\right)^i\left(\frac{1}{1 - \lambda\theta}\right)(m_{t-1} - (1 - \theta)m_{t-1-i}),$$

given an initial price level p_0. In the case of a constant money supply of $\overline{m} = m_t$ for all t, this solution simplifies to

$$p_t = \left(\frac{1 - \lambda\theta - \theta}{1 - \lambda\theta}\right)^t p_0 + \sum_{i=0}^{t-1}\left(\frac{1 - \lambda\theta - \theta}{1 - \lambda\theta}\right)^i\left(\frac{1}{1 - \lambda\theta}\right)\theta\overline{m}.$$

In this case the long-run value of the price level with a constant money supply is

$$\begin{aligned}\lim_{t\to\infty} p_t &= \lim_{t\to\infty}\left(\frac{1 - \lambda\theta - \theta}{1 - \lambda\theta}\right)^t p_0 + \sum_{i=0}^{\infty}\left(\frac{1 - \lambda\theta - \theta}{1 - \lambda\theta}\right)^i\left(\frac{1}{1 - \lambda\theta}\right)\theta\overline{m} \\ &= 0 + \frac{1}{1 - ((1 - \lambda\theta - \theta)/(1 - \lambda\theta))}\left(\frac{1}{1 - \lambda\theta}\right)\theta\overline{m} \\ &= \overline{m}.\end{aligned}$$

The stable character of the price process in the adaptive expectations model is a function of the form of the expectations hypothesis. An alternative hypothesis is that expectations are formed "rationally" and that

$$\pi_t = \Delta p_{t+1} = p_{t+1} - p_t.$$

This formulation is a type of rational expectations in which people have perfect foresight and correctly guess the actual inflation rate. In this case the money demand equation (13.12) can be rewritten in the form of the difference equation

$$m_t - p_t = \gamma - \lambda[p_{t+1} - p_t],$$

which can be rearranged to

$$p_t = \frac{\lambda}{1 + \lambda}p_{t+1} + \frac{1}{1 + \lambda}(m_t - \gamma).$$

This difference equation can be expressed in terms of the inflation rate and the expected rate of growth of the money supply, $\mu_t = m_{t+1} - m_t$, as

$$\pi_t = \frac{\lambda}{1 + \lambda}\pi_{t+1} + \frac{1}{1 + \lambda}\mu_t.$$

If we assume that the sequence $\{\mu_t\}$ is bounded, then this difference equation has the infinite forward solution

$$\pi_t = \sum_{i=0}^{\infty}\left(\frac{\lambda}{1 + \lambda}\right)^i\left(\frac{1}{1 + \lambda}\mu_{t+i}\right)$$

since $1 > \lambda/(1 + \lambda) > 0$. The actual inflation rate in any period, which equals the expected inflation rate, is a weighted average of the infinite forward sum of all of the expected money growth rates. A change in the expected rate of growth of money in any future period affects the inflation rate today, with larger effects arising from expected changes closer to the present. In the case of constant money growth equal to $\bar{\mu}$, the inflation rate is

$$\begin{aligned}\pi_t &= \sum_{i=0}^{\infty}\left(\frac{\lambda}{1+\lambda}\right)^i\left(\frac{\bar{\mu}}{1+\lambda}\right)\\ &= \frac{1}{1-(\lambda/(1+\lambda))}\left(\frac{\bar{\mu}}{1-\lambda}\right)\\ &= \bar{\mu}.\end{aligned}$$

This infinite forward solution sum is typical of many types of economic models in which expectations are formed rationally. Another such example is the subject of the next application.

The Determination of Stock Prices

The price of an asset reflects the value of both future payouts earned by holding that asset and possible increases in the price of that asset. The importance of the future price of an asset for its current price introduces a dynamic element into asset pricing equations. In fact, a typical asset price equation takes the form of a first-order linear difference equation.

To illustrate this, we consider a model of stock prices. Define p_t as the time-*t* price of one share of a stock. The return on the stock is the sum of two components. A stock pays a dividend in period $t + 1$ for holding the stock during period t, and we denote the expected value of this dividend as d_{t+1}^e. Another source of return to a stock is the price at which it can be sold in the next period. During period t people expect the price of the stock in period $t + 1$ to be p_{t+1}^e. The expected return from holding a share of a stock must equal the return from holding a bond in an asset market when investors can choose between either asset and when there is no difference in riskiness or liquidity between stocks and bonds. If the money spent on a share of stock were instead invested in a one-period bond paying an interest rate r, the return would be $(1 + r)p_t$. The expected return on the stock is equated to the return on a bond if

$$(1+r)p_t = p_{t+1}^e + d_{t+1}^e.$$

We assume that $p_{t+1}^e = p_{t+1}$ for all t. We then have the first-order linear difference equation

$$(1+r)p_t = p_{t+1} + d_{t+1}^e,$$

which can be solved with methods discussed earlier. Rearranging terms, we have

$$p_t = \left(\frac{1}{1+r}\right)p_{t+1} + \left(\frac{1}{1+r}\right)d_{t+1}^e.$$

The solution (13.11) shows that this equation has the forward solution

$$p_t = \sum_{i=0}^{\infty}\left(\frac{1}{1+r}\right)^i\left(\frac{d_{t+1+i}^e}{1+r}\right). \tag{13.13}$$

This solution assumes that the terminal value d^e_∞ is finite since, then,

$$\lim_{t\to\infty}\left(\frac{1}{1+r}\right)^t\cdot\left(\frac{d^e_\infty}{1+r}\right)=0.$$

The solution (13.13) predicts that the period-t price of a stock equals the present discounted value of its expected future stream of dividends. In particular, if the expected dividend is constant and equal to $\bar{d}$, then the current stock price equals

$$\begin{aligned}p_t &= \sum_{i=0}^{\infty}\left(\frac{1}{1+r}\right)^i\left(\frac{\bar{d}}{1+r}\right)\\ &= \frac{1}{1-(1/(1+r))}\left(\frac{\bar{d}}{1+r}\right)\\ &= \frac{\bar{d}}{r},\end{aligned}$$

which is the present discounted value of the stream of constant dividend payments.

The solution (13.13) implies that anything that affects the dividend payment in the future affects the current price of the stock. The effect is larger for a given change that is closer to the present. Stock prices move in response to news about dividend payments, and, thus, we would expect stock prices to be volatile.

In fact, actual stock prices appear to be too volatile to be consistent with this model. Robert Shiller shows that the time path of the prices of composite stock market indices are much more volatile than the time path predicted by this model when actual dividend payments are used for the sequence $\{d^e_t\}^n_{t=0}$. Work by Robert Barsky and J. Bradford DeLong, however, suggests that this model of the stock market may prove consistent with the data if investors must estimate the path of dividends since this introduces more volatility into the stock price sequence.[6]

Exercises 13.2

1. Consider the Keynesian income determination model presented earlier for the case where $\alpha = 100$, $G = 100$, $\lambda = \frac{1}{2}$, and $\beta = \frac{4}{5}$.
   (a) What is the steady state level of income in this case?
   (b) Draw a phase diagram for this case. Identify the steady state in the diagram. Use the diagram to show the time path of income if income is initially below the steady state.
2. The Keynesian model discussed in this section does not include international trade. Consider an extension of this model for an "open" economy, one which trades with the rest of the world. The aggregate demand equation is

$$Y_t = I_t + C_t + TB_t,$$

[6]The citations for these papers are Robert Shiller, "Do stock prices move too much to be justified by subsequent changes in dividends," *American Economic Review* 71 (1981): 421–435, and Robert B. Barsky and J. Bradford DeLong, "Why does the stock market fluctuate?" *Quarterly Journal of Economics* 108, no. 2 (May 1993): 291–312.

where TB_t is the trade balance in period t, which is the difference between exports and imports. The trade balance is a function of the exogenous real exchange rate, Q_t, as well as current and past domestic income, as shown by the equation

$$TB_t = Q_t - \phi Y_t - \frac{\phi}{2} Y_{t-1},$$

where Q_t is the price of foreign goods relative to the price of domestic goods.

(a) Determine the steady state value of income in this open economy model.

(b) Draw a phase diagram for this model.

(c) Use the phase diagram to consider the effect on income of a devaluation that increases the real exchange rate.

3. Determine the half-life of the deviation from the steady state, H, in each of the following difference equations. Also, in each case, determine the change in x between period 0 and period A, where A is the integer closest in value to the real number H. Compare the actual charge, $x_A - x_0$, to $(x_0 + x_\infty)/2$.
   (a) $x_t = 0.25x_{t-1} + 60$, with $x_0 = 0$.
   (b) $x_t = 0.75x_{t-1} + 20$, with $x_0 = 0$.
   (c) $x_t = 0.95x_{t-1} + 4$, with $x_0 = 0$.
4. Determine the formula for the "third-life" of the deviation from the steady state for a first-order difference equation that is stable with monotonic dynamics. The "third-life" is the number of periods, T, from the initial period such that a variable moves one-third of the way from the initial value towards the steady state. Then use your answer, as well as the solution presented in the application, to determine the half-life and the third-life of the following difference equations.
   (a) $x_t = 0.85x_{t-1} + 60$.
   (b) $x_t = 0.90x_{t-1}$.
   (c) $x_t = 0.99x_{t-1} + 1$.
5. In the next chapter we will learn about the "price-specie flow" model, first developed by David Hume in the eighteenth century. The application in that chapter uses continuous time analysis. We can present the model with discrete time analysis as well. Define the amount of gold held by the residents of a country in any period t as g_t, the price level in that period as p_t, and the country's balance of trade in that period as b_t. Assume that the price level is directly linked to the country's holdings of gold such that

$$p_t = g_t.$$

The balance of trade determines the change in the country's gold holdings; the country acquires gold from abroad when it runs a trade surplus, and it ships gold to other countries when it runs a trade deficit, as shown by the relationship

$$b_t = g_t - g_{t-1}.$$

The country's balance of trade is a function of the relationship between its price level and the price level of its trading partners, ϕ, as shown by the relationship

$$b_t = \beta(\phi - p_t),$$

where $\beta > 0$.

(a) What is the long-run (that is, steady state) price level in the economy?

(b) Suppose that initially the price level does not equal its long-run level. Will the price level move towards its long-run price level? Will the price level oscillate or move in a monotonic fashion?

6. Determine how each of the following affects the speed of convergence as measured by the half-life of the Keynesian income determination model presented earlier where $\alpha = 100$, $G = 100$, $\lambda = \frac{1}{2}$, and $\beta = \frac{4}{5}$.

(a) A change in the difference between the initial and the subsequent levels of government spending from $100(= 400 - 300)$ to 400. (That is, assume G goes from 300 to 700.)

(b) A change in λ from $\frac{1}{2}$ to $\frac{3}{4}$

(c) A change in β from $\frac{4}{5}$ to $\frac{9}{10}$

7. Find the steady state value of the price level by using the adaptive expectations model presented in the application about money and prices when $m_t = 100$ for all t and when $\lambda = \frac{1}{2}$ and $\theta = \frac{1}{2}$. Draw a phase diagram for this case. Use this phase diagram to trace out the time path of the price level in response to an increase in the money supply from $m_0 = 100$ to $m_1 = 200$. Assume that, at time $t = 0$, the price level is at its steady state value.

8. Draw a phase diagram for the determination of stock prices when $r = 0.10$ and $d_t = 250$ for all t. How does this phase diagram change from period 0 to period 1 when $d_0 = 250$ and $d_t = 300$ for all $t \geq 1$? What happens to the stock price in period 1? What is the time path of the stock price?

9. Use the model presented in this section to determine the effect on the price of a stock today of each of the following. Assume that $r = 0.10$ and $d_t = 250$ for all t initially.

(a) $d_t = 300$ for all $t \geq 0$

(b) $d_t = 250$ for $10 > t \geq 0$ and $d_t = 300$ for all $t \geq 10$

(c) $d_t = 250$ for all $t \geq 0$ except for $d_2 = 400$

(d) $d_t = 250$ for all $t \geq 0$ except for $d_{10} = 400$

(e) r changes from $r = 0.10$ to $r = 0.50$

13.3 SECOND-ORDER DIFFERENCE EQUATIONS AND SYSTEMS OF EQUATIONS

As discussed at the beginning of this chapter, a second-order linear difference equation with a constant value of y takes the form

$$x_t = ax_{t-1} + bx_{t-2} + y. \tag{13.14}$$

The solution method for this equation parallels that used earlier to find a general solution for a first-order linear difference equation. We first find a particular solution to the equation that represents its steady state level. We then find a solution to the homogeneous version of this equation, that is, the version of (13.14) where $y = 0$. The complete solution also requires the specification of x_t at two different time periods rather than just one, as is the case with a first-order difference equation. We specify two initial conditions, x_0 and x_1.

We find the particular solution for the steady state value x_∞ by solving (13.14) for $x_t = x_{t-1} = x_{t-2} = x_\infty$. This gives us

$$x_\infty = \frac{1}{1 - a - b} y,$$

if $a + b \neq 1$. If $a + b = 1$, then no constant steady state exists unless $x_0 = x_1 = 0$ and $y = 0$. This result is analogous to the result discussed earlier for a first-order linear difference equation when $a = 1$.

The general solution to (13.14) is comprised of the sum of this particular solution and the solution to the homogeneous equation

$$x_t - ax_{t-1} - bx_{t-2} = 0.$$

Given the earlier results, we conjecture a solution to this homogeneous equation

$$x_t = k^t,$$

where k is a constant to be determined. If this conjectured solution works, then we have

$$x_t - ax_{t-1} - bx_{t-2} = k^t - ak^{t-1} - bk^{t-2} = 0.$$

This can also be written as

$$(k^2 - ak - b)k^{t-2} = 0,$$

which implies, that for $k \neq 0$,

$$k^2 - ak - b = 0.$$

We can solve for k by using the quadratic formula (see Chapter 2) to get the values

$$k_1, k_2 = \frac{1}{2}a \pm \sqrt{\frac{1}{4}a^2 + b}.$$

There are three possible sets of values of k_1 and k_2, which are dictated by the relative values of a and b. These are as follows:

1. $a^2/4 > -b$, which implies that $k_1 \neq k_2$ and both k_1 and k_2 are real numbers
2. $a^2/4 = -b$, which implies that $k_1 = k_2$ and this single root is a real number
3. $a^2/4 < -b$, which implies that the roots are complex numbers

We discuss each of these cases next.

Distinct Real Roots

For the case of two distinct real roots, the solution to the homogeneous difference equation is

$$x_t = Ak_1^t + Bk_2^t,$$

where A and B are two constants and Ak_1^t and Bk_2^t are linearly independent for any value of t.[7] We can obtain a complete solution, including explicit values of A and B, through the use of the two initial values x_0 and x_1 by solving the two equation system

$$x_0 = A + B + x_\infty$$
$$x_1 = Ak_1 + Bk_2 + x_\infty .$$

The general solution in the case of distinct real roots when $a + b \neq 1$ is, therefore,

$$x_t = Ak_1^t + Bk_2^t + x_\infty ,$$

where $x_\infty = y/(1 - a - b)$ and A and B are determined through two exogenous values of x.

As an example of this solution method, consider the difference equation

$$x_t = \frac{1}{2}x_{t-1} + \frac{3}{16}x_{t-2} + 5 \tag{13.15}$$

with the given initial values $x_0 = 1$ and $x_1 = 2$. The particular solution is

$$x_\infty = \frac{5}{1 - 1/2 - 3/16} = 16.$$

The roots used in the solution to the homogeneous equation, k_1 and k_2 are

$$k_1, k_2 = \frac{1}{2} \cdot \frac{1}{2} \pm \sqrt{\frac{1}{4}\left(\frac{1}{2}\right)^2 + \frac{3}{16}}$$
$$= \frac{3}{4} \text{ and } -\frac{1}{4}.$$

The solution to this difference equation, thus, takes the form

$$x_t = A\left(\frac{3}{4}\right)^t + B\left(-\frac{1}{4}\right)^t + 16.$$

We can determine the constants A and B by using the two given initial values $x_0 = 1$ and $x_1 = 2$ and solving

$$1 = A\left(\frac{3}{4}\right)^0 + B\left(-\frac{1}{4}\right)^0 + 16 = A + B + 16 \text{ and}$$
$$2 = A\left(\frac{3}{4}\right)^1 + B\left(-\frac{1}{4}\right)^1 + 16 = \frac{3A}{4} - \frac{B}{4} + 16,$$

[7] To check for linear independence, consider the two cases $t = 0$ and $t = 1$ and the determinant

$$\begin{vmatrix} A & B \\ Ak_1 & Bk_2 \end{vmatrix}.$$

If this determinant does not equal zero, that is, if

$$AB(k_2 - k_1) \neq 0,$$

then Ak_1^t and Bk_2^t are linearly independent (see Chapter 4 for a discussion of determinants).

which gives us $A = -\frac{71}{4}$ and $B = \frac{11}{4}$. Thus the complete solution to this difference equation is

$$x_t = \left(-\frac{71}{4}\right)\cdot\left(\frac{3}{4}\right)^t + \left(\frac{11}{4}\right)\cdot\left(-\frac{1}{4}\right)^t + 16. \tag{13.16}$$

This equation is stable since the absolute values of both $k_1 = \frac{3}{4}$ and $k_2 = -\frac{1}{4}$ are less than 1, and, therefore,

$$\lim_{x\to\infty} x_t = \lim_{x\to\infty}\left[\left(-\frac{71}{4}\right)\cdot\left(\frac{3}{4}\right)^t + \left(\frac{11}{4}\right)\cdot\left(-\frac{1}{4}\right)^t + 16\right] = 16.$$

The sequence corresponding to (13.15), which has the solution (13.16), is presented in Figure 13.7.

Repeated Real Roots

The solution for the case of distinct real roots must be modified when the roots are repeated since the two terms in the homogeneous equation are not linearly independent (see footnote 7). Instead, in the repeated root case, the solution to the homogeneous second-order difference equation is

$$x_t = (A + Bt)k^t,$$

where A and B are constants to be determined from two given values of x, such as x_0 and x_1. To demonstrate a solution in this case, consider the second-order difference equation

$$x_t = x_{t-1} - \frac{1}{4}x_{t-2} + \frac{5}{4}. \tag{13.17}$$

The particular solution is

$$x_\infty = \frac{5/4}{1 - 1 + 1/4} = 5.$$

The single root is

$$k = \frac{1}{2}\cdot 1 \pm \sqrt{\frac{1}{4}(1)^2 - \frac{1}{4}} = \frac{1}{2}.$$

The complete solution to this equation requires the specification of two values of x. We assume that $x_0 = 10$ and $x_1 = 8$. This implies that

$$10 = A + 5 \quad \text{and}$$

$$8 = (A + B)\frac{1}{2} + 5,$$

which implies $A = 5$ and $B = 1$. Thus the complete solution is

$$x_t = (5 + t)\left(\frac{1}{2}\right)^t + 5. \tag{13.18}$$

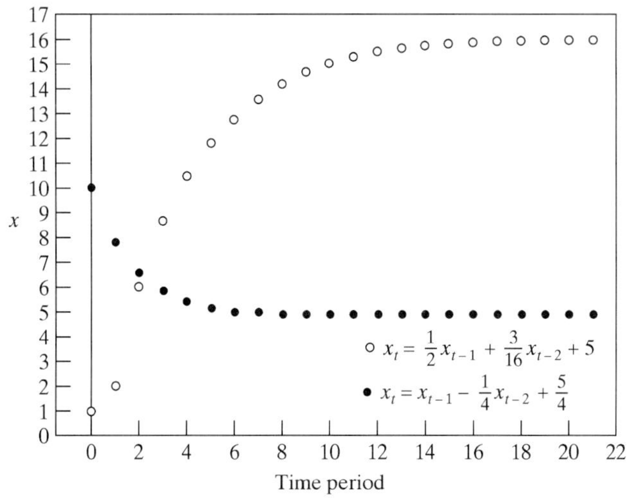

FIGURE 13.7 Second-Order Difference Equations (13.15) and (13.17)

This solution is stable because

$$\begin{aligned}\lim_{t\to\infty} x_t &= \lim_{t\to\infty}(5+t)\left(\frac{1}{2}\right)^t + 5\\ &= \lim_{t\to\infty} 5\left(\frac{1}{2}\right)^t + \lim_{t\to\infty} t\left(\frac{1}{2}\right)^t + 5\\ &= 5.\end{aligned}$$

This result is a particular case of the general property that

$$\lim_{t\to\infty} t(a^t) = 0 \quad \text{if} \quad |a| < 1.$$

The sequence corresponding to (13.17), which has the solution (13.18), is presented in Figure 13.7.

Complex Roots

In the case where $a^2/4 < -b$, the roots are complex numbers. In general, a complex number takes the form

$$r + m\sqrt{-1},$$

where r is called the real part and m is called the imaginary part of the number. In this case, where the roots are

$$k_1, k_2 = \frac{1}{2}a \pm \sqrt{\frac{a^2}{4} + b},$$

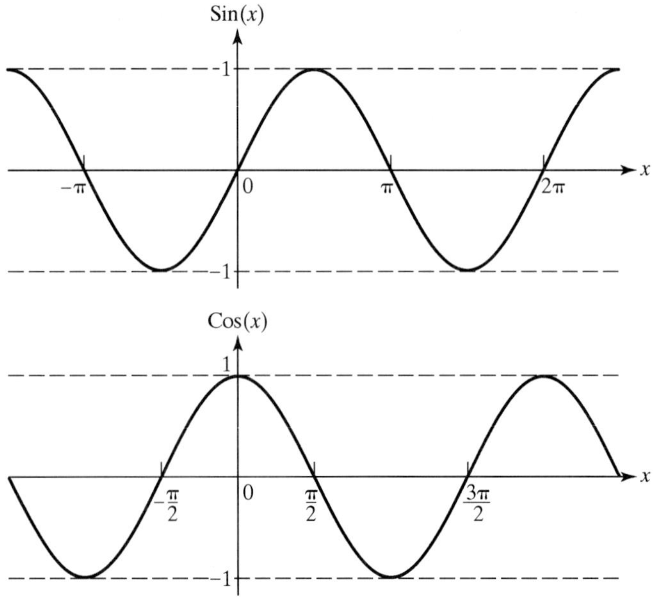

FIGURE 13.8 The Sine and Cosine Functions

the real part of each root is $a/2$. A detailed analysis of this case is beyond the scope of this book.[8] We note, however, that the solution in the complex root case is

$$x_t = A\left(\sqrt{-b}\right)^t \cos\left(\frac{at}{2\sqrt{-b}}\right) + B\left(\sqrt{-b}\right)^t \sin\left(\frac{at}{2\sqrt{-b}}\right) + x_\infty,$$

where $x_\infty = y/1 - a - b$, $\cos(x)$ is the cosine of x, $\sin(x)$ is the sine of x, and A and B are constants that are determined by the initial values of x. Note that $-b$ is necessarily positive. The sine and cosine functions are called periodic functions since their values oscillate, as shown in Figure 13.8. Figure 13.8 also shows that the values of the sine and cosine functions are bounded. These properties of the sine and cosine functions enable us to make two points. First, a second-order difference equation is stable if

$$\lim_{t\to\infty}\left(\sqrt{-b}\right)^t = 0.$$

This condition will hold if $-b < 1$. Since, in the complex root case, $a^2/4 < -b$, the condition that $-b < 1$ implies that $a^2/4 < 1$ or $a/2 < 1$. Thus the condition for stability is that the real part of the complex root, which is $a/2$, is less than one, a condition similar to those found for the case of real roots discussed earlier. Second, the sequence generated by the equation is oscillatory since the sine and cosine functions are oscillatory.

The solutions to these second-order linear difference equations give us the following results concerning stability.

---

[8]For a discussion of the case where the roots are complex see Carl P. Simon and Lawrence Blume, *Mathematics for Economists* (New York: W. W. Norton, 1994): 609–615.

Stability of a Second-Order Linear Difference Equation Stability of a second order linear difference equation with different types of roots is as follows.

Two Distinct Real Roots A second-order linear difference equation with two distinct real roots is stable if the absolute value of each root is less than 1.

A Single Repeated Root A second-order linear difference equation with one repeated root is stable if the absolute value of that root is less than 1.

Two Distinct Complex Roots A second-order linear difference equation with two complex roots is stable if the absolute value of the real part of each root is less than 1.

A second-order linear difference equation can generate a rich set of dynamics, as shown in the following application.

Multiplier-Accelerator Model

The simple Keynesian model presented in Section 13.2 was extended by Paul Samuelson to include an "accelerator" relationship in investment, whereby investment in one period depends upon the growth of income in the previous period.[9] For example, consider the accelerator relationship

$$I_t = \frac{1}{10}(Y_{t-1} - Y_{t-2}).$$

We can combine this with the other equations of the Keynesian model given in Section 13.2 to determine the contribution to the dynamics of this accelerator relationship. We first modify the national income equation by including investment to get

$$Y_t = C_t + I_t + G_t.$$

We again assume that period-t consumption is a function of permanent income in that period and that the parameter values are the same as in the example presented in Section 13.2. This gives us

$$C_t = 200 + \frac{4}{5}\left(\frac{1}{2}Y_t + \frac{1}{2}Y_{t-1}\right).$$

We also assume that $G = 400$. After substitution and some algebra, we get the second-order linear difference equation

$$Y_t = \frac{5}{6}Y_{t-1} - \frac{1}{6}Y_{t-2} + 1000.$$

[9] Paul A. Samuelson, "Interactions between the multiplier analysis and the principle of acceleration," *Review of Economic Statistics* 21 (1939): 75–78.

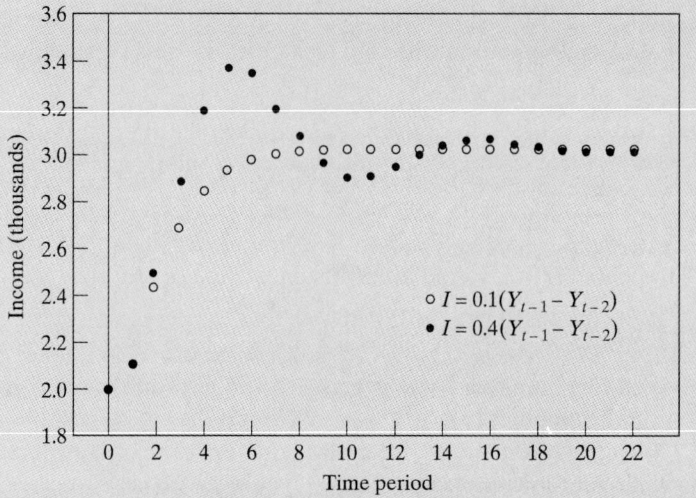

FIGURE 13.9 Multiplier Accelerator Model with Two Different Accelerator Specifications

The steady state here, as in the case discussed in Section 13.2, is $Y_\infty = 3000$. The roots of this difference equation are

$$k_1, k_2 = \frac{1}{2} \cdot \frac{5}{6} \pm \sqrt{\frac{1}{4}\left(\frac{5}{6}\right)^2 - \frac{1}{6}}$$

$$= \frac{1}{2}, \frac{1}{3}.$$

Therefore the solution to this second-order difference equation takes the form

$$Y_t = A\left(\frac{1}{2}\right)^t + B\left(\frac{1}{3}\right)^t + 3000.$$

We assume that the initial values are $Y_0 = 2000$ and $Y_1 = 2100$. We then have two equations in two unknowns,

$$2000 = A + B + 3000$$

$$2100 = \frac{1}{2}A + \frac{1}{3}B + 3000,$$

which gives us $A = -3400$ and $B = 2400$ for the complete solution

$$Y_t = (-3400)\left(\frac{1}{2}\right)^t + (2400)\left(\frac{1}{3}\right)^t + 3000.$$

The sequence corresponding to this solution with the two given initial values is illustrated in Figure 13.9.

This model generates oscillatory dynamics if the accelerator equation is

$$I_t = \frac{2}{5}(Y_{t-1} - Y_{t-2}),$$

and, otherwise, the model is the same. In this case the second-order linear difference equation is

$$Y_t = \frac{4}{3}Y_{t-1} - \frac{2}{3}Y_{t-2} + 1000.$$

This equation also has the same steady state value of $Y_\infty = 3000$, but its two roots are complex numbers since

$$\begin{aligned} k_1, k_2 &= \frac{1}{2} \cdot \frac{4}{3} \pm \sqrt{\frac{1}{4}\left(\frac{4}{3}\right)^2 - \frac{2}{3}} \\ &= \frac{2}{3} \pm \sqrt{-\frac{2}{9}} \\ &= \frac{2}{3} \pm \left(\sqrt{\frac{2}{9}} \cdot \sqrt{-1}\right). \end{aligned}$$

The analytic solution, in this case, involves the periodic functions sine and cosine, which give rise to oscillatory dynamics. Again, we can illustrate the dynamics by assuming that $Y_0 = 2000$ and $Y_1 = 2100$ and solving the sequence through repeated iteration. This sequence is also shown in Figure 13.9. As shown in that figure, the sequence of income oscillates in its movement towards its steady state value.

Systems of Difference Equations

In a system of difference equations, the value of an endogenous variable in one period depends upon both its value in another period and the value of one or more other endogenous variables. We illustrate the method for solving a system of difference equations by considering the system

$$\begin{aligned} p_t &= ap_{t-1} + by_{t-1} + m \\ y_t &= cp_{t-1} + dy_{t-1} + g, \end{aligned}$$

where p and y are the endogenous variables price and income, respectively, m is the money supply, g is government spending, and a, b, c, and d are parameters. This system can be expressed in matrix format as

$$\begin{bmatrix} p_t \\ y_t \end{bmatrix} = \begin{bmatrix} a & b \\ c & d \end{bmatrix} \cdot \begin{bmatrix} p_{t-1} \\ y_{t-1} \end{bmatrix} + \begin{bmatrix} m \\ g \end{bmatrix}$$

or, more compactly, as the system

$$n_t = An_{t-1} + x,$$

where

$$n_i = \begin{bmatrix} p_i \\ y_i \end{bmatrix} \quad \text{for} \quad i = t, t-1, \quad A = \begin{bmatrix} a & b \\ c & d \end{bmatrix}, \quad \text{and} \quad x = \begin{bmatrix} m \\ g \end{bmatrix}.$$

We solve this system by transforming it to a diagonal system representing a pair of univariate difference equations and using the characteristic roots and characteristic vectors of the 2 × 2 matrix. As shown in Section 5.3, we can diagonalize this system if its two characteristic roots are real and distinct. In this case

$$H^{-1}AH = \Lambda$$

where H is a 2 × 2 matrix of the characteristic vectors of A and Λ is a 2 × 2 diagonal matrix with its diagonal elements equal to the two characteristic roots of A, λ_1 and λ_2. As discussed in Chapter 5, the characteristic roots solve the characteristic equation

$$\lambda^2 - (a + d)\lambda + (ad - bc) = 0,$$

which gives us the two characteristic roots

$$\lambda_1, \lambda_2 = \frac{(a + d) \pm \sqrt{(a + d)^2 - 4(ad - bc)}}{2}.$$

In Chapter 5 we also showed that the 2 × 1 characteristic vectors h_i associated with the ith characteristic root has the property that

$$Ah_i = h_i\lambda_i$$

and H is the 2 × 2 matrix consisting of the two 2 × 1 column vectors h_1 and h_2, so $H = [h_1, h_2]$. We define

$$s = H^{-1}x \quad \text{and} \quad u_i = H^{-1}n_i \quad \text{for} \quad i = t, t - 1,$$

where

$$u_i = \begin{bmatrix} u_{1,i} \\ u_{2,i} \end{bmatrix} \quad \text{for} \quad i = t, t - 1.$$

Premultiplying the original system by H^{-1} and also introducing $HH^{-1} = I$, where I is a 2 × 2 identity matrix, we have

$$H^{-1}n_t = H^{-1}AHH^{-1}n_{t-1} + H^{-1}x$$

or

$$u_t = \Lambda u_{t-1} + s$$

since $H^{-1}AH = \Lambda$. This system represents the pair of first-order difference equations

$$u_{1,t} = \lambda_1 u_{1,t-1} + s_1$$
$$u_{2,t} = \lambda_2 u_{2,t-1} + s_2,$$

where s_i represents the ith element of the vector s and $u_{i,j}$ represents the ith element of the vector u for time period j. We can solve these two first-order difference equations by using the methods discussed earlier and then transform them back to a form in terms of p_t and y_t by premultiplying the solution by the matrix H since $Hu_t = HH^{-1}n_t = n_t$.

As a numerical example of this method, consider the system

$$\begin{bmatrix} p_t \\ y_t \end{bmatrix} = \begin{bmatrix} 0.3 & 0.1 \\ 0.2 & 0.2 \end{bmatrix} \cdot \begin{bmatrix} p_{t-1} \\ y_{t-1} \end{bmatrix} + \begin{bmatrix} 900 \\ 300 \end{bmatrix}.$$

The characteristic equation for the 2×2 matrix is

$$\lambda^2 - 0.5\lambda + 0.04 = 0,$$

which has the roots

$$\lambda_1, \lambda_2 = \frac{0.5 \pm \sqrt{0.25 - 0.16}}{2} = 0.4, 0.1.$$

A characteristic vector associated with the characteristic root 0.4 is

$$\begin{bmatrix} 1 \\ 1 \end{bmatrix}$$

since this solves $Ah = h \times (0.4)$, which is

$$\begin{bmatrix} 0.3 & 0.1 \\ 0.2 & 0.2 \end{bmatrix} \begin{bmatrix} 1 \\ 1 \end{bmatrix} = \begin{bmatrix} 0.4 \\ 0.4 \end{bmatrix}.$$

Likewise, a characteristic vector associated with the characteristic root 0.1 is

$$\begin{bmatrix} 1 \\ -2 \end{bmatrix}$$

since this solves $Ah = h \times (0.1)$, which is

$$\begin{bmatrix} 0.3 & 0.1 \\ 0.2 & 0.2 \end{bmatrix} \begin{bmatrix} 1 \\ -2 \end{bmatrix} = \begin{bmatrix} 0.1 \\ -0.2 \end{bmatrix}.$$

Thus, in this case, we have

$$H = \begin{bmatrix} 1 & 1 \\ 1 & -2 \end{bmatrix},$$

and, therefore,

$$H^{-1} = \begin{bmatrix} \frac{2}{3} & \frac{1}{3} \\ \frac{1}{3} & -\frac{1}{3} \end{bmatrix}.$$

We can use these results to transform the original system into an equivalent diagonal system. The endogenous vector of the original system is

$$H^{-1}n_t = \begin{bmatrix} \frac{2}{3} & \frac{1}{3} \\ \frac{1}{3} & -\frac{1}{3} \end{bmatrix} \begin{bmatrix} p_t \\ y_t \end{bmatrix} = \begin{bmatrix} u_{1,t} \\ u_{2,t} \end{bmatrix},$$

and the vector of exogenous variables is

$$H^{-1}x = \begin{bmatrix} \frac{2}{3} & \frac{1}{3} \\ \frac{1}{3} & -\frac{1}{3} \end{bmatrix} \begin{bmatrix} 900 \\ 300 \end{bmatrix} = \begin{bmatrix} 700 \\ 200 \end{bmatrix}.$$

The transformed system consists of the two first-order difference equations

$$u_{1,t} = 0.4u_{1,t-1} + 700$$
$$u_{2,t} = 0.1u_{2,t-1} + 200.$$

Given initial values of prices and income equal to p_0 and y_0, respectively, with corresponding initial values for the transformed system

$$\begin{bmatrix} u_{1,0} \\ u_{2,0} \end{bmatrix} = H^{-1}\begin{bmatrix} p_0 \\ y_0 \end{bmatrix},$$

Equation (13.8) shows that the solution to the transformed system is

$$u_{1,t} = 0.4^t u_{1,0} + \frac{1 - 0.4^t}{0.6}700$$
$$u_{2,t} = 0.1^t u_{2,0} + \frac{1 - 0.1^t}{0.9}200.$$

Note that this is a stable solution in the transformed variables since the absolute values of both of the characteristic roots are less than 1.

We can premultiply through by H to express the solution in terms of the original variables p and y. This gives us

$$H\begin{bmatrix} u_{1,t} \\ u_{2,t} \end{bmatrix} = H\begin{bmatrix} 0.4^t u_{1,0} \\ 0.1^t u_{2,0} \end{bmatrix} + H\begin{bmatrix} \frac{1-0.4^t}{0.6}700 \\ \frac{1-0.1^t}{0.9}200 \end{bmatrix}$$

or, if we recognize that $Hu = HH^{-1}n = n$ and use the values for the elements of H,

$$\begin{bmatrix} p_t \\ y_t \end{bmatrix} = \begin{bmatrix} \frac{p_0}{3}(2\cdot 0.4^t + 0.1^t) + \frac{y_0}{3}(0.4^t - 0.1^t) \\ \frac{2p_0}{3}(0.4^t - 0.1^t) + \frac{y_0}{3}(0.4^t + 2\cdot 0.1^t) \end{bmatrix} + \begin{bmatrix} \frac{1 - 0.4^t}{0.6}700 + \frac{1 - 0.1^t}{0.9}200 \\ \frac{1 - 0.4^t}{0.6}700 - 2\left(\frac{1 - 0.1^t}{0.9}200\right) \end{bmatrix}.$$

Note that the transformed system, and therefore the original system, are stable since

$$\lim_{t\to\infty} u_{1,t} = \frac{700}{0.6} = 1166.7$$
$$\lim_{t\to\infty} u_{2,t} = \frac{200}{0.9} = 222.2$$
$$\lim_{t\to\infty} p_t = \frac{700}{0.6} + \frac{200}{0.9} = 1388.9$$
$$\lim_{t\to\infty} y_t = \frac{700}{0.6} + \frac{400}{0.9} = 722.2$$

The stability of this system occurs because the absolute values of both of the characteristic roots are less than 1. A 2×2 system would be unstable if the absolute value of either characteristic root were greater than or equal to 1 since, then, the solution would include the term λ^t, which approaches either infinity or negative infinity as t approaches infinity.

A Second-Order Difference Equation as a System of Equations

We close this section by noting that a second-order difference equation can be solved as a system of two first-order difference equations. Consider again the multiplier accelerator model discussed earlier, which gives us the second-order difference equation

$$Y_t = \frac{5}{6}Y_{t-1} - \frac{1}{6}Y_{t-2} + \frac{2500}{3}.$$

Define the variable $Z_t = Y_{t-1}$. Then this single second-order difference equation can be expressed as the pair of first-order difference equations

$$\begin{aligned} Y_t &= \frac{5}{6}Y_{t-1} - \frac{1}{6}Z_{t-1} + \frac{2500}{3} \\ Z_t &= Y_{t-1}, \end{aligned}$$

which has the matrix representation

$$\begin{bmatrix} Y_t \\ Z_t \end{bmatrix} = \begin{bmatrix} \frac{5}{6} & -\frac{1}{6} \\ 1 & 0 \end{bmatrix} \begin{bmatrix} Y_{t-1} \\ Z_{t-1} \end{bmatrix} + \begin{bmatrix} \frac{2500}{3} \\ 0 \end{bmatrix}.$$

This system can be solved with the diagonalization techniques described earlier. We can check the stability of the system by solving for the roots of the characteristic equation, which, in this case, is

$$\lambda^2 - \frac{5}{6}\lambda + \frac{1}{6} = 0,$$

which gives us

$$\begin{aligned} \lambda_1, \lambda_2 &= \frac{5/6 \pm \sqrt{(5/6)^2 - 4/6}}{2} \\ &= \frac{1}{2}, \frac{1}{3} \end{aligned}$$

as we found earlier. The remainder of the solution of this model follows the method outlined previously.

Exercises 13.3

1. Consider the second-order difference equation

$$x_t = \frac{8}{9}x_{t-1} - \frac{7}{81}x_{t-2} + \frac{32}{9}$$

(a) What is the steady state value x_∞?
(b) Will this equation converge to its steady state value?
(c) What is the solution to this system if $x_0 = 3$ and $x_1 = 5$?

2. Consider the second-order difference equation

$$x_t = \frac{2}{3}x_{t-1} - \frac{1}{9}x_{t-2} + 4.$$

(a) What is the steady state value x_∞?
(b) Is this a stable or an unstable difference equation?
(c) What is the solution to this difference equation if the two initial values are $x_0 = 5$ and $x_1 = 6$?

3. Consider the second-order difference equation

$$x_t = 0.20x_{t-1} - 0.65x_{t-2}.$$

Characterize the dynamics of this equation.

4. Consider the homogeneous system

$$\begin{bmatrix} x_t \\ y_t \end{bmatrix} = \begin{bmatrix} 0.75 & 0.5 \\ 0.5 & 0.75 \end{bmatrix} \cdot \begin{bmatrix} x_{t-1} \\ y_{t-1} \end{bmatrix}.$$

(a) What are the two characteristic roots of the 2×2 matrix of this system?
(b) Find the characteristic vector associated with each of the characteristic roots.
(c) Use the matrix of characteristic vectors to transform this system into a diagonal system.
(d) Solve the diagonal system. Is the solution stable or unstable?
(e) Express the solution in terms of its original variables.

5. Consider the general homogeneous 2×2 system

$$\begin{bmatrix} x_{1,t} \\ x_{2,t} \end{bmatrix} = \begin{bmatrix} a_{11} & a_{12} \\ a_{21} & a_{22} \end{bmatrix} \cdot \begin{bmatrix} x_{1,t-1} \\ y_{2,t-1} \end{bmatrix},$$

where the two endogenous variables are x_1 and x_2. This can be expressed in compact matrix notation as

$$x_1 = Ax_2.$$

(a) What is the characteristic equation for the matrix A?
(b) Determine the conditions under which this system will be stable, expressed in terms of the trace of A (that is, $a_{11} + a_{22}$) and the determinant of A (that is, $a_{11}a_{22} - a_{12}a_{21}$). Assume that

$$(a_{11} + a_{22})^2 > 4(a_{11}a_{22} - a_{12}a_{21}).$$

Summary

This chapter introduces dynamic analysis with a presentation of difference equations. In dynamic analysis, models explicitly include the time at which events occur or the time at which decisions are made. Difference equations treat time as discrete units called periods. Applications in this chapter illustrate the use of difference equations in a range of economic models.

The results in this chapter are derived through the use of algebra and summation operators. But even though these tools are relatively simple, the concepts introduced in this chapter are more subtle. These include the nature of a solution to a dynamic model, the steady state, and monotonic versus oscillatory dynamics. These concepts are generally applicable to continuous time dynamic analysis, which is the subject of the next chapter. Therefore a solid grounding in this chapter will serve you well as you move onto the next chapter.

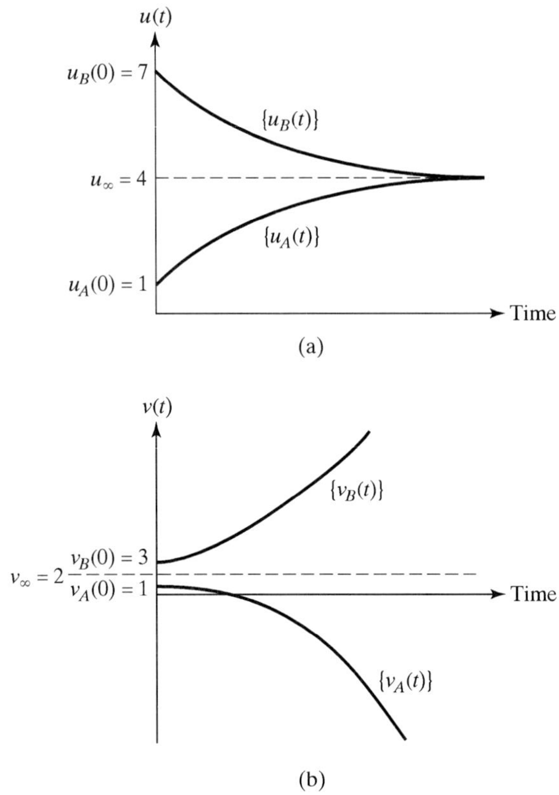

FIGURE 14.2 Time Paths of Variables for Equations (14.6) and (14.7)

As in the linear case, the points where the graph of a differential equation cross the horizontal axis in a phase diagram represent the equation's steady states. We can determine the stability of these steady states by generalizing the linear case. As in the examples discussed previously, the arrows of motion corresponding to the portion of the differential equation above the horizontal axis point to the right since $\dot{x}(t) > 0$ in this range, and the arrows of motion corresponding to the differential equation below the horizontal axis point to the left since $\dot{x}(t) < 0$ in this range. This implies that any steady state point where the differential equation crosses the horizontal axis from above, moving from left to right, is stable, and any steady state point where the differential equation crosses the horizontal axis from below is unstable.

We illustrate the qualitative analysis of nonlinear differential equations with reference to the continuous time version of the Solow growth model.[1] This model consists of several relationships. The core dynamic relationship in this model involves the instantaneous change in the stock of capital per capita, $\dot{k}(t)$, as the difference between investment

[1] You may recall that we discussed a discrete time version of the Solow growth model in Chapter 13.

per capita, $i(t)$, and depreciation. The model includes the assumption that a constant proportion δ of capital wears out each period. Therefore we have the equation

$$\dot{k}(t) = i(t) - \delta k(t).$$

National income accounting dictates that savings per capita equals investment per capita at each moment in an economy that does not lend to or borrow from the rest of the world.

$$s(t) = i(t)$$

Savings per capita is assumed to be a constant proportion of income per capita,

$$s(t) = \sigma y(t),$$

where $1 > \sigma > 0$. Income per capita is assumed to be determined by the intensive Cobb-Douglas production function

$$y(t) = k(t)^{\alpha}$$

where $1 > \alpha > 0$. Substituting these relationships into the first equation gives us the nonlinear differential equation

$$\dot{k}(t) = \sigma k(t)^{a} - \delta k(t).$$

As shown in Figure 14.3, this equation crosses the horizontal axis at two points, $k(t) = 0$ and $k(t) = (\sigma/\delta)^{1/(1-\alpha)}$. The steady state of 0 is unstable. The other steady state, labeled k_{∞} in the figure, is stable since the differential equation crosses the horizontal axis from above, moving from left to right. Thus the nonzero steady state of the continuous time Solow growth model, $k_{\infty} = (\sigma/\delta)^{1/(1-\alpha)}$, is stable.

Solution to an Equation with a Time-Varying Term

In this section we derive the solution to (14.1),

$$\dot{x}(t) = ax(t) + b(t),$$

when $b(t)$ is time-varying. This derivation uses integration. To make the use of integration more transparent in this context and to reinforce the intuition behind the

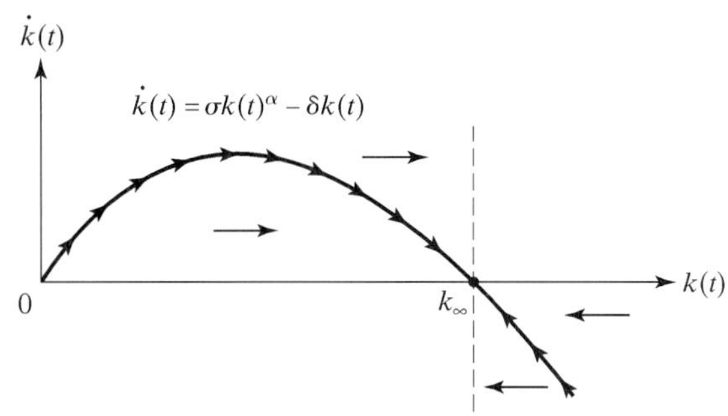

FIGURE 14.3 The Solow Growth Model

solutions (14.4) and (14.5), we first use integration to derive the solutions in the homogeneous case (14.3) and the constant term case (14.2).

To use integration for the homogeneous case, first consider (14.3) at some moment s. Dividing each side of (14.3) defined at moment s by $x(s)$ and multiplying each side by the differential ds, we get

$$\frac{dx(s)}{ds} \cdot \frac{1}{x(s)} \cdot ds = a\,ds$$

or

$$\frac{1}{x(s)} dx(s) = a\,ds.$$

The definite integral of each side of this equation from time 0 to time t (see Chapter 12) is

$$\int_{s=0}^{t} \frac{1}{x(s)}\,dx(s) = \int_{s=0}^{t} a\,ds,$$

where we assume $x(s) > 0$. Evaluating these integrals, we get

$$\ln(x(t)) - \ln(x(0)) = at - a \cdot 0 = at.$$

Adding $\ln(x(0))$ to each side of this expression and then taking the exponential of each side, we have

$$e^{[\ln(x(t))]} = e^{[\ln(x(0)) + at]}$$

or

$$x(t) = x(0) \cdot e^{at},$$

which is the same as the solution (14.4).

To use integration to derive the solution in the constant-term case, we consider (14.2) at moment s and multiply each side of this equation by the differential ds to get

$$dx(s) = ax(s)\,ds + b\,ds.$$

Then multiplying each side of this expression by e^{-as} and rearranging, we get

$$e^{-as}dx(s) - ax(s)e^{-as}ds = be^{-as}ds. \tag{14.8}$$

Note that the left-hand side of (14.8) can be written as

$$d[x(s)e^{-as}].$$

Substituting this into (14.8), we get

$$d[x(s)e^{-as}] = be^{-as}ds.$$

We take the definite integral of each side from time 0 to time t to get

$$\int_{s=0}^{t} d[x(s)e^{-as}] = \int_{s=0}^{t} b \cdot e^{-as}ds. \tag{14.9}$$

By the Fundamental Theorem of Calculus, the left-hand side of (14.9) is

$$x(t)e^{-at} - x(0)e^{-a\cdot 0} = x(t)e^{-at} - x(0).$$

Evaluating the integral on the right-hand side of (14.9) gives us

$$\int_{s=0}^{t} b\cdot e^{-as}ds = -\frac{b}{a}(e^{-at} - e^{-a\cdot 0}) = \frac{b}{a}(1 - e^{-at}).$$

Combining the left-hand side and the right-hand side of (14.9), we then have

$$x(t)e^{-at} - x(0) = \frac{b}{a}(1 - e^{-at}).$$

Multiplying each side of this expression by e^{at} and rearranging terms, we get

$$x(t) = \left(x(0) + \frac{b}{a}\right)\cdot e^{at} - \frac{b}{a},$$

which is the same as the solution (14.5).

We now turn to the case of (14.1), which includes a time-varying term. Note that (14.1) can be rearranged to be written in a form similar to (14.8). To do this, we consider (14.1) at moment s, multiply each side of this equation by the differential ds, and also multiply each side by the e^{-as}. After rearranging, we get

$$e^{-as}dx(s) - a\cdot x(s)e^{-as}ds = b(s)\cdot e^{-as}ds, \tag{14.10}$$

which only differs from (14.8) because the term $b(s)$ rather than b appears on the right-hand side. As discussed previously, the left-hand side of this expression equals $d[x(s)e^{-as}]$. Taking the definite integral of the left-hand side evaluated from time 0 to time t gives us

$$\int_{s=0}^{t} d[x(s)e^{-as}] = x(t)e^{-at} - x(0)e^{-a0} = x(t)e^{-at} - x(0),$$

where we assume that $x(0)$ is a given initial value. The definite integral of the right-hand side of (14.10) cannot be further evaluated without a specification of the function $b(s)$. Therefore a solution to (14.1) is

$$x(t)e^{-at} - x(0) = \int_{s=0}^{t} b(s)\cdot e^{-as}ds.$$

Multiplying each side of this equation by e^{at} and rearranging terms, we have

$$x(t) = x(0)\cdot e^{at} + e^{at}\cdot\int_{s=0}^{t} b(s)\cdot e^{-as}ds.$$

Note that e^{at} does not depend upon the variable of integration, s, and can therefore be moved inside the integral. We then get the solution to (14.1)

$$x(t) = x(0)\cdot e^{at} + \int_{s=0}^{t} b(s)\cdot e^{a(t-s)}ds. \tag{14.11}$$

This is a **backward solution** because $x(t)$ depends upon the current and past values of the independent variable $b(s)$. This solution is a generalization of the solutions (14.4) and (14.5). Solution (14.4) constitutes a special case in which $b(s) = 0$ for all s. Solution (14.5) is a special case where $b(s) = b$ for all s. In that case the integral in (14.11) equals $(b/a)(e^{at} - 1)$.

The solution (14.11) can be thought of as consisting of two parts. The part $x(0) \cdot e^{at}$ reflects the effect of the initial value $x(0)$ on the value of the variable at time t. If $a < 0$, then this effect dies out over time. If $a > 0$ and $x(0) \neq 0$, then this effect grows over time, and $x(t)$ approaches positive or negative infinity as t approaches infinity. The second part of the solution, the integral in (14.11), reflects the discounted past accumulated effects of the time path of $b(s)$ from time 0 to time t. As t approaches infinity,

$$\lim_{t \to \infty} \int_{s=0}^{t} b(s) \cdot e^{a(t-s)} \, ds$$

is finite for a bounded time path $\{b(s)\}$ if $a < 0$. If $a > 0$, the integral may not converge as $t \to \infty$, even if the time path $\{b(s)\}$ is bounded. Thus a sufficient condition for the backward solution (14.11) to be finite for any t is that $a < 0$.

When the relevant period extends infinitely far into the past and $a < 0$, then, given a bounded $x(\tau)$, the backward solution is

$$\begin{aligned} x(t) &= \lim_{\tau \to -\infty} \left[x(\tau) \cdot e^{a(t-\tau)} + \int_{s=\tau}^{t} b(s) \cdot e^{a(t-s)} \, ds \right] \\ &= \int_{s=-\infty}^{t} b(s) \cdot e^{a(t-s)} \, ds \end{aligned}$$

assuming $\{b(s)\}$ is bounded.

In Chapter 13 we found that a difference equation that does not have a finite backward solution may have a finite forward solution. A similar result holds in the case of differential equations. A finite **forward solution** can be obtained for (14.1) when $a > 0$ and the time path $\{b(s)\}$ is bounded. The definite integral of (14.10) evaluated in the limit as the terminal moment in time $\tau \to \infty$ is

$$\lim_{\tau \to \infty} \left[\int_{s=t}^{\tau} (e^{-as} \, dx(s) - a \cdot x(s) e^{-as}) \, ds \right] = \lim_{\tau \to \infty} \int_{s=t}^{\tau} b(s) \cdot e^{-as} \, ds. \tag{14.12}$$

Using previous results and assuming that the terminal value

$$\lim_{\tau \to \infty} x(\tau)$$

is finite, we find that the left-hand side of this expression is

$$\begin{aligned} \lim_{\tau \to \infty} \left[\int_{s=t}^{\tau} d[x(s)e^{-as}] \right] &= \lim_{\tau \to \infty} [x(\tau)e^{-a\tau} - x(t)e^{-at}] \\ &= -x(t)e^{-at}, \end{aligned}$$

where the expression in the second line reflects the fact that

$$\lim_{\tau \to \infty} x(\tau)e^{-a\tau} = 0$$

if we assume the terminal value $\lim_{\tau \to \infty} x(\tau)$ is finite and $a > 0$. Therefore, multiplying the left-hand side of (14.12) by $-e^{at}$, we get

$$-x(t)e^{-at}(-e^{at}) = x(t).$$

Multiplying the right-hand side of (14.12) by $-e^{at}$, we get the improper integral

$$-e^{at} \cdot \int_{s=t}^{\infty} b(s) \cdot e^{-as}\, ds = -\int_{s=t}^{\infty} b(s) \cdot e^{-a(s-t)}\, ds.$$

Thus the forward solution to (14.1), if we assume $a > 0$, $\lim_{\tau \to \infty} x(\tau)$ is finite and $\{b(s)\}$ is bounded, is

$$x(t) = -\int_{s=t}^{\infty} b(s) \cdot e^{-a(s-t)}\, ds. \tag{14.13}$$

The solution (14.13) represents a discounted infinite forward sum of the values of $b(s)$ from $s = t$ to $s \to \infty$. The integral converges since $a > 0$ and $(s - t)$ is nonnegative for the limits of integration. Thus, as with a difference equation, a differential equation that has a nonconvergent backward solution may have a convergent forward solution and conversely.

Both backward solutions and forward solutions are found in economic models. The applications in the following section demonstrate some of the uses of differential equations in a variety of economic contexts.

Exercises 14.1

1. Describe each function as homogeneous or nonhomogeneous and stable or unstable.

   (a) $\dfrac{dx(t)}{dt} = 10x(t) + 5$

   (b) $\dot{x}(t) = -2x(t)$

   (c) $\dot{x}(t) = -\dfrac{2}{3}x(t) + 2$

   (d) $\dfrac{dx(t)}{dt} = x(t) - 8$

2. Determine the steady state value of each of the four equations in question 1.
3. Determine the steady state value of each second-order differential equation.

(a) $\frac{d^2x(t)}{dt^2} = \frac{1}{2}\frac{dx(t)}{dt} - \frac{2}{3}x(t) + 30$

(b) $3\ddot{y}(t) - 2\dot{y}(t) + y(t) = 7$

4. Find the solution to each differential equation for each of the specified initial values.

(a) $\frac{dx(t)}{dt} = 10x(t) + 5, x(0) = -1$ and $x(0) = 5$

(b) $\dot{x}(t) = -2x(t), x(0) = 0$ and $x(0) = 3$

(c) $\dot{x}(t) = -\frac{2}{3}x(t) + 2, x(0) = 0, x(0) = 3$ and $x(0) = 5$

(d) $\frac{dx(t)}{dt} = x(t) - 8, x(0) = 4, x(0) = 8$ and $x(0) = 12$

5. For each of the solutions to the differential equations in question 4, determine $\lim_{t\to\infty} x(t)$. In which cases does $\lim_{t\to\infty} x(t)$ not depend upon the choice of the initial value? Why?

6. Draw a phase diagram as well as a time path for each equation when the initial value is greater than the steady state value.

(a) $\dot{x}(t) = -3x(t) + 12$

(b) $\dot{x}(t) = \frac{1}{2}x(t) - 8$

(c) $\dot{x}(t) = -\frac{1}{3}x(t) + 5$

7. The half-life of a differential equation, which we denote as H, is the amount of time it takes to move half way from its initial value $x(0)$ to its steady state value x_∞. Therefore, at time H,

$$x(H) = \frac{x_\infty + x(0)}{2}.$$

(a) Find the general formula for H as a function of a, $x(0)$, and b for the differential equation

$$\dot{x}(t) = ax(t) + b,$$

where $a < 0$.

(b) Does the initial distance between $x(0)$ and x_∞ affect H?

8. Solve each differential equation.

(a) $\frac{d\ln(Y(t))}{dt} = 0.02$ and $Y(0) = \$2$ billion

(b) $\frac{d\ln(E(t))}{dt} = -0.1$ and $E(0) = 125$ yen per dollar

9. Solve each differential equation.

(a) $\dot{x}(t) = -2x(t) + b(t)$, where $b(t) = 0$ for $0 \le t < 10$ and $b(t) = 100$ for $t \ge 10$, and $x(0) = 1$

(b) $\dot{x}(t) = 3x(t) + g(t)$, where $g(t) = 6$ for $5 \geq t > 0$, $g(t) = 3$ for $t > 5$, and $x(0) = 2$

(c) $\dot{x}(t) = 10x(t) + h(t)$, where $h(t) = e^{-2t} + 10$ and $x(0) = 3$

10. Plot the phase diagram for each equation. Identify the steady state points and characterize them as stable or unstable.

(a) $\dot{s}(t) = -4(s(t)^2) + 8s(t)$

(b) $\dot{m}(t) = m(t)^3 - 15(m(t)^2) + 36m(t)$

14.2 APPLICATIONS OF SINGLE DIFFERENTIAL EQUATIONS

The material presented in Section 14.1 shows how to solve linear first-order differential equations. The three applications in this section show some ways in which these equations are used in economic analysis.

The Price-Specie Flow Mechanism

One of the oldest models in international economics is the **price-specie flow mechanism.** This model was developed by the Scottish economist David Hume in the mid-eighteenth century to argue against mercantilist policies that advocated hoarding gold, which would be obtained by running persistent trade surpluses.[2] Hume showed that an effort to hoard gold would bid up prices and deteriorate national competitiveness. This would ultimately lead to a gold outflow through balance of trade deficits.

Hume did not present his model in an explicit mathematical framework, but the logic of his argument easily lends itself to one.[3] There are two basic relationships in the price-specie flow mechanism. The first is the price relationship dictated by the quantity theory of money. In its simplest form, this relationship specifies that the price level is proportional to the money supply. If we take the money supply to be fully backed by gold, then this equation is

$$g(t) = p(t),$$

where $g(t)$ is the natural logarithm of the stock of gold at moment t and $p(t)$ is the natural logarithm of the domestic price level at time t.

The specie flow relationship in this model reflects the change in the gold stock that arises with an imbalance in the trade account. A trade surplus increases a country's holdings of gold, while a trade deficit causes a country to lose some of its gold

---

[2] See David Hume, "Of the Balance of Trade," in his *Essays Moral, Political and Literary* (London: Longmans Green, 1898). This essay is reprinted in abridged form in Barry Eichengreen, ed., *The Gold Standard in Theory and History* (London: Methuen Publishers, 1985): 39–48.

[3] For a mathematical presentation of Hume's analysis in a two-country setting, see Maurice Obstfeld, "International Finance," *The New Palgrave: A Dictionary of Economics*, John Eatwell, Murray Milgate, and Peter Newman, eds. (London: The Macmillan Press, Ltd., 1987): 898–906.

holdings. This relationship is formalized in the equation

$$\frac{dg(t)}{dt} = b(q(t)),$$

where $b(q(t))$ represents the trade balance. The trade balance at time t is a function of the logarithm of the real exchange rate at that moment, $q(t)$. The real exchange rate represents the relative price of foreign goods to domestic goods and is given by the quotient $E \cdot P^*/P(t)$, where E is the fixed exchange rate expressed as units of domestic currency per ounce of gold and P^* is the foreign price level, which is assumed exogenous and constant (the product EP^* is the foreign price level expressed in domestic currency units). The logarithm of the real exchange rate is therefore

$$q(t) = \ln\left(\frac{EP^*}{P(t)}\right) = (\varepsilon + p^* - p(t)),$$

where $\ln(E) = \varepsilon$ and $\ln(P^*) = p^*$. We assume that the trade balance is a linear function of $q(t)$, as shown by

$$b(q(t)) = \beta\,(\varepsilon + p^* - p(t)),$$

where $\beta > 0$. Substituting the trade balance relationship into the relationship describing the change in the gold stock and using the price relationship gives us the nonhomogeneous linear differential equation

$$\frac{dg(t)}{dt} = -\beta g(t) + \beta\,(\varepsilon + p^*).$$

The solution for a nonhomogeneous linear differential equation with a constant term, which is given in (14.5), shows that the solution to this equation is

$$g(t) = (g(0) - (\varepsilon + p^*))e^{-\beta t} + (\varepsilon + p^*),$$

where $g(0)$ is the initial stock of gold holdings. This is a stable solution since, regardless of the value of $g(0)$,

$$\begin{aligned}\lim_{t\to\infty} g(t) &= \lim_{t\to\infty}[(g(0) - (\varepsilon + p^*))e^{-\beta t} + (\varepsilon + p^*)],\\ &= (\varepsilon + p^*),\end{aligned}$$

which is the steady state value of the equation.

Hume worked through the thought experiment of the effects of the overnight destruction of four-fifths of Britain's money supply. We can analyze this with reference to the solution given above or by using Figure 14.4. The steady state point, $g_\infty = \varepsilon + p^*$, is represented in the figure, and the slope of the line representing the differential equation is $-\beta < 0$. Suppose we start at the steady state point g_∞. A destruction of four-fifths of the money supply of Britain is represented in the figure by a change from the steady state point g_∞ to point H, where $H = \ln(G_\infty/5) = g_\infty - \ln(5)$. At this point, $dg(t)/dt$ is positive, and Britain begins to run trade surpluses. The source of the trade surpluses is the increase in the competitiveness of British goods due to the fall in the British price level accompanying the destruction of gold (since $p = g$ and g falls from

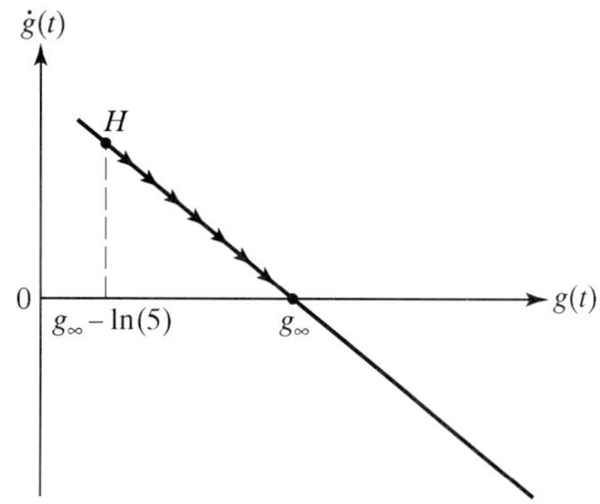

FIGURE 14.4 The Price-Specie Flow Mechanism

g_∞ to $g_\infty - \ln(5)$). Over time, however, the increase in the British gold stock due to the persistent trade surpluses raises the price level to the point where it asymptotically approaches its original level of g_∞. Thus Hume's analysis demonstrates the automatic mechanism by which the gold holdings of a country are determined. By extension, this model shows that efforts to maintain a persistent surplus in the trade balance are bound to fail due to the natural workings of an economy.

Stability in Monetary Models

In many intertemporal models, it is necessary to specify how expectations are formed. The particular specification of expectations formation in monetary models has important stability implications. Early on, monetary models incorporated the assumption of **adaptive expectations.** Under this assumption, the expected inflation rate is a function of inflation in the past. This assumption allows for the possibility that people consistently underestimate or overestimate the level of inflation. Economists became uncomfortable with the fact that this assumption is consistent with people not using all available information. An alternative assumption, known as **rational expectations,** assumes that people use all available information and consequently, on average, guess inflation correctly.

The central relationship in the monetary models discussed here is the money demand equation

$$m(t) - p(t) = -\lambda\pi(t),$$

where $m(t)$ is the logarithm of the money supply, $p(t)$ is the logarithm of the price level, and $\pi(t)$ is the logarithm of the expected inflation rate, all at moment t, and λ is a positive constant.[4] This is not a differential equation since $\pi(t)$ is the derivative of the expected price level with respect to time and not the derivative of the actual price level

[4] A discrete time version of this money demand relationship is used in the application about money and prices in Chapter 13.

with respect to time (which is $dp(t)/dt \equiv \dot{p}(t)$). Thus it is also necessary to specify a relationship between actual inflation, $\dot{p}(t)$, and expected inflation, $\pi(t)$.

A continuous time equation that reflects the assumption of adaptive expectations is

$$\dot{\pi}(t) = \alpha(\dot{p}(t) - \pi(t)),$$

where α reflects the speed with which expected inflation responds to the difference between actual and expected inflation ($\alpha > 0$). This equation shows that if actual inflation, $\dot{p}(t)$, is greater than expected inflation, $\pi(t)$, then there is an increase in expected inflation.[5] This equation can be written as

$$\dot{p}(t) = \frac{1}{\alpha}\dot{\pi}(t) + \pi(t).$$

We obtain a differential equation in actual inflation and the price level by substituting into this equation the value of $\pi(t)$ from the money demand equation and substituting the value of $\dot{\pi}(t)$ obtained from first differentiating the money demand equation with respect to time,

$$\dot{m}(t) - \dot{p}(t) = -\lambda\dot{\pi}(t).$$

After some simple algebra, we get the first-order differential equation

$$\dot{p}(t) = -\frac{\alpha}{1 - \alpha\lambda}p(t) + \frac{\alpha}{1 - \alpha\lambda}m(t) + \frac{1}{1 - \alpha\lambda}\dot{m}(t),$$

which is plotted as the line CC in the phase diagram in Figure 14.5(a). This differential equation has a negative slope and is therefore stable if (as assumed) $\alpha\lambda < 1$. It crosses the horizontal axis at the steady state value labeled $\bar{p}_\infty$. The stability of the equation ensures that the price level converges over time to its steady state value from any initial price level. For example, consider the case where $\dot{m}(t) = 0$ for all t and there is a one-time discrete jump in the money supply from $\bar{m}$ to $\tilde{m}$. The new differential equation line is labeled $C'C'$. If we begin at the original steady state $\bar{p}_\infty$, the inflation rate jumps from zero to A, and the price level slowly evolves to its new long-run level of $\tilde{p}_\infty$. The money demand equation shows that, during the transition from $\bar{p}_\infty$ to $\tilde{p}_\infty$, expected inflation equals $(1/\lambda)(p(t) - \tilde{m})$. Expected inflation is always negative during the transition since the steady state value of the price level is $\tilde{p}_\infty = \tilde{m}$ and, up until the steady state is reached, $p(t) < \tilde{m}$. Actual inflation, however, is positive during the transition, so, in this model, people consistently expect a lower inflation rate than the one that occurs.

If we assume that people have rational expectations, then the dynamics of the price level are quite different. A particular type of rational expectations is perfect foresight in which people's expectation about the future value of a variable exactly equals

[5] This represents a continuous time version of the adaptive expectations framework developed in discrete time by Philip Cagan in his paper "The Monetary Dynamics of Hyperinflation," *Studies in the Quantity Theory of Money,* Milton Friedman ed., (Chicago: University of Chicago Press, 1956). This paper is the subject of a discrete time difference equation application in Chapter 13.

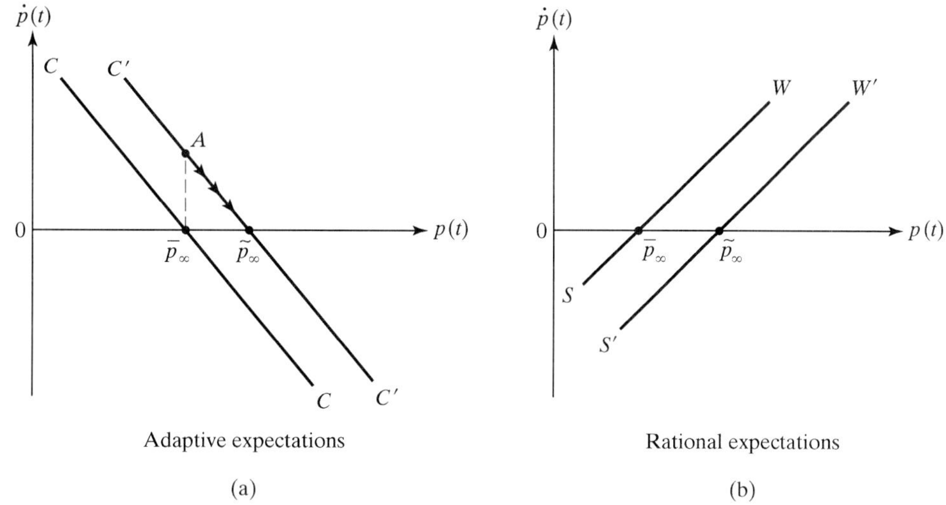

FIGURE 14.5 Stability in Monetary Models

the actual outcome. Thomas Sargent and Neil Wallace studied the determination of prices in a perfect foresight model with fully flexible prices.[6] The assumption of perfect foresight in this context is $\pi(t) = \dot{p}(t)$. Substituting this equation for expected inflation into the money demand equation, we get the differential equation

$$\dot{p}(t) = \frac{1}{\lambda}p(t) - \frac{1}{\lambda}m(t).$$

This differential equation is plotted as the line SW in Figure 14.5(b), which assumes that $m(t) = \bar{m}$. The line SW crosses the horizontal axis at the steady state value of the differential equation $\bar{p}_\infty = \bar{m}$. Its positive slope indicates that it is an unstable difference equation. To investigate the dynamics of this equation, suppose that the money supply initially meets $\bar{m}$ and prices initially equal their steady state value $\bar{p}_\infty$. Now consider what happens when the money supply increases to $\tilde{m}$. The differential equation line shifts to $S'W'$, which has the steady state value of the price level $\tilde{p}_\infty = \tilde{m}$. A simple analysis of the phase diagram would suggest that there is permanent and increasing deflation as we move down the $S'W'$ schedule, even though the money supply is constant. A more economically sensible result suggested by Sargent and Wallace is that the price level jumps from $\bar{p}_\infty$ to $\tilde{p}_\infty$ and there are no on-going dynamics. If the price level did not fully increase to $\tilde{p}_\infty$ at the moment the money supply changes from $\bar{m}$ to $\tilde{m}$, then a one-time increase in the money supply would lead to a price level that is either increasing or decreasing at an accelerating rate forever. We confirm this by noting that

[6] Thomas Sargent and Neil Wallace, "The stability of models of money and perfect foresight," *Econometrica* 41 (1973): 1043–1048.

the solution to the perfect foresight model with a constant money supply m is

$$p(t) = (p(0) - m)\, e^{1/\lambda} + m,$$

which has the positive coefficient $1/\lambda$ multiplying t in the exponential term. If $p(0)$ does not equal m, then the price level either goes to positive infinity if $p(0) > m$ or negative infinity if $p(0) < m$, even though the money supply is constant. Thus a sensible assumption is that the price level jumps such that $p(t) = m$ at any moment.

We can obtain the solutions to both the adaptive expectations and perfect foresight models with time-varying levels of the money supply by applying the results in Section 14.1. A straightforward application of the forward solution given in Section 14.1 shows that the logarithm of the price level in the perfect foresight model at time t equals

$$p(t) = \frac{1}{\lambda}\int_{s=t}^{\infty} m(s)e^{(t-s)/\lambda}\, ds.$$

This solution shows that the price at any moment represents the discounted value of the time path of the expected future money supply. Any expected future increase in the money supply will increase the current price level. The effect of an expected increase in the money supply on the current price level is larger, the closer to the present it occurs. An application of the backward solution (14.12) to the differential equation for the price level in the adaptive expectations case where the relevant period extends infinitely far into the past gives us the solution to the adaptive expectations model

$$p(t) = \frac{1}{1 - \alpha\lambda} = \int_{s=-\infty}^{t} [\alpha \cdot m(s) + \dot{m}(s)]e^{(\alpha/(1-\alpha\lambda))(s-t)} ds.$$

The Monetary Model of Exchange-Rate Determination

International investors move funds across countries in great quantities and at a rapid speed in search of the highest return. These international capital flows are a primary determinant of exchange rates. One model of exchange-rate determination in the presence of international capital mobility is the **monetary model of exchange-rate determination.**[7]

The central relationship in the monetary model of exchange-rate determination is **interest parity.** Interest parity is an arbitrage relationship (that is, one of no excess profit) that states that bonds denominated in different currencies provide the same return when that return is denominated in a common currency. The free flow of capital across national boundaries ensures that this arbitrage relationship holds. Interest parity requires that the interest rate offered on domestic bonds at moment t, $i(t)$, equals the sum of the interest rate offered on foreign bonds at that moment, i^* (which we

[7]For a full discussion of this model, see the chapter by Maurice Obstfeld and Alan Stockman titled "Exchange-Rate Dynamics" *Handbook of International Economics,* Vol. 2, Ronald Jones and Peter Kenen, eds. (Amsterdam: North Holland, 1985.)

assume is constant over time) and the expected rate of depreciation of the domestic currency. We assume perfect foresight so the expected rate of depreciation is identical to the actual rate of depreciation. The instantaneous rate of depreciation is $(dE(t)/dt)(1/E(t))$, where $E(t)$ is the exchange rate (units of domestic currency per unit of foreign currency, so an increase in $E(t)$ represents a depreciation of the currency). Denoting $\ln(E(t)) = \varepsilon(t)$, which implies that $(dE(t)/dt)(1/E(t)) = d\varepsilon(t)/dt$, the interest parity relationship requires $i(t) = i^* + d\varepsilon(t)/dt$. The intuition here is that foreign bonds are attractive both because of the interest they provide, i^*, and because of the prospect for capital gains they offer if the domestic currency depreciates relative to the foreign currency (that is, if $d\varepsilon(t)/dt > 0$). Arbitrage requires that the return on domestic bonds, i, equals the expected return on foreign bonds, which is approximately equal to the sum of the interest rate, i^*, and the expected depreciation of the domestic currency, $d\varepsilon(t)/dt$.[8]

This model has two other relationships. One is the money demand equation

$$m(t) - p(t) = -\lambda i(t),$$

where $m(t)$ is the logarithm of the money supply at time t and $p(t)$ is the logarithm of the price level at that moment. This equation reflects the fact that the nominal interest rate represents the opportunity cost of holding money, and therefore, money demand decreases with an increase in the nominal interest rate.[9] This model also assumes that the real exchange rate (EP^*/P in terms of the price-specie flow application) is constant. A simple equation that reflects this assumption sets the real exchange rate, as well as the foreign price level, equal to 1, and therefore, $E(t) = P(t)$ or, in terms of logarithms,

$$\varepsilon(t) = p(t).$$

Combining these relationships and rearranging terms, we have the first-order linear differential equation

$$\frac{d\varepsilon(t)}{dt} = \frac{1}{\lambda}\varepsilon(t) - \frac{1}{\lambda}m(t) - i^*.$$

The positive coefficient $1/\lambda$ on the homogeneous term $\varepsilon(t)$ indicates that this is an unstable differential equation. This can be seen most easily by considering the case where $m(t) = \overline{m}$, which is depicted by the line MM in the phase diagram in Figure 14.6. This line crosses the horizontal axis at the steady state value of $\overline{\varepsilon}_\infty = \overline{m} + \lambda i^*$. The slope of the line in the phase diagram is positive and equal to $1/\lambda$. The only stable solution is that the exchange rate always jumps to its steady state value since, otherwise, there is either a permanent and increasingly large depreciation or a permanent and increasingly large appreciation. Thus when the money supply increases to $\tilde{m}$, which

---

[8] For a full discussion of interest parity see Paul Krugman and Maurice Obstfeld, *International Economics*, 5th ed. (Reading, MA: Addison-Wesley, 2000), Chapter 13.

[9] The Fisher equation shows that $i(t) = r(t) + \pi(t)$, where $i(t)$ is the nominal interest rate and $r(t)$ is the real interest rate. Therefore this money demand equation is the same as the one presented earlier if the real interest rate, r, is taken to be equal to zero.

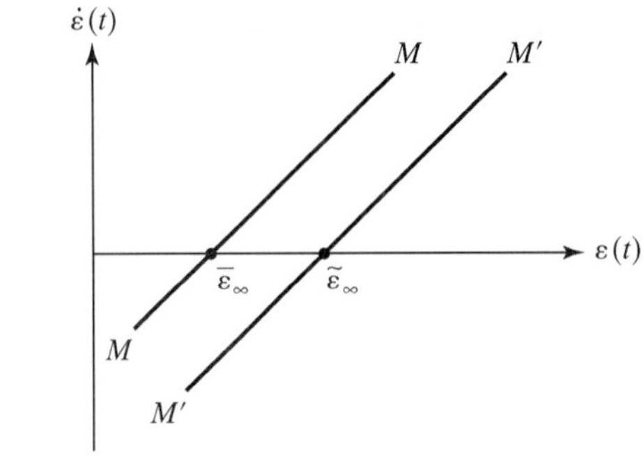

FIGURE 14.6 The Monetary Model of Exchange-Rate Determination

causes the phase diagram line to shift to $M'M'$, the only stable (and the only economically sensible) solution is that the exchange rate immediately jumps to $\tilde{\epsilon}_\infty$.

When the money supply is not constant, the solution for the exchange rate at moment t includes an improper integral. Equation (14.13) shows that this forward solution is

$$\varepsilon(t) = \int_{s=t}^{\infty} \left(\frac{m(s)}{\lambda} + i^* \right) \cdot e^{-(1/\lambda)(s-t)}\, ds.$$

We can simplify this integral by separating the integrand into the sum

$$\frac{m(s)}{\lambda} e^{-(1/\lambda)(s-t)} + i^* e^{-(1/\lambda)(s-t)}$$

and evaluating the second integral. This gives us the solution

$$\varepsilon(t) = i^*\lambda + \frac{1}{\lambda}\int_{s=t}^{\infty} m(s) \cdot e^{-(1/\lambda)(s-t)}\, ds.$$

The integral in this solution shows that the exchange rate at time t is a function of the discounted value of the infinite forward integral of the time path of the expected future money supply. Any expected increase in the money supply in the future causes the exchange rate to depreciate today. The depreciation caused by a given increase in the money supply is larger, the closer to the present that increase occurs. For example, if $i^* = 0$ and $m(s) = 1$ from $s = t$ to $s = t + 1$ and $m(s) = 0$ for $s > t + 1$, then the exchange rate in period t equals

$$\begin{aligned} \varepsilon(t) &= \frac{1}{\lambda}\int_{s=1}^{t+1} e^{-(1/\lambda)(s-t)}\, ds \\ &= 1 - e^{-1/\lambda}. \end{aligned}$$

In a second case, where $i^* = 0$ and $m(s) = 1$ from $s = t + 1$ to $s = t + 2$ and $m(s) = 0$ for both $t < s < t + 1$ and $s > t + 2$, then the exchange rate in period t is more appreciated (that is, $\varepsilon(t)$ is lower) than in the earlier case where $m(s) = 1$, as shown by the evaluation of the integral

$$\begin{aligned}\varepsilon(t) &= \frac{1}{\lambda}\int_{s=1}^{t+1} e^{-(1/\lambda)(s-t)}\,ds \\ &= e^{-1/\lambda} - e^{-2/\lambda} \\ &= e^{-1/\lambda}\cdot(1 - e^{-1/\lambda}).\end{aligned}$$

Exercises 14.2

1. Solve for expected inflation, $\pi(t)$, as a function of actual inflation by using the adaptive expectation equation

$$\dot{\pi}(t) = \alpha(\dot{p}(t) - \pi(t)),$$

treating the sequence $\{\dot{p}(t)\}$ as given, and assuming that, initially, actual inflation equals expected inflation.

2. Consider the money demand function

$$m(t) - p(t) = -\frac{1}{2}\pi(t),$$

where $m(t)$ is the natural logarithm of the money supply, $p(t)$ is the natural logarithm of the price level, and $\pi(t)$ is expected inflation. Suppose that there is perfect foresight, so $\dot{p}(t) = \pi(t)$. Find $p(0)$ in each case.

(a) $m(s) = 10$ for $s \geq 0$

(b) $m(s) = 10$ for $20 > s \geq 0$ and $m(s) = 15$ for $s \geq 20$

(c) $m(s) = 10$ for $20 > s \geq 0$, $m(s) = 15$ for $30 > s \geq 20$, and $m(s) = 10$ for $s \geq 30$

3. Study the effect of a devaluation that raises the domestic price of gold, E, in the price-specie flow model. Assume that the economy starts off in a steady state. Discuss the change (if any) in the steady state, as well as the time path of prices and gold holdings in the economy.

4. Consider a two-country version of the price-specie flow model. In this model, the world gold stock, $\overline{G}$, is allocated across the two countries, home and foreign, with G^H held at home and G^F held at foreign. Therefore $\overline{G} = G^H + G^F$.

(a) Recall that $G^H = M^H = P^H$ and $G^F = M^F = P^F$. Given

$$\dot{G}^H = \beta(P^F - P^H),$$

what is the solution for the home price level at any moment?

(b) In the late 1800s, there was a gold rush in Alaska, greatly increasing the gold supply of the United States. Employing the model developed in the first part of this problem, describe the effect of the discovery of gold in Alaska on the gold holdings and the price levels in the United States and in the rest of the world. Consider the United States to be the home country and the rest of the world to be the foreign country in the two-country model.

5. Consider the money demand function

$$m(t) - p(t) = -0.8i(t),$$

where $m(t)$ is the natural logarithm of the money supply, $p(t)$ is the natural logarithm of the price level, and $i(t)$ is the nominal interest rate. For convenience, assume that the real interest rate is zero and the foreign nominal interest rate is also zero. Also assume that $\varepsilon(t) = p(t)$, where $\varepsilon(t)$ is the natural logarithm of the exchange rate. Find the current spot exchange rate, $\varepsilon(0)$, when the Central Bank follows a constant money supply rule and annual money growth is $dm(t)/dt = 0.10$ and $m(0) = 0$.

6. Consider an extension of the monetary model of exchange-rate determination in which the interest parity relationship is modified to include a risk premium, $\rho(t)$, such that

$$i(t) = i^* + \frac{d\varepsilon(t)}{dt} + \rho(t).$$

The risk premium reflects the excess return that the domestic asset must pay to compensate for its riskiness. The risk premium may or may not be time-varying. Assume $i^* = 0$.

(a) Determine the value of the exchange rate at time 0 when the money supply is constant and equal to $\tilde{m}$ and the risk premium is constant and equal to $\tilde{\rho}$.

(b) Determine the value of the exchange rate at time 0 when the money supply is constant and equal to $\tilde{m}$ and the risk premium is time-varying and equal to $\rho(t)$.

(c) Determine the value of the exchange rate at time 0 when the money supply is time-varying and equal to $m(t)$ and the risk premium is time-varying and equal to $\rho(t)$.

14.3 SYSTEMS OF DIFFERENTIAL EQUATIONS

Continuous-time dynamic economic models may have more than one endogenous variable and more than one differential equation. In this section we extend the analysis in Section 14.1 by considering systems of differential equations. We begin with finding an explicit solution for systems where we can use the technique for diagonalizing matrices presented in Chapter 5. This technique was also used to solve systems of difference equations in Chapter 13. Diagonalization transforms the original system in which the time derivative of a variable depends upon one or more endogenous variables into a system consisting of a series of differential equations each with a single endogenous variable like those analyzed in Section 14.1. We then present the solutions to two cases where the systems cannot be diagonalized. We also present a phase diagram technique for analyzing a system of two differential equations with two endogenous variables. Throughout this section we focus on two-dimensional systems since those are the most prevalent cases found in economic analysis.

Diagonalizable Systems

We consider two-dimensional differential equation systems that take the general form

$$\begin{aligned}\dot{x}(t) &= ax(t) + by(t) + \alpha \\ \dot{y}(t) &= cx(t) + dy(t) + \beta,\end{aligned} \tag{14.14}$$

where a, b, c, d, α, and β are parameters. This system can be written in matrix form as

$$\begin{bmatrix}\dot{x}(t)\\ \dot{y}(t)\end{bmatrix} = A\begin{bmatrix}x(t)\\ y(t)\end{bmatrix} + \begin{bmatrix}\alpha\\ \beta\end{bmatrix}, \tag{14.15}$$

where

$$A = \begin{bmatrix}a & b\\ c & d\end{bmatrix}.$$

At the center of our strategy for solving this system is the relationship

$$A = H\Lambda H^{-1},$$

where Λ is the 2×2 diagonal matrix

$$\Lambda = \begin{bmatrix}\lambda_1 & 0\\ 0 & \lambda_2\end{bmatrix},$$

λ_1 and λ_2 are the two distinct characteristic roots of A, and H is a 2×2 matrix in which each column is a characteristic vector of A (see Section 5.3 for a discussion of characteristic roots and characteristic vectors). Recall from Chapter 5 that a 2×2 matrix A is diagonalizable if its two characteristic roots are real and distinct. As discussed in Chapter 5, the characteristic roots λ_1 and λ_2 solve the characteristic equation

$$\lambda_i^2 - (a + d)\lambda_i + (ad - bc) = 0$$

for $i = 1, 2$. The quadratic formula (see Chapter 2) shows that the two characteristic roots are

$$\lambda_1, \lambda_2 = \frac{(a + d) \pm \sqrt{(a + d)^2 - 4(ad - bc)}}{2}.$$

It is shown in Chapter 5 that the 2×1 characteristic vector h_i associated with the ith characteristic root has the property

$$Ah_i = h_i\lambda_i$$

and H is the 2×2 matrix consisting of the two 2×1 column vectors h_1 and h_2, so $H = [h_1, h_2]$. We define the two variables $u(t)$ and $v(t)$, which are linear combinations of $x(t)$ and $y(t)$, as

$$\begin{bmatrix}u(t)\\ v(t)\end{bmatrix} = H^{-1}\begin{bmatrix}x(t)\\ y(t)\end{bmatrix},$$

which therefore means

$$\begin{bmatrix} \dot{u}(t) \\ \dot{v}(t) \end{bmatrix} = H^{-1} \begin{bmatrix} \dot{x}(t) \\ \dot{y}(t) \end{bmatrix}.$$

Premultiplying each side of the original system (14.15) by H^{-1}, we obtain an equivalent system in the variables $u(t)$ and $v(t)$.

$$\begin{aligned} \begin{bmatrix} \dot{u}(t) \\ \dot{v}(t) \end{bmatrix} &= H^{-1}A \begin{bmatrix} x(t) \\ y(t) \end{bmatrix} + H^{-1} \begin{bmatrix} \alpha \\ \beta \end{bmatrix} \\ &= H^{-1}H\Lambda H^{-1} \begin{bmatrix} x(t) \\ y(t) \end{bmatrix} + H^{-1} \begin{bmatrix} \alpha \\ \beta \end{bmatrix} \end{aligned}$$

Since $H^{-1}H = I$, where I is a 2×2 identity matrix and defining

$$\begin{bmatrix} \theta \\ \phi \end{bmatrix} = H^{-1} \begin{bmatrix} \alpha \\ \beta \end{bmatrix},$$

we then have the system

$$\begin{bmatrix} \dot{u}(t) \\ \dot{v}(t) \end{bmatrix} = \Lambda \begin{bmatrix} u(t) \\ v(t) \end{bmatrix} + \begin{bmatrix} \theta \\ \phi \end{bmatrix}. \tag{14.16}$$

This transformed system consists of the two nonhomogeneous differential equations

$$\begin{aligned} \dot{u}(t) &= \lambda_1 u(t) + \theta \\ \dot{v}(t) &= \lambda_2 v(t) + \phi. \end{aligned} \tag{14.17}$$

The discussion in Section 14.1 shows that the solutions to the two equations in (14.17) are

$$\begin{aligned} u(t) &= k_1 e^{t \cdot \lambda_1} - \frac{\theta}{\lambda_1} \\ v(t) &= k_2 e^{t \cdot \lambda_2} - \frac{\phi}{\lambda_2}, \end{aligned}$$

where k_1 and k_2 are constants to be determined. To convert these solutions back into the original variables $x(t)$ and $y(t)$, we premultiply each side of this solution by the matrix H. The elements in each column of the matrix H are only defined up to multiplying by an arbitrary constant. Denoting these two arbitrary constants as s_1 and s_2, and noting that we can solve for the elements of H by using the relationship $AH = H\Lambda$ (see Section 5.3), we have[10]

$$H = \begin{bmatrix} \dfrac{s_1 b}{\lambda_1 - \alpha} & \dfrac{s_2 b}{\lambda_2 - a} \\ S_1 & S_2 \end{bmatrix}.$$

[10] See Section 5.3 for a full discussion of the determination of the elements of the matrix of characteristic vectors. This parallels the technique in Section 13.3 for solving a system of difference equations.

Premultiplying the solution in $u(t)$ and $v(t)$ by H, we have the general solution to (14.14) in terms of the original variables

$$\begin{aligned} x(t) &= \frac{k_1 s_1 b}{\lambda_1 - a} \cdot e^{t \cdot \lambda_1} + \frac{k_2 s_2 b}{\lambda_2 - a} \cdot e^{t \cdot \lambda_2} + \frac{\beta b - \alpha d}{ad - bc} \\ y(t) &= k_1 s_1 \cdot e^{t \cdot \lambda_1} + k_2 s_2 \cdot e^{t \cdot \lambda_2} + \frac{\alpha c - \beta a}{ad - bc}. \end{aligned} \tag{14.18}$$

The steady state for this system is the point (x_∞, y_∞) where

$$\begin{aligned} x_\infty &= \frac{\beta b - \alpha d}{ad - bc} \\ y_\infty &= \frac{\alpha c - \beta a}{ad - bc}. \end{aligned} \tag{14.19}$$

We obtain a specific solution by solving for $k_1 s_1$ and $k_2 s_2$. The specific solution depends upon two given values for the dependent variables, such as the initial values $x(0)$ and $y(0)$, and the assumptions about stability, which, as shown by the solution, depends upon the two characteristic roots of A. Next we turn to this point.

Stability Analysis

The stability of the two-variable system (14.14) depends upon the signs of the two characteristic roots of the matrix A since λ_1 and λ_2 appear in the exponential terms in the solution (14.18). The characteristic roots can be expressed in terms of the trace of the matrix A, which equals $(a + d)$, and the determinant of this matrix, which equals $(ad - bc)$, as

$$\lambda_1, \lambda_2 = \frac{\operatorname{tr}(A) \pm \sqrt{\operatorname{tr}(A)^2 - 4 \det(A)}}{2},$$

where $\operatorname{tr}(A)$ is the trace of A and $\det(A)$ is the determinant of A. Drawing on the result first presented in Chapter 5, we find that there are three possible outcomes for the signs of the characteristic roots of A.

Signs of the Characteristic Roots Let A be a 2×2 matrix with the two real and distinct characteristic roots λ_1 and λ_2, which requires that $\operatorname{tr}(A)^2 > 4 \det(A)$. Then

$$\begin{aligned} &\lambda_1 > 0 \quad \text{and} \quad \lambda_2 > 0 \quad \text{if} \quad \operatorname{tr}(A) > 0 \quad \text{and} \quad \det(A) > 0, \\ &\lambda_1 < 0 \quad \text{and} \quad \lambda_2 < 0 \quad \text{if} \quad \operatorname{tr}(A) < 0 \quad \text{and} \quad \det(A) > 0 \quad \text{and} \\ &\lambda_i > 0 \quad \text{and} \quad \lambda_j < 0 \quad \text{if} \quad \det(A) < 0 \quad (i = 1, j = 2 \quad \text{or} \quad i = 2, j = 1). \end{aligned}$$

We only consider solutions that are stable. This restriction is one factor in determining the relevant values for $k_1 s_1$ and $k_2 s_2$ when we use the solution (14.18). There are three types of stable systems, corresponding to the three possible sign patterns for the real characteristic roots of A. We consider each in turn.

Globally Stable

When λ_1 and λ_2 are each negative, then the system is **globally stable,** and, regardless of the initial values $x(0)$ and $y(0)$, the system eventually returns to its steady state values of x_∞ and y_∞ given in (14.19). In this case the point (x_∞, y_∞) is a **stable tangent node.** The general solution to this system is (14.18). We can determine the values of k_1s_1 and k_2s_2 for any given values of $x(0)$ and $y(0)$ since, for $t = 0$,

$$x(0) = \frac{k_1s_1b}{\lambda_1 - a} + \frac{k_2s_2b}{\lambda_2 - a} + \frac{\beta b - \alpha d}{ad - bc}$$

$$y(0) = k_1s_1 + k_2s_2 + \frac{\alpha c - \beta a}{ad - bc}.$$

These two equations can be solved for the two unknowns k_1s_1 and k_2s_2. Substituting these values into (14.18) gives the specific solution for (14.14).

Globally Unstable

When λ_1 and λ_2 are each positive, then the system is **globally unstable,** and the variables $x(t)$ and $y(t)$ approach either negative infinity or positive infinity unless the system is always at its steady state, that is, $x(t) = x_\infty$ and $y(t) = y_\infty$ for all t. Therefore we must have $k_1 = 0$ and $k_2 = 0$ to avoid an unstable solution, and, thus, the solution to (14.14) is

$$x(t) = \frac{\beta b - \alpha d}{ad - bc}$$

$$y(t) = \frac{\alpha c - \beta a}{ad - bc},$$

and this point is called an **unstable tangent node.** There are no on-going dynamics in this system. Instead the only stable solution involves the variables $x(t)$ and $y(t)$ "jumping" to their new steady state values whenever there is an exogenous change in α or β.

Saddlepath Stable

In two-variable models that assume rational expectations or its variant, perfect foresight, it is typically the case that one characteristic root (say, λ_1) is positive and the other characteristic root (say, λ_2) is negative. This situation gives rise to a model that is **saddlepath stable,** and the point (x_∞, y_∞), given in (14.19), is a **saddle point.** A saddlepath stable solution requires that $k_1 = 0$ if λ_1 is the positive root. Therefore the general solution in this case is

$$x(t) = \frac{k_2s_2b}{\lambda_2 - a} \cdot e^{t \cdot \lambda_2} + \frac{\beta b - \alpha d}{ad - bc}$$

$$y(t) = k_2s_2 \cdot e^{t \cdot \lambda_2} + \frac{\alpha c - \beta a}{ad - bc}.$$

The term $k_2 s_2 \cdot e^{t \cdot \lambda_2}$ is common to the solutions for $x(t)$ and $y(t)$. Thus we can find the joint time path of $x(t)$ and $y(t)$ by solving to remove this term. This gives us the unique linear **saddlepath**

$$y(t) = \frac{(\lambda_2 - a)}{b} \cdot x(t) + \left[\frac{\alpha bc - \beta ab - (\lambda_2 - a)(\beta b - \alpha d)}{(ad - bc)b}\right],$$

which shows the relationship between $x(t)$ and $y(t)$ for any t. One of the variables in this system may evolve slowly and the other must jump such that the saddlepath relationship between the two variables is always satisfied. Notice that the dynamics of this system are monotonic since there is a linear relationship between $y(t)$ and $x(t)$ along the saddlepath.

We can obtain the specific solution to this model, given an initial value, such as $x(0)$, and by solving for $k_2 s_2$. For example, evaluating the solution at $t = 0$, given $x(0)$, we have

$$k_2 s_2 = \frac{(\lambda_2 - a)}{b} x(0) - \frac{(\lambda_2 - a)(\beta b - \alpha d)}{b(ad - bc)}.$$

This value for $k_2 s_2$ can be used in the general solution to get a specific solution.

Systems That Are Not Diagonalizable

The previous results depend upon our ability to find a matrix that, when multiplied by A, results in a diagonal matrix. In general, we cannot find a diagonal matrix when the two characteristic roots of A are identical because $\mathrm{tr}(A)^2 = 4 \det(A)$. In this case the single characteristic root is

$$\lambda = \frac{\mathrm{tr}(A)}{2} = \frac{a + d}{2}.$$

For example, the system

$$\dot{x}(t) = x(t) + y(t) + \alpha$$
$$\dot{y}(t) = y(t) + \beta$$

cannot be diagonalized since the trace of the matrix of the system is 2 and the determinant of the matrix of the system is 1 and $\mathrm{tr}^2 - 4 \cdot \det = 0$.

In general, the solution to the system (14.14) when there is a repeated characteristic root because $(a + d)^2 = 4(ad - bc)$ is

$$\begin{aligned} x(t) &= k_1 e^{t\lambda} + k_2 t e^{t\lambda} + \frac{\beta b - \alpha d}{ad - bc} \\ y(t) &= \left[\left(\frac{\lambda - a}{b}\right)(k_1 + k_2 t) + \frac{k_2}{b}\right] + \frac{\alpha c - \beta a}{ad - bc} \end{aligned} \tag{14.20}$$

for $b \neq 0$. The system will be globally stable if $\lambda = (a+d)/2 < 0$. In this case the pair of values defining the steady state is called a **stable node** or a **stable focus.** If $\lambda = (a + d)/2 > 0$, then the system is globally unstable, and the pair of values defining the steady state is called an **unstable node** or an **unstable focus.**

In the case where $\text{tr}(A)^2 < 4\det(A)$, the system will include two complex roots since they will include the term $\sqrt{-1}$. For example, if the matrix of the system is

$$A = \begin{bmatrix} -\frac{1}{2} & -9 \\ \frac{1}{4} & -\frac{1}{2} \end{bmatrix},$$

then the two characteristic roots are

$$\lambda_1, \lambda_2 = \frac{-1 \pm \sqrt{1 - 4(1/4 + 9/4)}}{2} = -\frac{1}{2} \pm 3\sqrt{-1}.$$

These two roots are complex numbers. As discussed in Chapter 13, a complex number takes the form

$$r + m\sqrt{-1},$$

where r is called the real part and m is called the imaginary part of the number. Thus, for the two roots given above, each has a real part equal to $-\frac{1}{2}$, while the imaginary part of one of the roots is 3 and the imaginary part of the other root is -3. A detailed study of the analytic solution in this case is beyond the scope of this book, but we note two important results, which we draw on in the next section where we discuss qualitative solutions with phase diagrams. First, a system of differential equations with complex roots is stable if the real parts of the characteristic roots of the system are negative. Second, the dynamics of the system are oscillatory. We can verify these results by noting that the solution to the system in the case of two complex roots is

$$x(t) = e^{rt}[k_1 \cos(vt) + k_2 \sin(vt)] + \frac{\beta b - \alpha d}{ad - bc}$$

$$y(t) = e^{rt}\left[\frac{(r-a)k_1 + vk_2}{b}\cos(vt) + \frac{(r-a)k_2 - vk_1}{b}\sin(vt)\right] + \frac{ac - ba}{ad - bc},$$

where k_1 and k_2 are constants that will depend upon the initial conditions and

$$v = \frac{1}{2}\sqrt{4\det(A)^2 - \text{tr}(A)^2},$$

which is a real number. The important point with respect to stability is that the sine function, $\sin(vt)$, and the cosine function, $\cos(vt)$, are bounded; therefore, $x(t)$ and $y(t)$ are bounded if $r < 0$, and $x(t)$ and $y(t)$ are not bounded if $r > 0$ (see Figure 13.8, which presents a graph of the sine function and the cosine function). If $r < 0$, then the steady state point is called the **stable focus** or **spiral sink,** and both $x(t)$ and $y(t)$ move toward the steady state point over time from any initial point. The steady state point is called an **unstable focus** or **source** if $r > 0$, and both $x(t)$ and $y(t)$ move away from the steady state point over time from any initial point other than the steady state point. Also, the sine and cosine functions are periodic functions, that is, the values of the functions oscillate. Therefore the presence of these functions in the solution means that there will be an oscillatory path for $x(t)$ and $y(t)$. Next we investigate the qualitative aspects of the dynamics in the case of roots that are complex numbers, along with the other cases discussed here, by using a two-dimensional phase diagram.

Two-Variable Phase Diagram

We can study a system of two differential equations by using a two-variable phase diagram. A phase diagram is drawn in a plane with $y(t)$ on one axis and $x(t)$ on the other axis. The combination of points $x(t)$ and $y(t)$ such that $\dot{x}(t) = 0$ represents one line in the phase diagram, and the combination of points such that $\dot{y}(t) = 0$ represents another line in the diagram. The point where these two schedules cross represents the steady state point of the system, (x_∞, y_∞). We can analyze dynamic stability in a phase diagram by considering the four regions defined by the $\dot{x}(t) = 0$ schedule and the $\dot{y}(t) = 0$ schedule. In Figure 14.7 we study three different phase diagrams and consider the dynamics in the regions we refer to as *N, E, S,* and *W,* representing the directions north, east, south, and west of the steady state point.

In each of the phase diagrams in Figure 14.7, the $\dot{x}(t) = 0$ schedule is positively sloped, and the $\dot{y}(t) = 0$ schedule is negatively sloped. Therefore, in terms of the elements of A in (14.15), a and b are of different signs and c and d are of the same sign. The phase diagrams differ in the individual parameters of A, a difference that gives rise to a different type of dynamic stability in each case.

The phase diagram in Figure 14.7(a) is globally stable since the sign pattern of the elements of A is

$$\begin{array}{ll} a < 0 & b > 0 \\ c < 0 & d < 0, \end{array}$$

and, therefore, the trace of A, which equals $a + d$, is negative and its determinant, which equals $ad - bc$, is positive. In regions N and W, the dynamics force x to increase, and, in regions S and E, the dynamics force x to decrease. In regions N and E, the dynamics force y to decrease, and, in regions S and W, the dynamics force y to increase. Any initial point, like that labeled 1 in the figure, leads to a movement toward the steady state point at the intersection of the $\dot{x}(t) = 0$ and $\dot{y}(t) = 0$ schedules. The figure includes a possible time path from point 1 to the steady state.

The phase diagram in Figure 14.7(b) is globally unstable since the sign pattern of the elements of A is

$$\begin{array}{ll} a > 0 & b < 0 \\ c > 0 & d > 0, \end{array}$$

and, therefore, the trace of A is positive and its determinant is positive. In regions N and W, the dynamics force x to decrease, and, in regions S and E, the dynamics force x to increase. In regions N and W, the dynamics force y to increase, and, in regions S and E, the dynamics force y to decrease. At any initial point other than the steady state where the $\dot{x}(t) = 0$ and $\dot{y}(t) = 0$ schedules intersect, the dynamics force $x(t)$ and $y(t)$ away from the steady state. Thus the only stable solution in models that are globally unstable is an immediate jump to the new steady state with a change in any exogenous

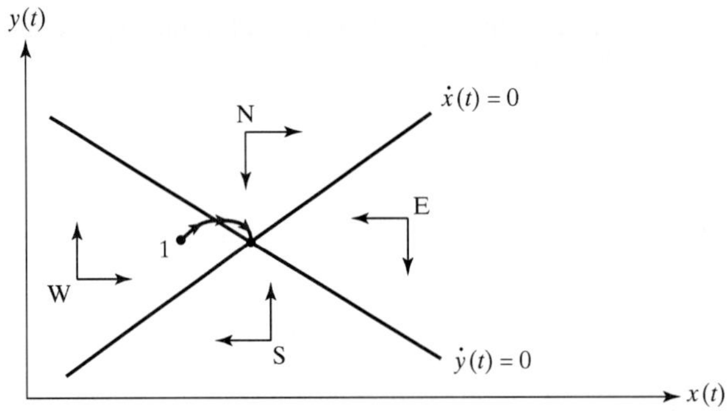

Globally Stable, ($\lambda_1 < 0,\ \lambda_2 < 0$)

(a)

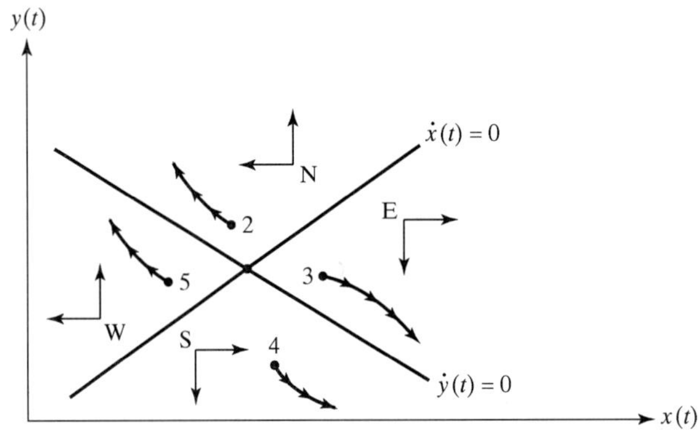

Globally Unstable, ($\lambda_1 > 0,\ \lambda_2 > 0$)

(b)

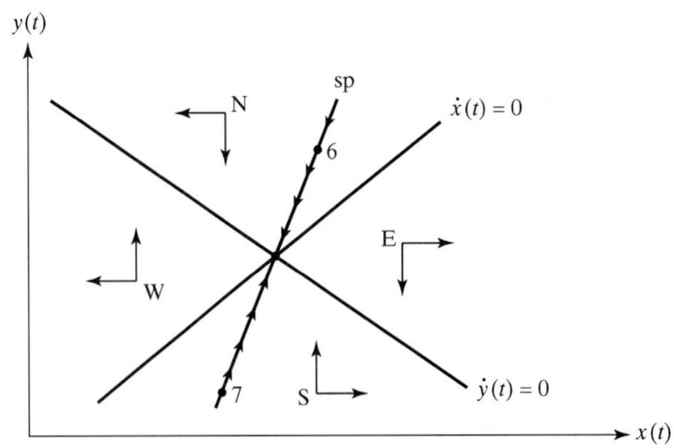

Saddlepath Stable, ($\lambda_1 < 0,\ \lambda_2 > 0$)

(c)

FIGURE 14.7 Two-Variable Phase Diagram

variables. Any other initial point, such as the points labeled 2, 3, 4, or 5, result in a time path diverging from the steady state as shown in the figure.

The phase diagram in Figure 14.7(c) is saddlepath stable since the sign pattern of the elements of A is

$$\begin{array}{ll} a > 0 & b < 0 \\ c < 0 & d < 0, \end{array}$$

and, therefore, the determinant of A is negative. In regions N and W, the dynamics force x to decrease, and, in regions S and E, the dynamics force x to increase. In regions S and W, the dynamics force y to increase, and, in regions N and E, the dynamics force y to decrease. This figure also includes the saddlepath, which passes through the steady state point represented by the intersection of the $\dot{x}(t) = 0$ and $\dot{y}(t) = 0$ schedules. The forces of motion dictate the arrows of motion drawn on the saddlepath. The slope of the saddlepath is

$$\frac{dy(t)}{dx(t)} = \frac{\lambda_2 - a}{b},$$

which is positive since the characteristic root is negative, a is positive, and b is negative. At any moment, the pair of values of $x(t)$ and $y(t)$ are on the saddlepath and either at the steady state or moving toward it. For example, points 6 and 7 are on the saddlepath, and the subsequent time path from either of these points is along the saddlepath toward the steady state.

The dynamics in the globally stable and saddlepath cases are monotonic. In the cases where the system cannot be diagonalized, the dynamics may be oscillatory. The two graphs in Figure 14.8 illustrate possible stable trajectories for a system with one repeated root. Figure 14.8(a) illustrates the trajectories for the homogeneous system

$$\begin{bmatrix} \dot{x}(t) \\ \dot{y}(t) \end{bmatrix} = \begin{bmatrix} \lambda & 1 \\ 0 & \lambda \end{bmatrix} \begin{bmatrix} x(t) \\ y(t) \end{bmatrix},$$

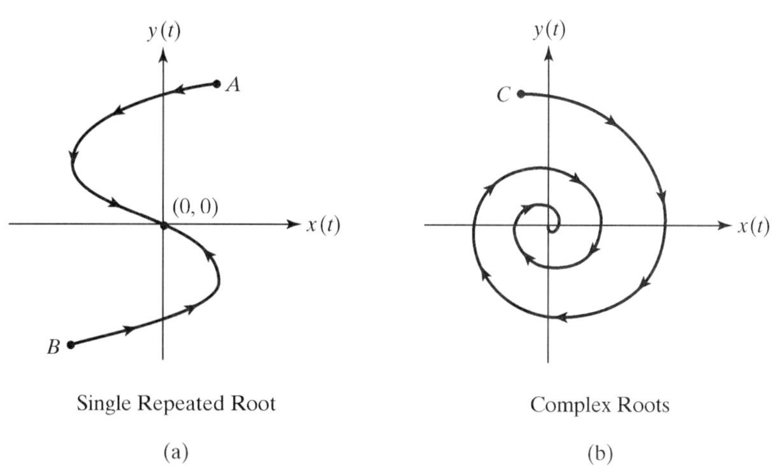

FIGURE 14.8 Oscillatory Dynamics

where $\lambda < 0$. The steady state of this system is the origin. The two possible initial points are labeled A and B. Note that, along either one of these trajectories, from A to $(0, 0)$ or from B to $(0, 0)$, the time path of $x(t)$ oscillates, while the time path of $y(t)$ is monotonic. Figure 14.8(b) illustrates the time path of a homogeneous system with two complex roots that have negative real parts. The trajectories in this figure spiral in from the initial point C towards the steady state point $(0, 0)$. This spiral trajectory represents oscillatory paths for both $x(t)$ and $y(t)$.

Phase diagrams with saddlepath properties are used frequently in macroeconomic models that assume perfect foresight. One such model is presented in the following application.

Exchange Rate Overshooting

The flexible price exchange-rate model presented in the application in Section 14.2 has the property that a given change in the money supply leads to a proportional change in the exchange rate. Exchange rates are very volatile, however, a characteristic not well captured by the flexible price exchange-rate model. An alternative model developed by Rudiger Dornbusch is able to account for exchange-rate volatility.[11]

The simplest version of Dornbusch's model consists of four equations. We assume perfect foresight, so there is no distinction between the expected value of a variable and its actual value. The interest parity relationship

$$i(t) = i^* + \dot{\varepsilon}(t),$$

where $i(t)$ is the nominal interest rate at moment t, i^* is the foreign interest rate, which is assumed constant, and $\dot{\varepsilon}(t)$ is the derivative of the exchange rate with respect to time. The exchange rate is defined as units of domestic currency per one unit of foreign currency, so an increase in ε represents a depreciation of the domestic currency. The money demand equation

$$m - p(t) = -\mu i(t)$$

where m is the logarithm of the money supply and $p(t)$ is the logarithm of the price level at time t, is similar to the one presented in Section 14.2. The simplest version of an income determination equation

$$y(t) = \beta(\varepsilon(t) + p^* - p(t))$$

has income as a function of the logarithm of the real exchange rate, which is the sum of the logarithm of the nominal exchange rate and the foreign price level, p^*, minus the domestic price level. An increase in the real exchange rate, which represents a real depreciation of the currency, stimulates output by making exports cheaper and by making imports more expensive. The final equation is a Phillips curve–type relationship that links inflation, $\dot{p}(t)$, to the difference between actual income, $y(t)$, and potential income, $\bar{y}$,

$$\dot{p}(t) = \theta(y(t) - \bar{y}),$$

[11] Rudiger Dornbusch, "Expectations and exchange-rate dynamics," *Journal of Political Economy* (December 1976): 1161–1176.

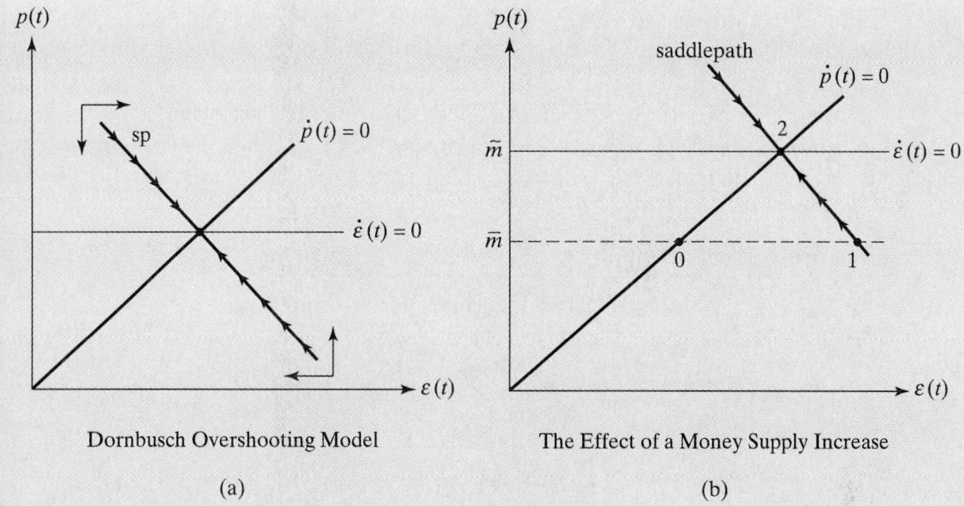

FIGURE 14.9 Dornbusch Overshooting Model and Effect on Money Supply

where θ is a parameter that reflects the responsiveness of inflation to excess aggregate demand. We simplify the algebra by setting i^*, p^*, and $\bar{y}$ equal to zero. After some algebra, we express this model as the system

$$\begin{bmatrix} \dot{\varepsilon}(t) \\ \dot{p}(t) \end{bmatrix} = \begin{bmatrix} 0 & \dfrac{1}{\mu} \\ \beta\theta & -\beta\theta \end{bmatrix} \cdot \begin{bmatrix} \varepsilon(t) \\ p(t) \end{bmatrix} + \begin{bmatrix} -\dfrac{m}{\mu} \\ 0 \end{bmatrix}.$$

The determinant of the matrix of this system is $-\beta\theta/\mu$. The fact that the determinant is negative indicates that the dynamics are characterized by saddlepath stability. The exchange rate is the jump variable, and the price level is the slowly evolving variable.

The phase diagram of this system is presented in Figure 14.9(a). The $\dot{\varepsilon}(t) = 0$ schedule is horizontal and intersects the vertical axis at the point where $p(t) = m$. The $\dot{p}(t) = 0$ passes through the origin, and its slope equals 1. The saddlepath passes through the steady state point $(\varepsilon_\infty, p_\infty)$. We can determine this steady state point by solving the system when $\dot{\varepsilon}(t) = 0$ and $\dot{p}(t) = 0$, which gives us

$$\varepsilon_\infty = p_\infty = m.$$

The slope of the saddlepath is

$$\frac{dp(t)}{d\varepsilon(t)} = \lambda_2 \mu,$$

where λ_2 is the negative root of the system. This shows that the saddlepath has a negative slope since μ is positive.

Figure 14.9(b) shows the effect of an increase in the money supply from $\bar{m}$ to $\tilde{m}$. This change causes the $\dot{\varepsilon}(t) = 0$ schedule to shift up and the saddlepath to shift up and to the right. At the moment the money supply increases, the exchange rate jumps to point 1 from its initial steady state of point 0. Over time the system moves along the saddlepath to the new steady state point 2, with the exchange rate falling (that is, appreciating) and the price level rising. Thus the exchange rate overshoots its new steady state level of $\varepsilon_\infty = \tilde{m}$ in the short run. This overshooting, which does not occur in the flexible price monetary model presented in Section 14.2, is a possible reason for the observed volatility in exchange rates.

A Note on Second-Order Differential Equations

A second-order linear differential equation takes the form

$$\frac{d^2x(t)}{dt^2} = a\frac{dx(t)}{dt} + bx(t) + c$$

or, equivalently, with the "dot" notation,

$$\ddot{x}(t) = a\dot{x}(t) + bx(t) + c.$$

This equation can be solved with the techniques developed in this section. Define the new variable $y(t)$, where $y(t) = dx(t)/dt$. Using this definition, we can rewrite the single second-order linear differential equation as the system of first-order differential equations

$$\frac{dy(t)}{dt} = ay(t) + bx(t) + c$$

$$\frac{dx(t)}{dt} = y(t)$$

or, in matrix form, as

$$\begin{bmatrix} \dot{x}(t) \\ \dot{y}(t) \end{bmatrix} = \begin{bmatrix} 0 & 1 \\ b & a \end{bmatrix} \cdot \begin{bmatrix} x(t) \\ y(t) \end{bmatrix} + \begin{bmatrix} 0 \\ c \end{bmatrix}.$$

This system can be solved with the techniques discussed in this section.

The stability of the solution to a second-order differential equation follows from the results described previously. Define the 2×2 matrix in the above system as A and, consider the case where there are two distinct real roots. The trace of A is negative and its determinant is positive if $a < 0$ and $b < 0$. In this case both characteristic roots are negative, and the solution to the second-order differential equation is globally stable. The trace of A is positive and its determinant is positive if $a > 0$ and $b < 0$. In this case both characteristic roots are positive, and the solution to the second-order differential equation is globally unstable. The determinant of A is negative if $b > 0$. In this case one characteristic root is positive, and one is negative. As $t \to \infty$, the positive characteristic root will dominate the solution, and $x(t) \to \infty$ or $x(t) \to -\infty$.

Exercises 14.3

1. Determine the steady state values for the variable $x(t)$ and $y(t)$ for each system of equations.

(a) System I:

$$\dot{x}(t) = -x(t) + 4$$
$$\dot{y}(t) = 3x(t) - 6y(t) - 6$$

(b) System II:

$$\dot{x}(t) = \frac{1}{2}x(t) - \frac{1}{4}y(t)$$
$$\dot{y}(t) = 13x(t) + 7\frac{1}{2}y(t) - 56$$

(c) System III:

$$\dot{x}(t) = \frac{5}{2}x(t) + \frac{7}{2}y(t) - 25$$
$$\dot{y}(t) = \frac{1}{2}x(t) - \frac{1}{2}y(t) + 1$$

2. What are the stable dynamics of each system presented in question 1? Construct a phase diagram for each system, and show the path to the steady state that would result from some point away from the steady state, if such a path exists.
3. Determine the explicit stable solution to System II presented in question 1.
4. Find the stable solution to System III in question 1 when the initial value of the system is $x = 0$, $y = 8$.
5. Consider a variant of the Dornbusch overshooting model in which the money demand equation is

$$m(t) - p(t) = -\mu i(t) + \varphi y(t)$$

and otherwise the model is the same as in the text.

(a) Determine the conditions under which the model is saddlepath stable.
(b) Is it possible to have "undershooting" rather than "overshooting" in this model (that is, can the saddlepath have a positive slope)?

6. Consider the macroeconomic model

$$\dot{u}(t) = -\beta(\overline{m} - p(t)) + \sigma(\overline{u} - \theta(t))$$
$$\dot{p}(t) = \theta(\overline{u} - \theta(t)),$$

where $u(t)$ is the unemployment rate, $p(t)$ is the logarithm of the price level, $\overline{m}$ is the exogenously determined money supply, and $\overline{u}$ is the natural rate of unemployment. The first equation shows that unemployment responds to monetary policy and also, all else equal, unemployment tends towards its natural rate. The second equation is a Phillips curve.

(a) Determine the steady state of the model.
(b) What type of dynamics characterize this model?
(c) Construct a phase diagram for this model.
(d) Use your phase diagram to trace out the effects of a one-time increase in the money supply from $\overline{m}$ to $\tilde{m}$.

7. Calculate the characteristic roots of the following second-order linear differential equations. Determine whether each equation is stable or unstable.

(a) $\ddot{x}(t) = -4\dot{x}(t) + \frac{7}{4}x(t) + 5$

(b) $\ddot{y}(t) = 2\dot{y}(t) + \frac{3}{4}y(t) + 2$

(c) $\ddot{z}(t) = 2\dot{z}(t) - \frac{5}{4}z(t) + 1$

Summary

This chapter has continued our study of dynamic analysis with a study of differential equations. Differential equations are found in fields of economics in which the value of variables at different moments in time is important, such as finance, macroeconomics, and international economics. Many of the concepts discussed in this chapter are similar to those discussed in Chapter 13 in which dynamic analysis is studied in the context of discrete time models.

Differential equations and phase diagrams are important for the material presented in the next chapter in which we solve for the optimal time path of variables in dynamic problems.

Chapter 15

Dynamic Optimization

Several of the applications of constrained optimization presented in Chapter 11 are two-period discrete-time optimization problems. The objective function in these intertemporal consumption problems is the discounted sum of utility in each period. The intertemporal constraints in these problems link actions taken in the one period with actions taken in the other period. For example, if consumption is higher in the first period, then, all else equal, the budget constraint requires that it is lower in the second period. These intertemporal constraints make these **dynamic optimization** problems more complicated than a simple sequence of one-period optimization problems. Nevertheless, we are able to obtain solutions to these problems by simply applying the standard techniques of constrained optimization after setting up the problem in an appropriate manner. As shown in the first section of this chapter, the extension of these methods to settings of more than two periods is relatively straightforward.

The extension of these techniques to continuous time dynamic optimization problems is not as straightforward. The greater part of this chapter is devoted to techniques for finding the optimal time path of variables in a continuous time framework. In particular, we consider dynamic optimization problems in which the constraints include one or more differential equations. The technique for solving these types of problems, which is called **optimal control theory,** was developed in the 1950s by the Soviet mathematician L.S. Pontryagin and his associates and, independently, by the American mathematician Richard Bellman.[1] Optimal control theory allows consideration of the optimal time path of a set of variables rather than just the identification of a stationary equilibrium. By way of analogy to the material on differential equations in Chapter 14, a full characterization of the solution to many types of dynamic problems requires the determination of the path to the steady state, as well as the steady state itself.

In this chapter we introduce the elements of optimal control theory in order to provide a working knowledge of its basic results.[2] In Section 15.1 we set up and solve a

---

[1] L. S. Pontryagin et al., *The Mathematical Theory of Optimal Processes*, K. N. Trirogoff, trans. (New York: Interscience Publishers, 1962) and Richard Bellman, *Dynamic Programming,* (Princeton: Princeton University Press, 1957).

[2] A full exposition of dynamic optimization is beyond the scope of this book. A reader interested in more detail and more general results than those presented here can consult Chapter 8 of Akira Takayama, *Mathematical Economics,* 2d ed. (Cambridge, England: Cambridge University Press, 1985), 600–719 and the references therein.

discrete time dynamic optimization problem and interpret its solution. In Section 15.2 we present a continuous time version of the discrete time problem and present the conditions that solve this problem. Section 15.3 concludes this chapter with some extensions of the basic results presented in the previous section and some economic applications. An appendix to the chapter presents a heuristic derivation of the necessary conditions for a continuous time dynamic optimization problem.

15.1 DYNAMIC OPTIMIZATION IN DISCRETE TIME

Discrete time dynamic optimization problems can be solved with the Lagrange multiplier method presented in Chapter 11. In this section we extend the results from the two-period model, which are discussed in Chapter 11, to the case where there are more general functions and the problem includes more than two periods. The intuition and results from this discrete time analysis will serve us well when we turn to the continuous time case in the next section.

Consider the problem facing the managers of a firm who wish to maximize total profits from time $t = 0$ to time $t = T$. Profits at any moment t depend upon two variables, the amount spent on labor during that moment and the capital available to the firm at the beginning of the period. The amount spent on labor is called the **control variable,** which we denote as c_t. The value of the control variable can be selected each period. Control variables take the form of flows, such as the flow of consumption or the flow of labor services. Given a choice of the time path of the control variable, the managers cannot independently choose the time path of capital, which is the **state variable,** since the amount spent on labor implicitly determines the amount of revenues left over for investment in capital. State variables are stocks, such as the stock of capital, the stock of available oil, or the stock of gold. In this problem, k_t represents the stock of capital from the end of period $t - 1$ to the end of period t.

We define an instantaneous profit function $\pi(c_t, k_t, t)$, which is assumed to be twice-differentiable and concave for all values of its arguments. The profit function describes an instantaneous flow of profits, and, therefore, total profits accrued over an entire period equals the value of the profit function during that period times the length of the period, which we denote as m.[3] The goal of the managers of the firm is to maximize the profit of the firm over the time period $t = 0$ to T. The profit over this period is represented by the sum

$$\sum_{t=0}^{T} m \cdot \pi(c_t, k_t, t). \tag{15.1}$$

This problem also includes an intertemporal constraint on the accumulation of capital. Investment in period t, which is the change in the capital stock from period t to period $t + 1$ (absent depreciation), is assumed to be determined by the function

$$k_{t+1} - k_t = m \cdot f(c_t, k_t, t), \tag{15.2}$$

[3] We use instantaneous functions here, which must be multiplied by m to give a value over a period, in anticipation of extending this example to the continuous time case in the next section.

where $f(c_t, k_t, t)$, like $\pi(c_t, k_t, t)$, is an "instantaneous" function and must be multiplied by m to get the cumulative change in capital for an entire period. We also assume that there is an initial given stock of capital equal to $\underline{k}$ and that, at the end of period T, the capital stock must equal $\bar{k}$. Thus the Lagrangian function associated with this problem (see Chapter 11) is

$$L = \sum_{t=0}^{T} [m \cdot \pi(c_t, k_t, t) - \lambda_t(k_{t+1} - m \cdot f(c_t, k_t, t) - k_t)] - \mu_0(k_0 - \underline{k}) - \mu_T(k_T - \bar{k}), \tag{15.3}$$

where the λ_t's represent $T + 1$ Lagrange multipliers on the constraint imposed by the capital accumulation equation and μ_0 and μ_T represent the Lagrange multipliers on the constraints due to the initial condition and the terminal condition, respectively. The λ_t's are called **costate variables** or, more descriptively, **dynamic Lagrange multipliers.** As discussed in Chapter 11, the solution to this problem requires simultaneously solving first-order conditions. These first-order conditions include

$$\frac{\partial L}{\partial c_t} = m \cdot [\pi_c(c_t, k_t, t) + \lambda_t \cdot f_c(c_t, k_t, t)] = 0 \quad \text{for} \quad t = 0, 1, \ldots, T, \tag{15.4}$$

$$\frac{\partial L}{\partial \lambda_t} = k_{t+1} - m \cdot f(c_t, k_t, t) - k_t = 0 \quad \text{for} \quad t = 0, 1, \ldots, T, \tag{15.5}$$

$$\frac{\partial L}{\partial \mu_0} = k_0 - \underline{k} = 0, \quad \text{and} \tag{15.6}$$

$$\frac{\partial L}{\partial \mu_T} = k_T - \bar{k} = 0, \tag{15.7}$$

where $\pi_c(c_t, k_t, t)$ and $f_c(c_t, k_t, t)$ represent the partial derivatives of the respective functions with respect to c_t. The first-order condition (15.4) requires that c_t in each period maximizes the term in square brackets in (15.3), given the amount of capital for that period. The first-order condition (15.5) represents the difference equation that governs the evolution of the capital stock, (15.2).[4] The first-order conditions (15.6) and (15.7) require that the initial condition and the terminal condition are satisfied.

The final first-order condition for this problem requires us to take the partial derivative of L with respect to the capital stock. Both k_t and k_{t+1} appear in the Lagrangian function. To obtain the first-order condition with respect to the capital stock in any one period, it is useful to note that

$$\sum_{t=0}^{T} -\lambda_t(k_{t+1} - k_t) = -\lambda_0(k_1 - k_0) - \lambda_1(k_2 - k_1) - \cdots - \lambda_T(k_{T+1} - k_T)$$
$$= \left[\sum_{t=1}^{T} k_t(\lambda_t - \lambda_{t-1})\right] + k_0\lambda_0 - k_{T+1}\lambda_T.$$

[4] In Chapter 11 we discussed the equivalence of the condition $\partial L/\partial\lambda$ and the condition that the equality constraint holds exactly.

This result allows us to rewrite (15.3) as

$$L = \sum_{t=1}^{T} [m \cdot \pi(c_t, k_t, t) + \lambda_t \cdot m \cdot f(c_t, k_t, t) + k_t(\lambda_t - \lambda_{t-1})] + k_0\lambda_0 - k_{T+1}\lambda_T$$
$$+ m \cdot \pi(c_0, k_0, 0) + \lambda_0 \cdot m \cdot f(c_0, k_0, 0) - \mu_0(k_0 - \underline{k}) - \mu_T(k_T - \bar{k}). \tag{15.8}$$

Then we can more easily obtain the first-order condition with respect to k_t, which is

$$\frac{\partial L}{\partial k_t} = m \cdot [\pi_k(c_t, k_t, t) + \lambda_t \cdot f_k(c_t, k_t, t)] + (\lambda_t - \lambda_{t-1}) = 0 \quad \text{for}$$
$$t = 1, 2, \ldots, T, \tag{15.9}$$

where $\pi_k(c_t, k_t, t)$ and $f_k(c_t, k_t, t)$ represent the partial derivatives of the functions with respect to k_t.

We can interpret the first-order condition (15.9) by remembering that the Lagrange multiplier represents the effect of a small change in the constraint on the optimal value of the objective function.[5] In this context, the Lagrange multiplier λ_t represents the amount by which the maximum attainable value of the sum of profits is increased if an additional unit of capital is obtained at the end of the tth period at no cost in foregone spending on labor (that is, as if the capital were a pure gift). Thus λ_t is the shadow price of capital, and it reflects the marginal value of capital at the end of the tth period. Therefore $-(\lambda_t - \lambda_{t-1})$ represents the rate at which capital depreciates in value. The first-order condition (15.9) requires that the depreciation in value of capital over an interval equals the sum of its contribution to profits during that interval, $m \cdot \pi_k(c_t, k_t, t)$, plus its contribution to enhancing the value of the capital stock at the end of the interval, $m \cdot \lambda_t \cdot f_k(c_t, k_t, t)$. As noted by Robert Dorfman, along the optimal time path, "a unit of capital loses value or depreciates as time passes at the rate at which its potential contribution to profits becomes its past contribution."[6]

An alternative way to present the first-order conditions (15.4), (15.5), and (15.9) involves the **Hamiltonian** function

$$H(c_t, k_t, \lambda_t, t) = \pi(c_t, k_t, t) + \lambda_t \cdot f(c_t, k_t, t). \tag{15.10}$$

The product $m \cdot H(c_t, k_t, \lambda_t, t)$ represents the total value of activity in period t since it is the sum of total profits earned over that period, $m \cdot \pi(c_t, k_t, t)$, plus the amount of capital accumulated during that period, $m \cdot f(c_t, k_t, t)$, times the marginal value of capital at that time, λ_t.

The Lagrangian function (15.3) can be rewritten with this Hamiltonian function as

$$L = \sum_{t=0}^{T} [m \cdot H(c_t, k_t, \lambda_t, t) - \lambda_t(k_{t+1} - k_t)] - \mu_0(k_0 - \underline{k}) - \mu_T(k_T - \bar{k}). \tag{15.11}$$

---

[5] See the discussion in Chapter 11. The following interpretation draws from Robert Dorfman, "An economic interpretation of optimal control theory," *American Economic Review* 59, no. 5 (December 1969): 817–831.

[6] Ibid., 821.

Along the optimal path where the Hamiltonian takes its maximum value, which we denote as $H(c_t^*, k_t^*, \lambda_t, t)$, the first-order condition (15.4) shows that

$$\frac{\partial L}{\partial c_t} = m \cdot \frac{\partial H(c_t^*, k_t^*, \lambda_t, t)}{\partial c_t} = 0 \quad \text{for} \quad t = 0, 1, \ldots, T. \tag{15.12}$$

The Envelope Theorem allows us to ignore terms that arise from the chain rule. For example, the term

$$\frac{\partial H(c_t^*, k_t^*, \lambda_t, t)}{\partial k_t^*} \cdot \frac{\partial k_t^*}{\partial c_t}$$

equals zero because, along the optimum path, $\partial k_t / \partial c_t = 0$. Since the Hamiltonian represents the total value of activity, the first-order condition (15.12) can be interpreted as requiring that consumption in each period maximizes the total value of activity in that period. The first-order condition (15.5) can be written as

$$\frac{\partial L}{\partial \lambda_t} = m \cdot \frac{\partial H(c_t^*, k_t^*, \lambda_t, t)}{\partial \lambda_t} - (k_{t+1} - k_t) = 0 \quad \text{for} \quad t = 0, 1, \ldots, T \tag{15.13}$$

when the partial derivative of the Hamiltonian is evaluated along the optimal path. This just restates the capital accumulation constraint (15.2) since, along the optimal path, $\partial H(c_t^*, k_t^*, \lambda_t, t)/\partial \lambda_t = f(c_t^*, k_t^*, t)$. Finally, substituting the Hamiltonian into the Lagrange function as it is written in (15.8) and taking the partial derivative with respect to k_t along the optimal path, we have the restatement of (15.9) as

$$\frac{\partial L}{\partial k_t} = m \cdot \frac{\partial H(c_t^*, k_t^*, \lambda_t, t)}{\partial k_t} + (\lambda_t - \lambda_{t-1}) = 0 \quad \text{for} \quad t = 1, 2, \ldots, T. \tag{15.14}$$

This problem has a specified terminal value k_T. An alternative situation arises when the terminal value can be chosen optimally. In this case the term $-\mu_T(k_T - \bar{k})$ is not included in the Lagrangian functions (15.3) and (15.8), and the first-order condition (15.7) is omitted. In its place is the first-order condition

$$\lambda_T k_T = 0, \tag{15.7$'$}$$

which is known as the **transversality condition.** This condition meets the requirement that

$$\frac{\partial L}{\partial k_{T+1}} = -\lambda_T = 0$$

if k_T does not equal zero. The intuition behind the transversality condition is that if there is any capital left at the end of the relevant time period ($k_T \neq 0$), then its shadow price must be zero.[7] Alternatively, if there is a positive shadow price at the end of the relevant time period, then there must be no capital left. If the transversality condition

[7] The relevant time period in this problem ends with period T; but the state equation dictates a value for k_{T+1} given k_T, and the optimal value c_T^*.

is not met, then profits could have been higher had there been a different allocation of spending between labor and capital.

These first-order conditions constitute the **maximum principle** for discrete time dynamic optimization problems. As we will see in the next section, there is a similar set of conditions that constitute the maximum principle for problems in continuous time.

Exercises 15.1

1. Consider a firm with the profit function

$$\Pi_t = F(K_t, L_t) - w_t L_t - I_t,$$

where Π_t is profits, K_t is capital, L_t is labor, w_t is the (exogenous) wage, and I_t is investment. Subscripts refer to the time period. The production function, $F(K_t, L_t)$ has continuous first partial derivatives with $F_i > 0$ and $F_{ii} < 0$ for $i = K, L$. The managers of the firm wish to maximize the present discounted value of profits from the present (period 0) to period T, which equals

$$V_0 = \sum_{s=0}^{T} \left(\frac{1}{1+r}\right)^s \Pi_s.$$

The capital accumulation constraint facing the firm is

$$K_{t+1} = (1 - \delta)K_t + I_t,$$

where δ is the depreciation rate. The firm initially has no capital, and in period T the firm must have capital equal to $\underline{K}$. Set up the Hamiltonian for this problem. Solve for the optimal amount of labor to hire and the optimal amount of investment in each period.

2. Consider a variant of question 1 in which there is a cost to installing capital, C_t, which is

$$C_t = \frac{\gamma I_t^2}{2K_t}$$

and therefore the total cost of investment is

$$I_t + C_t = I_t + \frac{\gamma I_t^2}{2K_t}.$$

The firm's profit in any period is

$$\Pi_t = F(K_t, L_t) - w_t L_t - I_t - \frac{\gamma I_t^2}{2K_t}.$$

Assume that the capital accumulation equation is

$$K_{t+1} = K_t + I_t$$

that, as in the previous example, $K_0 = 0$, and that at the terminal period $T, K_T = \underline{K}$.

(a) Set up the Hamiltonian in this case.

(b) Does the first-order condition for labor differ from that in question 1?

(c) Solve for the first-order conditions for capital and investment.

(d) Denoting the Lagrange multiplier λ_t, define $q_t = \lambda_t(1 + r)^t$. Show that the optimal solution includes the condition

$$q_t(1 + r) = F_K(K_{t+1}, L_{t+1}) + \frac{\gamma I_{t+1}^2}{K_{t+1}^2} + q_{t+1}.$$

3. In Chapter 11 we discussed a two-period intertemporal consumption problem. Consider a T-period version of that problem. A consumer attempts to maximize, at time 0,

$$\sum_{t=0}^{T} \beta^t U(C_t),$$

where C_t is consumption in period $t(C_t > 0)$, β is a subjective discount rate $(1 > \beta > 0)$, and the utility function has the properties

$$U'(C_t) > 0, U''(C_t) < 0, U(0) = -\infty.$$

The consumer enjoys an exogenous sequence of income $\{Y_s\}_{t=0}^{T}$ and faces the budget constraint

$$(1 + R)B_t + Y_t = C_t + B_{t+1},$$

where R is the real interest rate and B_t is the consumer's portfolio of bonds in period t. We assume $B_0 = 0$ and require $B_{T+1} = 0$.

(a) Set up the Hamiltonian function for this problem.

(b) Use the first-order conditions to solve for the optimal relationship between marginal utility in any two adjacent periods.

(c) Compare this solution to the one obtained for the two-period problem in Chapter 11.

4. Consider an extension of question 3 in which consumers must produce their income using capital which they accumulate through investment. The budget constraint in any period t is

$$(1 + R)B_t + F(K_t) = C_t + B_{t+1} + I_t,$$

where $F(K_t)$ is a production function with a continuous first derivative, $F' > 0$ and also $F'' < 0$, and I_t is investment in period t. The capital accumulation equation is

$$K_{t+1} = I_t + K_t.$$

Again consider this problem from period 0 to period T with $B_0 = 0$, $K_0 = 0$, $B_T = 0$, and $K_T = \underline{K}$, and assume the representative consumer wishes to maximize, at time 0,

$$\sum_{t=0}^{T} \beta^t U(C_t),$$

where C_t is consumption in period $t (C_t > 0)$, β is a subjective discount rate $(1 > \beta > 0)$, and the utility function has the properties

$$U'(C_t) > 0, \quad U''(C_t) < 0, \quad \text{and} \quad U(0) = -\infty.$$

(a) Set up the Hamiltonian in this case. The Hamiltonian must include a set of Lagrange multipliers for capital and another set of Lagrange multipliers for bonds.

(b) Use the first-order conditions to determine the condition for the optimal amount of capital each period, a condition which will use $F'(K_t)$.

15.2 OPTIMAL CONTROL THEORY

Optimal control theory shows how to solve continuous time maximization problems in which the objective function includes an integral and the constraints include a differential equation. In this section we build on the intuition developed in the discrete time problems discussed in the previous section to present the main results of optimal control theory. Although a formal proof of the continuous time maximum principle is well beyond the scope of this book, the appendix to this chapter presents a heuristic argument for the necessary conditions for an optimal time path.

The continuous time version of the problem facing the managers of the firm discussed in the previous section involves the optimal selection of a time path of the control variable $c(t)$, which represents the flow of expenditures on labor. In general, the path of the control variable in an optimal control problem must be **piecewise continuous.** This condition requires that the path of the control variable is continuous but for (possibly) some finite number of jump discontinuities and that the size of the jumps is finite. This problem also includes a constraint on the accumulation of the state variable, capital $k(t)$. The state variable in an optimal control problem must be continuous and **piecewise differentiable,** that is, the path can have a finite number of "corners" or points where its derivative is not defined. Figure 15.1(a) illustrates the time path of a piecewise continuous variable, and Figure 15.1(b) illustrates the time path of a piecewise differentiable variable.

The profit of the firm over the time period $t = 0$ to T is a function of both the control variable and the state variable, as well as time itself, and is given by the integral

$$\int_{t=0}^{T} \pi(c(t), k(t), t)\, dt, \tag{15.15}$$

where $\pi(c(t), k(t), t)$ is the instantaneous profit function. This integral is the continuous time analogue to the sum in (15.1). The continuous time analogue to the difference equation (15.2) that describes the evolution of the capital stock is the differential equation

$$\dot{k}(t) = f(c(t), k(t), t), \tag{15.16}$$

where $\dot{k}(t) \equiv dk(t)/dt$. The functions $\pi(c(t), k(t), t)$ and $f(c(t), k(t), t)$ are assumed to be continuous in all their arguments and to have continuous first-order partial

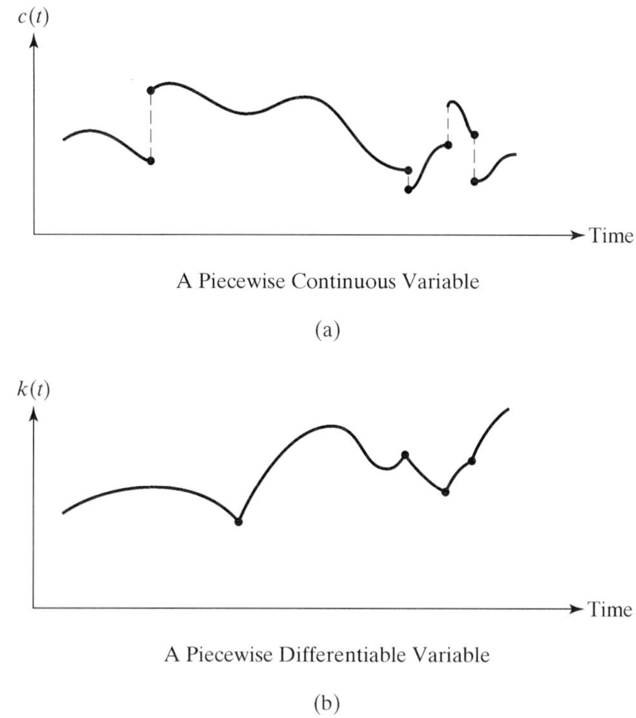

FIGURE 15.1 Piecewise Continuous and Piecewise Differentiable Variables

derivatives with respect to $k(t)$ and t, but not necessarily with respect to $c(t)$. The initial condition mirrors that in the problem in Section 15.1, with

$$k(0) = \underline{k}. \tag{15.17}$$

We consider two possible cases with respect to the terminal condition, the fixed terminal condition case where

$$k(T) = \overline{k}$$

as well as the case where $k(T)$ is chosen optimally.

The **maximum principle** (also known as **Pontryagin's maximum principle**) provides a set of conditions that are necessary for obtaining the maximum value of the objective function subject to the constraints.

The Maximum Principle If $c(t)$ and $k(t)$ maximize

$$\int_{t=0}^{T} \pi(c(t), k(t), t)\, dt$$

subject to the state equation

$$\dot{k}(t) = f(c(t), k(t), t),$$

where

- $\pi(c(t), k(t), t)$ is piecewise continuous,
- $f(c(t), k(t), t)$ is continuous and piecewise differentiable,
- both $\pi(c(t), k(t), t)$ and $f(c(t), k(t), t)$ have continuous first-order partial derivatives with respect to $k(t)$ and t, and
- the initial condition $k(0) = \underline{k}$ holds,

then, for the Hamiltonian function

$$H(c(t), k(t), \lambda(t), t) = \pi(c(t), k(t), t) + \lambda(t) \cdot f(c(t), k(t), t),$$

the following maximum principle conditions must be met at the optimal values $c^*(t)$ and $k^*(t)$:

(i) $H(c^*(t), k^*(t), \lambda(t), t) \geq H(c(t), k^*(t), \lambda(t), t)$ for all t

(ii) $\dfrac{\partial H(c^*(t), k^*(t), \lambda(t), t)}{\partial k(t)} = -\dot{\lambda}(t)$

(iii) $\dfrac{\partial H(c^*(t), k^*(t), \lambda(t), t)}{\partial \lambda(t)} = \dot{k}(t)$

(iv) $k(0) = k$,

where the notation used in conditions (ii) and (iii) means that the partial derivatives are evaluated along the optimal path.

One of the following conditions must also be met:

(v) If the terminal value of the state variable must equal $\bar{k}$, then $k(T) = \bar{k}$.

(vi) If the terminal value of the state variable is not given, then $\lambda(T) = 0$. ■

We also note the following.

- If $c^*(t)$ is in the interior (rather than at a boundary) of the admissable region for the control variable and if the Hamiltonian is continuously differentiable in $c(t)$, then condition (i) implies

$$\frac{\partial H(c^*(t), k^*(t), \lambda(t), t)}{\partial c(t)} = 0.$$

- We can solve a problem that requires the minimization of the integral of an instantaneous objective function, $v(c(t), k(t), \lambda(t), t)$, in the same fashion as the maximum problem by simply defining a function

$$w(c(t), k(t), \lambda(t), t) = -v(c(t), k(t), \lambda(t), t)$$

and finding the maximum of the problem by using the function $w(c(t), k(t), \lambda(t), t)$.

We illustrate the use of the maximum principle with the following example, which has a simple geometric interpretation. Consider the problem of choosing the optimum path of the control $c(t)$ to maximize

$$\int_{t=0}^{10} -\sqrt{1 + c(t)^2} \; dt$$

subject to the constraints

$$\frac{dk(t)}{dt} = c(t),$$
$$k(0) = 4, \quad \text{and}$$
$$k(10) = 24,$$

where $k(t)$ is the state variable. We form the Hamiltonian

$$H(c(t), k(t), \lambda(t)) = -\sqrt{1 + c(t)^2} + \lambda(t) \cdot c(t).$$

The maximum principle shows that the first order-conditions are

$$\frac{\partial H(c(t), k(t), \lambda(t))}{\partial c(t)} = -\frac{c(t)}{\sqrt{1 + c(t)^2}} + \lambda(t) = 0, \tag{15.18}$$

$$\frac{\partial H(c(t), k(t), \lambda(t))}{\partial k(t)} = 0 = -\dot{\lambda}(t), \tag{15.19}$$

$$\frac{\partial H(c(t), k(t), \lambda(t))}{\partial \lambda(t)} = c(t) = \dot{k}(t), \tag{15.20}$$

$$k(0) = 4, \quad \text{and} \tag{15.21}$$

$$k(10) = 24. \tag{15.22}$$

The condition (15.19) shows that the costate variable is constant since $\dot{\lambda}(t) = 0$. This result, combined with (15.18), shows that the control variable $c(t)$ is also constant, and, therefore, we denote it as c. To solve for the optimal value c, we integrate condition (15.20) to obtain

$$\int_{t=0}^{10} \frac{dk}{dt} dt = \int_{t=0}^{10} c \cdot dt$$
$$k(10) - k(0) = c \cdot 10 - c \cdot 0 = 10 \cdot c.$$

The conditions (15.21) and (15.22) show that $k(10) - k(0) = 24 - 4 = 20$, and, therefore, the optimal value of the control variable is $c = 20/10 = 2$.

This example has the geometric interpretation of finding the minimum distance between the two points (0, 4) and (10, 24) in a graph of the function $k = f(t)$. Figure 15.2 presents these two points along with an arbitrary function $f(t)$. The distance between the line segment connecting any two points i and $i + m$ on the function $f(t)$, is given by the Pythagorean Theorem to be

$$s_i = \sqrt{(\Delta t)^2 + (\Delta k(i))^2},$$

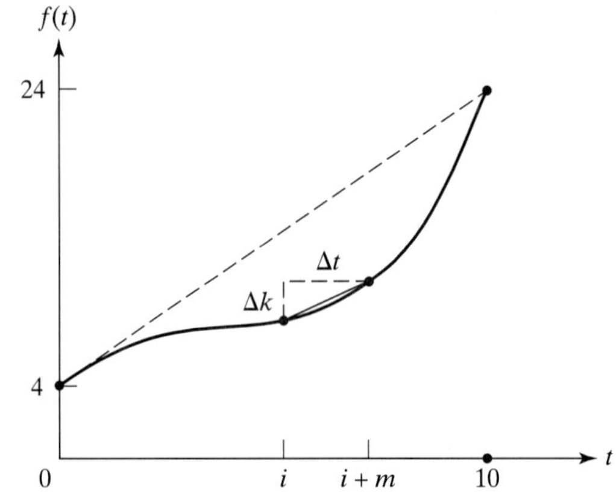

FIGURE 15.2 A Minimum Distance Problem

where $\Delta t = (i + m) - i = m$ and $\Delta k(i) = k(i + m) - k(i)$. This is equal to

$$s_i = \left(\sqrt{1 + \left(\frac{\Delta k(i)}{\Delta t}\right)^2}\right) \cdot \Delta t.$$

If the distance 0 to 10 is divided up into M sections, then the total distance of the function $f(t)$ can be approximated by

$$\sum_{i=0}^{M} s_i = \sum_{i=0}^{M} \left(\sqrt{1 + \left(\frac{\Delta k(i)}{\Delta t}\right)^2}\right) \cdot \Delta t.$$

In the limit, as $\Delta t \rightarrow 0$, this sum equals the integral

$$\int_{t=0}^{10} \sqrt{1 + \left(\frac{dk}{dt}\right)^2} \cdot dt.$$

Given the state equation $dk(t)/dt = c(t)$, the integrand is $\sqrt{1 + c(t)^2}$. The solution to the optimal control problem shows that the optimal value of c is the constant 2. Therefore the function that minimizes the distance is the straight line

$$k(t) = 2t + A,$$

where A is a constant. The terminal condition shows that $k(10) = 24$, and, therefore, $A = 24 - 20 = 4$. Thus the function that minimizes the distance between the points is

$$k(t) = 2t + 4.$$

As you may have suspected, and as the maximum principle confirms, the shortest distance between two points is a straight line.

The conditions that provide for a maximum in the continuous time case closely resemble those of the discrete-time case. While a complete proof of these conditions is beyond the scope of this book, the discussion in the appendix provides heuristic support for the maximum principle.

Sufficient Conditions

In the discussion of the static optimization problems in Chapters 10 and 11, we show that the concavity of the objective function is a sufficient condition for identifying an interior critical point as a maximum. In a dynamic optimization framework, O. L. Mangasarian shows that if the functions $\pi(c(t), k(t), t)$ and $f(c(t), k(t), t)$ are both concave in $c(t)$ and $k(t)$ and if the optimal solution has $\lambda(t) \geq 0$ for the case where $f(c(t), k(t), t)$ is nonlinear in $c(t)$ or $k(t)$, then the necessary conditions are also sufficient conditions. More generally, Kenneth Arrow and Mordecai Kurz show that if $H^*(k(t), \lambda(t), t)$ is the maximum of the Hamiltonian with respect to $c(t)$, given $k(t)$, $\lambda(t)$, and t, then, if $H^*(k(t), \lambda(t), t)$ is concave in $k(t)$, for given $\lambda(t)$ and t, the necessary conditions are also sufficient. This more general result, however, requires checking the concavity of the derived function $H^*(k(t), \lambda(t), t)$ rather than the functions that are basic to the problem, $\pi(c(t), k(t), t)$ and $f(c(t), k(t), t)$.[8]

Exercises 15.2

1. Consider the following problem involving the control variable $y(t)$ and the state variable $x(t)$. The objective is to maximize

$$\int_{t=0}^{40} -\frac{y(t)^2}{2}\, dt,$$

where the state variable is governed by the differential equation

$$\dot{x}(t) = y(t);$$

$x(0) = 20$ and $x(40) = 0$, and $t = 40$ is the terminal time.

(a) Set up the Hamiltonian.

(b) Find the conditions that satisfy the maximum principle.

(c) Solve for the explicit solution for the control variable, $y(t)$.

2. Consider the optimal control problem involving the control variable $y(t)$ and the state variable $x(t)$. The objective is to maximize

$$\int_{t=0}^{10} -\left(2x(t)y(t) + y(t)^2\right) dt$$

when the state variable is determined by

$$\dot{x}(t) = y(t);$$

the initial value of the state variable is $x(0) = 10$, while its terminal value is $x(10) = 100$.

(a) Set up the Hamiltonian.

(b) Find the conditions that satisfy the maximum principle.

(c) Solve for the explicit solution for the control variable.

---

[8] O. L. Mangasarian, "Sufficient conditions for the optimal control of nonlinear systems," *Journal of SIAM Control,* 4 (February 1966): 139–152 and Kenneth Arrow and Mordecai Kurz, *Public Investment, the Rate of Return, and Optimal Fiscal Policy* (Baltimore: Johns Hopkins University Press, 1970).

3. Consider the optimal control problem in which we want to find the maximum value of

$$\int_{t=0}^{1} \ln(y(t))\,dt$$

where $y(t)$ is the control variable and $x(t)$ is the state variable. The state variable has the initial value $x(0) = 0$ and the terminal value $x(1) = 30$; its value over time is determined by

$$\dot{x}(t) = -3y(t).$$

(a) Set up the Hamiltonian.

(b) Find the conditions that satisfy the maximum principle.

(c) Solve for the explicit solution for the control variable.

4. The managers of the firm Orange Computers want to maximum profits over the next five years before the firm goes public. This goal corresponds to maximizing

$$\int_{t=0}^{5} \left(K(t) - K(t)^2 - \frac{I(t)^2}{2} \right) dt,$$

where $K(t)$ is the capital stock of the firm and $I(t)$ is its investment. Because of the nature of the computer industry, capital depreciates very quickly as new technologies come on line, and therefore the capital accumulation equation is

$$\frac{dK(t)}{dt} = I(t) - \frac{K(t)}{2}.$$

The firm initially has no capital, and at the time the firm goes public, the managers want $K(5) = 10$.

(a) Set up the Hamiltonian for this problem.

(b) Show that the solution is saddlepath stable. What are the two characteristic roots of the system?

5. Show that the solution to the optimal control problem of maximizing

$$\int_{t=0}^{T} -\gamma \frac{y(t)^2}{2}\,dt$$

subject to

$$\dot{x}(t) = \alpha x(t) + \beta y(t)$$

is saddlepath stable. In this problem, $y(t)$ is the control variable, $x(t)$ is the state variable, the parameters α, β, and γ are all positive, and there is an initial condition and a terminal condition for the state variable.

15.3 EXTENSIONS AND APPLICATIONS OF OPTIMAL CONTROL THEORY

This section continues our discussion of optimal control theory by linking the maximum principle to the older technique of the calculus of variations, as well as by extending the framework discussed in several different ways. This section includes several economic applications that illustrate these extensions.

The Calculus of Variations

Optimal control theory is a generalization of an older technique called the calculus of variations. The calculus of variations shows how to solve the problem of maximizing the integral

$$\int_{t=a}^{b} f(\dot{x}(t), x(t), t)\, dt$$

subject to the conditions $x(a) = \underline{x}$ and $x(b) = \bar{x}$. We can easily express this in terms of an optimal control problem by defining

$$u(t) = \dot{x}(t)$$

and rewriting the integral as

$$\int_{t=a}^{b} f(u(t), x(t), t)\, dt.$$

Consider $u(t)$ as the control variable and $x(t)$ as the state variable. The Hamiltonian for this problem is

$$H(u(t), x(t), \lambda(t)) = f(u(t), x(t), t) + \lambda(t)u(t).$$

The first-order conditions from the maximum principle then show that the solution to this problem includes

$$\frac{\partial H(u(t), x(t), t)}{\partial u(t)} = \frac{\partial f(u(t), x(t), t)}{\partial u(t)} + \lambda(t) = 0$$

and

$$\frac{\partial H(u(t), x(t), t)}{\partial x(t)} = \frac{\partial f(u(t), x(t), t)}{\partial x(t)} = -\dot{\lambda}(t).$$

Taking the derivative with respect to time of the first condition, we have

$$\frac{d}{dt}\left(\frac{\partial f(u(t), x(t), t)}{\partial u(t)}\right) + \dot{\lambda}(t) = 0.$$

Recalling that $\dot{x}(t) = u(t)$, we can solve to remove $\dot{\lambda}(t)$ to obtain **Euler's equation** for the solution to this calculus of variation problem

$$\frac{\partial f(\dot{x}(t), x(t), t)}{\partial x(t)} = \frac{d}{dt}\left(\frac{\partial f(\dot{x}(t), x(t), t)}{\partial \dot{x}(t)}\right).$$

discount rate. The Bests' optimal consumption path is characterized by a steadily rising level of consumption if the real interest rate is greater than their subjective discount rate. The Bests' optimal consumption path is characterized by a steadily decreasing level of consumption if their subjective discount rate is greater than the real interest rate.

The Bests' consumption path must also satisfy an intertemporal budget constraint. Multiplying each side of the third optimality condition by e^{-rt} and then integrating with respect to time, we have, in present value terms, the budget constraint

$$\int_{t=0}^{50} (w(t) + ra(t) - c(t))e^{-rt}dt = \int_{t=0}^{50} \frac{da(t)}{dt}e^{-rt}dt.$$

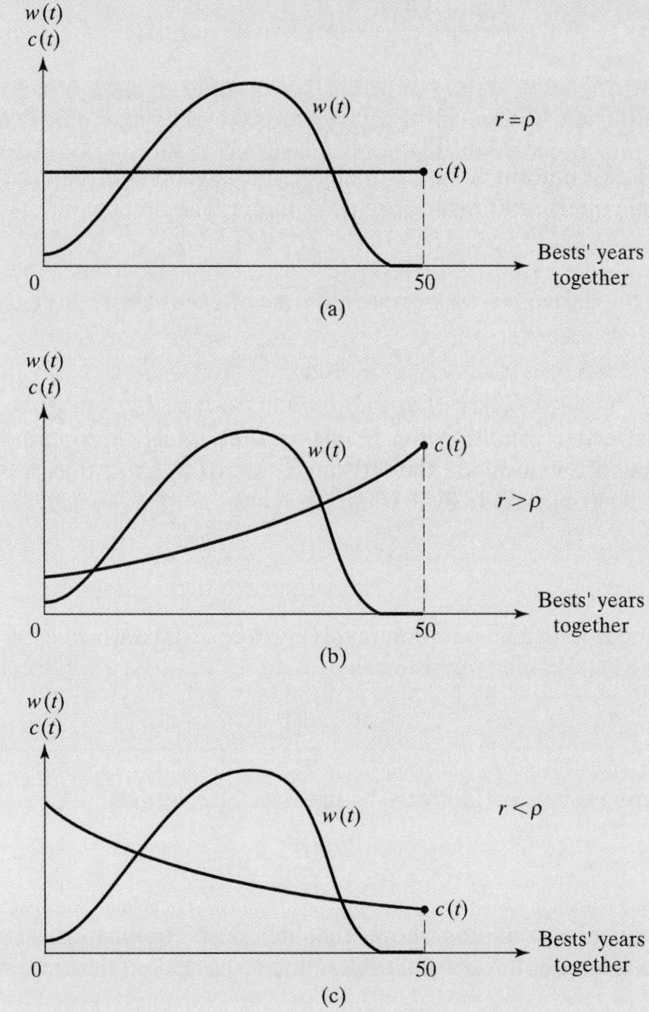

FIGURE 15.3 Optimal Lifetime Consumption Paths

We can further simplify the budget constraint for this problem by using the initial and terminal conditions. These conditions require that

$$\int_{t=0}^{50} \frac{da(t)}{dt} e^{-rt} dt = \int_{t=0}^{50} e^{-rt} da(t) = a(50)e^{-r \cdot 50} - a(0) = 0.$$

The terminal and initial conditions of this problem also require that

$$\int_{t=0}^{50} ra(t)e^{-rt} dt = 0.$$

Therefore the intertemporal budget constraint requires that

$$\int_{t=0}^{50} w(t)e^{-rt} dt = \int_{t=0}^{50} c(t)e^{-rt} dt,$$

that is, that the present value of the lifetime stream of wage income equals the present value of the lifetime stream of consumption.

A typical lifetime pattern of savings and consumption consistent with the life-cycle theory includes borrowing in the early part of one's life, paying back that debt and acquiring assets in mid-life, and living off accumulated savings at the end of one's life. We illustrate this type of pattern by showing the optimal consumption paths for the Bests under three different scenarios concerning the relative size of r and ρ in Figure 15.3(a), (b), and (c). In each of these cases, the path of wages is the same. Each case satisfies the intertemporal budget constraint. Therefore the discounted value of the area under the consumption path equals the discounted value of the area under the wage path. In Figure 15.3(a), where $r = \rho$ consumption is constant, and the Bests borrow money at the beginning of their married lives, pay this back and accumulate assets during the middle of their lives, and live off their savings in their final years. We compare this constant-consumption baseline case to the cases where the real interest rate does not equal the subjective discount rate. In Figure 15.3(b) where $r > \rho$ the Bests' consumption grows steadily over time. As compared to the constant-consumption case, the Bests' borrow less in their early lives and consume more at the end of their lives. Figure 15.3(c) illustrates the case where $r < \rho$, and consumption decreases over time. In this case, as compared to the constant-consumption case, the Bests borrow more at the beginning of their lives together and consume less at the end of their lives.

Infinite Horizon

The planning horizon in the problems previously discussed is finite with a fixed terminal date. In many contexts it is reasonable to consider the relevant planning horizon as the entire future. In this case the objective function, corresponding to (15.15), is

$$\int_{t=0}^{\infty} \pi(c(t), k(t), t)\, dt.$$

The terminal condition in an infinite horizon problem where the state variable must asymptotically approach some value $\bar{k}$ is simply

$$\lim_{t\to\infty}(k(t)) = \bar{k}.$$

The terminal condition in an infinite horizon problem where the state variable can be chosen optimally at all moments is

$$\lim_{t\to\infty}(\lambda(t)k(t)) = 0. \tag{15.24}$$

This transversality condition requires that if $k(t)$ remains nonzero and finite asymptotically, then $\lambda(t)$ must asymptotically approach zero. If $k(t)$ grows forever at some positive rate, then $\lambda(t)$ must approach zero at a faster rate such that the transversality condition is satisfied.

This transversality condition is not necessary when the subjective discount rate equals zero, that is, when, in an integral like (15.23), $\rho = 0$. In this case the necessary transversality condition is

$$\lim_{t\to\infty}(H^*(t)) = 0,$$

where $H^*(t)$ represents the value of the Hamiltonian along the optimal path at time t.[11]

Many problems in economics are cast in terms of an infinite horizon, reflecting the assumption that the appropriate terminal date is in the very distant future. For example, the life spans of corporations exceed the life spans of their current directors. It is also appropriate to cast intertemporal consumption problems in the framework of an infinite horizon if we assume that the current generation values the utility of future generations.

To illustrate this, we modify our optimal consumption example above by assuming Mr. and Mrs. Best have children (who themselves have children, and so on). The Bests value the utility of future generations, and, therefore, the appropriate discounted utility is represented by the improper integral

$$\int_{t=0}^{\infty} 2\sqrt{c(t)}e^{-\rho t}dt.$$

The only other distinction between this problem and the one previously presented is the replacement of the terminal condition $a(50) = 0$ with the transversality condition

$$\lim_{t\to\infty}(\lambda(t)a(t)) = \lim_{t\to\infty}(q(t)e^{\rho t}a(t)) = 0.$$

The solution to this problem includes the same equation for the growth of consumption as that in the finite-horizon case. In this case, however, the intertemporal budget constraint is

$$\int_{t=0}^{\infty}(w(t) + ra(t) - c(t))e^{-rt}dt = \int_{t=0}^{\infty} e^{-rt}da(t).$$

[11] See Phillipe Michel, "On the transversality condition in infinite horizon optimal problems," *Econometrica* 50, no. 4 (July 1982): 975–985.

With the initial condition $a(0) = 0$, this intertemporal budget constraint implies

$$\int_{t=0}^{\infty} w(t)e^{-rt}\,dt = \int_{t=0}^{\infty} c(t)e^{-rt}\,dt.$$

Unlike the previous case where $a(50) = 0$, this case allows for the possibility that the Bests leave a bequest to their children. This would be optimal if the current generation has relatively much higher income than subsequent generations. Alternatively, if later generations have relatively high incomes, then the optimal outcome is one where the current generation leaves a debt that future generations repay.

The following application provides another example of optimal consumption with an infinite time horizon.

Optimal Growth

The framework of the Solow growth model has been used in this book to analyze the optimal long-run savings rate (in the application about the Golden Rule in Chapter 9) as well as the time path of the economy (in the discussions in Chapters 13 and 14). In this application we turn to this model once again to analyze the optimal consumption path for an economy.

As discussed in Chapters 9, 13, and 14, the Solow growth model is based on some simple macroeconomic identities and some assumptions about the aggregate production function for the economy. The basic macroeconomic identity is $Y(t) = C(t) + I(t)$, where $Y(t)$ represents income, $C(t)$ represents consumption, and $I(t)$ represents investment. Another central relationship is that the change in the capital stock equals investment minus depreciation. Modeling depreciation as a constant proportion δ of the capital stock gives us the equation

$$\dot{K}(t) = I(t) - \delta K(t).$$

We frame this model in per capita terms and define income per capita, the capital stock per capita, and consumption per capita as $y(t)$, $k(t)$, and $c(t)$, respectively. Differentiation shows that the instantaneous change in the capital stock per capita at any moment t is

$$\dot{k}(t) = \frac{\dot{K}(t)}{N(t)} - \frac{\dot{N}(t)}{N(t)} \cdot \frac{K(t)}{N(t)}.$$

We assume that population growth $\dot{N}(t)/N(t)$ is constant and equal to n. Combining these relationships, we get the equation

$$\dot{k}(t) = y(t) - c(t) - (n + \delta)k(t).$$

We also assume that production (which equals income) is determined by a Cobb-Douglas production function that can be written in intensive form as $y(t) = k(t)^{\alpha}$ (see the discussion of the Golden Rule in Chapter 9). Thus the state equation in this problem is

$$\dot{k}(t) = k(t)^{\alpha} - c(t) - (n + \delta)k(t).$$

The extension of the Solow model required for analyzing the question of optimal growth requires the inclusion of an objective function. An objective function studied in the literature on optimal growth is

$$U = \int_{t=0}^{T} u(c(t)) \cdot e^{-\rho t} dt,$$

where $u(c(t))$ is the instantaneous utility function associated with the "representative" consumer and ρ is a discount factor with $\rho > 0$. The standard assumptions require that $u'(c(t)) > 0$ (nonsatiation, or utility always increases with an increase in consumption); $u''(c(t)) < 0$ (diminishing marginal utility); and $\lim_{c(t)\to 0} u'(c(t)) = -\infty$ (it is necessary to avoid extremely low levels of consumption). We also require that consumption is strictly positive. In this example we consider the instantaneous utility function

$$u(c(t)) = \ln(c(t)),$$

which has the required characteristics.

The current-value Hamiltonian function for this problem is

$$\hat{H}(c(t), k(t), \lambda(t)) = \ln(c(t)) + q(t) \cdot (k(t)^{\alpha} - c(t) - (n + \delta)k(t)).$$

The maximum principle shows that the first-order conditions are

$$\hat{H}_c = \frac{1}{c(t)} - q(t) = 0,$$
$$\hat{H}_k = q(t)(\alpha k(t)^{\alpha-1} - (n + \delta)) = \rho q(t) - \dot{q}(t), \quad \text{and}$$
$$\hat{H}_q = k(t)^{\alpha} - c(t) - (n + \delta)k(t) = \dot{k}(t),$$

and this problem also requires that the initial condition $k(0) = \underline{k}$ and the transversality condition

$$\lim_{t\to\infty} (q(t)e^{-\rho t}k(t)) = 0$$

are satisfied.

The first condition can be rewritten as $c(t)q(t) = 1$. Taking the derivative of each side of this expression with respect to time, we obtain

$$\dot{c}(t) \cdot q(t) + c(t) \cdot \dot{q}(t) = 0.$$

Dividing this expression by $c(t) \cdot q(t)$ and rearranging, we have

$$\frac{\dot{c}(t)}{c(t)} = -\frac{\dot{q}(t)}{q(t)},$$

which is similar to the first-order condition in the life-cycle consumption problem presented earlier.

As in the life-cycle model, we next solve for consumption growth as a function of variables other than the costate variable. To do so, we use the condition $\hat{H}_k = \rho q(t) - \dot{q}(t)$. After some manipulation of this condition, we have

$$\alpha k(t)^{\alpha-1} - (n + \delta) - \rho = -\frac{\dot{q}(t)}{q(t)},$$

which shows that consumption along the optimal path satisfies the condition

$$\frac{\dot{c}(t)}{c(t)} = \alpha k(t)^{\alpha-1} - (n + \delta) - \rho.$$

This condition, known as the **Keynes-Ramsey Rule,** was derived by Frank Ramsey in a 1928 article that includes an explanation attributed to John Maynard Keynes.[12] This rule implies that consumption increases over time if the marginal product of capital net of population growth and depreciation,

$$\alpha k(t)^{\alpha-1} - n - \delta,$$

is greater than the rate of time preference, ρ. Intuitively, this condition shows that when the marginal product of capital is relatively high, there is a larger benefit from depressing current consumption, which leads to a larger subsequent rate of growth of consumption.

Phase Diagram Depiction

Analysis of solutions to many types of continuous time dynamic optimization problems is aided by the development of an appropriate phase diagram. Here we show how to use a phase diagram to illustrate the solution to the optimal growth problem previously discussed.

The solution to the optimal growth problem can be expressed as two nonlinear differential equations in the two variables: consumption per worker, $c(t)$, and capital per worker, $k(t)$.[13] The two relevant equations are

$$\dot{k}(t) = k(t)^{\alpha} - c(t) - (n + \delta)k(t)$$

and

$$\dot{c}(t) = (\alpha k(t)^{\alpha-1} - (n + \delta) - \rho)c(t).$$

One way to analyze the solution to this problem, or to many other types of dynamic optimization problems, is to use a two-variable phase diagram like the type discussed in Chapter 14.

The two-variable phase diagram for this problem is depicted in Figure 15.4. The vertical axis of this figure is the amount of consumption, and the horizontal axis is the amount of capital. The figure includes a vertical line that shows the set of points where $\dot{c}(t) = 0$. The horizontal intercept of this line is the amount of capital k_G where

$$\frac{\alpha}{k_G^{1-\alpha}} - (n + \delta) - \rho = 0.$$

[12] Frank P. Ramsey, "A mathematical theory of savings," *Economic Journal* 38, no. 152 (December 1928): 543–559. For a discussion of representative agent macroeconomic models that are solved with optimal control theory, see Olivier Blanchard and Stanley Fischer, *Lectures on Macroeconomics* (Cambridge, Mass.: M.I.T. Press, 1989), Chapter 2. Blanchard and Fischer discuss the Keynes-Ramsey Rule on pages 41–43.

[13] Alternatively, the solution can be expressed as two nonlinear differential equations in $k(t)$ and $\lambda(t)$.

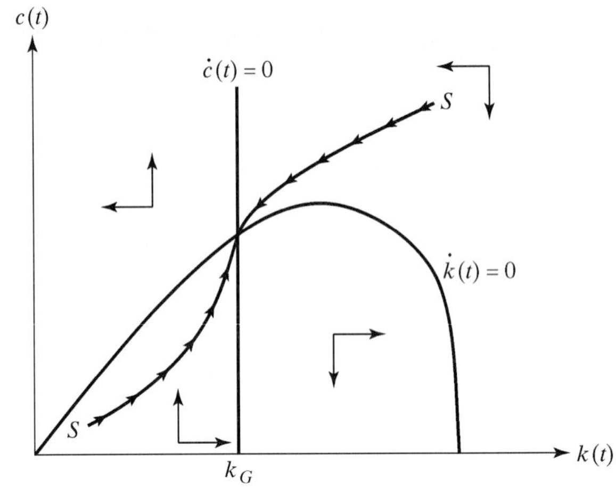

FIGURE 15.4 Phase Diagram of Optimal Consumption

For any amount of capital less k_0 than k_G, consumption rises since

$$\dot{c}(t) = (\alpha k_0^{\alpha - 1} - (n + \delta) - \rho)c(t) > 0,$$

and, for any amount of capital greater than k_G, consumption falls. This result gives us the vertical arrows that depict the forces of motion of the system when $k(t)$ does not equal k_G. These arrows point up to the left of the line $\dot{c}(t) = 0$ and point down to the right of the line $\dot{c}(t) = 0$.

The phase diagram in Figure 15.4 also includes a curve that depicts the points where $\dot{k}(t) = 0$. This curve begins at the point $(0, 0)$ and has a positive slope up to the point where $\alpha k(t)^{\alpha-1} - (n + \delta)$ equals zero and, thereafter, has a negative slope until it crosses the horizontal axis at the point where

$$k(t)^\alpha = (n + \delta)k(t).$$

Below this schedule, the level of consumption is less than the level that would cause $\dot{k}(t) = 0$ for the associated level of capital, and, since consumption enters the state equation negatively, the arrows of motion in this region point to the right. Above this schedule, the arrows of motion point to the left since the consumption-capital pairs in this region are associated with a decreasing capital stock per worker.

The intersection of the $\dot{c}(t) = 0$ and the $\dot{k}(t) = 0$ schedules represents the steady state value of consumption per worker and capital per worker. The system of nonlinear differential equations is saddlepath stable. The saddlepath, labeled as *SS* in Figure 15.4, passes through the point that represents the steady state value of consumption per worker and capital per worker. Given any initial positive capital stock, the saddlepath shows the unique path that consumption per worker and capital per worker must follow to be consistent with all the maximum principle conditions, including the transversality condition. The positive slope of the saddlepath indicates that if consumption per worker is growing, then investment per worker is positive (that is, $\dot{k}(t)$ is positive) and conversely.[14]

The Value of the Hamiltonian Over Time

The conditions of the maximum principle enable us to find a simple expression for the value of the Hamiltonian over time when it is evaluated along the optimal path. The total derivative of the Hamiltonian with respect to time, evaluated along its optimal path, equals

$$\frac{dH(c^*(t), k^*(t), \lambda(t), t)}{dt} = H_c^* \cdot \dot{c}(t) + H_k^* \cdot \dot{k}(t) + H_\lambda^* \cdot \dot{\lambda}(t) + \frac{\partial H^*}{\partial t},$$

where H_i^* represents the partial derivative of the Hamiltonian with respect to its ith argument, evaluated at its optimal value. The maximum principle requires that $H_c^* = 0$, $H_k^* = -\dot{\lambda}(t)$, and $H_\lambda^* = \dot{k}(t)$. Therefore

$$\frac{dH(c^*(t), k^*(t), \lambda(t), t)}{dt} = 0 \cdot \dot{c}(t) - \dot{\lambda}(t) \cdot \dot{k}(t) + \dot{k}(t) \cdot \dot{\lambda}(t) + \frac{\partial H^*}{\partial t}$$

$$= \frac{\partial H^*}{\partial t}.$$

In the **nonautonomous case,** where time is a separate argument in the Hamiltonian, as with $H(c(t), k(t), \lambda(t), t)$, the total derivative of the Hamiltonian with respect to time equals its partial derivative with respect to time since the other terms arising from the chain rule cancel out. In the **autonomous case,** where the Hamiltonian does not include time as an explicit and separate argument, although it may include the discounting term $e^{-\rho t}$ as with $H(c(t), k(t), \lambda(t))$, the Hamiltonian is constant along the optimal time path.

This property of the Hamiltonian along the optimal path is used in problems of finding the optimal time to undertake an action, as shown in the following discussion.

Optimal Time

A variant of the maximum principle previously presented can be used for problems in which one component of the solution involves the determination of the terminal time. In problems in which the terminal value of the control $x(T)$ is given, but the terminal time, T, must be determined, the Hamiltonian evaluated along the optimal path must satisfy the condition

$$H(x^*(T), g^*(T), \lambda(T), T) = 0.$$

[14] Saddlepath stability can be shown by a linearization of the solution around the steady state. Linearization through the use of a Taylor series is discussed in Chapter 7. Saddlepath stability is discussed in Chapter 14. For more on the dynamics of this problem and a more detailed analysis of the phase diagram, see Chapter 2 of Blanchard and Fischer, *Lectures on Macroeconomics* or Chapter 2 of Robert Barro and Xavier Sala-i-Martin, *Economic Growth.*

This general result holds in both the nonautonomous and the autonomous cases. In the latter case, we previously show that the Hamiltonian is constant over time. Therefore, in the autonomous case, along the optimal path, the Hamiltonian must satisfy the condition

$$H(x^*(t), g^*(t), \lambda(t)) = 0 \quad \text{for} \quad 0 \leq t \leq T,$$

where the initial time is $t = 0$. This result is used in the following application.

Optimal Depletion of an Exhaustible Resource

Suppose that in your capacity as the manager of a gold mine you must determine the optimal rate at which gold should be extracted from the mine.[15] The instantaneous rate of extractions is $x(t)$, which is nonnegative. With the stock of gold in the mine equal to $g(t)$ at time t

$$x(t) = -\dot{g}(t).$$

The rate of extraction is the control variable in this problem, and the stock of gold is the state variable. The extraction equation is the state equation. We assume that the appropriate planning horizon is the entire future and future payments are discounted at the rate ρ. We also assume that the price of gold follows an exogenous time path with the price equal to $p(t)$ at time t. Finally, we assume that any amount up to a maximum $x_{\max}$ can be extracted from the mine costlessly at any moment. In this case the problem you face is to maximize the present value of the stream of payments

$$\int_{t=0}^{\infty} p(t)x(t)e^{-\rho t}\,dt$$

subject to the state equation

$$\dot{g}(t) = -x(t).$$

The initial stock of gold at time zero, $g(0)$, is

$$g(0) = \underline{G},$$

and we assume that $\underline{G} > x_{\max}$. At some time T, when the mine yields its last ounce of gold,

$$g(T) = 0.$$

This problem involves solving for the optimal T given the exogenous path of prices $p(t)$.

The Hamiltonian for this problem,

$$H(x(t), g(t), \lambda(t)) = p(t)x(t)e^{-\rho t} - \lambda(t)x(t),$$

is autonomous. One of the first-order conditions is

$$\frac{\partial H(x(t), g(t), \lambda(t))}{\partial \lambda(t)} \equiv H_{\lambda} = -x(t) = \dot{g}(t),$$

[15]This example is drawn from Colin Clark, *Mathematical Bioeconomics: The Optimal Management of Renewable Resources* (New York: John Wiley, 1976).

which gives us the state equation. Another first-order condition is

$$\frac{\partial H(x(t), g(t), \lambda(t))}{\partial g(t)} \equiv H_g = \dot{\lambda}(t),$$

but, noting that $H_g = 0$, we find that $\dot{\lambda}(t) = 0$ and, therefore, the costate variable λ is constant across time.

The maximum value of the Hamiltonian cannot be found by setting its partial derivative with respect to $x(t)$ equal to zero since the Hamiltonian, which can be written as

$$H(x(t), g(t), \lambda) = [p(t)e^{-\rho t} - \lambda]x(t),$$

is linear in $x(t)$. Instead, we find that the Hamiltonian is maximized if we choose an extraction policy such that

$$\begin{aligned} x(t) &= 0 \quad \text{if} \quad p(t)e^{-\rho t} < \lambda \\ x(t) &= x_{\max} \quad \text{if} \quad p(t)e^{-\rho t} \geq \lambda \end{aligned}$$

since $x(t)$ must be nonnegative.

The condition that the Hamiltonian equals zero for $0 \leq t \leq T$ enables us to solve for λ. At the moment when the mine becomes fully depleted of gold, that is, at time T, when $x(T) = x_{\max}$,

$$H(x(T), g(T), \lambda) = [p(T)e^{-\rho T} - \lambda]x_{\max} = 0,$$

which implies

$$\lambda = p(T)e^{-\rho T}.$$

We use this result in developing the conditions for the maximization of the Hamiltonian.

$$\begin{aligned} x(t) &= 0 \quad \text{if} \quad p(t) < p(T)e^{\rho(t-T)} \\ x(t) &= x_{\max} \quad \text{if} \quad p(t) \geq p(T)e^{\rho(t-T)}. \end{aligned}$$

This is called a **bang-bang solution** since it involves the control being either fully "on" when $x(t) = x_{\max}$ or the control being fully "off" when $x(t) = 0$. The optimal solution may involve several intervals when mining takes place at full capacity, followed by intervals when the mine is left dormant.

Given the terminal date T, we can determine the date at which mining begins, T_S, by using the conditions $g(0) = \underline{G}$ and $g(T) = 0$, along with the state equation

$$\dot{g}(t) = -x(t).$$

In the case where mining continues unabated from T_S to T, these conditions imply

$$\begin{aligned} \underline{G} &= -(g(T) - g(0)) \\ &= -\int_{t=0}^{T} dg \\ &= -\int_{t=0}^{T} \frac{dg}{dt}\, dt \end{aligned}$$

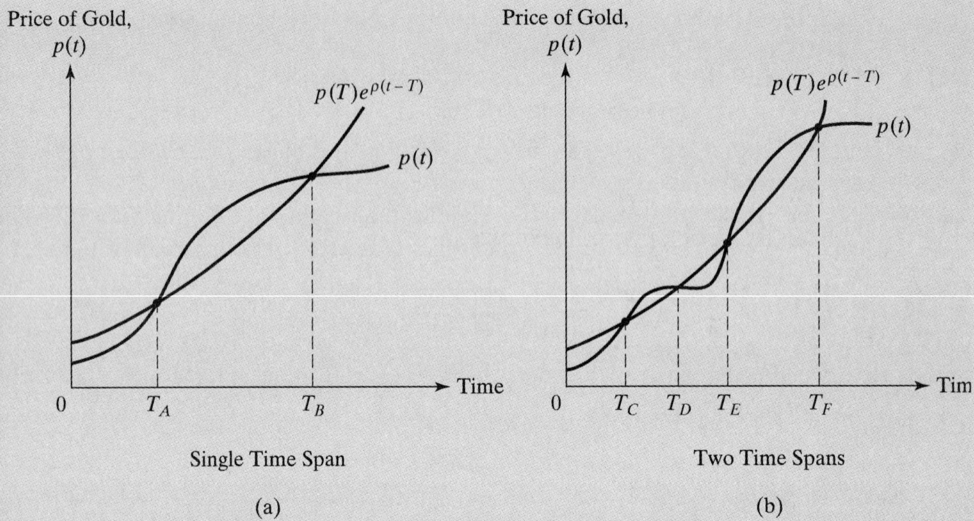

FIGURE 15.5 Phase Diagrams of Optimal Mining Times

$$
\begin{aligned}
&= \int_{t=0}^{T} x(t)\,dt \\
&= \int_{t=0}^{T_S} 0 \cdot dt + \int_{t=T_S}^{T} x_{\max}\,dt \\
&= (T - T_s)x_{\max}.
\end{aligned}
$$

For example, if $\underline{G} = 20$ tons, then, with $x_{\max} = 4$ tons/year, the period T_S to T is five years.

It may be the case that the optimal solution is one where the mine is alternatively opened and closed as the path of prices rises above and then falls below $p(T)e^{\rho(t-T)}$. In a case like this, where the mine is open from time T_C to time T_D, closed for a time, and then reopened from time T_E to time T_F, the analogue to the condition given previously is

$$
\underline{G} = \int_{t=T_C}^{T_D} x_{\max}\,dt + \int_{t=T_E}^{T_F} x_{\max}\,dt.
$$

Figure 15.5(a) and (b) illustrates two different solutions to this problem corresponding to two different paths of the price of gold. The price path in each of these graphs is depicted by the line labeled $p(t)$ These graphs also include the line representing $p(T)e^{\rho(t-T)}$. An optimal solution is one in which T is chosen such that $p(T)e^{\rho(t-T)}$ intersects the price path for an interval sufficiently long to just exhaust the total supply of gold. In Figure 15.5(a) this interval consists of the single time span $[T_A, T_B]$. In Figure 15.5(b) this interval consists of the two time spans $[T_C, T_D]$ and $[T_E, T_F]$ Each of these diagrams is drawn for the case where $\underline{G} = 20$ and $x_{\max} = 4$ tons/year, and, therefore, $T_B - T_A = (T_D - T_C) + (T_F - T_E) = 5$.

Exercises 15.3

1. In his 1928 paper "A Mathematical Theory of Savings," Frank Ramsey set up a problem in which the utility of future consumption was not discounted since he believed doing so would be "ethically indefensible." Instead, he solved the problem of choosing a capital stock, $k(t)$, to minimize the difference between the utility of consumption, $u(c(t))$, and a "bliss" level of utility, B. A simple version of his optimization problem is to maximize

$$-\int_{t=0}^{\infty} [B - u(c)]\, dt,$$

where

$$u'(c) > 0, \quad u''(c) < 0, \quad \text{and} \quad u(0) = -\infty$$

subject to the constraint

$$c(t) = f(k(t)) - \frac{dk(t)}{dt},$$

where $dk(t)/dt$ represents investment and $f(k(t))$ is a production function with $f' > 0$ and $f'' < 0$.

(a) Use the calculus of variations to show that the first-order condition for this problem is

$$-f'(k(t)) = \frac{d[u'(c(t))/dt]}{u'(c(t))}.$$

(b) Consider the special case of $f(k(t)) = k(t)^{\alpha}$ with $1 > \alpha > 0$ and $u(c(t)) = \ln(c(t))$. Find the first-order condition in this case. Compare it to the Keynes-Ramsey Rule presented in the text.

2. Suppose that Mr. and Mrs. Best receive a wedding gift of \$20,000.

(a) How does this alter their lifetime consumption profile in the case where they leave no bequests?

(b) Suppose Mr. and Mrs. Best, having received a wedding gift of \$20,000, want to leave a bequest of \$20,000. Is their lifetime consumption any different from the case where they received no wedding gift and leave no bequest?

3. You have an inventory of G gold coins. You want to sell these coins at a time that maximizes the integral

$$\int_{t=0}^{\infty} p(t) G e^{-\rho t}\, dt,$$

where $p(t)$ is the exogenous time path of the price of one gold coin. What is the optimal time to sell these coins? (*Hint*: Consider the gold mine application where $x_{\max} > \underline{G}$, and use a graph like the one presented in the text for the gold-mining example.)

Summary

This chapter presents the elements of dynamic optimization and optimal control theory. The discrete time analysis in Section 15.1 is a straightforward extension of the types of two-period problems in Chapter 11. The multiperiod problem presented in this section provides the intuition for the solution to the continuous time problem in Section 15.2. In that section we present the maximum principle, which provides necessary conditions for the identification of the optimal time path. In Section 15.3 we extend the discussion by considering some properties of the optimal solution, alternative frameworks for the problem, and the use of the phase diagram to depict the optimal solution.

Optimal control theory can be thought of as one intertemporal version of the constrained optimization problems discussed in Chapter 11. Constrained optimization problems are at the heart of economic analysis. Likewise, optimal control provides a very important set of tools for those areas in economics in which decisions that are made at different moments in time are central to our understanding of the relevant economic issues.

Appendix to Chapter 15: Heuristic Derivation of Maximum Principle

We can replicate the results from the maximum principle by using the Lagrangian multiplier approach in the special case when there is a continuous first-order partial derivative of the Hamiltonian with respect to the control variable. In this case the Hamiltonian has a continuous first-order partial derivative with respect to $c(t)$, and its maximum value is not at the boundary of the control variable. Under these conditions, consider the problem of maximizing (15.15) subject to the state equation (15.16), with a given initial value $k(0) = \underline{k}$. The Lagrangian-type function corresponding to this is

$$L = \int_{t=0}^{T} \pi(c(t), k(t), t)\, dt - \int_{t=0}^{T} \lambda(t)[\dot{k}(t) - f(c(t), k(t), t)]\, dt - \mu(k(0) - \underline{k}), \quad (15.A1)$$

where $L \equiv L(c(t), k(t), \lambda(t), t, \mu)$; $\lambda(t)$ is the costate variable, which serves as a dynamic Lagrange multiplier; and μ is the Lagrange multiplier associated with the initial condition. We want to write (15.A1) to explicitly include the Hamiltonian function defined above. To do this, we first rewrite the second integral in (15.A1) as

$$-\int_{t=0}^{T} \lambda(t)[\dot{k}(t) - f(c(t), k(t), t)]\, dt = \int_{t=0}^{T} \lambda(t) \cdot f(c(t), k(t), t)\, dt - \int_{t=0}^{T} \lambda(t) \cdot \dot{k}(t)\, dt.$$

Noting that

$$\frac{d[\lambda(t)k(t)]}{dt} = \dot{\lambda}(t)k(t) + \lambda(t)\dot{k}(t),$$

we can write

$$\lambda(t)\dot{k}(t) = \frac{d[\lambda(t)k(t)]}{dt} - \dot{\lambda}(t)k(t).$$

Integrating both sides of this expression from $t = 0$ to $t = T$, we have

$$\int_{t=0}^{T} \lambda(t)\dot{k}(t)\,dt = \int_{t=0}^{T} \frac{d[\lambda(t)k(t)]}{dt}\,dt - \int_{t=0}^{T} \dot{\lambda}(t)k(t)\,dt.$$

Since

$$\int_{t=0}^{T} \frac{d[\lambda(t)k(t)]}{dt}\,dt = \lambda(T)k(T) - \lambda(0)k(0),$$

we can rewrite the previous expression as

$$\int_{t=0}^{T} \lambda(t)\dot{k}(t)\,dt = \lambda(T)k(T) - \lambda(0)k(0) - \int_{t=0}^{T} \dot{\lambda}(t)k(t)\,dt.$$

We can now write the Lagrangian (15.A1) as

$$L = \int_{t=0}^{T} [\pi(c(t), k(t), t) + \lambda(t)f(c(t), k(t), t)]\,dt + \int_{t=0}^{T} \dot{\lambda}(t)k(t)\,dt$$
$$- \lambda(T)k(T) + \lambda(0)k(0) - \mu(k(0) - \underline{k}\ ).$$

Defining the Hamiltonian

$$H(c(t), k(t), \lambda(t), t) = \pi(c(t), k(t), t) + \lambda(t)f(c(t), k(t), t)$$

enables us to rewrite this Lagrangian as

$$L = \int_{t=0}^{T} [H(c(t), k(t), \lambda(t), t) + \dot{\lambda}(t)k(t)]\,dt$$
$$- \lambda(T)k(T) + \lambda(0)k(0) - \mu(k(0) - \underline{k}). \tag{15.A2}$$

Denote the optimal time paths of the control and state variables as $c^*(t)$ and $k^*(t)$, respectively. Suppose that we deviate from the optimal path for the control by the arbitrary function

$$c(t, \epsilon) = c^*(t) + \epsilon \cdot p_1(t).$$

The state equation requires that there is some function that shows the corresponding deviation from the optimal path for the state variable

$$k(t, \epsilon) = k^*(t) + \epsilon \cdot p_2(t).$$

There is also a corresponding deviation from the optimal terminal value

$$k(T, \epsilon) = k^*(T) + \epsilon \cdot dk(T).$$

With the introduction of ϵ, we write the Lagrangian function (15.A2) as

$$L = \int_{t=0}^{T} [H\,(c(t, \epsilon), k(t, \epsilon), \lambda(t), t) + \dot{\lambda}(t)k(t, \epsilon)]\,dt$$
$$-\lambda(T)k(T, \epsilon) + \lambda(0)k(0) - \mu(k(0) - \underline{k}), \tag{15.A3}$$

where now we define $L \equiv L(c(t, \epsilon), k(t, \epsilon), \lambda(t), t, \mu)$. If, in fact, $c^*(t)$ is optimal, then a very small deviation from this path does not affect the value of the Lagrangian function (15.A3); that is,

$$\frac{\partial L(c(t, \epsilon), k(t, \epsilon), \lambda(t), t, \mu)}{\partial \epsilon} = 0.$$

This result allows us to determine the necessary conditions of the maximum principle. The partial derivative of (15.A3) with respect to ϵ, when evaluated at the optimal value of the control and state variables, is comprised of several component parts. The partial derivative will equal zero if each of these component parts equals zero, a result that yields several conditions. One of these conditions is

$$\frac{\partial}{\partial \epsilon}[\lambda(T)k^*(T, \epsilon)] = 0. \tag{15.A4}$$

Using the perturbation equation for the state variable, we see that the condition (15.A4) requires that

$$\frac{\partial}{\partial \epsilon}[\lambda(T)k^*(T, \epsilon)] = \frac{\partial}{\partial \epsilon}[\lambda(T) \cdot (k^*(T) + \epsilon \cdot dk(T))] = \lambda(T)\,dk(T) = 0,$$

which is satisfied by the transversality condition $\lambda(T) = 0$. Another required condition is

$$\frac{\partial}{\partial \epsilon}\left[\int_{t=0}^{T} [H^* + \dot{\lambda}(t)k^*(t, \epsilon)]\,dt\right] = 0, \tag{15.A5}$$

where, to avoid clutter, we define $H^* \equiv H(c^*(t, \epsilon), k^*(t, \epsilon), \lambda(t), t)$. This condition is satisfied when

$$\int_{t=0}^{T}\left[\frac{\partial H^*}{\partial \epsilon} + \frac{\partial \dot{\lambda}(t)k^*(t, \epsilon)}{\partial \epsilon}\right]dt = 0.$$

Using the chain rule and the equations showing the deviation from the optimal path, we find

$$\frac{\partial H^*}{\partial \epsilon} = \frac{\partial H^*}{\partial c} \cdot p_1(t) + \frac{\partial H^*}{\partial k} \cdot p_2(t)$$

and

$$\frac{\partial \dot{\lambda}(t)\,k^*(t, \epsilon)}{\partial \epsilon} = \frac{\partial \dot{\lambda}(t)\,k^*(t, \epsilon)}{\partial k} \cdot p_2(t) = \dot{\lambda}(t) \cdot p_2(t).$$

Thus, for any arbitrary functions $p_1(t)$ and $p_2(t)$, the expression

$$\left[\frac{\partial H^*}{\partial \epsilon} + \frac{\partial \dot{\lambda}(t)k^*(t, \epsilon)}{\partial \epsilon}\right] = \frac{\partial H^*}{\partial c} \cdot p_1(t) + \frac{\partial H^*}{\partial k} \cdot p_2(t) + \dot{\lambda}(t) \cdot p_2(t)$$

equals zero when

$$\frac{\partial H^*}{\partial c} = 0$$

and

$$\frac{\partial H^*}{\partial k} + \dot{\lambda}(t) = 0.$$

These two conditions correspond to condition (i) when there is a continuous first-order partial derivative of the Hamiltonian with respect to the control variable and to condition (ii) of the maximum principle. Condition (iii) of the maximum principle simply requires that the state equation is satisfied.

Solutions

Chapter 2

Section 2.1

1. (a) $(-5, 0)$
   (b) $[-5, 0)$
   (c) $(-\infty, 100)$
   (d) $T(-\infty, 100]$
   (e) $(0, \infty)$
   (f) $(-\infty, \infty)$
3. (a) yes
   (b) yes
   (c) no
   (d) no
5. (a) When $Q = 10$, $TC = 125$. When $Q = 25$, $TC = 200$. When there is no production ($Q = 0$), $TC = 75$.
   (b) linear graph
   (c) domain: [0.50]; range: [75, 325]
7. (a) $\lim_{x \to \infty} = 2$
   (b) $\lim_{x \to 7^+} = \infty$
   (c) $\lim_{x \to 7^+} = 7$
   (d) $\lim_{x \to 1} = 0$
9. The function presented in question 8(c),

$$y = -3 + \frac{1}{x + 7},$$

is not continuous over the domain $(-\infty, 0]$ since the function is undefined at the point $x = -7$.

Section 2.2

1. (a) strictly monotonic
   (b) nonmonotonic
   (c) strictly monotonic
   (d) monotonic
3. (a) $x = f^{-1}(y) = \dfrac{y-14}{7}$
   (b) This function does not have an inverse unless we restrict the domain to $y \geq 6$, in which case the inverse is $x = f^{-1}(y) = \sqrt{y-6}$
   (c) This function does not have an inverse unless we restrict the domain to $y \geq 0$ in which case the inverse is $x = f^{-1}(y) = y^2$
   (d) $x = f^{-1}(y) = y^{1/3}$
5. (a) no
   (b) yes
   (c) either two minima and one maximum or two maxima and one minimum
7. (a) average rate of return = 12
   (b) average rate of return = 16
   (c) average rate of return = − 12
   (d) average rate of return = 0
9. (a) $y' = 5$
   (b) The slope of the secant line is

$$\frac{f(x_A) - f(x_B)}{x_B - x_A} = -4.$$

   The value of the slope of the secant line represents the average rate of change of a function over the interval defined by the two endpoints of the secant line.
   (c) The function is strictly convex over the given interval since the secant line lies wholly above the function.
11. (a) $A \Leftarrow B$
   (b) $A \Leftarrow B$
   (c) $A \Rightarrow B$
   (d) $A \Leftrightarrow B$, and this set satisfies the necessary and sufficient condition.

Section 2.3

1. (a) x^{-1}
   (b) $(xy)^4$
   (c) x^{20}
   (d) x^3y^2 (no further simplification possible)
   (e) $\left(\dfrac{1}{xy}\right)^6$

3. (a) 8
   (b) $2^{12} = 4096$
   (c) $\frac{1}{2}$
   (d) $\frac{x+3}{x+2}$
   (e) $(x+1)^{25}$
5. (a) $x = \frac{6}{5}$
   (b) $x = 1, \ -6$
   (c) $x = -3$ (two equal roots)
   (d) $f(x) = (x+1)(x^2 - 3x + 2) = (x+1)(x-1)(x-2) = 0$ so $x = (-1, 1, 2)$
7. Some points:

x	0	$\frac{1}{4}$	$\frac{1}{2}$	$\frac{3}{4}$	1
$2x^2$	0	$\frac{1}{8}$	$\frac{1}{2}$	$\frac{9}{8}$	2
2^x	1	1.19	1.41	1.68	2

The two functions do not share a y-intercept but do have a common value when $x = 1$.

9. Some points:

x	0	1	2	3	4
$\left(\frac{1}{2}\right)2^x$	$\frac{1}{2}$	1	2	4	8
$\left(\frac{1}{2}\right)4^x$	$\frac{1}{2}$	2	8	32	128

The two curves share a y-intercept in both cases when $x = 0$, $y = \frac{1}{2}$. When $A = \frac{1}{4}$, the curves no longer share a common y value since the graph of the first function shifts down.

11. (a) i $= c$
    (b) ii $= d$
    (c) iii $= a$
    (d) iv $= e$
    (e) v $= b$

Chapter 3

Section 3.1

1. (a) $X_t = 100$
   (b) $X_{t+5} = 115.93$

(c) $X_{t+1} = 200$
(d) $X_{t+50} = 710.67$

3. (a) $X_t = 22.22$
(b) $X_t = 20.4$
(c) $X_t = 17.82$
(d) $X_t = 25$
(e) $X_t = 27.6$

5. (a) \$52,500
(b) \$56,784
(c) \$80,549

7. The levels of national income in 2010, Y_{2010}, under different assumptions about the rate of growth beginning in 1992 and given Y_{1992}, the level of income in 1992:

$$\text{growth rate of 2.5\%:} \quad Y_{2010} = (e^{18 \times 0.025})\, Y_{1992} = 1.57Y_{1992}$$
$$\text{growth rate of 3.0\%:} \quad Y_{2010} = (e^{18 \times 0.030})\, Y_{1992} = 1.72Y_{1992}$$
$$\text{growth rate of 3.5\%:} \quad Y_{2010} = (e^{18 \times 0.035})\, Y_{1992} = 1.88Y_{1992}$$

The ratios of national income in 2010 under different scenarios concerning the rate of growth:

$$\text{growth rate of 3.0\% compared to 2.5\%:} \quad \frac{1.72Y_{1992}}{1.57Y_{1992}} = 1.10$$
$$\text{growth rate of 3.5\% compared to 2.5\%:} \quad \frac{1.88Y_{1992}}{1.57Y_{1992}} = 1.20$$

9. $100(1.02)^5 = 110.41$; $100(1.03)^{-5} = 86.26$

Section 3.2

1. (a) $X_{t+1} = 21.65$
(b) $X_{t+1} = 20.1$
(c) $X_{t+1} = 22.1$

3. Choose Bank B, which will offer a 0.25% better return (\$3,916).

5. (a) $X_{t+3} = 98.25$
(b) $X_{t+0.5} = 75.94$
(c) $X_{t-2} = 60.19$
(d) $X_{t+0.25} = 76.13$
(e) $X_{t+0.75} = 73.33$

7. For Indonesia

$$207\,(e^{11 \times 0.0175}) = 250.9,$$

and for China

$$1{,}250\,(e^{11 \times 0.0104}) = 1{,}401.5.$$

The percentage difference between the continuous compounding calculation and the discrete compounding calculation is 0.16% for Indonesia and 0.06% for China.

9. $PV = 5{,}578$
11. (a) $L(0) = 1$
    (b) $\lim_{t \to \infty} L(t) = 2$
    (c) $L(2) - L(1) = 1.181 - 1.095 = 0.086$. $L(11) - L(10) = 1.667 - 1.632 = 0.035$. This represents diminishing marginal advances in productivity over time.

Section 3.3

1. (a) 100
   (b) 0
   (c) $-5 \log_{10} x$
   (d) $\log_2 (a + b)$
   (e) $a + bx + cz$
   (f) $3 \ln 4x = 3(\ln 4 + \ln x)$
   (g) $-5 + 2(\alpha \ln x - \beta \ln y)$
3. Assuming that $x > 1$ and since $e > 2$, $\ln 32 < \log_2 32$. Note that $\ln 32 = 3.47$ and $\log_2 32 = 5$.
5. $U = \sum_{i=1}^{n} q_i^{\beta_i}$
7. The ratio of health care in 1999 (H_{1999}) to GDP in 1999 (Y_{1999}) is $H_{1999}/Y_{1999} = 0.10$. With health care growing at a continuously compounded annual rate of 4.8% and GDP growing at a continuously compounded rate of 2%, we would have, after 30 years,

$$\frac{H_{2029}}{Y_{2029}} = \frac{H_{1999} e^{30 \times 0.048}}{Y_{1999} e^{30 \times 0.02}} = 0.10 e^{30 \times 0.028} = 0.23$$

   and health care would command almost a quarter of GDP. It is likely, however, that economic forces rein in the rise in health care costs before they reach this proportion of national income.
9. When n is bigger, the Rule-of-70 appears to hold better.
   (a) $n = 69.66$, Rule-of-70 = 70
   (b) $n = 14.21$, Rule-of-70 = 14
   (c) $n = 7.27$, Rule-of-70 = 7
   (d) $n = 3.10$, Rule-of-70 = 2.8
   (e) $n = 1$, Rule-of-70 = 0.7
11. $n = \dfrac{\ln 1.5}{0.05} = 8.1$ years

Chapter 4

Section 4.1

1. (a) $(w, x, y) = \left(\frac{1}{4}, 4, 4\right)$
   (b) $(w, x, y) = (-19, -232, -116)$
   (c) $(w, x, y) = (3, 6, 14)$
   (d) $(w, x, y) = \left[\left(\frac{6 - 4g - b - 2h}{5}\right), (8 - 5g - b - 4h), (8 - 5g - b - 4h)\right]$
3. (a) $(x, y, z) = [(8a - 9h - 2), (8a - 9h - 2), (2a - 2h - 2)]$
   (b) $(\Delta x, \Delta y, \Delta z) = (-9\Delta h, -9\Delta h, -2\Delta h)$
   (c) $(\Delta x, \Delta y, \Delta z) = (-27, -27, -6)$
5. (a) $Y = 12{,}000$, $C = 11{,}000$
   (b) $Y = 10{,}500$, $C = 10{,}000$
7. (a) $Y = 20{,}500$, $R = 0.05$
   (b) For $\Delta M = 400$, $\Delta Y = 2000$ and $\Delta R = -0.2$.
9. In solving the model, we found the common wage to be

$$W = \frac{\beta_B Y - L_B}{\gamma}$$

and therefore

$$\Delta W = \frac{\beta_B \, \Delta Y - \Delta L_B}{\gamma}.$$

Using the solution for ΔL_B, we obtain, after some manipulation,

$$\Delta W = \frac{\beta_A + \beta_B}{2\gamma} \Delta Y.$$

Section 4.2

1. (a) $\sum_{i=1}^{5} ax_i = ax_1 + ax_2 + ax_3 + ax_4 + ax_5$
   (b) $\sum_{i=1}^{n} = b_i x^i = b_1 x^1 + b_2 x^2 + \cdots + b_n x^n$
   (c) $\left(\sum_{i=2}^{3} x_{i+1}\right)\left(\sum_{i=2}^{3} y_{i-1}\right) = (x_3 + x_4)(y_1 + y_2) = x_3 y_1 + x_3 y_2 + x_4 y_1 + x_4 y_2$
   (d) $\sum_{i=1}^{3} i x_i (x_i + 2) = x_1(x_1 + 2) + 2x_2(x_2 + 2) + 3x_3(x_3 + 2)$
   (e) $\sum_{i=-1}^{-4} x^i = \frac{1}{x} + \frac{1}{x^2} + \frac{1}{x^3} + \frac{1}{x^4}$
3. (a) $a_{22} = -100$
   (b) $b_{13} = m$

(c) $c_{21} = -1$
(d) $d_{23} = \theta$

5. (a) not conformable
(b) conformable; solution dimension is 1×1.
(c) not conformable
(d) conformable; solution dimension is $1 \times l$.

7. (a) $S = \begin{bmatrix} 7a & 7b & 7c & 7d \\ 9a & 9b & 9c & 9d \\ 4a & 4b & 4c & 4d \end{bmatrix}$
(b) $S = \begin{bmatrix} 1 & 2 & 4 \\ 3 & 7 & 16 \end{bmatrix}$
(c) $S = \begin{bmatrix} 7 & 5 & 4 & 2 \end{bmatrix}$
(d) $S = \begin{bmatrix} a - g + 7h & 4g + 2h \\ x - w + 7p & 4w + 2p \\ b - c + 7d & 4c + 2d \end{bmatrix}$

9. The four equations which comprise the model:

$$AD = C + I$$
$$C = 2000 + \frac{3}{4}Y$$
$$I = 500 - 1000r$$
$$AD = Y$$

Section 4.3

1. (a) $\begin{bmatrix} 1 & 0 \\ 0 & 1 \end{bmatrix}$
(b) $\begin{bmatrix} 2 - a \\ 1 - b \end{bmatrix}$
(c) $\begin{bmatrix} -3 & 9 & 25 & 5 \end{bmatrix}$

3. (a) $M \cdot L \cdot K$
(b) $(M \cdot L)K = M(L \cdot K)$

5. (a) $X' = \begin{bmatrix} 4 & 1 \\ 6 & 2 \end{bmatrix}, \quad Y' = \begin{bmatrix} -3 & 7 \\ 5 & 2 \\ 0 & -4 \\ 1 & 3 \end{bmatrix}$
(b) $(XY)' = Y'X' = \begin{bmatrix} 30 & 11 \\ 32 & 9 \\ -24 & -8 \\ 22 & 6 \end{bmatrix}$

Section 4.4

1. (a) nonsingular
   (b) singular
   (c) nonsingular
   (d) nonsingular
3. The only system which can be solved is that in question 2(a).
5. (a) adj $A = \begin{bmatrix} 7 & -3 \\ -4 & 2 \end{bmatrix}$

   (b) adj $A = \begin{bmatrix} -4 & -1 \\ -9 & -3 \end{bmatrix}$

   (c) adj $A = \begin{bmatrix} 1 & -2 \\ 2 & 0 \end{bmatrix}$

   (d) adj $A = \begin{bmatrix} 4 & -6 \\ 3 & \frac{1}{2} \end{bmatrix}$

7. (a) $A^{-1} = \begin{bmatrix} \frac{10}{44} & \frac{4}{44} \\ \frac{-6}{44} & \frac{2}{44} \end{bmatrix}$

   (b) $A^{-1} = \begin{bmatrix} 0 & -1 \\ 1 & 1 \end{bmatrix}$

   (c) singular so no inverse

   (d) $A^{-1} = \begin{bmatrix} \frac{\beta}{-\beta^2} & \frac{\beta}{\beta^2} \\ \frac{1}{\beta^2} & \frac{1-\beta}{-\beta^2} \end{bmatrix}$

   (e) singular so no inverse

   (f) $A^{-1} = \begin{bmatrix} \frac{d-\lambda}{a(d-\lambda)-\lambda(d-\lambda)-cb} & \frac{-b}{a(d-\lambda)-\lambda(d-\lambda)-cb} \\ \frac{-c}{a(d-\lambda)-\lambda(d-\lambda)-cb} & \frac{a-\lambda}{a(d-\lambda)-\lambda(d-\lambda)-cb} \end{bmatrix}$

   (g) $A^{-1} = \begin{bmatrix} \frac{7}{2} & -\frac{3}{2} \\ -2 & 1 \end{bmatrix}$

   (h) $A^{-1} = \begin{bmatrix} \frac{4}{23} & \frac{3}{23} \\ \frac{9}{23} & -\frac{1}{23} \end{bmatrix}$

(i) $A^{-1} = \begin{bmatrix} \frac{1}{4} & -\frac{1}{2} \\ \frac{1}{2} & 0 \end{bmatrix}$

(j) $A^{-1} = \begin{bmatrix} \frac{4}{20} & -\frac{6}{20} \\ \frac{3}{20} & \frac{1}{20} \end{bmatrix}$

9. (a) $\begin{bmatrix} 1 & \frac{1}{2} \\ \frac{1}{2} & 1 \end{bmatrix} \cdot \begin{bmatrix} A \\ B \end{bmatrix} = \begin{bmatrix} F \\ G \end{bmatrix}$
   (b) $A = B = 37.50$
   (c) $A = 0, B = 112.50$

Chapter 5

Section 5.1

1. (a) $|B| = -54$
   (b) $|B| = 0$
   (c) $|B| = -\lambda$
3. (a) $|B| = -54$
   (b) $|B| = 0$
   (c) $|B| = -\lambda$
5. (a) $|A| = 10.50$
   (b) $|A| = 441$
   (c) $|A| = 4$
7. $|T| = t_{11} \cdot t_{22} \cdot t_{33} \cdot t_{44} \cdot t_{55}$

Section 5.2

1. (a) $\text{adj}(A) = \begin{bmatrix} 25 & 35 & -17 \\ -20 & 15 & 5 \\ 40 & -30 & 33 \end{bmatrix}$
   (b) $\text{adj}(A) = \begin{bmatrix} bc - a^2 & -(bc - ac) & ab - bc \\ -(c^2 - ab) & ac - bc & -(a^2 - c^2) \\ ac - b^2 & -(a^2 - b^2) & ab - bc \end{bmatrix}$

(c) $\text{adj}(A) = \begin{bmatrix} 6 & -92 & -4 & 16 \\ 30 & -82 & -20 & 80 \\ 78 & 64 & 11 & -44 \\ -192 & 298 & 128 & -134 \end{bmatrix}$

(d) $\text{adj}(A) = \begin{bmatrix} 18 & -4 & -32 & -8 \\ -18 & 0 & 36 & 0 \\ 216 & -56 & -412 & -40 \\ -162 & 42 & 300 & 30 \end{bmatrix}$

3. (a) $\begin{bmatrix} 1 & -1 & -1 \\ -0.8 & 1 & 0 \\ 0 & 0 & 1 \end{bmatrix} \cdot \begin{bmatrix} Y \\ C \\ I \end{bmatrix} = \begin{bmatrix} G \\ 200 \\ 1000 - 2000R \end{bmatrix}$

(b) $A^{-1} = \begin{bmatrix} 5 & 5 & 5 \\ 4 & 5 & 4 \\ 0 & 0 & 1 \end{bmatrix}$

(c) $\Delta Y = -250$. The change in income due to a change in government spending is more in this scenario than in Section 4.1 in Chapter 4 since money demand is not included in this model and there is no crowding out.

5. (a) $(x, y) = (4, 0)$

(b) $(x, y) = \left(\frac{320}{17}, \frac{28}{17}\right)$

(c) $(x, y, z) = \left(\frac{53}{9}, \frac{44}{9}, \frac{152}{9}\right)$

(d) $(x, y, z) = \left(\frac{38}{28}, \frac{96}{28}, \frac{72}{28}\right)$

7. If the matrix A is nonsingular, a homogeneous equation system yields the solution that $x_1 = x_2 = \cdots = x_n = 0$. Using Cramer's rule, which, in this case, replaces the first column of matrix A with a column of zeroes, suggests that $|A_j| = 0$. The value of $|A|$ must therefore be non-zero in order for there to be a defined solution since $x_j = |A_j|/|A| = 0/|A| = 0$. If matrix A were singular, then its determinant would be zero which would make the solution of x_j undefined.

Section 5.3

1. (a) $\lambda^2 - 6\lambda + 5 = 0; \lambda_1, \lambda_2 = 1, 5; |A| = 8 - 3 = 5$
   (b) $\lambda^2 + 4\lambda + 3 = 0; \lambda_1, \lambda_2 = -1, -3; |A| = 3 - 0 = 3$
   (c) $\lambda^2 - 3\lambda - 4 = 0; \lambda_1, \lambda_2 = -1, 4; |A| = -10 - (-6) = -4$
3. (a) In matrix format,

$$\begin{bmatrix} 2 & 6 \\ 1 & -3 \end{bmatrix} \begin{bmatrix} x_1 \\ x_2 \end{bmatrix} = \begin{bmatrix} 20 \\ 4 \end{bmatrix}$$

(b) The characteristic equation is $\lambda^2 + \lambda - 12 = 0$, $\lambda_1, \lambda_2 = 3, -4$.

(c) Associated with the characteristic root 3,

$$\begin{bmatrix} 2 & 6 \\ 1 & -3 \end{bmatrix} \begin{bmatrix} p_1 \\ p_2 \end{bmatrix} = \begin{bmatrix} 3p_1 \\ 3p_2 \end{bmatrix},$$

which gives us $p_1 = 6p_2$. Associated with the characteristic root -4,

$$\begin{bmatrix} 2 & 6 \\ 1 & -3 \end{bmatrix} \begin{bmatrix} p_1 \\ p_2 \end{bmatrix} = \begin{bmatrix} -4p_1 \\ -4p_2 \end{bmatrix},$$

which gives us $p_1 = -p_2$. So the matrix P is (up to a multiplicative constant)

$$P = \begin{bmatrix} 6 & 1 \\ 1 & -1 \end{bmatrix}.$$

(d) We have

$$P^{-1} = \begin{bmatrix} \frac{1}{7} & \frac{1}{7} \\ \frac{1}{7} & -\frac{6}{7} \end{bmatrix},$$

and by matrix multiplication, we find $P^{-1}AP = \Lambda$, where Λ is a diagonal matrix with the elements 3 and -4.

5. The characteristic equations and characteristic roots (found by using the quadratic formula) are as follows;

(a) $\lambda^2 - 0.5\lambda + 0.0225 = 0$; $\lambda_1, \lambda_2 = 0.05, 0.45$. This is stable.

(b) $\lambda^2 - \lambda - 0.3125 = 0$; $\lambda_1, \lambda_2 = -0.25, 1.25$. This is not stable.

(c) $\lambda^2 - 1.5\lambda + 0.3125 = 0$; $\lambda_1, \lambda_2 = 0.25, 1.25$. This is not stable.

Chapter 6

Section 6.2

1. (a) $\dfrac{\Delta y}{\Delta x} = 5$

(b) $\dfrac{\Delta y}{\Delta x} = -15$

(c) $\dfrac{\Delta y}{\Delta x} = 2 + 12x_0 + 6\,\Delta x$

(d) $\dfrac{\Delta y}{\Delta x} = -2x_0 - \Delta x$

3. (a) $\dfrac{\Delta z}{\Delta x} = 3gx_0^2 + 3gx_0\,\Delta x + g\,\Delta x^2$

   (b) $\dfrac{\Delta w}{\Delta x} = b + 2cx_0 + c\,\Delta x + 3gx_0^2 + 3gx_0\,\Delta x + g\,\Delta x^2$

5.

	$x_0 = 1, \Delta x = 1$	$x_0 = 2, \Delta x = 1$	$x_0 = 2, \Delta x = 2$
(a) $y = 10x - 4$	$\dfrac{\Delta y}{\Delta x} = 10$	10	10
(b) $y = 3x^2 + 6x - 5$	$\dfrac{\Delta y}{\Delta x} = 15$	21	24
(c) $y = x^3 + 4x^2 - 6x + 12$	$\dfrac{\Delta y}{\Delta x} = 13$	33	46

   Changing the values of x_0 and Δx has no impact on (a) since it is linear. Doubling the value of x_0 has a greater impact on the quadratic and cubic functions than does doubling the value of Δx.

7. (a) $TR = 10Q - 0.5Q^2$
   (b) $\Delta TR/\Delta Q = 10 - Q - 0.5\,\Delta Q$. When $\Delta Q = 1$ and $Q_0 = 5$, the impact on total revenue of a one unit change in Q is 4.5.
   (c) The impact on total revenue is 6.5 when $Q_0 = 3$ and $\Delta Q = 1$.
   (d) The impact on total revenue is 6 when $Q_0 = 3$ and $\Delta Q = 2$.

Section 6.3

1. (a) $f'(x) = 30$
   (b) $f'(x) = 16x - 6$
   (c) $f'(x) = 0$
   (d) $f'(x) = -4x$
3. $R'(t) = 25 - 150$; $t_m = 0.167$. An increase in the tax rate beyond t_m would decrease tax revenue since the effect of lower sales on tax revenue more than offsets the effect of the higher tax rate, so higher taxes would reduce consumption.
5. Equal average tax rates: at a given level of income, the tax systems should have secant lines drawn from the origin with the same slope. Equal marginal tax rates: the line tangent to each of the three tax functions at a given level of income should have the same slope.
7. $C'(q) = 4q$; $AC(q) = 10/q + 2q$. The total cost curve, $C(q) = 10 + 2q^2$, where $q \geq 0$, is a convex function. Therefore, the marginal cost, which is measured as the slope of a line tangent to the total cost function at a given point, is greater than the slope of the secant line from the origin to that same point. An increase in output will increase the slope of the secant line, but the slope of the marginal cost curve will always be greater than that of the secant line.
9. The roots of the equation $y = 4x^2 - 8x + 3$ are $\frac{12}{8}, \frac{1}{2}$, which means that the value of the function at these values of x equals zero. The following ordered pairs can be plotted for this function: (0, 3), (1, −1), (2, 3)

(a) $f'(x) = 8x = 8$. When $f'(x) = 0, x = 1$. The extreme value is a global minimum.

(b) The graph is a convex curve with y-intercept $(0, 3)$. It reaches a global minimum at $(1, -1)$ and passes through the x-axis at $\left(\frac{1}{2}, 0\right)$ and $\left(\frac{12}{8}, 0\right)$.

11. The derivative of this function is

$$\frac{dP}{d\ln Y} = -58.2 + 7.8\ln Y.$$

(a) This derivative equals zero for $\ln Y = 58.2/7.8 = 7.46$, which corresponds to a level of income of $e^{7.46} = \$1{,}737$.

(b) Evaluating this derivative at $\ln Y = 7.04$, we obtain -3.29. Evaluating this derivative at $\ln Y = 8.60$, we obtain 8.88. A sketch of this function, then, shows that it is "flatter" than the function presented in the application (and, because the value of $\ln Y$ where the derivative is equal to zero is smaller in this function, the minimum point of the function is to the left of the minimum point of the function in the application. The association of the minimum point of a function with the point where the derivative equals zero is discussed in detail in Chapter 9).

Section 6.4

1. (a) $dy = (14x - 3)\,dx$

(b) $dy = \left(10 - \dfrac{1}{2}x\right)dx$

(c) $dy = (-2x)\,dx$

(d) $dy = (3x^2 + 3)\,dx$

3. (a) $dy = \left(6x + \dfrac{1}{3}\right)dx$. When $\Delta x = 0.5$, $\Delta y = 6\dfrac{1}{6}$. When $\Delta x = 2$, $\Delta y = 24\dfrac{2}{3}$

(b) $dy = (x)\,dx$. When $\Delta x = \dfrac{1}{4}$, $\Delta y = \dfrac{1}{2}$. When $\Delta x = 10$, $\Delta y = 20$

(c) $dy = (3x^2 - 4)\,dx$. When $\Delta x = 8$, $\Delta y = 64$. When $\Delta x = 0.2$, $\Delta y = 1.6$

5. (a) The derivative of the consumption function is $dC/dY = 0.8$, which in economic terms is the marginal propensity to consume or the portion of current income which is consumed in a given period.

(b) Using the differential approximation, $\Delta C = f'(y) \cdot \Delta y = 800$, which in this case equals the actual difference in consumption due to the ΔY since the consumption function is linear.

7. The roots of the function are $x_1, x_2 = -1, 11$. The differential equation is $dy = (10 - 2x)\,dx$

	Actual	Estimate	Difference
$\Delta x = 0.5$	22.75	24	5.5%
$\Delta x = 1$	27	28	3.7%
$\Delta x = 1.75$	30.94	34	9.9%
$\Delta x = 3$	35	44	26%

The percentage difference should be read as how much bigger the differential estimate is than the actual value of y. The differential approximation becomes a less accurate estimate for the actual value of y as the Δx gets larger.

Chapter 7

Section 7.1

1. (a) $f'(x) = \frac{3}{2}x^{1/2}$
   (b) $f'(x) = 0$
   (c) $f'(x) = -7x^{-5}$
   (d) $f'(x) = 16x + \frac{3}{2\sqrt{x}}$
   (e) $f'(x) = -\frac{2}{3}x^{-3} - 2$
3. $f'(x) = 0$ is the derivative of a constant function such as $f(x) = 5$. $f'(x_0) = 0$ is the derivative of a function evaluated at $x = 0$, such as $f(x) = 2x^2$ whose derivative is $f'(x) = 4x$. At point $x = 0$, the derivative also equals zero.
5. $TR = AR \cdot Q = f(Q) \cdot Q$, so the derivative of TR, marginal revenue (MR), is
$$MR = f'(Q) = Qf'(Q) + f(Q).$$
7. (a) $f'(x) = 20 - 8x; f'(-1) = 28; f'(1) = 12$, so the derivative is decreasing
   (b) $f'(x) = 2e^{2x}; f'(0) = 2; f'(2) = 109$, so the derivative is increasing
   (c) $f'(x) = \frac{3}{x}; f'(4) = \frac{3}{4}; f'(6) = \frac{1}{2}$, so the derivative is decreasing
   (d) $f'(x) = 4(x + 1); f'(-5) = -16; f'(1) = 8$, so the derivative is increasing
9. $d(M/P)/di = -\lambda e^{(-\lambda i)}$; When the interest rate rises, people want to hold fewer real balances and more of other assets that earn interest, so M/P falls as i rises.

Section 7.2

1. (a) $f'(x) = 4x^3 - 9x^2 + 14x + 3$
   (b) $f'(x) = 198(2x + 4)^{98}$
   (c) $f'(x) = (200x + 200)(5x^2 + 10x + 3)^{19}$
   (d) $f'(x) = abe^{abx}$
   (e) $f'(x) = b(e^{x^a})^{b-1} \times (ax^{a-1}e^{x^a})$
   (f) $f'(x) = (e^{a+bx+cx^2})^{10} \cdot 10(b + 2cx)$

3. (a) The derivative of average cost is

$$A'(x) = \frac{(f'(x)x) - 1(f(x))}{x^2} = \frac{1}{x}\left[f'(x) - \frac{f(x)}{x}\right] = \frac{1}{x}\,[f'(x) - A(x)],$$

where the last term in brackets is marginal cost minus average cost times $1/x$.

(b) When the derivative of average cost is less than zero, then it is decreasing. Marginal cost is less than average cost.

(c) When the derivative of average cost is more than zero, then it is increasing. Marginal cost is greater than average cost.

(d) If marginal cost equals average cost, then $A'(x) = 0$, which is a point of horizontal tangency

5. $$\frac{dY_f}{dDef} = \frac{dY_f}{dTB_B} \times \frac{dTB_A}{e_d} \times \frac{de_d}{dK_f} \times \frac{dK_f}{di_d} \times \frac{di_d}{dDef}.$$
$(+)\qquad(+)\qquad(+)\qquad(+)\quad(+)\qquad(+)$

A $(+)$ indicates a positive relationship between the two variables, and a $(-)$ indicates a negative relationship between the variables. In the case of dTB/e_d, where the exchange rate is measured in units of domestic currency, a strengthening currency is measured as a decrease in the exchange rate since it takes fewer units of domestic currency to purchase one unit of foreign currency. A stronger exchange rate has a dampening effect on Country A's trade balance, since it encourages imports, but it has a strengthening effect on Country's B's trade balance by stimulating that country's exports. The ultimate effect of an increase in Country A's budget deficit, therefore, is to increase Country B's income.

7. (a) $f'(x) = \dfrac{2}{\ln 2(2x + 3)}$

(b) $f'(x) = \dfrac{2}{x \ln 4}$

(c) $f'(x) = 3x^2 \log_2 x + \dfrac{x^2}{\ln 2}$

(d) $f'(x) = \dfrac{1/\ln 3 - \log_2 x}{2x^2}$

9. (a) $\varepsilon = -4$ and therefore elastic. Elasticity changes because of the linear function.

(b) $\varepsilon = -1.2$ and therefore elastic. Elasticity changes with changes in x and y.

(c) $\varepsilon = -0.5$, which is inelastic and constant.

(d) $\varepsilon = -2$, which is elastic and constant.

11. (a) $Q_M = 10$; $P_M = 20$. If $Q_M = 8$, $P_M = 24$ and demand is elastic. If Q_M rises to 11, this part of the demand curve is inelastic.

(b) $E_{q,p} = -0.5$ which is inelastic. Because elasticity is constant, it will not change when quantity demanded changes.

13. (a) $P = 7.389$; $Q = 403.4$
    (b) $\varepsilon^D = -2$
    (c) $\varepsilon^S = 0.5$
    (d) response of P_P to a change in $T = -0.8$; response of P_C to change in $T = 0.2$
    (e) The price facing consumers rises by more than the price facing producers for a given increase in the tax because the elasticity of demand is less than the elasticity of supply in absolute value terms. With $T = 1$, the new $P_C = 7.589$ and the new $P_P = 6.589$. The new Q is approximately 381.

Section 7.3

1. (a) $f''(x) = 14 - 6x$
   (b) $f''(x) = 10x^{-3}$
   (c) $f''(x) = -x^{-2}$
   (d) $f''(x) = 2e^x + 4xe^x + x^2e^x$
   (e) $f''(x) = 600x^{-26}$
3. (a) $f''(x) = 2$; convex since the second derivative is constant.
   (b) $f''(x) = \dfrac{-3}{2\sqrt{x^3}}$; concave since the second derivative is always negative.
   (c) $f''(x) = 6x - 12$, concave and convex portions since the second derivative changes sign.
   (d) $f''(x) = -3x^{-2}$; concave since the second derivative is always negative.
5. $f''(x) = 30x^4$, so the second derivative is unambiguously positive, and the function is strictly convex since a secant line connecting two points lies wholly below the function itself. When evaluated at $f(x_0)$, the second derivative equals zero, but the function remains strictly convex.

7.
$$\frac{d\ln U}{dq_i} = \frac{\beta_i}{q_i - \gamma_i} > 0$$

   A positive marginal utility implies that the total utility is a monotonically increasing function, as consumer demand theory requires.

$$\frac{d^2\ln U}{dq_i^2} = \frac{-\beta_i}{(q_i - \gamma_i)^2} < 0$$

   The function exhibits diminishing marginal utility and is concave.
9. Coefficient of relative risk aversion, αx; coefficient of absolute risk aversion, α
11. The relationship between the actual function and its approximations:

		$x = 2$	$x = 2.1$
(a)	Actual	$f(x) = 3$	$f(x) = 3.73$
	Linear	$h(x) = 3 + 7(x - 2)$	$h(x) = 3.7$
	Quadratic	$j(x) = 3 + 7(x - 2) + 3(x - 2)^2$	$j(x) = 3.73$

		$x = 2$	$x = 2.1$
(b)	Actual	$f(x) = 1.3863$	$f(x) = 1.4351$
	Linear	$h(x) = \ln 4 + \frac{1}{2}(x - 2)$	$h(x) = 1.4363$
	Quadratic	$j(x) = \ln 4 + \frac{1}{2}(x - 2) - \frac{1}{4}(x - 2)^2$	$j(x) = 1.4338$

		$x = 2$	$x = 2.1$
(c)	Actual	$f(x) = 403.4$	$f(x) = 544.6$
	Linear	$h(x) = e^6 + 3e^6(x - 2)$	$h(x) = 566.8$
	Quadratic	$j(x) = e^6 + 3e^6(x - 2) + \frac{9}{2}e^6(x - 2)^2$	$j(x) = 591.3$

Chapter 8

Section 8.2

1. (a) $\frac{\partial y}{\partial x_1} = 48x_1^3 - 12x_1x_2; \frac{\partial y}{\partial x_2} = -6x_1^2 + 12x_2^2$

   (b) $\frac{\partial y}{\partial x_1} = 6x_1x_2 + 24x_1 + 5x_2 + 20; \frac{\partial y}{\partial x_2} = 3x_1^2 + 5x_1 + 1$

   (c) $\frac{\partial y}{\partial x_1} = \frac{2x_2^2 - 14}{(x_1 - 2)^2}; \frac{\partial y}{\partial x_2} = \frac{-2x_1x_2}{x_1 - 2}$

   (d) $\frac{\partial y}{\partial x_1} = 6x_2^2e^{(3x_1)}; \frac{\partial y}{\partial x_2} = 4x_2e^{(3x_1)}$

   (e) $\frac{\partial y}{\partial x_1} = \frac{-2}{x_1}; \frac{\partial y}{\partial x_2} = \frac{-4}{x_2}$

   (f) $\frac{\partial y}{\partial x_1} = 2x_1 + 2\sqrt{x_2}; \frac{\partial y}{\partial x_2} = \frac{x_1}{\sqrt{x_2}} - 4$

3. (a) $\frac{\partial y}{\partial x_1} = 0; \frac{\partial y}{\partial x_2} = 186$

   (b) $\frac{\partial y}{\partial x_1} = 88; \frac{\partial y}{\partial x_2} = 9$

   (c) $\frac{\partial y}{\partial x_1} = 18; \frac{\partial y}{\partial x_2} = 8$

   (d) $\frac{\partial y}{\partial x_1} = 1928; \frac{\partial y}{\partial x_2} = 321$

(e) $\frac{\partial y}{\partial x_1} = -2; \frac{\partial y}{\partial x_2} = -1$

(f) $\frac{\partial y}{\partial x_1} = 6; \frac{\partial y}{\partial x_2} = -\frac{7}{2}$

5.

$$f_w(w,x,y,z) = \tau\alpha w^{\tau-1}; f_{ww}(w,x,y,z) = \tau(\tau-1)\alpha w^{\tau-2}$$

$$f_x(w,x,y,z) = \frac{\beta}{\theta y} \cdot \ln(\phi z); f_{xx}(w,x,y,z) = 0$$

(a) $f_y(w,x,y,z) = -\theta\frac{\beta x}{(\theta y)^2} \cdot \ln(\phi z); f_{yy}(w,x,y,z) = 2\theta^2\frac{\beta x}{(\theta y)^3} \cdot \ln(\phi z)$

$f_z(w,x,y,z) = \frac{\beta x}{\theta y} \cdot \frac{1}{z}; f_{zz}(w,x,y,z) = -\frac{\beta x}{\theta y} \cdot \frac{1}{z^2}$

(b) $f_{xz}(w,x,y,z) = \frac{\beta}{\theta y} \cdot \frac{1}{z}; f_{wy}(w,x,y,z) = 0$

(c) According to Young's Theorem, this function has six cross partial derivatives.

7. The partial derivative is

$$f_x(x,y,z) = \frac{1}{z+x} - \frac{y+x}{(z+x)^2} = \frac{z-y}{(z+x)^2},$$

which is positive if $z > y$, negative if $y > z$, and 0 if $y = z$.

9. (a) $\frac{r_{India}}{r_{US}} = \left(\frac{2}{3}\right)^{2.5} \cdot \left(\frac{1}{15}\right)^{-1.5} \approx 21.08$

(b) $\frac{\partial(r_I/r_{US})}{\partial(A_I/A_{US})} = \frac{1}{1-\alpha}\left(\frac{A_I}{A_{US}}\right)^{-\alpha/(1-\alpha)} \cdot \left(\frac{Q}{L}\right)^{-\alpha/(1-\alpha)}$

11. (a) The demand varies with price according to the relationship

$$\frac{\partial Q_D}{\partial P} = -0.25e^4P^{-1.25} \text{ in September}$$

$$\frac{\partial Q_D}{\partial P} = -0.25e^{3.5}P^{-1.25} \text{ in January}$$

$$\frac{\partial Q_D}{\partial P} = -0.25e^3P^{-1.25} \text{ in May.}$$

(b) The demand varies with the number of months since September according to the relationship

$$\frac{dQ_D}{dt} = -0.125e^4P^{-0.25}e^{-0.125t}.$$

Section 8.3

1. (a) $\frac{dy}{dz} = 40x - 8w$

   (b) $\frac{dy}{dz} = \left(12x^2 + \frac{1}{4}z^2\right)(-2z^{-3}) + \left(\frac{1}{2}xz - 2\right)$

   (c) $\frac{dy}{dz} = \frac{\partial y}{\partial v} \cdot \frac{dv}{dz} + \frac{\partial y}{\partial w} \cdot \frac{dw}{dz} + \frac{\partial y}{\partial z}$

   (d) $\frac{dy}{dz} = \frac{4xt^2 + 10t}{z} + \frac{2x^2t + 5x}{\sqrt{z}}$

3. (a) $\frac{dTB}{dM} = f_E \frac{dE}{dM} - g_E \frac{dE}{dM} - g_{Y_{US}} \frac{dY_{US}}{dM}$

   (b) $\frac{dTB}{dM} = f_E \frac{dE}{dM} - g_E \frac{dE}{dM} - g_{Y_{US}} \frac{dY_{US}}{dM} \gtreqless 0$

   $\frac{dTB}{dY_J} = f_{Y_J} > 0$

5. (a) Partial derivatives are homogeneous of degree -1. For example,

$$f_x(sx, sy, sw) = sw^{-1} = s^{-1}(w^{-1})$$

   (b) Partial derivatives are homogeneous of degree 0. For example,

$$f_x(sx, sy, sw) = 2sx^1sw^{-1} = s^0(2x^1w^{-1})$$

   (c) Partial derivatives are homogeneous of degree 2. For example,

$$f_x(sx, sy, sw) = 3s^2x^2s^1y^1s^{-1}w^{-1} + 2s^1y^1s^1w^1 = s^2(3x^2yw^{-1}) + s^2(2yw)$$

   (d) Partial derivatives are homogeneous of degree 0. For example,

$$f_x(sx, sy) = \frac{s^1}{\sqrt{s^2x^2 + s^2y^2}} = \frac{s^1x^1}{s^1 \cdot \sqrt{x^2 + y^2}}$$

7. (a) The function is homogeneous of degree $k = \frac{7}{12}$ since

$$f(sx_1, sx_2) = (sx_1)^{1/4}(sx_2)^{1/3} = s^{7/12}f(x_1, x_2)$$

   (b) The partial derivatives of the production function are

$$\frac{\partial y}{\partial x_1} = \frac{1}{4}x_1^{-3/4}x_2^{1/3} \quad \text{and} \quad \frac{\partial y}{\partial x_2} = \frac{1}{3}x_1^{1/4}x_2^{-3/4}$$

   where the f_i are homogeneous of degree $k - 1 = -\frac{5}{12}$ as follows:

$$f_1(sx_1, sx_2) = \frac{1}{4}(sx_1)^{-3/4}(sx_2)^{1/3} = s^{-5/12}f_1(x_1, x_2)$$

$$f_2(sx_1, sx_2) = \frac{1}{3}(sx_1)^{1/4}(sx_2)^{-2/3} = s^{-5/12}f_1(x_1, x_2)$$

(c) Euler's Theorem shows that

$$x_1\left(\frac{1}{4}(sx_1)^{-3/4}(sx_2)^{1/3}\right) + x_2\left(\frac{1}{3}(sx_1)^{1/4}(sx_2)^{-2/3}\right) = \frac{7}{12}s^{-5/12}(x_1, x_2),$$

where $f(x_1, x_2) = y = x_1^{1/4}x_2^{1/3}$.

9. (a) homogeneous of degree 2
   (b) homothetic but not homogeneous
   (c) homothetic and homogeneous of degree 2
   (d) homothetic and homogeneous of degree 4
   (e) homothetic but not homogeneous

Exercise 8.4

1. (a) $dw = \left(4x + \frac{1}{2}y\right)dx + \left(\frac{1}{2}x - 9y^2\right)dy$

   (b) $dy = \left(12x_1^2 - \frac{1}{x_1}\right)dx_1 + \left(6 - \frac{1}{x_2}\right)dx_2$

   (c) $dz = \left(\frac{2xy^3 + x^2y}{(y^3 + xy)^2}\right)dx - \left(\frac{3x^2y^2 + x^3}{(y^3 + xy)^2}\right)dy$

   (d) $dy = (4x_1e^{(3x_2)})\,dx_1 + (6x_1^2e^{(3x_2)})\,dx_2$

3. The function $y = 3x^2 - 2x + z^3 - 1.5z^2 - xz$, evaluated at $x, z = (2, 1) = 5.5$

	Actual (Δy)	Estimate (dy)	Difference
$\Delta x, \Delta z = 1$	11.5	7	40%
$\Delta x, \Delta z = 0.5$	4.5	3.5	22%
$\Delta x, \Delta z = 0.1$	0.74	0.7	5.4%

5. (a) .05
   (b) −50
   (c) 5
   (d) −2.50

7. (a) $-\frac{7K}{3L}$

   (b) Slope $= -7$; Slope $= -\frac{1}{2}$

   (c) MRTS is 7 and $\frac{1}{2}$, respectively.

9. (a) $MRS_{A,B} = -\frac{B}{A}$

   (b) $MRS_{A,B} = -\frac{B}{3A}$

11. For a given level of M,

$$\frac{dY}{dH} = -0.4\frac{Y}{H}.$$

Chapter 9

Section 9.1

1. (a) $x^* = 5$, which is a minimum
   (b) $x^* = (1, 2)$, which are maximum and minimum, respectively
   (c) $x^* = 0$, which is a maximum
   (d) $x^* = \frac{1}{2}$, which is a maximum
   (e) $x^* = (-1.80, 0.46)$, which are maximum and minimum, respectively
   (f) $x^* = \exp = 2.718$, which is a maximum
3. The maximum number of extreme points for the function is $n - 1$.
5. The general formula for determining the critical points of a quadratic function is $\beta + 2\gamma x = 0$. The general formula for the critical points of a cubic function is

$$\frac{-2\gamma \pm \sqrt{(2\gamma)^2 - 12\theta\beta}}{6\theta} = 0.$$

7. Substituting the functions, we get

$$V(R) = 9R - 2\left(\frac{R^2}{4}\right) = 9R - \frac{R^2}{2}.$$

The vote-maximizing use of resources is found by setting the derivative equal to zero,

$$V'(R) = 9 - R = 0,$$

so $R^* = 9$ and then $V(9) = 81 - \frac{81}{2} = 40.5$ percent of the vote; she loses anyway. This is a maximum since $V''(R) = -1$.

9. The profit function is also a cubic function with two bends. The first curvature is convex and crosses the x-axis at the quantity where the concave portion of the total cost curve intersects the total revenue curve. The profit function reaches a maximum at Q^*, the point where there is a maximum positive difference between the total revenue and total cost curves. The marginal revenue curve is a horizontal line. The marginal cost curve is a U-shaped convex curve, and the marginal profit curve is a concave curve.

Section 9.2

1. $\dfrac{d^2S}{d\pi^2} = (-2\lambda + \lambda^2\pi)\exp(-\lambda(\pi + r) + ay) = 0$

   Since the exponential term cannot equal zero, the first set of terms on the left must equal zero for the product to equal zero. The inflection point is $\pi = 2/\lambda$.

3. In order to maximize profits, the monopolist should produce at $Q = 5$, which corresponds to a price of $P = 2$.

5. (a) $\pi_A = (p_A - c)Q_A = (p_A - c)(a - p_A + bp_B)$;
   $\pi_B = (p_B - c)Q_B = (p_B - c)(a - p_B + bp_A)$

   (b) $p_A = \dfrac{a + c}{2} + \dfrac{b}{2}p_B = R_A; p_B = \dfrac{a+c}{2} + \dfrac{b}{2}p_A = R_B$

   (c) $p_A^* = p_B^* = \dfrac{a+c}{2-b}$

7. The intensive production function is $y = k^a$, which incorporates labor-augmenting technological progress, and $i = (\delta + n + g)k$. According to the Solow growth model, $c = y - i = k^a - (\delta + n + g)k$, so $dc/dk = 1/2\sqrt{k} - 0.145 = 0$ and $k = 11.91$, which is the Golden Rule level of capital accumulation that maximizes consumption per efficiency unit of labor. Labor-augmenting technological progress and population growth, or an increase in the labor force, have the same directional impact on k.

9. The cost-minimizing quantity is $Q = 14.47$. The original function has a y-intercept at $(0, 500)$, a local maximum at $Q = 5.53$, a local minimum at $Q = 14.47$, and an inflection point at $Q = 10$. The profit maximizing quantity is $Q = 12$, however, and if the firm produced the cost-minimizing quantity, it would be earning less than maximum profit.

Chapter 10

Section 10.1

1. (a) $(x, z) = \left(-2, \dfrac{1}{4}\right)$

   (b) $(x, z) = (4, 1)$

   (c) $(x, z) = \left(\dfrac{1}{64}, 9\right)$

   (d) $(x, z) = (0, 0)$

3. (a) $(a, b) = (-5, -3)$

   (b) $(a, b) = (0, 0)$

(c) $(a, b) = \left(-\frac{1}{4}, \frac{9}{4}\right)$

(d) $(a, b) = (1, 1)$

5. (a) The level of inflation that maximizes seigniorage revenue is

$$\pi = \frac{b(X - ct)}{2(a - bg)}.$$

(b) The tax rate that maximizes income tax revenues is

$$t = \frac{X + g\pi}{2c}.$$

(c) They choose different outcome.

$$\pi = \frac{b(X - ct) + gt}{2(a - bg)},$$

which is $gt/2(a - bg)$ bigger than the answer to question 4(a).

$$t = \frac{X + g\pi - bc\pi}{2c},$$

which is $b\pi/2$ smaller than the answer to question 4(b). R is higher in the cooperation case.

7. $(E, U) = (70, 30)$

9. (a) $A_C^* = 500$ and $A_M^* = 250$; $\pi_C = 187{,}500$ and $\pi_M = 62{,}500$; $\pi_C + \pi_M = 250{,}000$

(b) $A_C^* = \frac{3000}{7}$ and $A_M^* = \frac{1000}{7}$; $\pi_C + \pi_M = 306, 122.45$

(c) $A = 250$; $\pi_C + \pi_M = 250{,}000$

11. The critical points of this function are $(Q_B, Q_S) = \left(\frac{185}{26}, \frac{40}{13}\right)$.

Section 10.2

1. (a) Saddle point
   (b) Maximum
   (c) Minimum
   (d) Maximum
3. (a) Saddle point
   (b) Saddle point
   (c) Saddle point
   (d) Minimum

5.

$$\frac{\partial^2 C}{\partial E^2} = -4 < 0,$$
$$\frac{\partial^2 C}{\partial X^2} = -4 < 0,$$
$$\frac{\partial^2 C}{\partial E\,\partial X} = -2,$$

and $(-4)(-4) > (-2)^2$.

7. Confirming maximum profits in part (a),

$$-2\beta \cdot -2\theta > 0^2.$$

Confirming maximum profits in part (b),

$$(-2B - 2C)(-2\theta - 2C) = 4\beta\theta + 4\beta C + 4C\theta + 4C^2 > (-2C)^2.$$

9. The stationary point is $r^* = s^* = 0$. The second derivatives are $\partial^2 z/\partial r^2 = 2\theta$ and $\partial^2 z/\partial s^2 = 2\gamma$.
   (a) $\theta > 0$, $\gamma > 0$, so minimum
   (b) $\theta < 0$, $\gamma < 0$, so maximum
   (c) θ and γ are different, so saddle point

11. The first order conditions are

$$\frac{\partial y}{\partial x} = -4x - 4 + 4z = 0 \quad \text{and}$$
$$\frac{\partial y}{\partial z} = -z + 4 + 4x = 0$$

   (a) The stationary point is $x^* = -1$ and $z^* = 0$.
   (b) The second partial derivatives and the cross partial derivative are

$$\frac{\partial^2 y}{\partial x^2} = -4,$$
$$\frac{\partial^2 y}{\partial z^2} = -1, \quad \text{and}$$
$$\frac{\partial^2 y}{\partial x\,\partial z} = 4.$$

Thus, we have $\partial^2 y/\partial x^2 < 0$ and $\partial^2 y/\partial z^2 < 0$, two of the conditions needed for the stationary point to be a maximum, but the other condition is not met since $(\partial^2 y/\partial x^2)(\partial^2 y/\partial z^2) < (\partial^2 y/\partial x \partial z)^2$; therefore, this stationary point is neither a maximum nor a minimum.

Exercises 10.3

1. For this function, all three second partial derivatives $\partial^2 y/\partial x_i^2 = 2$ for $i = 1, 2, 3$, and all cross partial derivatives are zero. Therefore the stationary point, (0, 0, 0), is a minimum.

3. For a function with all cross partial derivatives equal to zero, a stationary point is a minimum if all second derivatives are positive when evaluated at the stationary point, and a stationary point is a maximum if all second partial derivatives are negative when evaluated at the stationary point. If some second partial derivatives are zero or if they are of different signs, then the stationary point is a saddle point.
5. $(x_1^*, x_2^*, x_3^*) = (4, 2, 4)$. The sufficient condition shows that these represent a local maximum

$$f_{11} = -1 > 0,$$
$$f_{11}f_{22} = 6 > (f_{12})^2 = 4, \quad \text{and}$$
$$f_{11}f_{22}f_{33} + 2f_{12}f_{23}f_{13} < f_{11}(f_{23})^2 + f_{22}(f_{13})^2 + f_{33}(f_{12})^2$$

7. In the matrix

$$A = \begin{bmatrix} a_{11} & a_{12} \\ a_{21} & a_{22} \end{bmatrix},$$

the two first-order principal minors are a_{11} and a_{22}, and the single second-order principal minor is the determinant of the matrix, $|A| = a_{11}a_{22} - a_{12}a_{21}$. This matrix is positive definite if the two leading principle minors, a_{11} and $|A|$, are positive. This matrix is positive semidefinite if $a_{11} \geq 0$, $a_{22} \geq 0$, and $|A| \geq 0$. This matrix is negative definite if $a_{11} < 0$ and $|A| > 0$. This matrix is negative semidefinite if $a_{11} \leq 0$, $a_{22} \leq 0$, and $|A| \geq 0$. Therefore, using these criteria, we find that the matrix in part (a) is negative definite, the matrix in part (b) is positive semidefinite, the matrix in part (c) is negative semidefinite, and the matrix in part (d) is positive definite.

Chapter 11

Section 11.1

1. (a) $(x, z) = (8, 0)$, minimum
   (b) $(x, z) = \left(\frac{1}{3}, \frac{2}{3}\right)$, minimum
   (c) $(x, z) = (4, 1)$, minimum
   (d) $(x, z) = \left(\frac{4}{3}, \frac{32}{3}\right)$, maximum
   (e) $(x, z) = \left(\frac{1}{2}, \frac{1}{2}\right)$, maximum
3. $R = 16$, $L = 8$ ($R = 0$ yields minimum)
5. (a) $\frac{S}{4} + \frac{V}{2} + \frac{J}{12} = 6$
   (b) $\overline{U}(V, J) = \frac{1}{3}\ln\left(24 - 2V - \frac{J}{3}\right) + \frac{1}{3}\ln(V) + \frac{1}{3}\ln(J)$. The ratio is $6V = J$

(c) $\overline{U}(S, J) = \frac{1}{3}\ln(S) + \frac{1}{3}\ln\left(12 - \frac{J}{6} - \frac{S}{2}\right) + \frac{1}{3}\ln(J)$. The ratio is $3V = J$

(d) The optimal amounts of soup, salad, and juice are $S = 8$, $V = 4$, and $J = 24$.

(e) The solution provides a maximum level of utility since each of the second-order conditions are negative.

7. $(x, y, z) = (1, 4, 9)$, saddle point.

9. The constraint is $T + P = 12$. Expressing this as $T = 12 - P$, substituting it into the revenue function, and taking the derivative, we find the first-order condition to be

$$R'(P) = -\frac{1}{2}(12 - P)^{-1/2} + \frac{1}{4}\left(\frac{P}{2}\right)^{-1/2} = 0.$$

Solving, we obtain the optimal level $P = 4$ and, using the constraint, $T = 8$. The second derivative of the internalized objective function is

$$U''(M) = -\frac{1}{4}(12 - P)^{-3/2} - \frac{1}{16}\left(\frac{P}{2}\right)^{-3/2} < 0$$

for $P = 4$. Therefore, this choice of P and T represents a maximum increase in revenues.

Section 11.2

1. (a) $(x, z, \lambda) = (12, 4, 15)$

(b) $(a, b, c, \lambda) = (12, 6, 1, 16)$

(c) $(x, z, \lambda) = \left(\frac{5100}{7}, \frac{136}{7}, \frac{4 \cdot (5100)^3 \cdot (136)^3}{7^6}\right)$.

(d) $(x, y, \lambda) = \left(4, 4, \frac{1}{32}\right)$.

3. $X = \frac{\ln 2 + 4}{3}$, $M = \frac{8 - \ln 2}{3}$, λ is the marginal utility regarding the increase in time you devote to these activities.

5. $(M, L) = (4, 8)$; GPA $= 4.0$

7. $(w, x, y) = (4, 4, 4)$

9. The Lagrangian function is

$$L = G^{1/3}U^{2/3} - \lambda(W_G G + W_U U - B),$$

where B is the total wage bill. The first-order conditions are

$$\frac{\partial L}{\partial G} = \frac{1}{3}G^{-2/3}U^{2/3} - \lambda W_G = 0$$

$$\frac{\partial L}{\partial U} = \frac{2}{3}G^{1/3}U^{-1/3} - \lambda W_U = 0$$

$$\frac{\partial L}{\partial \lambda} = W_G G + W_U U - B = 0.$$

(a) Solving the first-order conditions, we get

$$\frac{G}{U} = \frac{1}{2}\frac{W_U}{W_G}.$$

(b) If W_U rises, then G/U rises.
(c) With $B = 1500$, $W_G = 50$, and $W_U = 25$, we have $G = 10$ and $U = 40$.

Section 11.3

1. (a) $(x_1, x_2) = (15, 30)$
   (b) $(x_1, x_2) = (15, 30)$
   (c) $\lambda_a = 1/\sqrt{32} = 0.178$; $\lambda_b = 1/\sqrt{120} = 0.0083$. The value of the Lagrangian is different in each case despite the same values for x_1 and x_2 due to the differences in the functional form.
3. Solving the Lagrangian function $F(K, L, \lambda) = rK + wL - \lambda(K^\alpha \cdot L^{1-\alpha} - \overline{Q})$,

$$\lambda = \frac{r}{\alpha \cdot L^{1-\alpha} \cdot K^{\alpha-1}} = \frac{w}{(1-\alpha)L^{-\alpha} \cdot K^\alpha} \Leftrightarrow \frac{K}{L} = \frac{\alpha}{1-\alpha} \cdot \frac{w}{r}$$
$$\Leftrightarrow \ln\left(\frac{K}{L}\right) = \ln\left(\frac{\alpha}{1-\alpha}\right) + \ln\left(\frac{w}{r}\right).$$

Therefore, the elasticity of substitution σ is

$$\sigma = \frac{d\ln(K/L)}{d\ln(w/r)} = 1.$$

5. (a) $\dfrac{1}{C_1} = (1 + R) \cdot \dfrac{\beta}{C_2}$
   (b) $\dfrac{1}{1 - \gamma} = (1 + R) \cdot \dfrac{\beta}{1 - \gamma} \Leftrightarrow 1 = (1 + R) \cdot \beta$
   (c) $\exp(-\alpha C_1) = (1 + R) \cdot \beta \cdot \exp(-\alpha C_2)$
7. (a) Setting Y_1, C_1 as income and consumption at the first period,

$$A = Y_1 - C_1$$
$$(1 + r)A + Y_2 = C_2 + R + (E - S).$$

   A consolidated intertemporal budget constraint is $(1 + r - \alpha\theta)Y_1 + Y_2 = (1 + r - \alpha\theta)C_1 + C_2 + R + (1 - \alpha)E - \beta$.
   (b) Putting $(1 + r - \alpha\theta)Y_1 + Y_2 = \overline{Y}$, the Lagrangian function is written as

$$L = 2\sqrt{C_1} + 2\beta\sqrt{C_2} + 2\beta\sqrt{E} + 2\beta^2\sqrt{R}$$
$$- \lambda[(1 + r - \alpha\theta)C_1 + C_2 + R + (1 - \alpha)E - \beta - \overline{Y}].$$

Solving the Lagrangian function, we get

$$C_1 = \frac{(1-\alpha)\cdot(\overline{Y}+\beta)}{(1+r-\alpha\theta)[(1-\alpha)+(1+\beta^2)\cdot\beta^2\cdot(1-\alpha)\cdot(1+r-\alpha)+\beta^2\cdot(1+\rho-\alpha\theta)]},$$

$$C_2 = \frac{(1+r-\alpha\theta)\cdot\beta^2\cdot(1-\alpha)\cdot(\overline{Y}+\beta)}{(1-\alpha)+(1+\beta^2)\cdot\beta^2\cdot(1-\alpha)\cdot(1+r-\alpha\theta)+\beta^2\cdot(1+r-\alpha\theta)},$$

$$R = \frac{(1+r-\alpha\theta)\cdot\beta^4\cdot(1-\alpha)\cdot(\overline{Y}+\beta)}{(1-\alpha)+(1+\beta^2)\cdot\beta^2\cdot(1-\alpha)\cdot(1+r-\alpha\theta)+\beta^2\cdot(1+r-\alpha\theta)}, \quad \text{and}$$

$$E = \frac{(1+r-\alpha\theta)\cdot\beta^2\cdot(\overline{Y}+\beta)}{(1-\alpha)[(1-\alpha)+(1+\beta^2)\cdot\beta^2\cdot(1-\alpha)\cdot(1+r-\alpha\theta)+\beta^2\cdot(1+r-\alpha\theta)}.$$

(*Hint*: Express all variables in terms of C_2, and substitute them into the constraint. You will get

$$C_2\left[\frac{1}{\beta^2(1+r-\alpha\theta)}+1+\beta^2+\frac{1}{1-\alpha}\right]=b-\overline{Y}.)$$

9. (a) The optimal allocations:

$$A_1 = 3.75$$
$$A_2 = 2.50$$
$$w = 10.5$$
$$t_1 = 7.5$$
$$t_2 = 6.0$$

(b) $G_1 = 7.50$; $G_2 = 15$

(c) This technological change would reduce n_1 and thereby increase the relative amount of activity A_1.

(d) This improvement in "physical productivity" will reduce n_2 and thereby increase the relative amount of activity A_2.

(e) The increase in wages will decrease the consumption of the more time-intensive activity A_2.

Section 11.4

1. The Lagrangian function is

$$L = 2x^2 - y^2 - \lambda_1(x^2+y^2-1)+\lambda_2 x+\lambda_3 y,$$

and the solution that provides the maximum value must satisfy

$$\frac{\partial L}{\partial x} = 4x - 2\lambda_1 x + \lambda_2 = 0,$$

$$\frac{\partial L}{\partial y} = 2y - 2\lambda_1 y + \lambda_3 = 0,$$

$$\lambda_1(x^2+y^2-1) = 0,$$

$$\lambda_2 x = 0,$$

$$\lambda_3 y = 0,$$
$$\lambda_2 \geq 0, \lambda_3 \geq 0, \quad \text{and}$$
$$x^2 + y^2 = 1.$$

The optimal solution is $x = 1$, $y = 0$, which means that $\lambda_2 = 0$.

3. The Lagrangian function is

$$L = \frac{1}{3}\ln(S) + \frac{1}{3}\ln(V) + \frac{1}{3}\ln(J) - \lambda\left(\frac{S}{4} + \frac{V}{2} + \frac{J}{12} - 6\right) - \mu(S + J - 40),$$

and the solution that provides the maximum value must satisfy

$$\frac{\partial L}{\partial S} = \frac{1}{3S} - \frac{\lambda}{4} - \mu = 0,$$
$$\frac{\partial L}{\partial V} = \frac{1}{3V} - \frac{\lambda}{2} = 0,$$
$$\frac{\partial L}{\partial J} = \frac{1}{3J} - \frac{\lambda}{12} - \mu = 0,$$
$$\lambda\left(\frac{S}{4} + \frac{V}{2} + \frac{J}{12} - 6\right) = 0,$$
$$\mu(S + J - 40) = 0,$$
$$\lambda \geq 0, \quad \mu \geq 0, \quad \text{and}$$
$$\frac{S}{4} + \frac{V}{2} + \frac{J}{12} \leq 6, \quad S + J \leq 40.$$

The optimal solution has $\lambda \neq 0$, $\mu = 0$, with $S = 8$, $V = 4$, and $J = 24$.

5. The Lagrangian function is

$$L = u(x_1, x_2) - \lambda(p_1x_1 + p_2x_2 - m) - \mu(t_1x_1 + t_2x_2 - T),$$

and the solution that provides the maximum value must satisfy

$$L_1 = u_1 - \lambda p_1 - \mu t_1 = 0,$$
$$L_2 = u_2 - \lambda p_2 - \mu t_2 = 0,$$
$$\lambda(p_1x_1 + p_2x_2 - m) = 0,$$
$$\mu(t_1x_1 + t_2x_2 - T) = 0,$$
$$\lambda \geq 0, \quad \mu \geq 0, \quad \text{and}$$
$$m \leq p_1x_1 + p_2x_2, \quad T \leq t_1x_1 + t_2x_2.$$

It is not the case that $p_1x_1 + p_2x_2 = m$ and $t_1x_1 + t_2x_2 = T$ since if it were more of one or both goods could be consumed, which would raise utility. So it is unlikely that the solution is one where $\lambda = 0$ and $\mu = 0$. It is also unlikely that both $\lambda \neq 0$ and $\mu \neq 0$ since this would mean that both constraints would be binding. It is more likely that either $\lambda \neq 0$ and $\mu = 0$, in which case the budget constraint is binding and the time constraint is not binding, or $\lambda = 0$ and $\mu \neq 0$, in which case the time constraint is binding and the budget constraint is not binding.

Chapter 12

Exercises 12.1

1. (a) 1000
   (b) 941.76
   (c) overestimate equals 985; underestimate equals 955
   (d) overestimate equals 977.60; underestimate equals 963
   (e) overestimate equals 973.04; underestimate equals 968.19
   (f) continuous stream equals 970.61
3. The antiderivatives can be checked by taking the derivatives.
5. The values of the antiderivatives evaluated over the interval 1 to 5 are
   (a) -60
   (b) $41\frac{1}{3}$
   (c) $-18\frac{2}{3}$
   (d) 21.0675
   (e) 7.2^{10}
7. The stream of services is discounted by the interest rate to obtain the present value of services. The present value of a given stream of services decreases as the interest rate increases.
9. Marginal revenue equals

$$\frac{dz}{dx} = 4e^{0.5x} + \frac{x^2}{2} + C.$$

Exercises 12.2

1. (a) $F(x) = \frac{1}{4}x^4 + C$
   (b) $F(x) = x + C$
   (c) $F(x) = \frac{2}{7}x^{7/2} + C$
   (d) $F(x) = -3x^{-1} + C$
   (e) $F(x) = 2e^{2x} + C$
   (f) $F(x) = e^{x^2/4} + C$
   (g) $F(x) = \ln(6x^3 + 2) + C$
3. (a) $F(x) = \frac{x^4}{4} + \frac{2}{3}x^3 + 4x + C$
   (b) $F(x) = -e^{-2x} - \ln(3x^2 - 1) + 2x^{5/2}$
   (c) $F(x) = x^2 - 2x - 2\ln(x)$
   (d) $F(x) = \frac{2}{5}x^{5/2} + \frac{2}{3}x^{3/2} - \frac{2}{3}x^{-3/2}$

5. (a) $F(x) = x\ln(x) - x + C$
   (b) $F(x) = \frac{x^3}{3}\ln(x) - \frac{x^3}{9} + C$
   (c) This requires repeated use of integration by parts. Each time, let $dv = e^{4x}$, and therefore $v = 1/4e^{4x}$. The solution is

$$\frac{x^3}{4}e^{4x} - \frac{3x^2}{16}e^{4x} + \frac{3x}{32}e^{4x} - \frac{3}{128}e^{4x} + C.$$

   (d) Let $u = x^2/2$ and $dv = 2x\sqrt{1 + x^2}\,dx$. Then we have the solution

$$\frac{x^2}{3}(1 + x^2)^{3/2} - \frac{2}{15}(1 + x^2)^{5/2}.$$

7. The capital stock at the end of year 25 equals 104.
9. (a) 17,183
   (b) 19,651

Exercises 12.3

1. (a) Continuous payment equals \$1,014; payment at the end of the year equals \$979.
   (b) \$1,024
   (c) \$1,001.67
   (d) Parents should invest in the ten-year bond since the value of the longer term bond will increase more rapidly than that of the five-year bond given a change in interest rates.
3. (a) Producer's surplus increases by 65.
   (b) Producer's surplus increases by 158.
5. (a) Present value = $100V$, which, when $V = 0.0028$ of national income, equals 28% of a year's national income.
   (b) If the discount rate equals the rate of growth in the economy, the present value of the benefit of reducing inflation to zero is zero.
   (c) If the real discount rate exceeds the rate of growth, there is actually a cost to reducing inflation
7. (a) To find U, note that we need

$$\int_1^U \frac{1}{x}\,dx = \ln(U) - \ln(1) = \ln(U) = 1,$$

   and therefore $U = e$.
   (b) Given $U = e$,

$$\int_1^{e/2} \frac{1}{x}\,dx = \ln\left(\frac{e}{2}\right) - \ln(1) = 0.3 \text{ (approx.)}.$$

(c) Given $U = e$,

$$\int_{e/2}^{e} \frac{1}{x}\,dx = \ln(e) - \ln\left(\frac{e}{2}\right) = 0.7 \text{ (approx.)}.$$

(d) The mean is,

$$\int_{1}^{e} x \cdot \frac{1}{x}\,dx = e - 1 = 1.72 \text{ (approx.)}.$$

9. For the uniform distribution with lower limit a and upper limit b, the mean is $(a + b)/2$ and the variance is

$$\int_{0}^{1} \left(x - \frac{a+b}{2}\right)^2 \cdot \frac{1}{b-a}\,dx = \frac{(b-a)^2}{12}.$$

11. As shown in the application about measuring inequality, the Gini coefficient associated with this continuous Lorenz curve function $L(p)$ equals

$$G = 1 - 2\int_{0}^{1} L(p)\,dp = 1 - 2\int_{0}^{1} [p - 0.375\sqrt{p}(1 - p)]\,dp.$$

Evaluating the integral, we get

$$\begin{aligned}\int_{0}^{1} [p - 0.375\sqrt{p}(1 - p)]\,dp &= \frac{p^2}{2}\bigg|_0^1 - \int_{0}^{1} [0.375\sqrt{p}(1 - p)]\,dp \\ &= \frac{1}{2} - \frac{0.375p^{1.5}}{1.5}\bigg|_0^1 + \frac{0.375p^{2.5}}{2.5}\bigg|_0^1 \\ &= \frac{1}{2} - \frac{0.375}{1.5} + \frac{0.375}{2.5} = 0.4.\end{aligned}$$

Chapter 13

Section 13.1

1. The first six values for the difference equations are:
   (a) $v_0 = 200, v_1 = 205, v_2 = 209.4, v_3 = 213.2, v_4 = 216.6, v_5 = 219.5$
   (b) $w_0 = 50, w_1 = -4, w_2 = 6.8, w_3 = 4.6, w_4 = 5.1, w_5 = 5$
   (c) $x_0 = 120, x_1 = 90, x_2 = 82.5, x_3 = 80.6, x_4 = 80.2, x_5 = 80$
   (d) $y_0 = 30, y_1 = 10, y_2 = 30, y_3 = 10, y_4 = 30, y_5 = 10$
   (e) $y_0 = 0, y_1 = \frac{5}{2}, y_2 = \frac{15}{4}, y_3 = \frac{35}{8}, y_4 = \frac{75}{16}, y_5 = \frac{155}{32}$
3. (a) $v_\infty = 240$
   (b) $w_\infty = 5$

(c) $x_\infty = 80$
(d) y_∞ is not well defined
(e) $y_\infty = 10$

5. The first values of these equations are
   (a) $x_0 = 100, x_1 = 80, x_2 = 85, x_3 = 76.3, x_4 = 76.6, x_5 = 72.3$; stable
   (b) $y_0 = 100, y_1 = 90, y_2 = 76.7, y_3 = 76.6, y_4 = 72.3, y_5 = 71.3$; stable
   (c) $z_0 = 40, z_1 = 30, z_2 = 50, z_3 = 70, z_4 = 150, z_5 = 350$; unstable
7. The starting salary $s_0 = 40{,}000$. The equation showing the relationship in subsequent years is

$$s_t = 0.95s_{t-1} + 2500(1.1)^{t-1},$$

which gives the sequence $s_0 = 40{,}000$, $s_1 = 40{,}500$, $s_2 = 41{,}225$, $s_3 = 42{,}189$, $s_4 = 43{,}407$, $s_5 = 44,897$ and $s_6 = 46,678$. The percentage increases are, respectively, 1.25%, 1.79%, 2.34%, 2.89%, 3.43% and 3.97%.

9. The difference equation for the number of cars is

$$c_{t+1} = \frac{1}{11}c_t^2 + \frac{10}{11}.$$

   (a) The two steady states are found by finding the roots of $c_\infty^2 - 11c_\infty + 10 = 0$. These roots are $c_\infty = 1$, $c_\infty = 10$.
   (b) See Figure 13.1.9. The steady state $c_\infty = 1$ is stable, and the steady state $c_\infty = 10$ is unstable.
   (c) See Figure 13.1.9.

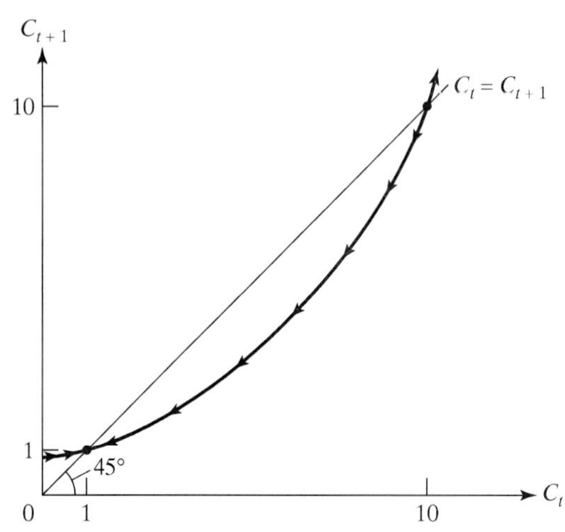

FIGURE 13.1.9.

Section 13.2

1. (a) The steady state level of income is \$1,000.
   (b) See Figure 13.2.1.

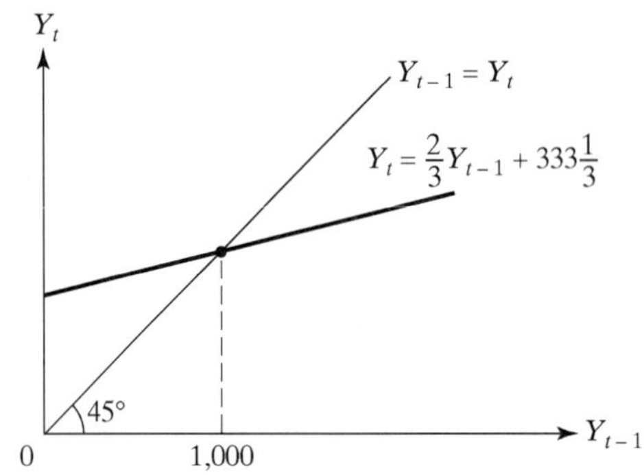

FIGURE 13.2.1.

3. Use the the fact that the steady state value, x_∞, is

$$x_\infty = \frac{y}{1 - a}$$

and that the half-life is calculated as

$$H = -\frac{\ln(2)}{\ln(a)} \approx -\frac{0.6931}{\ln(a)}.$$

(a) $H = -0.6931/\ln(0.25) = -0.6931/(-1.3863) = 0.50$ periods. We have $x_1 = 75$ so that the difference between x_0 and x_1 is 75. The steady state is

$$\frac{60}{1 - 0.25} = 80 \quad \text{and} \quad \frac{x_0 - x_\infty}{2} = 40.$$

(b) $H = -0.6931/\ln(0.75) = -0.6931/(-0.2877) = 2.41$ periods. We have $x_2 = 35$ so the difference between x_0 and x_2 is 35. The steady state is

$$\frac{20}{1 - 0.75} = 80 \quad \text{and} \quad \frac{x_0 + x_\infty}{2} = 40.$$

(c) $H = -0.6931/\ln(0.95) = -0.6931/(-0.0513) = 13.51$ periods. Using (13.8), we have

$$x_{14} = 0.95^{14} \times 0 + \frac{1 - 0.95^{14}}{1 - 0.95} \times 4 = 40.99$$

so that the difference betweeen x_0 and x_{14} is 40.99. The steady state is

$$\frac{4}{1 - 0.95} = 80 \quad \text{and} \quad \frac{x_0 + x_\infty}{2} = 40.$$

Note that $x_A - x_0$ is closer to $(x_0 + x_\infty)/2$ for large values of A.

5. We can use these equations to obtain a difference equation in p_t,

$$p_t = \frac{1}{a + \beta} p_{t-1} + \frac{\beta}{1 + \beta} \phi.$$

(a) The steady state value of p is

$$p_\infty = \frac{(\beta/(1 + \beta))\phi}{1 - 1/(1 + \beta)} = \phi.$$

(b) The coefficient on p_{t-1} is positive and less than 1. Therefore the dynamics are stable and monotonic.

7. The steady state value is $p_\infty = 100$. The slope of the line representing the difference equation in Figure 13.2.7 is $\frac{1}{3}$.

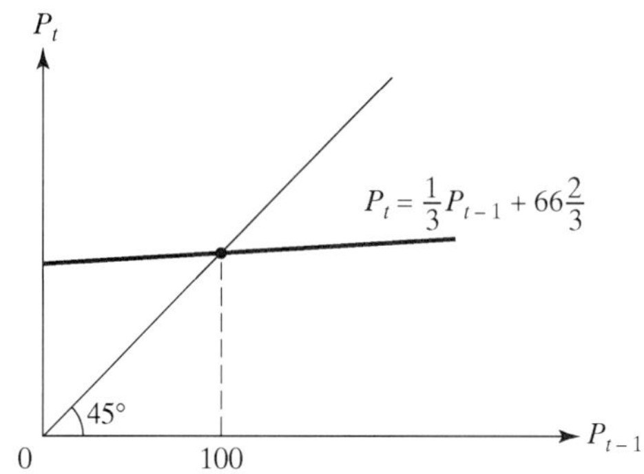

FIGURE 13.2.7.

9. Initially, with a constant stream of dividends equal to \$250 and $r = 0.1$, $p_0 = 250/0.1 = 2500$.

(a) $p_0 = 300/0.1 = 3000$.

(b) The easiest way to calculate this is to subtract from \$3000

$$\sum_{t=1}^{9} \left(\frac{1}{1 + r}\right)^i 50.$$

From the discussion in Section 13.1 we find

$$\sum_{t=1}^{9} \left(\frac{1}{1 + r}\right)^i 50 = 50\left(\frac{1 - (1/(1 + r))^{10}}{1 - 1/(1+r)} - 1\right) = 337.7$$

so $p_0 = \$2662$.

(c) $p_0 = 2500 + 150\left(\frac{1}{1 + r}\right)^2 = 2624.$

(d) $p_0 = 2500 + 150\left(\frac{1}{1 + r}\right)^{10} = 2558.$

(e) $p_0 = \frac{250}{0.5} = 500.$

Section 13.3

1. For the second-order difference equation

$$x_t = \frac{8}{9}x_{t-1} - \frac{7}{81}x_{t-2} + \frac{32}{9}$$

(a) The steady state is found by solving

$$x_\infty = \frac{8}{9}x_\infty - \frac{7}{81}x_\infty + \frac{32}{9}$$

which gives us $x_\infty = 4$

(b) The two roots are

$$k_1, k_2 = \frac{1}{2}\frac{8}{9} \pm \sqrt{\frac{(8/9)^2}{4} - \frac{7}{81}} = \frac{1}{9}, \frac{7}{9}.$$

The equation is stable since the roots are less than 1 in absolute value.

(c) To solve for the constants, note that at time 0 and at time 1, respectively,

$$3 = A + B + 4$$
$$5 = A\frac{7}{9} + B\frac{1}{9} + 4,$$

which can be solved to give us $A = 5/3$ and $B = -8/3$ so the solution to the equation is

$$x_t = \frac{5}{3}\left(\frac{7}{9}\right)^t - \frac{8}{3}\left(\frac{1}{9}\right)^t + 4.$$

3. The roots of this equation are

$$k_1, k_2 = 0.10 \pm \sqrt{\frac{1}{4}(0.04) - 0.65}$$
$$= 0.10 \pm 0.8\sqrt{-1}.$$

The real parts of the two complex roots are less than 1 so this is a stable, oscillatory equation.

5. (a) The characteristic equation is

$$\lambda^2 - (a_{11} + a_{22})\lambda + (a_{11}a_{22} - a_{12}a_{21}) = 0.$$

(b) The roots of the characteristic equation are

$$\lambda_1, \lambda_2 = \frac{(a_{11} + a_{22}) \pm \sqrt{(a_{11} + a_{22})^2 - 4(a_{11}a_{22} - a_{12}a_{21})}}{2}$$

or, in terms of the trace, $\text{tr}(A) = a_{11}a_{22}$ and determinant, $\det(A) = (a_{11}a_{22} - a_{12}a_{21})$

$$\lambda_1, \lambda_2 = \frac{\text{tr}(A) \pm \sqrt{\text{tr}(A)^2 - 4\det(A)}}{2}$$

When the roots are real, both roots are positive if $\text{tr}(A) > 0$ and $\det(A) > 0$, both roots are negative if $\text{tr}(A) < 0$ and $\det(A) > 0$. One root is positive and one is negative if $\det(A) < 0$. (see Chapter 14, Section 14.3 for a discussion of a related point in the context of differential equations).

Chapter 14

Section 14.1

1. (a) nonhomogeneous, unstable
   (b) homogeneous, stable
   (c) nonhomogeneous, stable
   (d) nonhomogeneous, unstable
3. (a) 45
   (b) 7
5. (a) for $x(0) = -1$, $\lim_{t\to\infty} x(t) = -\infty$; for $x(0) = 5$, $\lim_{t\to\infty} x(t) = \infty$; initial value matters.
   (b) for $x(0) = 0$, $\lim_{t\to\infty} x(t) = 0$; for $x(0) = 3$, $\lim_{t\to\infty} x(t) = 0$; initial value does not matter.
   (c) for $x(0) = 0$, $\lim_{t\to\infty} x(t) = 3$; for $x(0) = 3$, $\lim_{t\to\infty} x(t) = 3$; for $x(0) = 5$, $\lim_{t\to\infty} x(t) = 3$; initial value does not matter.
   (d) for $x(0) = 4$, $\lim_{t\to\infty} x(t) = -\infty$; for $x(0) = 8$, $\lim_{t\to\infty} x(t) = 8$; for $x(0) = 12$, $\lim_{t\to\infty} x(t) = \infty$; initial value matters.
7. (a) To find the half-life, which occurs at time H, first note that $\dot{x}(t) = ax(t) + b$, which is stable since $a < 0$, has the solution

$$x(t) = \left(x(0) + \frac{b}{a}\right)e^{at} - \frac{b}{a},$$

and at time H

$$x(H) = \left(x(0) + \frac{b}{a}\right)e^{aH} - \frac{b}{a} = \frac{x(0) + x_\infty}{2}.$$

Note that $x_\infty = -b/a$. Solving for H,

$$\left(x(0) + \frac{b}{a}\right)e^{aH} - \frac{b}{a} = \frac{x(0) - b/a}{2}.$$

Therefore

$$\left(x(0) + \frac{b}{a}\right)e^{aH} = \frac{x(0) + b/a}{2}$$

and

$$e^{aH} = \frac{1}{2} \quad \text{implying} \quad aH = \ln\left(\frac{1}{2}\right)$$

$$H \approx \frac{-0.69}{\alpha} \quad \text{since} \quad \ln\left(\frac{1}{2}\right) \approx -0.69.$$

(b) no, H is only a function of the parameter a.

9. (a) For $\dot{x}(t) = -2x(t) + b(t)$, where $b(t) = 0$ for $0 \leq t \leq 10$, $b(t) = 100$ for $t > 10$, and $x(0) = 1$ and for $t \leq 10$,

$$x(t) = e^{-2t}.$$

For $t > 10$,

$$\begin{aligned} x(t) &= e^{-2t} + \int_{s=0}^{t} 100e^{-2(t-s)}\, ds \\ &= e^{-2t} + 50(1 - e^{20-2t}). \end{aligned}$$

(b) For $\dot{x}(t) = 3x(t) + g(t)$, where $g(t) = 6$ for $0 \leq t \leq 5$, $g(t) = 3$ for $t > 5$, and $x(0) = 2$ and for $0 \leq t \leq 5$,

$$x(t) = 2e^{3t} + \int_{s=0}^{t} 6e^{3(t-s)}\, ds.$$

For $t > 5$,

$$\begin{aligned} x(t) &= 2e^{3t} + \int_{s=0}^{5} 6e^{3(5-s)}\, ds + \int_{s=5}^{t} 3e^{3(t-s)}\, ds \\ &= 2e^{3t} + 2(e^{15} - 1) + \int_{s=5}^{t} 3e^{3(t-s)}\, ds. \end{aligned}$$

(c) For $\dot{x}(t) = 10x(t) + h(t)$, where $h(t) = e^{-2t} + 10$ and $x(0) = 3$,

$$\begin{aligned} x(t) &= 3e^{10t} + \int_{s=0}^{t} (e^{-2t} + 10)e^{10(t-s)}\, ds \\ &= 3e^{10t} + \int_{s=0}^{t} e^{8t}e^{-10s}\, ds + 10\int_{s=0}^{t} e^{10(t-s)}\, ds \\ &= 3e^{10t} + \left(e^{10t} + \frac{e^{8t}}{10}\right)(1 - e^{-10t}). \end{aligned}$$

Section 14.2

1.

$$\pi(t) = \dot{p}(0)e^{-\alpha t} + \int_{s=0}^{t} \alpha\dot{p}(t)e^{-\alpha(t-s)}\,ds,$$

where $\dot{p}(0)$ is the initial level of actual inflation and equals the initial level of expected inflation $\pi(0)$.

3. The solution of the differential equation describing the behavior of domestic gold holdings is

$$g(t) = (g(0) - (\varepsilon + p^*))e^{-\beta t} + (\varepsilon + p^*),$$

with the steady state $g_\infty = \varepsilon + p^*$ and initially $g(0) = \varepsilon + p^*$. The effect of a devaluation is to increase ε to ε'. The new solution is

$$\begin{aligned} g(t) &= ((\varepsilon + p^*) - (\varepsilon' + p^*))e^{-\beta t} + (\varepsilon' + p^*) \\ &= (\varepsilon - \varepsilon')e^{-\beta t} + (\varepsilon' + p^*), \end{aligned}$$

with the steady state $g_\infty = \varepsilon' + p^*$.

5. With $m(t) - p(t) = -0.8i(t)$, we have

$$\dot{\varepsilon}(t) = 1.25\varepsilon(t) - 1.25m(t).$$

With $m(0) = 0$ and $dm(t)/dt = 0.10$, we have $m(t) = 0.10t$, and

$$\varepsilon(0) = \int_{s=0}^{\infty} 1.25 \cdot (0.10s)e^{-1.25s}\,ds.$$

we integrate by parts to get

$$\begin{aligned} \varepsilon(0) &= -\frac{0.125s}{1.25}e^{-1.25s}\Big|_0^\infty - \int_{s=0}^{\infty} -\frac{0.125}{1.25}e^{-1.25s}\,ds \\ &= 0.08. \end{aligned}$$

Section 14.3

1. The steady state values are found by setting $\dot{x}(t) = 0$ and $\dot{y}(t) = 0$ and solving.
   (a) $x_\infty = 4, y_\infty = 1$.
   (b) $x_\infty = 2, y_\infty = 4$.
   (c) $x_\infty = 3, y_\infty = 5$.
3. The only stable solution is that the system is at its steady state and therefore $x(t) = 2$ and $y(t) = 4$.
5. This system can be expressed as

$$\begin{bmatrix} \dot{\varepsilon}(t) \\ \dot{p}(t) \end{bmatrix} = \begin{bmatrix} \dfrac{\beta\varphi}{\mu} & \dfrac{1-\beta\varphi}{\mu} \\ \beta\theta & -\beta\theta \end{bmatrix} \cdot \begin{bmatrix} \varepsilon(t) \\ \dot{p}(t) \end{bmatrix} + \text{constant terms}$$

(a) The system is saddlepath stable if the determinant of the matrix is negative, that is, if

$$-\frac{\beta^2\varphi\theta}{\mu} - \left(\frac{1-\beta\varphi}{\mu}\right)\beta\theta < 0$$

or, equivalently, if $\beta\varphi + \theta > \beta\theta$.

(b) The slope of the saddlepath is

$$\frac{dp}{d\varepsilon} = \frac{\mu\lambda_2 - \beta\varphi}{\mu - \beta\varphi}$$

where λ_2 is the negative characteristic root. The saddlepath has a negative slope if $\mu > \beta\varphi$ and a positive slope if $\mu < \beta\varphi$. Either of these conditions could be consistent with saddlepath stability.

7. The characteristic roots for the second-order linear differential equation

$$\ddot{x}(t) = a\dot{x}(t) + bx(t) + c$$

are

$$\lambda_1, \lambda_2 = \frac{a \pm \sqrt{a^2 - 4b}}{2}.$$

(a) The equation is stable since the two roots are each negative, with $\lambda_1 = -\frac{1}{2}$ and $\lambda_2 = -\frac{7}{2}$.

(b) The equation is unstable since the two roots are positive, with $\lambda_1 = \frac{1}{2}$ and $\lambda_2 = \frac{3}{2}$.

(c) The equation is unstable since the one root is negative and one is positive, with $\lambda_1 = -\frac{1}{2}$ and $\lambda_2 = \frac{5}{2}$.

Chapter 15

Section 15.1

1. The Hamiltonian is

$$H_t = \left(\frac{1}{1+r}\right)^t (F(K_t, L_t) - wtL_t - I_t) + \lambda_t(I_t - \delta K_t).$$

The first-order conditions are

$$\frac{\partial H_t}{\partial L_t} = \left(\frac{1}{1+r}\right)^t (F_L(K_t, L_t) - w_t) = 0$$

$$\frac{\partial H_t}{\partial I_t} = -\left(\frac{1}{1+r}\right)^t + \lambda_t = 0$$

$$\frac{\partial H_t}{\partial K_t} = \left(\frac{1}{1+r}\right)^t F_K(K_t, L_t) - \delta\lambda_t = -(\lambda_t - \lambda_{t-1})$$

$$\frac{\partial H_t}{\partial \lambda_t} = (I_t - \delta K_t) = -(K_{t+1} - K_t)$$

The optimal amount of labor satisfies the condition $F_L(K_t, L_t) = w_t$ in each period. Making the substitution from the optimality conditions $\lambda_t = (1/(1+r))^t$, the optimal amount of capital satisfies the condition

$$\left(\frac{1}{1+r}\right)^t F_K(K_t, L_t) - \delta\left(\frac{1}{1+r}\right)^t = -\left(\left(\frac{1}{1+r}\right)^t - \left(\frac{1}{1+r}\right)^{t-1}\right)$$

or

$$F_K(K_t, L_t) = \delta + r.$$

3. (a) The Hamiltonian is

$$H_t = \beta^t U(C_t) + \lambda_t(RB_t + Y_t - C_t).$$

(b) The first-order conditions are

$$\frac{\partial H_t}{\partial C_t} = \beta^t U'(C_t) - \lambda_t = 0$$

$$\frac{\partial H_t}{\partial B_t} = \lambda_t R = -(\lambda_t - \lambda_{t-1}).$$

Solving, we find the optimal condition to be

$$(1 + R)\beta U'(C_t) = U'(C_{t-1}).$$

(c) This is the same as the condition for the two-period problem in Chapter 11.

Section 15.2

1. (a) The Hamiltonian is

$$H = -\frac{y(t)^2}{2} + \lambda(t)y(t).$$

(b) The maximum principle shows that the optimal conditions include

$$\frac{\partial H}{\partial y} = -y(t) + \lambda(t) = 0$$

$$\frac{\partial H}{\partial x} = 0 = \dot{\lambda}(t)$$

$$\frac{\partial H}{\partial \lambda} = y(t) = \dot{x}(t),$$

which shows that λ is constant and therefore y is constant.

(c) To solve for y, we use the initial and terminal conditions to obtain

$$\int_{t=0}^{40} \frac{dx}{dt}\, dt = x(40) - x(0) = -20$$

and

$$\int_{t=0}^{40} \frac{dx}{dt}\, dt = \int_{t=0}^{40} y\, dt = 40y = -20,$$

and, therefore, $y = -1/2$. Also, since $\dot{x} = y$, $x(t) = -1/2t + 20$.

3. (a) The Hamiltonian is

$$H = \ln(y(t)) - 3\lambda(t)y(t).$$

(b) The maximum principle shows that the optimal conditions include

$$\frac{\partial H}{\partial y} = \frac{1}{y(t)} - 3\lambda(t) = 0$$
$$\frac{\partial H}{\partial x} = 0 = -\dot{\lambda}(t)$$
$$\frac{\partial H}{\partial \lambda} = -3y(t) = \dot{x}(t),$$

which shows that λ is constant and, therefore, y is constant since $y = 1/3\lambda$.

(c) Using the initial and terminal conditions,

$$\int_{t=0}^{1} \frac{dx}{dt} dt = x(1) - x(0) = 30$$

and since $\dot{x}(t) = -3y$,

$$\int_{t=0}^{1} \frac{dx}{dt}\, dt = \int_{t=0}^{1} -3y\, dt = -3y = 30,$$

and therefore, $y = -10$. Also, since $\dot{x} = -3y$, $x(t) = 30t$.

5. The Hamiltonian in this problem is

$$H = -\gamma \frac{y(t)^2}{2} + \lambda(t)(\alpha x(t) + \beta y(t)).$$

The solution for this problem uses the optimal conditions

$$\frac{\partial H}{\partial y} = -\gamma y(t) + \beta\lambda(t) = 0$$
$$\frac{\partial H}{\partial x} = \alpha\lambda(t) = -\dot{\lambda}(t)$$
$$\frac{\partial H}{\partial \lambda} = ax(t) + \beta y(t) = \dot{x}(t).$$

Using the first condition, which shows that $\lambda(t) = (\gamma/\beta)y(t)$ along the optimal path, we can write this as a two-equation differential equation system in $y(t)$ and $x(t)$:

$$\begin{bmatrix} \dot{x}(t) \\ \dot{y}(t) \end{bmatrix} = \begin{bmatrix} \alpha & \beta \\ 0 & -\alpha \end{bmatrix} \cdot \begin{bmatrix} x(t) \\ y(t) \end{bmatrix}.$$

The trace of this matrix is 0, and its determinant is $-\alpha^2$; therefore its two characteristic roots are $\pm 2\alpha$, and the system is saddlepath stable.

Section 15.3

1. Let $V = B - u(c)$, and note that $c(t) = f(k(t)) - dk(t)/dt$. Consider the integrand as $V(c(k, \dot{k}))$.

(a) Note that

$$V_k = V_c \frac{\partial c}{\partial k} = -u'(c) \cdot f'(k)$$
$$V_{\dot{k}} = V_c \frac{\partial c}{\partial \dot{k}} = -u'(c) \cdot (-1) = u'(c).$$

Euler's equation shows that the first-order condition is $V_k = (d/dt)V_{\dot{k}}$, which gives us

$$-u'(c) \cdot f'(k) = \frac{d}{dt} u'(c),$$

which can be rewritten to obtain the equation in the text.

(b) In this case, $f'(k(t)) = \alpha k(t)^{\alpha-1}$, $u'(c(t)) = 1/c(t)$ and $(d/dt)\,u'(c(t)) = (d/dt)(c(t)^{-1}) = -\dot{c}(t)/c(t)^2$. The optimal condition is, therefore,

$$\alpha k(t)^{\alpha-1} = \frac{\dot{c}(t)}{c(t)},$$

which is the same as the condition in the text if $n = 0$, $\delta = 0$, and $\rho = 0$.

3. The entire stock of gold coins can be sold at once so the "extraction time" in this case is an instant. The optimal time for selling the gold coins is the time where the schedule $p(T)e^{\rho(t-T)}$ is tangent to the price path, $p(t)$, as shown in Figure 15.3.3.

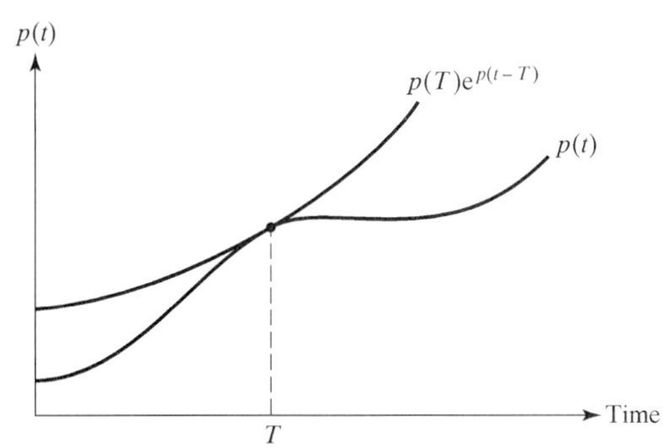

FIGURE 15.3.3.

Index

The Greek Alphabet

A	α	alpha
β	β	beta
Γ	γ	gamma
Δ	δ	delta
E	ε	epsilon
Z	ζ	zeta
H	η	eta
Θ	θ	theta
I	ι	iota
K	κ	kappa
Λ	λ	lambda
M	μ	mu
N	ν	nu
Ξ	ξ	xi
O	o	omicron
Π	π	pi
P	ρ	rho
Σ	σ	sigma
T	τ	tau
Υ	υ	upsilon
Φ	ϕ or φ	phi
X	χ	chi
Ψ	ψ	psi
Ω	ω	omega

Mathematical Symbols

$\equiv$	Identically equal to.
$\approx$	Approximately equal to.
(x, y)	Open interval from x to y, endpoints not included.
$[x, y]$	Closed interval from x to y, endpoints included.
$(x, y]$	Half-open (or half-closed) interval from x to y, x not included, y included.
$[x, y)$	Half-open (or half-closed) interval from x to y, x included, y not included.
$S = \{x, y, z\}$	Set S, including listed members.
$S = \{x \mid x \text{ has property } a\}$	Set S, members having property a.